The Options Course

Founded in 1807, John Wiley & Sons is the oldest independent publishing company in the United States. With offices in North America, Europe, Australia, and Asia, Wiley is globally committed to developing and marketing print and electronic products and services for our customers' professional and personal knowledge and understanding.

The Wiley Trading series features books by traders who have survived the market's ever changing temperament and have prospered—some by reinventing systems, others by getting back to basics. Whether a novice trader, professional, or somewhere in-between, these books will provide the advice and strategies needed to prosper today and well into the future.

For a list of available titles, visit our web site at www.WileyFinance.com.

The Options Course

High Profit & Low Stress Trading Methods

Second Edition

GEORGE A. FONTANILLS

WILEY

John Wiley & Sons, Inc.

Published by John Wiley & Sons, Inc., Hoboken, New Jersey.
Published simultaneously in Canada.

For general information on our other products and services, or technical support, please contact our Customer Care Department within the United States at 800-762-2974, outside the United States at 317-572-3993 or fax 317-572-4002.

Wiley also publishes its books in a variety of electronic formats. Some content that appears in print may not be available in electronic books.

For more information about Wiley products, visit our web site at www.wiley.com.

Library of Congress Cataloging-in-Publication Data:

Fontanills, George.
    The options course : high profit & low stress trading methods / George A.
Fontanills.—2nd ed.
      p. cm.
    Includes index.
    ISBN 0-471-66851-6 (cloth)
  1. Options (Finance) I. Title.
    HG6024.A3F66 2005
    332.64'53—dc22   2004028852

Printed in the United States of America.

10 9 8 7 6 5 4 3 2 1

To Charlene Fontanills—
the one true love of my life.

Contents

CHAPTER 12 Choosing the Right Broker 330

CHAPTER 13 Processing Your Trade 347

CHAPTER 14 Margin and Risk 371

CHAPTER 15 A Short Course in
Economic Analyses 382

CHAPTER 16 Mastering the Market 403

CHAPTER 17 How to Spot Explosive Opportunities 415

CHAPTER 18 Tools of the Trade 453

CHAPTER 19 Final Summary 466

APPENDIX A Trading Resources 485

APPENDIX B Important Charts and Tables 503

APPENDIX C Strategy Reviews 511

APPENDIX D Success Guides 527

Glossary 533

Index 557

Preface

An investment in knowledge always pays the best interest.

—Benjamin Franklin

Most new investors and traders, whether they are beginners or professionals, usually lose money for two reasons. First, they do not have a grasp of how the markets really work. Second, they are under too much stress when they trade because they fear losing money. Many times, traders liquidate good trades too quickly or have no idea when to take profits. But learning to trade successfully is not an impossible task. This book is designed to build your knowledge base of the markets to a professional level and to provide you with strategies that make money in the marketplace. My trading program is the result of many years of trading experience, as well as many years of research and development, all in the pursuit of developing the optimal methodologies to trade the stock, options, and futures markets.

Students often ask me how I got started as a full-time investor. Perhaps like you, I was looking for an opportunity that would allow me to achieve my financial dreams after a long road of despair. After attending high school in Miami, I felt a college career was necessary to become successful. Although I questioned what success really meant to me and whether college would bring me that success, I settled on the University of Florida in Gainesville for the wrong reasons. It was close to home and all my friends were going there.

One day, after just a few semesters, I woke up having difficulty breathing. I went to the university clinic and was told I had a mild case of pneumonia. After a week of useless medications, my breathing troubles increased. Finally X-rays were taken, and at the age of 18, I was diagnosed with Hodgkin's disease, a form of cancer. There is no news that can be more devastating to a young person and his family.

Perhaps the hardest thing I had to face was the loss of my physical prowess. Until that time, I was in exceptional shape, working out every day and participating in lots of sports. Over the next year, I was hospitalized and had to undergo chemotherapy treatments and radiation therapy. Throughout this dark time, I continued my studies at a community college.

At this point, I realized that life was too short to waste time, and that I needed to work as hard as I could to achieve everything I wanted to do. As my resolve to succeed took flight, I coined the phrase, "Out of adversity comes inspiration."

I slowly recovered and went on to attend New York University, graduating with honors with a bachelor's degree in accounting. I subsequently earned my CPA license and joined a large accounting firm. However, after spending several years in public accounting, I once again felt disillusioned. I needed something more. I applied and, to my surprise, was accepted at Harvard Business School. After two grueling years (but something I would do again without hesitation), I graduated.

Here I was, a bright and energetic young man with an MBA from the finest business school in the world with countless job offers others would never dream of turning down. But somehow I just couldn't get excited about any of the positions, no matter what they paid me. I had already traveled down that road and knew that it led to a dead end. Instead, I decided to go into business for myself.

Driven by my need for a more rewarding career, I started my first business. It failed. Strike one. Undaunted, I started a second business, which never even got off the ground. Strike two. On my third attempt—an attempt to strike gold in the real estate business—I realized that I could actually be good at something. Working with some wealthy individuals in Massachusetts, I was just able to keep my head above water. I would find great real estate deals and they would put up the money to buy them. Subsequently, I would get a small piece of each deal.

Unfortunately, I forgot one thing: I needed to eat and pay the rent without the benefit of a consistent salary. Finally, the day came when my landlord (one of my partners) came to collect my rent and I had no money to pay it. I hedged as best I could and asked him to give me a little more time. He turned me down, adding that he was going to throw me out regardless of how much money I made him in the past. I was shocked. At first I thought he was kidding around. But with a stern look on his face, he proved me wrong, stating unequivocally, "One day you will thank me for teaching you this lesson." At the time, I cockily replied that I'd be much happier with a wheelbarrow full of money. In hindsight, I realize that he was probably referring to my favorite personal proverb about finding inspiration in adversity. However, he is still waiting for me to thank him.

Crushed and downhearted, I went to my parents to borrow money to eat and live. Being a Harvard MBA and having to borrow money from your parents is very demoralizing. Having to listen to "Why don't you get a real job?" not only from them but from others made me decide to give corporate life another shot.

Soon after, I found a consulting job that lasted a whole 30 days. It was supposed to be a permanent job. But as I was being fired, I was told I had the wrong attitude. In fact, they said much more than that, but most of it could never be printed. Unfortunately, they were right. I did have the wrong attitude. I just didn't want to work for anyone but myself. I returned to real estate and started looking for new projects, but this time I was determined to control them. In this roundabout way, I was first introduced to the concept of an option. A real estate option allowed me to control a piece of property with very little cash for a specific period of time. As I later learned, stock and futures options are very similar.

My first deal was exciting. I found a great apartment complex going into foreclosure and convinced the owner I could buy the property. In fact, I had no cash at all. Even worse, my credit was destroyed and my shiny BMW had been repossessed. Since I was approximately $50,000 in debt, I did what I had to do: I convinced an investor to put up the option money and split the profits after the property was sold. I made a nice $35,000 profit on that deal—finally, a success.

After a series of profitable deals, the bottom fell out of the real estate market. There was no money available anywhere. Once again, I was left with a big question mark as to what I should be doing with my life. Luckily, serendipity intervened. One day, I received a small advertisement in the mail for a book on futures trading. Although I had no clue as to what futures trading was all about, I ordered the book. What struck me most were tales about making large amounts of money in a short period of time using very little cash. This sounded very similar to what I had been doing with real estate.

Why had I never learned any of this when I attended Harvard Business School? How could the great "boot camp of capitalism" neglect to teach me about futures markets? My interest was now piqued. I picked up a few more books. I began to watch the markets. I even played with a few introductory strategies; but although I found them interesting, they were not very profitable. My first big mistake was to convince my investment partners that we should begin trading by hiring experienced professionals. In less than 30 days, these so-called professionals lost about 30 percent of our capital. This was an extremely poor way to inspire confidence in my investors. I decided to fire everyone and learn to do it myself. I knew that I could lose at least 30 percent without even trying (even more if I really tried). I was determined to make a profit, and the trick was to get a competitive edge. That much I did learn at Harvard. To be successful, you need to have an edge.

I began to analyze where I could find this edge, focusing my attention on using computers to garner information faster than others did. I gained experience as a trader, even learning how to write my own computer programs. Eventually, this long and eventful journey gave birth to Optionetics. Today, I teach this system to individuals all over the world. Hopefully, this book will enable you to develop a better understanding of the markets and will assist you in learning how to profitably trade. In my opinion, there is no better lifestyle than that of a successful trader.

GEORGE A. FONTANILLS
Miami Beach, Florida
December 2004

Acknowledgments

I attribute my success as a teacher, trader, and businessman to the incredible support I receive each and every day from my friends, family, and colleagues. I am fortunate to be able to do the job I enjoy with some of the most extraordinary people in the business. I would like to thank everyone at Optionetics who has helped to build our company into a global one. Your hard work and team spirit allow me to do what I love to do: trade options. Without you, this book would not be possible. You are all simply the best. In particular, and in no order of importance, I would like to especially thank the following people:

Tom Gentile is the Chief Trader for Optionetics. I would like to thank him for contributing a lot of great material for the second edition of this book. We work so closely together as a trading group that I often cannot distinguish my original ideas from Tom's. Simply stated, Tom is a trading genius, and his nickname "the option guru" is well deserved.

Richard Cawood is the CEO of the Global Group and Optionetics and the mastermind who perhaps maintains the lowest public profile of our group while having the highest influence. I am very fortunate to have his business acumen leading our team. The success of our full-time trading endeavors is made possible only because Richard manages our business. And with that I have to acknowledge his right hand, Tony Clemendor, an old friend and groundbreaking COO. My partners—Tom Gentile, Richard Cawood, and Tony Clemendor—are the backbone of the company and deserve the bulk of the credit in building our company.

In addition, I wish to recognize Amy Morris, who has been with us since we started. Without her dedication and inspirational management skills, my life would be much more difficult. And of course, I send waves of gratitude to Kym Trippsmith, my Editor-in-Chief. Her resourcefulness, hard work, and determination are the reasons this book—as well as all the others—exist. Thank you, Kym!

My thanks also go to my trading family, writers, and friends. In particular, Frederic Ruffy and Jody Osborne are two of the most outstanding writers I have ever had the pleasure of working with. Their timely revisions to this edition of *The Options Course* were invaluable. Finally, I want to thank Kim Diehl, the Associate Editor, for her eagle eyes and editing acumen. There are many others and I hope they forgive me for not being able to list everyone.

My loving family has supported me in all my adventures over the years. I thank them for always believing in me even when I didn't believe in myself. When my battle with cancer occurred, they were always at my side and their prayers were answered with my recovery. I thank God for my second lease on life.

People continually ask me why I publish material. For the record, I enjoy passing on my knowledge to others. However, without my team supporting me, I would probably stick to trading full-time for a living. Thanks to the help of my incredible support team, I am able to do both of the things that I love: trade and teach.

Finally, I would like to thank my students, who inspire me to keep writing and publishing. Over the years, we have made numerous friends and received many great ideas from our students that have enhanced our own trading. I look forward to meeting you someday at one of my many speaking engagements or at an Optionetics seminar coming to a town near you. Until then, good luck and great trading.

G. A. F.

About the Author

Having struggled to overcome a life-threatening illness as a young man, George Fontanills is a true believer in the idea that pursuing your dreams is something that should never be put off until tomorrow. Like many people, George followed the typical educational and work-related path: From high school he went to college, and from college to an accounting job at the prestigious firm of Deloitte, Haskins Sells. Upon receiving his CPA license, George started work with Andersen Consulting. Not quite satisfied with where his life was headed, he left this job to attend Harvard Business School's MBA program.

After receiving his MBA, George decided to get off the treadmill of unsatisfying jobs. In the face of several high-paying job opportunities, George decided that he needed to start his own business. His first business failed. Undaunted, he started a second business that never left the starting gate. A survivor, he kept going. Running low on money, George became a real estate investor buying property with no money down. Finding a business he enjoyed, he quickly began to build a successful track record and increase his net worth. Just as he began to feel that he had found his lifelong career, the bottom fell out of the real estate market—strike three.

As George pondered his next move, he received a brochure on making money in the markets. After ordering the book, he began trading . . . and losing money. Rather than concentrating on his own losses, he began studying successful traders to see what they were doing differently. Using the analysis skills he developed at Harvard, George conducted a comprehensive investigation to determine what differentiated the winners from the losers. Risking the money he made in real estate, George tested his conclusions, eventually developing a unique approach to trading that involved utilizing managed risk strategies to strategically attack any market. By mathematically controlling risk every time a trade is placed, consistent profits can be made without the stress of unbridled losses. Fontanills called this trading style "Optionetics." As his net worth soared, he gained a reputation as an expert in nondirectional, managed-risk trading and has become a well-respected teacher and speaker at trading conferences all over the world. Today, Optionetics offers several of the best-attended trading courses in the world. George's straightforward and insightful approach to trading has enabled thousands of people to learn how to limit their risks and maximize their trading successes.

These days, Fontanills is President Emeritus of Global Investment Research Corp. and an active options and stock trader. George's reputation as "the dean of options trading" has led to numerous guest appearances on television and radio shows across the country. Most recently, he has been quoted in *The Wall Street Journal, Barron's, Research* magazine, CBS MarketWatch, and TheStreet.com. He also appears on CNBC, Bloomberg, and CNNfn, as well as numerous radio stations across the country. In addition, George Fontanills has written two best-sellers, *The Options Course* and *Trade Options Online*, and co-written with his partner, Tom Gentile, two others: *The Stock Market Course* and *The Volatility Course*. These "definitive guides to trading" have added to his critical acclaim as one of the best trading instructors in the world.

Introduction

Options are one of the most profitable tools available to traders today. They offer traders the ability to leverage positions, manage risk, and enhance returns on existing portfolios. To those who choose to trade options, this book provides the practical knowledge—from basic concepts to sophisticated techniques—necessary for successful options trading. It is designed to provide novice and intermediate traders with methods and strategies that will enhance profits and manage risk more effectively.

The investment world has gone through amazing gyrations since the first edition of *The Options Course* was released back in 1998. We have lived through the boom of the Internet along with the subsequent bust—when the dot-com became the dot-bomb. During this period, fortunes were made and lost virtually overnight. Traders who made money so fast they didn't know what to do with it turned around and lost it so fast it made their heads spin. It is always painful to see how fast investors can lose money—especially when techniques to limit risk could easily have been employed.

In addition to this wild time in early 2000, we saw a precipitous decline in the technology sector as well as in many blue-chip stocks. In the years following the collapse of the Internet bubble, almost everyone lost money. Even people with mutual funds saw tremendous drops in their monthly statements. Meanwhile, many small as well as institutional investors kept betting that the market would rebound, only to see it fall again and again. This continual drain destroyed the confidence of many stock market players.

Conversely, bond investors saw their yields rise dramatically as the Federal Reserve had to keep dropping interest rates. Apparently, the economic slowdown would not halt unless dramatic reductions in interest rates could spur economic recovery. It was a slow process and the American economy continues to slowly recover.

World events have also changed our lives dramatically. September 11, 2001, was one of the most horrific and unforgettable events in the history of humankind. Unfortunately, too many mothers, daughters, fathers, and sons as well as all the heroes of 9/11 will be remembered in history due to the horrible deeds of a few. As someone who was in New York and saw this event firsthand, I will never forget this day for the rest of my life. This event—along with surviving Hodgkin's disease when I was only 18—has led me to understand the importance of living life to its fullest every day. Undoubtedly it has woken us all up; we are now more fully aware of the global scope of the world we live in and the importance of appreciating the gift of life on this amazing planet.

As options traders, we have to focus on the many events that can make markets move in any one of three directions: up, down, or sideways. One of the most vital factors that must become part of your daily market approach is to pay close attention to volatility. How fast can an event drive the markets, and how can we take advantage of this event? What strategies can be employed when historical and implied volatility diverge? Options provide the knowledgeable investor or trader opportunities to create scenarios that others may not see. A stock investor can only buy or sell a stock, whereas an options trader can have a number of different strategies for different time frames. I like to say that we are playing a chess game with the markets. The market makes a move; I counter that move until, hopefully, I "checkmate" the market.

During the past 10 years of teaching individuals how to make money in the markets, I have had the opportunity to meet thousands of people, and they each seek ways to improve their lives—both for themselves and for their families. I hope that your own personal success will enable you to help your loved ones. Just remember that life is short and there are many roads it may take; but if we do our best to be good to others, then any path we take should also reward us many times over.

I certainly hope this book will help you to change your life in a positive way. The powerful strategies reviewed in it offer traders the ability to consistently make good returns when these trading approaches are solidly understood and strategically applied. Although at times it may seem like an insurmountable task to comprehend all aspects of options, I promise that it is well worth the effort. Just think back at how much time and money you spent in getting to where you are today. A little more consistent time and effort can reward you many times over.

The first question you need to ask yourself is: Why do you want to trade? The most common answer is to make more money. While trading can provide a great living, it's important to make sure you love what you do—no matter what it is. This will lead you to become more successful in the field of your choice. Once you have asked yourself why you want to trade, then ask yourself why you want to trade options. Most individuals want to trade options because these incredibly flexible instruments enable traders to control an asset for less money. For example, let's say I want to buy your house from you one year from today. I am willing to pay you the appraised value today plus another 10 percent on top of that. (If you don't take 10 percent, maybe I offer 15 percent or 25 percent.) Once you agree on the price and I pay you a deposit (known as the premium), I will have an option contract to purchase an asset (your house) at an agreed-to time (one year from today) at an agreed-to price. For this I pay you a premium. This is a simple example of a call option. The buyer (me) will have a right to buy the asset (your house) from the seller of the option (you), who will have an obligation to deliver the option (sell the house) to the option buyer.

If you want the right to sell an asset, you can employ the use of a put option. A good analogy can be the purchase of auto insurance, which provides the right to sell your car (the asset) to the seller of the put (the insurance company) if the value goes down due to an accident. Let's say you purchase a policy that values your car at $25,000 and you pay $1,000 for one year's coverage. What you have done is purchased the right to sell your car (the asset) for $25,000 for a one-year period in exchange for the premium of $1,000. If nothing happens in the year, your option will "expire worthless" and you will have to buy another put option (next year's insurance policy).

These relatively simple analogies are the initial steps to managing trading risk and leveraging your capital more effectively. In this book, you can learn how to use these amazing trading instruments in the volatile markets of the twenty-first century.

I have been fortunate to work with some of this country's best traders. This has enabled me to pass on an abundance of knowledge geared to help people become successful traders. This information comes from years of experience spanning from my first days as a novice trader through my experience running a floor trading operation at the American Stock Exchange and in the Chicago futures pits.

It is my sincere hope that you can learn to develop moneymaking trading acumen by reading this book. Most importantly, you will be able to avoid many of the costly errors commonly made in trading and investing and ascend your own learning curve in leaps and bounds. I have confidence that you will gain significant insight into the world of investing by studying the strategies in this book. By applying this knowledge to stocks, futures, and options markets, I have no doubt that you will find trading a lucrative endeavor.

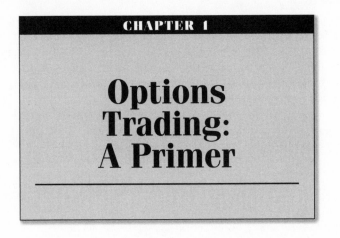

CHAPTER 1

Options Trading: A Primer

Trading is an elusive beast to the uninitiated, filled with mystery and complexity. Although trillions of dollars' worth of stocks, futures, and options change hands every day, learning to trade is a complicated puzzle that takes patience and perseverance to navigate effectively. Perhaps you have a friend who has made money or know other friends who have lost money playing the markets. Learning to trade can be the beginning of an exciting new career, especially if you master combining options with futures and stocks.

Many years of teaching and trading have taught me that the most successful investors are those who do not think of trading as work, but as play. Obviously, a love affair with anything you do will increase your chances of success dramatically. Perhaps that's why I like to call what I do "grown-up Nintendo." Making money is just a natural consequence of my daily play.

My systematic approach to trading emphasizes risk management. I know how to spot optimal moneymaking opportunities to increase my chances of high returns from low-risk investments. I share this trading knowledge with individuals throughout the world through seminars and various innovative products designed to foster a strong foundation in options trading in the stock and futures markets.

Stock, futures, and options trading provide investors with the best opportunity to find rewards that satisfy almost anyone's financial objectives. My investment philosophy is to make money any way we can, in any market we can. It's a matter of working with a matrix of trading strategies, developing a feel for how to trade profitably, and learning the tricks of the trade.

What separates those investors who make consistent returns year after year from those who can't ever seem to make a winning investment? Vision. Simply put, the winning investor has the vision to systematically spot good opportunities, while the losing investor simply never developed this insight. Can this vision be developed? Some say that a great investor has an innate sense that drives his or her ability to make money. However, I believe that although there may be a few individuals with this innate sense, most great investors learn by trial and error until they find what works best for them.

For example, many people refer to Warren Buffett as the greatest investor of all time. He appears to have a knack for turning anything he touches into gold. Is it because he is just so much smarter than everyone else, or has he developed a methodology over the years that works for him on a consistent basis? For someone as successful as he is, I would have to say that he has *both* innate skill and a formula for success. This formula for success can be developed by anyone. The problem is that most investors don't have the persistence and drive necessary to achieve success.

First and foremost, you have to learn how to invest and trade the right way. Typically, most new investors lose money when they first begin due to their lack of understanding of what it really takes to succeed. Many may listen to their stock or commodity broker from the outset and never develop an understanding of the markets. Many more lose money until they realize their main error is taking someone else's investment advice. A word of caution: Just because someone is licensed to take an order and execute a trade does not mean that person has the knowledge to invest your money wisely. Gaining the right kind of knowledge, however, is critical to trading success. Although there is risk in virtually all investments and trades, you can mitigate risks by learning how to protect yourself using innovative option strategies. Once you learn how to manage risk, the rewards come more easily.

If you intend to enter the markets, you'll need to decide what kind of investing/trading you want to engage in. Keep in mind that there is a big difference between investing and trading. An investor is an individual who takes a long-term perspective. For example, if you have $5,000 to invest and you place all the money in a mutual fund—a pool of investments managed by a professional manager—then you are taking a passive role for the long term. If you choose to set up an individual retirement account (IRA), you will more than likely keep it until retirement.

A trader, on the other hand, takes a more active role. Traders may make investments that last for seconds, minutes, hours, weeks, or even years, always looking for an opportunity to move the money around to capture a greater return. Typical traders actively make investment decisions on a continuous basis, never allowing anyone else to control the funds. As a trader, you need to focus on strategies that provide the best chance to create profitable trades. Combining stocks or futures with options provides you with extra leverage; but this extra leverage is a double-edged sword. Options give you the chance to make a very high return using smaller amounts of cash than futures or stocks require, but this leverage also creates an opportunity for you to lose money just as fast.

The losing traders are those who do not respect risk. To survive in this business and have the opportunity to enjoy the fruits of your labor, you must develop a very healthy respect for risk. Before entering any investment, you should ask yourself four questions:

1. How much profit can I make?
2. What is the maximum loss I can take?
3. At what point will I get out if I am wrong?
4. When should I take profits?

As you make the transition to becoming a motivated, knowledgeable, and successful trader, you will have to undertake a realistic examination of your personal goals, habits, dreams, and dislikes. This step is of utmost importance. Many individuals believe that they will enjoy a certain profession, but then give up before the opportunity to achieve success appears.

You must have a good understanding as to why you want to participate in any endeavor. Why are you taking the time to learn a new profession? What are your goals? What are your strengths? What are your weaknesses? Before you can become a serious and successful trader, you need to search for these answers. Make a list and add to it every day as more things become apparent. Try to be honest with yourself. Keep your highest goals in mind and work toward them one step at a time using your list of attributes to strengthen your willpower to succeed.

The three primary reasons for developing trading savvy are:

1. *To achieve more wealth.* The number one reason that most people want to become traders in the stock, futures, and options markets is to attain financial rewards. Stories about the large sums of money to be made and the successes of the rich and famous inspire a desire to achieve the same level of financial success. Just as it is a business's objective to produce more cash flow to pump up the bottom line, a trader's objective is to make more money from money. That is how a trader monitors progress. Although "money doesn't buy happiness," having plenty of money sure helps. However, there is no need to make having money your sole goal in life; as far as I'm concerned, that would undermine your development as a well-rounded individual.

2. *To improve family life.* The ultimate goal, other than trading just to make money, is to create a better life for yourself and your family. The success I have been fortunate enough to achieve through hard work has allowed me to help my family and friends financially when they needed it; I have found this ability to help others very enjoyable. Once you have achieved a financial level where you can live each day without worrying about which bills need to be paid, you will have more freedom to discover your true purpose in life. As an added bonus, you can also afford the time and energy to help others, which will make your life as an investor even more fulfilling.

3. *To gain greater autonomy in the workplace or be your own boss.* The third most common reason is the desire to break away from a day-to-day job that has been emotionally and/or financially unfulfilling. This is the main reason I started trading; I needed more than what real estate offered. As I like to ask my seminar students, "How many of you are here to try to get out of a real job?" More often than not, it's better to describe the day-to-day grind most people subject themselves to as an *unreal* job, since many cannot believe they have to go through the motions each day. In essence, it has become a nightmare.

Whether you enjoy what you are doing today and just want to supplement your income, or you are looking to become your own boss, there is no better profession than that of a trader. For example, I travel extensively and live in various locations. With a small laptop computer, Internet access, and a cell phone, I can conduct my business from almost anywhere, which maximizes my freedom. For me, trading is a dream come true.

THE ROAD TO SUCCESSFUL TRADING

Achieving trading success is not easy. In fact, just getting started can be an overwhelming process. The road to wealth can take many paths. To determine your optimal trading approach, start by making an honest assessment of your financial capabilities. Successful traders only use funds that are readily available and can be invested in a sound manner. It is also critical to accurately assess your time constraints to determine the style of trading that suits you best. If you want to trade aggressively, you can do so using various short-term strategies. If you want to take a hands-off approach, you can structure trades to meet that time frame. All of these choices are less difficult to make if you respect the following trading guidelines.

1. Gain the knowledge to succeed over the long run.
2. Start with acceptable trading capital.

3. Establish a systematic approach to the markets.
4. Be alert for trading opportunities at all times.
5. Develop the fine art of patience.
6. Build a strong respect for risk.
7. Develop a delta neutral trading approach.
8. Reduce your stress level.

Gain the Knowledge to Succeed over the Long Run

You have to have knowledge to succeed. Most new investors and traders enter this field expecting to immediately become successful. However, many have spent tens of thousands of dollars and many years in college learning a specific profession and still do not make much money. To be successful, you need to start your journey on the right path, which will increase your chance of reaching your final destination: financial security. To accomplish this goal, learn as much as you can about low-risk trading techniques and increase your knowledge base systematically.

Successful traders have an arsenal of trading tools that allows them to be competitive in the markets. I have used the word *arsenal* purposely. I believe that as an investor or trader, you need to recognize that each and every day in the marketplace is a battle. You must be ready to strategically launch an attack using all the resources in your arsenal. Your first weapon—knowledge—will enable you to make fast and accurate decisions regarding the probability of success in a specific investment. Is it incongruous to suggest that trading is war and also that to trade successfully one must reduce one's level of stress? I believe not. The most composed and well-armed opponents win wars. The same is true for traders. In most cases, winners will be more comfortable (less stressed) regarding their ability to win. Knowledge fosters confidence. If you are well armed, you will be confident as you go off to fight the battle of the markets. Increased confidence leads to lower stress and higher profits.

Start with Acceptable Trading Capital

Many investors start with less than $10,000 in their trading accounts. However, it is important to realize that the less you have in your account, the more cautious you have to be. Perhaps the toughest problem is to establish a sufficient capital base to invest effectively. If you begin investing or trading with very little capital, you will assure yourself of failure. Making money in the markets requires a learning curve, and incurring loss is part of the trading process. When it comes to trading, "you have to pay to play." You don't need to be a millionaire, but trading does require a certain amount of capital to get started. In many cases, the brokerage firm you choose will determine how much is required to put you in the game. However, no matter how much you begin with, it is a good idea to start out by trading conservatively. If you invest smartly, you can make very good returns and your financial goals will be realized.

Establish a Systematic Approach to the Markets

The third key to successful moneymaking in the markets is to develop a systematic approach that combines all the weapons in your arsenal to compete effectively in the marketplace. Then, and only then, will you be able to reduce your stress enough to believe in the plan and stick with it. A systematic approach diffuses the inherent madness of the marketplace, allowing you to make insightful trading decisions.

Be Alert for Trading Opportunities at All Times

By opening your receptivity to opportunity, you will be able to find many more promising trades than you thought possible. Where do you find opportunities? Everywhere. When you begin to train yourself to automatically look for trading opportunities in everything you do, you are on your way to being an up-and-coming successful trader.

Develop the Fine Art of Patience

Patience is one of the most difficult aspects of trading and investing and extremely hard to teach. I have to work at applying patience conscientiously each and every day, even after years of trading.

As a professional trader and investor, I have the opportunity to sit in front of computers all day long, day after day. This is another double-edged sword. Yes, I have the ability to look for promising trading opportunities because I have lots of information in front of me; however, I also have the opportunity to second-guess great trades due to fluctuations in the market that may be unimportant. Therefore, I have learned that the best investments are those in which I have thoroughly studied the risk and reward and have developed a time frame for the trade to work. For example, if I place a trade with options six months out, I try to stay with the trade for that period of time. This takes patience. Of course, if I reach my maximum profit level before that time, I take that profit and get out.

Do not feel that you are at a disadvantage if you cannot trade and invest full-time. This allows you to avoid the "noise" in the market that occurs each and every trading day. Many of my successful students make more money by not watching the markets too closely.

Build a Strong Respect for Risk

You must respect risk if you are to survive as an investor or a trader. Before you ever place an order with your broker, make sure you calculate the maximum potential risk and reward as well as the breakeven(s) of the trade. This will help you stay in the game so you can achieve your goals. Risk graphs, which are explored in later chapters, are important tools for assessing risk and reward.

Develop a Delta Neutral Trading Approach

Delta neutral trading is composed of strategies in which a trade is created by selecting a calculated ratio of short and long positions that balance out to an overall position delta of zero. The term *delta* refers to the degree of change in an option's price in relation to changes in the price of the underlying security. The delta neutral trading approach reduces risk and maximizes the potential return. Effectively applying these strategies in your own personal trading approach generally requires four steps:

1. *Test your trading systems by paper trading.* Paper trading is the process of simulating a trade without actually putting your money on the line. To become a savvy delta neutral options trader, you will need to practice strategies by placing trades on paper rather than with cash. Although it may not feel the same as putting your money on the line, it will help you to develop practical experience that will foster confidence in your abilities. This will come in very handy in the future. Since there is no substitute for personal experience, you should test all ideas *and* your ability to implement them properly prior to using real money.

2. *Discuss opening a brokerage account with several brokers.* Make sure you have a broker who is knowledgeable and fairly priced. Brokers can be assets or liabilities. Make certain your broker is an asset who will help make you richer, not "broker." Do not sacrifice service by selecting the broker with the lowest cost. Shop around for the right person or firm to represent your interests. Your broker will play a crucial role in your development as a successful trader. Take your time, and if you are not satisfied, find someone else.

3. *Open a brokerage account.* It's best to consider a brokerage firm that specializes in stocks, futures, and options. Then you can easily place trades in any market using the same firm. When it comes to trading, flexibility and precision are equally important. Today, some online brokers specialize in options. We provide examples in later chapters.

4. *Start small.* Any mistakes you make early in your trading career will obviously cost you money. If you start with small trades in the beginning, you will be able to gain the knowledge, experience, and confidence necessary to move on to bigger trades. The bottom line is that a mistake made in a small trade means a smaller loss of capital, which can help keep you in the game.

Reduce Your Stress Level

Successful traders have to find ways to reduce the stress commonly associated with trading. I reconstructed my trading style after experiencing more stress than I had thought I could ever handle. In a typical trading day with the S&P 500 (Standard & Poor's 500 Index, which represents the 500 largest companies in the United States), I found myself buying close to the high of the day. Immediately the market started to tumble so fast that I was down 100 points even before I got my buy filled (i.e., before my order was executed). I finally was able to regain my composure just enough to pick up the phone in a panic to sell as fast as possible. By then the market had tumbled almost 200 points. Worst of all, I had purchased too many contracts for the money I had in my account; and, to top it all off, it was my first trade ever in the S&P.

That was the point in my trading career that I experienced the panic and stress of losing more than 40 percent of my account in three minutes—more than one month's pay as an accountant. I did not trade again for more than two months while I tried to figure out whether I could really do this for a living. Luckily, I did start trading again; however, I reduced my trading size to one contract position at a time for more than a year.

Many professional floor traders and off-floor traders have had similar experiences. However, these kinds of stressful events must be overcome and used as lessons that needed to be learned. Simply put, stress produces incomplete knowledge access. Stress, by its nature, causes humans to become tense in not only their physical being but also their mental state. For years, physicians have made the public aware that stress can lead to many illnesses including hardening of the arteries with the possibility of a heart attack or other ailments. Reducing stress can lead to bigger rewards and can be accomplished by building a low-stress trading plan.

To create your own plan, follow this three-point outline:

1. Define your risk.
2. Develop a flexible investment plan.
3. Build your knowledge base systematically.

Define Your Risk   As a trader you have the ability to make large profits with the risk of potentially large losses. This is no secret. Unfortunately, that old maxim "cut your losses and let your profits run" is easier said than done. By defining your risk, you are assured that you cannot lose more money than the amount you have established as being the maximum position loss. You will also be able to develop strategies that create the potential for large rewards by predefining your acceptable risk parameters and by applying strategies that combine stocks and options on stocks, or futures and options on futures.

Develop a Flexible Investment Plan   The second step in reducing risk and stress is to develop an investment plan that is flexible. Flexibility allows a trader to cultivate a matrix of strategies with which to respond to market movement in any direction. Erratic market movement can change your position dramatically in seconds. Each price move (tick) rearranges everyone's assumptions about what the market is about to do. This dynamic environment borders on schizophrenia, where the bulls and bears do battle trying to outmaneuver each other. This, in turn, creates profitable opportunities for the knowledgeable investor with a smart and flexible investment plan and creates nightmares for the uninitiated trader without a plan, only a hunch as to where the market appears to be going. Investors and traders have to be entrepreneurial by nature to survive. One of the greatest attributes of entrepreneurs in any industry is the ability to recognize a roadblock and change direction when one is reached. Traders must also exhibit this flexibility if they are to survive in the marketplace.

Build Your Knowledge Base Systematically   The third step to creating a successful investment plan is to systematically build a solid base of innovative strategies from which to invest wisely. Most investors start the same way. They read a few books, open a small account, and lose everything very quickly. However, there is one way to differentiate the winners from the losers. Winners persist at learning as much as they can by starting slowly and collecting tools to beat the market consistently. Successful options traders first learn to walk, then to run. Usually traders begin with simplistic strategies such as going long or shorting the market, and using stops to limit losses. Some just listen to their brokers and follow their trading ideas. Once initiated, traders accelerate their learning at the right time to become successful.

Successful traders usually specialize in one area or just a few areas. This specialization allows the trader to develop strategies that consistently work in certain recognizable market conditions. A successful investor realizes that, in all likelihood, these situations will reoccur and the same strategies can be used profitably over and over again. At my alma mater, Harvard Business School, the same systematic approach is used. I never realized what the school was attempting to accomplish until after graduation when I had time to apply this approach to the real world—all those case studies on businesses I had no interest in fostered my ability to learn how to think in any environment. This systematic building of knowledge will enable you to quickly get up and running as a successful trader in the marketplace.

CONCLUSION

Options, the most flexible financial instrument that exists today, provide unique investment opportunities to knowledgeable traders on a regular basis. However, the entire options arena can be a very complex and confusing place in which to venture, especially for the novice trader. The primary reason for this complexity is the fact that options trading is a multidimensional process; and each dimension needs to be understood in order to trade successfully.

Prior to initiating an options position, there are three main issues to consider: direction, duration, and magnitude. Direction refers to whether the underlying security will move up, down, or sideways. Duration refers to how long it will take for the anticipated move to take place. Magnitude refers to how big the subsequent move will be. In order to make a profit, the options trader must be correct in all three of these categories. This is the primary reason that many people lose money when trading options. They do not accurately understand the three dimensions of an options position.

The first step in taking your options trading to another level is to understand and comprehend the interrelation of direction, duration, and magnitude. Additionally, the trader must use these three different variables in order to provide an edge in the market. It is imperative to be able to combine and exploit these three variables in order to give yourself an advantage; otherwise your trading will become no more than an exercise in giving your money away to other traders.

Many times it is necessary to work with combinations of options in order to give yourself an edge in the market as opposed to just buying a call or a put. This is where understanding spreads, straddles, and various option combinations is helpful. There are a few general rules that I always follow when looking for and constructing option positions. The first is that when I am going to bet on the future direction of a security, I want to give myself enough time to be right. That means I will usually choose long-term equity anticipation securities (LEAPS) for directional trades. LEAPS is a name given to options with expiration dates further than nine months away. The second rule is in regard to magnitude or volatility.

When combining different options together, I want to be a seller of expensive options (high volatility) and a buyer of cheap options (low volatility). The third rule is that I want to make time my friend as opposed to my enemy by purchasing options that have plenty of time left to expiration and selling shorter-term options. This allows me to take advantage of the time decay characteristic of an option. These guidelines are a brief summary of the issues that need to be understood when building trades that give you a competitive edge in the market.

To the beginner, these issues may seem complex and convoluted; but with a little bit of practice everything should become quite clear. If you take the time to understand the concepts of direction, duration, and magnitude, you'll soon be able to start experimenting with a variety of different options strategies. For example, if you want to be bullish on a particular stock, then you can take a longer-term perspective by placing a bull call spread using LEAPS. For shorter-term trades, you can take advantage of time decay by using credit spreads, calendar spreads, or butterfly strategies. Increased comprehension of these basic concepts will enable you to combine short- and long-term strategies together to help you become an even more proficient trader.

As you build experience as a trader, you will become more confident in your ability to make money. After a few successes, traders are more motivated to develop the perseverance necessary to stay with the winning trades and exit losing positions quickly. In the long run, you have a much better chance of becoming successful when you start by acquiring a solid foundation of the option basics. In addition, keep a journal of every trade you make—especially your paper trades—as a road map of where you've been and where you want to go on your journey to trading victory. Remember, patience and persistence are the keys to trading options successfully.

CHAPTER 2

The Big Picture

I n this book, our discussion of trading involves a variety of different investment vehicles in addition to options: stocks, futures, commodities, exchange-traded funds (ETFs), and indexes. These financial instruments can be assembled in an infinite number of combinations. My own trading focuses on stocks and options. Yet, an appreciation of all these tools can help build an integrated understanding of what is happening day to day in the financial marketplace. So, let's take a closer look at the fundamental components of each investment vehicle to see how one differs from the other.

Note: The word "market" can be used to describe the overall stock market or to refer to individual markets such as a specific stock, futures, or market sector.

STOCKS

Those of you just starting in the field of investment have most likely heard about one popular financial instrument: the stock. In fact, thousands of stocks are traded on the U.S. stock exchanges every day. But what exactly is a stock? Basically, a stock is a unit of ownership in a company. The value of that unit of ownership is based on a number of factors, including the total number of outstanding shares, the value of the equity of the company (what it owns less what it owes), the earnings the company produces now and is expected to produce in the future, as well as investor demand for the shares of the company.

For example, let's say you and I form a company together and decide that there will be only two shareholders (owners) with only one share each. If our company has only one asset of $10,000 and we have no liabilities (we don't owe any money), our shares should be worth $5,000 each ($10,000 ÷ 2 = $5,000). If the company were sold today, together we would have a net worth of $10,000 (assets = $10,000; liabilities = 0).

However, if it is projected that our company will make $100,000 this year, $200,000 next year, and so on, then the value goes up on a cash flow basis as we will have earnings. Investors would say that we have only $10,000 in net worth now, but they see this growing dramatically over the next five years. Therefore, they value us at $1 million—in this case, 10 times next year's projected earnings. This is very similar to how stocks are valued in the stock market.

Stocks are traded on organized stock exchanges like the New York Stock Exchange (NYSE) and through computerized markets, such as the National Association of Securities Dealers Automated Quotations (NASDAQ) system. Share prices move due to a variety of factors including assets, expected future earnings, and the supply of and demand for the shares of the company. Accurately determining the supply of and demand for a company's stock is very important to finding good investments. This is what creates momentum, which can be either positive or negative for the price of the stock.

For example, scores of analysts from brokerage firms follow certain industries and companies. They have their own methods for determining the value of a company and its price per share. They typically issue earnings estimates and reports to advise their clients. Analyst, or Wall Street, expectation will drive the value of the shares before the actual earnings report is issued. If more investors feel the company will beat analyst predictions, then the price of the shares will be bid up as there will be more buyers than sellers. If the majority of investors feels that the company's earnings will disappoint "the street," then the price will decline (also referred to as "offered down"). As stated earlier, the stock market is similar to an auction. If there are more bidders (buyers), prices will rise. This is referred to as "bidding up." If there are more people offering (sellers), prices will fall.

For example, let's say Citigroup (C) is expected by analysts to report earnings of $1 per share. If news starts to leak out that the earnings will be $1.25 per share, the share price will jump up in anticipation of the better-than-expected earnings. Then if Citigroup reports only $.75 per share, the stock price will theoretically fall dramatically, as the actual earnings do not meet initial expectations and are well below the revised expected earnings. The investors who bought the stock in anticipation of the better-than-expected earnings will sell it at any price to get out. This happens quite often in the market and causes sharp declines in the value of companies. It is not uncommon to see shares decline in price 25 to 50 percent in one day. Conversely, it is also common to see shares rise in value in a similar fashion.

Dividends

American companies may periodically declare cash and/or dividends on a quarterly or yearly basis. Dividends are provided to the shareholders— otherwise referred to as stockholders—as an income stream that they can rely on. This is quite similar to a bank paying interest on certificates of deposit (CDs) or savings accounts. There are a number of companies that boast that they have never missed a dividend or have always increased dividends.

Companies that distribute their income as dividends are usually in mature industries. You typically will not find fast-growing companies distributing dividends, as they may need the capital for future expansion and may feel they can reinvest the funds at a higher rate of return than the stockholders. As a stock trader, you need to know how this process affects your long or short investment. Basically, a company's board of directors will decide whether to declare a dividend, which is paid out and distributed to shareholders on a date set by the company. Also, some companies will declare a special dividend from time to time. This dividend is paid out and distributed to shareholders on a date set by the company, referred to as a payable date.

In order to qualify for a dividend, you must be a shareholder on record as of the record date (the date you are "recorded" as the owner of the shares) of the dividend. You can also sell the stock as soon as the next day after the payable date and still receive the dividend.

A beginner may think this is a profitable way to buy and sell shares: Buy the shares a few days before the record date and sell them on the day after the payable date. However, before you run out and open a stock brokerage account in order to implement this tactic, you may want to consider that, in most cases, the stock prices will be trading lower on the day that the dividend is payable. That's because on the dividend payable date (i.e., the date on which you get paid the dividend), the stock should trade at its regular price minus the dividend.

Let's consider an example. If IBM (IBM) declared a $1 per share dividend payable on June 30, and closed at $90 on June 29, then on June 30, IBM would open at $89. As a stock trader, it is important to be aware of dividends and how they can affect a stock. You can find stocks declaring dividends by looking in the newspaper financial pages or at various financial web sites.

Market Capitalization

Market capitalization is defined as the total dollar value of a stock's out-standing shares and is computed by multiplying the number of outstanding shares by the current market price. Thus, market capitalization is a measure of corporate size. With approximately 8,500 stocks available to trade on U.S. stock exchanges, many traders judge a company by its size, which can be a determinant in price and risk. In fact, there are four unofficial size classifications for U.S. stocks: blue chips, mid-caps, small caps, and micro-caps.

1. *Blue-chip stocks*. Blue chip is a term derived from poker, where blue chips in a card game hold the most value. Hence, blue-chip stocks are those stocks that have the most market capitalization in the marketplace (more than $5 billion). Typically they enjoy solid value and good security, with a record of continuous dividend payments and other desirable investment attributes.

2. *Mid-cap stocks*. Mid-caps usually have a bigger growth potential than blue-chip stocks but they are not as heavily capitalized ($500 million to $5 billion).

3. *Small-cap stocks*. Small caps can be potentially difficult to trade because they do not have the benefit of high liquidity (valued at $150 million to $500 million). However, these stocks, although quite risky, are usually relatively inexpensive and big gains are possible.

4. *Micro-cap stocks*. Micro-caps, also known as penny stocks, are stocks priced at less than $2 per share with a market capitalization of less than $150 million.

Some traders like to trade riskier stocks because they have the potential for big price moves; others prefer the longer-term stability of blue-chip stocks. In general, deciding which stocks to trade depends on your time availability, stress threshold, and account size.

Common versus Preferred Stock

Officially, there are two kinds of stocks: common and preferred. A company initially sells common stock to investors who intend to make money by purchasing the shares at a lower price and selling them at a higher price. This profit is referred to as capital gains. However, if the company falters, the price of the stock may plummet and shareholders may end up holding stock that is practically worthless. Common stockholders also have the opportunity to earn quarterly dividend payments as the company makes profits. For example, if a company announces a $1 dividend on each share and you own 1,000 shares, you can collect a healthy dividend of $1,000.

In contrast, preferred stockholders receive guaranteed dividends prior to common stockholders, but the amount never changes even if the company triples its earnings. Also, the price of preferred stock increases at a slower rate than that of common stock. However, if the company loses money, preferred stockholders have a better chance of receiving some of their investment back. All in all, common stocks are riskier than preferred stocks, but offer bigger rewards if the company does well. (See Table 2.1 for a comparison.)

Stock Classifications

Another way to classify a stock is by the nature of its objectives (see Table 2.2). The correct classification often is derived by looking at what a stock does with its profits. For example, if a company reinvests its profits to promote further growth, then it is known as a *growth* stock. A growth stock is a company whose earnings and/or revenues are expected to grow more rapidly than the average earnings of the overall stock market. Generally, growth stocks are extremely well managed companies in expanding industries that consistently show strong earnings. Their objective is to continue delivering the performance their investors expect by developing new products and services and bringing them to market in a timely fashion.

If a stock regularly pays dividends to its shareholders, then it is regarded as an *income* stock. Usually only large, fully established companies can afford to pay dividends to their shareholders. Although income stocks are fundamentally sound companies, they are often considered conservative investments. Growth stocks are more risky than income stocks but have a greater potential for big price moves. Don't be lured into an income stock simply because it pays a high dividend. During the late 1990s, many utility companies paid high dividends. Then problems surfaced in the industry and stocks in the utility sector became extremely volatile. Many suffered large percentage drops in their share prices. Therefore, even though these companies paid hefty dividends, many shareholders suffered losses due to the drop in the stock price.

Additionally, there has been a surge in the popularity of socially responsible or "green" stocks. Socially conscious investing entails investing in companies (or green mutual funds) that are socially and environmentally responsible and follow ethical business practices. Green investors seek to use the power of their money to foster social, environmental, and economic changes that will improve conditions on the earth.

TABLE 2.1 Comparison of Common and Preferred Stock

Common Shares	Preferred Shares

• Common shares offer larger potential rewards than preferred shares; shareholders share the rise in stock price more quickly than preferred shares.
• If a common stock declines in price, shareholders share these losses and the value of their shares may drop dramatically.
• Although shareholders of common stock are eligible to receive dividends, companies are not obligated to distribute a portion of the profits back to the shareholders (i.e., they do not offer investors guaranteed performance results).
	• Preferred shares are a hybrid between bonds and common stock. Due to their hybrid nature, the price of preferred shares does not act like the firm's bonds or the common stock. The more bondlike a preferred stock is, the more it will mirror the bond pricing; the more like common stock it is, the more closely it follows the price changes of the common stock.
	• The particular features of any one preferred stock are spelled out in the legalese of the issuance, as determined by management and approved by the common stockholders.
	• Features of preferred shares may or may not include such criteria as:
	  • Guaranteed dividends at regular intervals—cumulative or noncumulative.
	  • Limited dividend amount regardless of company's profits.
	  • Voting inferiority (or superiority) to common stock depending on the specific agreement.
	  • Possible convertibility into common stock or bonds.

Stock Sectors

Stock market activity is reported each day by certain indexes, which reflect the general health of the economy. Everyone has seen the Dow Jones Industrial Average (DJIA) mentioned on the nightly news as a key indicator of the day's trading performance. But what is the DJIA and how did it get started? In 1884, Charles Dow surveyed the average closing prices of nine railroad stocks and two manufacturing companies, which, in his opinion, represented the general trends in the national economy. He printed the results in his newspaper, a forerunner of today's *Wall Street Journal*. Over the next 12 years, he honed that list until he finally settled

TABLE 2.2 Types of Stocks

Stock Type	Characteristic	Examples
Growth stocks— aggressive	• Rarely pay out dividends to their shareholders because they prefer to reinvest their profits into future growth. • Two kinds of growth stocks: established growth and emerging growth. Established growth stocks have seen several years of successful expansion. In contrast, emerging growth stocks are the up-and-comers that are currently experiencing dramatic expansion, yet have limited previous growth experience. Both offer investors the potential to make dramatic gains or suffer heavy losses depending on market performance.	Cisco (CSCO) Dell Inc. (DELL) Home Depot (HD) Charles Schwab (SCH)
Income stocks— conservative	• Solid companies that offer slow, but steady growth. • Regularly pay out dividends to their shareholders. • Do not offer dramatic returns.	ExxonMobil (XOM) 3M (MMM) Bank of America (BAC) Duke Energy (DUK)
Cyclical stocks	• Fluctuate in relation to the economy, seasons, or events. • Provide an excellent gauge for the strength of the economy.	PPG Industries (PPG) Weyerhaeuser (WY) Alcoa (AA)
Turnaround stocks— aggressive	• Stocks that have suffered severe losses that are due for a turnaround—investors have to know when a stock has reached rock bottom and just what can make it turn around. • Offer explosive growth opportunities. • No guarantees and high risk. • Warren Buffett's favorite stock picking method.	Blockbuster (BBI) LSI Logic (LSI) Rite Aid Corp. (RAD)
Green stocks— vary	• Environmentally friendly and socially conscious stocks. • Spawned the concepts of socially "conscious investing" and "corporate accountability." • If saving the rain forests is high on your priority list of things to do, green stock investing is definitely worth checking out at www.greenmoneyjournal.com.	Canon (CAJ) Timberland (TBL) Whole Foods Market (WFMI)

on 12 industrial stocks. In 1896, Charles Dow began to publish this list and the overall average every day.

Today's DJIA reflects the performance of 30 major companies representing key manufacturing, technology, energy, financial, and service industries worth approximately 25 percent of the total value of all stocks listed on the New York Stock Exchange. It is widely regarded as an accurate assessment of the daily trends in the American economy. However, many investors believe the DJIA is too narrow with only 30 stocks in the index. The Standard & Poor's 500 Index (S&P 500) is followed very widely these days as it represents a more diversified portfolio of 500 different companies. However, if you track the performance of the DJIA to the S&P 500 you will find that they are highly correlated (prices move very similarly).

While the Dow Jones Industrial Average and the S&P 500 track the performance of the stock market as a whole, some indexes are used to track sectors. In fact, there is a wide variety of stock sectors from which to choose. The following list is a general outline of the most popular ones.

Sector Index	Symbol
MS Consumer Products Index	$CMR
Dow Jones Utility Average	$DUX
PHLX Bank Sector Index	$BKX
DJ Transportation Average	$DTX
AMEX Oil Index	$XOI
PHLX Defense Sector Index	$DFX
MS Cyclical Index	$CYC
AMEX Natural Gas Index	$XNG
AMEX Pharmaceutical Index	$DRG
MS Commodity-Related Index	$CRX
MS Retail Store Index	$MVR
PHLX Box-Maker Index	$BMX
AMEX Broker/Dealer Index	$XBD
PHLX Oil Service Index	$OSX
AMEX Networking Index	$NWX
PHLX Street.com Internet Index	$DOT
AMEX Biotechnology Index	$BTK
MS Oil Service Index	$MGO
GSTI Computer Software Index	$GSO
GSTI Computer Hardware Index	$GHA
CBOE Internet Index	$INX
PHLX Semiconductor Index	$SOX
PHLX Gold Mining Index	$XAU
AMEX Airline Index	$XAL
AMEX Disk Drive Index	$DDX

Instead of using indexes, some traders watch the performance of individual stocks to gauge trends in an industry or sector. Some sectors and gauges follow. For example, Intel (INTC) is often considered a gauge for the semiconductor group.

- **Technology:**

   Computers (e.g., Dell, Hewlett-Packard).

   Internet-related (e.g., Amazon.com, Yahoo!).

   Software-related (e.g., Microsoft, Adobe).

   Semiconductors (e.g. Intel, Applied Materials).

- **Health-related:**

   Pharmaceuticals (e.g., Merck, Pfizer).

   Biotech (e.g., Amgen, Biogen).

- **Defense industry** (e.g., Boeing, Lockheed Martin).

- **Retailers:**

   Clothing (e.g., Gap, Wal-Mart).

   Sportswear (e.g., Nike, Reebok).

   Automakers (e.g., General Motors, Ford).

- **Transportation** (e.g., Delta Air Lines, Continental).

- **Financial services** (e.g., Citigroup, J. P. Morgan).

This list is not meant to be an exhaustive list; rather, it is meant to reflect the diverse range of fields and individual stocks within each sector. This may very well be why many prospective investors shy away from making their own investment decisions. The plethora of opportunities can be overwhelming to many people.

The IPO System

The equities market generates wealth in several different ways. As private companies expand, they come to a point where they need more capital to finance further growth. Many times the solution to this problem is to offer stock in the company to the public through an initial public offering (IPO).

To do this the company hires the services of a brokerage firm to underwrite its stock, which means the brokerage will buy all the shares the company is offering for sale. The brokerage then charges a commission for managing the IPO and generates cash by selling the shares to investors. The commission is usually about 10 percent of the total value of all shares.

There is a misconception among many people who believe a company makes money every time a share of its stock is traded after its IPO, but that simply is not true. Companies get the IPO money, and that is it. From that point on, the money derived from the buying and selling of a company's stock is passed back and forth between the actual buyers and sellers.

The IPO is an avenue provided by the stock market for a company to fund expansion. If the expansion succeeds and the company prospers, it will hire more people and buy more raw materials from other companies. This process contributes to the expansion of the economy as a whole, generating wealth that would not have existed without the stock market.

Investors who profit from a successful IPO also create wealth for the overall economy. If they buy low and sell high, they have made a profit that improves their standard of living and their ability to buy goods and services. They also use stock profits to start small businesses, reinvest in the stock market, or add to their savings. This process of putting stock profits back into the economy helps the economy grow over the long term and is a vital component of economic prosperity.

If a company increases its profits year after year, its stock price will rise. The increase in price is the result of the law of supply and demand. When the company went public it issued a limited number of shares, called a float or the number of shares outstanding. As the demand for these shares increases, the supply decreases. In this situation, the price will rise.

Companies definitely benefit when their stocks are in great demand. A company's market capitalization, the value of all shares of its stock, will go up. Market capitalization is computed by multiplying the current stock price by the number of outstanding shares. The equities market is a powerful mechanism of the capitalist system. It has an enormous influence on the business cycle, because it creates wealth and stimulates investment in the future.

This is also why it should be no surprise that the stock market is so sensitive to economic news such as an interest rate change. The economy is a fluid system, one that evolves through predictable ups and downs. Investors will buy stocks when it appears that companies will be able to use the capitalist system to improve their earnings. They will sell stocks when it seems that economic woes are on the horizon.

This buying and selling is prompted by economic news that provides the clues to the direction the economy is taking. All that said, the IPO market is one of capitalism's greatest gifts because it provides a mechanism for companies to expand and create wealth in the future.

FUTURES

To the novice, futures contracts can be quite confusing; yet they offer a unique opportunity to make money in today's volatile markets. Futures markets consist of a variety of commodities (e.g., gold, oil, soybeans, etc.); financial trading instruments (e.g., bonds, currencies); indexes (e.g, S&P 500, Nasdaq 100); and most recently, single stock futures (Microsoft, Intel, Citigroup). A futures contract is the agreement to buy or sell a uniform quantity and quality of physical or financial commodities at a designated time in the future at a specific price. The contracts themselves are traded on the futures market.

Futures markets gave rise to two distinct types of traders: hedgers and speculators. Hedgers consist primarily of farmers and manufacturers. Futures contracts were initially used by farmers and manufacturers to protect themselves or lock in prices for a certain crop or product cycle. Hence, hedgers are primarily interested in actually selling or receiving the commodities themselves. Keep in mind that futures prices are directly driven by consumer supply and demand, which is primarily dependent on events and seasonal factors.

For example, if you are a farmer who grows wheat, soybeans, and corn, you can sell your products even though they have not yet been farmed. If the price of corn is at a level that you like, you can sell a corresponding number of futures contracts against your expected production. An oil company can do the same thing, locking in the price of oil at a level to guarantee the price it will receive. For instance, British Petroleum (BP) may sell crude oil futures one year away to lock in that specific price. To make a profit, a company has to predetermine the price of its production and plan accordingly.

The other players are the speculators. These traders play the futures markets to make a profit. Speculators do not expect to take delivery of a product or sell futures to lock in a crop price. Most contracts are now traded on a speculative basis. In other words, most people are in the futures market to try to make money on their best judgment as to the future price movement of the futures contract. For example, if you believe corn prices will rise in the next three months, you would buy—go long—the corn futures three months out. If you believe corn prices will fall during this same period, you will sell—go short—the corn futures contract three months out.

Hedgers and speculators have a symbiotic relationship. They need one another for futures trading to work. Hedgers try to avoid risk while speculators thrive on it. Together they keep the markets active enough for everyone to get a piece of the action. Unlike stocks, where profits depend on company growth, futures markets are a zero-sum game—for each buyer there is a seller and vice versa.

Physical commodities are raw materials, which are traded on futures exchanges; examples include grains, meats, metals, and energies. Financial commodities include debt instruments (such as bonds), currencies, single stock futures, and indexes. In these markets, money is the actual commodity being traded, and price depends on a variety of factors including interest rates and the value of the U.S. dollar.

Physical Commodities

A wide variety of commodities can be profitably traded. Some are seasonal in nature, such as grains, food and fiber, livestock, metals, and energies. Some fluctuate due to seasonal changes in climate. Others may change due to world events, such as an Organization of Petroleum Exporting Countries (OPEC) meeting. Each market is unique. Physical commodity markets include:

- Grains (e.g., soybeans, wheat, corn).
- Food and fiber (e.g., coffee, cocoa, sugar, orange juice, cotton).
- Livestock (e.g., feeder cattle, live cattle, lean hogs, pork bellies).
- Metals (e.g., copper, gold, silver).
- Energies (e.g., crude oil, natural gas, heating oil, unleaded gas).

Financial Commodities

Commodity trading goes beyond grains, energy, cattle, and pork bellies and includes a variety of more complex financial instruments that trade actively across the globe. These so-called financial commodities include debt instruments like government bonds as well as Eurodollars and foreign currency exchange. Entire books can be written about any of these investments. However, a basic understanding of the most important financial commodities can also help traders make sense of the daily happenings in the financial markets at home and abroad.

Debt Instruments   Just as there are instruments to trade stocks, either individually or collectively as an index, there are numerous instruments available to trade interest rates. Welcome to the world of debt instruments! The first response I usually get when I talk about trading interest rates is, "Who would want to trade interest rates?" The simple answer is banks and other lending institutions that have loans outstanding, as well as investors who have a great deal of exposure in interest rate investments.

Originally, the futures markets were primarily used to hedge—offset or mitigate—risk. Today, financial commodities, including all the interest rate instruments, are growing at a faster rate than traditional commodities. The interest rate markets have participants from all over the world trading interest rates for hedging purposes and speculation. If you have interest rate risk or you just want to speculate on the direction of interest rates, there are plenty of markets and opportunities awaiting you. These markets are also traded extensively in off-exchange markets such as those created by banks and securities trading firms, also referred to as the over-the-counter (OTC) market.

Bonds are one of the most popular forms of financial instruments. A bond is a debt obligation issued by a government or corporation that promises to pay its bondholders periodic interest at a fixed rate and to repay the principal of the loan at maturity at a specified future date. Bonds are usually issued with a value of $1,000 to $100,000, representing the principal or amount of money borrowed. Other popular financial instruments include:

- *Treasury bill (T-bill)*. These short-term government securities have maturities of no more than one year. Treasury bills are issued through a competitive bidding process at a discount from par; there is no fixed interest rate.
- *Treasury bond (T-bond)*. This marketable, fixed-interest U.S. government debt security has a maturity of more than 10 years. The most often quoted T-bond is the 10-year bond.
- *Treasury note (T-note)*. This is a marketable, fixed-interest U.S. government debt security with a maturity of between 1 and 10 years.
- *Eurodollars*. Eurodollars are dollars deposited in foreign banks. The futures contract reflects the rates offered between London branches of top U.S. banks and foreign banks.

Currency Markets   The currency markets are another very large market. Most countries have their own currencies. These currencies go up or down relative to each other based on a number of factors such as economic growth (present and future), interest rates, and supply and demand. Most major currencies are quoted against the U.S. dollar. Therefore, there will typically be an inverse relationship between the U.S. dollar and other currencies. The major currency futures traded at the Chicago Mercantile Exchange include the following:

- Euro (ECU or European currency unit).
- Swiss franc.
- British pound.

- Japanese yen.
- Canadian dollar.

If the U.S. dollar goes up, then the Japanese yen will drop along with other foreign currencies. Keep in mind that the Canadian and U.S. dollars move similarly due to their physical proximity and the closeness of their economies. Each of these currencies will then have a rate relative to each of the others. This cross-reference is referred to as the cross rate. The yen/pound, euro/dollar, and so on will have their own rates at which they may be traded.

Why are currencies traded? As you are probably aware, many products are sold across borders. A company may sell $100 million worth of computer equipment in Japan, and will likely be paid in yen. If the company prefers to be paid in U.S. dollars, it can go into the futures market or cash market—traded from bank to bank—to change its yen purchase. By selling yen futures contracts, the company can lock in its profits in U.S. dollars. Speculators are also active in the currency markets, buying and selling based on their predictions for the changes in cross rates. Trillions (yes, trillions) of dollars are traded each day in the currency markets, 24 hours a day.

Single Stock Futures The introduction of single stock futures (SSFs) in the United States on November 8, 2002, was one of the most anticipated events in today's financial world. Single stock futures offer widespread applications for both professionals and retail users. They were previously traded on the London Financial Futures and Options Exchange (which is now part of Euronext.liffe—the international derivatives business of Euronext), and the U.S. market continues to hold high promise for these unique instruments.

Single stock futures are futures contracts that are based on single stocks. As previously stated, a future is a contract to either buy or sell an underlying instrument at a predetermined price at a set date in the future. Unlike an option, the holder of the future has the obligation (as opposed to the right) to take delivery at expiration. One single stock futures contract represents 100 shares of stock, which will convert into stock if held to expiration. Like other futures contracts, SSFs have expiration months of March, June, September, and December. Speculators buy stock futures when they expect the share price to move higher, and sell futures when they want to profit from a move lower in the stock price. Hedgers can also use single stock futures to protect stock positions.

Currently, there are approximately 115 single stock futures available to trade, including IBM, Microsoft, Citigroup, and Johnson & Johnson. Trading is done through an electronic exchange called OneChicago, which is a joint venture between the Chicago Board Options Exchange, the Chicago Mercantile Exchange, and the Chicago Board of Trade. In addition, trades clear through the Options Clearing Corporation (OCC).

There are several things to consider when looking at single stock futures as opposed to the outright stock. First, while a future could be thought of as a price discovery tool for the stock, generally the stock and future will not trade at the same price. The price of an SSF is determined according to the following formula:

SSF = Stock price × (1 + time to expiration × interest rate) – dividends

Since SSFs have quarterly expirations, time to expiration is based on the remaining time until the end of the quarter. Normally the single stock future will trade above the stock; this is partially due to leverage of the future. Unlike stocks, SSFs require the buyer to put up margin of only a small portion of the underlying stock value in order to purchase, right now proposed to be about 20 percent of the cash value of the underlying stock. We should recognize here that margin in futures does not represent borrowed money, as in stocks. Futures margin is the cash that the investor must put up in order to hold a position. As the futures are marked to market at the end of the day, this amount may fluctuate. The only time the stock would trade over the future would be if there were a large dividend to be paid—investors would likely hold the stock to collect the dividend. Futures holders do not collect dividends paid by the underlying stock.

As options traders, we welcome the arrival of SSFs. Not only are they easier to execute than stock, but they are also less costly. For traders who trade stock, this added leverage will increase returns, whether the stock moves higher or lower in price. Prudent risk management and carefully thought out trading strategies, as always, will carry the day.

Index Markets   As noted earlier, an index is a tool used to measure and report value changes in a specific group of stocks or commodities. There is a variety of indexes tailored to reflect the performances of many different markets or sectors. Here are some of the most popular market indexes (also known as averages or market averages):

- *Dow Jones Industrial Average ($INDU).* The most widely followed index, the DJIA represents 30 blue-chip stocks and is used as an overall indicator of market performance.
- *Standard & Poor's 500 Index ($SPX).* A benchmark of U.S. common stock performance, this index includes 500 of the largest U.S. stocks—400 industrial companies, 40 utilities, 40 financial corporations, and 20 transportation companies.

- *NYSE Composite Index.* This index is composed of all the stocks traded on the New York Stock Exchange.
- *Nasdaq Composite Index ($COMPQ).* This index tracks the performances of all stocks traded on the Nasdaq Stock Market. The National Association of Securities Dealers Automated Quotations (NASDAQ) devised a computerized system that provides brokers and dealers with price quotations for securities traded over-the-counter as well as for many New York Stock Exchange–listed securities.
- *Nasdaq 100 Index ($NDX).* The top 100 nonfinancial stocks trading on the Nasdaq Stock Market.
- *S&P 100 Index ($OEX).* This index represents 100 of the largest U.S. stocks with listed options.
- *Wilshire 5000.* This market value–weighted index monitors 7,000 U.S.-based equities traded on the New York Stock Exchange, the American Stock Exchange, and the Nasdaq Stock Market, and is a popular indicator of the broad trend in stock prices.
- *Commodity Research Bureau Futures Price Index (CRB Futures).* This index tracks the commodity markets and is closely monitored as an indicator of economic inflation.
- *DAX.* Similar to the U.S. Dow Jones Industrial Average, this index tracks the performance of the top 30 German stocks. This is not a market capitalization–weighted index; each company has an equal weighting.
- *Financial Times Stock Exchange (FTSE) Index.* This index is composed of the top 100 companies (by market capitalization) in Great Britain.
- *Euro Stoxx 50.* This index tracks the top 50 stocks from the European Economic Community.
- *Nikkei 225.* This benchmark index is composed of 225 Japanese companies and is a popular indicator of the broad trend in stock prices.

As you can see from the wide variety of indexes listed, you can trade in virtually any type of market that interests you. Indexes like the ones listed can help to track and monitor changes not just in the U.S. market, but around the globe.

However, it is important to specialize in just one index to begin with and then continue learning various risk management techniques. There is a vast amount of information that everyone needs to sort out, and that's what makes investing so interesting. It is exciting to find the needle in the haystack—you just need to know where to begin looking and what to look for. Buying (going long) and selling (going short) are the simplest forms of trading in futures markets. They are also the most popular strategies because many individuals are not familiar with the more creative aspects of trading. However, by learning to combine stocks with options, you can create trades that limit risk and maximize your potential profits.

Exchange-Traded Funds   Another way to play the index market is through a relatively new investment vehicle, exchange-traded funds (ETFs). Despite their relative newness, ETFs have become among the most popular trading tools in the marketplace today. For example, you have probably heard of the Nasdaq 100 QQQ Index (QQQ). Not only is it the most actively traded exchange-traded fund today, it has one of the busiest options contracts. In addition, there are a host of different ETFs available to the option strategist today. Consequently, understanding what these investment vehicles are and how they trade can open up an enormous number of trading opportunities.

The American Stock Exchange pioneered the concept of ETFs when the exchange launched the S&P Depositary Receipts (SPY), or Spiders, in 1993. In a nutshell, ETFs trade like stocks, but represent specific indexes. Therefore, exchange-traded funds offer investors a way to buy and sell shares that represent entire baskets of stocks. In the case of Spiders, the basket of stocks represents the companies included within the Standard & Poor's 500 Index. When buying SPY shares, investors are really buying the entire S&P 500 Index. Dow Jones Diamonds (DIA), in turn, track the performance of the Dow Jones Industrial Average ($INDU) and started trading in 1998. The QQQ, also known as the Qs, is today's most popular exchange-traded fund and made its debut in March 1999. It tracks the performance of the Nasdaq 100 ($NDX). While QQQ options have been actively traded for several years, options on DIA made their debut earlier this year and there are no options yet available on the SPY.

The American Stock Exchange, however, has not been the sole player in the ETF market. Barclay's Global Investors introduced a series of ETFs in June 1996 called WEBs (now known as iShares). To date, the company has brought forth more than 60 of these so-called iShares, which trade on the American Stock Exchange. Holding Company Depositary Receipts (HOLDRS) are another type of exchange-traded fund. HOLDRS also trade on the American Stock Exchange and can be bought and sold in round lots of 100 shares. In addition, HOLDRS are available on a variety of different industry groups such oil service, biotechnology, semiconductors, and so on. Not all iShares and HOLDRS have options linked to their performance, however. In order to find those that do, option traders can visit the Chicago Board Options Exchange (www.cboe.com) and the American Stock Exchange (www.amex.com), where complete product specifications are available for HOLDRS and iShares.

The Nasdaq Stock Market also has plans to list its own family of exchange-traded funds. The exchange's list of ETFs will include the first-ever fund based on the performance of the widely watched Nasdaq Composite Index ($COMPQ). In addition, the family of exchange-traded funds is expected to include companies that trade on the Nasdaq from specific industries such as telecommunications, financial services, biotechnology, and so on. Furthermore, these investment vehicles will trade on the Nasdaq Stock Market. The launch of the new Nasdaq ETFs is expected to occur later this year.

While there are a number of different ETFs available for trading today, there is an important distinction between these investment vehicles and the more common cash-based index products. In fact, indexes and index options date back well before the development of exchange-traded funds. Charles Dow created the first index in 1884. It was known as the Dow Jones Railroad Average (today's Dow Jones Transportation Average [$TRAN]). Index options did not come into existence until almost a century later. To be specific, the Chicago Board Options Exchange (CBOE) was the first to list options on the S&P 100 Index ($OEX) in 1983. Since that time, options have been launched on a number of other indexes. Some, like the OEX, reflect the performance of the entire market. For instance, traders can buy and sell options on the S&P 500 Index ($SPX) and the Dow Jones Industrial Average ($DJX). These, of course, are familiar measures of the U.S. stock market. Other indexes are designed to gauge the performance of specific sectors. These include the PHLX Semiconductor Index ($SOX), the AMEX Biotechnology Index ($BTK), and the Morgan Stanley Oil Service Index ($MGO). There are a large number of other cash-based indexes and their complete specifications can be found on the web sites of the Chicago Board Options Exchange, the American Stock Exchange, or the Philadelphia Stock Exchange (www.phlx.com).

There is an important difference between ETFs like the Nasdaq 100 QQQ and cash-based indexes. Specifically, exchange-traded funds are physical delivery options (i.e., settle for shares), but index options involve cash settlement. For instance, a call writer (seller) who is faced with assignment on his or her Diamonds must deliver DIA shares. However, a call writer of DJX options must provide cash payment (equal to the difference between the exercise settlement value and the strike price of the index option). In addition, most index options settle European-style and, therefore, exercise can only take place at expiration. By contrast, ETFs settle American-style, which means that option writers can face assignment at any time prior to expiration.

OPTIONS

Options are probably the most versatile trading instrument ever invented. They provide a high-leverage approach to trading that can significantly limit the overall risk of a trade, especially when combined with stock or futures. As a result, understanding how to develop profitable strategies using options can be extremely rewarding, both personally and financially. The key is to develop an appreciation about how these investment vehicles work, what risks are involved, and the vast reward potential that can be unleashed with well-conceived and time-tested trading strategies.

First, it is important to differentiate between futures and options. A futures contract is a legally binding agreement that gives the holder the right to actually buy (and take delivery of) or sell (be obligated to deliver) a commodity or financial instrument at a specific price. In contrast, purchasing an option is the right, *but not the obligation*, to buy or sell a financial instrument (stock, index, futures contract, etc.) at a specific price. The key here is that *buying* an option is not a legally binding contract. In contrast, *selling* (writing or shorting) an option obligates the seller to provide (or buy) the instrument at the agreed-upon price if asked to do so.

So, option buyers have rights and option sellers have obligations. Option buyers have the right, but not the obligation, to buy or sell a stock, index, or futures contract at a predetermined price before a predefined expiration date. In contrast, option sellers, sometimes called writers, have the obligation to buy or sell the underlying stock shares (or futures contract) if an assigned option buyer or holder exercises the option.

There are two types of options contracts: puts and calls. A put option is an options contract that gives the owner the right to sell (or put) the underlying asset at a specific price for a predetermined period of time. Call options, in contrast, give the option holder the right, but not the obligation, to buy a stock at a predetermined price for a specific period of time.

Importantly, for every option buyer there is a seller. Buyers and sellers do not deal with one another directly, but through their respective brokerage firms. If an investor sells a call and the new owner exercises

Two Types of Options

Puts: A bearish type of options contract that gives the buyer the right, but not the obligation, to sell, or put, a specific asset (stock, index, or futures contract) at a specific price for a predetermined period of time.

Calls: A bullish type of options contract that gives the buyer the right, but not the obligation, to buy, or call, a specific asset (stock, index, or futures contract) at a specific price for a predetermined period of time.

the call, the call seller has the obligation to deliver the financial instrument to the option holder at the call strike price. The call seller will get notice from the broker that he or she must provide the stock or futures contract to the option holder. This is known as assignment. Once assigned, the option writer is obligated to fulfill the terms of the options contract.

A put seller, in contrast, has the obligation to accept delivery of the financial instrument from the option holder. If the put seller is assigned, the brokerage firm will notify the put seller that he or she must buy the financial instrument at the predetermined price. In Chapter 3 we explain how to anticipate the assignment of a short option. For now, it is important to understand that a put owner has the right to exercise the options contract and, if so, the option seller will face assignment on the option. Therefore, if you decide to write an options contract, you must be willing to face the prospect of assignment—which, as we later see, can involve significant risks.

To see how options work, let's consider an example using a stock option. Say that you believe the price of IBM is going to rise over the next three months. But instead of buying 100 shares of IBM, you decide to buy a call option. The IBM call gives you the right, but not the obligation, to buy 100 IBM shares for a specific price until a specific point in time. For this right you pay a price: the option premium. Furthermore, you can exercise the right at any time until the option expires—that is, unless you close the position before the option expires. You can close an option position at any time through an offsetting transaction. For example, if you buy an IBM call options contract, you can close the position at any time by selling an identical IBM call options contract.

In another example, suppose you do not own any options and you agree to sell or write a call option on IBM. Why would you do this? Well, some traders sell options in order to collect the premium and earn income. However, if the stock rises dramatically, the trader may be asked to sell IBM shares to the option holder at the call strike price, which is well below the current market price.

Knowing Your Options

Exercise: If you own a put or call, you can implement your right to *exercise* an option.

Assignment: If you are an option seller, you face the possibility of *assignment*.

Options on stocks, indexes, futures, and exchange-traded funds are similar. However, each option will have a different underlying asset. It is important to understand the underlying asset, how its price changes, and how those changes impact the price of the option. Options are derivatives, which means their price changes are derived from the value of another asset (stock, futures contract, index, etc.). The asset is known as the underlying security.

In addition to understanding the underlying asset, traders must also understand the trading terms used to describe an options contract. For example, every option has a strike price—a price at which the stock or future can be bought or sold until the option's expiration date. Options are available in several strike prices depending on the current price of the underlying asset. As a result, the profitability of an option depends primarily on the rise or fall in the price of the underlying stock or futures contract (and its relation to the strike price of the option). An option's premium also depends on the time left until expiration, volatility, and other factors discussed later in this book.

Stock Options

Not all stocks have options available to be traded. Currently in the United States there are more than 4,000 stocks that have tradable options. This number grows daily. Each stock option represents 100 shares of a company. Therefore, if you buy one XYZ stock option, it represents 100 shares of XYZ stock. If XYZ shares are trading at $10 per share, then you are controlling $1,000 worth of stock with one option ($10 per share × 100 shares). And you may be controlling this $1,000 amount with only $250, depending on the price of the option's premium. This would give you leverage equal to four to one—not too shabby odds.

Futures Options

Most futures markets have tradable options, including gold, silver, oil, wheat, corn, soybeans, orange juice, Treasury bonds, and so on. However, unlike stocks, each contract represents a unique quantity. Options on futures have the futures contract as the underlying instrument. It is the futures contract that is to be delivered in the event an option is exercised. Each futures contract represents a standardized quantity of the commodity. As you begin to trade futures, you have to become familiar with the specifics of each futures market. (If you have any questions, you can always call your broker.) For example, a gold futures contract is equal to 100 ounces of gold. With gold trading at $410 per ounce, the futures contract is worth $41,000: (100 ounces × $410 per ounce). Each futures

Option Characteristics

1. Options give you the right to buy or sell an underlying instrument at a specific price.
2. If you buy an option, you are not obligated to buy the underlying instrument; you simply have the right to exercise the option.
3. If you sell a call option, you are obligated to deliver the underlying asset at the price at which the call option was sold if the buyer exercises his or her right to take delivery. If you sell a put you must buy the underlying if exercised.
4. Options are good for a specified period of time after which they expire and the holder loses the right to buy or sell the underlying instrument at the specified price.
5. Options when bought are purchased at a debit to the buyer. That is, the money is debited from the brokerage account.
6. Options when sold are sold at a credit to the seller. Money is added to the brokerage account.
7. Options are available in several strike prices at or near the price of the underlying instrument.
8. The cost of an option is referred to as the option premium. The price reflects a variety of factors including the option's volatility, time left until expiration, and the price of the underlying asset.
9. There are two kinds of options: calls and puts. Calls give you the right to buy the underlying asset and puts give you the right to sell the underlying asset.
10. All the put or call options with the same underlying security are called a class of options. For example, all the calls for IBM constitute an option class.
11. All put and call options that are in one class and have the same strike price and expiration are called an option series.
12. Options are available on a variety of different underlying assets including stocks, futures, and indexes.

contract has its own unique specifications, and that can be quite confusing to a novice futures trader.

Options on Indexes and Exchange-Traded Funds

An index option is an option that represents a specific index—a group of items that collectively make up the index. We have already discussed the index markets and exchange-traded funds. Options on indexes and ETFs fluctuate with market conditions. Broad-based indexes cover a wide range of industries and companies. Narrow-based indexes cover stocks in one industry or economic sector.

Index options allow investors to trade in a specific industry group or market without having to buy all the stocks individually. The index is calculated as the average change of the stock price of each stock in the index. Each index has a specific mathematical calculation to determine the price change, up or down. An index or ETF option is an option that is tied directly to the change in the value of the index or exchange-traded fund.

Index options make up a very large segment of the options that are traded. Why are so many options traded on indexes? The explosive growth in index trading has occurred in recent years due to the increase in both the number of indexes and the number of traders who have become familiar with index trading. The philosophy of an index is that a group of stocks—a portfolio—will diversify the risk of owning just one stock. Hence, an index of stocks will better replicate what is happening in an industry or the market as a whole. This allows an investor or trader to participate in the movement of a specific industry, both to the upside and to the downside.

It appears that index and ETF options will continue to proliferate and trading volume will increase in many of the instruments. A word of caution: A number of these instruments do not have much liquidity. However, used wisely, index options can be an important instrument in your trading arsenal. Also, it is important to understand the difference between the way ETF options and index options settle. Namely, exchange-traded funds, which can be bought and sold like stocks, settle for shares. Cash indexes cannot be bought or sold. They settle for cash.

Liquidity

Liquidity is the ease with which a financial instrument can be traded. It can be defined as the volume of trading activity that enables a trader to buy or sell a security or derivative and receive fair value for it. A high volume of people trading a market is needed to make it rewarding. Liquidity provides the opportunity to move in and out of positions without difficulty. For example, at-the-money options often have excellent liquidity because they have a better chance of being profitable than out-of-the-money options. Therefore, they are easier to trade and many traders focus solely on the at-the-money contract.

When I first started trading, I visited the exchanges. A friend who was a floor trader walked me from one pit to another. In one pit, there were two guys sitting around reading the newspaper. Was there a lot of opportunity there? I didn't think so. I figured when an order hits that pit, everyone probably starts laughing at the poor sucker who placed it. Then I checked out the bond pit. There were 500 people fighting for an order. I quickly recognized that the bond market had high liquidity and plenty of opportunity. I went to the natural gas pit at the New York Mercantile Exchange. It was a madhouse. There were 200 people in a pit 10 feet wide (prior to moving to their new state-of-the-art building), yelling and screaming. I couldn't understand a thing they were saying, but once again I recognized high liquidity. To this day, I look for pits where there are plenty of people playing the game because plenty of players equals opportunity.

How can you avoid illiquid markets? Well, since you probably don't have the ability to actually visit an exchange, you can still check out the liquidity of a market by reviewing the market's volume to see how many shares or contracts have been traded. Both *The Wall Street Journal* and *Investor's Business Daily* report volume changes. It is vital for a trader to ascertain whether trading volume is high or low, increasing or decreasing. It's hard to quantify just how much volume is enough to qualify a market as one with liquidity. However, as a rule of thumb, I prefer to look for stocks that are trading at least 300,000 shares every day. Futures markets vary widely, and it is best to monitor activity daily and pick a market that trades many more contracts than you trade. Since there are no absolutes, there are situations when this rule can be tossed out the window in exchange for common sense. But until you have enough experience, this may be a good rule of thumb to follow. Bottom line, a plentiful number of buyers and sellers and an elevated volume of trading activity provide high liquidity, which gives traders the opportunity to move in and out of a market with ease. Illiquid markets can make the process much more difficult and more costly.

Volatility

Profitable markets are those markets that provide opportunity for making good returns on investments. Obviously, some markets are more trader-friendly than others. Opportunity in a market is contingent on a number of factors. Volatility is one of the most important and misunderstood of these factors. It measures the amount by which an underlying asset is expected to fluctuate in a given period of time. In more simple terms, volatility can be thought of as the speed of the change in the market.

There are two basic kinds of volatility: implied and historical. Historical volatility, often referred to as actual or statistical volatility, is computed using *past stock prices*. It can be calculated by using the standard deviation of a stock's price changes from close-to-close of trading going back a given number of days (10, 20, 90, etc.). High or low historical volatility also gives traders a clue as to the type of strategy that can best be implemented to optimize profits in a specific market. That is, strategies that work well in volatile markets will not generate big profits in a low-volatility environment. A variety of indicators, such as Bollinger bands, can be used to create historical volatility computations that are graphed on a chart.

Implied volatility (IV) is another type of volatility. It is calculated by using the actual market price of an option and an *option pricing model* (Black-Scholes for stocks and indexes; Black for futures). If the premium of an option increases without a corresponding change in the price of the underlying asset, the option's implied volatility will have increased also. Overpricing and undervaluing an option's premium can be caused by an inaccurate perception of the future movement in the price of an asset. For example, if implied volatility rises significantly for no reason (and there is no increase in historical volatility), the option may be overpriced. Traders can take advantage of changes in implied volatility by applying specific option strategies.

Note: Since volatility is such a complex issue, my partner, Tom Gentile, and I wrote an entire book on the subject entitled *The Volatility Course* (John Wiley & Sons, 2002). If you are going to trade options, you owe it to yourself to develop a strong understanding of volatility.

Options-Trading Discipline

Proper money management and patience in options trading are the cornerstones to success. The key to this winning combination is discipline. Now, discipline is not something that we apply only during the hours of trading, opening it up like bottled water at the opening bell and storing it away at the closing. Discipline is a way of life, a method of thinking. It is, most of all, an approach. If you have a consistent and methodical system, discipline leads to profits in trading. On the one hand, it means taking a quick, predefined loss because it is often better to exit a losing position rather than letting the losses pile up. On the other hand, discipline is holding your options position if you are winning, and not adjusting an options position when it is working in your favor.

It also entails doing a significant amount of preparatory work before market hours. This includes getting ready and situated before initiating a trade so that, in a focused state, you can monitor market events as they unfold.

Discipline can sometimes have a negative sound, but the way to freedom and prosperity is an organized, focused, and responsive process of trading. With that, and an arsenal of low-risk/high-profit options strategies, profits can indeed flow profusely. The consistent disciplined application of these strategies is essential to our success as professional traders. Plan your trade and trade your plan.

Finally, as option traders, in order to improve in the discipline arena we must identify and either change or rid ourselves of anything in our mental environment that doesn't contribute to the strictest execution of our well-planned trading approach. We have to stay focused on what we need to learn and do the work that is necessary. Your belief in what is possible will continue to evolve as a function of your propensity to adapt.

CONCLUSION

Almost every successful trader I know has an area of expertise. For some, it is trading futures. Others like trading commodities. Some traders specialize in trading the Nasdaq 100 QQQs. My experience is mostly related to stock options. Initially, traders tend to explore a large number of different vehicles and then narrow down their focus to a specific instrument and a small number of winning strategies.

Hopefully, this chapter has provided you with a better idea of what financial instruments are available for trading today and how they differ from one another. We discussed a number of different underlying assets including stocks, futures, exchange-traded funds, indexes, and options. All can be used in creating and implementing options trading strategies.

At this point, the readers should also understand that a futures contract is significantly different from an options contract. While both represent agreements between two parties, the contracts are structured in ways that are considerably different from one another. From here, we focus more on options and, in later chapters, discuss specific trading strategies that work in a variety of different market scenarios.

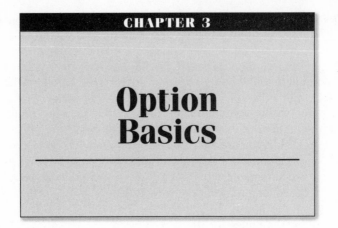

CHAPTER 3

Option
Basics

After I was introduced to the futures market I saw how, with a small amount of capital, I could increase my leverage and control much more of a particular commodity using less money. What I did not fully understand was the potential risk. Shortly into my futures trading career, it became evident to me exactly what could happen to an account when one was on the wrong side of the futures market. This resulted in a temporary setback referred to by many in the business as a *margin call*, which requires a trader to provide additional money to the broker as a guarantee to stay in the trade. Later that year, I returned to the futures market with a more disciplined approach that included trading options.

As a trader, I find options to be the most effective way to maintain consistent trading profits. They have become vitally important tools in my trading toolbox. However, like any tool, they are most effective when used properly and dangerous if not respected. There's an adage among savvy traders that says, "Options don't lose money; people do."

Most of my favorite trading strategies use put and call options to act as insurance policies in a wide variety of trading scenarios. You probably have insurance on your car or house because it is the responsible and safe thing to do. Options provide the same kind of safety net for your trades. They also allow you to control more shares of a certain stock without tying up a large amount of capital in your account.

In order to grasp the complex nature of trading options, it is important to build a solid foundation in option basics. In Chapter 2, we started building that foundation with a brief introduction to various financial markets and trading instruments. Now let's continue our discussion, but narrow our focus to the fascinating world of options.

WHAT IS AN OPTION?

Outside in the world beyond finance, an *option* is merely a choice. There is an infinite number of examples of options. Perhaps you are looking for a house to rent, but you are also interested in buying a house in the future. Let's say I have a house for rent and would be willing to sell the house. A 12-month lease agreement with an option to buy the house at $100,000 is written. As the seller, I may charge you $1,000 extra just for that 12-month option to buy the house. You now have 12 months in which to decide whether to buy the house for the agreed price. You have purchased a *call option*, which gives you the right to buy the house for $100,000, although you are in no way obligated to do so.

A variety of factors may help you decide whether to buy the house, including appreciation of the property, transportation, climate, local schools, and the cost of repairs and general upkeep. Housing prices may rise or fall during the lease period, which could also be a determining factor in your decision. Once the lease is up, you lose the option to buy the house at the agreed price. If you decide to buy the house, you are exercising your right granted by the terms of our contract. That's basically how a call option works.

So, in the options market, a call gives the owner the right to buy a stock (or index, futures contract, index, etc.) at a predetermined price for a specific period of time. The call owner could elect *not* to exercise the right and could let the option expire worthless. He or she might also sell the call at a later point in time and close the position. Regardless of what the owner decides to do, the call option represents an option to its owner.

Throughout the rest of this book, out discussion of options deals with the types of contracts that are traded on the organized options exchanges. Each day, millions of these contracts are bought and sold. Each contract can in turn be described using four factors:

1. The name of the underlying stock (or future, index, exchange-traded fund, etc.).
2. The expiration date.
3. The strike price.
4. Whether it is a put or call.

Therefore, when discussing an option, the contract can be described using the four variables alone. For example, "IBM June 50 Call" describes the call option on shares of International Business Machines (IBM) that expires in June and has a strike price of 50. The QQQ October 30 Put is the put option contract on the Nasdaq 100 QQQ that expires in October and has a strike price of 30.

DETERMINANTS OF OPTION PRICES

Options are sometimes called "wasting assets" because they lose value as time passes. This makes sense because, all else being equal, an option to buy or sell a stock that is valid for the next six months would be worth more than the same option that has only one month left until expiration. You have the right to exercise that option for five months longer! However, time is not the most important factor that will determine the value of an options contract.

The price of the underlying security is the most important factor in determining the value of an option. This is often the first thing new options traders learn. For example, they might buy calls on XYZ stock because they expect XYZ to move higher.

In order to really understand how option prices work, however, it is important to understand that the value of a contract will be determined largely by the relationship between its strike price and the price of the underlying asset. It is the difference between the strike price and the price of the underlying asset that plays the most important role in determining the value of an option. This relationship is known as *moneyness*.

The terms in-the-money (ITM), at-the-money (ATM), and out-of-the-money (OTM) are used with reference to an option's moneyness. A call option is in-the-money if the strike price of the option is below where the underlying security is trading and out-of-the-money if the strike price is above the price of the underlying security. A put option is in-the-money if the strike price is greater than the price of the underlying security and out-of-the-money if the strike price is below the price of the underlying security. A call or put option is at-the-money or near-the-money if the strike price is the same as or close to the price of the underlying security.

Price of Underlying Asset = 50

Strike Price	Call Option	Put Option
60	OTM	ITM
55	OTM	ITM
50	ATM	ATM
45	ITM	OTM
40	ITM	OTM

As noted earlier, the amount of time left until an option expires will also have an important influence on the value of an option. All else being equal, the more time left until an option expires, the greater the worth. As time passes, the value of an option will diminish. The phenomenon is known as time decay, and that is why options are often called wasting assets. It is important to understand the impact of time decay on a position. In fact, time is the second most important factor in determining an option's value.

The dividend is also one of the determinants of a stock option's price. (Obviously, if the stock pays no dividend, or if we are dealing with a futures contract or index, the question of a dividend makes no difference.) A dividend will lower the value of a call option. In addition, the larger the dividend, the lower the price of the corresponding call options. Therefore, stocks with high dividends will have low call option premiums.

Changes in interest rates can also have an impact on option prices throughout the entire market. Higher interest rates lead to somewhat higher option prices, and lower interest rates result in lower option premiums. The extent of the impact of interest rates on the value of an option is subject to debate; but it is considered one of the determinants throughout most of the options-trading community.

The volatility of the underlying asset will have considerable influence on the price of an option. All else being equal, the greater an underlying asset's volatility, the higher the option premium. To understand why, consider buying a call option on XYZ with a strike price of 50 and expiration in July (the XYZ July 50 call) during the month of January. If the stock has been trading between $40 and $45 for the past six years, the odds of its price rising above $50 by July are relatively slim. As a result, the XYZ July 50 call option will not carry much value because the odds of the stock moving up to $50 are statistically small. Suppose, though, the stock has been trading between $40 and $80 during the past six months and sometimes jumps $15 in a single day. In that case, XYZ has exhibited relatively high volatility and, therefore, the stock has a better chance of rising above $50 by July. The call option, or the right to buy the stock at $50 a share, will have better odds of being in-the-money at expiration and, as a result, will command a higher price since the stock has been exhibiting higher levels of volatility.

Understanding the Option Premium

New option traders are often confused about what an option's premium is and what it represents. Let's delve into the total concept of options premium and hopefully demystify it once and for all. The meaning of the word *premium* takes on its own distinction within the options world. It represents an option's price, and is comparable to an insurance premium.

If you are buying a put or a call option, you are paying the option writer a price for this privilege. This best explains why so often the terms *price* and *premium* are used interchangeably.

One of the most common analogies made for options is that they act like insurance policies, particularly the premium concept. For example, as a writer of an option, you are offering a price guarantee to the option buyer. Further, the writer plays the role of the insurer, assuming the risk of a stock price move that would trigger a claim. And just like an insurance underwriter, the option writer charges a premium that is nonrefundable, whether the contract is ever exercised.

From the moment an option is first opened, its premium is set by competing bids and offers in the open market. The price remains exposed to fluctuations according to market supply and demand until the option stops trading. Stock market investors are well aware that influences that cannot be quantified or predicted may have a major impact on the market price of an asset.

These influences can come from a variety of areas such as market psychology, breaking news events, and/or heightened interest in a particular industry. And these are just three illustrations where unexpected shifts in market valuations sometimes occur.

Although market forces set option prices, it does not follow that premiums are completely random or arbitrary. An option pricing model applies a mathematical formula to calculate an option's theoretical value based on a range of real-life variables. Many trading professionals and options strategists rely on such models as an essential guide to valuing their positions and managing risk.

However, if no pricing model can reliably predict how option prices will behave, why should an individual investor care about the principles of theoretical option pricing? The primary reason is that understanding the key price influences is the simplest method to establish realistic expectations for how an option position is likely to behave under a variety of conditions.

These models can serve as tools for interpreting market prices. They may explain price relationships between options, raise suspicions about suspect prices, and indicate the market's current outlook for this security. Floor traders often use the models as a decision-making guide, and their valuations play a role in the market prices you observe as an investor. Investors who are serious about achieving long-term success with options find it instrumental to understand the impact of the six principal variables in the theoretical establishment of an option's premium:

1. Price of underlying security.
2. Moneyness.

3. Time to expiration.
4. Dividend.
5. Change in interest rates.
6. Volatility.

UNDERSTANDING OPTION EXPIRATION

Although expiration is a relatively straightforward concept, it is one that is so important to the options trader that it requires a thorough understanding. Each option contract has a specific expiration date. After that, the contract ceases to exist. In other words, the option holder no longer has any rights, the seller has no obligations, and the contract has no value. Therefore, to the options trader, it is an extremely important date to understand and remember.

Have you ever heard someone say that 90 percent of all options expire worthless? While the percentage is open to debate (the Chicago Board Options Exchange says the figure is closer to 30 percent), the fact is that options do expire. They have a fixed life, which eventually runs out. To understand why, recall what an options contract is: an agreement between a buyer and a seller. Among other things, the two parties agree on a duration for the contract. The duration of the options contract is based on the expiration date. Once the expiration date has passed, the contract no longer exists. It is worthless. The concept is similar to a prospective buyer placing a deposit on a home. In that case, the deposit gives the individual the right to purchase the home. The seller, however, will not want to grant that right forever. For that reason, the deposit gives the owner the right to buy the home, but only for a predetermined period of time. After that time has elapsed, the agreement is void; the seller keeps the deposit, and can then attempt to sell the house to another prospective buyer.

While an options contract is an agreement, the two parties involved do not negotiate the expiration dates between themselves. Instead, option contracts are standardized contracts and each option is assigned an expiration cycle. Every option contract, other than long-term equity anticipation securities (LEAPS), is assigned to one of three quarterly cycles: the January cycle, the February cycle, or the March cycle. For example, an option on the January cycle can have options with expiration months of January, April, July, and October. The February cycle includes February, May, August, and November. The March cycle includes March, June, September, and December.

In general, at any point in time, a stock option will have contracts with four expiration dates, which include the two near-term months and two further-term months. Therefore, in early January 2005 a contract on XYZ will have options available on the months January, February, April, July and October. Index options often have the first three or four near-term months and then three further-term months. The simplest way to view which months are available is through an option chain (see pp. 58–59).

The actual expiration date for a stock option is close of business prior to the Saturday following the third Friday of the expiration month. For instance, expiration for the month of September 2005 is September 17, 2005. That is the last day that the terms of the option contract can be exercised. Therefore, all option holders must express their desire to exercise the contract by that date or they will lose their rights. (Although options that are in-the-money by one-quarter of a point or more will be subject to automatic exercise and the terms of the contract will automatically be fulfilled.) While the last day to exercise an option is the Saturday following the third Friday of the expiration month, the last day to trade the contract is the third Friday. Therefore, an option that has value can be sold on the third Friday of the expiration month. If an option is not sold on that day, it will either be exercised or expire worthless.

While the last day to trade stock options is the third Friday of the expiration month, the last trading day for some index options is on a Thursday. For example, the last full day of trading for Standard & Poor's 500 ($SPX) options is the Thursday before the third Friday of the month. Why? Because the final settlement value of the option is computed when the 500 stocks that make up the index open on Friday morning. Therefore, when trading indexes, the strategist should not assume that the third Friday of the month is the last trading day. It could be on the Thursday before.

According to the Chicago Board Options Exchange, more than 60 percent of all options are closed in the marketplace. That is, buyers sell their options in the market and sellers buy their positions back. Therefore, most option strategists do not hold an options contract for its entire duration. Instead, many either take profits or cut their losses prior to expiration. Nevertheless, expiration dates and cycles are important to understand. They set the terms of the contract and spell the duration of the option holder's rights and of the option seller's obligations.

SEVEN CHARACTERISTICS OF OPTIONS

Options are available on most futures, but not all stocks, indexes, or exchange-traded funds. In order to determine if a stock, index, or exchange-traded fund has options available, ask your broker, visit an options symbol directory, or see if an option chain is available.

Also, keep in mind that futures and futures options fall under a separate regulatory authority from stocks, stock options, and index options. Therefore, trading futures and options on futures requires separate brokerage accounts when compared to trading stocks and stock options. As a result, a trader might have one brokerage account with a firm that specializes in futures trading and another account with a brokerage firm that trades stocks and stock options. If you are new to trading, determine if you want to specialize in stocks or futures. Then find the best broker to meet your needs.

Whether trading futures or stock options, all contracts share the following seven characteristics:

1. Options give you the right to buy or sell an instrument.
2. If you buy an option, you are not obligated to buy or sell the underlying instrument; you simply have the right to exercise the option.
3. If you sell an option, you are obligated to deliver—or to purchase—the underlying asset at the predetermined price if the buyer exercises his or her right to take delivery—or to sell.
4. Options are valid for a specified period of time, after which they expire and you lose your right to buy or sell the underlying instrument at the specified price. Options expire on the Saturday following the third Friday of the expiration month.
5. Options are bought at a *debit* to the buyer. So the money is deducted from the trading account.
6. Sellers receive *credits* for selling options. The credit is an amount of money equal to the option premium and it is credited or added to the trading account.
7. Options are available at several strike prices that reflect the price of the underlying security. For example, if XYZ is trading for $50 a share, the options might have strikes of 40, 45, 50, 55, and 60. The number of strike prices will increase as the stock moves dramatically higher or lower.

The premium is the total price you have to pay to buy an option or the total credit you receive from selling an option. The premium is, in turn, computed as the current option price times a multiplier. For example, stock options have a multiplier of 100. If a stock option is quoted for $3 a contract, it will cost $300 to purchase the contract.

One more note before we begin looking at specific examples of puts and calls: An option does not have to be exercised in order for the owner to make a profit. Instead, an option position can, and often is, closed at a profit (or loss) prior to expiration. *Offsetting transactions* are used to close option positions. Basically, to offset an open position, the trader must sell an equal number of contracts in the exact same options contract. For example, if I buy 10 XYZ June 50 calls, I close the position by selling 10 XYZ June 50 calls. In the first case, I am buying to *open*. In the second, I am selling to *close*.

MECHANICS OF PUTS AND CALLS

As we have duly noted, there are two types of options: calls and puts. These two types of options can make up the basis for an infinite number of trading scenarios. Successful options traders effectively use both kinds of options in the same trade to hedge their investment, creating a limited-risk trading strategy. But, before getting into a discussion of more complex strategies that use both puts and calls, let's examine each separately to see how they behave in the real world.

Call Options

Call options give the buyer the right, but not the obligation, to purchase the underlying asset. A call option increases in value when the underlying asset rises in price, and loses value when the underlying falls in price. Thus, the purchase of a call option is a bullish strategy; that is, it makes a profit as the stock moves higher.

In order to familiarize you with the basics of call options, let's explore an example from outside the stock market. A local newspaper advertises a sale on DVD players for only $49.95. Knowing a terrific deal when you see one, you cut out the ad and head on down to the store to purchase one. Unfortunately, when you arrive you find out all of the advertised DVD players have already been sold. The manager apologizes and says that she expects to receive another shipment within the week. She gives you a rain check entitling you to buy a DVD player for the advertised discounted price of $49.95 for up to one month from the present day. You have just received a call option. You have been given the right, not the obligation, to purchase the DVD player at the guaranteed strike price of $49.95 until the expiration date one month away.

Later that week, the store receives another shipment and offers the DVD players for $59.95. You return to the store and exercise your call option to buy one for $49.95, saving $10. Your call option was in-the-money. But what if you returned to find the DVD players on sale for $39.95? The

call option gives you the right to purchase one for $49.95—but you are un-
der no obligation to buy it at that price. You can simply tear up the rain
check coupon and buy the DVD player at the lower market price of $39.95.
In this case, your call option was out-of-the-money and expired worthless.

Let's take a look at another scenario. A coworker says her DVD player
just broke and she wants to buy another one. You mention your rain
check. She asks if you will sell it to her so she can purchase the DVD
player at the reduced price. You agree to this, but how do you go about
calculating the fair value of your rain check? After all, the store might sell
the new shipment of DVD players for less than your guaranteed price.
Then the rain check would be worthless. You decide to do a little investigation on the store's pricing policies. You subsequently determine that
half the time, discounted prices are initially low and then slowly climb
over the next two months until the store starts over again with a new sale
item. The other half of the time, discounted prices are just a one-time
thing. You average all this out and decide to sell your rain check for $5.
This price is the theoretical value of the rain check based on previous
pricing patterns. It is as close as you can come to determining the call
option's fair price.

This simplification demonstrates the basic nature of a call option. All
call options give you the right to buy something at a specific price for a fixed
amount of time. The price of the call option is based on previous price patterns that only approximate the fair value of the option (See Table 3.1).

If you buy call options, you are "going long the market." That means
that you intend to profit from a rise in the market price of the underlying
instrument. If bullish (you believe the market will rise), then you want to
buy calls. If bearish (you believe the market will drop), then you can "go
short the market" by selling calls. If you buy a call option, your risk is the
money paid for the option (the premium) and brokerage commissions. If
you sell a call option, your risk is unlimited because, theoretically, there is
no ceiling to how high the stock price can climb. If the stock rises sharply,
and you are assigned on your short call, you will be forced to buy the
stock in the market at a very high price and sell it to the call owner at the

TABLE 3.1 Call Option Moneyness

In-the-money (ITM)	The market price of the underlying asset is more than your strike price.
At-the-money (ATM)	The market price of the underlying asset is the same as your strike price.
Out-of-the-money (OTM)	The market price of the underlying asset is less than your strike price.

much lower strike price. We will discuss the risks and rewards of this strategy in more detail later.

For now, it is simply important to understand that a call option is in-the-money (ITM) when the price of the underlying instrument is higher than the option's strike price. For example, a call option that gives the buyer the right to purchase 100 shares of IBM for $80 each is ITM when the current price of IBM is greater than $80. At that point, exercising the call option allows the trader to buy shares of IBM for less than the current market price. A call option is at-the-money (ATM) when the price of the underlying security is equal to its strike price. For example, an IBM call option with a strike price of $80 is ATM when IBM can be purchased for $80. A call option is out-of-the-money (OTM) when the underlying security's market price is less than the strike price. For example, an IBM call option with an $80 strike price is OTM when the current price of IBM in the market is less than $80. No one would want to exercise an option to buy IBM at $80 if it can be directly purchased in the market for less. That's why call options that are out-of-the-money by their expiration date expire worthless.

Price of IBM = 80

Strike Price	Call Option	Option Premium
100	OTM	.50
95	OTM	1.00
90	OTM	2.25
85	OTM	4.75
80	ATM	6.50
75	ITM	10.00
70	ITM	13.75
65	ITM	17.50
60	ITM	20.75

Purchasing a call option is probably the simplest form of options trading. A trader who purchases a call is bullish, expecting the underlying asset to increase in price. The trader will most likely make a profit if the price of the underlying asset increases fast enough to overcome the option's time decay. Profits can be realized in one of two ways if the underlying asset increases in price before the option expires. The holder can either purchase the underlying shares for the lower strike price or, since the value of the option has increased, sell (to close) the option at a profit. Hence, purchasing a call option has a limited risk because the most you stand to lose is the premium paid for the option plus commissions paid to the broker.

Let's review the basic fundamental structure of buying a standard call on shares using IBM. If you buy a call option for 100 shares of IBM, you get the right, but not the obligation, to buy 100 shares at a certain price. The certain price is called the strike price. Your right is good for a certain amount of time. You lose your right to buy the shares at the strike price on the expiration date of the call option.

Generally, calls are available at several strike prices, which usually come in increments of five. In addition, there normally is a choice of several different expiration dates for each strike price. Just pick up the financial pages of a good newspaper and find the options for IBM. Looking at this example, you will see the strike prices, expiration months, and the closing call option prices of the underlying shares, IBM.

Price of IBM = 80

Strike Price	January	April	July
75	6.40	7.50	8.30
80	2.00	3.90	4.80
85	.40	1.60	2.80

The numbers in the first column are the strike prices of the IBM calls. The months across the top are the expiration months. The numbers inside the table are the option premiums. For example, the premium of an IBM January 75 call is 6.40. Each $1 in premium is equal to $100 per contract (i.e., the multiplier is equal to 100) because each option contract controls 100 shares. Looking at the IBM January 75 call option, a premium of 6.40 indicates that one contract trades for $640: (6.40 × $100 = $640).

The table also shows that the January 80 calls are priced at a premium of $2. Since a call option controls 100 shares, you would have to pay $200 plus brokerage commissions to buy one IBM January 80 call: (2 × $100 = $200). A July 75 call trading at 8.30 would cost $830: (8.30 × $100) plus commissions:

- Cost of January IBM 80 call = 2 × $100 = $200 + commissions.
- Cost of July IBM 75 call = 8.30 × $100 = $830 + commissions.

All the options of one type (put or call) that have the same underlying security are called a *class* of options. For example, all the calls on IBM constitute an option class. All the options that are in one class and have the same strike price and expiration are called a *series* of options. For example, all of the IBM 80 calls with the same expiration date constitute an option series.

Put Options

Put options give the buyer the right, but not the obligation, to sell the underlying stock, index, or futures contract. A put option increases in value when the underlying asset falls in price and loses value when the underlying asset rises in price. Thus, the purchase of a put option is a bearish strategy. That is, the put option increases in value when the price of an underlying asset falls. Let's review the following analogy to become more familiar with the basics of put options.

You've decided to set up a small cottage industry manufacturing ski jackets. Your first product is a long-sleeved jacket complete with embroidered logos of the respective ski resorts placing the orders. The manager of the pro shop at a local ski resort agrees to purchase 1,000 jackets for $40 each, if you can deliver them by November. In effect, you've been given a put option. The cost of producing each jacket is $25, which gives you a $15 profit on each item. You have therefore locked in a guaranteed profit of $15,000 for your initial period of operation.

This guaranteed order from the resort is an in-the-money put option. You have the right to sell a specific number of jackets at a fixed price (strike price) by a certain time (expiration date). Just as November rolls around, you find out that a large manufacturer is creating very similar products for ski resorts for $30 each. If you didn't have a put option agreement, you would have to drop your price to meet the competition's price, and thereby lose a significant amount of profit. Luckily, you exercise your right to sell your jackets for $40 each and enjoy a prosperous Christmas season. Your competitor made it advantageous for you to sell your jackets for $40 using the put option because it was in-the-money.

In a different scenario, you get a call from another ski resort that has just been featured in a major magazine. The resort needs 1,000 jackets by the beginning of November to fulfill obligations to its marketing team and is willing to pay you $50 per jacket. Even though it goes against your grain to disappoint your first customer, the new market price of your product is $10 higher than your put option price. Since the put option does not obligate you to sell the jackets for $40, you elect to sell them for the higher market price to garner an even bigger profit.

These examples demonstrate the basic nature of a put option. Put options give you the right, but not the obligation, to sell something at a specific price for a fixed amount of time. Put options give the buyer of puts the right to "go short the market" (sell shares). If bearish (you believe the market will drop), then you could go short the market by buying puts. If you buy a put option, your maximum risk is the money paid for the option (the premium) and brokerage commissions.

Theoretically, if bullish (you believe the market will rise), then you

TABLE 3.2 Put Option Moneyness

In-the-money (ITM)	The market price of the underlying asset is less than your strike price.
At-the-money (ATM)	The market price of the underlying asset is the same as your strike price.
Out-of-the-money (OTM)	The market price of the underlying asset is more than your strike price.

could "go long the market" by selling puts—but make no mistake, this comes with high risk! If you sell a put option, your risk is unlimited until the underlying asset reaches zero because, if the stock falls precipitously and the short option is assigned, you will be forced to buy the stock at the previously higher strike price. You can then either hold it or sell it back into the market at a significantly lower price.

A put option is in-the-money (ITM) when the price of the underlying instrument is lower than the option's strike price (see Table 3.2). For example, a put option that gives the buyer of the put the right to sell 100 shares of IBM for $80 each is in-the-money when the current price of IBM is less than $80, because the option can be used to sell the shares for more than the current market price. A put option is at-the-money (ATM) when the price of the underlying shares is equal to its strike price. For example, an IBM put option with a strike price of $80 is at-the-money when IBM can be purchased for $80. A put option is out-of-the-money (OTM) when the underlying security's market value is greater than the strike price. For example, an IBM put option with an $80 strike price is out-of-the-money when the current price of IBM is more than $80. No one would want to exercise an option to sell IBM at $80 if it can be sold directly for more. That's why put options that are out-of-the-money by their expiration date expire worthless.

Price of IBM = 80

Strike Price	Put Option	Option Premium
100	ITM	20.80
95	ITM	17.50
90	ITM	13.80
85	ITM	10.00
80	ATM	6.50
75	OTM	4.75
70	OTM	2.30
65	OTM	1.00
60	OTM	.50

Purchasing put options is generally a bearish move. A holder who has purchased a put option benefits when there is a decrease in the price of the underlying asset. This enables the holder to buy the underlying asset at a lower price on the open market and sell it back at a higher price to the writer of the put option. A decrease in the underlying asset's price also promotes an increase in the value of the put option so that it can be sold for a higher price than was originally paid for it. The purchase of a put option provides unlimited profit potential (to the point where the underlying asset reaches zero). The maximum risk of the put option is limited to the put premium plus commissions to the broker placing the trade.

LEAPS

The acronym LEAPS stands for long-term equity anticipation securities. While the name seems somewhat arcane, LEAPS are nothing more than long-term options. Some investors incorrectly view these long-term options as a separate asset class. But in fact, the only real difference between LEAPS and conventional stock options is the time left until expiration. That is, while short-term options expire within a maximum of eight months, LEAPS can have terms lasting more than two and a half years. At the same time, however, while the only real distinction between conventional options and LEAPS is the time left until expiration, there are important differences to consider when implementing trading strategies with long-term equity anticipation securities. One of the most important factors is the impact of time decay.

The Chicago Board Options Exchange (CBOE) first listed LEAPS in 1990. The goal was to provide those investors who have longer-term time horizons with opportunities to trade options. Prior to that, only short-term options with a maximum expiration of eight months were available. The exchange labeled the new securities as long-term equity anticipation securities in order to differentiate between the new contracts and already existing short-term contracts. According to the exchange, "the name is not important. It is the flexibility that long-term options can add to a portfolio that is important."

In order to add flexibility to your portfolio using LEAPS, there are a number of important factors to consider. First, like conventional options, these options represent the right to buy (for calls) or sell (for puts) an underlying asset for a specific price (the strike price) until expiration. Each option contract represents the right to buy or sell 100 shares of stock. All LEAPS have January expirations, and new years are added as time passes. For example, the year 2007 LEAPS were created after the expiration of the May 2004 contract. Approximately one-third of the stocks that already had LEAPS were issued the 2007 LEAPS after the May expiration. The remaining two-thirds will be listed when June and July option contracts expire.

Not all stocks, however, will be assigned long-term options. In order to have long-term options, the stock must already have listed short-term options. In addition, according to the CBOE, long-term options are listed only on large, well-capitalized companies with significant trading volume in both their stock and their short-term options. In order to find out if a given stock has LEAPS, simply pull up an option chain on the Optionetics.com web site's home page and see if the stock has options expiring in January 2006 or January 2007. If so, the stock does indeed have long-term options available.

When long-term options become short-term options, they are subject to a process known as melding. During that time, the terms of the option contract (the strike price, the unit of trade, expiration date, etc.) do not change. The symbol assigned to the contract is the only thing that changes during the melding phase. The exchanges generally assign different trading symbols to long-term options to distinguish between the LEAPS and the short-term contracts. Therefore, for bookkeeping purposes, the long-term option is converted to a short-term option and the symbol changes from the LEAPS symbol to the symbol assigned to the conventional options. This melding process occurs after either the May, June, or July expiration that precedes the first LEAPS expiration. After that, the LEAPS status and special symbol are removed and the options begin trading like regular short-term options. In sum, the terms of the options contract such as the unit of trading, strike price, and expiration date do not change when LEAPS become short-term contracts. Therefore, neither will the option's price. It is merely a cosmetic change.

In trading, LEAPS can provide several advantages over short-term options. For example, when protecting a stock holding through the use of puts, the investor can purchase the options and not worry about adjusting the position for up to two and a half years—which means less in commissions. At the same time, bullish trades such as long calls and bull call spreads can be established using out-of-the-money LEAPS. Doing so can provide the investor a long-term operating framework similar to the traditional buy-and-hold stock investor, but without committing as much trading capital to the investment.

Another difference between long-term and short-term options will be the impact of time decay, which refers to the fact that options lose value as time passes and as expiration approaches. The process is not linear, however. Instead, time decay becomes greater as the option's expiration approaches. Therefore, all else being equal, an option with two years until expiration will experience a slower rate of decay than an option with two months until expiration. As a result, LEAPS can offer better risk/reward ratios when implementing strategies that require holding long-term options, such as calendar spreads or debit spreads, but not strategies that attempt to benefit from the impact of time decay—like the covered call.

I love LEAPS! Remember that these options are nothing more than stock or index options with very distant expiration dates. These long-term options are available on the most actively traded contracts like Microsoft, General Electric, and IBM. They allow traders more time for trades to work in their favor and have become among my favorite ways to play the long-term trends in the stock market. Bottom line: Don't overlook the power of LEAPS.

OPTION CHAINS

In order to view the various option prices at any given point in time, traders often use a tool known as *option chains*. Not only do option chains offer the current market prices for a series of options, they also tell of an option's liquidity, the available strike prices for the option contract, and the expiration months. In fact, option chains are so important that many brokerage firms offer them to their clients with real-time updates. At the same time, while chains can be extremely helpful tools to the options trader, they are also fairly easy to understand and use.

Today, option chains are readily found. Not long ago, they were available mostly to brokerage firms and other professional investors. Now, however, individual investors can go to a number of web sites and find option chains. Most online brokerage firms provide them, as do several options-related web sites. For instance, at the Optionetics.com home page, pulling up an option chain for any given stock is simply a matter of entering the stock ticker symbol in the quote box at the top of the screen and selecting "chain."

An example of an option chain from Optionetics.com appears in Figure 3.1. It is a snapshot of some of the Microsoft (MSFT) options with February 2004 expirations. It is not a complete list of all the options available at that time on MSFT. In fact, it is only a small fraction. Listing all of MSFT options would take more than 100 rows and a couple of pages.

Option chains like this one are split in two right down the middle. On the left side we have calls and on the right we see puts. On the left side of the table, each row lists a call option contract for MSFT, and on the right

Calls					Puts			
Symbol	Bid	Ask	Op.Int.	Strike	Symbol	Bid	Ask	Op.Int.
MQFBD	8.2	8.3	112	Feb04-20.000	MQFND	0	0.05	100
MQFBX	5.7	5.8	2256	Feb04-22.500	MQFNX	0	0.05	527
MSQBE	3.2	3.4	7789	Feb04-25.000	MSQNE	0	0.05	10504
MSQBY	1.05	1.1	89988	Feb04-27.500	MSQNY	0.25	0.3	78573
MSQBF	0.1	0.15	100937	Feb04-30.000	MSQNF	1.8	1.9	10002
MSQBZ	0	0.05	5164	Feb04-32.500	MSQNZ	4.2	4.3	766
MSQBG	0	0.05	160	Feb04-35.000	MSQNG	6.7	6.8	150

FIGURE 3.1 Microsoft Option Chain (*Source:* Optionetics © 2004)

side each row reflects a different put option. Separating the puts and
calls, we have a column with the heading "strike." This tells us the strike
price of both the puts and calls. For example, in the first row, we have the
February 2004 options with the strike price of 20. In this case, the strikes
occur at 2.5-point increments. So, as we move down the rows, we see the
strike prices of 22.5, 25, 27.5, and so on. Once we reach the end of the
February 2004 strike prices, the March 2004 options would appear next
on the chain.

Each column within the figure provides a different piece of information. On each side of the figure (call and put), the first column lists the option's symbol. For example, on the left half of the figure, the first row
shows the February 20 call, which has the ticker symbol MQFBD (we will
see how to create options symbols shortly).

As with stocks, options have a *bid* price and an *ask* price, which appear in columns two and three. The bid is the current price at which the
market will buy the option, and the ask is the price at which the option
can be bought. The next column indicates the option's *open interest*.
Open interest is the total number of contracts that have been opened and
not yet closed out. For instance, if an option trader buys (as an initial
transaction) five February 25 calls, the open interest will increase by five.
When he or she later sells those five calls (to close the transaction), open
interest will decrease by five. Generally, the more open interest, the
greater the trading activity associated with that particular option and,
hence, the better the liquidity. Open interest is updated only once a day.

The information included in an option chain will differ somewhat
depending on the source, but the variables in Figure 3.1 are usually
found. Some chains will include the last price, the day's volume, or other
bits of trading data. Regardless of the source, chains are important. They
allow traders to see a variety of different contracts simultaneously,
which can help the trader sort through and identify the option contract
with the most appropriate strike, expiration month, and market price for
any specific strategy.

OPTION SYMBOLS

Before we move on to the next chapter and the discussion of actual trading strategies, let's discuss one more basic element of the options market: the option symbol. In the stock market, stocks on the New York Stock Exchange and American Stock Exchange usually have symbols consisting of one, two, or three letters. For example, the symbol for Sears is simply S, Coca-Cola has the symbol KO, and International Business Machines is easy to remember—IBM. Nasdaq-listed stocks have symbols with four (and on rare occasions five or six) letters. That's why some traders refer to Nasdaq stocks as the "four-letter stocks."

Option contracts are a bit more complicated than stocks, however, and the ticker symbols include three pieces of information. The first part of an option symbol describes the underlying stock. It is known as the root symbol and is often similar to the actual ticker of the stock. For instance, the root symbol for International Business Machines is straightforward. It is the same as the stock symbol: IBM. Four-letter stocks, however, always have root symbols different from their stock symbols. For instance, while the stock symbol for Microsoft is MSFT, the option symbol is MSQ. Option root symbols can have one, two, or three letters, but never four. In the case of a stock price that has moved dramatically higher or lower, there may be two or more root symbols. For example, referring back to the option chain for Microsoft, we can see that it shows root symbols of MQF and MSQ.

The second part of an option symbol represents the month and defines whether the option is a put or a call. For example, a January call uses the letter A after the root symbol. Therefore, the IBM January call will have the root symbol IBM and then A, or IBMA. The February call is B, March C, and so on until December, which is the letter L (the twelfth letter in the alphabet). The expiration months for puts begin at the letter M. For instance, the IBM February put will have the letter N following the root symbol, or IBMN. Table 3.3 provides the symbol letter for each month.

The final element to an option symbol reflects the strike price. Generally, the number 5 is assigned the letter A, 10 to the letter B, 15 the letter C, and so on until 100, which is given the letter T. Therefore, the IBM January 95 call will have the symbol IBMAS. Table 3.3 provides the letters assigned to each strike price.

In conclusion, the symbol for any option contract will consist of three pieces of information. The first is the root symbol. It is often similar to the ticker symbol of the underlying stock, but not always. The root symbol can also vary based on the strike prices available for the option; whether it is a one-, two-, three-, or four-letter stock; and if it is a LEAPS or not. The second part of the symbol simply defines the expiration month. The final

TABLE 3.3 Option Symbol Letters

	Jan	Feb	Mar	Apr	May	Jun	Jul	Aug	Sept	Oct	Nov	Dec
Calls	A	B	C	D	E	F	G	H	I	J	K	L
Puts	M	N	O	P	Q	R	S	T	U	V	W	X

Symbol	A	B	C	D	E	F	G	H	I	J	K	L	M
Strike Price	5	10	15	20	25	30	35	40	45	50	55	60	65
	105	110	115	120	125	130	135	140	145	150	155	160	165

Symbol	N	O	P	Q	R	S	T	U	V	W	X	Y	Z
Strike Price	70	75	80	85	90	95	100	7.50	12.50	17.50	22.50	27.50	32.50
	170	175	180	185	190	195	200	107.50	112.50	117.50	122.50	127.50	132.50

element indicates the strike price of the option. Taken together the three pieces of information define the option symbol, which is used to pull up quotes and place orders.

EXPIRATION CYCLES REVISITED

Not all stocks have options available to trade. Among other rules, newly public companies—low-priced stocks and firms that do not have much trading volume in their stock—will not have options. Tradable options, those listed on the exchanges, are *solely* the creations of the exchanges. Companies have no ability to either create or eliminate options for their firms. Firms do create unique options as incentives for their key employees and sometimes as sweeteners or bonuses for the purchase of stock. Such options, which are issued by companies to their employees, are different from the options discussed throughout this book. Instead, we are talking about options that trade on the organized options exchanges and can be bought and sold through a brokerage firm.

The standard, tradable options on the options exchanges are all created by the exchanges themselves. To determine whether options exist for the stock you are contemplating trading, you can check out numerous web sites (including www.optionetics.com or the Chicago Board Options Exchange site, www.cboe.com); look in the option tables of the newspaper; or call your broker. Once you have determined that options are available, you can retrieve a quote or an option chain (see Figure 3.2). Let's review this now and consider the six issues that define an option.

1. Contract size.
2. Month of expiration.
3. Underlying stock.
4. Strike price.
5. Type of option (put or call).
6. Bid and ask price of the option.

The distinguishing factor of options is that they expire; unlike equities, options have a finite life. Thus, knowing the expiration date is critical. One of the great keys to the success of tradable options is the standardization of expiration dates. All stock options officially expire at 10:59 P.M. Central time on the Saturday following the third Friday of the designated month. However, for all practical purposes, the options expire at the close of business on the third Friday of the month because that is

Options Chains

Symbol: [AMZN] [Option Chain ▼] [**get info**] Symbol Lookup

Amazon.com Inc (AMZN)

| Miniquote (delayed) | | last: 21.36 | chg: 0.17 | %chg: 0.80% |

Calls

Symbol	Bid	Ask	Op. Int.
ZQNBQ	8.800	9.000	15
ZQNBC	6.300	6.500	616
ZQNBQ	3.800	4.000	2468
ZQNBD	1.300	1.450	6181
ZQNBS	0.000	0.050	15386
ZQNBC	0.000	0.050	4966
ZQNBR	0.000	0.050	507
ZQNBF	0.000	0.050	241
ZQNBZ	0.000	0.050	0

Strike

| Feb03-12.500 |
| Feb03-15.000 |
| Feb03-17.500 |
| Feb03-20.000 |
| Feb03-22.500 |
| Feb03-25.000 |
| Feb03-27.500 |
| Feb03-27.500 |
| Feb03-27.500 |

Puts

Symbol	Bid	Ask	Op. Int.
ZQNNO	0.000	0.050	281
ZQNNC	0.000	0.050	5114
ZQNNO	0.000	0.050	10695
ZQNND	0.000	0.050	22688
ZQNNE	1.100	1.200	5042
ZQNNE	3.500	3.700	749
ZQNNR	6.000	6.200	90
ZQNNF	8.500	8.700	14
ZQNNZ	11.000	11.200	0

FIGURE 3.2 Option Quote for Amazon.com (AMZN) February Call and Put Options (*Source:* Optionetics © 2004)

usually the last time to trade them. The final accounting (except for rare errors) is completed early Saturday morning.

As previously mentioned, optionable stocks are assigned to one of three expiration cycles (January, February, or March) by the exchange when the options are first created for the firm. The cycles, and their standard expiration months, are listed in Table 3.4.

All stocks with options have active options for the current month, the next month out, and then the next two cycle months. For instance, on March 30, a stock in each of the cycles would have options expiring on the third Friday of the months in Table 3.5.

In addition to the four months listed in Table 3.5 for all optionable stocks, the most active stocks also have LEAPS that will expire on January of the next two years. Those LEAPS become regular options when the January date is within nine months of expiration. A new LEAPS option is created each May, June, or July, depending on which cycle the particular stock is located in, for the subsequent year out.

TABLE 3.4 Cycles and Expiration Months

Cycle	January	February	March
Expiration months	January	February	March
	April	May	June
	July	August	September
	October	November	December

TABLE 3.5 Four Expiration Months for Optionable Stocks

Cycle	January	February	March
Current month	April	April	April
Next month	May	May	May
Next cycle month	July	August	June
Second cycle month	October	November	September

To further complicate matters, a given stock may not have options created if there will be some dramatic change in the stock that is known by the exchanges. For instance, if the firm is about to be acquired or delisted, the exchange may not create a particular set of options for the next normal month, awaiting events. In all cases, check with your broker, the CBOE, or even the Optionetics.com web site to be sure that a particular option exists.

The strike price, or exercise price, is designed to provide options that will attract trading volume. Thus, options are created that closely surround the current stock price. The norm is to set the strike prices in the following increments:

- For stock prices under $25, strikes will be $2.50 apart, starting at $5 (5, 7.5, 10, etc.).
- For stock prices between $25 and $200, strikes will be $5 apart (25, 30, 35, etc.).
- For stock prices greater than $200, strikes will be $10 apart (200, 210, 220, etc.).
- In 2003, options with one-point increments between strike prices started trading on some actively traded low-priced stocks. For example, a $5 stock might have strike prices of 5, 6, 7, and so on.

As the stock price moves up or down, new options are created around the new stock prices. However, the old options will remain in effect until expiration (they are not eliminated just because the stock price has moved).

As with most things in life, these rules are not absolute. Stock splits, for instance, can cause some strange strikes. If a company institutes a split, the option prices and numbers of contracts will also be affected. A 2-for-1 split would cause an option with a strike of 85 to turn into two options with a strike of 42.50. Similarly, a 3-for-1 split would cause the same option to become three options, each with a strike of 28.33.

Also, for stocks that move rapidly up and down, like the volatile technology stocks, there are often options only at 10-point increments, even though the stock is selling well under $200. This is particularly true of options that are several months from expiration. The reasoning is that with rapid stock price movements, if options were created for every standard strike, there could easily be 30 or 40 strikes for both puts and calls on that stock for each expiration month. The problem is that every time the stock price moves each of those options must be repriced, and the calculations and tracking required become humongous. Likewise, with a given volume of option trading for a particular stock, the more option choices available, the less volume any one option will likely have, resulting, of course, in decreased liquidity.

INTRINSIC VALUE AND TIME VALUE

Intrinsic value is defined as the amount by which the strike price of an option is in-the-money. It is a very important value to determine, since it is the portion of an option's price that is not lost due to the passage of time. For a call option, intrinsic value is equal to the current price of the underlying asset minus the strike price of the call option. For a put option, intrinsic value is equal to the strike price of the option minus the current price of the underlying asset. If a call or put option is at-the-money, the intrinsic value would equal zero. Likewise, an out-of-the-money call or put option has no intrinsic value. The intrinsic value of an option does not depend on how much time is left until expiration. It simply tells you how much real value you are paying for. If an option has no intrinsic value, then all it really has is time value, which decreases as an option approaches expiration.

Time value (theta) can be defined as the amount by which the price of an option exceeds its intrinsic value. Also referred to as extrinsic value, the time value of an option is directly related to how much time the option has until expiration. Theta decays over time. For example, if a call costs $5 and its intrinsic value is $1, the time value would be $5 − $1 = $4. Let's use the following table to calculate the intrinsic value and time value of a few options.

Price of IBM = 86

Call Strike	January	February	May
80	6.40	7.50	8.25
85	2.60	3.90	4.75
90	.90	1.60	2.75

Here are the calculations for the IBM February 85 calls if IBM is now trading at $86:

- Intrinsic value = underlying asset price minus strike price: $86 − $85 = $1.
- Time value = call premium minus intrinsic value: $3.90 − $1 = $2.90.

Now let's look at the intrinsic value of each option relative to its time value.

- The January 80 call has a minimum value of 6; therefore, you are paying .40 point of time value for the option (6.40 − 6 = .40).
- The February 80 call has a minimum value of 6; therefore, you are paying 1.50 points of time value for this option (7.50 − 6 = 1.50).
- The May 80 call has a minimum value of 6; therefore, you are paying 2.25 points of time value for this option (8.25 − 6 = 2.25).

As you can see, the intrinsic value of an option is the same, no matter what time is left until expiration. Now let's look at some options within the same month, but with different strike prices:

Price of IBM = 86

Strike	January
70	16.25
75	11.50
80	6.40

- The January 70 call has 16 points of intrinsic value (86 − 70 = 16) and .25 points of time value (16.25 − 16 = .25).
- The January 75 call has 11 points of intrinsic value (86 − 75 = 11) and .50 points of time value (11.50 − 11 = .50).
- The January 80 call has 6 points of intrinsic value (86 − 80 = 6) and .40 points of time value (6.40 − 6 = .40).

Obviously, an option with three months till expiration is worth more than an option that expires this month. Theoretically, the option with three months till expiration has a better chance of ending up in-the-money than the option expiring this month. That's why an OTM option consists of nothing but time value. The more out-of-the-money an option is, the less it costs. However, since it has no real (intrinsic) value, all you are paying for is time value (i.e., the time to let your OTM option become profitable due to a swing in the market). The probability that an extremely

OTM option will turn profitable is quite slim. To confirm this, just go to your local library and look up some options' prices in previous copies of a financial newspaper, such as *Investor's Business Daily*. Compare the present-day price of a particular option to prices in back issues of the same publication.

Since you can exercise an American-style call option anytime you want, its price should not be less than its intrinsic value. An option's intrinsic value is also called the minimum value primarily because it tells you the minimum the option should be selling for (i.e., exactly what you are paying for and how much time value you have left). What does this mean? Most importantly, it means that the cheaper the option, the less real value you are buying. Intrinsic value acts a lot like car insurance. If you buy a zero-deductible policy and you have an accident, even a fender bender, you're covered. You pay less for a $500-deductible policy, but if you have an accident the total damage must exceed $500 before the insurance company will pay for the remainder of the damages.

The prices of OTM options are low, and get even lower further out-of-the-money. To many traders, this inexpensive price looks good. Unfortunately, OTM options have only a slim probability that they will turn profitable. The following table demonstrates this slim chance of profitability.

Price of XYZ = 86

Call Strike	January	Intrinsic Value	Time Value
70	17.00	16.00	1.00
75	13.50	11.00	2.50
80	10.75	6.00	4.75
85	6.50	1.00	5.50
90	3.00	0	3.00

With the price of XYZ at 86, a January 90 call would have a price (premium) of 3. To be 3 points above the strike price, XYZ has to rise 7 points to 93 in order for you to break even. If you were to buy a January 75 call and pay 13.50 for it, XYZ would have to rise to 88.50 in order to break even (75 + 13.50 = 88.50). As you can see, the further out-of-the-money an option is, the less chance it has of turning a profit.

Theta (time value) correlates the change in the price of the option with respect to the time left until expiration. The passage of time has a snowball effect as well. If you've ever bought options and sat on them until the last couple of weeks before expiration, you might have noticed that at a certain point the market seems to stop moving anywhere. Option prices are exponential—the closer you get to expiration, the more money you're going to lose if the market doesn't move. On the expiration day, an option's worth is its intrinsic value. It's either in-the-money or it isn't.

Early in my options career, I realized that as you go deeper in-the-money with calls or puts, the options have less time value and more intrinsic value. This means that you are paying less for time; therefore, the option moves more like the underlying asset. This is referred to as the delta of an option. The delta is the key to creating delta neutral strategies and we will delve deeply into its properties and functions as we explore more advanced trading techniques throughout this book. Let's now explore various strike price trends.

Price of XYZ = 50

Call Strike	January	February	May
45	6.40	7.50	8.25
50	2.30	3.90	4.75
55	.90	1.60	2.75

Looking at the expiration months for XYZ, notice that in the January column, the price (premium) of a call is higher for lower strike prices. For example, the price of an XYZ January 45 call (6.40) is higher than the price of the XYZ January 50 call (2.30). That makes sense since the XYZ January 45 call allows you to buy a $50 stock (XYZ) for $45 per share, while the XYZ January 50 call allows you to buy it for $50. Also notice that the price of a call is lower for closer expirations. For example, the price of the XYZ May 50 call (4.75) is higher than the price of the XYZ January 50 call (2.30). This makes sense since the May 50 call allows you to buy XYZ at $50 until close of business prior to the third Saturday of May (a period of about four months from January). With the XYZ January 50 call, your right expires at close of business prior to the third Saturday of January. The only difference between these options is the amount of time the trader has to make a decision on the option and its probability of closing in-the-money. The same principle applies to puts. Less time to expiration means lower prices. The buyer has less time for the put to move in-the-money or to decide what to do with the option.

TIME DECAY

Have you ever heard the expression that options are "wasting assets"? Since options suffer from what is known as time decay, the option contract loses value with each passing day. Therefore, if a strategist buys a put or call and holds it in her account, even if the underlying stock or index makes no price movement at all, the portfolio will lose value. As a result, options strategists must carefully examine how time is affecting their options positions. This section explains how.

Options contracts are agreements between two parties as to the right to buy (in the case of call) or sell (with respect to puts) an underlying asset at a predetermined price. Each options contract has a fixed expiration date. Hence, an XYZ call option gives the owner the right to buy XYZ at a specific price (known as a strike price), and the XYZ put option gives the owner the right to sell 100 shares of XYZ stock at a predetermined price, but only until a certain expiration date.

A stock options contract is valid only until the Saturday following the third Friday of an expiration month. For example, the October 2004 options expire on October 16, 2004. The last day to trade these options is on the third Friday of October, which falls on October 15, 2004. The time left until the option expires is known as the life of the option. As expiration approaches, all else being equal, the life and the value of the option will decline. Some traders use the term *time value premium*. All else being equal, the greater the amount of time left until the option expires, the more valuable the options contract.

At the same time, the rate of time decay is not linear. As an option approaches expiration, the rate of decay becomes faster. For instance, an option with only three weeks left until expiration will lose time value premium at a faster rate than an equivalent option with 12 months of life remaining. Mathematically speaking, the rate of time decay is related to the square root of the life of the option. For instance, an option with three months of life left will lose value twice as fast as an option with nine months left (three being the square root of nine). Similarly, an option with 16 months left will decay at half the rate of an option with four months left.

The option's amount of time decay can be measured by one of the Greeks known as theta. The theta of an option is computed using an option pricing model. Alternatively, it can be found using the Optionetics.com Platinum site.

EXITING A TRADE

There are three ways to exit an option trade. An option can be offset or exercised, or it can simply expire. Experience is the best teacher when it comes to choosing the best alternative. In most cases, traders close options through offsetting trades. However, since each alternative has an immediate result, learning how to best close out a trade is a vital element to becoming a successful trader.

Offsetting

Offsetting is a closing transaction that cancels an open position. It is accomplished by doing the opposite of the opening transaction. There are four ways to offset an option transaction:

1. If you bought a call, you have to sell a call.
2. If you sold a call, you have to buy a call.
3. If you bought a put, you have to sell a put.
4. If you sold a put, you have to buy a put.

The best time to offset an option is when it is in-the-money and therefore will realize a profit. Offsetting can also be used to avoid incurring further losses. An option can be offset at any time—one second after it has been entered or one minute before expiration. Offsetting an option is the most popular technique of closing an option. In fact, 95 percent of all the options with value are offset.

Exercising

There are various reasons why a trader might choose to exercise an option versus offset it. Of the 5 percent that are exercised, 95 percent are exercised at expiration. Exercising will close your open call option position by taking ownership of the underlying stock. If you want to exercise a long (bought) stock option:

- Simply notify your broker, who will then notify the Options Clearing Corporation (OCC).
- By the next day, you will own (if exercising calls) or have sold (if exercising puts) the corresponding shares of the underlying asset.
- You can exercise an American option at any time; but primarily you will do it—if you do it at all—just prior to expiration.
- If the market rises, you may choose to exercise a call option. Your trading account will then be debited for 100 shares of the underlying stock (per option) at the call's strike price.
- If the market declines, you may choose to exercise a put option. You will then receive a credit to your account for 100 shares of underlying stock at the put strike price. This is called shorting the market and can be a risky endeavor.

An option seller cannot exercise an option. By selling an option, you are taking the risk of having a buyer exercise the option against you when market price movement makes it an in-the-money (ITM) option. The OCC randomly matches or assigns buyers and sellers to one another. If there is an excess of sellers by expiration, all open-position ITM short options are automatically exercised by the OCC. In order to avoid being automatically exercised, short option holders can choose to offset or close their options instead.

Letting It Expire

Letting an option expire is used when the option is out-of-the-money (OTM) or worthless as it approaches the expiration date. For short options, letting them expire is the best way to realize a profit. If you let a short option expire, you get to keep the credit received from the premium. Since a momentary fluctuation in price can mean the difference between opportunity and crisis, traders with open positions need to keep track of the price of the underlying asset very carefully. Luckily, computers make this process easier than ever before. There are plenty of web sites that provide detailed option and stock listings, including our own site (www.optionetics.com).

ASSIGNMENT

Assignment is one of the more confusing characteristics of an option. Although it occurs infrequently, it is an important part of basic option mechanics. As an option trader, you'll need to have a solid understanding of assignment in order to maximize your chances for success. Let's take a closer look.

Anticipating Assignment

As we have seen, selling puts or calls can involve significant risks. However, there are some strategies that carry relatively low risk, but also involve selling options. Many of these trades are more complex trades that we will explore in later chapters. For now, let's assume we sell an option, but we want to determine if there is a risk of assignment. Are all options assigned? When are the odds of assignment the greatest? While there is no way to know for certain when assignment will occur, there are some relatively certain ways to anticipate it before it happens.

Recall that sellers take on an obligation to honor the option contract.

Therefore, if you sell a call option, you agree to sell the stock at a predetermined price until the option expires. On the other hand, if you are a put seller, you have the obligation to buy the stock, or have it put to you, at the option's strike price until the option expires. When you have to fulfill your obligation to buy or sell a stock, you are "assigned." Therefore, assignment is the process of buying or selling a stock in accordance to the terms of the option contract. Once assigned, the option seller has no choice but to honor the contract. In other words, it is too late to try to buy the option contract back and close the position.

Although option sellers have an obligation to buy or sell a stock at a predetermined price, assignment will take place only under certain circumstances. How do you know if you are at risk of being assigned? First, exercise generally takes place only with in-the-money options. For example, a call option that has a strike price below the price of the underlying stock is ITM. If XYZ stock is currently trading for $55 a share, the March 50 call options will have an intrinsic value of $5 because the option buyer can exercise the option, buy the stock for $50, immediately sell it in the market for $55, and realize a $5 profit. A put option, on the other hand, will be ITM when the stock price is below the strike price. The put is in-the-money when its strike price is higher than its stock price. It is extremely rare for assignment to take place when options are not ITM. In addition, if an option is in-the-money at expiration, assignment is all but assured. In fact, the OCC automatically exercises any option contract that is one-quarter of a point ITM at expiration. That is, options that are in-the-money by one-quarter of a point or more are subject to automatic exercise.

The second important factor to consider when assessing the probability of assignment is the amount of *time value* left in the option. When an option is exercised before expiration, it is known as early or premature exercise. In general, if there is time value ($1/4$ point or more) left in the option, the option will usually not be exercised. Option sellers can expect assignment when the option has little to no time value remaining. Since the time value of an option decreases as time passes, the probability of early exercise increases as the expiration date approaches. To determine the amount of time value remaining in a call or put option, traders can use the following formulas:

- Call time value = call strike price + call option price – stock price.
- Put time value = stock price + put option price – put strike price.

Finally, this discussion of assignment applies to American-style options. American-style options can be exercised at any time prior to expiration, while European-style options can be exercised only at expiration. Most index options settle European-style. Stock options, on the other hand, exercise American-style. Therefore, stock option sellers can be assigned at any time before the option expires, and anticipating the assignment is important when using strategies that involve selling option contracts.

In sum, the probability of assignment increases as:

1. The option moves in-the-money.
2. The time value of the option drops below ¼ point.

There are odd times when assignment will take place with slightly out-of-the money options or options with time value remaining. These are the exception, however, and relatively low-probability events.

CASH OR MARGIN ACCOUNTS

Many options strategies require margin deposited with a broker. When we discuss the strategies in the next few chapters, we will explain what amount of margin is required for each position. But first, what exactly is margin?

Buying or selling stocks is referred to as a "trade." For instance, if you decide to buy 100 shares of XYZ and the stock price is $100, you are trading your money for the shares. In this case, the trade is $10,000 for 100 shares of XYZ stock.

The exact amount you *need* to make your first trade depends on a number of factors including:

- Your market selection.
- Size of the transaction (number of shares).
- Risk on the trade.

Your first trade also depends on whether you want to do your trade using a margin or cash account.

- *Cash trades* require you to put up 100 percent of the money in cash. All costs of the trade need to be in the account before the trade is placed. For example, to buy 100 shares of IBM at $100 per share, you would have to pay $10,000 plus commissions up front.
- *Margin trades* require traders to only put up half the total amount to purchase shares while their brokerage lends them the other half at a small interest rate. So for the same IBM example you would have to pay $5,000 plus commissions up front.

The term *margin* refers to the amount of money an investor must pay to enter a trade, with the remainder of the cash being borrowed from the brokerage firm. The shares you have purchased secure the loan. Most traders prefer a margin account because it allows them to better leverage assets in order to produce higher returns. In addition, a margin account is usually required for short positions and options trading.

Based on Securities and Exchange Commission (SEC) rules, the margin requirement to purchase stock equals 50 percent of the amount of the trade. At this rate, margin accounts give traders 2-for-1 buying leverage. If the price of the stock rises, then everyone wins. If the price of the stock falls below 75 percent of the total value of the initial investment, the trader receives a *margin* call from the broker requesting additional funds to be placed in the margin account.

Brokerages may set their own margin requirements, but it is never less than 75 percent—the amount required by the Fed. Brokerages are usually willing to lend you 50 percent of a trade's cost, but often require a certain amount of money be left untouched in your account to secure the loan. This money is referred to as the margin requirement.

Of course, brokers don't lend money for free. They charge interest on the loan amount over and above the commission on the trade. The interest and commissions are paid regardless of what happens to the price of the stock. The margin's interest rate is usually the broker call rate plus the firm's add-on points. This rate is cheaper than most loans, as it is a secured loan—they have your stock, and in most cases will get their cash back before you get your stock back.

Ultimately, there are no absolutes when it comes to margin. Combining the buying and selling of options and stocks may create a more complex margin calculation. However, these strategies usually have reduced margin requirements in comparison to just buying or shorting stocks alone. Since every trade is unique, margin requirements will depend on the strategy you employ and your broker's requirements.

Margin calls, which are demands from brokers for more money, are a reality that traders have to deal with every day. Unless you have a crystal ball that forecasts the future, there are no sure bets. Obviously, the larger your capital base becomes, the less you have to worry about margin. But it's always a good idea to keep margin in mind and not let yourself get overextended, no matter how enticing that "just one more" trade looks.

While stock trades usually require a 50 percent margin deposit from your account to place depending on your brokerage, margin requirements on futures markets vary from commodity to commodity. Similarly, the amount of margin in the options market depends on the nature and risk of the position as well as your brokerage's discretion.

CONCLUSION

The options market is a fascinating place that continues to grow in popularity today. Like any derivative, options can carry high risks when not respected or when used carelessly. At the same time, options on stocks, futures, and indexes can offer huge rewards to those savvy traders who have studied them well.

So far, we have covered only the mechanics of options trading. By now, you should understand the difference between a put and call, the factors that determine and influence option prices, why options are known as wasting assets, and how to use symbols to retrieve options quotes.

In the next chapter, we move on to the topic that really matters: how option strategies make money in the markets. As we will see, a profuse number of different strategies can be used to generate profits whether we expect a stock to move higher, move lower, or stay in a narrow price range. Some strategies are very simple, and some are more complex. Regardless, there are several important factors to be considered when reading through various options trading strategies. Which ones make the most sense to you? Which ones feel right? Which trading strategies are you most comfortable with? Try to identify only one or two, because in the beginning you will want to specialize and concentrate your efforts on just a few strategies. It can prove overwhelming if you try to master them all (to do so can take a lifetime), which is one of the major reasons I find options so fascinating.

CHAPTER 4

Basic Trading Strategies

Trading is a diverse activity that encompasses a wide variety of analysis techniques and innovative approaches. The optimal approach for you requires an assessment of both your time availability and your risk tolerance. Once these factors are determined, you're ready to specialize in those techniques that fit your parameters. There are three fundamental approaches on which all trading strategies are based: strategic trades, long-term trades, and delta neutral trades. Each has its own set of conditions and rules that foster a unique trading style.

Strategic trades are typically short-term trading opportunities geared especially for day traders and short-term traders who have the opportunity to monitor the markets very closely each day. Strategic trades are specific to certain markets and may be driven by economic data or events. Many strategic traders use the Standard & Poor's 500 as the key index on which they focus their attention when trading market-related instruments. The Dow Jones Industrial Average (the Dow) is also watched closely to tip off certain bond and currency trades. As a trader, you need to develop your own personal trading style based on the patterns you encounter in the markets. Consistently applying the use of a strategic trading approach fosters success.

Long-term trading methodologies differ greatly from strategic trades. Long-term traders do not look at trades from a second-to-second perspective. Instead, they approach trades from the perspective of a couple of days to a few months, or even into the next year. These trades are based more on market trends and seasonal factors. They take a while to blossom and bear fruit, which gives the long-term trader more time to develop the art of patience.

Delta neutral trades make up the third kind of trades, and probably the most complex. These strategies create hedged trades in which the overall position delta equals zero. As the market rises and falls, the overall position delta moves away from zero. Adjustments can then be made by purchasing or selling instruments in such a way as to bring the overall position delta back to zero. Each adjustment has profit-making potential. Most delta neutral trades can be structured in such a way that your total cost and risk are minimized.

Delta neutral trading strategies and longer-term trading opportunities are better suited for traders who are not able to sit in front of their computers all day watching the markets move. Successful delta neutral traders create a trading system with a time frame they feel comfortable working in. You can create trades that are three months out, two months out, one month out, or even only one day out. If you are the type of person who does not want to think about your trading every single day, simply take a longer-term approach.

Delta neutral strategies can be applied to any market. It can be advantageous to learn to trade both stocks and futures. Even if you think you want to trade just futures, you can make just as much money trading stocks if you use delta neutral strategies. In either case, the options strategies outlined in this book can be applied using stocks or futures. As you read about them, think about the ones that make the most sense to you and then specialize in those strategies.

RISK PROFILES

Before launching into our discussion of specific strategies, let's discuss one of the most important tools for viewing the profit and loss potential of any options strategy: the risk profile. Understanding and managing risk is the critical task of all traders. Very experienced traders and the mathematically adept may be able to intuitively understand what risk is being assumed by a given trade, but the rest of us work best with a visual picture of the risk we are taking. For that reason, the drawing and understanding of risk curves is an essential part of daily trading activities.

A risk profile is a graphic representation of the profit/loss of a position in relation to price changes in the underlying asset. The horizontal numbers at the bottom of the graph—from left to right—show the underlying stock prices. The vertical numbers from top to bottom show a trade's potential profit and loss. The sloping graph line indicates the theoretical profit and loss of the position at expiration as it corresponds to the price of the underlying shares. The zero line on the chart shows the trade's breakeven. By looking at any given market price, you can determine its corresponding profit or loss. Risk profiles enable traders to get a feel for the trade's probability for making a profit.

In order to get a better handle on what a risk curve is, let's use a hypothetical example. The first thing to understand is that the risk graph depicts the value an option or an options position in relation to changes in the underlying asset's price. As an example, let's consider call options on Wal-Mart Stores (WMT). Here, WMT is the underlying asset. Assume shares of Wal-Mart are trading for $60 each and one January 70 call can be purchased for $2.50 (or $250 per contract). Therefore, the underlying asset is Wal-Mart Stores and the option is the WMT January 70 call.

Table 4.1 shows the risk and reward of holding the WMT January 70 call. The prices are hypothetical prices that might exist at expiration on the third Friday in January. Notice that if the stock doesn't rise above $70 a share, the position loses $250 because the option expires worthless at or below $70 a share and yields no profit. If the stock climbs to $75, the options are worth $5 and the profit totals $250: [(75 − 70) − 2.50] × 100. At $80 a share, the profit equals $7.50 ($10 − $2.50). Notice that the position breaks even at $72.50 because $2.50 was the initial cost of the call when purchased.

Rather than creating a table for the risk/reward profile of the WMT January 70 call, we can create a risk graph. It plots the profit from the option (on the vertical axis) along with the price of the stock (along the horizontal axis). Figure 4.1 shows the risk graph of the Long WMT January 70 call in its standard form. The potential profit from the call is plotted along the vertical axis.

The classic view risk graph shown in Figure 4.2 was created using Optionetics.com Platinum software. The lowest of the four lines on the graph considers the potential profit and loss of the WMT January 70 call at expiration and contains the same information as the table. Just as we saw

TABLE 4.1 Risk/Reward Profile of WMT January 70 Call

Potential Profit and Loss from WMT January 70 Call Purchase

WMT at Expiration	January 70 Call at Expiration	Profit/Loss
$60.00	$ 0.00	−$250.00
$65.00	$ 0.00	−$250.00
$70.00	$ 0.00	−$250.00
$72.50	$ 2.50	$ 0.00
$75.00	$ 5.00	$250.00
$80.00	$10.00	$750.00

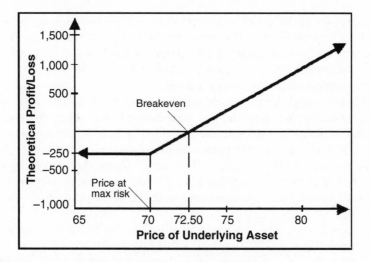

FIGURE 4.1 Standard Risk Graph for 1 Long WMT January 70 Call @ 2.50

on the table, the profits begin to accrue when WMT hits $72.50 a share. The breakeven point (at expiration) occurs where the straight black diagonal line intersects with the zero profit line. The other lines reflect the risk/reward with a specific number of days (as shown in the upper left-hand corner) remaining before expiration. The position of the profit/loss lines at various time intervals is based on the model's assumption that implied volatility remains constant. While this assumption doesn't reflect reality, it must still be made in order to produce the chart.

In addition to using Optionetics.com Platinum, you can also use other options pricing software or compute the graph manually. To actually draw the risk curve, your tools can be anything from a pencil and piece of graph paper to a computerized spreadsheet program such as Lotus 123 or Microsoft Excel. The steps will be the same. Drawing a risk curve for any trade, regardless of its complexity, consists of five basic steps:

1. Determine the stock prices for which you will have to calculate values of your trade at expiration.

2. Calculate the profit (or loss) at each of those points, and determine the breakeven level.

3. Sketch the two axes of your risk curve—the vertical axis will delineate the profit (or loss) of the trade, while the horizontal axis will depict the price of the underlying for which you have determined a profit or loss.

4. Actually plot the points that you calculated in step 2 onto the graph set up in step 3.

5. Draw lines connecting each point plotted in step 4.

This simple five-step process will permit you to calculate a risk curve (even without a computer), detailing the actual profit or loss that can be expected at any stock price upon expiration. Granted, you cannot estimate potential profit or loss prior to expiration, but a basic rule of thumb is that the profits will not be as high, nor the losses as great, at any time prior to expiration. If you don't have a sophisticated risk-graphing program available, this process will give you the basic outline of what your trade will look like. As you gain experience and your trading becomes more refined,

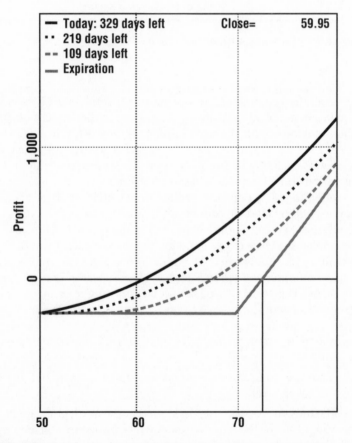

FIGURE 4.2   Wal-Mart January 70 Call Risk Curve (*Source:* Optionetics Platinum © 2004)

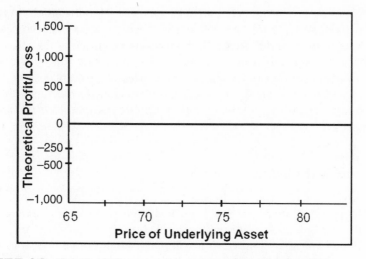

FIGURE 4.3 Risk Graph Framework for 1 Long WMT 70 Call @ 2.50

you will find yourself needing the power of the packaged programs. However, for the beginning trader, a simple risk curve at expiration like this one will help explain where profits can be made or lost. If you graph out the risk curve on every trade you are contemplating, the visual recognition of the risk will soon improve your trading in countless ways.

Skill Builder

Now it's your turn. Follow the five steps to see if you can manually create a risk graph (using the framework in Figure 4.3) for 1 Long WMT 70 Call @ 2.50. The complete risk graph can be found in Figure 4.1 if you want to check your work.

Breakeven	72.50
Maximum loss	–$250
Price at maximum loss	70
Profit @ 75	$250
Profit @ 80	$750

LONG STOCK

While the term *going long* might have you envisioning a football player going deep for a pass, in the financial markets going long is one of the most common investing techniques. It consists of buying stock, futures, or options in anticipation of a rise in the market price (or, in the case of a long put, a drop in the price). An increase in the price of the stock obviously adds value to a stock holding. To close this long position, a trader would sell the stock at the current price. A profit is derived from the difference between the initial investment and the closing price. A long stock position is completely at the mercy of market direction to make a profit.

Long Stock Mechanics

In this example, the trader is long 100 shares of XYZ (currently trading at $50). Remember, shares of stock do not have premium or time decay. Long stock has a one-to-one risk/reward ratio. This means that for every point higher the shares move, you will make $100. Conversely, for every point the shares fall below the purchase price, you will lose $100.

Figure 4.4 shows the risk profile of this long stock example. As you can see, when the share price rises, you make money; when it falls, you lose money. Notice how the profit/loss line for the stock position shows a 1-to-1 movement in price versus risk and reward. This means that the stock trade has an unlimited profit potential and limited risk as the price of the stock can fall only as far as zero.

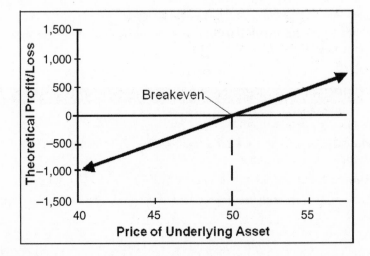

FIGURE 4.4   Long 100 Shares XYZ @ 50

Exiting the Position

When you purchase a stock, the only way to exit the position (without exercising options) is to simply sell the shares at the current market price. If the price of the stock rises, the trader makes a profit; if the price falls, then a loss is incurred. Thus, if XYZ rises to 60, 100 shares will yield a profit of $1,000: $(60 - 50) \times 100 = \$1,000$. If XYZ declines to 40, 100 shares create a loss of $1,000: $(50 - 40) \times 100 = \$1,000$.

Long Stock Case Study

Buying, or going long, stock is the easiest and most straightforward trading strategy available. However, this doesn't mean it is the best strategy to use. Going long stock consists of buying shares of a company outright and holding onto them as they (hopefully) gain in value. The positives to this strategy are that it is easy and figuring your profits and losses is straightforward. The stock can also be held forever, as long as the company remains a valid corporation and does not declare bankruptcy. However, the costs can be expensive, making it difficult to diversify.

There are many different ideas on how to pick a good stock, depending on your time frame. Technical analysis is often used for short-term trading decisions, while fundamental analysis is the main discipline for buying stocks over the long term. As with any trading strategy, it still is a good idea to have exit points set up in advance so that you aren't swayed by emotion.

A risk graph for a long stock trade is very easy to create, even by hand. It is a straight line, which shows that for every dollar gained in the security, you profit a dollar per share. The same holds true to the downside. It shows the dollar-for-dollar profit/loss that comes with this basic strategy.

Long Stock

Strategy: Buy shares of stock.

Market Opportunity: Look for a bullish market where a rise in the price of the stock is anticipated.

Maximum Risk: Limited to the price of the stock as it falls to zero.

Maximum Profit: Unlimited as the stock price rises above the initial entry price.

Breakeven: Price of the stock at initiation (not including commissions).

Margin: Usually 50 percent of the total cost of the shares.

Let's say we saw the Nasdaq 100 Trust (QQQ) break above resistance on May 1, 2004, and decided to buy 100 shares at $27.69. The risk graph of this trade is shown in Figure 4.5.

This trade proved to be a good investment decision, with the Qs moving higher right into 2004. We might have held onto this trade until the Qs started a downtrend in early 2004. Let's assume we got out at 36, when the Qs made a lower high and a lower low. By getting out at 36, we would have made $8.31 per share, or $831 overall. Not bad, but we had to invest $2,769 (or half this amount if we used margin)—a 30 percent return on investment. Of course, if the Qs had lost ground, we would have lost a dollar per share for each point the Qs fell.

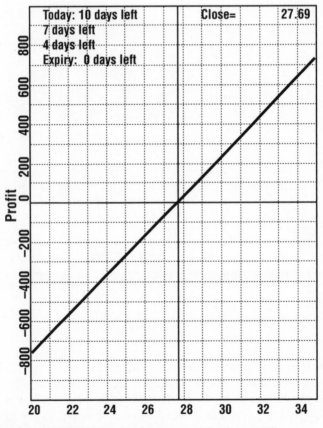

FIGURE 4.5 Risk Graph of Long 100 Shares of Stock on QQQ
(*Source:* Optionetics Platinum © 2004)

Long Stock Case Study

Strategy: With the security trading at $27.69 a share on May 1, 2004, buy 100 shares of the Nasdaq 100 Trust (QQQ).

Market Opportunity: Expect advance in shares on break of resistance.

Maximum Risk: Limited to initial debit of $2,769.

Maximum Profit: Unlimited to the upside. In this case, exiting at $36 a share garnered an $831 profit.

Breakeven: Initial entry price (not including commissions). In this case, $27.69.

Margin: None needed, but can be used to cover half the cost of initial entry.

SHORT STOCK

Traders can take advantage of a falling market by selling, or shorting, shares of stock. Initially, this process can be quite confusing. After all, most investors want to buy a stock at a lower price and sell it for a profit at a higher price. Short selling reverses this process. With short sales, the trader actually sells the stock first and hopes that it will decline in value, so that it can be bought back at a lower price. The difference between the selling price and the purchase price represents the profit or loss.

In order to sell a stock short, traders must first borrow the shares from their broker. This is not always going to be possible and will depend on the specific stock and the brokerage firm. In some cases, it might not be possible to find the stock. This is especially true of less liquid or actively traded shares.

Generally, a broker will look in one of four places for the shares to lend to the short seller. The most common source is from other customers who are long the stock in their margin accounts. Alternatively, the firm might look to one of three other places:

1. Its own inventory.
2. Securities borrowed from another brokerage firm.
3. Securities borrowed from institutional investors.

If the firm has exhausted these options and come up empty, the short seller will not be able to borrow and short that particular stock.

Once the stock is sold, the trader will profit if the stock moves lower. Keep in mind, however, that if any dividends are paid by the stock, then the lender, not the short seller, is entitled to them. The person holding an open short position must pay the amount of the dividend to the lender. In addition, the margin requirements call for a 150 percent deposit of the net proceeds from the short sale. Also, importantly, the lender generally retains the right to demand that the stock be returned to him or her at any time. So, one risk to short selling is that the lender may demand that the shares be returned before the stock has made a move lower. Undoubtedly, short selling stock comes with a variety of risks.

Short Stock Mechanics

An investor believes that the price of XYZ is too high and expects the stock to move southward. It is currently trading for $20 share. So, she instructs her broker to sell short 1,000 shares of XYZ at $20. The brokerage firm then lends the investor the securities and they are sold in the market for $20. The total credit received from the short sale equals $20,000. Now the money is in the account, but the customer owes the brokerage firm the 1,000 shares. The risk graph for this trade is shown in Figure 4.6.

If XYZ falls, the trader can book a profit. For example, let's say XYZ drops to $10 a share and the short seller instructs the broker to buy back 1,000 shares to close the position. The stock is purchased for $10 a share and the cost of the trade is $10,000 (plus commissions). She then returns the borrowed shares and closes the trade. The profit is equal to the difference between the purchase price and the selling price, or $10,000 (minus commissions). Suppose, though, XYZ appreciates to $30 a share and the trader decides that it's time to cut her losses. In this case, she must buy

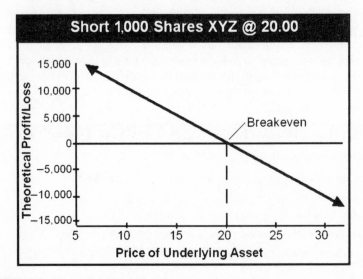

FIGURE 4.6 Short Stock Risk Graph

XYZ back for $30 per share, or $30,000, and return the borrowed stock to her brokerage. The loss is equal to the purchase price minus the sale price, or $10,000 (plus commissions).

Exiting the Position

When you sell shares short, the only way to exit the position (without applying options) is to buy back the shares at the current market price. In order to do so, you must instruct your broker to close the trade or to "buy to cover." Then, once the stock is purchased, the borrowed shares are moved out of the account and returned to the original owner.

Short Stock Case Study

Outside of trading options, there is only one method a trader has to make a profit during a downtrend in stocks: short selling stock. As previously discussed, going short is the process of borrowing shares from your broker and then replacing these shares at a future date when the stock has lost ground. If this occurs, a trader can profit on the decrease in price. However, shorting stock is extremely dangerous and cannot be done on all stocks and at all times.

It's vital to keep in mind that shorting stock requires a large amount of margin. This is because the risk is unlimited to the upside. If you borrow a stock from your broker at $50, expecting it to decline, but it instead moves higher, you are at risk the whole way up. If the stock hits $75, you have lost $25 for each share you are short. This means that a margin call would have occurred several times on this move up. A margin call is a Federal Reserve requirement that a customer deposit a specified amount of money or securities to keep a trade open when a sale or purchase is made in a margin account; the amount is expressed as a percentage of the

Short Stock

Strategy: Sell shares of stock.

Market Opportunity: Look for a bearish market where the stock is expected to fall sharply.

Maximum Risk: Unlimited as the stock moves higher.

Maximum Profit: Limited to the full stock price as it can only fall to zero.

Breakeven: Price of the stock at initiation (not including commissions).

Margin: Yes—usually 150 percent of short sale proceeds.

market value of the securities at the time of purchase. The deposit must
be made within one payment period.

Another negative to shorting stock is that it can only be done on
stocks that have large volume. Also, a stock can not be shorted on a
downtick. This means that if the market is falling hard and you want to
short a stock, it can't be done until the stock has traded at the same price
or higher.

Let's take a look at the risk graph in Figure 4.7, which depicts going
short 100 shares of the Nasdaq 100 Trust (QQQ) at $82.44 on November 6,
2000. The short sale of 100 shares produces a credit of $8,244. As you can
see, the risk graph for a short stock is the exact opposite of a risk graph

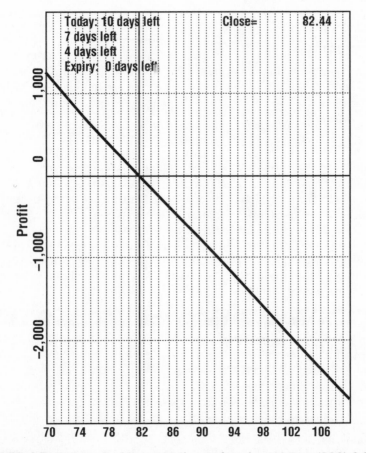

FIGURE 4.7   Risk Graph of Short 100 Shares of Nasdaq 100 Trust (QQQ) @ 82.44
(*Source:* Optionetics Platinum © 2004)

Short Stock Case Study

Strategy: With the security trading at $82.44 a share on November 6, 2000, sell 100 shares of the Nasdaq 100 Trust (QQQ).

Market Opportunity: Expect continued decline in shares.

Maximum Risk: Unlimited to the upside.

Maximum Profit: Unlimited down to zero. In this case, an exit at $40 a share would create a $4,244 profit.

Breakeven: Initial entry price (not including commissions). In this case, $82.44 (not including commissions).

Margin: Extensive; depends on broker requirements and SEC requirements.

for a long stock. Although the trade profits dollar-for-dollar as the stock moves lower, it is also at risk dollar-for-dollar if the stock price increases. Keep in mind that your broker will require a rather large sum of capital to cover the margin requirement with the firm—usually 150 percent.

Luckily, this trade proved to be a good investment decision, with the Qs moving lower and then sharply lower. If a trader had stayed short until the 200-day moving average was broken near 40, he or she would have made a significant profit. The Qs fell that year from 82.44 to 40 in about a 12-month period, which would have created a healthy profit for the savvy short seller!

LONG CALL

In the long call strategy, you are purchasing the right, but not the obligation, to buy the underlying shares at a specific price until the expiration date. This strategy is used when you anticipate an increase in the price of the underlying stock. A long call strategy offers unlimited profit potential with limited downside risk. It is often used to get high leverage on an underlying security that you expect to increase in price.

If you want to go long a call, your risk curve would look like the graph in Figure 4.8. When the underlying security price rises, you make money; when it falls, you lose money. This strategy provides unlimited profit potential with limited risk. It is often used to get high leverage on an underlying security that you expect to increase in price. Zero margin borrowing is allowed. That means that you don't have to hold any margin in your account to place the trade. You pay a premium (cost of the call), and this expenditure is your maximum risk.

Perhaps the only drawback is that options have deadlines, after which you cannot recoup the premium it cost to buy them. Thus, you need to buy calls with enough time till expiration for the underlying to

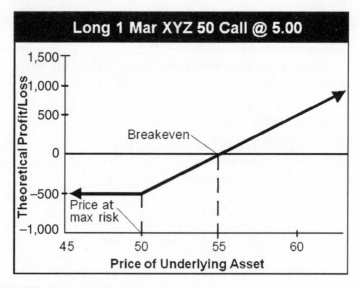

FIGURE 4.8 Long Call Risk Graph

move into the profit zone—at least 90 days—or simply purchase LEAPS with a year or two until expiration. In addition, it's best to buy calls with low implied volatility to lower the breakeven and minimize the debit to your account.

Long Call Mechanics

In this example, let's buy 1 March XYZ 50 Call @ 5.00, with XYZ trading at $50. This trade costs a total of $500 (5 × 100 = $500) plus commissions. The maximum risk is equal to the cost of the call premium or $500. The maximum reward is unlimited to the upside as underlying shares rise above the breakeven. The breakeven is calculated by adding the call premium to the strike price. In this example, the breakeven is 55 (50 + 5 = 55), which means the underlying shares have to rise above 55 for the trade to start making a profit.

In Figure 4.8, note how the numbers that run from top to bottom indicate the profit and loss of this trade. The numbers that run left to right indicate the price of the underlying asset. The sloping line indicates the theoretical profit or loss of the call option at trade expiration according to the price of the underlying asset. Note how the loss is limited to the premium paid to purchase the call option.

The risk graph of the long call shows unlimited profit potential and a limited risk capped at $500 (see Figure 4.8). The breakeven is calculated by adding the call premium to the strike price. The long call breakeven is slightly higher than the breakeven on the stock, but this is the trade-off a trader takes for opting for a position with less risk and a higher return on investment.

Exiting the Position

A long call strategy offers two distinct exit scenarios. Each scenario primarily depends on the movement of the underlying shares, although volatility can have a major impact as well.

- *XYZ rises above the breakeven (55):* Offset the position by selling a call option with the same strike price and expiration at an acceptable profit; or exercise the option to purchase shares of the underlying market at the lower strike. You can then hold these shares as part of your portfolio or sell them at a profit at the current higher market price.
- *XYZ falls below the breakeven (55):* If a reversal does not seem likely, contact your broker to offset the long call by selling an identical call to mitigate your loss. The most you can lose is the initial premium paid for the option.

In this example, let's say XYZ rises 10 points to 60. There are two ways to take advantage of it: exercise or offset it. By exercising the March 50 call, you will become the owner of 100 shares of XYZ at the lower price of $50 per share. You can then sell the shares for the current price of $60 a share and pocket the difference of $1,000. But since you paid $500 for the option, this process reaps only a $500 profit ($1,000 – $500 = $500) minus commissions. The more profitable technique is to sell the March 50 call for the new premium of 14.75, an increase of 9.75 points. By offsetting the March 50 call, you can make a profit of $975 ($1,475 – $500 = $975)—a 195 percent return!

Conversely, if you had bought 100 shares of XYZ at $50 per share, you would have made a profit of $1,000 (not including commissions) when the shares reached $60 per share—an increase of 10 points. The profit on the long stock position is slightly higher than the profit on the long call—a big $25. However, the return on investment is much higher for the long call position because the initial investment was significantly lower than the initial capital needed to buy the stock shares. While both trades offered profit-making opportunities, the long call position offered a significantly lower risk approach and the power to use the rest of the available trading capital in other trades. For an initial investment of $5,000, you could have

Long Call

Strategy: Buy a call option.

Market Opportunity: Look for a bullish market where a rise above the breakeven is anticipated.

Maximum Risk: Limited to the amount paid for the call.

Maximum Profit: Unlimited as the price of the underlying instrument rises above the breakeven.

Breakeven: Call strike price + call option premium.

Margin: None.

purchased 10 call options and made a total profit of $9,750—now, that's a healthy return.

The ability of a call option to be in-the-money by expiration is primarily determined by the movement of the underlying stock. It is therefore essential to know how to analyze stock markets so that you can accurately forecast future price action in order to pick the call with the best chance of making a profit. Understanding market movement is not an easy task. Although it takes time to accumulate market experience, you can learn how various strategies work without risking hard-earned cash by exploring paper trading techniques.

Long Call Case Study

In order to illustrate how the long call works in the real world, let's consider an example using a familiar name—Intel (INTC). Suppose you were studying some research notes on Intel and it seemed to you that the stock price had fallen too far given the outlook for the company's semiconductor sales. The chart pattern also seemed to suggest that the stock was due to move higher. With shares trading near $15.75, you expect it to move above $20 by year-end. So, you decide to establish a bullish trade on the chipmaker.

Instead of buying shares, you decide to buy the INTC January 17.50 call. That is, you will buy the call option on Intel that has the strike price of 17.50 and has an expiration month of January. The current premium is $2.55 per contract and you buy 10 contracts. The total cost of the trade is therefore $2,550: (2.55 × 10) × 100 = 2,550. Since Intel is trading near $16 a share at the time, this call is out-of-the-money. Many call buyers prefer to use out-of-the-money calls because they provide the most leverage. It is a very aggressive way to trade the market.

To calculate the breakeven, we add the option's strike price to the contract price, or 17.50 plus 2.55. The breakeven equals $20.05 a share. Often,

traders will exit the long call strategy before expiration if the stock moves
dramatically higher or falls too far below the breakeven. Recall that time
decay is the greatest during the last 30 days of an option's life. Therefore,
it is best not to hold an option like the long call during that time. In addition, many traders will exit the position if it does not move in the anticipated direction. For example, if INTC drops below $15 a share, the trader
might choose to close the trade. In that case, the $15 level would be con-
sidered a *stop loss*, or a predetermined price point where the trader exits a
losing trade. In any case, rarely will the long call be exercised when it is
purchased in anticipation of a move higher in the underlying security. Instead, the position is closed through an offsetting transaction. Specifically,
you will sell 10 INTC January 17.50 calls to close.

The chart in Figure 4.9 shows the risk graph for the INTC January

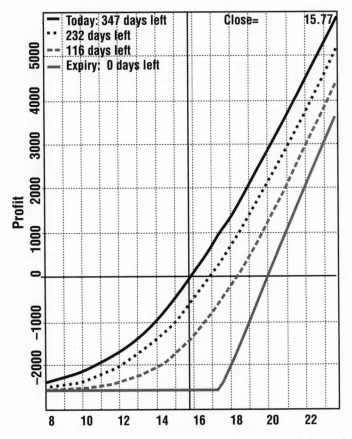

FIGURE 4.9 Risk Graph of Long INTC Call (*Source:* Optionetics Platinum © 2004)

Long Call Case Study

Strategy: With the stock trading near $16 a share in February 2003, buy 10 INTC January 17.50 calls @ $2.55 and hold until the end of the year.

Market Opportunity: The stock looks bullish and is expected to rise above $20 a share by January.

Maximum Risk: Limited to the amount paid for 10 calls or $2,550.

Maximum Profit: Unlimited as the price of the underlying instrument rises above the breakeven. In this case, the INTC January 17.50 call topped $30 a contract for an 11-month gain of 600 percent.

Breakeven: Strike price + call option premium. In this case, 20.05: (17.50 + 2.55).

Margin: None.

17.50 long call at the time the trade was established. We can see that if the stock falls the call will lose value. In contrast, profits begin to build as the stock moves higher. The maximum risk is equal to the premium, or $255 per contract. The upside potential is quite large. In fact, in this case, Intel not only rose above $20 a share that year, it topped $30. As a result, by the end of the year, the INTC January 17.50 call was worth $17.50 a contract— for an 11-month 600 percent gain!

Long Call versus Long Stock

As you can see, a long call strategy has many advantages compared with buying stock. For clarity's sake, let's review these advantages.

- *Cost.* The premium of an option is significantly lower than the amount required to purchase a stock.
- *Limited risk.* Since the maximum risk on a long call strategy is equal to the premium paid for the option, you know before entering the trade exactly how much money you could potentially lose.
- *Unlimited reward.* Once you hit breakeven (call strike price + call option premium = breakeven), you have unlimited reward potential as in a stock purchase.
- *Increased leverage.* Less initial investment also means that you can leverage your money a great deal more than the 2-for-1 leverage buying stock on margin offers.

The only drawback is that options have a limited time until they expire. But even this disadvantage can be seen as an advantage if you consider the opportunity cost of waiting months and sometimes years for a stock that has taken a bearish turn to reverse direction.

SHORT CALL

In a short call trade, you are selling call options on futures or stock contracts. This strategy is placed when you expect the price of the underlying instrument to fall. If you want to go short a call, your risk curve would look like the graph in Figure 4.10. If you want to short a stock, your risk curve would fall from the upper left-hand corner to the lower right-hand corner (see Figure 4.10). Notice how the horizontal line slants upward from right to left, providing insight as to its bearish nature. When the underlying instrument's price falls, you make money; when it rises, you lose money. This strategy provides limited profit potential with unlimited risk. It is often used to get high leverage on an underlying security that you expect to decrease in price.

Selling a call enables traders to profit from a decrease in the underlying market. If the underlying stock stays below the strike price of the short call until the option's expiration, the option expires worthless and the trader gets to keep the credit received. But if the price of the underlying stock rises above the short call strike price before expiration, the short option will be assigned to an option buyer. A call buyer (as discussed in the previous section on long calls) has the right to buy the underlying asset at the call strike price at any time before expiration by exercising the call. If the assigned call buyer exercises the option, the option seller is obligated to deliver 100 shares of the underlying stock to the

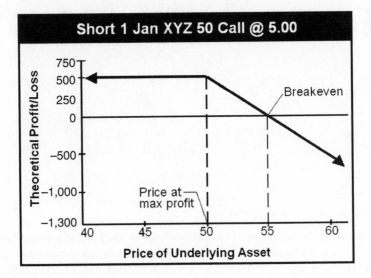

FIGURE 4.10 Short Call Risk Graph

option buyer at the short call strike price. This entails buying the underlying stock at the higher price and delivering it to the option buyer at the lower price. The difference between these two prices constitutes the seller's loss and the buyer's open position profit. This can be a huge loss in fast markets, which is why we never recommend selling short, or "naked," options.

Selling naked calls is not allowed by many brokerages. Some may require you to have at least $50,000 as a margin deposit. This speaks volumes about just how risky this strategy can be. However, since a short call is very useful in hedging and combination options strategies, it is important to understand its basic properties.

In the case of selling options, be advised that you will initially receive money into your account in the form of a credit. This is the premium for which you sold the option. This strategy is used to generate income from the short sale of an option, since it provides immediate premium to the seller. In addition, it's best to short calls when the implied volatility of the option is high; that way, you maximize the premium received. This is vital since the profit on a short call is limited to the premium received, and the position has an unlimited upside risk. As you can see by looking at the risk graph in Figure 4.10, this is a very risky strategy because it leaves the trader completely unprotected.

Short Call Mechanics

Let's create an example that shows the trader going short 1 Jan XYZ 50 Call @ 5.00. The trader collected $500 (5 × 100 = 500) minus commissions for this trade. The maximum reward is limited to the credit the trader receives at the trade's initiation. Conversely, the risk on this trade is unlimited as the price of the underlying asset rises above the breakeven. The breakeven of a short call equals the strike price of the call option plus the call premium. In this trade, the breakeven at expiration is 55: (50 + 5 = 55). As the market drops, the position increases until it hits the maximum credit (i.e., the amount of premium taken in for the call). Please note that a short call comes with unlimited risk to the upside. It is very important that you learn how to create covered positions (i.e., sell an option and buy an option) to limit your risk and protect against unlimited loss.

Figure 4.10 shows the risk profile of the short call position. When the underlying stock reaches a price of 50, the position's profit hits a maximum of $500 (the credit received). The call's potential loss is unlimited and continues to increase as the price of the underlying asset rises above the $55 breakeven. If the market price of the underlying asset doesn't rise, you get to keep the credit. However, this is the most that can be made on the trade.

Exiting the Position

A short call strategy offers three distinct exit scenarios. Each scenario primarily depends on the movement of the underlying shares.

- *XYZ falls below the call strike price (50):* This is the best exit strategy. The call expires worthless at expiration. This means you get to keep the premium, which is the maximum profit on a short call position.
- *XYZ rises above the call strike price (50):* The call will be assigned to a call holder. In this scenario, the call seller is obligated to deliver 100 shares of XYZ at $50 per share to the assigned option holder by purchasing 100 shares of XYZ at the current market price. The difference between the current market price and the delivery price of $50 a share constitutes the loss (minus the credit of $500 initially received for shorting the call).
- *XYZ starts to rise above the breakeven (55):* You may want to offset the position by purchasing a call option with the same strike price and expiration to exit the trade because assignment becomes increasingly likely once the time value of an option falls below $1/4$ point.

Short Call Case Study

When looking for short call candidates, what we want to see is a stock that has run into resistance and that is expected to move lower before option expiration. Since we are selling the call, we also want to use time decay to our advantage by selling front month options. Lastly, we are looking for a stock that has options that are showing high implied volatility (IV) compared to the past. The higher the IV, the larger the premium we receive up front. Let's look at a real-world example for a short call.

In late May 2003, we could have run a search for stocks that had options showing high implied volatility. One stock that would have shown up

Short Call

Strategy: Sell a call option.

Market Opportunity: Look for a bearish or stable market where you anticipate a fall in the price of the underlying below the breakeven.

Maximum Risk: Unlimited as the stock price rises above the breakeven.

Maximum Profit: Limited to the credit received from the call option premium.

Breakeven: Call strike price + call option premium.

Margin: Required. Amount subject to broker's discretion.

was Northrop Grumman (NOC). On May 26, NOC spiked higher, but ran into resistance near $90.

By entering a short call, we have unlimited risk to the upside. This means that if the stock moves sharply higher, we have to come up with the money to cover the call. However, we get a credit immediately from the sale of the call, though margin will be needed. In our example, NOC was at $87.96 as of the close of trading on May 27. At that time, we could have sold the June 90 call for $1.10, or $110 per contract. In this case, our maximum risk is unlimited as the stock rises and our maximum profit is the initial credit received. Our breakeven point is found by adding the credit we received (1.10) to the strike price of 90: (1.10 + 90 = 91.10). Thus, the breakeven point as of expiration is at $91.10.

By looking at the risk graph in Figure 4.11, notice how the profit area

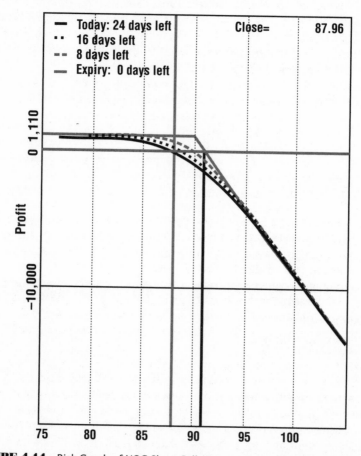

FIGURE 4.11   Risk Graph of NOC Short Call (*Source:* Optionetics Platinum © 2004)

Short Call Case Study

Strategy: With the stock trading near $88 a share on May 27, 2003, sell 10 June 90 calls @ 1.10 and hold until expiration.

Market Opportunity: NOC has run into resistance and looks like it is in a downtrend.

Maximum Risk: Unlimited to the upside above the breakeven.

Maximum Profit: Net credit initially received. In this case, $1,110: ($110 × 10 = $1,110).

Breakeven: Strike price + call option credit. In this case, 91.10: (90 + 1.10).

Margin: Extensive.

is small when compared to the loss area. This occurs because the trade has unlimited risk as the stock rises. For most traders, this type of trade is too risky to undertake and it requires a lot of capital to be held in margin. Nonetheless, for the trader who has the funds and uses appropriate money management, a short call can be profitable.

In our example, shares of NOC remained below $90 all the way through June expiration on June 20. In fact, the stock was making a move higher when expiration hit, but this trade still would have closed with a maximum profit of $110 per contract.

COVERED CALL

Covered call writing (selling) is the strategy that seems to be promoted most by the investment community. Many stockbrokers use this technique as their primary options strategy, perhaps because it is the one technique they are trained to share with their clients. It is also widely used by many so-called professional managers. Nevertheless, it can be a dangerous strategy for those who do not understand the risks involved. A few publications describe this technique as a "get rich quick" method for investing in the stock market, but it can become a "get poor quick" strategy if done incorrectly.

What is this technique all about? The purpose of the covered call is to increase cash income from a long stock or futures position. It provides some protection against decreases in the price of a long underlying position or increases in the price of a short underlying position. A covered call has limited profit potential and can result in substantial losses; but these potential losses are less than those for an unprotected long stock or futures position.

A covered call write is composed of the purchase of a stock (or futures contract) and the sale of a call option against the purchased underlying asset. Remember, the buyer of a call option has the right to call the option seller (writer) to deliver the stock at the price at which the option was purchased. Therefore, if you write an option you are the seller, and you are responsible for delivering the stock at the strike price at which the option was sold to the purchaser if the option is exercised. At the inception of the transaction, you receive a premium, which pays you for the time value of the option as well as any intrinsic value the option may have at that time.

You may be wondering what is wrong with the whole concept of covered call writing. Why are so many people incorrect when they use this strategy? Many traders simply do not know the risks they are assuming when they implement this overused technique. If you placed covered calls in stocks that only go up, you could make out very well. However, how many people pick stocks that only go up?

A range-bound stock exhibits price action between two specified points: resistance and support. Resistance is the point at which prices stop rising and tend to start to drop. Support is the point at which prices stop dropping and tend to start to rise. When a stock rises, it hits a certain price where the sellers rush in, outnumbering the buyers, and thereby causing prices to start to fall off. The support level is the place where the price has become low enough for buyers to start to outnumber the sellers and the price begins to rise again. If this recurs over a specified period of time (e.g., six months), strong support and resistance levels have probably been established. Stocks that exhibit these tendencies can be excellent candidates for covered call writing. However, you must be aware that nontrending stocks also can begin trends, and many may begin trending to the downside.

Covered Call Mechanics

Let's create a hypothetical example using a technology stock with the name XYZ Computer Corp. The ticker symbol for shares is XYZ and the company is one of the world's leading computer sellers. The company has performed exceptionally well, with shares rising more than 400 percent in a one-year period! Let's say XYZ Computer is trading at $49 per share after numerous stock bonuses, and we decide to place a covered call trade.

Let's buy 100 shares of XYZ at $49 each. This part of the trade costs $4,900 ($49 × 100 = $4,900). The amount of margin (the capital required) would be half this amount, or $2,450. In a covered call strategy, a trader offsets the purchase cost of shares with the sale of a call option. The covered call consists of selling one call for each 100 shares owned. The call can have any strike price and any expiration; however, this step can be difficult. You have to choose which option to sell. You have a multitude of choices: near-term, long-term, in-the-money, out-of-the-money, at-the-money, and so on. Many covered call writers sell options one or two strikes out-of-the-money (OTM) because they want the shares to have a little room to run up before reaching the strike price at which the option was sold.

Let's say that on September 9, XYZ is trading at $49, and the October 50 and 55 call options (which have 40 days to expiration) have the following option premiums:

- October 50 Call @ 2.75.
- October 55 Call @ 1.75.

In this example, let's go long 100 shares of XYZ at $49 and short 1 XYZ October 50 call at $2.75. This transaction has two sides, the debit (purchase of shares) and the credit (sale of option). The debit equals $4,900 ($49 × 100 = $4,900); however, the amount of margin (the capital required to place the trade) would be half this amount, or $2,450. In addition, you would receive a $275 credit (2.75 × $100 = $275) for the short option on 100 shares of stock. The risk profile for this trade is shown in Figure 4.12.

If the stock rises from $49 to $50, the strike price of the option, you

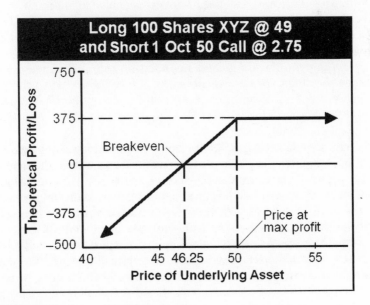

FIGURE 4.12 Covered Call Risk Graph

make an additional $100. You also get to keep the $275 credit you received. In total, your profit will be $375. If the stock goes to $55 you still get $375. If the shares go to $100 you still get only $375. In both these instances, you have to deliver the shares to the assigned purchaser of the option as it will be exercised at expiration since the option is in-the-money (i.e., the share price is greater than the strike price of the option). That means that for an investment of $2,075: ($2,450 – $375 = $2,075), you can make $375 if the stock rises to at least $50 by expiration—a 17 percent return in only 40 days.

Lastly, the breakeven of a covered call is calculated by subtracting the credit received on the short call from the price of the underlying security at trade initiation. In this trade, the breakeven is 46.25: (49 – 2.75 = 46.25).

In Figure 4.12, the risk graph for the covered call example, notice how the profit line slopes upward from left to right, conveying the trader's desire for the market price of the stock to rise slightly. It also shows the trade's limited protection. As XYZ declines beyond the breakeven (47.25), the value of the stock position plummets as it falls to zero. Thus, the inherent risk in this strategy rears its ugly head.

Overall, the covered call offers a slightly better approach than if you simply purchase the stock at $49 and watch it drop, because you have reduced your breakeven price by 2.75 points. XYZ must drop below this new breakeven price (46.25) to start losing money at expiration. But once it falls below the breakeven, losses can accumulate quickly.

Now let's say you sell the October 55 calls at 1.75; then your breakeven price is higher at $47.25 ($49 less the 1.75 received for selling the 55 call). By selecting the higher strike call option to sell, you will receive less of a credit and will raise your breakeven price for the stock. However, then you have a greater potential return on the investment if and when the stock goes up. Obviously, you lose money when the stock goes below the breakeven price. Bottom line: each option has a certain trade-off for the option writer. You have to decide which one best fits the market you are trading.

As mentioned previously, if the price of XYZ stock has been going up significantly over the past year, covered call writing would not have hurt you. You may not have received the 400 percent gain stock purchasers received, but perhaps you could have slept better at night, as you would have reduced your breakeven point. Unfortunately, traders may select stocks that have just begun a tailspin and lose 50 percent of their value overnight. In these cases, a covered call strategy will not help. These traders may get to keep the short option's credit, but that will not go very far in light of losing 50 percent or more on the total price of the stock. There are numerous examples of companies losing 30 percent, 40 percent, 75 percent, or all their value in one day. *Do not count on this strategy to save you from losing large sums of money if the stock makes a big drop.* Writing covered calls can work. However, you must find stocks that meet one of two criteria: trending upward or maintaining a trading range.

As exhibited with XYZ, covered calls work well with stocks on the rise. Unfortunately, even stocks with upward trends have moments in which they make sharp corrections. These periods are difficult for covered call writers as they watch their accounts shrink, because the covered call does not offer comprehensive protection to the downside. However, in many cases good stocks will rebound. If you do choose to write covered calls, do so only in high-grade stocks that have been in a consistent uptrend and have exhibited strong growth in earnings per share.

To protect yourself from severe down moves, you can combine covered calls with buying puts for protection. If you purchase long-term puts (over six months), you can continue to write calls month after month, but you will have the added protection of the right to sell the underlying stock at a specific price.

Exiting the Position

Since a covered call protects only a stock within a specific range, it is vital to monitor the daily price movement of the underlying stock. Let's investigate optimal exit strategies for the first covered call example, the sale of the 50 call.

- *XYZ rises above the short strike (50):* The short call is assigned. Use the 100 shares from the original long stock position to satisfy your obligation to deliver 100 shares of XYZ to the option holder at $50 a share. This scenario allows you to take in the maximum profit of $375.
- *XYZ falls below the short strike (50), but stays above the initial stock price (49):* The short call expires worthless and you get to keep the premium ($275) received. No losses have occurred on the long stock position and you can place another covered call to offset the risk on the long stock position if you wish.
- *XYZ falls below the initial stock price (49), but stays above the breakeven (46.25):* The long stock position starts to lose money, but this loss is offset by the credit received from the short call. If XYZ stays above 46.25, the position will break even or make a small profit.
- *XYZ falls below the breakeven (46.25):* Let the short option expire worthless and use the credit received to partially hedge the loss on the long stock position.

Covered calls are one of the most popular option strategies used in today's markets. If you want to gain additional income on a long stock

Covered Call

Strategy: Buy the underlying security and sell an OTM call option.

Market Opportunity: Look for a bullish to neutral market where a slow rise in the price of the underlying is anticipated with little risk of decline.

Maximum Risk: Limited to the downside below the breakeven as the stock falls to zero.

Maximum Profit: Limited to the credit received from the short call option + (short call strike price − price of long underlying asset) × 100.

Breakeven: Price of the underlying asset at trade initiation − short call premium.

Margin: Amount subject to broker's discretion.

position, you can sell a slightly OTM call every month. The risk lies in the strategy's limited ability to protect the underlying stock from major moves down and the potential loss of future profits on the stock above the strike price. Covered calls can also be combined with a number of bearish options strategies to create additional downside protection.

Covered Call Case Study

Covered calls are often used as an income strategy on stocks that we are holding long-term. They also can be used as a short-term profit maker by purchasing the stock and selling the call at the same time. The idea is to sell a call against stock that is already owned. If we do not want to give up the stock, we must be willing to buy the option back if it moves in-the-money. However, if we feel the stock will not rise above our strike price, we would benefit by selling the call.

On December 1, 2003, shares of Rambus (RMBS) were falling back after an attempt to break through resistance at $30. The stock rose to a high of $32.25, but ultimately ended flat on the session right at $30 a share. Viewing the chart, we might have decided that $30 would hold and that entering a covered call strategy might work well.

By entering a short call, we have unlimited risk to the upside. However, by owning the stock, we mitigate this risk because we could use the stock to cover the short call. Let's assume we didn't already own Rambus, so we need to purchase 500 shares at $30 and sell 5 December 30 calls at $2.05 each. Our maximum profit for this trade is $1,025 [(2.05 × 5) × 100] and this occurs if the stock is at or above 30 on December 19. The maximum risk is still large because the amount of the credit for selling the calls does little for a major drop in the stock. Our breakeven point is at 27.95, which is figured by taking the credit received and subtracting it from the price of the underlying at trade initiation (30 – 2.05). Figure 4.13 shows the risk graph for this trade.

Though we have limited our upside risk by using stock to cover the short call, we still have significant risk to the downside if the stock were to fall sharply. However, if the stock remains near $30, we get to keep the entire credit, even though there wasn't a loss in the shares of stock. Since the passage of time erodes the value of the option, it's best to use short-term options.

In our example, shares of RMBS did try several times to break higher, but each time resistance held and the stock ultimately closed at $26.37 on

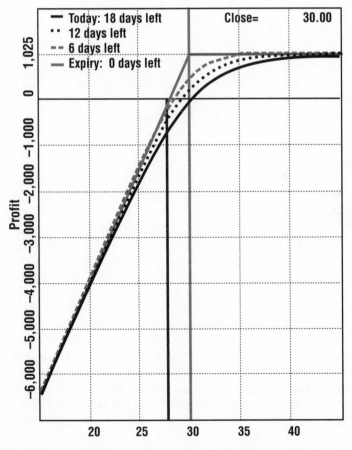

FIGURE 4.13 Risk Graph of Covered Call on RMBS (*Source:* Optionetics Platinum © 2004)

Covered Call Case Study

Strategy: With the stock trading at $30 a share on December 1, sell 5 December 30 calls @ 2.05 and buy 500 shares of Rambus stock.

Market Opportunity: Expect consolidation in shares after failure to break out.

Maximum Risk: Limited as the stock moves lower (as the stock can only fall to zero). In this case, the loss is $790.

Maximum Profit: Credit initially received. In this case, 5 calls @ 2.05 each = $1,025.

Breakeven: Price of the underlying asset at trade initiation – call option credit. In this case, 27.95: (30 – 2.05).

Margin: None.

expiration December 19. At expiration, the stock position was down $3.63 a share, or $1,815: (3.63 × 500). However, the loss was offset by the $1,025 received from the credit from the short calls. So, the trade results in a $790 loss. A trader could continue to sell calls against the stock each month if it is felt the stock will remain near the strike price.

LONG PUT

In the long put strategy, you are purchasing the right, but not the obligation, to sell the underlying stock at a specific price until the expiration date. This strategy is used when you anticipate a fall in the price of the underlying shares. A long put strategy offers limited profit potential (limited because the underlying asset can fall no further than zero) and limited downside risk. It is often used to get high leverage on an underlying security that you expect to decrease in price.

If you want to go long a put, your risk curve would look like the graph in Figure 4.14. Note how the profit/loss line for a long put strategy slopes upward from right to left. When the underlying instrument's price falls, you make money; when it rises, you lose money. Note how the profit on a long put is limited as the price of the underlying asset can only fall to zero.

The long put strategy is often used to get high leverage on an underlying security that is expected to decrease in price. It requires a fairly small investment and consists of buying one or more puts with any strike and any expiration. The buyer of put options has limited risk over the life of the option, regardless of the movement of the underlying asset. The put

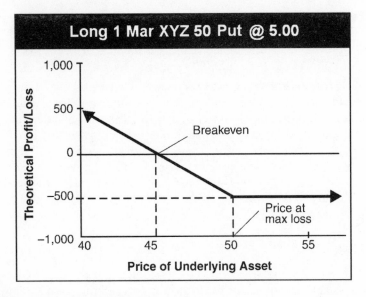

FIGURE 4.14 Long Put Risk Profile

option buyer's maximum risk is limited to the amount paid for the put. Profits are realized as the put increases in value as the underlying asset's value falls. Buying a put is a limited-risk bearish strategy that can be used instead of shorting stock. It is best placed when the option is exhibiting low implied volatility. Keep in mind that the further away the expiration date is, the higher the premium. But the cost that time contributes to a put premium must be balanced out by the need for sufficient time for the underlying shares to move into a profitable position.

Long Put Mechanics

Let's create an example by going long 1 January XYZ 50 Put @ 5. The cost of this position is $500 (5 × 100 = $500) plus commissions. The maximum risk for this trade is limited to the premium of the put option while the reward is limited to the downside until the underlying asset reaches zero. Looking at the risk graph in Figure 4.14, notice how potential profit and loss values correspond to underlying share prices. Can you see the breakeven point? The breakeven is calculated by subtracting the put premium from the put strike price. In this trade, the breakeven is 45 (50 – 5 = 45), which means that XYZ would have to fall below 45 for the trade to start making a profit.

Exiting the Position

Choosing an exit strategy depends on the movement of the underlying shares as well as changes in volatility.

- *XYZ falls below the breakeven (45):* Either offset the long put by selling a put option with the same strike and expiration at an acceptable profit or exercise the put option to go short the underlying market. You can hold this short position or cover the short by purchasing the shares back at the current lower price for a profit.
- *XYZ rises above the breakeven (45):* You can wait for a reversal or offset the long put by selling an identical put option and using the credit received to mitigate the loss. The most you can lose is the initial premium paid for the put.

In this example, let's say the price of XYZ falls from $50 to $40. This results in a rise in the premium of the October 50 put to 13.75. You now have a decision to make. To exit a long put, you can offset it, exercise it, or let it expire. To offset this position, you can sell the March 50 put and reap a profit of $875: (13.75 – 5) × 100 = $875. If you choose to exercise the position, you will end up with a short position of 100 shares of XYZ at $50. This would bring in an additional credit of $5,000 (minus commissions). However, you would then be obligated to cover the short sometime in the future by purchasing 100 shares of XYZ at the current price. If you covered the short with the shares priced at $40, you would make a profit of $500: (5,000 – 4,000 = $1,000 for the stock minus $500 for the cost of the put). Therefore, offsetting the option yields a higher profit. In fact, you almost never want to exercise an option with time value remaining because it will be more profitable to simply sell the option. In addition, exercising the long put requires enough money in your trading account to post the required margin to short the shares.

Long Put

Strategy: Buy a put option.

Market Opportunity: Look for a bearish market where you anticipate a fall in the price of the underlying below the breakeven.

Maximum Risk: Limited to the price paid for the put option premium.

Maximum Profit: Limited below the breakeven as the stock price can only fall to zero.

Breakeven: Put strike price – put premium.

Margin: None.

Long Put Case Study

A long put involves the purchase of just one option strike and one expiration month. Buying a long put is a strategy that benefits from a decline in the underlying security. However, unlike selling stock short, there isn't a need to use margin and entering the put is an easy process. As with any long debit strategy, a long put will suffer from time decay, so we want to use options that have at least 60 days, and preferably more, until expiration.

By entering a long put, we have limited our risk to the initial cost of the put. At the same time, we have limited reward to the downside as the underlying can only fall to zero. Let's go back to the fall of 2000 and see how entering a put on the Nasdaq 100 Trust (QQQ or Qs) would have worked following a triple top formation.

The Qs moved above 100 on August 31, but then formed a bearish pattern on September 1. At this time, it seemed that a break back below 100 would be bearish for the Qs. Thus, on September 5, an option trader could have entered a long put when the Qs closed at $99.50.

The December 100 puts could be purchased for $8 each. Our maximum risk would then be $4,000 if we were to buy five contracts. Figure 4.15 shows the risk graph for long puts on the Qs.

The risk graph shows that as the Qs fall, the puts increase in worth. Of course, if this trade were to be held until expiration, the price of the Qs would need to be below 92 to make a profit. However, the quicker the Qs drop, the larger the profit in the near term. In order to see a double in this trade, a move to about 85 would need to occur.

At the close of trading the very next day (September 6), these puts were worth $9.38, a gain of nearly $700 in one day. The Qs continued to fall during the next several months, leading to a sharp decline for security, but a large increase in the long puts. Selling continued after the Qs fell

---

Long Put Case Study

Strategy: With the security trading at $99.50 a share on September 5, 2000, buy 5 December 100 puts @ 8.00 on the Nasdaq 100 Trust (QQQ).

Market Opportunity: Expect decline in shares following bearish chart pattern.

Maximum Risk: Limited to initial debit of $4,000.

Maximum Profit: $46,000 if Qs were to go to zero. In this case, the puts increased to $17 each for a profit of $4,500.

Breakeven: Strike minus the initial cost per put. In this case, 92: (100 – 8).

Margin: None.

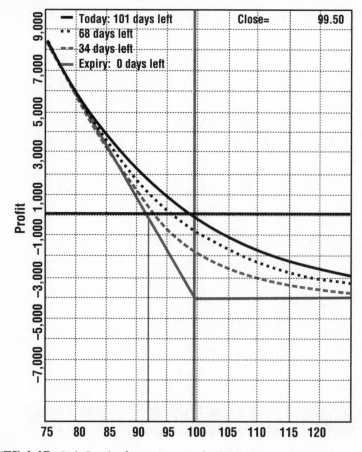

FIGURE 4.15 Risk Graph of Long Puts on the QQQ (*Source:* Optionetics Platinum © 2004)

through their 200-day moving average and were unable to recapture this prior support level. On the close of trading October 3, 2000, the Qs were at 84 and the puts were now selling for $17 each. At this time, the long puts could have been sold for a profit of $4,500: [(17 – 8) × 5] × 100 = $4,500.

SHORT PUT

A short put strategy offers limited profit potential and limited, yet high risk. It is best placed in a bullish market when you anticipate a rise in the price of the underlying market beyond the breakeven. By selling a put option, you will receive the option's premium in the form of a credit into your trading account. The premium received is the maximum reward for a short put position. In most cases, you are anticipating that the short put will expire worthless.

If you want to go short a put, your risk curve would look like the graph in Figure 4.16. A short put strategy creates a risk profile that slants downward from right to left from the limited profit. Notice that as the price of the asset falls, the loss on the short put position increases (until the price of the underlying stock hits zero). Additionally, the profit is limited to the initial credit received for selling the put. When the underlying instrument's price rises, you make money; when it falls, you lose money. This strategy provides limited profit potential with limited risk (as the underlying can only fall to zero). It is often used to get high leverage on an underlying security that you expect to increase in price.

As explained earlier, when you sell options, you will initially receive the premium for which you sold the option in the form of a credit into your account. The premium received is the maximum reward. The maximum loss is limited to the downside until the underlying asset reaches zero.

What kind of a view of the market would you have to sell puts? You would have a bullish or neutral view. The breakeven for initiating the trade is the strike price at which the puts are sold minus the premium received. If the market were to rise, the position would increase in value to the amount of premium taken in for the puts. Looking at the risk graph, notice that as the price of the asset falls, the loss of your short put

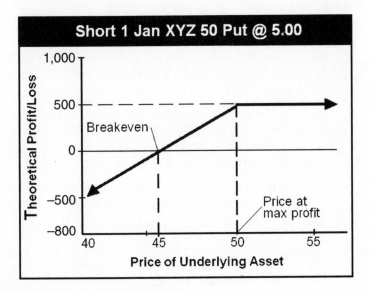

FIGURE 4.16 Short Put Risk Graph

position increases (see Figure 4.16). This strategy requires a heavy margin deposit to place and is best placed using short-term options with high implied volatility, or in combination with other options.

Short Put Mechanics

Let's create an example by going short 1 January XYZ 50 Put @ 5. The maximum profit on this trade is equal to the amount received from the option premium, or $500 (5 × 100 = $500) minus commissions. To calculate the breakeven on this position, subtract the premium received from the put strike price. In this case, the breakeven is 45 (50 – 5 = 45). If XYZ rises above $45, the trade makes money. You earn the premium with the passage of time as the short option loses value.

A short put strategy creates a risk profile that slants downward from right to left (see Figure 4.16). Notice that as the price of the asset falls, the loss of your short put position increases until the price of the underlying stock hits zero. This signifies that the profit increases as the market price of the underlying rises.

Exiting the Position

A short put strategy offers three distinct exit scenarios. Each scenario primarily depends on the movement of the underlying shares.

- *XYZ rises above the put strike price (50):* This is the best exit strategy. The put expires worthless and you get to keep the premium, which is the maximum profit on a short put position.
- *XYZ reverses and starts to fall toward the breakeven (45):* You may want to offset the position by purchasing a put option with the same strike price and expiration to exit the trade.
- *XYZ falls below the put strike price (50):* The short put is assigned and the put writer is obligated to buy 100 shares of XYZ at $50 per share from the put holder. The short put seller now has a long shares position and can either sell the XYZ shares at a loss or wait for a reversal. The maximum loss occurs if the price of XYZ falls to zero. The short put writer then loses $5,000 (100 shares × 50 = $5,000) less the $500 credit received from the premium, or a total loss of $4,500 (5,000 – 500 = $4,500).

Short Put Case Study

When we buy a put, we want the underlying security to move lower. Thus, when we sell a put, we want the stock to rise. However, our maximum

Short Put

Strategy: Sell a put option.

Market Opportunity: Look for a bullish or stable market where a rise above the breakeven is anticipated.

Maximum Risk: Limited as the stock price falls below the breakeven until reaching a price of zero.

Maximum Profit: Limited to the credit received from the put premium.

Breakeven: Put strike price – put premium.

Margin: Required. Amount subject to broker's discretion.

profit is the premium we receive for selling the put, so if we expect a large move higher in the stock, we would be better off to buy a call. Selling a put is best used when we expect a slightly higher price or consolidation to take place.

When a stock falls sharply to support in one or two sessions, this is often a good time to look at selling puts. If we expect that the stock might start to consolidate following a decline, selling a put could provide nice profits. However, the risk remains rather high because the stock could continue to fall and a put seller is at risk the whole way down to zero.

On July 31, 2003, shares of Cardinal Health (CAH) fell $10 to about $55 a share. This drop might have seemed overdone given the circumstances and a trader could have entered a short put near the close of the session. The August 55 put could be sold for $1.65, which means selling five contracts would bring in $825. We want to use the front month option because time value works in our favor. If CAH were to stay at $55 or move higher by August 15, the trader would receive the maximum profit.

The risk graph shown in Figure 4.17 details how the risk in this trade is rather high compared with the reward. This means that margin will be an issue and that a large amount of margin will be needed to enter this type of trade. The breakeven point for this trade is calculated by subtracting the credit received from the strike price (55 – 1.65 = 53.35). Thus, even a slight move lower would still generate a profit in this trade, but if CAH were to fall below $53.35 the losses would start to grow.

Fortunately, shares of CAH did move higher after this decline, leaving the trader with the maximum profit of $825 from the sale of five puts. Later, we will talk about a less risky way to profit using spreads instead of naked options.

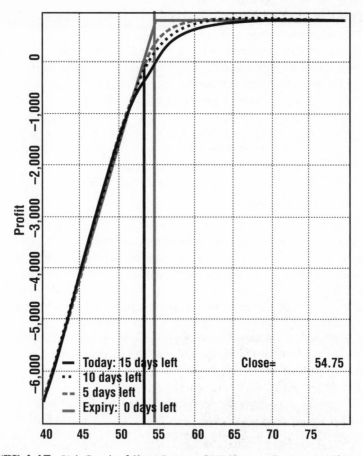

FIGURE 4.17 Risk Graph of Short Puts on CAH (*Source:* Optionetics Platinum © 2004)

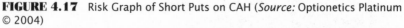

Short Put Case Study

Strategy: With the stock trading at $54.75 a share on July 31, 2003, sell 5 August 55 puts @ 1.65 each on Cardinal Health (CAH).

Market Opportunity: Expect CAH to consolidate or move higher following large one-day drop in shares.

Maximum Risk: Unlimited as stock falls all the way to zero.

Maximum Profit: Initial credit received. In this case, $825: (5 × 1.65) × 100.

Breakeven: Strike price minus the initial credit per put. In this case, 53.35: (55 − 1.65).

Margin: Extensive.

COVERED PUT

You can also use a covered put in a bearish market to profit from a possible increase in a short stock or futures position. A covered put consists of selling the underlying futures or stock position and selling a put to cover the underlying asset's position. This trade can be very risky, because it involves short selling a stock, which requires a high margin. The reward on a covered put is limited to the difference in the initial price of the short underlying asset minus the strike price of the short put plus the credit received for the option premium.

Covered Put Mechanics

In this example, let's go short 100 shares of XYZ @ 50 and short 1 June XYZ 45 Put @ 2.50. The risk graph below shows a covered put position at expiration. Once the market moves to the upside above the breakeven, there is unlimited risk. Margin is $7,500 (stock price plus 50 percent more); however, the credit on the short stock is $5,000. In addition, the credit on the short put is $250. Total credit is $5,250. The maximum reward on this trade occurs if XYZ closes at or below 45 at expiration. The maximum profit for this trade is $750: (50 – 45) + 2.50 × 100 = $750. Figure 4.18 shows the risk profile for the covered put example.

As with most short strategies, this trade is hazardous because it

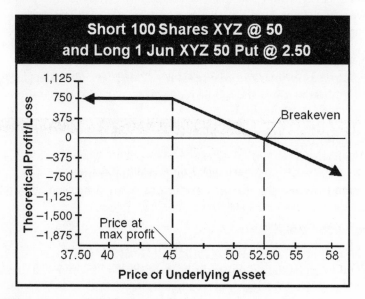

FIGURE 4.18 Covered Put Risk Graph

comes with unlimited risk. The breakeven of a covered put strategy equals the price of the underlying asset at trade initiation plus the option premium. In this trade, the breakeven is 52.50: (50 + 2.50 = 52.50). That means that if XYZ moves above $52.50, the trade will lose $100 for each point it rises. In fact, the higher the underlying asset climbs, the more money will be lost (see Figure 4.18).

Exiting the Position

Since a covered put protects a stock only within a specific range, it is vital to monitor the daily price movement of the underlying stock. Let's investigate optimal exit strategies in the following scenarios:

- *XYZ declines below the short strike price (45):* The short put is assigned and you are obligated to buy 100 shares of XYZ from the option buyer at $45 per share. However, you can unload these shares for the short share price of $50. This exit process garners the maximum profit of $750.
- *XYZ declines below the initial stock price (50), but remains above the short strike price (45):* The short put expires worthless and you get to keep the premium received. No losses have occurred on the short stock position and you are ready to place another covered put to bring in additional profit on the position if you wish.
- *XYZ rises above the initial stock price (50) but stays below the breakeven (52.50):* The short stock position starts to lose money, but this loss is offset by the credit received from the short put. As long as the stock stays below the breakeven, the position will break even or make a small profit.
- *XYZ rises above the breakeven (52.50):* Let the short put expire worthless and use the credit received to partially hedge the loss on the short stock position.

Both covered calls and covered puts are high-risk strategies, although they can be used to try to increase the profit on a trade. It is essential to be aware of the risks involved and to be extremely careful in selecting the underlying markets for your covered call or put writing strategies.

Covered Put Case Study

A covered put can be used to profit in the short term by going short a stock and then selling a put to bring in additional income. The reason a covered put is not a suggested strategy for most traders is because it has unlimited risk. The sale of the put does help offset the cost of the short stock, but if the stock rises, this income might mean very little. Let's use Rambus (RMBS) once again to show how a covered put would have worked for this stock when compared to a covered call.

By entering a short put, we have limited risk to the downside all the way to zero. At the same time, we have unlimited risk to the upside and a large margin requirement for selling the stock short. Let's assume we didn't already own Rambus, so we need to sell short 500 shares at $30 and sell five December 30 puts. Remember, RMBS shares were trading right at $30 a share, so we would be able to keep the entire premium from the put if the stock closes at or above this point. However, as the stock declines, we profit from being short on Rambus.

The December 30 puts could be sold for 2.10 each and Rambus shares could be sold short for $30 a share. Thus, we would receive a credit of $16,050 for entering the covered put. However, the maximum profit would be limited to just $1,050. The best way to see this is by looking at a risk graph of the trade shown in Figure 4.19. Notice how the risk continues to grow as the stock moves higher. This is because the amount of money brought in from selling the put does little to offset the potential loss obtained from selling RMBS shares short. However, no matter how low the stock moves, our maximum profit is achieved because the gain in the short stock will offset the loss in the short put.

In our example, shares of RMBS did try several times to break higher, but each time resistance held and the stock ultimately closed at 26.37 on expiration (December 19). This would have resulted in the maximum profit of $1,050. The short put would have had a value of 3.70 to buy back on expiration. This results in a loss of 1.60 each (or $800 for five contracts) for the put. However, the 500 shares of RMBS sold short are now

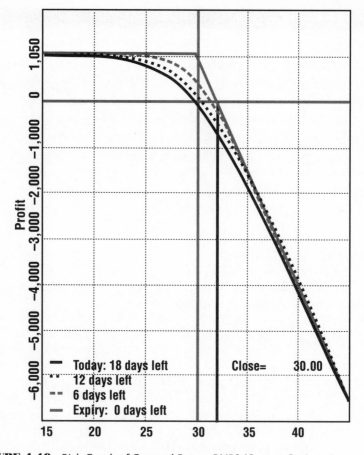

FIGURE 4.19 Risk Graph of Covered Put on RMBS (*Source:* Optionetics Platinum © 2004)

showing a profit of 3.63: (30 − 26.37). This means the profit from the short stock is $1,815: (3.63 × 500). If the option were not bought back, the trader would be forced to buy shares to cover the short, but the net result would still be a profit.

This might seem like a good way to bring in premium on a stock expected to move lower. However, the margin required would be large and the risk is normally just too high to be a consistently profitable strategy.

Covered Put Case Study

Strategy: With the stock trading at $30 a share on December 1, sell 5 December 30 puts @ 2.10 each and sell short 500 shares of Rambus stock.

Market Opportunity: Expect consolidation in shares after failure to break out.

Maximum Risk: Unlimited to the upside above the breakeven.

Maximum Profit: Limited to the credit received on the short put option + the price of security sold – put option strike price × 100. In this case, the maximum profit is $1,050: (5 × 210) + (30 – 30) × 100 = $1,050.

Breakeven: Strike price + put option credit. In this case, 32.10: (30 + 2.10).

Margin: Significant.

STRATEGY ROAD MAPS

For your convenience, the following subsections provide step-by-step analyses of the basic strategies discussed in this chapter.

Long Call Road Map

In order to place a long call, the following 13 guidelines should be observed:

1. Look for a low-volatility market where a rise in the price of the underlying stock is anticipated.
2. Check to see if this stock has liquid options available.
3. Review options premiums with various expiration dates and strike prices. Use options with more than 90 days until expiration.
4. Investigate implied volatility values to see if the options are overpriced or undervalued. Look for options with low implied volatility.
5. Review price and volume charts over the past year to explore price trends and liquidity.
6. Choose a long call option with the best profit-making probability. Determine which call option to purchase by calculating:
   - **Limited Risk:** Limited to the initial premium required to purchase the call.
   - **Unlimited Reward:** Unlimited to the upside as the underlying stock rises above the breakeven.
   - **Breakeven:** Call strike + call premium.
7. Create a risk profile for the trade to graphically determine the trade's feasibility. The long call's risk profile slants upward from left to right.

8. Write down the trade in your trader's journal before placing the trade with your broker to minimize mistakes made in placing the order and to keep a record of the trade.

9. Make an exit plan before you place the trade. Determine a profit and loss percentage that will trigger an exit of the position. Close out the entire trade by 30 days to expiration.

10. Contact your broker to buy the chosen call option. A margin deposit is not required.

11. Watch the market closely as it fluctuates. If the market continues to rise, hold onto the call option until you have made a satisfactory profit or a reversal seems imminent.

12. If the underlying market gives a dividend to its stockholders, this will have a negative effect on the price of a call option because a dividend usually results in a slight decline in the price of a stock.

13. Choose an exit strategy based on the price movement of the underlying stock and the effects of changes in the implied volatility of the call option:

- *The market rises above the breakeven:* Offset the position by selling a call option with the same strike price and expiration at an acceptable profit; or exercise the option to purchase shares of the underlying market at the lower strike. You can then hold these shares as part of your portfolio or sell them at a profit at the current higher market price.

- *The market falls below the breakeven:* If a reversal does not seem likely, contact your broker to offset the long call by selling an identical call to mitigate your loss. The most you can lose is the initial premium paid for the option.

Short Call Road Map

In order to place a short call, the following 13 guidelines should be observed:

1. Look for a high-volatility market where a fall in the stock's price is anticipated.

2. Check to see if this stock has liquid options available.

3. Review options premiums with various expiration dates and strike prices. Options with less than 45 days until expiration are best.

4. Investigate implied volatility values to see if the options are overpriced or undervalued. Look for options with high implied volatility and, thus, a higher premium.

5. Review price and volume charts over the past year to explore price trends and liquidity.

6. Choose a short call option with the best profit-making probability. Determine which call option to sell by calculating:

   - **Unlimited Risk:** Unlimited to the upside as the underlying stock rises above the breakeven.
   - **Limited Reward:** Limited to the initial call premium received as a credit.
   - **Breakeven:** Call strike + call premium.

7. Create a risk profile for the trade to graphically determine the trade's feasibility. A short call's risk profile slants down from left to right showing the limited profit and unlimited risk as the stock rises.

8. Write down the trade in your trader's journal before placing the trade with your broker to minimize mistakes made in placing the order and to keep a record of the trade.

9. Make an exit plan before you place the trade. Determine a profit and loss percentage that will trigger an exit of the position. For example, a 50 percent profit or loss is an easy signal to exit the position.

10. Contact your broker to go short (sell) the chosen call option. Margin is required to place a short call, the amount of which depends on your broker's discretion.

11. Watch the market closely as it fluctuates. If the price of the underlying stock rises above the strike price of the short call option, it is in danger of being assigned. If exercised, the option writer is obligated to deliver 100 shares (per option) of the underlying asset at the short call strike price to the option holder.

12. If the underlying market gives a dividend to its stockholders, this will usually cause the price of the call option to decline slightly, which works in favor of the short call strategy.

13. Choose an exit strategy based on the price movement of the underlying stock and the effects of changes in the implied volatility of the call option:

    - *The market falls below the strike price:* Wait for the call to expire worthless and keep the credit received from the premium.
    - *The market reverses and begins to rise above the call strike price:* Exit the position by offsetting it through the purchase of an identical call option (same strike price and expiration date) to avoid assignment.

Covered Call Road Map

In order to place a covered call, the following 13 guidelines should be observed:

1. A covered call is a conservative income strategy designed to provide limited protection against decreases in the price of a long underlying stock position. Look for a range-bound market or a bullish market where you anticipate a steady increase in the price of the underlying stock.

2. Check to see if the stock has liquid options.

3. Review call option premiums and strike prices no more than 45 days out.

4. Investigate implied volatility values to see if the options are overpriced or undervalued. Look for expensive options to get the most out of selling the call.

5. Explore past price trends and liquidity by reviewing price and volume charts over the past year.

6. Choose a higher strike call no more than 45 days out to sell against long shares of the underlying stock and then calculate the maximum profit, which is limited to the credit received from the sale of the short call plus the profit made from the difference between the stock's price at initiation and the call strike price.

7. Determine which spread to place by calculating:

   - **Limited Risk:** Limited to the downside as XYZ can only fall below the breakeven to zero.
   - **Limited Reward:** Limited to the credit received from the short call plus the strike price minus the initial stock price.
   - **Breakeven:** Calculated by subtracting the short call premium from the price of the underlying stock at initiation.

8. Create a risk profile of the most promising option combination and graphically determine the trade's feasibility. Note the unlimited risk beyond the breakeven.

9. Write down the trade in your trader's journal before placing the trade with your broker to minimize mistakes made in placing the order and to keep a record of the trade.

10. Make an exit plan before you place the trade. You must be willing to sell the long stock at the short call's strike price in case the call is assigned.

11. Contact your broker to buy and sell the chosen options. Place the trade as a limit order so that you limit the net debit of the trade.

12. Watch the market closely as it fluctuates. The profit on this strategy is unlimited—a loss occurs if the underlying stock closes at or below the breakeven points. You can also adjust the position back to a delta neutral to increase profit potential.

13. Choose an exit strategy depending on the movement of the underlying stock:

    - *The price of the stock rises above the short strike:* The short call is assigned and exercised by the option holder. You can then use the 100 shares from the original long stock position to satisfy your obligation to deliver 100 shares of the underlying stock to the option holder at the short call strike price. This scenario allows you to take in the maximum profit.

    - *The price of the stock falls below the short call strike price, but stays above the initial stock price:* The short call expires worthless and you get to keep the premium received. No losses have occurred on the long stock position and you are ready to sell another call to offset your risk.

    - *The stock falls below the initial stock price but stays above the breakeven:* The long stock position starts to lose money, but this loss is offset by the credit received from the short call. As long as the stock does not fall below the breakeven, the position will break even or make a small profit.

    - *The stock falls below the breakeven:* Let the short option expire worthless and use the credit received to partially hedge the loss on the long stock position.

Long Put Road Map

In order to place a long put, the following 13 guidelines should be observed:

1. Look for a low-volatility market where a steady decrease in price is anticipated.

2. Check to see if this stock has liquid options available.

3. Review options premiums with various expiration dates and strike prices. Use options with more than 90 days to expiration.

4. Investigate implied volatility values to see if the options are overpriced or undervalued. Look for options with low implied volatility.

5. Review price and volume charts over the past year to explore past price trends and liquidity.

6. Choose a long put option with the best profit-making probability. Determine which option to buy by calculating:

   - **Limited Risk:** Limited to the initial premium required to purchase the put option.

   - **Limited Reward:** Limited to the downside as the underlying stock can only fall to zero.

   - **Breakeven:** Put strike – put premium.

7. Create a risk profile for the trade to graphically determine the trade's feasibility. The profit/loss line slopes up from right to left.

8. Write down the trade in your trader's journal before placing the trade with your broker to minimize mistakes made in placing the order and to keep a record of the trade.

9. Make an exit plan before you place the trade. Determine a profit and loss percentage that will trigger an exit of the position. Close out the entire trade by 30 days to expiration.

10. Contact your broker to buy the chosen put option. A margin deposit is not required.

11. Watch the market closely as it fluctuates. If the market continues to fall, hold onto the put option until you have hit your target profit or a reversal seems imminent.

12. If the underlying market gives a dividend to its stockholders, this will have a positive effect on the price of a put option because a dividend usually results in a slight decline in the price of a stock.

13. Choose an exit strategy based on the price movement of the underlying stock and the effects of changes in the implied volatility of the put option:

    - *The underlying stock falls below the breakeven:* Either offset the long put by selling a put option with the same strike and expiration at an acceptable profit or exercise the put option to go short the underlying market. You can hold this short position or cover the short by buying the shares back at the current lower price for a profit.

    - *The underlying stock rises above the breakeven:* You can wait for a reversal or offset the long put by selling an identical put option and using the credit received to mitigate the loss. The most you can lose is the initial premium paid for the put.

Short Put Road Map

In order to place a short put, the following 13 guidelines should be observed:

1. Look for a high-volatility market where an increase or steady rise is anticipated.
2. Check to see if this stock has liquid options available.
3. Review options premiums with various expiration dates and strike prices. Options with less than 45 days to expiration are best.
4. Investigate implied volatility values to see if the options are over-priced or undervalued. Look for options with high implied volatility, and thus a higher premium.
5. Review price and volume charts over the past year to explore past price trends and liquidity.
6. Choose a short put option with the best profit-making probability. Determine which put option to sell by calculating:

   - **Limited Risk:** Limited to the downside below the breakeven as the underlying stock can only fall to zero.
   - **Limited Reward:** Limited to the initial put premium received as a credit.
   - **Breakeven:** Put strike – put premium.

7. Create a risk profile for the trade to graphically determine the trade's feasibility. The risk graph slopes down from right to left, showing a limited profit.
8. Write down the trade in your trader's journal before placing the trade with your broker to minimize mistakes made in placing the order and to keep a record of the trade.
9. Make an exit plan before you place the trade. Determine a profit and loss percentage that will trigger an exit of the position.
10. Contact your broker to sell the chosen put option. This strategy requires a margin deposit; the amount depends on your broker's discretion.
11. Watch the market closely as it fluctuates. If the price of the underlying stock falls below the short strike price, it will most likely be assigned. If exercised, the option writer is obligated to purchase 100 shares of the underlying asset at the short strike price (regardless of the decrease in the price of the underlying stock) from the option holder.

12. If the underlying market gives a dividend to its stockholders, this will have a negative effect on the price of a short put because a dividend usually results in a slight decline in the price of a stock.

13. Choose an exit strategy based on the price movement of the underlying stock and the effects of changes in the implied volatility of the put option:

   • *The underlying stock continues to rise or remains stable:* Wait for the option to expire worthless and keep the credit received from the premium.

   • *The underlying stock reverses and starts to fall:* Exit the position by offsetting it through the purchase of an identical put option (same strike price and expiration date) to avoid assignment.

Covered Put Road Map

In order to place a covered put, the following 13 guidelines should be observed:

1. Look for a range-bound market or bearish market where you anticipate a slow decrease in the price of the underlying stock.

2. Check to see if this stock has options.

3. Review put option premiums and strike prices no more than 45 days out.

4. Explore past price trends and liquidity by reviewing price and volume charts over the past year.

5. Investigate implied volatility values to see if the options are overpriced or undervalued.

6. Choose a lower strike put no more than 45 days out to sell against short shares of the underlying stock.

7. Determine which trade to place by calculating:

   • **Unlimited Risk:** The maximum risk is unlimited to the upside above the breakeven. Requires margin to place.

   • **Limited Reward:** The maximum profit is limited to the credit received from the sale of the short put option plus the profit made from the difference between the stock's price at initiation and the short put strike price.

- **Breakeven:** Calculated by adding the short put premium to the price of the underlying stock at initiation.

8. Risk is unlimited to the upside as the underlying asset rises above the breakeven. Create a risk profile for the trade to graphically determine the trade's feasibility.

9. Write down the trade in your trader's journal before placing the trade with your broker to minimize mistakes made in placing the order and to keep a record of the trade.

10. Choose your exit strategy in advance. How much money is the maximum amount you are willing to lose? How much profit do you want to make on the trade?

11. Contact your broker to sell the stock and sell the chosen put option against it. Choose the most appropriate type of order (market order, limit order, etc.). This strategy will require a large margin to place, depending on your brokerage's requirements.

12. Watch the market closely as it fluctuates. The profit on this strategy is limited. Keep in mind that an unlimited loss occurs if and when the underlying stock rises above the breakeven point.

13. Choose an exit strategy:

- *The price of the stock falls below the short put strike price:* The short put is assigned to an option holder. You can then use the 100 shares you are obligated to buy at the short put strike price to cover the original short stock position. This scenario allows you to take in the maximum profit.

- *The price of the stock rises above the short strike, but stays below the initial stock price:* The short put expires worthless and you get to keep the premium received. No losses have occurred on the short stock position and you are ready to place another short put position to bring in additional profit on the short stock position if you wish.

- *The price of the stock rises above the initial stock price, but stays below the breakeven:* The short stock position starts to lose money, but this loss is offset by the credit received from the short put. As long as the stock doesn't rise above the breakeven, the position will break even or make a small profit.

- *The price of the stock rises above the breakeven:* Let the short put expire worthless and use the credit received to partially hedge the increasing loss on the short stock position.

CONCLUSION

Having been involved in teaching options strategies for more than a decade, I'm still amazed by the lack of knowledge pertaining to what I believe is the most flexible investment vehicle available: the option. The number one question I receive from publications, individual investors, and almost everyone I meet is: Why should anyone trade options? After all, options are so risky. This line of reasoning makes me cringe. It's obvious that educators, brokers, and the overall investment community simply haven't done a good enough job informing investors of the benefits of trading options. Yes, there are risks if you haven't taken the time to learn how to trade options. But that goes for stocks, too! Knowledge is power. In my opinion, every trader should attain enough knowledge to be able to make informed decisions about whether to include options as part of their investment arsenals.

The initial eight strategies covered in this chapter—long stock, short stock, long call, short call, covered call, long put, short put, and covered put—are the fundamental building blocks of intermediate and advanced trading techniques. It is absolutely essential to your success as an options trader to develop a solid understanding of these basic strategies. Your knowledge level is what will ultimately determine how successful you will be. The primary reason that beginning traders do not last is because they do not educate themselves enough. The more knowledge you have in your field, the more confidence you have, and that will inevitably enhance your trading results. I am still learning and trying to increase my trading savvy on a daily basis. This is the type of hunger for knowledge that you need to have—not only to thrive, but also to survive in the volatile markets of the twenty-first century.

Covered calls are the most popular option strategy used in today's markets. If you want to gain additional income on a long stock position, you can sell a slightly OTM call every month. The risk lies in the strategy's limited ability to protect the underlying stock from major moves down and the potential loss of future profits on the stock above the strike price. Covered calls, however, can be combined with a number of bearish options strategies to create additional downside protection.

While covered calls are a very popular strategy, covered puts enable traders to bring in some extra premium on short positions, but with high risk involved. Once again, you can keep selling a put against the short shares every month to increase your profit. However, shorting stock is a risky trade no matter how you look at it because there is no limit to how much you can lose if the price of the stock rises above the breakeven. There are many other ways to take advantage of a stock's bearish movement, using options to limit the trade's risk and maximize the leveraging ability of your trading account. In fact, we will cover 19 additional strategies in this book.

Covered writes also enable traders to weather moderate price fluctuations without accumulating losses. This should help reduce stress; any technique that helps to reduce stress is a worthwhile addition to a trader's arsenal. To gain added protection, try buying a long put against a covered call or a long call against a covered put. The extra outlay of premium acts as an insurance policy, and that could mean the difference between losing a little on the premium versus taking a heavy loss in a volatile market.

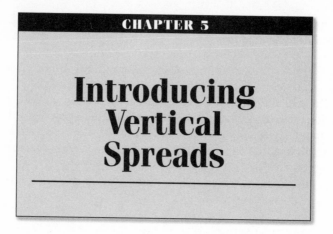

CHAPTER 5

Introducing Vertical Spreads

Since all markets have the potential to fluctuate beyond their normal trend, it is essential to learn how to apply strategies that limit your losses to a manageable amount. A variety of options strategies can be employed to hedge risk and leverage capital. Each strategy has an optimal set of circumstances that will trigger its application in a particular market. Vertical spreads are basic limited risk strategies, and that's why I tend to introduce them first. These relatively simple hedging strategies enable traders to take advantage of the way option premiums change in relation to movement in the underlying asset.

Vertical spreads offer limited potential profits as well as limited risks by combining long and short options with different strike prices and like expiration dates. The juxtaposition of long and short options results in a net debit or net credit. The net debit of a bull call spread and a bear put spread correlates to the maximum amount of money that can be lost on the trade. Welcome to the world of limited-risk trading! However, the net credit of a bull put spread and a bear call spread is the maximum potential reward of the position—a limited profit. Success in this kind of trading is a balancing act. You have to balance out the risk/reward ratio with the difference between the strikes—the greater the strike difference, the higher the risk.

One of the keys to understanding these managed risk spreads comes from grasping the concepts of intrinsic value and time value—variables that provide major contributions to the fluctuating price of an option. Although changes in the underlying asset of an option may be hard to forecast, there are a few constants that influence the values of options premiums. The following constants provide a few insights into why

130

vertical spreads offer a healthy alternative to traditional bullish and bearish stock trading techniques:

- Time value continually evaporates as an option approaches expiration.
- OTM and ATM options have no intrinsic value—they are all time value and therefore lose more premium as expiration approaches than ITM options.
- The premiums of ITM options have minimum values that change at a slower pace than OTM and ATM options.
- Vertical spreads take advantage of the differing rates of change in the values of the options premiums.

The four vertical spreads that we use can be broken down into two kinds of categories: debit and credit spreads, each with a bullish or bearish bias. The success of these strategies depends on being able to use options to exploit an anticipated directional move in a stock. As usual, timing is everything. To become good at forecasting the nature of a directional trend, try to keep track of a stock's support and resistance levels. Remember, a breakout beyond a stock's trading range can happen in either direction at any time. Limiting your risk is a great way to level the playing field.

VERTICAL SPREAD MECHANICS

Vertical spreads are excellent strategies for small investors who are getting their feet wet for the first time. Low risk makes these strategies inviting. Although they combine a short and a long option, the combined margin is usually far less than what it would cost to trade the underlying instrument. If you are new to the options game, take the time to learn these four strategies by paper trading them first. The rest of this chapter is designed to help you become familiar with these innovative strategies.

There are two kinds of debit spreads: the bull call spread and the bear put spread. As their names announce, a bull call spread is placed in a bullish market using calls and a bear put spread is placed in a bearish market using puts. Debit spreads use options with more than 60 days until expiration. The maximum risk of a debit spread is limited to the net debit of the trade.

In contrast, the maximum profit of a credit spread is limited to the net credit of the trade. There are two kinds of credit spreads: the bull put spread and the bear call spread. The bull put spread is placed in a bullish

TABLE 5.1 Vertical Spread Definitions

Type	Strategy	Components
Debit	Bull call spread	Long lower strike call and short higher strike call(s)
	Bear put spread	Long higher strike put(s) and short lower strike put(s)
Credit	Bull put spread	Long lower strike put(s) and short higher strike put(s)
	Bear call spread	Long higher strike call(s) and short lower strike call(s)

market using puts and a bear call spread is placed in a bearish market using calls. In general, credit spreads have lower commission costs than debit spreads because additional commissions are avoided by simply allowing the options to expire worthless. Since credit spreads offer a limited profit, make sure that the credit received is worth the risk before placing the trade.

To determine which strategy is the most appropriate, it is important to scan a variety of strike prices and premiums to find the optimal risk-to-reward ratio. This is accomplished by calculating the maximum risk, maximum reward, and breakeven of each potential spread to find the trade with the best probability of profitability. Choosing the type of trade (debit or credit) depends on whether you prefer to pay for a trade out-of-pocket or take the credit and ride the bear or bull all the way to expiration (see Table 5.1).

BULL CALL SPREAD

The bull call spread, also called the long call spread, is a debit strategy created by purchasing a lower strike call and selling a higher strike call with the same expiration dates. The shortest time left to expiration often provides the most leverage, but also provides less time to be right. This strategy is best implemented in a moderately bullish market. Over a limited range of stock prices, your profit on this strategy can increase by as much as 1 point for each 1-point increase in the price of the underlying asset. However, the total investment is usually far less than the amount required to buy the stock shares. The bull call strategy has both limited profit potential and limited downside risk.

The maximum risk on a bull call spread is limited to the net debit of the options. To calculate the maximum profit, multiply the difference in the strike prices of the two options by 100 and then subtract the net debit. The maximum profit occurs when the underlying stock rises above the strike price of the short call causing it to be assigned and exercised. You can then exercise the long call, thereby purchasing the underlying stock at the lower strike price and delivering those shares to the option holder at the higher short price. The breakeven of a bull call spread is calculated by adding the net debit to the lower strike price.

Choosing the Options

In order to choose the options with the best probability of profitability for a debit spread, it is important to balance out four factors:

1. The options need at least 60 days until expiration in order to give the underlying stock enough time to move into a profitable position.
2. Keep the net debit as low as possible to make the trade worthwhile.
3. Make the difference in strikes large enough to handle the net debit so that the maximum profit is worthwhile.
4. Make sure the breakeven is within the trading range of the underlying shares.

Bull Call Spread Mechanics

With XYZ trading at $51, let's create an example by going long 1 XYZ September 50 Call @ 3.50 and short 1 XYZ September 55 Call @ 1.50. The difference between the premium for the long 50 call and the credit received from the short 55 call leaves a net debit of 2 points. The maximum risk for this trade is the debit paid for the spread, or $200: $(3.50 - 1.50) \times 100 = \$200$. The maximum reward for the trade is calculated by subtracting the debit paid from the differences in the strike: $[(55 - 50) - 2] \times 100 = \$300$. The breakeven on this strategy occurs when the underlying asset's price equals the lower strike plus the net debit. In this case, the net debit is 2 points, so the breakeven is 52: $(50 + 2 = 52)$. Thus, the trade makes money (theoretically) as long as the underlying asset closes above 52 by expiration. The risk profile for this trade is shown in Figure 5.1.

The risk profile for a bull call spread visually reveals the strategy's limited risk and profit parameters. Notice how the maximum profit occurs at the short call strike price.

To find a market that is appropriate for placing a bull call spread, look for any markets that are trending up nicely or have reached their support level and are poised for a rebound. Your intention is for the market to rise as high as the strike price of the short call. That way, if the short call is exercised early, you can make the maximum return on the trade by exercising the long call and pocketing the difference.

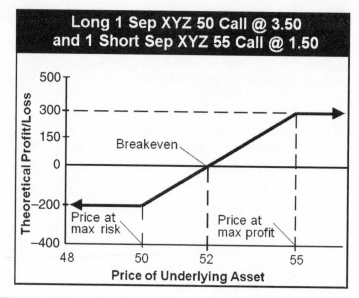

FIGURE 5.1   Bull Call Spread Risk Graph

Exiting the Position

To exit a bull call spread, it is important to monitor the daily price movement of the underlying stock and the fluctuating options premiums. Let's explore what happens to the trade in the following scenarios:

- *XYZ rises above the short strike (55):* The short call is assigned and you are obligated to deliver 100 shares of XYZ to the option holder at $55 a share. By exercising the long call, you can buy 100 shares of XYZ at $50 a share and pocket the difference of $500 (not including commissions). By subtracting the cost of the trade ($200), the net profit on the spread is $300—the maximum profit available.
- *XYZ rises above the breakeven (52), but not as high as the short strike (55):* Offset the options by selling a 50 call at a profit and buying a 55 call back at a slight loss, pocketing a small profit.
- *XYZ remains below the breakeven (52), but above the long strike (50):* Sell a 50 call at a profit and buy a 55 call at a loss, pocketing a small profit; or wait until expiration and sell the long call at a slight profit to offset the trade's net debit and let the short option expire worthless.
- *XYZ falls below the long strike (50):* Let the options expire worthless, or sell a 50 call prior to expiration to mitigate some of the loss.

Bull Call Spread

Strategy: Buy a call at a lower strike price. Sell a call at a higher strike price. Both options must have identical expiration dates.

Market Opportunity: Look for a moderately bullish to bullish market where you expect an increase in the price of the underlying asset above the price of the call option sold.

Maximum Risk: Limited to the net debit paid for the spread. Maximum risk results when the market closes at or below the strike price of the long call.

Maximum Profit: Limited. (Difference in strike prices − net debit paid) × 100. Profit results when the market closes above the breakeven.

Breakeven: Strike price of lower call + net debit paid.

Margin: Required. Amount subject to broker's discretion.

Bull Call Spread Case Study

A bull call spread is used when a trader is moderately bullish on a stock or index. By using a spread, the up-front cost to enter the trade is lower, but the offset is that the maximum reward is limited. Even so, when we expect to sell a stock at a given price anyway, it makes sense to lower the cost and thereby limit the risk to a manageable amount.

A bull call spread consists of buying a call and selling a higher strike call. The sale of the higher strike call brings in premium to offset the cost of buying the lower strike call. What we then have is a limited risk, limited reward strategy.

On October 24, 2003, the Semiconductor HOLDRS (SMH) put in a bottom formation. This was a good time to enter a bull call spread on SMH shares, looking for about a 6-point move in the shares. As of the close on this day, SMH shares were priced at $38.55. The January 40 calls could be purchased for $2.05 and the January 45 call could be sold for $0.50. This left us with a debit of $1.55 a contract to enter a bull call spread. The risk graph for this trade is shown in Figure 5.2.

When trading a bull call spread, it's best to see a 2-to-1 reward-to-risk ratio. This trade meets this qualification. The maximum reward is calculated by subtracting the net debit (1.55) from the difference between strikes (45 − 40 = 5) and then multiplying this number by 100. Thus, the maximum reward on this trade is $345: (5 − 1.55) × 100 = $345. By entering five contracts, this trade would have cost $775, with a maximum reward of $1,725. The breakeven point is found by adding the net debit to the lower strike price. In this case, the breakeven is 41.55: (40 + 1.55 = 41.55). The risk graph of this trade is shown in Figure 5.2.

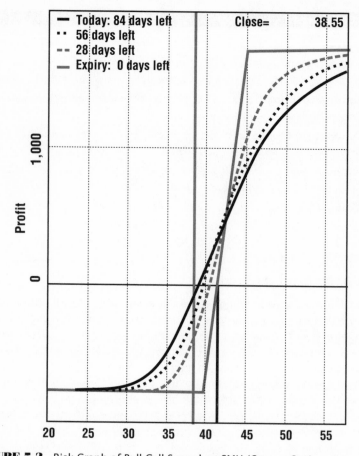

FIGURE 5.2   Risk Graph of Bull Call Spread on SMH (*Source:* Optionetics Platinum © 2004)

On November 7, 2003, shares of SMH closed at $43.99 after trading slightly higher during the session. Since $44 was our price target, we could have sold on this day for nearly a 100 percent profit. The January 40 call could be sold for $5.30 and the January 45 call could be purchased back for $2.40. This equates to credit of $2.90 a share, but we then need to subtract the initial debit of $1.55. Thus, our total profit was $135 a contract, or $675 overall.

Though buying a call outright would have created a larger profit, the risk also would have been greater. If SMH shares had fallen lower following the entry into this trade, a bull call spread would have seen a much smaller loss than a straight call.

Bull Call Spread Case Study

Strategy: With the security trading at $38.55 a share on October 24, 2003, buy 5 January 40 calls @ 2.05 and sell 5 January 45 calls @ .50 on Semiconductor HOLDRS (SMH).

Market Opportunity: Expect a move higher in shares following a bounce from support.

Maximum Risk: Limited to initial net debit of $775: [(2.05 – .50) × 5] × 100.

Maximum Profit: (Difference in strikes – net debit) × 100. In this example, the maximum profit is $1,725 and the actual realized profit is $675.

Breakeven: Lower strike + net debit paid. In this case, the breakeven is 41.55: (40 + 1.55).

BEAR PUT SPREAD

A bear put spread, or long put spread, is a debit spread that is created by purchasing a put with a higher strike price and selling a put with a lower strike price. Both options must expire in the same month. This is a bearish strategy and should be implemented when you expect the market to close below the strike price of the short put option—the point of maximum reward (at expiration).

This high-leverage strategy works over a limited range of stock and futures prices. Your profit on this strategy can increase by as much as 1 point for each 1-point decrease in the price of the underlying asset. Once again, the total investment is usually far less than that required to short sell the stock. The bear put spread has both limited profit potential and limited upside risk. Puts with the shortest time left to expiration usually provide the most leverage, but also reduce the time frame you have for the market to move to the maximum reward strike price.

The maximum risk of a bear put spread is limited to the net debit of the trade. The maximum profit depends on the difference in strike prices minus the net debit. It is important to find a combination of options that provides a high enough profit-to-risk ratio to make the spread worthwhile.

Bear Put Spread Mechanics

With XYZ currently trading at $56, let's create a bull put spread by going long 1 XYZ September 55 Put @ 2 and short 1 XYZ September 50 Put @ .50. The difference between the long 55 put premium of 2 ($200) and the credit received for the short 50 put (.50 or $50) is a net debit of $150. The net debit is the maximum risk for a bear put spread. The maximum reward for the trade is calculated by subtracting the net debit paid from the difference between strike prices: $(55 - 50) - 1.50 \times 100 = \$350$. Even though the reward is limited to \$350, the sale of the 50 put has lowered the breakeven on this position. The breakeven occurs when the underlying asset's price equals the higher strike price minus the net debit. In this case, the breakeven would be 53.50: $(55 - 1.50 = 53.50)$. The risk graph for this trade is shown in Figure 5.3.

The risk profile (see Figure 5.3) of a bear put spread slants upward from right to left, displaying its bearish bias. Once the underlying stock falls to the price of the short put, the trade reaches its maximum profit potential. Conversely, if the price of the underlying stock rises to the strike price of the long put, you will lose the maximum limited amount. Once again, it is important to monitor this trade for a reversal or a breakout to avoid losing the maximum amount.

Exiting the Trade

To exit a bear put spread, you have to monitor the daily price movement of the underlying stock and the fluctuating options premiums. Let's explore what you can do to profit on a bear put spread if one of the following scenarios occurs.

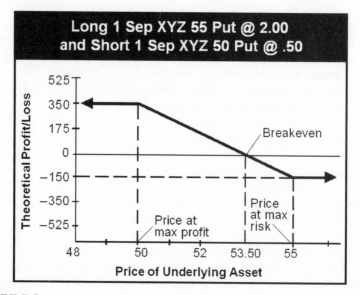

FIGURE 5.3 Bear Put Spread Risk Graph

Bear Put Spread

Strategy: Buy a higher strike put and sell a lower strike put with the same expiration date.

Market Opportunity: Look for a bearish market where you anticipate a modest decrease in the price of the underlying asset below the strike price of the short put option.

Maximum Risk: Limited to the net debit paid.

Maximum Profit: Limited. (Difference in strike prices – net debit) × 100.

Breakeven: Higher put strike price – net debit paid.

Margin: Required. Amount subject to broker's discretion.

- *XYZ falls below the short strike (50):* The short put is assigned and you are obligated to purchase 100 shares of XYZ from the option holder at $50 a share. By exercising the long put, you can turn around and sell those shares at $55 a share and pocket the difference of $500. By subtracting the cost of the trade ($150), the profit on the spread is $350—the maximum profit available.
- *XYZ falls below the breakeven (53.50), but not as low as the short strike (50):* Offset the trade by selling a 55 put at a profit and buying a 50 put at a loss, pocketing a small profit.
- *XYZ remains above the breakeven (53.50), but below the long strike (55):* Sell a 55 put at a profit and buy a 50 put at a loss, pocketing a small profit, or wait until expiration and sell the long put at a slight profit to offset the trade's net debit and let the short option expire worthless.
- *XYZ rises above the long strike (55):* Let the options expire worthless, or sell the 55 put at expiration to mitigate some of the loss.

Bear Put Spread Case Study

A bear put spread is used when a trader is moderately bearish on a stock or index. By using a spread, the up-front cost to enter the trade is lower, but the offset is that the maximum reward is also lower. Even so, when we expect to cover short stock at a given price anyway, it makes sense to lower our cost.

A bear put spread consists of buying a put and selling a lower strike put. The sale of the lower strike put brings in premium to offset the cost of buying the higher strike put. What we then have is a limited risk, limited reward strategy.

On June 5, 2003, shares of Cigna (CI) were showing bearish tendencies. The stock closed the session on June 5 at $52 and a trader might have anticipated a move lower to support near $40. The move was expected to occur within the next few months, so a trader could have used the October options. By purchasing a 50 put and selling a 40 put, the trader would have entered a bear put spread for a total of $3.05 per contract. The long put would have cost $4.00 and the short put could have been sold for $0.95. In this case, let's assume the trader decides to place a trade for five bull call spreads. The risk graph for this trade is shown in Figure 5.4.

Just like a bull call spread, we want to see a reward-to-risk ratio of at least 2-to-1. For this trade, the maximum risk is the initial debit of $305, or $1,525 for 5 contracts. The maximum reward is calculated by subtracting

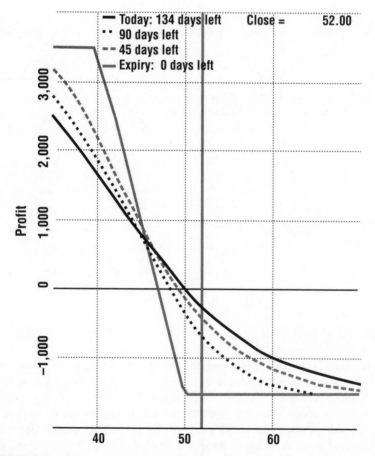

FIGURE 5.4 Risk Graph of Bear Put Spread on CI (*Source:* Optionetics Platinum © 2004)

Bear Put Spread Case Study

Strategy: With the security trading at $41.04 a share on June 5, 2003, buy 5 October 50 puts @ 4.00 and sell 5 October 40 puts @ .95 on Cigna (CI).

Market Opportunity: Expect a moderate decline in the price of the underlying stock.

Maximum Risk: Limited to initial net debit. In this case, $1,525: [5 × (4 − .95)] × 100.

Maximum Profit: (Difference in strikes − net debit) × 100. In this example, the maximum risk is $3,475 and the actual realized profit is $1,875.

Breakeven: Upper strike minus the net debit paid. In this case, the breakeven is 46.95: (50 − 3.05).

the debit (3.05) from the difference in strike prices (50 − 40 = 10). Thus, the maximum reward of this trade is $695: (10 − 3.05) × 100 = $695 per contract, or $3,475 for all five contracts. This creates a reward-to-risk ratio of 2.28 to 1 (6.95/3.05).

On July 15, 2003, shares of CI closed at $41.04, leaving this trade with a very nice gain. Though the price target of $40 hadn't quite been reached, the trade was up more than 100 percent and this would have been a good time to take profits. The October 50 put could be sold for $9.50 and the October 40 put could be purchased back for $2.70. This equates to a credit of $6.80 a share, but we then need to subtract out the initial debit of $3.05. Thus, our total profit was $3.75 a share, $375 a contract, and $1,875 for all five contracts—a gain of 123 percent.

Though buying a put outright would have created a larger profit, the risk also would have been greater. If CI shares had risen following the entry into this trade, a bear put spread would have seen a much smaller loss than a straight put.

BULL PUT SPREAD

A bull put spread is a credit spread created by the purchase of a lower strike put and the sale of a higher strike put using the same number of options and identical expirations. The maximum reward of this strategy is limited to the credit received from the net premiums and occurs when the market closes above the strike price of the short put option. Therefore, this strategy is implemented when you are bullish and expect the market to close above the strike price of the put option sold.

The maximum profit of a bull put spread is limited to the net credit received on the trade. The maximum risk is calculated by subtracting the net credit from the difference in strikes and then multiplying this number by 100. The breakeven of a bull put spread is calculated by subtracting the net credit from the higher strike put.

Choosing the Options

In order to choose the options with the best probability of profitability for a credit spread—bull put and bear call spreads—it is important to balance out five factors:

1. The profit on these strategies depends on the options expiring worthless; therefore, it is best to use options with 45 days or less until expiration to give the underlying stock less time to move into a position where the short put will be assigned and the maximum loss occur.
2. Since the maximum profit is limited to the net credit initially received, keep the net credit high enough to make the trade worthwhile.
3. Keep the short strike at-the-money—try to avoid selling an in-the-money put.
4. The difference between strikes must be small enough so that the maximum risk is low enough to make the trade worthwhile.
5. Make sure the breakeven is within the underlying shares' trading range.

Bull Put Spread Mechanics

Let's say you are bullish on XYZ, currently trading at 44. You expect a move upward for a close above 50 by next month. To initiate a bull put spread, you sell a higher strike XYZ June 50 put at $7.50 and purchase a lower strike XYZ June 45 put at $3. Both strikes are close enough to allow XYZ to reach the projected strike price of 50. Remember, the object of this strategy is to have both options expire worthless and be able to keep the net credit. In this example, the maximum reward is the net credit of 4.50, or $450 per contract. The breakeven occurs when the underlying asset's price equals the higher strike price minus the net credit. In this case, the breakeven equals 45.50: (50 − 4.50 = 45.50).

This trade makes the maximum profit if XYZ closes at or above 50 at expiration. You get to keep a lesser portion if the trade closes between 45.50 and 50. As long as XYZ closes above the breakeven point of 45.50, you won't lose money. The maximum risk is calculated by subtracting the net credit from the difference between strike prices multiplied by 100. In this trade the maximum risk is $50: (50 − 45) − 4.50 × 100 = $50. Therefore, if XYZ closes below 45, you lose $50. The risk profile for this bull put spread example is shown in Figure 5.5.

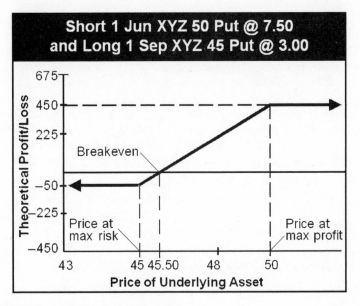

FIGURE 5.5 Bull Put Spread Risk Graph

The risk profile of a bull put spread slants upward from left to right displaying its bullish bias. If the underlying shares rise to the price of the short put, the trade reaches its maximum profit potential. Conversely, if the price of the underlying stock falls to the strike price of the long put, the maximum limited loss occurs. Always monitor the underlying stock for a reversal or a breakout to avoid the maximum loss.

Exiting the Trade

To exit a bull put spread, you have to monitor the daily price movement of the underlying stock and the fluctuating options premiums. Although each trade is unique, let's explore what happens to the trade in the example in the following scenarios:

- *XYZ rises above the short strike (50):* Let the options expire worthless and keep the maximum credit received when the trade was initiated ($450).
- *XYZ stays above the breakeven (45.50), but does not rise above the short strike (50):* The short put is assigned and you are obligated to purchase 100 shares of XYZ from the option holder at $50 a share. You can sell the shares at the current price, which is above the strike price of the long put and incur a small loss that can be offset

by the initial credit received. You can also offset the long put by selling it to garner an additional profit.

- *XYZ falls below the breakeven (45.50), but stays above the long strike (45):* Once again, the short put is assigned and you are obligated to purchase 100 shares of XYZ from the option holder at $50 a share. You can sell the shares at the current price, which is slightly above the strike price of the long put. In this case, the loss on the shares will not be balanced out by the credit received. Selling the long put may bring in additional money to mitigate some of the loss.
- *XYZ falls below the long strike (45):* The short put is assigned and you are obligated to purchase 100 shares of XYZ from the option holder at $50 a share. You can now exercise the long put to sell the shares at $45 each, incurring the maximum loss of $500, which is balanced by the $450 credit received at initiation for a total loss of $50 (plus commissions).

Bull Put Spread Case Study

A bull put spread is a credit strategy that benefits when the underlying security trades sideways or higher. Stocks often hit support, which sends the stock higher. At these times, using an at-the-money credit spread can bring in profits. A credit spread profits if the stock moves in two of the possible three directions a stock can move. Both a bear call spread and a bull put spread benefit from sideways movement, with the former benefiting from a down move and the latter from an up move.

A bull put spread consists of selling a put and buying a lower strike put. The sale of the higher strike put brings in premium, which is larger than the cost of purchasing the lower strike put. What we then have is a

Bull Put Spread

Strategy: Buy a put at a lower strike price. Sell a put at a higher strike price. Both options must have identical expiration dates.

Market Opportunity: Look for a moderately bullish to bullish market where you expect an increase in the price of the underlying asset above the strike price of the put option sold.

Maximum Risk: Limited. (Difference in strikes − net credit) × 100.

Maximum Profit: Limited to the net credit received. Profit is made when the market closes above the strike price of the short put option. This is a credit trade when initiated.

Breakeven: Higher put strike price − net credit received.

Margin: Required. Amount subject to broker's discretion.

limited risk/limited reward strategy. Unlike a debit spread, though, the risk is often higher than the reward while the odds of success are usually very high.

On December 11, 2003, shares of Inco Limited (N) formed a bullish formation. The stock closed the session at $34.86, but it looked as if the stock would move higher and use $35 as support. Using this forecast, a bull put credit spread could have been implemented. Since a credit spread benefits from time decay, it's usually best to use front month options. However, the December option had just six days left, so we would have used the January options. By selling the January 35 put for 1.65 and buying the January 30 put for 0.35, this bear call spread would have brought in a credit of $1.30 per contract. The risk graph for this trade is shown in Figure 5.6.

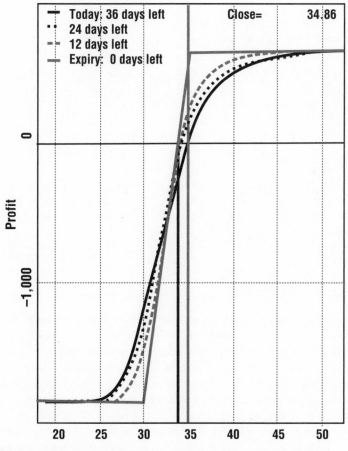

FIGURE 5.6 Risk Graph of Bull Put Spread on N (*Source:* Optionetics Platinum © 2004)

Bull Put Spread Case Study

Strategy: With the security trading at $34.86 a share on December 12, 2003, sell 5 January 35 puts @ 1.65 and buy 5 January 30 puts @ 0.35 on Inco Limited (N).

Market Opportunity: Expect a moderate move higher in the underlying or at least consolidation above $35.

Maximum Risk: (Difference in strikes − net credit) × 100. In this case, $370: [(35 − 30) − 1.30] × 100 or $1,850 for 5 contracts.

Maximum Profit: Net credit received. In this case, $650: (5 × 1.30) × 100.

Breakeven: Higher strike minus the initial credit per contract. In this case, 33.70: (35 − 1.30).

This bullish credit spread would see the maximum profit achieved as long as shares of N were at or above $35 on February 20, which was options expiration. The maximum risk is calculated by subtracting the net credit per contract of $1.30 from the difference between strikes (30 − 25 = 5). Therefore, the maximum risk is $370 per contract [(5 − 1.30) × 100 = $370] or $1,850 for five contracts. The breakeven is calculated by subtracting the net credit of 1.30 from the higher strike of 35. Thus, the breakeven for this trade was at $33.70. Once again, let's assume the trade consists of five contracts for a maximum profit of $650.

Shares of N did indeed move higher from this point, leaving the trader with the maximum profit of $650. In this example, the trader had to do nothing but watch the options close worthless, leaving the entire credit in the trader's account.

BEAR CALL SPREAD

A bear call spread consists of selling a lower strike call and buying a higher strike call using the same number of options and identical expiration dates. This is a credit trade when initiated and makes money when the market closes below the strike of the short option. This strategy is used when you have a bearish view of a market. It offers a limited profit potential with limited risk. The maximum reward is achieved when the closing price of the underlying security is below the lower strike call, yielding the full net credit for the trade. Therefore, this trade should be implemented by selling options that have a high probability of expiring worthless so you can keep the net credit.

The maximum risk is equal to the difference between strike prices minus the net credit times 100. The maximum risk occurs when the stock or futures contract closes at or above the strike price of the option purchased. This means that the short option will have increased in value while the one purchased has not increased in value as much. The breakeven is calculated by adding the strike price of the lower call to the net credit received.

Bear Call Spread Example

Let's say XYZ is trading at $51 and you think it's ready for a correction. You decide to initiate a bear call spread by going short 1 XYZ June 50 Call @ 3.50 and long 1 XYZ June 55 Call @ 1.00. When you initiate this trade, you receive a credit of 2.50, or $250 per contract: $(3.50 - 1.00) \times 100 = \$250$. This is the maximum reward that would be earned at expiration if XYZ closes at or below $50 per share.

Since the maximum risk is equal to the difference between strike prices minus the net credit, the most you can lose in this example is $250: $(55 - 50) - 2.50 \times 100 = \$250$. Maximum risk occurs if XYZ closes at or above 55. The short option would have a value of 5: $(55 - 50 = 5)$. The long 55 call would expire worthless; therefore, your position would lose 5 points, or $500 if the position closes at the higher strike price. However, you received a credit of $250; therefore, your risk is a net $250: ($500 − $250 = $250). The breakeven on this trade occurs when the underlying stock price equals the lower strike price plus the net credit. In this trade, the breakeven is 52.50: $(50 + 2.50 = 52.50)$. The trade breaks even or makes money as long as XYZ does not go above 52.50 at expiration. The risk graph of this trade is shown in Figure 5.7.

The risk graph of a bear call spread slants downward from left to right, displaying its bearish bias. If the underlying shares fall to the strike price of the short call, the trade reaches its maximum profit potential. Conversely, if the price of the underlying shares rises to the strike price of the long call, the maximum limited loss occurs. Always monitor the underlying shares for a reversal or a breakout to avoid incurring a loss.

Exiting the Trade

- ***XYZ rises above the long strike (55):*** The short call is assigned and you are obligated to deliver 100 shares of XYZ to the option holder at $50 per share. By exercising the long call, you can turn around and buy those shares at $55 each, thereby losing $500. This loss is mitigated by the initial $250 credit received for a total loss of $250 (not including commissions).

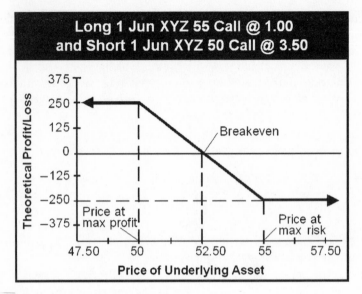

FIGURE 5.7 Bear Call Spread Risk Graph

- *XYZ falls below the long strike (55), but not below the breakeven (52.50):* The short call is assigned and you are obligated to deliver 100 shares of XYZ to the option holder at $50 a share by purchasing XYZ at the current price. This loss is mitigated by the initial $250 credit received. You can also sell the 55 call to offset and further reduce the loss.
- *XYZ falls below the breakeven (52.50), but not as low as the short strike (50):* The short call is assigned and you are obligated to deliver 100 shares of XYZ to the option holder at $50 a share by purchasing XYZ at the current price. The loss is offset by the initial $250 credit received. Selling the 55 call can bring in some additional money to offset the loss.
- *XYZ falls below the short strike (50):* Let the options expire worthless to make the maximum profit of $250.

Bear Call Spread Case Study

A bear call spread is a credit strategy that benefits from the underlying security trading sideways or lower. Stocks often run into resistance, which impedes higher movement. At these times, using an at-the-money credit spread can bring in profits. A credit spread profits if the stock moves in

Bear Call Spread

Strategy: Buy a call at a higher strike price. Sell a call at a lower strike price. Both options must have identical expiration dates

Market Opportunity: Look for a moderately bearish to bearish market where you expect a decrease in the price of the underlying asset below the strike price of the call option sold.

Maximum Risk: Limited. (Difference in strikes – net credit) × 100. Maximum risk results when the market closes at or above the strike price of the long option.

Maximum Profit: Limited to the net credit received. Maximum profit is made when the market closes below the strike price of the short calls. This is a credit trade when initiated.

Breakeven: Strike price of lower call + net credit received.

Margin: Required. Amount subject to broker's discretion.

two of the possible three directions a stock can move. A bear call spread benefits from sideways movement as well as a decline in prices.

Let's review: A bear call spread consists of selling a call and buying a lower strike call. The sale of the higher strike call brings in premium that is larger than the amount it costs to buy the lower strike call, thereby creating a limited risk/limited reward strategy. However, unlike a debit spread, the potential loss on a credit spread is almost always higher than the potential profit. However, the odds of success are very high, which is why these strategies are worthy of additional study.

On September 23, 2003, shares of Monster Worldwide (MNST) were showing bearish tendencies. The stock closed the session on September 24 at $27.74 and it looked likely that $25 would be broken. During the next session, it was possible to enter a bear call spread for a nice credit. Since a credit spread benefits from time decay, it's important to use front month options. By selling the October 25 call for 3.10 and buying the October 30 call for 0.70, this bear call spread would have brought in a credit of $2.40 per contract. The maximum risk would be $2.60 per contract, which is a rather good reward-to-risk ratio for a credit spread. The risk graph for this trade is shown in Figure 5.8.

In two out of every three cases, credit spreads expire with the trader keeping the entire credit. This is because traders of bear call spreads profit if the stock stays constant or moves down. For this example, the maximum reward is the credit received, which for five contracts would be $1,200. The maximum risk is found by subtracting the credit per contract from the difference between strikes (30 − 25 = 5).

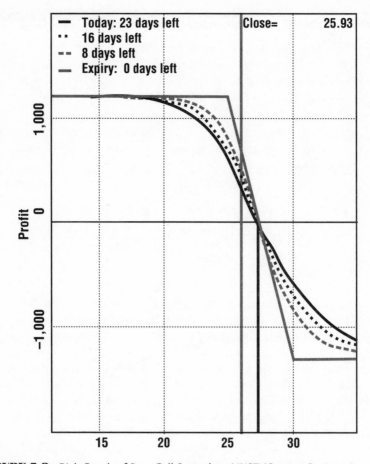

FIGURE 5.8 Risk Graph of Bear Call Spread on MNST (*Source:* Optionetics Platinum © 2004)

Thus, the maximum risk is $260 per contract [(5 – 2.40) × 100 = $260)] or $1,300 for five contracts, and the reward/risk ratio is 0.92 to 1.00. The breakeven is determined by adding the initial credit to the lower strike, or 27.40: (25 + 2.40 = 27.40).

So let's take a look at what happened in the real world. Shares of MNST traded near $25 for the next week, but on October 10, they shot sharply higher. However, the upper strike was not penetrated, with the high of the session coming at $29.35. During the next week, shares of MNST fell and on expiration Friday, October 17, the stock traded as low as $25 and the short call could have been purchased back for anywhere from $0.25 to $1.70. In this case, the October 25 call was purchased back for $0.45, leaving a profit of $195 per contract or $975 for all five contracts.

Bear Call Spread Case Study

Strategy: With the security trading near $27 a share on September 24, 2003, sell 5 October 25 calls @ 3.10 and buy 5 October 30 calls @ 0.70 on Monster Worldwide (MNST).

Market Opportunity: Expect a moderate decline in the underlying stock price.

Maximum Risk: (Difference in strikes × 100) – net credit. In this case, $1,300: $5 \times \{[(30 - 25) \times 100] - 240\} = \$1,300$.

Maximum Profit: Net credit = Short premium – long premium. In this case, $1,200: $5 \times (3.10 - .70) = \$1,200$.

Breakeven: Lower strike plus the initial credit per contract. In this case, 27.40: (25 + 2.40).

GETTING FILLED

Now that you've been introduced to spread trading, there are a few mechanical realities that must be dealt with—namely, getting your spread order filled at a price you can live with. There are many factors involved between the time you hit the send button and the time you receive confirmation that your spread has been "filled." Before you hit send, make sure you assess the bid/ask price of the spread. The bid is the highest price a prospective buyer (trader or dealer) is prepared to pay for a specified time for a trading unit of a specified security. Thus, the bid is also the price at which an investor can sell to a broker-dealer. The ask is the lowest price acceptable to a prospective seller (trader or dealer) of the same security. The ask, therefore, is the price at which an investor can buy from a broker-dealer. Together, the bid and ask prices constitute a quotation or quote and the difference between the two prices is the bid-ask spread. Sometimes you may have a hard time cutting the bid/ask on a spread, and even miss getting filled at or above the asking price. What I'm talking about is a common occurrence that goes something like this:

You like stock XYZ, which is trading at 110. You decide you'd like to go four months out on the 100/120 bull call spread. The bid on the spread is 5.50 and the ask is 6.50. In other words, if you owned the spread, it would have a selling value of 5.50. If you were buying the spread it would have an asking price of 6.50. Not wanting to pay what the market is asking, you put in a limit order of 6 on the buy side, meaning that you'll pay up to $600 for the spread. As the day wears on, you check your account online and see you haven't been filled. The stock dips some, and you check the bid/ask on the spread again; it's now 5.75 bid, 6.75 ask. Still you haven't been filled, and you're feeling frustrated! What's going on?

Here's the explanation: In order to complete a spread as a single transaction, the traders on the floor must find market makers to match up both sides of the spread in a single transaction. There has to be someone willing to sell a 100 call while someone else buys a 120 call. This is a much more difficult task than simply selling or buying calls as individual transactions. So, even though you may only be trying to cut the bid/ask by a small amount, it can be difficult to get a market maker to take this as a combination order. This is especially true in fast moving markets where scores are being reeled off in hundreds of individual contracts. Now the trader who has your ticket has the market maker stop, calculate the net amounts, and then make a decision.

I had an interesting and frustrating event a few months back that will shed some light on this topic. I wanted the August YHOO 55/65 bull call spread at 5.50. The bid/ask was approximately 5 and 6, so I was trying to shave a small amount, half a point. Hours went by and I checked again. YHOO had dipped intraday as I expected, and I was looking for my fill confirmation. The ask was now 5.75 and I still didn't have my order filled! I had the head of my brokerage office call down to the floor and I learned that in a fast moving market (as it was) no one wants to stop to calculate a spread when individual calls and puts are flying back and forth in lots of 20, 50, or 100 contracts on a stock like YHOO. I could have legged in, but I have a rule that I trade a vertical spread only as a limit order on the cost of the overall spread—no legging in. So I missed the trade.

However, sometimes this situation can work to your advantage. Let's say you offer 8.50 on a spread that was bid/ask at 7.50 and 9.50. Then the underlying stock, XYZ, starts to fall; the ask on the spread had fallen to 7.75. You decide to cancel and try the trade again when it's on the way up. You hold your breath, hoping you didn't already get filled as the asking price passed down through your offer of 8.50. Sure enough, you get your cancel confirmation in a little while and breathe a sigh of relief. Sure, XYZ will likely come back, but it would be better to place the bull call spread buy on the way up than on the way down—unless you're specifically targeting a certain price.

One more piece of advice: Don't chase the market. I sometimes wish I had raised my offer on YHOO; but I won on that transaction anyway because I stuck to my principles. Besides, the money I would have put in YHOO is working for me in another trade. If you wish to leg in (buying the lower call, then selling the higher call), be sure you've solidly confirmed the market direction first.

BID-ASK SPREAD: A CLOSER LOOK

From the first moment we are exposed to a real options quote, we realize that options do not trade at just one price. There is a bid price and an ask (or offer) price. For example, the Cisco (CSCO) October 20 calls do not trade for 55 cents. Instead, you may see a quote similar to this: CSCO 22.50 Calls: .50–.60.

In this example of the CSCO 22.50 calls, $.50 is the bid and $.60 is the ask (or offer). That means that everyone who is interested in selling CSCO 22.50 calls can do so at $.50 and all interested buyers of CSCO 22.50 calls can own them for $.60. Since we are not market makers, in order to guarantee ourselves a fill, we must pay the ask and sell the bid.

To illustrate the meaning of these two prices, imagine walking into a car dealership. A dealer has two prices on a car. There is a dealer invoice and a sticker price. A car dealer is willing to buy cars for dealer invoice, and is happy when they're sold at sticker price. Unless the dealer is trying to pad the sales numbers to meet some quota, we will not be lucky enough to drive a car off a lot for dealer invoice. However, in buying cars as well as in trading options, we try our best not to pay sticker price. Of course, this means the dealer can refuse to sell us the car, just as a market maker can refuse to trade with us. Only by paying the full no-haggle price can we be assured a fill on a trade.

In trading options, the reality is that while the quoted best ask in CSCO 22.50 calls may read $.60, someone in the CSCO pit may be willing to sell those calls for less. A car dealer may be willing to sell you a car for less than sticker price, but why pass on the chance that you or someone else might pay full fare? So the ask price will remain $.60 until someone tests it—namely with a limit order between the two amounts that define the bid/ask spread.

A limit order is an order to buy or sell a financial instrument (stock, option, etc.) at or below a specified price. For instance, you could tell a broker to "Buy me one January XYZ call at $8 or less" or "Sell 100 shares of XYZ at $20 or better."

I bring up the example of CSCO because of the incredible liquidity in that stock. That liquidity in the stock and in its corresponding options allows the bid-ask spread to be very tight—10 cents wide, in this case. So the question then arises: Is there anything that keeps the market makers from creating wider spreads? In the case of less liquid stocks, is there a chance that spreads can become too wide? Is there anything to protect us from abusively wide spreads? Actually, there is! It may not seem like it at times, but there exist legal width limits for options. This practice was instituted by the exchanges to keep the market makers in check and to entice retail customers to trade more. These limits are based on the option price—the higher the price of the option, the higher the allowable width of the bid-ask spread. The limits are shown in Table 5.2.

One small note: For option prices $3 and up, options no longer trade in nickels. The smallest denomination for those options is dimes. So do

TABLE 5.2 Option Values and Limits

Option Values	Limit
$0 to $1.95	25 cents
$2 to $5	40 cents
$5.10 to $10	50 cents
$10.10 to $20	80 cents
$20.10 and up	1 dollar

not try to pay $3.65 for an option. We must make up our mind to make our purchase price either $3.60 or $3.70. A pet peeve of many market makers is a retail customer who does not know this information.

Now let's look at a practical application of legal widths and how they can affect us. Let us revisit those same CSCO October 22.50 calls with a bid-ask of .50–.60. If we decide to be aggressive and pay the ask, we are incurring 10 cents of slippage (the difference between the bid price and the ask price). Now let's say we were right and CSCO shoots up $5; our calls are now worth somewhere around $5.50! As we look to exit our trade, we may look forward to a market quote of 5.40–5.60. However, the limit on the width of those options is 50 cents. Hence the real quote facing us may be closer to 5.20–5.70. Fifty cents of slippage is quite possible. We may console ourselves with the fact that we made some money in our trade, but that's no excuse for giving up so much on our exit. We can usually diminish the problem by testing the market and placing limit orders inside of the bid-ask spread.

STRATEGY ROAD MAPS

For your convenience, the following subsections provide step-by-step analyses of the vertical spreads discussed in this chapter.

Bull Call Spread Road Map

In order to place a bull call spread, the following guidelines should be observed:

1. Look for a bullish market where you anticipate a modest increase in the price of the underlying stock.
2. Check to see if this stock has options available.
3. Review call options premiums per expiration dates and strike prices. Bull call spreads are best placed on stocks that have at least

60 days until expiration. The utilization of LEAPS options is a good choice for this strategy. LEAPS give you the opportunity to put time on your side.

4. Investigate implied volatility values to see if the options are over-priced or undervalued.

5. Explore past price trends and liquidity by reviewing price and volume charts over the past year.

6. Choose a lower strike call to buy and a higher strike call to sell. Both options must have the same expiration date. In general, a good combi-nation is relatively low "buy" strikes combined with higher "sell" strikes. Get the breakeven low enough so that you can sleep at night. The lower buy strikes lower the breakeven point. Give yourself plenty of room to profit if the stock runs. This is accomplished by choosing higher sell strikes.

7. Determine the specific trade you want to place by calculating:

   - **Limited Risk:** The most that can be lost is the net debit of the two options.
   - **Unlimited Reward:** Calculated by subtracting the net debit from the difference in strike prices times 100.
   - **Breakeven:** Calculated by adding the lower strike price to the net debit.
   - **Return on Investment:** Reward/risk ratio.

8. Create a risk profile for the trade to graphically determine the trade's feasibility. The risk profile for a bull call spread visually reveals the strategy's limited risk and profit parameters. Notice how the maxi-mum profit occurs at the short call strike price.

9. Write down the trade in your trader's journal before placing the trade with your broker to minimize mistakes made in placing the order and to keep a record of the trade.

10. Create an exit strategy before you place the trade.

   - Consider doing two contracts at once. Try to exit half the trade when the value of the trade has doubled or when enough profit ex-ists to cover the cost of the double contracts. Then the other trade will be virtually a free trade and you can take more of a risk, allow-ing it to accumulate a bigger profit.
   - If you have only one contract, exit the remainder of the trade when it is worth 80 percent of the maximum possible value of the spread.

The reason for this rule is that it usually takes a very long time to see the last 20 percent of value in a profitable vertical spread. It's better to take the trade off and look for new trades where the money can be put to better use. We recommend exiting the trade prior to 30 days before expiration.

11. Contact your broker to buy and sell the chosen call options. Place the trade as a limit order so that you limit the net debit of the trade.

12. Watch the market closely as it fluctuates. The profit on this strategy is limited—a loss occurs if the underlying stock closes below the breakeven point.

13. Choose an exit strategy based on the price movement of the underlying stock:

- ***The underlying stock rises above the short strike:*** The short call is assigned and you are obligated to deliver 100 shares (per call) to the option holder at the short strike price. Exercise the long call to buy the underlying stock at the lower strike and deliver these shares to the option holder. The resulting profit is the maximum profit available.

- ***The underlying stock rises above the breakeven, but not as high as the short strike:*** Sell a call with the long call strike and buy a call with the short strike. There should be a small profit remaining.

- ***The underlying stock remains below the breakeven, but above the long strike:*** Offset the options by selling a call with the long strike and buying a call with the short strike to partially mitigate the initial debit or allow you to pocket a small profit; or wait until expiration and sell the long call to offset the trade's net debit and let the short option expire worthless.

- ***The underlying stock falls below the long option:*** Let the options expire worthless, or sell the long call prior to expiration to mitigate some of the loss.

Bear Put Spread Road Map

In order to place a bear put spread, the following guidelines should be observed:

1. Look for a bearish market where you anticipate a modest decrease in the price of the underlying stock.

2. Check to see if this stock has options available.

3. Review put options premiums per expiration dates and strike prices. Buy options with at least 60 days until expiration.

4. Investigate implied volatility values to see if the options are overpriced or undervalued. These spreads are best placed when volatility is low.

5. Explore past price trends and liquidity by reviewing price and volume charts over the past year. Look for chart patterns over the past one to three years to determine where you believe the stock should be by the date of expiration.

6. Choose a higher strike put to buy and a lower strike put to sell. Both options must have the same expiration date. Determine the specific trade you want to place by calculating:

   - **Limited Risk:** The most that can be lost on the trade is the net debit of the two option premiums.
   - **Unlimited Reward:** Calculated by subtracting the net debit from the difference in strike prices times 100.
   - **Breakeven:** Calculated by subtracting the net debit (divided by 100) from the long strike price.
   - **Return on Investment:** Reward/risk ratio.

7. Create a risk profile for the trade to graphically determine the trade's feasibility. If the underlying stock increases or exceeds the price of the short put, the trade reaches its maximum risk (loss) potential. Conversely, if the price of the underlying stock decreases or falls below the strike price of the long put, the maximum reward is attained.

8. Write down the trade in your trader's journal before placing the trade with your broker to minimize mistakes made in placing the order and to keep a record of the trade.

9. Make an exit plan before you place the trade.

   - Consider doing two contracts at once. Try to exit half the trade when the value of the trade has doubled or when enough profit exists to cover the cost of the double contracts. Then the other trade will be virtually a free trade and you can take more of a risk allowing it to accumulate a bigger profit. If the spread doubles, exit half of the position.
   - If you have only one contract, exit the remainder of the trade when it is worth 80 percent of its maximum value.
   - Exit the trade prior to 30 days before expiration.

10. Contact your broker to buy and sell the chosen put options. Place the trade as a limit order to limit the net debit of the trade.

11. Watch the market closely as it fluctuates. The profit on this strategy is limited—a loss occurs if the underlying stock rises above break-even point.

12. Choose an exit strategy based on the price movement of the underlying stock.

   - *The underlying stock falls below the short strike:* The short put is assigned and you are obligated to purchase 100 shares (per option) of the underlying stock from the option holder at the short put strike price. By exercising the long put, you can turn around and sell the shares received from the option holder at the higher long put strike and pocket the difference—the maximum profit available.

   - *The underlying stock falls below the breakeven, but not as low as the short strike:* Sell a put with the long put strike and buy a put with the short strike. There should be a small profit remaining.

   - *The underlying stock remains above the breakeven, but below the long strike:* Sell a put with the long strike and buy a put with the short strike, which will partially offset the initial debit or allow you to pocket a small profit; or wait until expiration and sell the long put to offset the trade's net debit and let the short option expire worthless.

   - *The underlying stock rises above the long option:* Let the options expire worthless, or sell the long put prior to expiration to mitigate some of the loss.

Bull Put Spread Road Map

In order to place a bull put spread, the following guidelines should be observed:

1. Look for a bullish market where you anticipate a modest increase in the price of the underlying stock.

2. Check to see if this stock has options available.

3. Review put options premiums per expiration dates and strike prices. Look for combinations that produce high net credits. The Optionetics.com Platinum site allows for searches that will quickly qualify candidates for you. Since the maximum profit is limited to the net credit

initially received, try to keep the net credit as high as possible to make the trade worthwhile.

4. Investigate implied volatility values to see if the options are over-priced or undervalued. Look for options with forward volatility skews—where the higher strike option you are selling has higher IV than the lower strike option you are purchasing.

5. Explore past price trends and liquidity by reviewing price and volume charts over the past year or two.

6. Choose a lower strike put to buy and a higher strike put to sell. Both options must have the same expiration date. Keep the short strike at-the-money. Try to avoid selling an in-the-money put because it is already in danger of assignment.

7. Place bull put spreads using options with 45 days or less until expiration. Since the profit on this strategy depends on the options expiring worthless, it is best to use options with 45 days or less until expiration to put time decay on your side.

8. Determine the specific trade you want to place by calculating:

   - **Limited Risk:** The most you can lose is the difference between strikes minus the net credit received times 100.
   - **Limited Reward:** The net credit received from placing the combination position.
   - **Breakeven:** Calculated by subtracting the net credit from the short put strike price. Make sure the breakeven is within the underlying stock's trading range.
   - **Return on Investment:** Reward/risk ratio.

9. Create a risk profile for the trade to graphically determine the trade's feasibility. The diagram will show a limited profit above the upside breakeven and a limited loss below the downside breakeven. In the best scenario, the underlying stock moves above the higher strike price by expiration and the short options expire worthless.

10. Write down the trade in your trader's journal before placing the trade with your broker to minimize mistakes made in placing the order and to keep a record of the trade.

11. Make an exit plan before you place the trade.

   - Consider doing two contracts at once. Try to exit half the trade when the value of the trade has doubled or when enough profit exists to cover the cost of the double contracts. Then the other trade will be virtually a free trade and you can take more of a risk, allow-ing it to accumulate a bigger profit.

- If you have only one contract, exit the remainder of the trade when it is worth 80 percent of the maximum possible value of the spread. The reason for this rule is that it usually takes a very long time to see the last 20 percent of value in a profitable vertical spread. It's better to take the trade off and look for new trades where the money can be put to better use.

12. Contact your broker to buy and sell the chosen put options. Place the trade as a limit order so that you maximize the net credit of the trade.

13. Watch the market closely as it fluctuates. The profit on this strategy is limited—a loss occurs if the underlying stock falls below the breakeven point.

14. Choose an exit strategy based on the price movement of the underly-ing stock:

- *The underlying stock rises above the short strike:* Options expire worthless and you keep the initial credit received (maxi-mum profit).

- *The underlying stock rises above the breakeven, but not as high as the short strike:* The short put is assigned and you are then obligated to purchase 100 shares from the option holder of the underlying stock at the short strike price. You can either keep the shares in hopes of a reversal or sell them at the current price for a small loss, which is not completely balanced out by the initial credit received. To bring in additional money, sell the long put.

- *The underlying stock remains below the breakeven, but above the long strike:* The short put is assigned and you are then obligated to purchase 100 shares of the underlying stock from the option holder at the short strike price. You can either keep the shares in hopes of a reversal or sell them at the current price for a small loss, which is not completely balanced out by the initial credit received. To mitigate this loss, sell the long put.

- *The underlying stock falls below the long option:* The short put is assigned and you are then obligated to purchase 100 shares of the underlying stock from the option holder at the short strike price. By exercising the long put, you can sell these shares at the long strike price. This loss is partially mitigated by the initial credit received and results in the trade's maximum loss.

Bear Call Spread Road Map

In order to place a bear call spread, the following guidelines should be observed:

1. Look for a moderately bearish market where you anticipate a modest decrease in the price of the underlying stock—not a large move.
2. Check to see if this stock has options.
3. Review call options premiums per expiration dates and strike prices. Look for combinations that produce high net credits. The Optionetics.com Platinum site allows for searches that will quickly qualify promising candidates for you. Since the maximum profit is limited to the net credit initially received, keep the net credit as high as possible to make the trade worthwhile.
4. Investigate implied volatility values to see if the options are overpriced or undervalued. Look for options with a reverse volatility skew—lower strike options have higher implied volatility and higher strike options have lower implied volatility.
5. Explore past price trends and liquidity by reviewing price and volume charts over the past year or two.
6. Choose a higher strike call to buy and a lower strike call to sell. Both options must have the same expiration date. Place bear call spreads using options with 45 days or less until expiration.
7. Determine the specific trade you want to place by calculating:

   - **Limited Risk:** The most you can lose is the difference in strike prices minus the net credit times 100.
   - **Limited Reward:** The maximum reward is the net credit received from placing the combination position.
   - **Breakeven:** Lowest strike price plus net credit received
   - **Return on Investment:** Reward/risk ratio.

8. Create a risk profile for the trade to graphically determine the trade's feasibility. The risk graph of a bear call spread slants downward from left to right, displaying its bearish bias. If the underlying stock falls to or past the price of the short put, the trade reaches its maximum profit potential. Conversely, if the price of the underlying stock rises to or exceeds the strike price of the long put, the maximum limited loss occurs.
9. Write down the trade in your trader's journal before placing the trade with your broker to minimize mistakes made in placing the order and to keep a record of the trade.

10. Make an exit plan before you place the trade.

- Consider doing two contracts at once. Try to exit half the trade when the value of the trade has doubled or when enough profit exists to cover the cost of the double contracts. Then the other trade will be virtually a free trade and you can take more of a risk, allowing it to accumulate a bigger profit.

- If you have only one contract, exit the remainder of the trade when it is worth 80 percent of its maximum value.

11. Contact your broker to buy and sell the chosen call options. Place the trade as a limit order so that you maximize the net credit of the trade.

12. Watch the market closely as it fluctuates. The profit on this strategy is limited—a loss occurs if the underlying stock rises above the breakeven point.

13. Choose an exit strategy based on the price movement of the underlying stock:

- ***The underlying stock falls below the short strike:*** Let the options expire worthless to make the maximum profit (the initial credit received).

- ***The underlying stock falls below the breakeven, but not as low as the short strike:*** The short call is assigned and you are then obligated to deliver 100 shares of the underlying stock to the option holder at the short strike by purchasing these shares at the current price. The loss is offset by the initial credit received. By selling the long call, you can bring in an additional small profit.

- ***The underlying stock remains above the breakeven, but below the long strike:*** The short call is assigned and you are then obligated to deliver 100 shares of the underlying stock to the option holder at the short strike price by purchasing these shares at the current price. This loss is mitigated by the initial credit received. Sell the long call for additional money to mitigate the loss.

- ***The underlying stock rises above the long option:*** The short call is assigned and you are then obligated to deliver 100 shares of the underlying stock to the option holder at the short strike. By exercising the long call, you can turn around and buy those shares at the long call strike price regardless of how high the underlying stock has risen. This limits your loss to the maximum of the trade. The loss is partially mitigated by the initial credit received on the trade.

CONCLUSION

The four vertical spreads covered in this chapter—bull call spread, bear put spread, bull put spread, and bear call spread—are probably the most basic option strategies used in today's markets. Since they offer limited risk and limited profit, close attention needs to be paid to the risk-to-reward ratio. Never take the risk unless you know it's worth it! Each of these strategies can be implemented in any market for a fraction of the cost of buying or selling the underlying instruments straight out.

In general, vertical spreads combine long and short options with the same expiration date but different strike prices. Vertical trading criteria include the following steps:

1. Look for a market where you anticipate a moderately directional move up or down.
2. For debit spreads, buy and sell options with at least 60 days until expiration. For credit spreads, buy and sell options with less than 45 days until expiration.
3. No adjustments can be made to increase profits once the trade is placed.
4. Exit strategy: Look for 50 percent profit or get out before a 50 percent loss.

In general, volatility increases the chance of a vertical spread making a profit. By watching for an increase in volatility, you can locate trending directional markets. In addition, it can often be more profitable to have your options exercised if you're in-the-money than simply exiting the trade. This isn't something you really have any control over, but it is important to be aware of any technique for increasing your profits.

These strategies can be applied in any market as long as you understand the advantage each strategy offers. However, learning to assess markets and forecast future movement is essential to applying the right strategy. It's the same as using the right tool for the right job; the right tool gets the job done efficiently and effectively. Each of the vertical spreads has its niche of advantage. Many times, price will be the deciding factor once you have discovered a directional trend.

The best way to learn how these strategies react to market movement is to experience them by paper trading markets that seem promising. You can use quotes from *The Wall Street Journal* or surf the Internet to a number of sites including www.cboe.com (for delayed quotes) or www.optionetics.com. Once you have initiated a paper trade, follow it each day to learn how market forces affect these kinds of limited risk strategies.

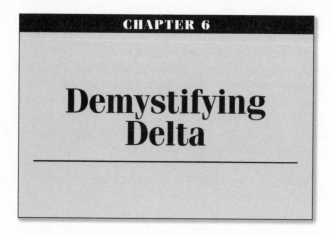

CHAPTER 6

Demystifying Delta

D elta neutral trading is the key to my success as an options trader. Learning how to trade delta neutral provides traders with the ability to make a profit regardless of market direction while maximizing trading profits and minimizing potential risk. Options traders who know how to wield the power of delta neutral trading increase their chances of success by leveling the playing field. This chapter is devoted to providing a solid understanding of this concept as well as the mechanics of this innovative trading approach.

In general, it is extremely hard to make any money competing with floor traders. Keep in mind that delta neutral trading has been used on stock exchange floors for many years. In fact, some of the most successful trading firms ever built use this type of trading. Back when I ran a floor trading operation, I decided to apply my Harvard Business School skills to aggressively study floor trader methods. I was surprised to realize that floor traders think in 10-second intervals. I soon recognized that we could take this trading method off the floor and change the time frame to make it successful for off-floor traders. Floor traders pay large sums of money for the privilege of moving faster and paying less per trade than off-floor traders. However, changing the time frame enabled me to compete with those with less knowledge. After all, 99 percent of the traders out there have very little concept of limiting risk, including money managers in charge of billions of dollars. They just happen to have control of a great deal of money so they can keep playing the game for a long time. For example, a friend once lost $10 million he was managing. Ten minutes later I asked him, "How do you feel about losing all that money?" He casually replied, "Well, it's not my money." That's a pretty sad story; but it's the truth. This kind of mentality is a major reason why it's important to manage your accounts using a limited risk trading approach.

Delta neutral trading strategies combine stocks (or futures) with options, or options with options in such a way that the sum of all the deltas in the trade equals zero. Thus, to understand delta neutral trading, we need to look at "delta," which is, in mathematical terms, the rate of change of the price of the option with respect to a change in price of the underlying stock.

An overall position delta of zero, when managed properly, can enable a trade to make money within a certain range of prices regardless of market direction. Before placing a trade, the upside and downside breakevens should be calculated to gauge the trade's profit range. A trader should also calculate the maximum potential profit and loss to assess the viability of the trade. As the price of the underlying instrument changes, the overall position delta of the trade moves away from zero. In some cases, additional profits can be made by adjusting the trade back to zero (or delta neutral) through buying or selling more options, stock shares, or futures contracts.

If you are trading with your own hard-earned cash, limiting your risk is an essential element of your trading approach. That's exactly what delta neutral trading strategies do. They use the same guidelines as floor trading but apply them in time frames that give off-floor traders a competitive edge in the markets.

Luckily, these strategies don't exactly use rocket science mathematics. The calculations are relatively simple. You're simply trying to create a trade that has an overall delta position as close to zero as possible. I can look at a newspaper and make delta neutral trades all day long. I don't have to wait for the S&Ps to hit a certain number, or confuse myself by studying too much fundamental analysis. However, I do have to look for the right combination of factors to create an optimal trade.

An optimal trade uses your available investment capital efficiently to produce substantial returns in a relatively short period of time. Optimal trades may combine futures with options, stocks with options, or options with options to create a strategy matrix. This matrix combines trading strategies to capitalize on a market going up, down, or sideways.

To locate profitable trades, you need to understand how and when to apply the right options strategy. This doesn't mean that you have to read the most technically advanced books on options trading. You don't need to be a genius to be a successful trader; you simply need to learn how to make consistent profits. One of the best ways to accomplish this task is to pick one market and/or one trading technique and trade it over and over again until you get really good at it. If you can find just one strategy that works, you can make money over and over again until it's so boring you just have to move on to another one. After a few years of building up your trading experience, you will be in a position where you are constantly redefining your strategy matrix and markets.

Finding moneymaking delta neutral opportunities is not like seeking the holy grail. Opportunities exist each and every day. It's simply a matter of knowing what to look for. Specifically, you need to find a market that has two basic characteristics—volatility and high liquidity—and use the appropriate time frame for the trade.

THE DELTA

To become a delta neutral trader, it is essential to have a working understanding of the Greek term *delta* and how it applies to options trading. Almost all of my favorite option strategies use the calculation of the delta to help devise managed risk trades. The delta can be defined as the change in the option premium relative to the price movement in the underlying instrument. This is, in essence, the first derivative of the price function, for those of you who have studied calculus. Deltas range from minus 1 through zero to plus 1 for every share of stock represented. Thus, because an option contract is based on 100 shares of stock, deltas are said to be "100" for the underlying stock, and will range from "−100" to "+100" for the associated options.

A rough measurement of an option's delta can be calculated by dividing the change in the premium by the change in the price of the underlying asset. For example, if the change in the premium is 30 and the change in the futures price is 100, you would have a delta of .30 (although to keep it simple, traders tend to ignore the decimal point and refer to it as + or − 30 deltas). Now, if your futures contract advances $10, a call option with a delta of 30 would increase only $3. Similarly, a call option with a delta of 10 would increase in value approximately $1.

One contract of futures or 100 shares of stock has a fixed delta of 100. Hence, buying 100 shares of stock equals +100 and selling 100 shares of stock equals −100 deltas. In contrast, all options have adjustable deltas. Bullish option strategies have positive deltas; bearish option strategies have negative deltas. Bullish strategies include long futures or stocks, long calls, or short puts. These positions all have positive deltas. Bearish strategies include short futures or stocks, short calls, or long puts; these have negative deltas. Table 6.1 summarizes the plus or minus delta possibilities.

As a rule of thumb, the deeper in-the-money your option is, the

TABLE 6.1 Positive and Negative Deltas	
Market Up (Positive Deltas)	**Market Down (Negative Deltas)**
Buy calls.	Sell calls.
Sell puts.	Buy puts.
Buy stocks.	Sell stocks.
Buy futures.	Sell futures.

higher the delta. Remember, you are comparing the change of the futures or stock price to the premium of the option. In-the-money options have higher deltas. A deep ITM option might have a delta of 80 or greater. ATM options—these are the ones you will be probably working with the most in the beginning—have deltas of approximately 50. OTM options' deltas might be as small as 20 or less. Again, depending how deep in-the-money or out-of-the-money your options are, these values will change. Think of it another way: Delta is equal to the probability of an option being in-the-money at expiration. An option with a delta of 10 has only a 10 percent probability of being ITM at expiration. That option is probably also deep OTM.

When an option is very deep in-the-money, it will start acting very much like a futures contract or a stock as the delta gets closer to plus or minus 100. The time value shrinks out of the option and it moves almost in tandem with the futures contract or stock. Many of you might have bought options and seen huge moves in the underlying asset's price but hardly any movement in your option. When you see the huge move, you probably think, "Yeah, this is going to be really good." However, if you bought the option with a delta of approximately 20, even though the futures or stock had a big move, your option is moving at only 20 percent of the rate of the futures in the beginning. This is one of the many reasons that knowing an option's delta can help you to identify profitable opportunities. In addition, there are a number of excellent computer programs geared to assist traders to determine option deltas, including the Platinum site at Optionetics.com.

Obviously, you want to cover the cost of your premium. However, if you are really bullish on something, then there are times you need to step up to the plate and go for it. Even if you are just moderately friendly to the market, you still want to use deltas to determine your best trading opportunity. Now, perhaps you would have said, "I am going to go for something a little further out-of-the-money so that I can purchase more options." Unless the market makes a big move, chances are that these OTM options will expire worthless. No matter what circumstances you encounter, determining the deltas and how they are going to act in different scenarios will foster profitable decision making.

When I first got into trading, I would pick market direction and then buy options based on this expected direction. Many times, they wouldn't go anywhere. I couldn't understand how the markets were taking off but my options were ticking up so slowly they eventually expired worthless. At that time, I had no knowledge of deltas. To avoid this scenario, remember that knowing an option's delta is essential to successful delta neutral trading. In general, an option's delta:

- Estimates the change in the option's price relative to the underlying security. For example, an option with a delta of 50 will cost less than an option with a delta of 80.
- Determines the number of options needed to equal one futures contract or 100 shares of stock to ultimately create a delta neutral trade with an overall position delta of zero. For example, two ATM call options have a total of +100 deltas; you can get to zero by selling 100 shares of stock or one futures contract (−100 deltas).
- Determines the probability that an option will expire in-the-money. An option with 50 deltas has a 50 percent chance of expiring in-the-money.
- Assists you in risk analysis. For example, when buying an option you know your only risk is the premium paid for the option.

To review the delta neutral basics: The delta is the term used by traders to measure the price change of an option relative to a change in price of the underlying security. In other words, the underlying security will make its move either to the upside or to the downside. A *tick* is the minimum price movement of a particular market. With each tick change, a relative change in the option delta occurs. Therefore, if the delta is tied to the change in price of the underlying security, then the underlying security is said to have a value of 1 delta. However, I prefer to use a value of 100 deltas instead because with an option based on 100 shares of stock it's easier to work with.

Let's create an example using IBM options, with IBM currently trading at $87.50.

- Long 100 shares of IBM = +100 deltas.
- Short 100 shares of IBM = −100 deltas.

Simple math shows us that going long 200 shares equals +200 deltas, going long 300 shares equals +300 deltas, going short 10 futures contracts equals −1,000 deltas, and so on. On the other hand, the typical option has a delta of less than 100 unless the option is so deep in-the-money that it acts exactly like a futures contract. I rarely deal with options that are deep in-the-money as they generally cost too much and are illiquid.

All options have a delta relative to the 100 deltas of the underlying security. Since 100 shares of stock are equal to 100 deltas, all options must have delta values of less than 100. An Option Delta Values chart can be found in Appendix B outlining the approximate delta values of ATM, ITM, and OTM options.

VOLATILITY

Volatility measures market movement or nonmovement. It is defined as the magnitude by which an underlying asset is expected to fluctuate in a given period of time. As previously discussed, it is a major contributor to the price (premium) of an option; usually, the higher an asset's volatility, the higher the price of its options. This is because a more volatile asset offers larger swings upward or downward in price in shorter time spans than less volatile assets. These movements are attractive to options traders who are always looking for big directional swings to make their contracts profitable. High or low volatility gives traders a signal as to the type of strategy that can best be implemented to optimize profits in a specific market.

I like looking for wild markets. I like the stuff that moves, the stuff that scares everybody. Basically, I look for volatility. When a market is volatile, everyone in the market is confused. No one really knows what's going on or what's going to happen next. Everyone has a different opinion. That's when the market is ripe for delta neutral strategies to reap major rewards. The more markets move, the more profits can potentially be made.

Volatility in the markets certainly doesn't keep me up at night. For the most part, I go to bed and sleep very well. Perhaps the only problem I have as a 24-hour trader is waking up in the middle of the night to sneak a peek at my computer. If I discover I'm making lots of money, I may stay up the rest of the night to watch my trade.

As uncertainty in the marketplace increases, the price for options usually increases as well. Recently, we have seen that these moves can be quite dramatic. Reviewing the concept of volatility and its effect on option prices is an important lesson for beginning and novice traders alike. Basically, an option can be thought of as an insurance policy—when the likelihood of the "insured" event increases, the cost or premium of the policy goes up and the writers of the policies need to be compensated for the higher risk. For example, earthquake insurance is higher in California than in Illinois. So when uncertainty in an underlying asset increases (as we have seen recently in the stock market), the demand for options increases as well. This increase in demand is reflected in higher premiums.

When we discuss volatility, we must be clear as to what we're talking about. If a trader derives a theoretical value for an option using a pricing model such as Black-Scholes, a critical input is the assumption of how volatile the underlying asset will be over the life of the option. This volatility assumption may be based on historical data or other factors or analyses. Floor and theoretical traders spend a lot of money to make sure the volatility input used in their price models is as accurate as possible. The validity of the option prices generated is very much determined by this theoretical volatility assumption.

Whereas theoretical volatility is the input used in calculating option prices, implied volatility is the actual measured volatility trading in the market. This is the price level at which options may be bought or sold. Implied volatilities can be acquired in several ways. One way would be to go to a pricing model and plug in current option prices and solve for volatility, as most professional traders do. Another way would be to simply go look it up in a published source, such as the Optionetics Platinum site.

Once you understand how volatilities are behaving and what your assumptions might be, you can begin to formulate trading strategies to capitalize on the market environment. However, you must be aware of the characteristics of how volatility affects various options. Changes in volatility affect at-the-money option prices the most because ATM options have the greatest amount of extrinsic value or time premium—the portion of the option price most affected by volatility. Another way to think of it is that at-the-money options represent the most uncertainty as to whether the option will finish in-the-money or out-of-the-money. Additional volatility in the marketplace just adds to that.

Generally changes in volatility are more pronounced in the front months than in the distant months. This is probably due to greater liquidity and open interest in the front months. However, since the back month options have more time value than front month options, a smaller volatility change in the back month might produce a greater change in option price compared to the front month. For example, assume the following (August is the front month):

- August 50 calls (at-the-money) = $3.00; Volatility = 40%
- November 50 calls (at-the-money) = $5.00; Volatility = 30%

Following an event that causes volatility to increase we might see:

- August 50 calls = $4.00; Volatility = 50%
- November 50 calls = $6.50; Volatility = 38%

We can see that even though the volatility increased more in August, the November options actually had a greater price increase. This is due to the greater amount of time premium or extrinsic value in the November options. Care must be taken when formulating trading strategies to be aware of these relationships. For example, it is conceivable that a spread could capture the volatility move correctly, but still lose money on the price changes for the options.

Changes in volatility may also affect the skew: the price relationship between options in any given month. This means that if volatility goes up in the market, different strikes in any given month may react differently. For example, out-of-the-money puts may get bid to a much higher relative volatility than at-the-money puts. This is because money managers and investors prefer to buy the less costly option as disaster protection. A $2 put is still cheaper than a $5 put even though the volatility might be significantly higher.

So how does a trader best utilize volatility effects in his/her trading? First, it is important to know how a stock trades. Events such as earnings and news events may affect even similar stocks in different ways. This knowledge can then be used to determine how the options might behave during certain times. Looking at volatility graphs is a good way to get a feel for where the volatility normally trades and the high and low ends of the range.

A sound strategy and calculated methodology are critical to an option trader's success. Why is the trade being implemented? Are volatilities low and do they look like they could rally? Remember that implied volatility is the market's perception of the future variance of the underlying asset. Low volatility could mean a very flat market for the foreseeable future. If a pricing model is being used to generate theoretical values, do the market volatilities look too high or low? If so, be sure all the inputs are correct.

The market represents the collective intelligence of the option players' universe. Be careful betting against smart money. Watch the order flow if possible to see who is buying and selling against the market makers. Check open interest to get some indication of the potential action, especially if the market moves significantly. By keeping these things in mind and managing risk closely, you will increase your odds of trading success dramatically.

RELATIONSHIP BETWEEN VOLATILITY AND DELTA

One of the concepts that seems to confuse new options traders is the relationship between volatility and delta. First, let's quickly review each topic separately. Volatility represents the level of uncertainty in the market and the degree to which the prices of the underlying are expected to change over time. When there is more uncertainty or fear, people will pay more for options as a risk control instrument. So when the markets churn, investors get fearful and bid up the prices of options. As people feel more secure in the future, they will sell their options, causing the implied volatility to drop.

Delta can be thought of as the sensitivity of an option to movement in the underlying asset. For example, an option with a delta of 50 means that for every $1 move in the underlying stock the option will move $0.50. Options that are more in-the-money have higher deltas, as they tend to move in a closer magnitude with the stock. Delta can also be thought of as the probability of an option finishing in-the-money at expiration. An option with a delta of 25 has a 25 percent chance of finishing in-the-money at expiration.

An increase in volatility causes all option deltas to move toward 50. So for in-the-money options, the delta will decrease; and for out-of-the-money options, the delta will increase. This makes intuitive sense, for when uncertainty increases it becomes less clear where the underlying might end up at expiration. Since delta can also be defined as the probability of an option finishing in-the-money at expiration, as uncertainty increases, all probabilities or deltas should move toward 50–50. For example, an in-the-money call with a delta of 80 under normal volatility conditions might drop to 65 under a higher-volatility environment, reflecting less certainty that the call will finish in-the-money. Thus, by expiration, volatility is zero since we certainly know where the underlying will finish. At zero volatility, all deltas are either 0 or 1, finishing either out-of-the-money or in-the-money. Any increase in volatility causes probabilities to move away from 0 and 1, reflecting a higher level of uncertainty.

It is always important to track volatility, not only for at-the-money options but also for the wings (out-of-the-money) options as well. A trade may have a particular set of characteristics at one volatility level but a completely different set at another. A position may look long during a rally but once volatility is reset, it may be flat or even short. Knowing how deltas behave due to changes in volatility and movement in the underlying is essential for profitable options trading.

APPROPRIATE TIME FRAME

The next step is to select the appropriate time frame for the kind of trade you want to place. Since I am no longer a day trader, I'm usually in the 30- to 90-day range of trading. And for the most part, I prefer 90 days. Since I don't want to sit in front of a computer all day long at this point in my trading career, I prefer to use delta neutral strategies. They allow me to create trades with any kind of time frame I choose.

Delta neutral strategies are simply not suitable for day trading. In fact, day trading doesn't work in the long run unless you have the time and the inclination to sit in front of a computer all day long. Day trading takes a specific kind of trader with a certain kind of personality to make it work. My trading strategies are geared for a longer-term approach.

If you're going to go into any business, you have to size up the competition. In my style of longer-term trading, my competition is the floor trader who makes money on a tick-by-tick basis. But I choose not to play that game. I've taken the time frame of a floor trader—which is tick-by-tick—and expanded it to a period floor traders usually don't monitor. Applying my strategies in longer time frames than day-to-day trading is my way of creating a trader's competitive edge.

CONCLUSION

Delta neutral trading combines options with stocks (or futures) and options with options to create trades with an overall position delta of zero. To set up a balanced delta neutral trade, it is essential to become familiar with the delta values of ATM, ITM, and OTM options. Deltas provide a scientific formula for setting up trading strategies that give you a competitive edge over directional traders. Experience will teach you how to use this approach to take advantage of various market opportunities while managing the overall risk of the trade efficiently. I cannot stress enough the importance of developing a working knowledge of the deltas of options.

Professional options traders think in terms of spreads and they hedge themselves to stay neutral on market direction. The direction of the underlying stock is less important to them than the volatility of the options (implied volatility) and the volatility of the underlying stock (statistical or historical volatility).

Professional options traders also let the market tell them what to do. They recognize the market is saying that the appropriate strategy is to sell premium when option volatility is high (options are expensive). Conversely, they understand the market is saying that the low-risk strategy is to buy premium when implied volatility is low (options are cheap).

The most difficult aspect of delta neutral options trading is learning to stay focused on volatility. The reason it's psychologically hard to trade on volatility considerations is because it's natural to look at a price chart, draw conclusions about future market direction, and be tempted to bias your positions in the direction you feel prices will move.

However, the point of delta neutral trading is that you want to make money based on how accurately you forecast volatility; you don't want to run the risk of losing money by forecasting market direction incorrectly. That's why you should initiate your spreads delta neutral. It's also why you should adjust them back to neutral if they later become too long or short— which brings us to the second most difficult aspect of delta neutral options trading: acting without hesitation when the market tells you to act.

If your position becomes too long or short, you must mechanically adjust it without hoping for the price to move in the direction of your delta bias. While it's natural to want to give the market a chance to go your way, the fact of the matter is that the market has already proven you wrong, so it would only be wishful thinking to expect it will suddenly move the way you want. Every delta neutral trader knows the feeling of having a weight lifted from his shoulders the moment he or she does the right thing by executing an adjustment to get neutral.

When you buy premium, be prepared to take action if the market makes a big move so you can lock in profits. When you sell premium, don't expect volatility to collapse right away. You will probably need to be patient. You hope the underlying asset won't move a lot while you're waiting. However, time decay helps you while you're waiting.

As you can see, the concept of delta neutral is not one trade, but rather a method of advanced thinking. If you can master the basics of delta neutral thinking, then you can create delta neutral trades from any combination of assets. The concept is to be able to make a profit regardless of where the stock moves.

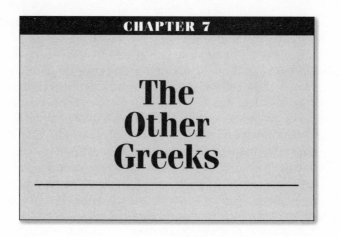

CHAPTER 7

The Other Greeks

T o create a delta neutral trade, you need to select a calculated ratio of short and long positions that combine to create an overall position delta of zero. To accomplish this goal, it is helpful to review a variety of risk exposure measurements. The option Greeks are a set of measurements that can be used to explore the risk exposures of specific trades. Since options and other trading instruments have a variety of risk exposures that can vary dramatically over time or as markets move, it is essential to understand the various risks associated with each trade you place.

DEFINING THE GREEKS

Options traders have a multitude of different ways to make money by trading options. Traders can profit when a stock price moves substantially or trades in a range. They can also make or lose money when implied volatility increases or decreases. To assess the advantage that one spread might have over another, it is vital to consider the risks involved in each spread. When making these kinds of assessments, options traders typically refer to the following risk measurements: delta, gamma, theta, and vega. These four elements of options risk are referred to as the option "Greeks." Let's take a deeper look at the most commonly used Greeks and how they can be used in options trading.

First, I would like to go over a couple of technical issues in regard to the Greeks. These numbers are calculated using higher-level mathematics and the Black-Scholes option pricing model. My objective is not to explain those computations, but to shed some light on the practical uses of these concepts. Additionally, I would suggest using an options software program to calculate these numbers so that you are not wasting precious time on tedious mathematics. Lastly, it is important to realize that these numbers are strictly theoretical, meaning that model values may not be the same as those calculated in real-world situations.

Each risk measurement (except vega) is named after a different letter in the Greek alphabet—delta, gamma, and theta. In the beginning, it is important to be aware of all of the Greeks, although understanding the delta is the most crucial to your success. Comprehending the definition of each of the Greeks will give you the tools to decipher option pricing as well as risk. Each of the terms has its own specific use in day-to-day trading by most professional traders as well as in my own trading approach.

- *Delta.* Change in the price (premium) of an option relative to the price change of the underlying security.
- *Gamma.* Change in the delta of an option with respect to the change in price of its underlying security.
- *Theta.* Change in the price of an option with respect to a change in its time to expiration.
- *Vega.* Change in the price of an option with respect to its change in volatility.

Each of these risk measurements contains specific important trading information. As you become more acquainted with the various aspects of options trading, you will find more and more uses for each of them. For example, they each make a unique contribution to an option's premium. The two most important components of an option's premium are intrinsic value and time value (extrinsic value).

In an effort to understand the elements that influence the value of an option, various option pricing models were created, including Black-Scholes and Cox-Rubinstein. To comprehend the Greeks, we must understand that they are derived from these types of theoretical pricing models. The values that are needed as inputs into the option pricing models are related to the Greeks. However, the inputs for the models are not the Greeks themselves. A common mistake among options traders is to refer to vega as implied volatility. When we refer to the Greeks, we are talking about risk that will ultimately affect the option's price. Therefore, a more accurate description of vega would be the option's price sensitivity to implied volatility changes.

Delta

The concept of the option's *delta* seems to be the first Greek that everyone learns. It's basically a measure of how much the value of an option will change given a change in the underlying stock. When the strike price of the option is close or at-the-money, the delta of the option will be around 50 for long call options and –50 for long put options. In the case of a call option, the option's delta could be higher if the value of the stock has exceeded the option's strike price significantly. If our call option's strike price were much higher than the price of the shares, the value of the delta would be smaller. For example, if XYZ stock is trading for $50 per share and I own the $60 strike price call, my delta may be around 30. Recall that delta is computed using an option pricing model. It will vary based on the difference between the stock price and the strike price of the option as well as the time left until expiration. In this case, let's assume the delta of this option is 30, or .30. Therefore, my position will theoretically make $30 for every $1 increase in XYZ stock based on the option's delta.

There are many ways that traders can use the delta, or hedge ratio, in their options analysis. A very basic way to use delta is in hedging a shares position. Let's suppose that I have 500 shares of XYZ and that I want to purchase some puts to protect my position. Most traders would purchase five at-the-money puts. This creates a synthetic call position. The idea is that the trader can exercise the puts if the market moves against him. In this respect the purchased options become like insurance for the stock trader. However, there is another way to look at this scenario. If I have 500 shares of XYZ stock, I can hedge the delta of the stock by purchasing 10 of the XYZ at-the-money puts. Since the delta of each share of stock is 1 and the delta of each at-the-money put is –50, I would need 10 puts to hedge the deltas of the long stock position. The results are similar to a straddle.

Example

Long 500 shares of XYZ	Delta = +500
Long 10 ATM puts	Delta = –500
Net delta	0

Gamma

Gamma tells us how fast the delta of the option changes for every 1 point move in the underlying stock. For this reason, some traders refer to gamma as the delta of the delta. However, gamma is different from delta in that it is always expressed as a positive number regardless of whether it relates to a put or a call. If the price of the stock increases $1 and the delta increases or decreases by a value of 15 then the gamma is 15. Remember, we are using our option pricing model to make this determination. Another interesting characteristic of gamma is that it is largest for the at-the-money options. This means that the deltas for the at-the-money options are more sensitive to a change in the price of the underlying stock.

While I have been talking about delta and gamma in relation to the underlying stock price, it is important to note that they are also influenced by time and volatility. Statistical (or historical) volatility is a measure of the fluctuation of the underlying stock. As I have already noted, delta is a measure of how the options price will change when the underlying stock changes. Therefore, the delta of the options will be generally higher for a higher-volatility stock versus a lower-volatility stock. This is due to the fact that the stock's volatility and the option's delta are related to the movement of the stock. Also, ITM and ATM option deltas fall faster than OTM options as they approach expiration.

Theta

The *theta* of an option is a measure of the time decay of an option. Theta can also be defined as the amount by which the price of an option exceeds its intrinsic value. Generally speaking, theta decreases as an option approaches expiration. Theta is one of the most important concepts for a beginning option trader to understand for it basically explains the effect of time on the premium of the options that have been purchased or sold. The less time that an option has until expiration, the faster that option is going to lose its value. Theta is a way of measuring the rate at which this value is lost. The further out in time you go, the smaller the time decay will be for an option. Therefore, if you want to buy an option, it is advantageous to purchase longer-term contracts. If you are using a strategy that profits from time decay, then you will want to be short the shorter-term options so that the loss in value due to time decay happens quickly.

Since an option loses value as time passes, theta is expressed as a negative number. For example, an option (put or call) with a theta of –.15 will lose 15 cents per day. As noted earlier, time decay is not linear. For that reason, options with less time until expiration will have a higher (negative) theta than those with only a few days of life remaining.

Vega

Vega tells us how much the price of the options will change for every 1 percent change in implied volatility. So, if we purchased the XYZ option for $100 and its vega is 20, we can expect the cost of the option to increase by $20 when implied volatility moves up by 1 percent. Vega tends to be highest for options that are at-the-money and decreases as the option reaches its expiration date. It is interesting to note that vega does not share the correlation to the stock's fluctuation that delta and gamma do. This is because vega is dependent on the measure of implied volatility rather than statistical volatility. This is an important distinction for traders who like to trade options straddles.

We all know that there is time value associated with the value of an option. The rate at which the option's time premium depreciates on a daily basis is called theta. It is typically highest for at-the-money options and is expressed as a negative value. So, if I have an option that has a theta of −.50, I can expect the value of my option to decrease 50 cents per day until the option's expiration. This characteristic of the option's time premium has particular interest to the trader of credit spreads.

ASSESSING THE RISKS

As options traders become more experienced with creating spreads, they should become more aware of the types of risks involved with each spread. To reach this level of trading competence, options traders should combine the values of the Greeks used to create the optimal options spread. The result will allow the trader to more accurately assess the risks of any given options spread.

Understanding the relative impact of the Greeks on positions you hold is indispensable. Here are six of the more salient mathematical relationships of these Greek variables:

1. The delta of an at-the-money option is about 50. Out-of-the-money options have smaller deltas and they decrease the farther out-of-the-money you go. In-the-money options have greater deltas and they increase the farther in-the-money you go. Call deltas are positive and put deltas are negative.
2. When you sell options, theta is positive and gamma is negative. This means you make money through time decay, but price movement is undesirable. So profits you're trying to earn through option time decay when you sell puts and calls may never be realized if the stock moves quickly in price. Also, rallies in price of the underlying asset will cause your overall position to become increasingly delta-short and to lose money. Conversely, declines in the underlying asset price will cause your position to become increasingly delta-long and to lose money.
3. When you buy options, theta is negative and gamma is positive. This means you lose money through time decay but price movement is desirable. So profits you're attempting to earn through volatile moves of

the underlying stock may never be realized if time decay causes losses. Also, rallies in price result in your position becoming increasingly delta-long and declines result in your position becoming increasingly delta-short.

4. Theta and gamma increase as you get close to expiration, and they're greatest for at-the-money options. This means the stakes grow if you're short at-the-money because either the put or the call can easily become in-the-money and move point-for-point with the equity. You can't adjust quickly enough to accommodate such a situation.

5. When you sell options, vega is negative. This means if implied volatility increases, your position will lose money, and if it decreases, your position will make money. When you buy options, vega is positive, so increases in implied volatility are profitable and decreases are unprofitable.

6. Vega is greatest for options far from expiration. Vega becomes less of a factor while theta and gamma become more significant as options approach expiration.

TIME DECAY'S EFFECT ON STRATEGY SELECTION

Since the rate of time decay varies from one options contract to the next, the strategist generally wants to know how time is impacting the overall position. For instance, a straddle, which involves the purchase of both a put and a call, can lose significant value due to time decay. In addition, given that the rate of time decay is not linear, straddles using short-term options are generally not advised. Instead, longer-term options are more suitable for straddles and the trade should be closed well before (30 days or more before) expiration. (The straddle strategy is explored in Chapter 8.)

Some strategies, on the other hand, can use time decay to the option trader's advantage. Have you ever heard that 85 percent of options expire worthless? While that is probably not entirely true, a large number of options do expire worthless each month. As a result, some traders prefer to sell, rather than buy, options because, unlike the option buyers, the option seller benefits from forces of time decay.

The simplest strategy that attempts to profit from time decay is the covered call—or buying shares of XYZ Corp. and selling XYZ calls. Perhaps a better alternative, however, is the calendar spread (see Chapter 10). This type of spread involves purchasing a longer-term call option on a stock and selling a shorter-term call on the same stock. The goal is to hold the long-term option while the short-term contract loses value at a faster rate due to the nonlinear nature of time decay. There are a number of different ways to construct calendar spreads. Some diagonal spreads, butterflies, and condors are examples of other strategies that can benefit from the loss of time value. In each instance, the strategist is generally not interested in seeing the underlying asset make a dramatic move higher or lower, but rather seeing the underlying stock trade within a range while time decay eats away at the value of its options.

VOLATILITY REVISITED

Volatility can be defined as a measurement of the amount by which an underlying asset is expected to fluctuate in a given period of time. It is one of the most important variables in options trading, significantly impacting the price of an option's premium as well as contributing heavily to an option's time value.

As previously mentioned, there are two basic kinds of volatility: implied and historical (statistical). Implied volatility is computed using the actual market prices of an option and one of a number of pricing models (Black-Scholes for shares and indexes; Black for futures). For example, if the market price of an option increases without a change in the price of the underlying instrument, the option's implied volatility will have risen. Historical volatility is calculated by using the standard deviation of underlying asset price changes from close-to-close of trading going back 21 to 23 days or some other predetermined period. In more basic terms, historical volatility gauges price movement in terms of past performance. Implied volatility approximates how much the marketplace thinks prices will move. Understanding volatility can help you to choose and implement the appropriate option strategy. It holds the key to improving your market timing as well as helping you to avoid the purchase of overpriced options or the sale of underpriced options.

In basic terms, volatility is the speed of change in the market. Some people refer to it as confusion in the market. I prefer to think of it as insurance. If you were to sell an insurance policy to a 35-year-old who drives a basic Honda, the stable driver and stable car would equal a low insurance premium. Now, let's sell an insurance policy to an 18-year-old, fresh out of high school with no driving record. Furthermore, let's say he's driving a brand-new red Corvette. His policy will cost more than the policy for the Honda. The 18-year-old lives in a state of high volatility!

The term *vega* represents the measurement of the change in the price of the option in relation to the change in the volatility of the underlying asset. As the option moves quicker within time, we have a change in volatility: Volatility moves up. If the S&P's volatility was sitting just below 17, perhaps now it's at 17.50. You can equate that .50 rise to an approximate 3 percent increase in options. Can options increase even if the price of the underlying asset moves nowhere? Yes. This frequently happens in the bonds market just before the government issues the employment report on the first Friday of the month. Before the Friday report is released, demand causes option volatility to increase. After the report is issued, volatility usually reverts to its normal levels. In general, it is profitable to buy options in low volatility and sell them during periods of high volatility.

When trading options, you can use a computer to look at various indicators to assess whether an option's price is abnormal when compared to the movement of the underlying asset. This abnormality in price is caused mostly by an option's implied volatility, or perception of the future movement of the asset. Implied volatility is a computed value calculated by using an option pricing model for volume, as well as strike price, expiration date, and the price of the underlying asset. It matches the theoretical option price with the current market price of the option. Many times, option prices reflect higher or lower option volatility than the asset itself.

The best thing about implied volatility is that it is very cyclical; that is, it tends to move back and forth within a given range. Sometimes it may remain high or low for a while, and at other times it might reach a new high or low. The key to utilizing implied volatility is in knowing that when it changes direction, it often moves quickly in the new direction. Buying options when the implied volatility is high causes some trades to end up losing even when the price of the underlying asset moves in your direction. You can take advantage of this situation by selling options and receiving their premium as a credit to your account instead of buying options. For example, if you buy an option on IBM when the implied volatility is at a high you may pay $6.50 for the option. If the market stays where it is, the implied volatility will drop and the option may then be priced at only $4.75 with this drop in volatility.

I generally search the computer for price discrepancies that indicate that an option is very cheap or expensive compared to its underlying asset. When an option's actual price differs from the theoretical price by any significant amount, I take advantage of the situation by purchasing options with low volatility and selling options with high volatility, expecting the prices to get back in line as the expiration date approaches.

To place a long volatility trade, I want the volatility to increase. I look for a market where the implied volatility for the ATM options has dropped down toward its historic lows. Next, I wait for the implied volatility to turn around and start going back up.

In its most basic form, volatility means change. It can be summed up just like that. Markets that move erratically—such as the energy markets in times of crisis, or grains in short supply—command higher option premiums than markets that lag. I look at volatilities on a daily basis and many times find options to be priced higher than they should be. This is known as *volatility skew*. Most option pricing models give the trader an edge in estimating an option's worth and thereby identifying skew. Computers are an invaluable resource in searching for these kinds of opportunities.

For example, deeply OTM options tend to have higher implied volatility levels than ATM options. This leads to the overpricing of OTM options based on a volatility scale. Increased volatility of OTM options occurs for a variety of reasons. Many traders prefer to buy two $5 options than one $10 option because they feel they are getting more bang for their buck. What does this do to the demand for OTM options? It increases that demand, which increases the price, which creates volatility skew. These skews are another key to finding profitable option strategy opportunities.

Although I strongly recommend using a computer to accurately determine volatility prices, there are a couple of techniques available for people who do not have a computer. One way is to compare the S&P against the Dow Jones Industrial Average. You can analyze this relationship simply by watching CNBC, looking at *Investor's Business Daily* or *The Wall Street Journal*, or going online to consult our web site (www.optionetics.com). A 1-point movement in the S&P generally corresponds to 8 to 10 points of movement in the Dow. For example, if the Dow drops 16 to 20 points, but the S&P is still moving up a point, then S&P volatility is increasing. On the other side, if you are consistently getting 1-point movement in the S&P for more than 10 points movement in the Dow, then volatility on the S&P is decreasing. This is one way to determine volatility.

Another way to determine volatility is to check out the range of the markets you wish to trade. The range is the difference between the high for the cycle and the low value for whatever cycle you wish to study (daily, weekly, etc.). For example, try charting the daily range of a stock and then keep a running average of this range. Then, compare this range to the range of the Dow or the S&P. If the range of your stock is greater than the Dow/S&P average, then volatility is increasing; if the range is less than the average, then volatility is decreasing. Determining the range or checking out the Dow/S&P relationship are two ways of gauging volatility with or without a computer. You can use these techniques to your advantage to determine whether you should be buying, initiating a trade, or just waiting. Remember, option prices can change quite dramatically between high and low volatility.

TYPES OF VOLATILITY RE-EXAMINED

In order to stack the odds in your favor when developing options strategies, it is important to clearly distinguish between two types of volatility:

implied and historical. Implied volatility (IV) as we have already noted, is the measure of volatility that is embedded in an option's price. In addition, each options contract will have a unique level of implied volatility that can be computed using an option pricing model. All else being equal, the greater an underlying asset's volatility, the higher the level of IV. That is, an underlying asset that exhibits a great deal of volatility will command a higher option premium than an underlying asset with low volatility.

To understand why a volatile stock will command a higher option premium, consider buying a call option on XYZ with a strike price of 50 and expiration in January (the XYZ January 50 call) during the month of December. If the stock has been trading between $40 and $45 for the past six weeks, the odds of the option rising above $50 by January are relatively slim. As a result, the XYZ January 50 call option will not carry much value. But say the stock has been trading between $40 and $80 during the past six weeks and sometimes jumps $15 in a single day. In that case, XYZ has exhibited relatively high volatility, and therefore the stock has a better chance of rising above $50 by January. A call option, which gives the buyer the right to purchase the stock at $50 a share, will have better odds of being in-the-money and as a result will command a higher price if the stock has been exhibiting higher levels of volatility.

Options traders understand that stocks with higher volatility have a greater chance of being in-the-money at expiration than low-volatility stocks. Consequently, all else being equal, a stock with higher volatility will have more expensive option premiums than a low-volatility stock. Mathematically, the difference in premiums between the two stocks owes to a difference in implied volatility—which is computed using an option pricing model like the one developed by Fischer Black and Myron Scholes, the Black-Scholes model. Furthermore, IV is generally discussed as a percentage. For example, the IV of the XYZ January 50 call is 25 percent. Implied volatility of 20 percent or less is considered low. Extremely volatile stocks can have IV in the triple digits.

Sometimes traders and analysts attempt to gauge whether the implied volatility of an options contract is appropriate. For example, if the IV is too high given the underlying asset's future volatility, the options may be overpriced and worth selling. On the other hand, if IV is too low given the outlook for the underlying asset, the option premiums may be too low, or cheap, and worth buying. One way to determine whether implied volatility is high or low at any given point in time is to compare it to its past levels. For example, if the options of an underlying asset have IV in the 20 to 25 percent range during the past six months and then suddenly spike up to 50 percent, the option premiums have become expensive.

Statistical volatility (SV) can also offer a barometer to determine whether an options contract is cheap (IV too low) or expensive (IV too high). Since SV is computed as the annualized standard deviation of past prices over a period of time (10, 30, 90 days), it is considered a measure of historical volatility because it looks at past prices. If you don't like math, statistical volatility on stocks and indexes can be found on various web sites like the Optionetics.com Platinum site. SV is a tool for reviewing the past volatility of a stock or index. Like implied volatility, it is discussed in terms of percentages.

Comparing the SV to IV can offer indications regarding the appropriateness of the current option premiums. If the implied volatility is significantly higher than the statistical volatility, chances are the options are expensive. That is, the option premiums are pricing in the expectations of much higher volatility going forward when compared to the underlying asset's actual volatility in the past. When implied volatility is low relative to statistical volatility, the options might be cheap. That is, relative to the asset's historical volatility, the IV and option premiums are high. Savvy traders attempt to take advantage of large differences between historical and implied volatility. In later chapters, we will review some strategies that show how.

APPLYING THE GREEKS

Now the challenge for the options strategist and particularly the delta neutral trader is to effectively interpret and manage these Greeks not only at trade initiation but also throughout the life of the position. The first thing to realize is that changes in the underlying instrument cause changes in the delta, which then impact all the other Greeks.

Keep these three rules in mind when evaluating the Greeks of your position.

1. The deltas of out-of-the-money options are smaller and they continue to decrease as you go further out-of-the-money. When the options strategist purchases options, theta is negative and gamma is positive. In this situation the position would lose money through time decay but price movement has a positive impact.

2. When the trader sells option premium then theta is positive and gamma is negative. This position would make money through time decay but price movement would have a negative effect. Also, theta and gamma both increase, the closer the position gets to expiration. In addition, theta and gamma are larger for at-the-money options.

3. When selling options, vega is negative; if implied volatility rises the position loses money and if it declines the position makes money.

Conversely, when a trader purchases options, vega is positive, so a rise in implied volatility is profitable and decreases have a negative impact on the position's profitability.

To be an effective options strategist, particularly if you want to make delta neutral type adjustments, understanding these Greek basics and being able to apply them to your options strategies is paramount to your success. These very important measurement tools coupled with the position's risk graph can provide the necessary information that will allow you to consistently execute profitable trades and send your equity curve sharply upward.

CONCLUSION

Many times when you have conversations with options traders, you will notice that they refer to the delta, gamma, vega, or theta of their positions. This terminology can be confusing and sometimes intimidating to those who have not been exposed to this type of rhetoric. When broken down, all of these terms refer to relatively simple concepts that can help you to more thoroughly understand the risks and potential rewards of option positions. Having a comprehensive understanding of these concepts will help you to decrease your risk exposure, reduce your stress levels, and increase your overall profitability as a trader. Learning how to integrate these basic concepts into your own trading programs can have a powerful effect on your success. Since prices are constantly changing, the Greeks provide traders with the means to determine just how sensitive a specific trade is to price fluctuations. Combining an understanding of the Greeks with the powerful insights risk profiles provide can help you take your options trading to another level.

Option pricing is based on a variety of factors. Each of these factors can be used to help determine the correct strategy to be used in a market. Volatility is a vital part of this process. Charting the volatility of your favorite markets will enable you to spot abnormalities that can translate into healthy profits. Since this is such a complicated subject, a great deal of time, money, and energy is spent to explore its daily fluctuations and profitable applications. The Platinum site at Optionetics.com provides access to these insights as well as daily trading information.

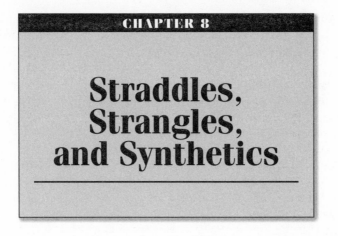

CHAPTER 8

Straddles, Strangles, and Synthetics

T he successful delta neutral trader looks at a market scenario with a discerning eye. Delta neutral trading involves hunting for the optimal mathematical relationship among strikes, premiums, and expiration months. The final strategy creates the highest probability of profitability and enables the trader to enjoy consistent returns on investments. For example, if I'm going to buy stock shares, I'm also going to buy or sell something in the options pit. When I put on one trade, I simultaneously put on another. These kinds of multiple trade strategies require a trader to consider the market from three directions.

1. What if the market goes up?
2. What if it goes down?
3. What if it doesn't go anywhere at all?

Do not confuse assessing these possibilities with trying to forecast market direction. Delta neutral traders do not need to guess which way the market will move because they have assessed in advance their reactions to market direction. They set up trades that maximize profits and minimize risk by balancing the delta of the overall position—and then they can make money regardless of market direction.

DELTA NEUTRAL MECHANICS

Setting up a delta neutral trade requires selecting a calculated ratio of short and long positions to create an overall position delta of zero. As noted in the preceding chapter, the delta of 100 shares of stock or one futures contract equals plus or minus 100. Thus, if you're buying 100 shares of stock or one futures contract, you are +100 deltas; if you are selling 100 shares of stock or one futures contract, you are –100 deltas. That's a pretty simple number to work with. It is not an abstract number. It's +100 or –100, and that's it. You can easily do that much in your head once you get the hang of it. No matter what stock or futures contract it is—S&Ps, bonds, currencies, soybeans, IBM, Dell, or Intel—it has a delta of plus or minus 100.

Options deltas are a little more complex. They depend on what kind of option you are trading—at-the-money (ATM), in-the-money (ITM), or out-of-the-money (OTM)—which is determined by the option's strike price and its relationship to the price of the underlying asset. Let's develop an example using shares of XYZ currently trading at $90. XYZ has options at 80, 85, 90, 95, and 100 (each $5 increment); the 90s are the ATM options. ATM options have deltas of about +50 or –50. Once again, this is a pretty easy calculation. It could be off a little bit, but plus or minus 50 is the general rule for an ATM option. This also means that there is a 50–50 chance of an ATM option closing in-the-money. It's similar to a coin flip—it can go either way.

Using these values, let's create a delta neutral trade. If we buy 100 shares of stock, we have +100 deltas. To get to delta neutral, we have to balance out the +100 deltas by finding –100 deltas, perhaps in the form of two short ATM options, which produce the required –100 deltas. This would bring our overall position delta to zero.

However, how do you determine which options equal –50? If you buy an ATM call, do you think you're +50 or –50? Well, since the purchase of a call is a bullish sign, buying an ATM call has a delta of +50, while the purchase of a put is a bearish strategy with a delta of –50. The plus and minus just mean that you expect the market to move up or down. In the easiest of terms, buying calls creates a positive delta; selling calls creates a negative delta. Buying puts creates a negative delta; selling puts creates a positive delta. These rules govern all delta neutral trading opportunities.

Positive Deltas— Market Expectation Up	Negative Deltas— Market Expectation Down
Buy calls.	Sell calls.
Sell puts.	Buy puts.
Buy stock.	Sell stock.
Buy futures.	Sell futures.

Let's return to our quest for a delta neutral trade. The easiest trade to make comes in the form of a straddle: the purchase of an ATM call and an

ATM put with the same strike and expiration date. Figure 8.1 shows the generic risk graph for this popular delta neutral strategy. The lower breakeven is the point where the trade will start to generate a profit as the stock continues downward; the upper breakeven is the point at which the trade will become profitable as the stock moves upward.

As can be readily seen from Figure 8.1, the straddle will be profitable in both significant up moves and down moves. The only place where there is a potential problem is when the stock does not move. Thus, the major problem with a straddle is that we are purchasing both options ATM; thus, the entire value of the two premiums is time value. As time value is not "real" in that there is no inherent value in it, and time value decreases to zero as the option approaches expiration, we have the crux of the problem with a straddle: The stock must move, and move soon, to recover the money that is being lost by the erosion of time in the trade.

There are two ways the trade will be profitable. The first is the obvious one of the stock moving significantly, which will increase the value of one option while simultaneously decreasing the value of the other option, although at a slower rate. The other is for both options to increase in value. The only way both options will increase in value simultaneously is to have the volatility of the options increase. All other variables in the Black-Scholes option pricing model will affect puts and calls in opposite directions. If the volatility of the options increases, then the option premiums will increase, and the possibility of the stock moving will also increase (the basic concept of what volatility is measuring). Thus, if you can find a stock with relatively low volatility that is increasing, the value of the

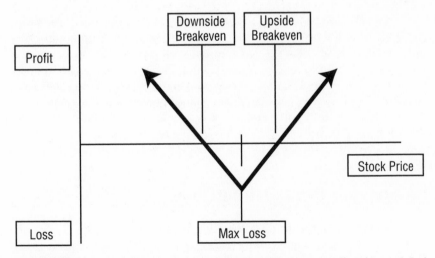

FIGURE 8.1 Risk Graph of a Delta Neutral Straddle (Long 1 Call and Long 1 Put)

straddle will increase and also the stock will be likely to move either up or down—a double chance for profit.

To be successful in trading straddles, we need to find a stock whose volatility is low but about to increase as the stock begins to move. This may sound like real guessing at first, but in reality it is not too hard to discover promising candidates. The primary, most reliable reason for an increase in volatility and for the stock price to move is news. News can be anything from court decisions to new product discoveries to accounting irregularities to earnings announcements. Of the various news possibilities, earnings reports are the easiest to predict, and the most common. Every quarter, each publicly traded company is required by the Securities and Exchange Commission (SEC) to report its earnings. Thus, each publicly traded firm will have four earnings reports each year—four chances for the stock to move unpredictably. Further, each announcement will tend to be made at approximately the same point in each quarter.

The natural state of things is for the stock's price movement, and hence volatility, to be relatively low until some announcement, or the anticipation of an announcement, triggers an upsurge in the volatility. Between announcements a firm's volatility tends to be low, and then it will rise as the earnings date approaches, dropping back down after the announcement and subsequent stock movement.

Thus, to enter a successful straddle trade, a trader only needs to determine far enough in advance just when the earnings announcement will be made, enter the trade, and then wait for the announcement date. In the normal case, on or about the announcement date the volatility will spike up and the stock will make its move one way or the other. At that point you exit the trade.

What if you went to sleep and waited for the options to expire? Since the trade is really designed to take advantage of a quick uptick in price movement and volatility, it's doubtful that you would want to stay in the position until expiration. More than likely, you'll want to exit the trade as soon as the news breaks; that's when the volatility ticks up and the stock should move. If you wait much longer, volatility will calm back down and the stock may return to its previous price, sucking all of your profits from the trade.

COMBINING STOCK WITH OPTIONS

Now let's take a look at trading delta neutral by combining stock with options. Let's say we've entered the market with +100 deltas by purchasing 100 shares of stock. To make the overall trade delta neutral, we have two choices using ATM options. We can either buy two ATM puts or sell two ATM calls. The question becomes whether it is better to sell ATM calls or buy ATM puts to get the necessary –100 deltas. When you sell an option, what happens to your account? You receive a credit for the total premiums of the options you sold. In other words, you have put money in your pocket. However, you have also assumed more risk. As usual, there's no such thing as a free lunch. Although putting money in your pocket sounds like a good thing, the unlimited risk you have to assume can be a harrowing experience.

So far, setting up a delta neutral trade has been quite simple. However, it takes experience and skill to know which strategy has the greater chance of making money. Since delta neutral trades do not rely on market direction, a profit is possible in most cases regardless of whether the market goes up or down.

Let's say we create a delta neutral trade by purchasing 100 shares of stock and buying two ATM put options. If the market swings up, the shares make money. However, we are out the premium paid on the two long puts. If the market takes a dive, our stock may lose money, but we'll make a profit on the two puts by using one as protection and making money on the other one. In other words, the deltas of my two puts will increase faster than the delta of the stock. Obviously, a major ingredient to profit making is setting up trades in such a way that your profits outweigh your losses.

However, options aren't always at-the-money. You can trade a wide variety of options with many different expiration dates. Many traders get cold feet deciding which options to work with. In general, ATM options are the easiest to work with, but not necessarily the most profitable. How do I determine which options to use? Once again, I need to visually see the profit and loss potentials of each trade by setting up its respective risk profile. So, let's set up an example of a delta neutral trade that consists of going long 100 shares of XYZ at $50 and simultaneously buying two long 50 ATM puts at $5. This strategy is called a *long synthetic straddle* and offers risk that is limited to the double premium paid for the ATM puts. The purchase of 100 shares of stock creates +100 deltas and the purchase of two ATM puts creates –100 deltas.

The risk curve visually details the trade's limited risk and unlimited potential profit in either direction. The risk graph for this trade (shown in Figure 8.2) creates a curve that is U-shaped. This is what an optimal risk curve looks like—one with limited risk and unlimited reward in either direction. In this example, the maximum risk at option expiration is $1,000: $(5 \times 2) \times 100$.

You can also create a long synthetic straddle by selling 100 shares of stock and buying 2 ATM calls. This trade has a relatively low margin

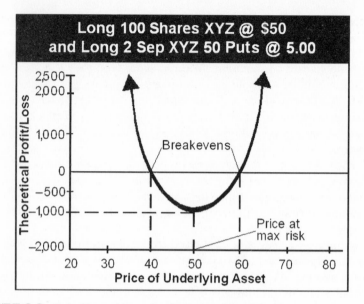

FIGURE 8.2   Delta Neutral Long Synthetic Straddle Risk Graph

requirement and moderate risk. The risk graph for this trade is similar to the one shown in Figure 8.2. Its U-shaped curve reflects unlimited profit potential and risk that is limited to the total premium paid or $1,000: $(5 \times 2) \times 100$.

Thus, as long as you are buying the options, the strategy is known as a long synthetic straddle. Conversely, you can create a *short synthetic straddle* by either purchasing 100 shares of stock and selling two ATM calls or selling 100 shares of stock and selling two ATM puts. With this strategy, your profit is limited to the credit received on the short puts and the risk is unlimited in either direction. Thus, the risk curve of a short synthetic straddle looks like an upside-down U. These trades involve shorting options, which can be extremely risky. If the market crashes you stand to lose a great deal of money. Conversely, if it moves up quickly you will also lose money. I prefer to teach traders to create trades with U-shaped curves, not upside-down U-shaped curves. Although the latter can be profitable, they often require traders to move quickly when things are not working out right. Typically, I favor buying stocks and buying puts.

Although all four of these examples are delta neutral trades, I urge you to avoid unlimited risk until you are have developed a strong track record. There are a variety of factors that you need to be familiar with to help you to determine which strategy has the best profit-making potential for a particular market. Once the underlying instrument moves far enough away from its initial position, you should be able to make money on one of the legs in your trade. Additionally, multiple contract positions enable traders to make positive or negative adjustments depending on how many deltas your overall position has moved and how many contracts make up the trade.

Which strategy do I prefer? In general, I prefer lower-risk trades. They are much less stressful. However, before I would place a trade either way, I would set up a risk profile of each possible strategy. This is by far the best way to find an answer to the question of buying versus selling options. In general, whenever you are buying options as part of a delta neutral trade, you are creating a risk graph with a U-shaped curve; and whenever you are selling options as part of a delta neutral trade, you are creating an upside-down U-shaped curve. I prefer to work with trades with upward U-shaped curves because they feature limited risk—a much safer strategy, especially for beginners. However, as you progress up your own trader's learning curve, opportunities will present themselves where you may want to take a higher risk in order to receive a potentially higher reward. Remember, every trade is unique.

LONG STRADDLE STRATEGY

For many traders, straddles have become a staple trading strategy in today's unforgiving market conditions. The idea of risking $500 a week on a position to make $250 (or a 50 percent return) in three to four weeks definitely works for me. A straddle is an innovative strategy that can truly benefit traders looking for a continuous income stream and it's probably the easiest of the delta neutral trades to create. A straddle consists of being long one ATM call and long one ATM put, both with the same strike price and expiration date. By calculating the deltas, you will note that they add up to zero (long ATM call = +50; long ATM put = −50). Thus, the strike prices of the straddle must be purchased at-the-money for the trade to be delta neutral. If the strikes are at anything other than the stock price, then the trade will not be delta neutral; it will have either a negative or a positive delta bias depending on whether the strikes are above or below the stock price.

The idea behind the straddle is that as the stock moves upward in price, the long call becomes more valuable. Although the long put will lose value at the same time, it will not lose value as fast as the call will gain value. In addition, there is a lower limit as to just how much value the put can lose—it can fall only to zero. Thus, as the stock rises in price, the net effect is that the straddle gains in value.

Of course, if the stock falls in price, the opposite will happen. The long put will continue to gain in value while the long call will lose value, but only until it reaches zero as well. Thus, if the stock loses value, the total straddle position will gain in value. Since buying a straddle involves buying both an ATM call and an ATM put (with identical strike prices and expiration months), buying a straddle can be fairly expensive. Your total risk on the position is the cost of the double premiums. For you to gain a profit, the market has to move sufficiently to make up the cost of that double premium. However, at least there are no margin requirements to worry about.

To place a long straddle, you need to locate a market with impending high volatility. For example, you might want to buy shares ahead of an earnings report or during a period of low volatility in anticipation of a period of high volatility. One of the most volatile days of the month for the stock market is the first Friday of each month when the employment report is released. This is the mother of all economic reports and has the ability to move the market in an absolutely psychotic fashion, typically resulting in a highly volatile day. The volatility might even pick up starting on Thursday, so I often place a straddle on the previous Wednesday. One important thing to remember about straddles is that you don't have to predict market direction. Regardless of whether it moves up or down, you can make some money. The essential factor is volatility.

Two other reports have an effect on market volatility, especially the financial markets: the Consumer Price Index (CPI) and the Producer Price Index (PPI). Unfortunately, these reports do not have a fixed date of release, although they usually come out the week after the employment report (i.e., the second week of the month). You should mark these dates on your calendar as a reminder. Actually, any report can move the market if the information is unexpected regarding housing starts, durable goods, or any of the leading economic indicators. However, the ones to pay particular attention to are the previously mentioned big three. You may have an opportunity to buy a straddle a couple of days before they are released and make some money.

The major disadvantage of a straddle is time decay. There is a substantial time premium to be lost if you do not choose your maturities properly and follow the rules for how long to hold these positions. The other disadvantage to straddles is that if the implied volatility of the options declines (a.k.a. vega risk), you are faced with a substantial penalty because you have had to pay the double premium of the options. That's why it's so important to buy cheap (low volatility) options in the first place.

Long Straddle Mechanics

Let's create a long straddle by going long 1 September XYZ 50 Call @ 2.50 and long 1 September XYZ 50 Put @ 2.50 with XYZ currently trading for

$50 a share. The maximum profit of this trade is unlimited. Both options have the same expiration month and the same strike price. Let's take a look at a long straddle's risk profile. To visualize the risk profile of a straddle, it can be helpful to imagine what each leg of the trade looks like. As previously defined, buying a straddle requires the purchase of a call and a put at the same strike price and the same expiration period. Since risk curves of complex strategies are only combinations of more basic trades, the risk profile of a long straddle is a combination of a long call risk curve and a long put risk curve. When combined, they create a V-shaped curve (see Figure 8.3). This important factor tells us that long straddles have unlimited profit potential and limited risk (the price of the two premiums).

When you create a long straddle, it is very important to determine the trade's range of profitability. To accomplish this, you need to calculate the upside breakeven and the downside breakeven. The upside breakeven occurs when the underlying asset's price equals the strike price plus the total premium. In this example, the upside breakeven is 55: 50 + (2.50 + 2.50) = 55. The downside breakeven occurs when the underlying asset's price equals the strike price minus the total premium. In this case, the downside breakeven equals 45: 50 − (2.50 + 2.50) = 45. XYZ has to move below $45 or above $55 for the straddle to make money by expiration.

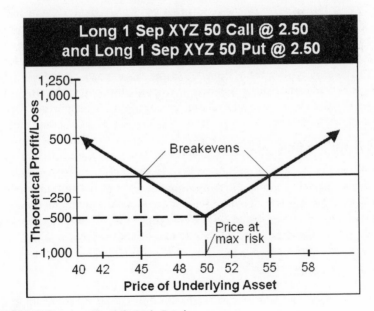

FIGURE 8.3 Long Straddle Risk Graph

Long Straddle

Strategy: Purchase an ATM call and an ATM put with the same strike price and the same expiration date.

Market Opportunity: Look for a market with low implied volatility options where a sharp volatility increase is anticipated.

Maximum Risk: Limited to the net debit paid.

Maximum Profit: Unlimited to the upside and limited to downside (as the underlying can only fall to zero) beyond the breakevens. Profit requires sufficient market movement but does not depend on market direction.

Upside Breakeven: ATM strike price + net debit paid.

Downside Breakeven: ATM strike price − net debit paid.

Exiting the Position

The following exit strategies can be applied to the long straddle example:

- *XYZ falls below the downside breakeven (45):* You can offset the put by selling a put for a profit. You can hold the essentially worthless call for a possible stock reversal.
- *XYZ falls within the downside (45) and upside (55) break-evens:* This is the range of risk and will cause you to close out the position at a loss. Simply sell the ATM options to exit the trade. The maximum risk is equal to the double premiums paid out or $500.
- *XYZ rises above the upside breakeven (55):* You are in your profit zone again. You can close the call position for a profit and hold the worthless put for a possible stock reversal.

Long Straddle Case Study

A long straddle is the simultaneous purchase of a call and a put using the same strike and the same expiration month. Since it involves the purchase of a double premium, the cost to enter is often high. This being the case, a long straddle should be used on options that have low implied volatility. When a trader expects a large move in a stock, but isn't sure about the directional bias of the move, a straddle is a good strategy to employ.

A straddle is a limited risk, unlimited reward strategy that relies on a strong move in the underlying security. The maximum risk is the total debit paid to enter the trade. In order to find the breakeven points, we have to add the debit of the trade onto the strike price for the upside breakeven and subtract it from the strike for the downside breakeven. In order to see how this works, let's look at a real-life example.

At the beginning of 2003, shares of Cisco (CSCO) started to form a chart pattern called a descending triangle. This formation often precedes a major move in a stock, but the direction of the move is hard to determine. Therefore, an options trader might want to use a straddle to benefit from a move in *either* direction. On April 10, 2003, Cisco shares closed at $13.21 after bouncing from the support. The triangle was becoming smaller, telling us that the stock was about to break out—yet the direction of the break was still hard to determine. Therefore, we entered a straddle.

The October 12.50 puts could be purchased for 1.55 a share and the October 12.50 calls could be purchased at 2.25. Buying five contracts would cost $1,900: $[5 \times (1.55 + 2.25)] \times 100$. This is also our maximum risk. The nice thing about a straddle is that if the stock doesn't move as expected, the straddle owner can get out without much of a loss as long as the options are not held until expiration. This is because time decay is light when an option is several months away from expiration.

Looking at the risk graph for this trade in Figure 8.4, notice how the maximum loss occurs only if CSCO shares close at $12.50 on expiration day. (Each line provides an idea of what the trade would be worth given a move within a certain time period; the lowest line shows the trade at expiration.)

To calculate the breakevens for this trade, add the net debit per contract of 3.80 to the strike of 12.50 to get an upside breakeven of $16.30. The downside breakeven is found by subtracting 3.80 from the strike of 12.50 to get 8.70.

Long Straddle Case Study

Strategy: With CSCO at $13.04 a share on April 10, Long 5 October 12.50 CSCO Puts @ 1.55 and Long 5 October CSCO 12.50 Calls @ 2.25.

Market Opportunity: Expect a breakout from consolidation.

Maximum Risk: Limited to initial debit. In this case, the maximum risk is $1,900: $[5 \times (1.55 + 2.25)] \times 100$.

Maximum Profit: Unlimited to the upside and limited to the downside (the underlying asset can only fall to zero). In this case, the trade garnered a profit of $1,200 on June 19.

Downside Breakeven: ATM strike price minus the initial cost per contract. In this case, the downside breakeven is 8.70: (12.50 – 3.80).

Upside Breakeven: ATM strike price plus the initial cost per contract. In this case, the upside breakeven is 16.30: (12.50 + 3.80).

Margin: None.

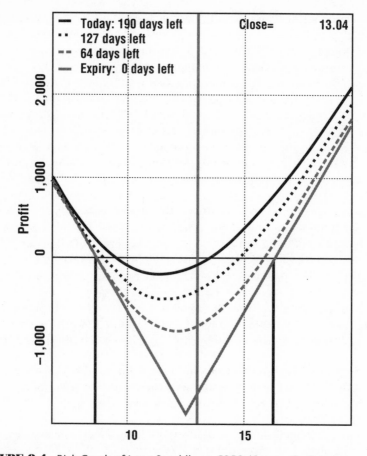

FIGURE 8.4 Risk Graph of Long Straddle on CSCO (*Source:* Optionetics Platinum © 2004)

CSCO shares did indeed break out and did so to the upside. On June 19, the daily chart formed a bearish formation and the owner of this straddle might have decided this was the point to exit. CSCO shares closed the session at $18.56, with the October 12.50 calls worth $620 a contract. Thus, the value of the five calls was $3,100. Once we subtract the debit of $1,900, we have a healthy profit of $1,200—a return on investment of 63 percent.

Profitable Straddle Selection Tactics

Purchasing a straddle allows the trader to make large potential profits if the stock moves far enough in either direction. To profitably implement this selection strategy, we need to discuss the importance of implied and historical volatility, time decay, breakeven points, and upcoming news events. Finally, we will tie all this information together into a high-profit/low-risk straddle selection blueprint.

First, the stock has to have low implied volatility compared to its historical volatility. The assumption here is that more often than not the implied volatility will return to its historical volatility reading. As traders, we always want to stack the probabilities in our favor, and this volatility "rubber band effect" is a terrific way of doing so. When volatility rises while we are in the trade, the value of our position will increase. We also want to see some price consolidation in recent weeks coupled with this low implied volatility.

Second, given that options are wasting assets, it is vital to always account for time decay. In general, you should allow more than 30 days to still be remaining after you plan to close your straddle position. This is due to the fact that time value decay accelerates in the final 30 days before expiration. Following this rule will help you to reduce risk; any losses due to time value decay are limited to very small amounts.

Third, knowing your breakeven points is important so you can properly set profit targets and stop loss levels. Let's review: To calculate the upside breakeven point, take the strike price and add it to the cost per straddle; to calculate the downside breakeven point, simply subtract the double premium of the options from the strike price. Breakevens are important in all option strategies and they are mentioned here not as a selection criterion, but rather to emphasize their key role in the trade management process.

Fourth, for the straddle to be profitable you have to select the right stock. It is absolutely essential that the company have an impending announcement coming within the next month that historically has caused implied volatility to rise in anticipation. The news events could be new product announcements, stock splits, takeovers, key management changes, or the more predictable quarterly earnings announcements. If the news has already come out, then entering a straddle position is very risky due to the likelihood of a drop-off in volatility.

In summary, here is a recap of the four key straddle trade selection rules:

1. Find a stock with low implied volatility that has a tight trading range spanning the past few weeks.
2. Allow at least 30 days to still be remaining after exiting the straddle position. This is usually right after the key announcement has been made.

3. Know your breakeven points and use them to set profit targets and stop-loss levels.

4. Make sure the company is planning a key announcement in the next three to six weeks and that historically the stock has reacted with exaggerated price movement due to speculation of the impending news event.

Hopefully, these straightforward yet powerful screening techniques will help you find some profitable straddle trades. Following these basic straddle selection rules will place the odds of being profitable squarely in the trader's corner. There are, of course, numerous other straddle selection techniques as well as adjustments that can be made during the trade; and I would encourage all serious traders to learn and explore the wide range of possibilities this innovative strategy offers. Traders can get stock volatility information from numerous resources on the Internet, but for the most comprehensive options data coverage the Optionetics Platinum site is hard to beat. (Do yourself a favor and take the tour sometime.)

Tools of the Trade: The ADX Index

Although straddles enable traders entering the stock options arena to have the opportunity to make income on a more short-term basis, straddles can be expensive if you are wrong. The key is finding the right market conditions that make straddles more likely to be profitable. In addition to the basic ideas of looking for stocks with consolidation patterns, earnings reports right around the corner, and options that have low implied volatility (i.e., cheap), I have seen some benefit in following and finding specific ADX patterns.

What is the ADX? The Average Directional Movement Index is a momentum indicator—an oscillator developed by Welles Wilder that seeks to measure the strength of a current trend. The key to successful straddles is finding a stock that will make a breakout move. To be successful, we don't care what direction the stock moves; we just need a solid move. The ADX is another tool to add to your trader's toolbox in selecting the right stock candidates for straddles.

The ADX is derived from two other indicators, also developed by Wilder, called the Positive Directional Indicator (+DI) and the Negative Directional Indicator (−DI). The ADX fluctuates between 0 and 100, although readings above 60 are rare. Readings below 20 indicate a weak trend often seen as range trading. Readings above 40 indicate a strong directional trend. Though the ADX does not indicate a trend as bullish or bearish, a reading above 40 clearly indicates there is strength in the current trend. In other words, if you find a stock with a high reading, say above 40, this indicates a strong trend but does not identify it as an upward or downward trend. However, by looking at the stock's chart you can usually easily identify it. For a straddle, I am looking for the weak, nonexistent trend that appears to be ready to move into a directional breakout. Now doesn't that sound like a nice straddle opportunity?

So, we can use the ADX to identify potential changes in a stock from nontrending to trending. How is this task accomplished? A good gauge occurs when the ADX begins to strengthen by rising from below 20 to above 20. Based on what I have seen, it is a sign that the range trading is ending and a trend could be developing—be it upward or downward. This kind of scenario is a perfect straddle candidate. The ADX can also indicate that a strong trend is ending and it's time to take your profits.

If you combine this process with looking for consolidation patterns, earnings reports within four to eight weeks, and cheap options, you are raising the odds in your favor. Over the years, I have become a strong technical analysis advocate. It has increased my odds tremendously. As a person becomes more committed to the idea of trading successfully, finding the right combination of trading tools is vital to your success. Be it fundamental or technical analysis or a combination of both, you need the right tools for your trading style to better gauge market opportunities.

Figure 8.5 shows a chart of the Oil Service HOLDRS (OIH) along with the 14-day ADX as well as two directional lines, +DI and –DI. When used together, these three lines are part of the Directional Moving Index (DMI) trading system. Basically, traders will be watching the ADX line to see if it is high or low. Standard use of the ADX includes the idea that an ADX line rising above 20 signals a trending market, while an ADX line falling below 40 signals the start of a nontrending environment.

On the chart, we can see ADX rising in November 2003 and crossing above 20 and both directional lines. This signals that a period of quiet trading is ending and the OIH is ready to see a period of greater volatility. The rising ADX served as an alert that a new trend was on the way. In this case, a straddle makes sense. The OIH has been trading quietly, but a volatile move is expected. This is an ideal environment for placing a straddle. Then when ADX rose to high levels and began falling in March 2004, that signaled that the trend in the OIH was reaching an end. At that time, the strategist would want to close the straddle.

The ADX is available in several software packages including Advanced GET and Profit Source, which allow you to set search parameters to produce a list of stocks that meet the requirement of crossing over an ADX of 20. With this list, you can look through the other criteria to find a strong candidate and increase your odds for placing a successful straddle.

Given the current market uncertainty, a straddle is an ideal trading

FIGURE 8.5 OIH Price Chart with ADX Line (*Source:* Optionetics © 2004)

strategy to deploy. Here's hoping that all your straddle trades encounter the most tumultuous of news events.

SHORT STRADDLE STRATEGY

A short straddle involves selling both a put and a call with identical strike prices and expiration months. This strategy is useful should the underlying futures remain fairly stable. It is attractive to the aggressive strategist who is interested in selling large amounts of time premium in hopes of collecting all or most of this premium as profit. In general, this is a neutral strategy with limited profit potential (the total credit from the short options) and unlimited risk. There is a significant probability of profit making but the risk can be very large, which is why I do not recommend placing a short straddle.

Short Straddle Mechanics

Let's imagine you are selling a straddle on XYZ Corp. and shares are trading for $50 a share in December. The short March 50 call option is trading at $2.50 and the short March 50 put option is trading at $2.50. You forecast that XYZ is going to continue trading in a narrow range, which results in a decrease in volatility. Again, if you are expecting a decrease in volatility, you want to sell options. You want to sell high volatility and buy low volatility.

Remember, XYZ is trading at $50 in this example. You have collected 5 points of net premium from the short options. The danger in this trade is that your maximum risk is unlimited to the upside and limited to the downside (as the underlying can only fall to zero). Remember, the safest trades have limited risk and unlimited reward potential or limited reward with a high probability of being correct. Although it's unlikely, XYZ could go to zero, the call side has unlimited risk. Luckily, at expiration, only one side could be wrong. They cannot both be wrong.

Anytime you sell an option, the net credit you receive is the maximum profit. Remember, when you sell options, you do not want market movement. You want the market to stabilize and go in a straight line. In this trade, you have collected $500. If XYZ stays between 55 and 45, you will make a profit. This is referred to as the profit range. When you sell straddles, it is vital to identify this range by calculating the upside and downside breakevens. This will enable you to determine the point at which the trouble starts. The upside breakeven occurs when the underlying asset's price equals the option strike price plus the net premium. The downside breakeven occurs when the underlying asset's price equals the option strike price minus the net premium. For example, the net premium for this trade is 5. Therefore, the upside breakeven is calculated by adding 5 to 50 to get 55. The downside breakeven is calculated by subtracting 5 from 50, which equals 45. Thus, your profit range exists between 55 and 45.

As you can see by looking at the risk profile in Figure 8.6, a short straddle looks like the opposite of a long straddle's risk graph. Since a long straddle has a V-shaped curve, a short straddle has an upside-down V-shaped curve because it is the combination of a short call and a short put. This shape clues us in to the fact that short straddles have limited profit potential and unlimited risk. If a market moves significantly from the centerline, you have unlimited potential to make profits when buying a straddle and unlimited risk when selling the straddle. Maximum profit is achieved if the market closes exactly at 50 by the expiration date. However, I do not recommend taking on this kind of risk. I include these examples so that you can understand the mechanics of this trade and be aware of the dangers inherent in shorting options.

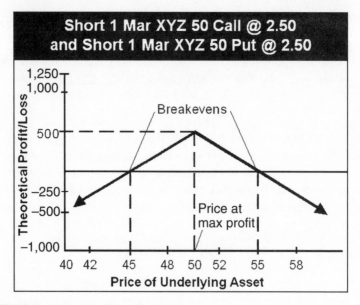

FIGURE 8.6   Short Straddle Risk Graph

Exiting the Position

The following exit strategies can be applied for the short straddle example:

- *XYZ falls below the downside breakeven (45):* You will want to close out the put position for a loss due to the chance that the put will be assigned.
- *XYZ falls within the downside (45) and upside (55) breakevens:* This is the range of profitability. The maximum profit occurs when the underlying stock is equal to the strike price (50). Options expire worthless and you get to keep the credit.
- *XYZ rises above the upside breakeven (55):* You will want to close out the call position for a loss due to the chance that the call will be assigned.

Selling straddles is a risky trade unless you find markets that are not likely to move away from a centerline. However, there are methods that can be utilized to substantially reduce the risks associated with this strategy. For example, you may want to purchase a strangle against it, thereby creating a condor (which is covered in Chapter 10). However, due to the fact that a short straddle comes with unlimited risk, I do not recommend its use and primarily teach it for educational purposes only.

Short Straddle

Strategy: Sell an ATM call and an ATM put with the same strike price and the same expiration date.

Market Opportunity: Look for a wildly volatile market where you anticipate a period of low volatility.

Maximum Risk: Unlimited above the upside and limited to the downside (as the underlying can only fall to zero) beyond the breakevens.

Maximum Profit: Limited to the net credit received. Profit is possible if the market stays between the breakevens.

Upside Breakeven: ATM strike price + net credit received.

Downside Breakeven: ATM strike price − net credit received.

Margin: Required. Extensive.

Short Straddle Case Study

A short straddle is a limited reward, unlimited risk strategy that profits if the underlying security trades sideways. Though profits can be made using this strategy, it is not one we at Optionetics suggest. Entering unlimited risk strategies is usually not a good idea and the short straddle is one of these. Since a long straddle requires a large move for the underlying security, it makes sense that a short straddle needs a sideways-moving, range-bound stock. However, because a short straddle consists of going short two options, the risk is high and the margin required to enter this strategy would be very large. Nonetheless, let's look at a real-life example of how a short straddle works.

On December 1, 2003, Home Depot (HD) was trading just under $37 a share. At this time, a trader might have believed the stock was set to trade sideways until late January when retail sales data for the month would be tabulated. As a result, a short straddle could be entered. A short straddle profits as long as the stock closes at expiration near the strike used. Since this strategy benefits from time decay, short-term options are typically used. In the case of HD, January 2004 options were used. However, because HD is in between strikes, the trader needs to decide whether the stock will move slightly higher or slightly lower by expiration. Let's use the 37.50 strike for this example.

The January 37.50 calls can be sold for 0.85 and the January 37.50 puts can be sold for 1.60. If five contracts were entered, the total credit would be $2.45 per contract or $1,225, with unlimited risk. The breakeven points are found by taking the credit of $2.45 per contract and subtracting it from the strike price for the lower breakeven and adding it for the higher breakeven. Thus, our breakeven points are at 35.05 and 39.95. If HD were to close in between these points at expiration in January, a profit would be made.

The risk graph in Figure 8.7 shows us exactly the opposite of what we normally want to see. The profit zone is a very small portion of the graph, with the loss section quite large. This type of risk profile normally means a large amount of margin will be needed, and this is definitely the case with a short straddle.

Home Depot did in fact trade sideways until January expiration, but the move was slightly to the downside, with the stock closing at $34.96. As

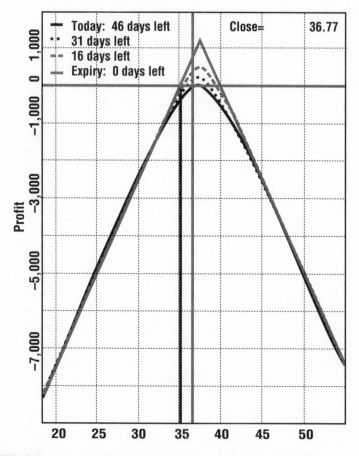

FIGURE 8.7   Risk Graph of Short Straddle on HD (*Source:* Optionetics Platinum © 2004)

Short Straddle Case Study

Strategy: With HD at $36.77 a share on December 1, Short 5 January HD 37.50 Calls @ 0.85 and Short 5 January HD 37.50 Puts @ 1.60.

Market Opportunity: Expect HD to trade sideways.

Maximum Risk: Unlimited risk to the upside and limited risk to the down-side (as the underlying can only fall to zero). In this case, a loss of –$55 at January expiration.

Maximum Profit: Limited to the net credit of the short options. In this case, $1,225: [5 × (.85 + 1.60)] × 100.

Downside Breakeven: ATM strike price minus the initial cost per con-tract. In this case, the DB is 35.05: (37.50 – 2.45).

Upside Breakeven: ATM strike price plus the initial cost per contract. In this case, the UB is 39.95: (37.50 + 2.45).

Margin: Extensive.

a result, this trade would have lost about $55. If the 35 strike had been used, nearly the maximum profit would have been achieved. This is the major difference between straddles and strangles. A strangle has a wider trading range, but brings in a smaller credit. A straddle has a larger credit, but a much smaller profit zone.

LONG STRANGLE STRATEGY

Strangles are quite similar to straddles, except they use OTM options, which changes the dynamics of the trade entirely. To construct a long strangle, you want to buy both an OTM call and an OTM put with the same expiration month but different strike prices. The best time frame to use for this options strategy is at least 60 days. Since the maximum risk is lim-ited to the double premium for the long options, a strangle should be viewed with respect to how expensive the options are. More often than not, one side will be underpriced and the other side will be overpriced.

The strike prices of the options used are the main difference between a straddle and a strangle strategy. A strangle has strikes that are slightly out-of-the-money, while straddles use ATM options. For example, if XYZ was trading at about $97, then the XYZ 100 calls and the XYZ 95 puts could be purchased to create a long strangle. The advantage of this strategy is that the potential loss—should XYZ remain at $97 at expiration—is less than that of a straddle. The disadvantage is that the stock needs to move even further than a straddle for the position to become profitable. Despite the fact that the strangle might look much cheaper than the straddle, it also carries more risk.

Long Strangle Mechanics

Let's create an example with XYZ priced once again at $50 per share. Let's select a strangle by going long a September 55 call for $2.50 and a September 45 put for $2.50 (see Figure 8.8). Once again, although you have no margin requirement, you are still going to have to pay both premiums. However, you are going to pay less than if you bought a straddle, because a strangle uses OTM options. Unfortunately, even though they cost less, you will need the market to make even greater moves to ever get your money out. This trade is delta neutral because the OTM options combine to create an overall position delta of zero (OTM call = +30; OTM put = –30). The maximum risk on this trade is the cost of the double premiums, which equals $500: ($2.50 + $2.50) × 100 = $500. Your maximum profit is unlimited. As shown by the long strangle's U-shaped risk curve, this strategy has unlimited profit potential and limited risk. The upside breakeven occurs when the underlying asset equals the call strike price plus the net debit paid. In this case, the upside breakeven equals 60: (55 + 5 = 60). The downside breakeven occurs when the underlying asset equals the put strike price minus the net debit. The downside breakeven equals 40: (45 – 5 = 40).

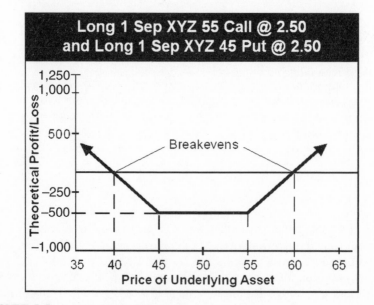

FIGURE 8.8   Long Strangle Risk Graph

Long Strangle

Strategy: Buy an OTM call and an OTM put with the same expiration date.

Market Opportunity: Look for a stable market where you anticipate a large volatility spike.

Maximum Risk: Limited to the net debit paid.

Maximum Profit: Unlimited to the upside and limited to the downside (as the underlying can only fall to zero) beyond the breakevens.

Upside Breakeven: Call strike price + net debit paid.

Downside Breakeven: Put strike price – net debit paid.

Margin: None.

The profit zones are therefore above 60 and below 40. Unfortunately, profit depends on a large move in the underlying instruments. A market with extremely high volatility might give you the necessary kick to harvest a profit from a long strangle strategy.

Exiting the Position

The following list provides some practical guidelines for exiting a strangle:

- *XYZ falls below the downside breakeven (40):* You can close the put position for a profit. You can hold the worthless call for a possible stock reversal.
- *XYZ falls within the downside (40) and upside (60) breakevens:* This is the range of risk and will cause you to close out the position at a loss. The maximum risk is the double premiums paid out of $500.
- *XYZ rises above the upside breakeven (60):* You are in your profit zone again and can close the call position for a profit. You can hold the worthless put for a possible stock reversal.

Long Strangle Case Study

A long strangle is the simultaneous purchase of a call and a put using different strikes, but the same expiration month. Since it involves the use of a long call and a long put, the cost to enter is high, but less than when using a straddle. This is because we are buying a call that is slightly out-of-the-money as well as a put that is slightly out-of-the-money. As with a straddle, a long strangle should be used on options that have low implied volatility. When a stock has been trading in a range and a break is expected, a long strangle is one way to profit without predicting the direction of the move.

In order to see how this works, let's look at a real-life example. At the end of 2003, shares of Cisco (CSCO) started to consolidate once again and this led to the belief that a breakout would soon occur. On December 26, CSCO shares closed at $23.75. The idea was that if the stock broke 25 to the upside or 22.50 to the downside, a major move would occur. So, a strangle using the April 25 call and the April 22.50 put was entered. The April 25 calls cost $1.05, as did the April 22.50 puts. Buying five contracts would cost $1,050, which was also the maximum risk of this multiple-contract position.

The nice thing about a strangle, as with a straddle, is that if the stock doesn't move as expected, the straddle owner can get out without much of a loss as long as he or she will not hold onto the options until expiration. This is because time decay is light when an option is still several months away from expiration.

By looking at the risk graph in Figure 8.9, you might notice how the maximum loss is wider than the maximum loss for a straddle. This is because the maximum loss occurs if the underlying closes within the strikes at expiration. The breakevens for this trade are found by adding the debit per contract of 2.10 to the strike of 25, which is $27.10 to the upside. The downside is found by subtracting 2.10 from the strike of 22.50, or 20.40.

Cisco did break out of this consolidation and did so to the upside. Once the $25 mark was passed, the gains came fast. The stock reached its peak on January 20 at $29.39, but the bearish pattern on January 21 would have taken us out of the strangle. At that point, Cisco was trading at $28.60 and the total profit for the strangle was $1,075—a 102 percent return on investment.

Long Strangle Case Study

Strategy: With the CSCO @ $23.75 a share on December 26, Long 5 April CSCO 25 Calls @ 1.05 and Long 5 April CSCO 22.50 Puts @ 1.05.

Market Opportunity: Expect a breakout from consolidation.

Maximum Risk: Limited to initial debit. In this case, the maximum risk is $1,050: (5 × 2.10) × 100.

Maximum Profit: Unlimited to the upside and limited to the downside (as the underlying can only fall to zero). In this case, $1,075 on January 21.

Downside Breakeven: Lower strike price minus the initial cost per contract. In this case, the DB is 20.40: (22.50 − 2.10).

Upside Breakeven: Higher strike price plus the initial cost per contract. In this case, the UB is 27.10: (25.00 + 2.10).

Margin: None.

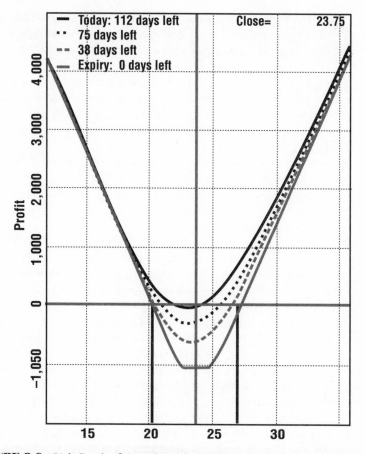

FIGURE 8.9 Risk Graph of Long Strangle on CSCO (*Source:* Optionetics Platinum © 2004)

SHORT STRANGLE STRATEGY

A short strangle is simply the opposite of a long strangle—you sell an OTM call and an OTM put with different strike prices and the identical expiration month. A short strangle has an upside-down U-shaped risk curve, which tells us that it has limited profit potential and unlimited risk (see Figure 8.10). In fact, your potential profits are less than when you place a short straddle because OTM premiums cost less than ATM premiums and deliver a reduced overall credit to the seller. However, your risk is also a little less than with the straddle because the market has to make a bigger move against you to reach the limits of your profit range. In most cases,

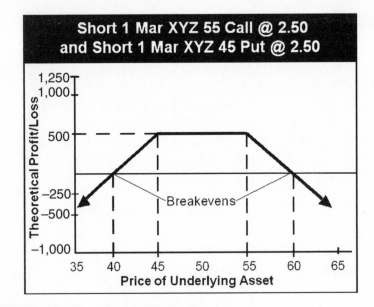

FIGURE 8.10   Short Strangle Risk Graph

you will have a margin requirement on this kind of trade. Short strangles are market neutral strategies as are short straddles. If the market doesn't move, you get to keep the premium. If you were expecting a huge move, with lots of volatility, would you sell a straddle or a strangle? Neither, not unless you have a death wish. Increasing volatility is a signal for long straddles and strangles.

Short Strangle Example

Using XYZ trading at $50 a share in February, let's create an example by selling one March 55 call at 2.50 and selling one March 45 put at 2.50. This is a classic example of selling a strangle. Figure 8.10 shows a risk profile of this short strangle example. Your maximum reward is the net credit of the option premiums or $5, which equals $500 a contract: (2.50 + 2.50) × 100 = $500. The maximum risk is unlimited. The upside breakeven occurs when the underlying asset equals the call strike price plus the net credit. The upside breakeven for this trade is 60: (55 + 5 = 60). The downside breakeven occurs when the underlying asset equals the put strike price minus the net credit, which is 40: (45 − 5 = 40) in this trade. Therefore the profit range is between 40 and 60.

Short Strangle

Strategy: Sell an OTM call and an OTM put with the same expiration date.

Market Opportunity: Look for a wildly volatile market where you anticipate a drop-off into a very stable market with low volatility.

Maximum Risk: Unlimited to the upside and limited to the downside (as the underlying can only fall to zero) beyond the breakevens.

Maximum Profit: Limited to the net credit received.

Upside Breakeven: Call strike price + net credit received.

Downside Breakeven: Put strike price – net credit received.

Margin: Required. Extensive.

Exiting the Position

Let's take a look at possible exit strategies for the short strangle example:

- *XYZ falls below the lower breakeven (40):* You will want to close out the position for the loss since the put is ITM and in danger of assignment.
- *XYZ falls within the lower (40) and higher (60) breakevens:* This is the range of profitability. Both options expire worthless and you get to keep the double premiums or maximum profit of $500 (minus commissions).
- *XYZ rises above the higher breakeven (60):* You will want to close out the position since the call is ITM and in danger of assignment.

The short strangle strategy is best used in combinations of spreads and butterflies and other option strategies. They can be added to these types of trades for extra protection. Once again, we do not recommend selling a strangle due to the unlimited risk that comes with it; however, it is essential to understand how they work so that you can integrate them into other trades.

Short Strangle Case Study

A short strangle is a limited reward, unlimited risk strategy that profits if the underlying security trades sideways. Though profits can be made using this strategy, it is not one I usually recommend. I'll say it again: Entering unlimited risk strategies is rarely a good idea! However, it's important to understand how the short strangle strategy works.

A long strangle requires a large move for the underlying security, so it makes sense that a short strangle needs a sideways-moving, range-bound stock. However, because we are short two options, the risk is high and the margin required to enter this strategy would be very large. Nonetheless, let's look at a real-life example of how a short strangle works.

On December 10, 2003, shares of the Nasdaq 100 Trust (QQQ) were trading at $34.56 each. At this time, a trader might have believed the stock was set to trade sideways during the holidays, as the chart had been moving sideways for several months. As a result, a short strangle could be entered. A short strangle profits as long as the stock closes at expiration in between the two strikes. Because this strategy benefits from time decay, usually short-term options are used. In the case of QQQ, January 2004 options were used.

The January 36 calls could be sold for 0.50 and the January 33 puts could be sold for 0.55. If five contracts were entered, the total credit of the option premiums would be $1.05, or $525 for the five contracts, with unlimited risk. The downside breakeven is calculated by subtracting the credit of $1.05 per contract from the lower strike price. The upside breakeven is calculated by adding the credit to the higher strike. In this example, the breakeven points are at 31.95 and 37.05. If the Qs were to close in between these points at expiration in January, a profit would be made.

The graph in Figure 8.11 shows us exactly the opposite of what we normally want to see. The profit zone is a very small portion of the graph, with the loss section much larger. This type of risk profile normally means a large amount of margin will be needed, and this is definitely the case with a short strangle.

Short Strangle Case Study

Strategy: With the security trading at $34.56 a share on December 10, 2003, sell 5 January 36 calls at 0.50 and 5 January 33 puts at 0.55 on the Nasdaq 100 Trust (QQQ).

Market Opportunity: Expect QQQ to trade sideways.

Maximum Risk: Unlimited to the upside and limited to the downside (as the underlying can only fall to zero) beyond the breakevens.

Maximum Profit: Limited to the initial credit received. In this case, $525: [5 × (.50 + .55)] × 100.

Downside Breakeven: Lower strike – the initial cost per contract. In this case, the DB is 31.95: (33 – 1.05).

Upside Breakeven: Higher strike + the initial cost per contract. In this case, the UB is 37.05: (36 +1.05).

Margin: Extensive.

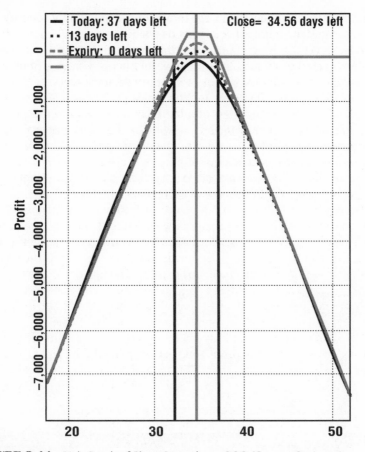

FIGURE 8.11 Risk Graph of Short Strangle on QQQ (*Source:* Optionetics Platinum © 2004)

In this case, the Qs did not stay in their range, as they broke out to new highs in early January. However, a smart trader probably would have looked to get out on December 29 when the Qs broke above resistance at 36. At this point, the risk would have been minimal, but if the holder of this short strangle were to hold on until expiration, a large loss would have occurred.

LONG SYNTHETIC STRADDLES

One of my favorite delta neutral strategies is the long synthetic straddle. It can be especially profitable because you can make adjustments as the market moves to increase your return. In this kind of straddle, you are combining options with stock; and as the market moves up or down, you can make money both ways. Perhaps this seems like a magic trick, especially if you are short stock and long calls. Obviously one leg of the trade will lose money as the other makes a profit. The difference between the profit and loss determines how much you are going to be able to pocket in profits with certain types of positions. Many factors govern the amount of profit, including the size of your account, the size of the trade, and whether you can adjust the trade to put yourself back to delta neutral after the market makes a move.

So, to review, there are at least three good reasons that a trader might prefer a synthetic straddle position as opposed to simply buying or selling stock outright.

1. The synthetic position is less costly, either in cash or margin requirements.

2. A synthetic position actually improves some element(s) of the base position that you are looking to enter.

3. The synthetic position will permit easier adjustments to the trade as conditions change.

In all, the synthetic straddle is a very powerful trading vehicle. When we account for costs of carry, put and call synthetic straddles are identical and can be used interchangeably. Stockholders and short sellers alike will be able to adjust the risk picture of a directional stock position to a delta neutral position, thus giving them the opportunity to make money in either direction.

Example #1: Long Synthetic Straddle Using Puts

Let's set up a long synthetic straddle by going long 100 shares of XYZ at $50 a share and long two September XYZ 50 puts with three months until expiration at $2.50 a contract. The risk profile for this trade is shown in Figure 8.12.

In this trade, when the market goes up, you have a profit on the stock and a smaller loss on the options (because their delta decreased). This leaves a net profit. When the market goes down, you have a loss on the underlying asset against a bigger profit on the options (because their delta increased), so again you have a net profit. Either way, when the market moves you can make additional profits by adjusting the trade back to delta neutral. The risk is due to the time decay of the options. Risk on this example is the cost of the options, or $500: $(2 \times \$2.50) \times 100 = \$500$. Total

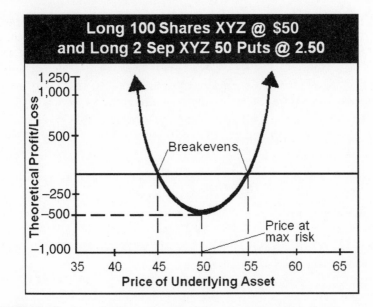

FIGURE 8.12 Long Synthetic Straddle (Using Long Puts) Risk Graph

risk is assumed only if you hold the position to expiration and the underlying asset does not move (or you fall asleep and never make an adjustment). The maximum profit is unlimited.

The upside breakeven of a long synthetic straddle is calculated by adding the net debit paid for the options to the price of the underlying asset. In this case, the upside breakeven is 55: (50 + 5 = 55). The downside breakeven is a little trickier. It is calculated using the following equation: [(2 × option strike price) – price of underlying stock at initiation] – net debit of options. In this trade, the downside breakeven is $45: [(2 × 50) – 50] – 5 = $45. Thus, this trade makes money if the price of the underlying moves above $55 a share or below $45, assuming you make no adjustments on the trade. Long synthetic straddles are best employed when you expect a significant move in the price of the underlying in either direction.

Exiting the Position

Let's investigate exit strategies for the long synthetic straddle with puts:

- ***XYZ falls below the downside breakeven (45):*** If the stock's price falls below the downside breakeven, you can exercise one of the puts to mitigate the loss on the stock and sell the other long put for a profit.

Long Synthetic Straddle with Puts

Market Opportunity: Look for a market with low volatility where you anticipate a volatility increase resulting in stock price movement in either direction beyond the breakevens.

Long Stock and Long Puts

Strategy: Buy 100 shares of underlying stock and buy two long ATM puts.

Maximum Risk: [Net debit of options + (price of underlying stock at initiation − option strike price)] × number of shares.

Maximum Profit: Unlimited to the upside and limited to the downside (as the underlying can only fall to zero) beyond the breakevens.

Upside Breakeven: Price of underlying stock at initiation + net debit of options.

Downside Breakeven: [(2 × option strike price) − price of underlying stock at initiation] − net debit of options.

Margin: None. 50% on stock is possible.

- *XYZ falls within the downside (45) and upside (55) breakevens:* This is the range of risk and will cause you to consider closing out the entire position at a loss or selling just the put options. The maximum risk is the cost of the double premium or $500 paid out for the puts.
- *XYZ rises above the upside breakeven (55):* If the stock's price rises above the upside breakeven, you will be making money on the stock and losing money on the put options. You can sell the stock to garner the profit and either sell the puts at a loss or hold onto them in case of a reversal.

Long Synthetic Straddle Using Puts Case Study

In this example, we want to find a stock or market that has been trading quietly, but could make an explosive move higher or lower. Studying the chart of the PHLX Semiconductor Index ($SOX) in April 2003, we arrive at the conclusion that the chip index is due for an explosive move in the near future. We are not sure of the direction and decide to set up a delta neutral strategy. However, it is not possible to set up a synthetic straddle on the Semiconductor Index. Why? It's a cash index. Instead, we decide to implement this trade on the Semiconductor HOLDRS (SMH), which is an exchange-traded fund that holds a basket of semiconductor stocks.

Holding Company Depositary Receipts (HOLDRS) are exchange-traded funds that hold baskets of stocks from specific industry groups. HOLDRS trade on the American Stock Exchange and can be bought or sold in lots of 100 shares. For example, investors can buy or sell Biotechnology HOLDRS (BBH), Semiconductor HOLDRS (SMH), or Oil Service HOLDRS (OIH). In all, the American Stock Exchange offers trading in 17 different HOLDRS. Options are also available on these exchange-traded funds and can be used to profit from trends related to specific sectors or industry groups.

First, we notice that the SMH is trading for \$26.50 a share during the month of April. We establish a long synthetic straddle by purchasing two near-the-money puts and 100 shares of Semiconductor HOLDRS. The near-the-money puts have a strike price of 25 and expire in January 2004. The put premium is initially \$3.20 and the trade is entered for a net debit of \$3,290.

The SMH synthetic straddle will have a slightly bullish bias due to the fact that the put options are slightly out-of-the-money. The delta of one January 25 put at initiation is approximately 32. As a result, this position has a positive delta of roughly 36. We could make the position almost perfectly delta neutral by purchasing three January 25 puts. But for the purposes of illustration, let's assume the trade is established using the aforementioned number of shares and contracts.

The risk curve in Figure 8.13 shows the profit and loss potential associated with this trade until expiration. The maximum profit is unlimited to the upside as SMH moves higher. The maximum risk is limited and equal to the net debit, or \$640 plus the difference in price between the SMH and the strike price multiplied by the number of shares, or \$1.50 × 100. Therefore, the maximum risk is \$790, but will occur only if the options are held until expiration. The upside breakeven is computed as the stock price plus the net debit of the options, or 32.90: (26.50 + 6.40). The downside breakeven is equal to 2 times the strike price minus the price of the stock minus the net debit of the options. In this case, 17.10: (50 − 26.50) − 6.40 = 17.10. Therefore, the trade requires a large move, above 32.90 or below 17.10, to earn a profit at expiration.

In all likelihood, the strategist would not hold this position until expiration because time decay is greatest 30 days before expiration. Let's suppose instead, the trade was closed 60 days before expiration, or on November 21, 2003. How would this trade have fared? At the time the position was closed, the Semiconductor HOLDRS were well above the entry price and near \$41 a share. The puts were deep out-of-the-money and practically worthless. The strategist could take the profits, which equal the value of the shares minus the cost of the trade, or \$4,100 minus \$3,290 or \$810 (25 percent), and then hold onto the two put options as lottery tickets.

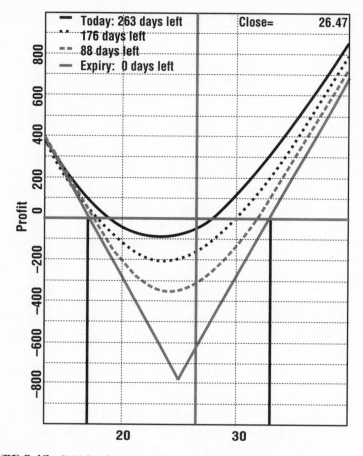

FIGURE 8.13 SMH Synthetic Straddle with Two Puts (*Source:* Optionetics Platinum © 2004)

Example #2: Long Synthetic Straddle with Calls

You can also create a long synthetic straddle by selling short the stock and buying call options to create an overall delta neutral position. When the market goes up, you have a loss on the underlying asset, but again you have a bigger profit on the options (their delta increases). When the market goes down, you have a profit on the underlying stock and a smaller loss on the options (their delta decreases). Either way, as long as the market moves beyond the breakevens, the trade harvests a net profit. Both trades are placed in markets where a rise in volatility is anticipated and the stock and options are liquid—that is, they have a sufficient number of shares (or contracts) trading that there is no problem entering or exiting the trade.

Long Synthetic Straddle with Puts Case Study

Market Opportunity: Look for a market with low volatility where you anticipate a volatility increase resulting in stock price movement in either direction beyond the breakevens.

Long Stock and Long Puts

Strategy: Buy 100 shares of Semiconductor HOLDRS for $26.50 and sell 2 SMH January 25 puts @ $3.20. Entry debit equals $3,290.

Maximum Risk: [Net debit of options + (price of underlying stock at initiation – option strike price)] × number of shares. In this case, the max risk is $790: [$6.40 + ($26.50 – 25)] × 100.

Maximum Profit: Unlimited to the upside and limited to the downside (as the underlying can only fall to zero). In this example, $810.

Upside Breakeven: Price of underlying at trade initiation + net debit of options. In this case, the UB is 32.90: (26.50 + 6.40).

Downside Breakeven: [(2 × option strike price) – price of underlying at trade initiation] – net debit of options. In this case, the DB is 17.10: [(2 × 25) – 26.50] – 6.40.

Let's examine a long synthetic straddle by shorting the stock and buying two September XYZ 50 calls @ 2.50 against XYZ trading at $50 per share. The maximum risk is limited to the net cost of the calls plus the difference in the call strike price minus the price of the stock at trade initiation. In this example, the maximum loss is limited to $500: [(2 × 2.50) + (50 – 50)] × 100 = $500. The reward is unlimited above the upside and below the downside breakevens. The downside breakeven is calculated by subtracting the net debit of the options from the stock price at trade initiation. In this example, the downside breakeven is 45: (50 – 5 = 45). The upside breakeven is calculated by adding net debit of the options to two times the strike price minus the initial stock price. In this example, the upside breakeven is 55: [(2 × 50) – 50] + 5 = 55. So, the trade theoretically will make a profit if the underlying rises above the upside breakeven (55) or falls below the downside breakeven (45). The risk profile of this trade is shown in Figure 8.14. As you can see, this risk graph is identical in format to the put synthetic straddle. Both offer a visual look at the strategy's unlimited reward beyond the upside and downside breakevens.

Note: Although Figure 8.14 is identical to the risk profile for the example of the long synthetic straddle using puts (Figure 8.12), this is due to the similarity of the option premium values as well as the cost of the underlying asset.

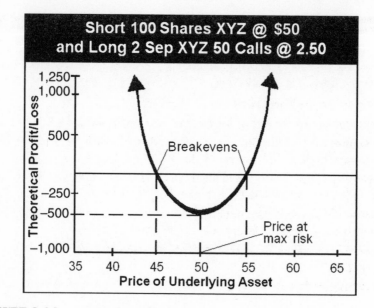

FIGURE 8.14 Long Synthetic Straddle (Using Long Calls) Risk Graph

Exiting the Position

Let's investigate exit strategies for the long synthetic straddle:

- *XYZ falls below the downside breakeven (45):* If the stock's price falls below the downside breakeven, you can purchase the shorted stock and let the calls expire worthless.

- *XYZ falls within the downside (45) and upside (55) breakevens:* This is the range of risk and will cause you to consider closing out the entire position at a loss or purchasing back the shorted stock and possibly holding the call options. The maximum risk for the entire position is the net cost of $500.

- *XYZ rises above the upside breakeven (55):* If the stock's price rises above the upside breakeven, you will be making money on the call options faster than you are losing on the shorted stock. You can close out the shorted stock and one call option and hold the additional option for additional revenue.

Long Synthetic Straddle with Calls

Market Opportunity: Look for a market with low volatility where you anticipate a volatility increase resulting in stock price movement in either direction beyond the breakevens.

Short Stock and Long Calls

Strategy: Sell 100 shares of underlying stock and buy 2 long ATM calls.

Maximum Risk: [Net debit of options + (option strike price – price of underlying at initiation)] × number of shares.

Maximum Profit: Unlimited to the upside and limited to the downside (as the underlying can only fall to zero) beyond the breakevens.

Upside Breakeven: [(2 × option strike price) – price of underlying stock at initiation] + net debit of options.

Downside Breakeven: Price of underlying stock at initiation – net debit of options.

Margin: Required on the short stock.

Long Synthetic Straddle with Calls Case Study

In this example, we want to trade the oil service in anticipation of an explosive move higher or lower, but we are not sure about direction. This time, the underlying asset is the Oil Service HOLDRS (OIH), which is an exchange-traded fund that holds a basket of oil drilling companies. In April 2003, with the OIH trading for $56 a share, we initiate a synthetic straddle by purchasing two October 2003 55 calls for $5.70 and selling short 100 OIH shares.

The risk graph of the OIH synthetic straddle appears in Figure 8.15. The trade is established for a credit equal to the difference between the short sale price minus the premium, or $4,460: (56 – 11.40) × 100. Success depends on the OIH making a move dramatically higher or lower. The upside breakeven is $65.40, or two times the strike price, minus the stock price, plus the options premium. The downside breakeven is simply the price paid for OIH minus the options premium, or $44.60. The maximum possible loss is $1,040, but will be incurred only if the trade is held until expiration.

Just as in the other example of a long synthetic straddle using puts, the strategist will not want to hold this trade until expiration. Instead, we will exit the trade before the last 30 days, or during that period of time when time decay is at its greatest. So, let's assume we exit the trade 45 days before the October calls expire. In this case, on August 30, 2003, the OIH was trading for $60 a share and the two calls were each quoted for $6

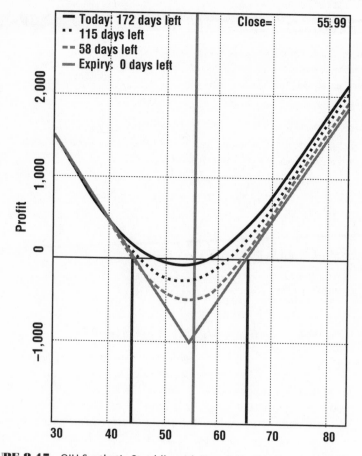

FIGURE 8.15 OIH Synthetic Straddle with Two Calls (*Source:* Optionetics Platinum © 2004)

a contract. So, the stock position resulted in a $4 per share loss, or $400, and the options moved only modestly higher. The strategist could book a $60 profit by closing out the long calls.

So, time decay hurt this position. In the end, the trade lost $360. It needed a larger move in the underlying asset and perhaps more time to work in the strategist's favor. Rather than closing the position entirely, the strategist could roll the position forward using longer-term options.

Long Synthetic Straddle with Calls Case Study

Market Opportunity: Look for a market with low volatility where you anticipate a volatility increase resulting in stock price movement in either direction beyond the breakevens.

Short Stock and Long Calls

Strategy: Sell 100 shares of OIH for $56 and buy 2 long October 2003 55 calls for $5.70 a contract.

Maximum Risk: [Net debit of options + (option strike price – price of underlying at trade initiation)] × 100. In this case, the max risk is $1,040: [$11.40 + (55 – $56)] × 100.

Maximum Profit: Unlimited to the upside and limited to the downside (as the underlying can only fall to zero) beyond the breakevens. In this example, $60.

Upside Breakeven: [(2 × option strike price) – price of underlying at initiation] + net debit of the options. In this case, 65.40: (2 × 55) – 56 + 11.40.

Downside Breakeven: Price of the underlying at trade initiation – net debit of options. In this case, 44.60: (56 – 11.40).

STRATEGY ROAD MAPS

Long Straddle Road Map

In order to place a long straddle, the following 14 guidelines should be observed:

1. Look for a market with low volatility about to experience a sharp increase in volatility that moves the stock price in either direction beyond one of the breakevens. The best long straddle opportunities are in markets that are experiencing price consolidation as they are often followed by a breakout. To find these consolidating markets, look through your charts for familiar ascending, descending, or symmetric triangles. As the stock price approaches the apex (point) of these triangles, they build up energy, much like a coiled spring. At some point this energy needs to be released and results in the price moving quickly. You don't care in which direction because you are straddling!

2. Check to see if this stock has options available.

3. Review options premiums per expiration dates and strike prices.

4. Investigate implied volatility values to see if the options are overpriced or undervalued. Look for cheap options at the low end of their implied volatility range, priced at less than the volatility of the underlying stock.

5. Explore past price trends and liquidity by reviewing price and volume charts over the past year.

6. A long straddle is composed of the simultaneous purchase of an ATM call and an ATM put with the same expiration month.

7. Place straddles with at least 60 days until expiration. You can also use LEAPS except the premiums are often very high and would be profitable only with a very large movement in the underlying stock.

8. Determine which spread to place by calculating:

   - **Limited Risk:** The most that can be lost on the trade is the double premiums paid.

   - **Unlimited Reward:** Unlimited to the upside and limited to the downside (the underlying can only fall to zero).

   - **Upside Breakeven:** Calculated by adding the call strike price to the net debit paid.

   - **Downside Breakeven:** Calculated by subtracting the net debit from the put strike price.

9. Create a risk profile of the most promising option combination and graphically determine the trade's feasibility. A long straddle will have a V-shaped risk profile showing unlimited reward above and limited profit to the downside.

10. Write down the trade in your trader's journal before placing the trade with your broker to minimize mistakes made in placing the order and to keep a record of the trade.

11. Make an exit plan before you place the trade. For example, exit the trade when you have a 50 percent profit at least 30 days prior to expiration on the options. If you have a winner, you do not want to see it become a loser. In this case, exit with a reasonable 50 percent gain. If not, then you should exit before the major amount of time decay occurs, which is during the option's last 30 days. If you have a multiple contract position, you can also adjust the position back to a delta neutral to increase profit potential.

12. Contact your broker to buy and sell the chosen options. Place the trade as a limit order so that you limit the net debit of the trade.

13. Watch the market closely as it fluctuates. The profit on this strategy is unlimited—a loss occurs if the underlying stock closes between the breakeven points.

14. Choose an exit strategy based on the price movement of the underlying and fluctuations in the implied volatility of the options.

- *The underlying shares fall below the downside breakeven:* You can close the put position for a profit. You can hold the worthless call for a possible stock reversal.
- *The underlying shares fall within the downside and upside breakevens:* This is the range of risk and will cause you to close out the position at a loss. The maximum risk is equal to the double premiums paid.
- *The underlying shares rise above the upside breakeven:* You are in your profit zone again and can close the call position for a profit. You can hold the worthless put for a possible stock reversal.

Long Strangle Road Map

In order to place a long strangle, the following 14 guidelines should be observed:

1. Look for a relatively stagnant market where you expect an explosion of volatility that moves the stock price in either direction beyond one of the breakevens. The best long strangle opportunities are in markets that are experiencing price consolidation because consolidating markets are often followed by breakouts.
2. Check to see if this stock has options available.
3. Review options premiums per expiration dates and strike prices.
4. Investigate implied volatility values to see if the options are overpriced or undervalued. Look for cheap options at the low end of their implied volatility range, priced at less than the volatility of the underlying stock.
5. Explore past price trends and liquidity by reviewing price and volume charts over the past year.
6. A long strangle is composed of the simultaneous purchase of an OTM call and an OTM put with the same expiration month.
7. Look at options with at least 60 days until expiration to give the trade enough time to move into the money.
8. Determine which spread to place by calculating:
   - **Limited Risk:** The most that can be lost on the trade is the double premiums paid for the options.
   - **Unlimited Reward:** Unlimited to the upside and limited to the downside (as the underlying can only fall to zero).
   - **Upside Breakeven:** Calculated by adding the call strike price to the net debit paid.

- **Downside Breakeven:** Calculated by subtracting the net debit from the put strike price.

9. Create a risk profile of the most promising option combination and graphically determine the trade's feasibility. A long strangle will have a U-shaped risk profile showing unlimited reward above the upside breakeven and limited profit below the downside breakeven.

10. Write down the trade in your trader's journal before placing the trade with your broker to minimize mistakes made in placing the order and to keep a record of the trade.

11. Make an exit plan before you place the trade. For example, exit the trade when you have a 50 percent profit or at least 30 days prior to expiration on the options. Exit with a reasonable 50 percent gain. If not, then you should exit before the major amount of time decay occurs, which occurs during the option's last 30 days.

12. Contact your broker to buy and sell the chosen options. Place the trade as a limit order so that you limit the net debit of the trade.

13. Watch the market closely as it fluctuates. The profit on this strategy is unlimited—a loss occurs if the underlying stock closes at or below the breakeven points. You can also adjust the position back to a delta neutral to increase profit potential if you have a multiple contract position.

14. Choose an exit strategy based on the price movement of the underlying stock and fluctuations in the implied volatility of the options:

   - *The underlying shares fall below the downside breakeven:* You can close the put position for a profit. You can hold the worthless call for a possible stock reversal.

   - *The underlying shares fall within the upside and downside breakevens:* This is the range of risk and will cause you to close out the position at a loss. The maximum risk is limited to the premiums paid.

   - *The underlying shares rise above the upside breakeven:* You are in your profit zone again and can close the call position for a profit. You can hold the worthless put for a possible stock reversal.

Long Synthetic Straddle Road Map

In order to place a long synthetic straddle with puts or calls, the following 14 guidelines should be observed:

1. Look for a market with low volatility about to experience a sharp increase in volatility that moves the stock price in either direction

beyond one of the breakevens. The best long synthetic straddle opportunities are in markets that are experiencing price consolidation as they are often followed by a breakout.

2. Check to see if this stock has options available.

3. Review options premiums per expiration dates and strike prices.

4. Investigate implied volatility values to see if the options are overpriced or undervalued. Look for cheap options. Those are options that are at the low end of their implied volatility range, priced at less than the volatility of the underlying stock.

5. Explore past price trends and liquidity by reviewing price and volume charts over the past year.

6. A long synthetic straddle can be composed by going long two ATM put options per long 100 shares or by purchasing two ATM call options against 100 short shares. Either technique creates a delta neutral trade that can be adjusted to bring in additional profit when the market moves up or down.

7. Place synthetic straddles using options with at least 60 days until expiration. You can also use LEAPS except the premiums are often very high and may be profitable only with a very large movement in the underlying stock.

8. Determine which spread to place by calculating:

   • **Limited Risk:** For a long synthetic straddle using puts, add the net debit of the options to the stock price at initiation minus the option strike price and then multiply this number by the number of shares. For a long synthetic straddle using calls, add the net debit of the options to the option strike price minus the price of the underlying at trade initiation, and then multiply this number by the number of shares. This is assumed only if you hold the position to expiration and the underlying stock closes at the option strike price.

   • **Unlimited Reward:** Unlimited to the upside and limited to the downside (as the underlying can only fall to zero).

   • **Upside Breakeven:** Calculated by adding the price of the underlying stock at initiation to the net debit of the options.

   • **Downside Breakeven:** Calculated by subtracting the stock purchase price plus the double premium paid for the options from twice the option strike price.

9. Create a risk profile of the most promising option combination and graphically determine the trade's feasibility. A long synthetic straddle

will have a U-shaped risk profile, showing unlimited reward and limited risk between the breakevens.

10. Write down the trade in your trader's journal before placing the trade with your broker to minimize mistakes made in placing the order and to keep a record of the trade.

11. Make an exit plan before you place the trade. For example, exit the trade when you have a 50 percent profit at least 30 days prior to expiration on the options. If not, then you should exit before the major amount of time decay occurs, which is during the option's last 30 days. You can also adjust the position back to a delta neutral to increase profit potential depending on how many contracts you are trading.

12. Contact your broker to buy and sell the chosen options. Place the trade as a limit order so that you limit the net debit of the trade.

13. Watch the market closely as it fluctuates. The profit on this strategy is unlimited—a loss occurs if the underlying stock closes between the breakeven points.

14. Choose an exit strategy based on the price movement of the underlying shares and fluctuations in the implied volatility of the options.

Exiting the long synthetic straddle with puts:

• *The underlying shares fall below the downside breakeven:* If the stock's price falls below the downside breakeven, you can exercise one of the puts to mitigate the loss on the stock and sell the other put for a profit.

• *The underlying shares fall within the downside and upside breakevens:* This is the range of risk and will cause you to consider closing out the entire position at a loss or selling just the put options. The maximum risk is the cost of the double premium paid out for the puts.

• *The underlying shares rise above the upside breakeven:* If the stock's price rises above the upside breakeven, you will be making money on the stock and losing money on the put options. You can sell them at a loss or hold onto them in case of a reversal.

Exiting the long synthetic straddle with calls:

• *The underlying shares fall below the downside breakeven:* If the stock's price falls below the downside breakeven, you can purchase the shorted stock and let the calls expire worthless.

• *The underlying shares fall within the downside and upside breakevens:* This is the range of risk and will cause you to consider closing out the entire position at a loss or purchasing back the shorted stock and possibly holding the call options.

- ***The underlying shares rise above the upside breakeven:*** If the stock's price rises above the upside breakeven, you will be making money on the call options faster than you are losing on the shorted stock. You can close out the shorted stock and one call option and hold the additional option for additional revenue.

CONCLUSION

Every trader, no matter how new or experienced, has wished they had bought the opposite side of a trade at one time or another. Maybe we felt strongly about earnings for a company and found out that though the news was good, the stock fell on the actual report. There are several different technical patterns that signal a strong move is likely, but the direction is hard to predict. Fortunately, there are a number of option strategies—straddles, strangles, and synthetic straddles—that take advantage of large moves without the need to predict market direction.

A straddle is a delta neutral strategy that is made up of buying an ATM call and an ATM put. A strangle is similar but uses OTM options instead. The obvious question new traders have is how do these types of trades make money? Any price movement means either a call value gain and a put loss, or a put gain and a call loss. However, the delta will increase more on the side of the trade that gains than it will decrease on the side that is losing value.

The other way we profit in a straddle is if implied volatility increases for the options. Since we are buying both sides of the trade, a rise in IV will benefit both the put and the call. However, this can also work in reverse, so we need to be confident that IV will either rise or at least stay constant. IV increases on pending news events, like earnings or FDA decisions. However, once the news has been announced, IV usually implodes and can lead to a volatility crush.

A straddle is a limited risk/unlimited reward strategy, but traders should still set profit goals. Many straddle traders look to make 50 percent profit on a straddle, but might use adjustments to lower risk, while holding on for higher profits. For example, once one side of a straddle pays for the whole trade, we can sell this side and hold on for a gain in the other side of the straddle. Of course, this would be contingent on the belief the stock was about to reverse course.

The strategist purchases straddles and strangles when there are expectations that the stock will make a significant move higher or lower, but the direction is uncertain. A sideways-moving stock will result in losses to the straddle or strangle holder. However, although a stock needs to make a rather large move to make a profit on a straddle (or a strangle), we also can get out without much of a loss if the stock doesn't move within a given time frame. However, this is only the case if we purchase options with enough time left until expiration. Time decay is the biggest enemy we have with a straddle, and time decay picks up speed the last 30 days of an option's life.

A long synthetic straddle consists of long stock and long puts or short stock and long calls to create a delta neutral trade. Most of the time, a long synthetic straddle utilizes at-the-money (ATM) options. Remember, ATM options normally have a delta near 50, or in this case –50. However, the maximum risk is not the entire debit, just the cost of the options. Risk occurs if the stock does not move by expiration and the time value of the long options erodes away.

The benefit to trading a long synthetic straddle is the adjustments that can be made. As the stock moves up and down, we can adjust the trade back to delta neutral to lock in profits. Many traders make adjustments when the total delta of the trade is up or down 100. We can make these adjustments by selling or buying stock or by selling or buying the options. This strategy is a great long-term tool, but make sure you understand the risks before entering this type of trade.

Used appropriately, the nondirectional strategies reviewed in this chapter can be nice profit producers, without a lot of risk. However, it is important to understand the basic rules and to know the associated risks. As with any strategy, a risk graph should always be created before entering the trade.

When you put on a long synthetic straddle, you are placing a hedge trade. All you are paying for is the cost of the options. If your broker requires you to have margin on the stock side, then try to find someone who will give you a cross-margin account. There are companies out there that offer cross margining, although it is a relatively new concept to the public. Putting on a synthetic straddle is not new; just the concept of looking at it as a low-risk trade from the brokerage firm side is new.

These trades are referred to as synthetic primarily because the two ATM options behave like the underlying stock (two ATM options = +100 or –100 deltas). They create a synthetic instrument that moves as the underlying asset changes. When you initiate the position, you are completely offsetting the other side to create a perfect delta neutral trade. As the market moves, you will gain more on the winning side of the trade or in adjustment profits than you will relinquish on the losing portions of the trade. It works because you are combining a fixed delta with a variable delta. Adjustments can be made when the market makes a move. If the market moves so that the overall trade is +100 deltas, then you can sell short 100 shares of stock. If the market moves and the overall position delta becomes –100, you can buy another futures contract or 100 shares of stock. Either way, the trade returns to delta neutral.

As a beginner, you should play it safe and place trades that offer limited risk. Although it may be tempting to go short options since a sale places money directly in your trading account over time, I do not recommend selling options until you are truly well-versed in delta neutral trading. Remember that when you sell options you do get a credit, but you only earn this credit as the options lose value over time.

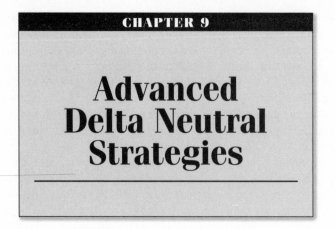

CHAPTER 9

Advanced Delta Neutral Strategies

U nderstanding the mechanics of a variety of delta neutral strategies is vital to becoming a profitable nondirectional trader. Instead of being overwhelmed by the complex nature of market dynamics, you can implement a delta neutral strategy that takes advantage of market conditions. Determining which strategy best fits the situation can easily be deduced through the use of risk profiles and relatively easy mathematical calculations. Delta neutral trading is all about empowering traders to maximize their returns and minimize their losses. Although professional traders have used delta neutral strategies on the major exchanges for years, off-floor traders are rarely aware of these strategies.

We have already explored the basic delta neutral trading techniques. It's time to turn the spotlight on some advanced strategies: ratio spreads and ratio backspreads. Ratio spreads are interesting strategies that provide a wide profit zone; however, they also have unlimited risk. Ratio backspreads, in contrast, offer limited risk with unlimited reward potential.

RATIO CALL SPREAD

A ratio spread is a strategy in which an uneven number of contracts with the same underlying instrument are bought and sold. Unlike straddles and strangles, which use a 1-to-1 ratio of the same kind of options, ratio spreads offset an uneven number of different types of options. A ratio call spread is useful when a trader sees a slight rise in a market followed by a sell-off. If this trade is done at a credit, the chance for success increases.

234

Although a ratio spread simply involves the buying and selling of an uneven number of contracts, there are a variety of complex ways to implement this strategy. For example, you can buy one OTM call option and sell two call options that are even further out-of-the-money. You can also use a ratio other than 1-to-2. For instance, you might buy two ATM options and sell three OTM options.

Many traders are willing to take the risk involved in shorting OTM options because they believe that the probability of the market moving that much is slim. Meanwhile, they are taking in a lot of premium. However, a volatile market can easily move enough to lose money on the uncovered short option. For that reason, we do not recommend this strategy, but we present it here in order to lead up to one of our favorite strategies—the ratio backspread.

Ratio Call Mechanics

For example, during the month of February, let's say you decide to create a ratio call spread by purchasing one July ATM 50 call at $4.50 and selling two July XYZ 55 calls at $2.50. This trade will not cost you any money to place because you're spending $450 (4.50 × 100) to buy the 50 call and receiving $500 [(2 × 2.50) × 100] in credit for selling the 55 calls. Thus, you are receiving a credit of $50 to place the trade. This trade has limited profit and unlimited risk. One of the short July OTM 55 calls is covered by the long 50 call. If the market goes to 60, you would make 10 points on the long call, lose 5 on the first call, to lock in a net profit of 5 points. However, the second 55 call is uncovered and even though it was an OTM option when the trade was initiated, there is some margin and risk on it. If the market rises to 60, the second 55 call loses 5 points, reducing the net profit to 0 points: (10 − 5 − 5 = 0).

The maximum profit of a ratio call spread is calculated using the following equation:

$$\text{Number of long contracts} \times (\text{difference in strike prices} \times 100)$$
$$+ \text{ net credit (or } - \text{ net debit)}$$

In this trade, the maximum profit is limited to $550: (55 − 50) × 100 + $50 = $550. However, the risk is unlimited to the upside above the breakeven point. The upside breakeven is calculated by using the following equation:

$$\text{Lower call strike price} + (\text{difference in strikes} \times \text{number of short contracts})$$
$$\div (\text{number of short calls} - \text{number of long calls})$$
$$+ \text{ net credit (or } - \text{ net debit)}$$

In this case, the upside breakeven is 60.50: $50 + [(55 - 50) \times 2] \div (2 - 1) + .50 = 60.50$. There is no risk to the downside because the trade was entered as a credit. This trade is best entered during times of high volatility with expectation of decreasing volatility. The risk graph for this example is shown in Figure 9.1.

Ratio Call Spread

Strategy: Buy a lower strike call and sell a greater number of higher strike calls.

Market Opportunity: Look for a volatile market where you expect a slight decline or a small rise not to exceed the strike price of the short options.

Maximum Risk: Unlimited to the upside above the breakeven.

Maximum Profit: Limited. [Number of long contracts × (difference in strikes × 100) + net credit (or − net debit)].

Upside Breakeven: Lower call strike price + [(difference in strikes × number of short contracts) ÷ (number of short calls − number of long calls)] + net credit (or − net debit).

Margin: Required. Extensive due to the naked call.

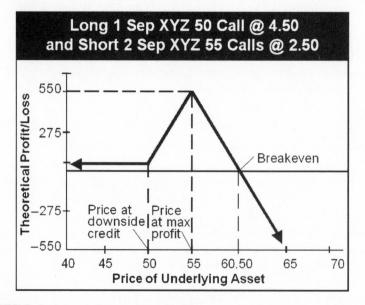

FIGURE 9.1 Ratio Call Spread Risk Profile

Ratio Call Spread Case Study

Eastman Kodak (EK) has been trading in a range and you expect the stock to either stay in that range or make a modest move higher. The stock is trading for $29.50 per share during the month of June. In order to profit from the stock's sideways trading, let's create a ratio call spread by selling two October 35 calls for $1.75 each and buying one October 30 call for $3. You earn a credit of 50 cents or $50 when establishing this trade.

Ideally, after establishing the trade, the stock will move only gradually higher. If it rises above $33, but below $35, the short options will expire worthless and you can book a profit on the long EK October 30 call. The maximum gain occurs at exactly $35 a share at expiration. At that point, both EK October 35 calls expire worthless and the long call is worth $5. In that case, the trader keeps the $350 for selling the two short calls and earns another $200 in profits from the long call. The total maximum gain is therefore $550. The risk profile for this trade is shown in Figure 9.2.

If EK falls sharply, the trader can do nothing but let the calls expire worthless. In this example, that's exactly what happened: The trade generated a $50 return. The upside breakeven is equal to 40.50: [30 + (5 × 2)] +.50 = 40.50. Losses begin to develop as the stock moves above the breakeven and are unlimited due to the naked short call. A move to $50 a share, for instance, would result in a $950 loss. Therefore, the strategist is taking a significant risk in order to earn a maximum of $550.

Ratio Call Spread Case Study

Strategy: Long 1 EK Oct 30 call @ $3.00 and Short 2 Oct 35 calls @ $1.75 for a credit of $50.

Market Opportunity: EK is expected to move modestly higher, but not explode to the upside.

Maximum Risk: Unlimited to the upside above the breakeven of $40.50 a share.

Maximum Profit: Number of long contracts × (difference in strikes × 100) + net credit (or − net debit). In this case, the max profit is $550: 1 × (5 × 100) + 50.

Upside Breakeven: Lower strike + [(difference in strikes × number of short options) ÷ (number of short calls − number of long calls) + net credit (or − net debit). In this case, the UB is 40.50: 30 + [(35 − 30) × 2 ÷ (2 − 1)] +.50.

Margin: Yes, due to sale of naked call.

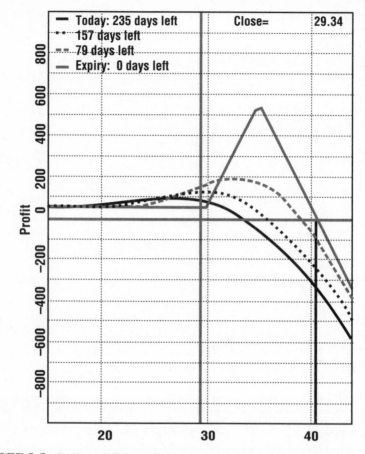

FIGURE 9.2   EK Ratio Call Spread (*Source:* Optionetics Platinum © 2004)

RATIO PUT SPREADS

A ratio put spread involves buying a higher strike put option and selling a greater number of lower strike OTM put options and should be implemented in a bullish market. The maximum profit of a ratio put spread is calculated by multiplying the difference in strike prices by 100 and then adding the net credit received. The maximum risk is limited to the stock going to zero and equals the lower strike price minus the difference between the two strike prices plus the net credit times 100. The downside breakeven is calculated by dividing the difference in strike prices times the number of short contracts by the number of short contracts minus the number of long contracts and subtracting that number from the higher put strike price. Then, subtract the net credit received or add the net debit paid.

A ratio put spread can be implemented when a slight fall in the market is anticipated followed by a sharp rise. This strategy works well in the stock market, as stocks generally tend to move up in price. However, it is important to place this trade on only high-quality stocks. If the company has reported lower than expected earnings or bad news is released, exit the position. A ratio put spread also works well in many futures markets, especially during seasonal periods when prices tend to go up (such as heating oil in the winter months).

The main risk in ratio spreads comes from the uncovered short call or put. These options have unlimited risk. Watch the market closely and exit or adjust the trade if the market moves to the strike price of the short options.

Ratio Put Spread Mechanics

Let's create an example with XYZ trading at $50 a share in February that consists of going long one July XYZ 50 put at $4.50 and two short July XYZ 45 puts at $2.50 each. This trade creates a net credit of .50 or $50: $[(2 \times 2.50) - 4.50] \times 100 = \$50$. The maximum profit of a ratio put spread is calculated by using the following formula:

$$\text{(Difference in strike prices} \times 100) + \text{net credit (or} - \text{net debit)}$$

In this trade, the maximum profit is limited to $550: $(50 - 45) \times 100 + \$50 = \$550$. The maximum risk is limited because the stock can only fall to zero and is calculated using the following formula:

$$\text{Lower strike price} - \text{(difference in strikes} - \text{net credit)} \times 100$$

In this example, the maximum risk is $3,950: $45 - [(50 - 45) - .50] \times 100 = \$3,950$. The downside breakeven is calculated by using the following formula:

$$\text{Higher strike price} - [\text{(difference in strikes} \times \text{number of short contracts)}$$
$$\div \text{(number of short contracts} - \text{number of long}$$
$$\text{contracts)}] - \text{net credit (or} + \text{net debit)}$$

In this example the downside breakeven is 39.50: $50 - [(50 - 45) \times 2] \div (2 - 1) - .50 = 39.50$. The risk graph for this trade is shown in Figure 9.3.

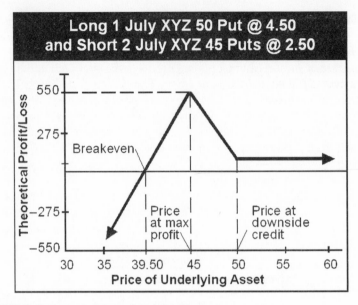

FIGURE 9.3 Ratio Put Spread Risk Profile

Ratio Put Spread Case Study

General Electric (GE) has been performing well and the stock is expected to take a pause or perhaps trade lower. With shares near $23.40 in February 2003, let's short sell two January GE 20 puts at $2 and go long 1 January 25 put at $4. The sale of the puts offsets the cost of the long put and the trade is executed at even (without a debit or credit).

Ratio Put Spread
Strategy: Buy a higher strike put and sell a greater number of lower strike puts.
Market Opportunity: Look for a market where you expect a rise or slight fall not to exceed the strike price of the short options.
Maximum Risk: Limited to the downside below the breakeven (as the stock can only fall to zero). Lower strike price – (difference in strikes – net credit) × 100.
Maximum Profit: Limited. (Difference in strikes × 100) + net credit (or – net debit).
Downside Breakeven: Higher strike price – [(difference in strikes × number of short contracts) ÷ (number of short contracts – number of long contracts)] – net credit (or + net debit).
Margin: Required. Extensive due to the naked put.

After establishing the trade, the strategist wants to see shares of General Electric edge lower. The maximum gain occurs at expiration if the stock is trading for $20 a share. At that point, both GE January 20 puts expire worthless and the long put is worth $5 a contract, or $1 more than the entry price. If so, the strategist earns $1 in profits with the long call and keeps the $4 in premium for selling the short puts. The maximum gain is therefore $500. The risk graph of this trade is shown in Figure 9.4.

If GE rises sharply, the strategist can do nothing but let the puts expire worthless. In that case, the loss is equal to the commissions paid for the trade. On the other hand, if the stock falls sharply, the losses can be substantial. The downside breakeven is equal to: higher strike price – [(difference in strike prices × number of short contracts) ÷ (number of

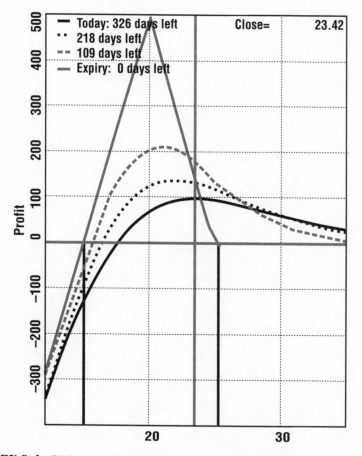

FIGURE 9.4   GE Ratio Put Spread (*Source:* Optionetics Platinum © 2004)

Ratio Put Spread Case Study

Strategy: Long 1 GE 25 Put @ $4.00 and Short 2 GE 20 Puts @ $2.00. Net debit/credit equals zero.

Market Opportunity: Look for GE to trade modestly lower or sideways.

Maximum Risk: Limited to the downside below the breakeven (as the stock can only fall to zero). Lower strike price − (difference in strikes − net credit) × 100. In this case, the max risk is $1,500: [20 − (25 − 20) − 0] × 100.

Maximum Profit: Limited. (Difference in strikes + net credit) × 100. In this case, the max profit is $500: {5 × [(25 − 20) + 0]} × 100.

Downside Breakeven: Higher strike − [(difference in strikes × number of short puts) ÷ (number of short puts − number of long puts)] − net credit. In this case, the DB is 15: 25 − [(5 × 2) ÷ 1] − 0.

Margin: Required. Extensive due to the naked put.

short contracts − number of long contracts)] − net credit (or + net debit), or $15: [25 − (5 × 2)] ÷ (2 − 1) − 0 = $15]. Losses begin to develop as the stock moves below the breakeven and are limited to the stock falling to zero. In this case, if the stock falls to zero, one short put will cover the long put and result in a $5 profit. The other put will probably be assigned for a $20 loss. The total loss would therefore be $1,500. Therefore, the strategist is risking $1,500 to earn $500 from this trade.

EXIT STRATEGIES FOR RATIO SPREADS

Whether trading call or put ratio spreads, it is important to remember that these strategies involve substantial risk for limited reward. The strategist wants to be careful because these types of spreads involve more short than long options and therefore involve naked options. In a call ratio spread, the risk is unlimited to the upside. If the underlying stock moves beyond the short strike price before expiration, the strategist might want to consider closing the position by buying back the short calls and selling the long call. If the stock drops, do nothing, let the options expire, and keep the net credit received for establishing the trade.

In the case of the put ratio spread, the opposite holds true. In that case, a sharp move lower in the stock can result in substantial losses. If the stock falls below the short strike price before expiration, the strategist might consider closing the position by purchasing back the short puts and selling the long put. If the stock moves higher, do nothing, let the options expire, and keep the credit.

CALL RATIO BACKSPREADS

Ratio backspreads are one of my favorite strategies for volatile markets. They are very powerful strategies that will enable you to limit your risk and receive unlimited potential profits. These strategies do not have to be monitored very closely as long as you buy and sell options with at least 90 days (the longer the better) until expiration. I like to call them "vacation trades" because I can place a ratio backspread, go on vacation, and not even worry about it. For some traders, ratio backspread opportunities are hard to find. Perhaps they are looking in the wrong places. It is difficult to find ratio backspread opportunities in highly volatile markets with expensive stocks or futures. For example, you will rarely find them in the S&P 500 futures market. This index is simply too volatile and the options are too expensive. Focus on medium-priced stocks (between $25 and $75) or futures. These trades can be quite profitable, so be persistent. They're out there—just keep looking.

Additionally, when looking for the right market for a call ratio backspread, scan for markets exhibiting a reverse volatility skew. In these markets, the lower strike options (the ones you want to sell) have higher implied volatility and can be overpriced. The higher strike options (the ones you want to buy) enjoy lower implied volatility and are often underpriced. By finding markets with a reverse volatility skew, you can capture the implied volatility differential between the short and long options.

A ratio backspread strategy involves buying one leg and selling another in a disproportionate ratio that does not create a net debit. The following seven rules must be diligently observed to create an optimal ratio backspread trade:

1. Choose markets where volatility is expected to increase in the direction of your trade.

2. Avoid markets with consistent low volatility. If you really want to place a ratio backspread in a market that does not move, pay close attention to rule 4.

3. Do not use ratios greater than .67—use ratios that are multiples of 1:2 or 2:3.

4. If you choose to trade a slow market, a .75 ratio or higher is acceptable only by buying the lower strike and selling the higher. However, there is more risk.

5. To create a call ratio backspread, sell the lower strike call and buy a greater number of higher strike calls.

6. To create a put ratio backspread, sell the higher strike put and buy a greater number of low strike puts.

7. Try to avoid debit trades. But if you do place a ratio backspread with a debit, you must be able to lose that amount.

Call Ratio Backspread Mechanics

As previously stated, a call ratio backspread involves selling the lower strike call and buying a greater number of higher strike calls. For example, let's pick a fictitious market (it doesn't matter which market as long as it is volatile) with strikes starting at 40, 45, 50, 55, and 60. The ATM calls are at 50, which means that the current price of the underlying market equals $50 also. Now, according to rule 5, the first part of a call ratio backspread is to sell the lower strike call. Which is the lowest strike call here? The 40 is the lowest strike call. Now, the other part of the rule tells me to buy a greater number of higher strike calls. Let's buy an option to buy this market at $60 because we think the market is going to reach $65. Am I going to pay less for this call than for the 40, or more? I'm going to pay less because now I'm speculating that the market mood is bullish. Speculating on market direction is one of the main reasons why many people lose money when they trade options. However, I'm going to go ahead and speculate that the market is going to go to 65, even though it's only at 50 right now. Furthermore, I'm going to pay less for a 60 option than a 55 strike. As the strike price goes up, the premiums of the ITM options also go up, as they are more and more valuable. If our market is currently trading at 50 but it's starting to rise, the price of the 60-strike option will also rise.

Now let's introduce the delta into this situation. The delta is the probability an option has of closing in-the-money at expiration. If a 50-strike option is at-the-money, which way can the market go? The market can move in either direction, which means there is a 50 percent probability of it closing in-the-money. Obviously, a price that's already in-the-money has a higher probability of closing in-the-money than something that's out-of-the-money. Therefore, the delta for an ITM option is higher than the delta for the ATM option or an OTM option. The higher the probability an option has of closing in-the-money, the higher its premium. This relationship enables a trader to create trades that are virtually free of charge. Ratio backspreads take full advantage of this relationship. It's a relatively simple concept. As the underlying instrument's price changes, the option deltas change accordingly. For example, our 40-strike option has a higher delta than one with a 60-strike, and therefore a higher premium as well.

Let's set up a call ratio backspread using XYZ, which is currently trading at 50. To satisfy the rules, let's sell a 40 call and buy more of the 60 calls in a ratio of 2-to-3 or less. This trade would receive a credit on the short 40 call and a debit on the long 60 calls. However, we have limited the risk of the short 40 call by offsetting it with one of the long 60 calls and can still profit from the other long 60 call.

As previously stated, determining risk is the most important part of setting up any trade. The risk of this trade can be calculated using the following option premiums:

Call	Price
60	$ 60
55	$ 70
50	$ 80
45	$ 90
40	$100

If we sell one 40-strike call option and buy two of the 60-strike call options, we have a debit of $20: $100 - (2 \times 60) = -\$20$. But if the prices rise, we'll make more money on the 60-strike calls than on the 40-strike call. If the market falls, the out-of-pocket cost of placing the trade is the maximum risk. The most we can lose is $20 on the downside.

The trick to creating an optimal trade is to avoid risk by using a ratio that makes the trade delta neutral. In this way, it is possible to place a trade for free at no net debit. That's right! You can create ratio backspreads that don't cost a penny (except for commissions) and still make healthy profits. You can do this by offsetting the credit side with the debit side so that they cancel each other out and you don't have to spend any money out-of-pocket. In this example, you can create a 2×3 ratio backspread at a $10 credit: $[(2 \times 100) - (3 \times 60)] = +\$20$. This is the best kind of trade to place (especially if you're 100 percent wrong about market direction), because you won't lose any money. In this case, as long as the market breaks down below the 40 strike, both options expire worthless. However, there is some risk between the 40 and 60 strike prices because the trade could lose more than it profits.

To figure out the most effective ratio, you have to accurately calculate the net credit of a trade. This can be accomplished by calculating the full credit realized from the short options and dividing it by the debit of one long option. You can then use up as much of the credit as you can to make the most profitable ratio.

Credit = Number of short contracts × short option premium × 100

Debit = Number of long contracts × long option premium × 100

Once you have figured out the best ratio of the trade, you still have to calculate your risk.

Risk = [(Number of short contracts × difference in strikes) × 100]
+ net debit paid (or – net credit)

Let's use these equations to determine an optimal call ratio backspread using XYZ trading at $50 during the month of February. Let's create a call ratio backspread by going short 1 XYZ January 50 call for $8.50 and going long 2 January 60 calls for $4.25 each. In this case, we are using long-term equity anticipation securities, or LEAPS. Our short calls give us a credit of $850: (8.50 × 100) = $850. The two long calls also cost $850: (2 × 4.25) × 100 = $850. Therefore, this trade can be placed at even.

While the call ratio backspread using one short 50 call and two long 60 calls can be set up at even, let's consider what happens when we increase it to a 2-to-3 ratio. By going short two XYZ January 50 calls at $8.50 and going long three XYZ January 60 calls at $4.25, we'll receive $1,700 from the sale of the short calls and pay only $1,275 to buy the long calls for a net credit of $425: (2 × 8.50) – (3 × 4.25) = $425. Actually, we could also buy four XYZ January 60 calls against the credit received for selling the three XYZ January 50 calls ($1,700 ÷ 425 = 4), but the ratio of 2 to 3 is recommended in the guidelines as a more optimal ratio for a ratio backspread. Therefore, let's create a ratio backspread with a 2-to-3 ratio, which satisfies rule 3 and garners a net credit of $425.

The next step is to take a look at this trade's risk profile. This risk graph (see Figure 9.5) shows the trade's unlimited potential reward if XYZ moves higher. It also reveals that the maximum risk of $1,575 is realized only if the underlying instrument is at the strike price of the long option (60) at expiration. The maximum risk is computed using the following formula:

[(Number of short calls × difference in strikes) × 100] – net credit

In this case, the maximum risk equals $1,575: [(2 × 10) × 100] – 425 = $1,575. Now let's calculate the upside breakeven of this example using the following equation:

Higher strike call + [(difference in strikes × number of short calls)
÷ (number of long calls – number of short calls)]
– net credit

In this case, the upside breakeven is $75.75: 60 + {[(60 – 50) × 2] ÷ (3 – 2)} – 4.25 = $75.75. The downside breakeven is simply computed by adding the lower strike price of the short options to the net credit divided by the number of short options. If a call ratio backspread is entered with a net

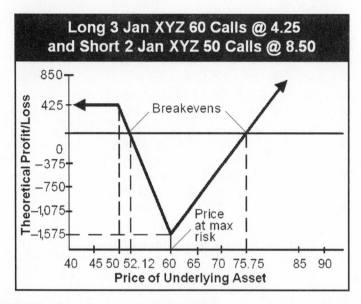

FIGURE 9.5 Call Ratio Backspread Risk Profile

debit, there is no downside breakeven. In this trade, the downside breakeven is $52.12: 50 + (4.25 ÷ 2) = 52.12. That means this trade makes money as long as the price of the underlying closes above the upside breakeven. Call ratio backspreads are best implemented during periods of low volatility in a highly volatile market that shows signs of increasing activity to the upside. The risk profile of this trade can be found in Figure 9.5.

Call Ratio Backspread

Strategy: Sell lower strike calls and buy a greater number of higher strike calls (the ratio must be less than .67).

Market Opportunity: Look for a market where you anticipate a sharp rise with increasing volatility; place as a credit or at even.

Maximum Risk: Limited. [(Number of short calls × difference in strikes) × 100] – net credit (or + net debit).

Maximum Profit: Unlimited to the upside above the upside breakeven.

Upside Breakeven: Higher strike call + [(difference in strikes × number of short calls) ÷ (number of long calls – number of short calls)] – net credit (or + net debit).

Downside Breakeven: Lower strike call + (net credit ÷ number of short calls)]. No downside breakeven exists if the trade is entered with a net debit.

Margin: Varies by brokerage firm policy.

Call Ratio Backspread Case Study

Let's say you're bullish on eBay (EBAY) and want to set up a strategy that has limited risk, but high profit potential. During the month of February 2003, the stock is trading for $75.25 a share. A call ratio backspread can be created by going short 2 EBAY January 80 calls at $11 and going long three EBAY January 90 calls at $6.50. The trade yields a net credit of $250. The risk graph shown in Figure 9.6 details the risk/reward profile of this trade.

Now, let's do the math. The maximum risk will occur at expiration if the stock moves to $90 a share. At that point, the short calls are worth $10 each and the long calls expire worthless. So, we lose $2,000 per contract minus the net credit $250, for a maximum risk of $1,750. Since you want to avoid this possibility at all costs, if the stock does not move above that

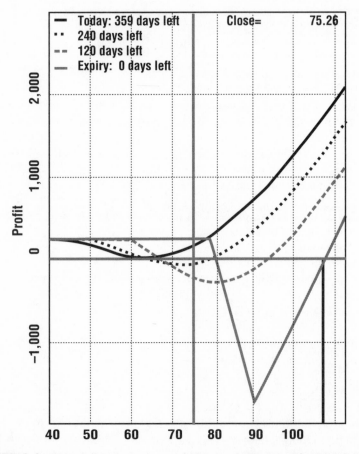

FIGURE 9.6 EBAY Call Ratio Backspread (*Source:* Optionetics Platinum © 2004)

Call Ratio Backspread Case Study

Strategy: Short 2 EBAY January 80 calls @ $11 and long 3 EBAY January 90 calls @ $6.50. The net credit equals $250.

Market Opportunity: EBAY looks set for an explosive move higher, but the strategist wants downside protection.

Maximum Risk: Limited. [(Number of short calls × difference in strikes) × 100] – net credit. In this case, $1,750: [(2 × 10) × 100] – $250.

Maximum Profit: Unlimited to the upside beyond the breakeven. In this case, the profit is $1,410.

Upside Breakeven: Higher strike call + [(difference in strikes × number of short calls) ÷ (number of long calls – number of short calls)] – net credit. In this case, $107.50: 90 + [(10 × 2) ÷ (3 – 2)] – 2.50.

Downside Breakeven: Lower strike call + (net credit ÷ number of short calls). In this case, $81.25: 80 + (2.50 ÷ 2).

level within a reasonable period of time, close the trade and move on. If the stock fails to rise or falls sharply, there's little we can do other than keep the credit and let the options expire worthless.

Ideally, however, the stock will move higher. The upside breakeven at expiration is equal to $107.50: 90.00 + [(10 × 2) ÷ (3 – 2) – 2.50 = $107.50. However, we do not intend to hold this position until expiration. Instead, we want to exit the position at least 30 days before expiration or after a reasonable profit has accrued.

In this case, eBay did indeed move higher. Six months later, the stock was trading near $110 a share. Although you would have probably booked profits long before that time, at $110 a share in August 2003, the long calls would have sold for $25.30 (a profit of $5,640) and the short calls could have been bought to close at $33.40 (a loss of $4,480). Thus, the net profit would have been $1,160 plus the original credit of $250, or $1,410.

PUT RATIO BACKSPREADS

The implementation of a put ratio backspread is a great way to play a bear market. A put ratio backspread is a delta neutral (nondirectional risk trade), which allows us to profit substantially from strong downward movement; however, we can also hedge and protect ourselves from upward movement. Thus, if we are incorrect and the stock goes against us, we are in a position where we won't lose anything, or we may even realize a small profit, depending on how we enter into the trade. I like to use a put ratio backspread when I can identify a stock with a bearish bias and expect the stock to make a significant move. If we are correct and the stock makes a strong move to the downside, we'll be in a position with limited profit potential (the stock can only fall to zero). If we are wrong and the stock moves against us, we can let the options expire worthless, not have to pay commissions to exit, and not lose any money or even make a little if the trade is placed with a net credit.

Placing put ratio backspreads on strong, downtrending stocks will further increase your chances of success. As compared with buying stock, they can offer the same unlimited reward potential but also provide you with limited downside risk. Compared with just buying calls, they can offer the same unlimited reward potential with a lower breakeven and less cost. Also, this trade helps to counter some of the impact from volatility in the markets, which allows us to place the trade after news has already come out on a particular stock.

A put ratio backspread strategy is created by selling a certain number of higher strike puts and simultaneously buying multiples of a lower strike put. This position is created in a ratio such that you sell fewer calls than you buy in a ratio of .67 or less. For instance, a 1×2 consists of one short put and two long puts. Similarly, you can create a 2×3, 3×5, or any combination trade with a ratio less than .67.

Put ratio backspreads are best placed in markets with a forward volatility skew. In these markets, the higher strike options (the ones you want to sell) have higher implied volatility and can be overpriced. The lower strike options (the ones you want to buy) enjoy lower implied volatility and are often underpriced. By trading the forward volatility skew, you can capture the implied volatility differential between the short and long options.

We want to make sure we give ourselves enough time to be right in this trade. The more time we can buy the better. With diligent research we can pinpoint good put ratio backspread trades with longer time frames and many times can even use LEAPS. Also, if we can't get in at even or for a small credit, then we shouldn't take the trade.

Although this trade can be entered for a small credit, there is still a window of risk. The maximum risk occurs when the stock is at the long strike on the expiration date. The broker will require and hold the risk amount as collateral in your account through the duration of the trade as protection from the worst-case scenario at expiration.

You can use the put ratio backspread to protect any long-term bullish positions and even sell out-of-the-money calls to create an appreciating collar position—a very nimble strategy indeed (covered in Chapter 10).

Taking into account the put ratio backspread advantages, which are potentially large profits on the downside, you can control the risk by how long you stay in the trade. And having a much lower risk than a long put directional trade, along with the flexibility of using it to create a collar, makes this a strategy worth evaluating when looking for bearish and protective strategies.

To reduce confusion, let's use the same numbers as the XYZ call ration backspread example to demonstrate a put ratio backspread. Using this strategy, we'll sell a higher strike put and buy a greater number of lower strike puts. The strikes are the same as before: 40, 45, 50, 55, and 60. The 60 put is the highest strike and comes with the highest intrinsic value and 40 is the lowest.

Using this scenario, I could place a wide variety of put ratio backspreads. To further complicate the situation, I could do different ratios on each combination. For this example, I'm going to sell the 60 put and buy a greater number of 55 puts. If the market crashes, I'll lose money to the 55 point; but below 55 I'll be making more on the 55 puts than I lose on the 60 puts because I have more of the 55 puts.

This actually happened to me once in the S&P 500 futures market. If you think the S&P 500 futures market is moving into lofty levels and you don't want to gamble a lot, you could do a put ratio backspread. I was lucky. The market moved down so fast that month that I made a lot of money. Similarly, if you had placed a put ratio backspread the day the market crashed back in 1987, you wouldn't need to read this book. You'd be in Aruba, the Bahamas, or somewhere equally relaxing. You'd be laughing all the way to the bank.

Put Ratio Backspread Mechanics

Let's take a look at the mechanics of a put ratio backspread. A put ratio backspread is composed of the sale of a higher strike put and the purchase of a greater number of lower strike puts. This strategy is best implemented at periods of low volatility in a highly volatile market when you anticipate increasing market activity to the downside (bearish).

In placing these kinds of trades, it is essential to create the most effective ratio in markets with increasing volatility, liquidity, and flexibility. Let's create a new put ratio backspread trade using XYZ at $50 a share during the month of February and look at the January LEAPS two years out. Strike prices on the LEAPS are available at 5-point increments. For example, with XYZ trading at $50, the available strikes are 40, 45, 50, 55, and so on. Any put options with strikes above 50 are in-the-money; put options with strikes below 50 are out-of-the-money.

Let's create a put ratio backspread by selling two January 2005 50 puts at $8 and buying five January 2005 40 puts at $3. The short puts generate a credit of $1,600: $(2 \times \$8) \times 100 = \$1,600$. The long puts cost only $300 each or a $1,500 debit. If we divide $1,600 by $300 a contract, we can afford to purchase five long put options and still have a net credit of $100. This generates a ratio of 2-to-5, which satisfies the rule of creating ratios less than .67. To calculate the risk, multiply the number of short contracts (2) by the difference in strike prices (10), by the multiplier (100), plus any debit paid (0) or minus any credit received ($100). This gives us a maximum risk of $1,900: [(2 × 10) × 100] – 100 = $1,900). The risk profile of this trade is shown in Figure 9.7.

As you can see, we have created a trade with limited reward (the stock can only fall to zero) and a maximum risk of $1,900. Once again, the maximum risk will be realized only if the underlying stock at the time of expiration is equal to the long strike price. The upside breakeven is the higher strike put option minus the net credit divided by the number of short puts. In this case, the upside breakeven is 49: [50 – (1 ÷ 2) = 49.50]. If the stock closes above $50 a share, the options expire worthless, but you can keep the credit. The downside breakeven is calculated using the following equation: Lower strike minus the number of short contracts times the difference in strike prices divided by the number of long options minus the number of short options plus the net credit (or subtract the net debit). In this trade, the downside breakeven is 34.33: 40 – [(50 – 40) × 2] ÷ (5 – 2) + 1 = 34.33. This trade makes money as long as the price of the underlying closes below the downside breakeven. If the trade had been entered with a net debit, the upside breakeven would not exist.

This put ratio backspread works because the further the market gets away from the strike where you originally purchased the options, the more money the trade will make. As each level of option gets further in-the-money,

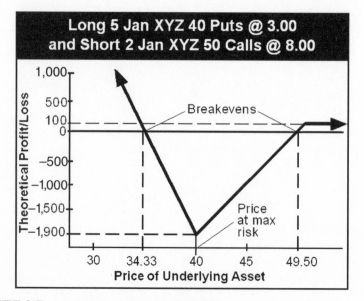

FIGURE 9.7 Put Ratio Backspread Risk Profile

> **Put Ratio Backspread**
>
> **Strategy:** Sell higher strike puts and buy a greater number of lower strike puts with a ratio less than .67.
>
> **Market Opportunity:** Look for a market where you anticipate a sharp decline with increased volatility; place as a credit or at even.
>
> **Maximum Risk:** Limited [(number of short puts × difference in strikes) × 100] − net credit (or + net debit).
>
> **Maximum Profit:** Limited to the downside below the breakeven (as the underlying can only fall to zero).
>
> **Upside Breakeven:** Higher strike put − (net credit ÷ number of short puts). No upside breakeven exists if the trade is entered with a net debit.
>
> **Downside Breakeven:** Lower strike price − [(number of short puts × difference in strikes) ÷ (number of long puts − number of short puts)] + net credit (or − net debit).
>
> **Margin:** Varies by brokerage firm policy.

the delta of the options purchased will become greater than the delta of the options sold. In other words, the further an option is in-the-money, the more it acts like a stock. The risk graph of this example is shown in Figure 9.7.

Put Ratio Backspread Case Study

In this chapter's final case study, we are considering a put ratio backspread on Intel (INTC). In this case, it's February 2004 and we're worried that the stock is due for a sharp fall. However, if we're wrong, we don't want to lose our shirt.

The stock is trading for exactly $30 a share and we set up a 1-to-2 put ratio backspread composed of the purchase of two INTC January 2005 25 puts @ $1.50 and the sale of one January 2005 30 put @ $3.50. The trade yields a $50 credit. If the stock rallies rather than falls, we can do nothing, keep the credit, and let the puts expire worthless.

Ideally, however, the stock will move below the downside breakeven. At expiration, the downside breakeven is equal to the lower strike price minus the difference in strike prices times the number of short puts plus the credit, which equals $20.50: $25 − (5 × 1) + .50 = $20.50. The maximum risk occurs if the stock closes at the lower strike price at expiration. At that point, the short call is $5 in-the-money, but the long call expires worthless. However, just as with the call ratio backspread, we do not want to hold this position until expiration. Instead, we want to exit the position 30 days before expiration or after a reasonable profit. The risk profile of this trade is shown in Figure 9.8.

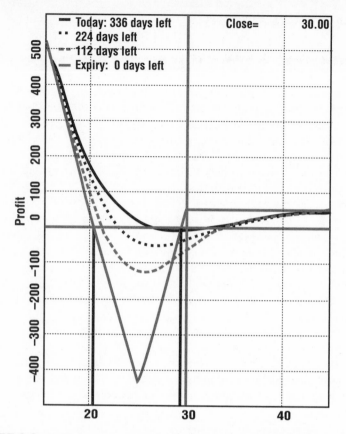

FIGURE 9.8   INTC Put Ratio Backspread (*Source:* Optionetics Platinum © 2004)

Put Ratio Backspread Case Study

Strategy: Short 1 INTC January 30 Put @ $3.50 and Long 2 January 25 Puts @ $1.50. The net credit equals $50.

Market Opportunity: We want to hedge in case Intel moves lower, but not lose if it continues to move northward.

Maximum Risk: Limited [(number of short puts × difference in strikes) × 100] – net credit. In this case, $450: [(1 × 5) × 100] – $50.

Maximum Profit: Limited to the downside beyond the breakeven (as the stock can only fall to zero) plus the credit.

Upside Breakeven: Higher strike – (net credit ÷ number of short puts). In this case 29.50: [30 – (.50 ÷ 1)].

Downside Breakeven: Lower strike – (number of short puts × difference in strikes) ÷ (number of long puts – number of short puts) + net credit. In this case, the DB is 20.50: 25 – [(1 × 5) ÷ (2 – 1)] + .50.

EXIT STRATEGIES FOR RATIO BACKSPREADS

Whether trading call or put ratio backspreads, the strategist wants to consider the possibility of early assignment on the short options. This can occur if the short options have little time value left. As a general rule, an option with a quarter point or less of time value will have a relatively high probability of assignment. At that point, it might be wise to close the backspread. In addition, we generally recommend exiting ratio backspreads 30 days prior to the options' expiration.

Here are a few exit rules to follow when dealing with put or call backspreads. First, if the trade has a reasonable profit (50 percent or more), consider closing out an equal number of short and long positions. Then, the remaining long option is working with free money and can be held for additional profits. Second, if the underlying stock rises between the upside and downside breakevens, exit the entire position with 30 days or less left until expiration. To do so, buy the short options back and sell the long options. In that case, try to mitigate the loss. Third, it is recommended that you close out the position before 30 days of expiration unless you feel strongly that the stock will continue to increase (in a call backspread) or decrease (in a put backspread). If the underlying stock falls below the downside breakeven in a call ratio backspread or above the upside breakeven in a put ratio backspread, let the options expire worthless.

VOLATILITY SKEWS

There are two types of volatility skews that can develop in an options class. The first type is known as a time skew and arises when the implied volatility of one month is significantly different from the other months. This often happens when there is a takeover rumor or some other event that causes the implied volatility of the short-term options to move higher relative to longer-term options. When this happens, the strategist can attempt to take advantage of the time skew with a calendar spread, which involves buying the options with the low implied volatility (IV) and selling the options with the high IV. The strike prices of the two options contracts are the same, but the expiration months are different.

The second type of volatility skew is known as a price skew. With this type of skew, the expiration months are the same. However, there is a significant difference in implied volatility along the various strike prices. For example, if the at-the-money options have a much higher implied volatility than the out-of-the-money options, the result is a price skew.

Going further, there are two types of price skews. With a forward price skew, the options with the higher strike prices have higher levels of implied volatility than the options with lower strike prices. A reverse volatility skew, in contrast, occurs when the lower strike prices have a higher volatility skew than the options with the higher strike price.

Traders can sometimes use forward and reverse volatility skews to their advantage. The goal is to sell those options with the higher implied volatility and buy the ones that have the lower IV because the ones with the higher implied volatility are considered more expensive. For instance, if a strategist identifies a forward volatility skew, they can attempt to profit with a put ratio backspread, which involves buying the options with the lower strike price and selling the options with the higher strikes. Call ratio backspreads make more sense when the strategist identifies a reverse skew. At that point, they would want to sell the options with the lower strike price and buy a greater number of the higher strike options.

STRATEGY ROAD MAPS

Ratio Call Spread Road Map

In order to place a call ratio spread, the following 12 guidelines should be observed:

1. Look for a market where you expect a decline (to keep the net credit) or a slight rise not to exceed the strike price of the short options.
2. Check to see if this stock has options available.
3. Explore past price trends and liquidity by reviewing price and volume charts over the past year.
4. Review options premiums per expiration dates and strike prices. Place the position as a credit or as close to at-even as you can. Use options with greater than 90 days until expiration. LEAPS options are a good choice since they provide an opportunity for time to work in your favor.
5. Investigate implied volatility values to see if the options are overpriced or undervalued. This strategy is best placed in markets with a reverse volatility skew. In this environment, the higher strike options (the ones you want to sell) have higher implied volatility and can be overpriced. The lower strike options (the ones you want to buy) enjoy lower implied volatility and are often underpriced. By trading the reverse volatility skew, you can capture the implied volatility differential between the short and long options.

6. A ratio call spread is composed of buying the lower strike call (ITM or ATM) and selling a greater number of higher strike calls (OTM). Determine which spread to place by calculating:

   - **Unlimited Risk:** Unlimited to the upside above the breakeven.

   - **Limited Reward:** Limited. [Number of long contracts × (difference in strikes × 100)] + net credit (or – net debit).

   - **Upside Breakeven:** Lower call strike price + [(difference in strikes × number of short contracts) ÷ (number of short calls – number of long calls)] + net credit (or – net debit).

   - **Downside Breakeven:** None when established for a credit.

7. Create a risk profile of the most promising option combination and graphically determine the trade's feasibility. A call ratio spread risk profile shows an unlimited risk above the upside breakeven and a limited reward.

8. Write down the trade in your trader's journal before placing the trade with your broker to minimize mistakes made in placing the order and to keep a record of the trade.

9. Make an exit plan before you place the trade. How much money is the maximum amount you are willing to lose? How much profit do you want to make on the trade? For example, exit the trade when the stock moves above the maximum profit level at any time prior to 30 days before expiration.

10. Contact your broker to buy and sell the chosen options. Place the trade as a limit order so that you limit the net credit/debit of the trade.

11. You do have to watch the market closely on this type of trade. The profit on this strategy is limited, but the risk is unlimited.

12. Choose an exit strategy based on the price movement of the underlying stock and fluctuations in the implied volatility of the options:

   - *The underlying stock exceeds the short strike price:* Once the stock has made a move higher, watch carefully for any further moves higher. Exit the strategy if the stock moves either (1) above the maximum profit level or (2) above the upside breakeven.

   - *The underlying stock falls below the downside breakeven:* Keep the credit and let the options expire.

Ratio Put Spread Road Map

In order to place a ratio put spread, the following 12 guidelines should be observed:

1. A ratio put spread can be implemented when a slight fall in the market is anticipated followed by a sharp rise.

2. Explore past price trends and liquidity by reviewing price and volume charts over the past year.

3. Check to see if this stock has options available.

4. Review options premiums per expiration dates and strike prices.

5. Investigate implied volatility values to see if the options are overpriced or undervalued. This strategy is best placed in markets with a forward volatility skew. In this environment, the lower strike options (the ones you want to sell) have higher implied volatility and can be overpriced. The higher strike options (the ones you want to buy) have lower implied volatility and are often underpriced. By trading this type of volatility skew, you can capture the implied volatility differential between the short and long options.

6. A ratio put spread is created by buying a higher strike put (ITM or ATM) and selling a greater number of lower strike puts (OTM). Determine which spread to place by calculating:

   - **Limited Risk:** Limited to the downside below the breakeven as the stock can only fall to zero. Lower strike price – (difference in strikes – net credit) × 100. Although limited, the risk can be significant.
   - **Limited Reward:** Limited. (Difference in strikes × 100) + net credit (or – net debit].
   - **Upside Breakeven:** None.
   - **Downside Breakeven:** Higher strike price – [(difference in strikes × number of short contracts) ÷ (number of short contracts – number of long contracts)] – net credit (or + net debit).

7. Create a risk profile of the most promising option combination and graphically determine the trade's feasibility.

8. Write down the trade in your trader's journal before placing the trade with your broker to minimize mistakes made in placing the order and to keep a record of the trade.

9. Make an exit plan before you place the trade. If the stock falls below the maximum profit point, consider closing the position. The position begins losing money if it falls below the breakeven.

10. Contact your broker to buy and sell the chosen options. Place the trade as a limit order so that you limit the net credit/debit of the trade.

11. You do have to watch the market closely on this type of trade. Losses can be substantial if the stock falls sharply.

12. Choose an exit strategy based on the price movement of the underlying stock and fluctuations in the implied volatility of the options:

   - *If the underlying stays the same or rises:* Do nothing, let the puts expire worthless and keep the net credit.
   - *The underlying stock falls below the short strike price:* You should consider exiting the entire position for a small gain.
   - *The underlying stock falls below the downside breakeven:* You should close the position and take the loss.

Call Ratio Backspread Road Map

In order to place a call ratio backspread, the following 14 guidelines should be observed:

1. Look for a bullish market where you anticipate a large increase in the price of the underlying stock. Choose stocks that are leaders in their fields and have an increasing stream of earnings and quarter-over-quarter growth.

2. Check to see if this stock has options available.

3. Explore past price trends and liquidity by reviewing price and volume charts over the past year.

4. Review options premiums per expiration dates and strike prices. Place the position as a credit or as close to at-even as you can. Use options with greater than 90 days until expiration. LEAPS options are a good choice since they provide ample opportunity for time to work in your favor.

5. Investigate implied volatility values to see if the options are overpriced or undervalued. This strategy is best placed in markets with a reverse volatility skew. In this environment, the lower strike options (the ones you want to sell) have higher implied volatility and can be overpriced. The higher strike options (the ones you want to buy) enjoy lower implied volatility and are often underpriced.

By trading the reverse volatility skew, you can capture the implied volatility differential between the short and long options.

6. A call ratio backspread is composed of selling the lower strike call (ITM or ATM) and buying a greater number of higher strike calls (OTM). It is not usually recommended to place positions with ratios greater than .67; use ratios that are a multiple of 1-to-2 (the most common) or 2-to-3. All options must have the same expiration date.

7. Look at options with at least 90 days until expiration to give the trade enough time to move into the money.

8. Determine which spread to place by calculating:

   • **Limited Risk:** Limited. [(Number of short calls × difference in strikes) × 100] – net credit (or + net debit).

   • **Unlimited Reward:** Unlimited to the upside above the upside breakeven.

   • **Upside Breakeven:** Higher strike call + [(difference in strikes × number of short calls) ÷ (number of long calls – number of short calls)] – net credit (or + net debit).

   • **Downside Breakeven:** Lower strike price + (net credit ÷ number of short calls)]. A downside breakeven does not exist if the trade is entered with a net debit.

9. Create a risk profile of the most promising option combination and graphically determine the trade's feasibility. A call ratio backspread risk profile shows an unlimited reward above the upside breakeven and a limited reward (if entered for a net credit) below the downside breakeven.

10. Write down the trade in your trader's journal before placing the trade with your broker to minimize mistakes made in placing the order and to keep a record of the trade.

11. Make an exit plan before you place the trade. How much money is the maximum amount you are willing to lose? How much profit do you want to make on the trade? For example, exit the trade when you have a 50 percent profit or at least 30 days prior to expiration on the options before the major amount of time decay occurs.

12. Contact your broker to buy and sell the chosen options. Place the trade as a limit order so that you limit the net debit of the trade.

13. You do not have to watch the market closely on this type of trade. The profit on this strategy is unlimited.

14. Choose an exit strategy based on the price movement of the underlying stock and fluctuations in the implied volatility of the options:

- *The underlying stock exceeds the upside breakeven:* Once you have made a reasonable profit (50 percent), you should close out an equal number of short calls and long positions. Since the remaining long option is now working with free money, you can afford to hold onto it for additional profit. It is recommended that you close out the position before 30 days to expiration unless you feel strongly that the stock will continue to increase.

- *The underlying stock rises between the upside and downside breakevens:* You should exit the entire position—buy the short calls back and sell the long calls—and try to mitigate the loss.

- *The underlying stock falls below the downside breakeven:* Let the options expire worthless, or sell the long call at expiration to mitigate any losses.

Put Ratio Backspread Road Map

In order to place a put ratio backspread, the following 14 guidelines should be observed:

1. Look for a bearish, low implied volatility market where you anticipate a sharp decline in the price of the underlying stock with increased volatility.

2. Explore past price trends and liquidity by reviewing price and volume charts over the past year.

3. Check to see if this stock has options available.

4. Review options premiums per expiration dates and strike prices. Ideally use options with at least 90 days until expiration. LEAPS options are also a good alternative for put ratio backspreads.

5. Investigate implied volatility values to see if the options are overpriced or undervalued. This strategy is best placed in markets with a forward volatility skew. In this environment, the higher strike options (the ones you want to sell) have higher implied volatility and can be overpriced. The lower strike options (the ones you want to buy) enjoy lower implied volatility and are often underpriced. By trading the forward volatility skew, you can capture the implied volatility differential between the short and long options.

6. A put ratio backspread is created by selling a higher strike put (ITM or ATM) and buying a greater number of lower strike puts (OTM). It is

not recommended to place positions with ratios greater than .67. Use ratios that are a multiple of 1 to 2 (the most common) or 2 to 3. All options must have the same expiration date.

7. Look at options with at least 90 days until expiration to give the trade enough time to move into the money.

8. Determine which spread to place by calculating:

- **Limited Risk:** [(Number of short puts × difference in strikes) × 100] – net credit or + net debit.

- **Limited Reward:** Limited to the downside below the downside breakeven (as the underlying can only fall to zero).

- **Upside Breakeven:** Higher strike put – (net credit ÷ number of short puts). An upside breakeven does not exist if the trade is entered with a net debit.

- **Downside Breakeven:** Lower strike price – [(number of short puts × difference in strikes) ÷ (number of long puts – number of short puts)] + net credit (or – net debit).

9. Create a risk profile of the most promising option combination and graphically determine the trade's feasibility.

10. Write down the trade in your trader's journal before placing the trade with your broker to minimize mistakes made in placing the order and to keep a record of the trade.

11. Make an exit plan before you place the trade. How much money is the maximum amount you are willing to lose? How much profit do you want to make on the trade? For example, exit the trade when you have a 50 percent profit or at least 30 days prior to option expiration.

12. Contact your broker to buy and sell the chosen options. Place the trade as a limit order so that you limit the net credit/debit of the trade.

13. You do not have to watch the market closely on this type of trade. The profit on this strategy is unlimited.

14. Choose an exit strategy based on the price movement of the underlying stock and fluctuations in the implied volatility of the options:

- *The underlying stock falls below the downside breakeven:* Once you have made a reasonable profit (50 percent +), you should close out an equal number of short and long puts. Since the other long option is now working with free money, you can afford to hold onto it for additional profit. It is recommended that you close out the position before 30 days until expiration unless you feel strongly that the stock will continue to decrease.

- *The underlying stock rises between the downside and upside breakevens:* You should exit the entire position and take the loss.

CONCLUSION

Ratio backspreads are great strategies that when ideally placed provide a credit for the position with unlimited reward potential. In general, these type of strategies consist of selling one or more options that are at-the-money and simultaneously buying a larger number of options that are further out-of-the-money where all options have the same expiration date and underlying stock or index.

Ratio backspreads are quite popular. The key to finding one lies in identifying the correct volatility conditions that will allow you to place them for a credit (or even). The Optionetics.com Platinum web site offers a variety of great tools to help search for these conditions.

Vacation trading criteria include the following issues.

- Look for a market where you anticipate a large directional move:
  - Up with a reverse volatility skew—call ratio backspreads.
  - Down with a forward volatility skew—put ratio backspreads.
- Buy and sell options with at least 90 days or greater till expiration. LEAPS are ideal as the time factor will work for you.
- Once you are deep in-the-money, you may want to consider an adjustment by closing out one long and one short position and continuing to hold one long position.
- Exit strategy: Look for your target profit and exit before 30 days to expiration. Your maximum risk is usually very low, so you can chose to stay in the trade and look for a turnaround or get out before a large percentage loss.

Volatility plays a key role in ratio backspreads. By searching for the right volatility combination you can create a position that gives you a high probability for a healthy reward. Developing a good feel for volatility is an important part of being able to pick the right market and the optimal strategy. Markets that go up rapidly most likely will come down fast. The faster they go down, the faster they go up. If you are in a market that is going straight to the moon, start looking for opportunities for put ratio backspreads. Why? When the markets are going straight up, traders pump up the call prices because of increased volatility. This also means that the market may very well be positioning itself for a severe correction to the downside. Many times you can get better prices on the put side of a trade, because people tend to buy calls when volatility increases. There is simply a greater demand for calls in a fast-moving market to the upside. If the market is going down and you expect continuation, do a put ratio backspread. If you expect a reversal, do a call ratio backspread.

The best way to learn how these strategies react to market movement is to experience them by paper trading markets that seem promising. Once you have initiated a paper trade, revisit the trade every week to learn how market forces affect these kinds of limited risk/unlimited reward strategies.

One of the most important actions in trading is exiting a trade. Paper trading is also a practical way of learning how to exit a trade by monitoring the market for profits or losses. Any fictitious losses can be chalked up to experience (rather than a real loss) and all winning trades will inspire confidence.

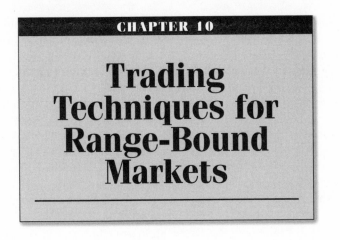

CHAPTER 10

Trading Techniques for Range-Bound Markets

A large percentage of markets trend sideways within a consistent trading range throughout the trading year. In many cases, you may find stock shares or futures that have been trading sideways for some time. While these markets do not produce much in the way of profits for the traditional buy-and-hold stock trader, they do provide options traders with amazing limited risk opportunities. This chapter takes a close look at these options strategies and how they can be employed to exploit sideways movement as well as the time value of options (otherwise known as the time premium).

As previously discussed, option pricing includes time value and intrinsic value. The intrinsic value of an option is the value an in-the-money (ITM) option has if it were exercised at that point. For example, if I own an IBM 70 December call option, and IBM is trading at $80, the option has $10 of intrinsic value. This is due to the fact that the strike price of the call option is below the current trading price of the underlying asset. If the option has a market price of $12, then the remaining $2 of the call option is the time value.

Furthermore, if an IBM 90 put option costs $13, it would have $10 of intrinsic value and $3 of time value. Intrinsic value is not lost due to the passage of time. Intrinsic value is lost only when the underlying asset—in this case IBM—moves against your option's position. In this example, if IBM moves down, the call options lose intrinsic value. If IBM moves up, the put options lose intrinsic value.

Time value is lost due to time decay (also referred to as the theta decay) of the option. Options lose the most time value in the last 30 days of the life of the option—the closer the expiration date, the faster the theta decay. Therefore, the last day will have the fastest loss of value due to time.

Since options lose value over time if markets do not move, this basic option characteristic can be used to create strategies that work in markets that are moving sideways. Before we can explore the specific strategies, however, you need to be able to spot a sideways (or range-bound) market.

A sideways market is a market that has traded between two numbers for a specified period of time. The minimum time frame I prefer to use is two months. However, for our purposes, a longer time frame can mean a more stable sideways market. As previously reviewed, these two numbers are referred to as the support and resistance levels. For example, if every time IBM dips to around $70 per share it rebounds, this would establish the support. If IBM would then trade up in price to reach $90 and then sell off again, this would establish the resistance. These two levels can then be used to employ an effective options strategy that would allow us to collect time premium.

How do you find these range-bound markets? I like to scan the various markets by eyeballing the charts. If I spot a market that appears to be going sideways, I take a ruler and try to draw a support and resistance line. If this is easily accomplished, I then look for the most effective options strategy to take advantage of the given market. Three of my favorite sideways strategies are the long butterfly, long condor, and long iron butterfly spreads. Additionally, we will also explore three more advanced range-trading strategies: the calendar spread, the diagonal spread, and the collar spread.

LONG BUTTERFLY

The long butterfly is a popular strategy that traders use when they expect the stock or market to trade within a range. The butterfly can be structured using calls, puts, or a combination of puts and calls. In this book, we will focus on the long butterfly using only call options. In that respect, the long butterfly includes three strike prices and can be thought of as a combination of a bull call spread and a bear call spread. Lower and middle strike prices are used to create the bull spread and middle and higher strike prices are used to create a bear call spread. Sometimes, traders refer to the middle strike prices, which are generally at-the-money, as the *body* and call the higher and lower strike prices the *wings*.

The long butterfly is a limited risk/limited reward strategy. It works well when the underlying stock makes relatively little movement. The strategy generates the maximum profits when the price of the underlying asset is equal to the strike price of the short options at expiration. The risks arise when the underlying asset moves dramatically higher or lower. However, the maximum risk is equal to the net debit paid for the trade. For that reason, the strategist will implement the long butterfly when expecting the underlying asset to stay within a range until the options expire.

As a side note, although we will be using calls in our next example, the long butterfly can also be created using puts. In this case, the strategist will establish the position by purchasing one OTM put (wing), selling two ATM puts (body), and buying one ITM put (wing). This would be a combination of a bull put spread and a bear put spread.

Some strategists prefer to use the so-called long iron butterfly, a trade that is created as a combination of a bear call spread (a short ATM call and a long OTM call) and a bull put spread (a long OTM put and a short ATM put). The short put should have a lower strike price than the short call. Therefore, unlike the long butterfly, the iron butterfly includes four strike prices instead of three. In any case, whether trading long butterflies with puts and calls or trading long iron butterflies, the goal is to see the underlying stock trade sideways and for the short options to lose value due to time decay and expire.

Long Butterfly Mechanics

To illustrate, let's consider an example using a hypothetical company, XYZ. During the month of January, shares are trading for $70 and have been trading in a range between $65 and $75 during the past several months. So, the strategist believes the stock will remain within that range and gravitate toward $70 from now until May expiration. As a result, a long butterfly is created using calls on XYZ.

In this case, the strategist goes long one May XYZ 65 call for $8, buys one May XYZ 75 call for $2, and sells two XYZ 70 calls for $4.50 each. The net debit of the trade is $1, or $100 for one long butterfly, which also represents the maximum risk. The maximum reward is equal to the difference between the middle and highest strike prices, minus the net debit times 100. In this example, the maximum profit equals $400 [(5 − 1) × 100 = $400] per contract. This will occur if the XYZ is trading for $70 a share at expiration. The risk graph of this trade is shown in Figure 10.1.

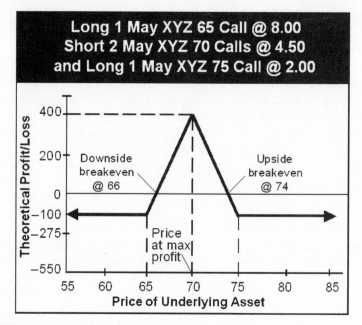

FIGURE 10.1   Long Butterfly Risk Graph

Exiting the Position

- *The underlying asset falls below the downside breakeven (66):* The strategist will generally want to let the options expire worthless and incur the maximum loss.

- *The stock is in between the breakevens (66 and 74):* The trade is in the profit zone and the strategist should let the short options expire. If possible, sell the long option with a lower strike price for a profit.

- *The stock makes a dramatic move higher than the upside breakeven (74):* Exit the position or, if the short options are assigned, exercise the long options to offset them.

Long Butterfly Case Study

A long butterfly is a strategy best used when a trader expects sideways movement in a stock or index. A long butterfly can use either all calls or all puts and is the combination of two spreads. If calls are used, we are combining a bull call spread and a bear call spread. For puts, it is the combination of a bull put spread and a bear put spread. The idea of the butter-

Long Butterfly

Strategy: Buy lower strike option, sell two higher strike options, and buy a higher strike option (all calls and puts) with the same expiration date.

Market Opportunity: Look for a range-bound market that is expected to stay between the breakeven points for an extended period of time.

Maximum Risk: Limited to the net debit paid. [(Long premiums – short premiums) × 100].

Maximum Profit: Limited. (difference between the middle strike price and the higher strike price – net debit) × 100. Max profit occurs at the short strike price.

Upside Breakeven: Higher strike price – net debit.

Downside Breakeven: Lower strike price + net debit.

Margin: The broker will generally require the collateral equal to the debit for both the bear call spread and the bull call spread.

---

fly is derived from the purchase of the "wings" of the trade and the sale of the "body."

A butterfly is a limited risk, limited reward strategy. The initial entry fee into a butterfly creates a net debit, which is also the maximum risk of the position. The maximum reward is calculated by subtracting the net debit from the difference between strike prices. For example, if we enter a 35-40-45 call butterfly, we would buy a 35 call, sell two 40 calls, and buy a 45 call. If our net debit was $3, our maximum risk would be $300 and our maximum reward would be $200: $(5 – 3) \times 100 = \$200$. The maximum profit occurs if the underlying security closes at the middle strike price at expiration.

In mid-October 2003, a trader might have looked at IBM and expected it to trade sideways through November's option expiration on the 21st. On October 16, IBM closed at $89.28 and it seemed likely that the stock would consolidate near $90 after a significant decline. As a result, we could have entered a butterfly using the 85-90-95 put options or call options. However, let's use the calls because they offered just a slightly better entry. Since this trade benefits from time erosion and because we don't want to give the stock too much time to move out of its range, it's usually best to use front month options when trading a butterfly.

The November 85 call could be purchased for $5.20. The 90 calls could be sold for $2. The 95 call would cost 0.60, leaving us with a total debit of $1.80. Let's say we decide to place a total of five contracts; the net debit would be $900, which is also the maximum risk. The maximum profit is found by subtracting the debit of 1.80 from the difference in spreads (5 points) to get $320: (5 – 1.80) × 100 = $320. Thus, if IBM were to close at $90 on expiration, the maximum profit of $320 per contract, or $1,600, would be achieved from an initial $900 investment.

Notice how the risk graph in Figure 10.2 shows the trade's limited reward and limited risk. The risk graph also points out that the maximum profit is impossible to achieve until expiration. This strategy rarely sees a trader get out with a profit at the beginning of the trade. This is because a butterfly benefits from time erosion. We normally would like to see at least a 2-to-1 reward-to-risk ratio when trading a butterfly. For this trade, our reward-to-risk ratio was about 1.8 to 1, but we could have easily gotten a 2-to-1 ratio by getting a price somewhere between the bid and the ask.

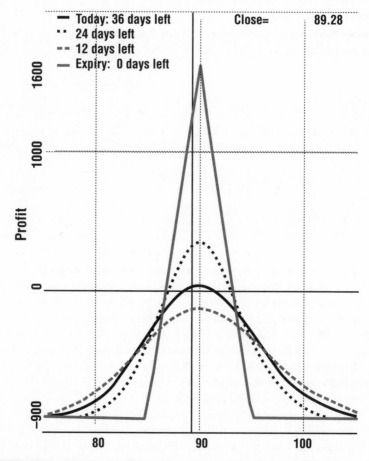

FIGURE 10.2   Risk Graph of Long Butterfly on IBM (*Source:* Optionetics Platinum © 2004)

Long Butterfly Case Study

Strategy: With the security trading at $89.28 a share on October 16, 2003, go long 5 November 85 calls @ 5.20, go short 10 November 90 calls @ 2, and go long 5 November 95 calls @ 0.60 on IBM.

Market Opportunity: Expect stock to stay in narrow range through November expiration.

Maximum Risk: Limited to the net debit. In this case, the max risk is $900: [(5.20 + .60) – (2 + 2)] × 5 × 100.

Maximum Profit: Limited to difference in strikes less initial debit. In this case, $1,600: [(95 – 90) – 1.80] × 100 = 320; (320 × 5).

Downside Breakeven: Lower strike plus the initial cost per contract. In this case, 86.80: (85 + 1.80).

Upside Breakeven: Upper strike minus the initial cost per contract. In this case, 93.20: (95 – 1.80).

IBM shares did indeed trade sideways through November expiration, closing at $88.63 on November 21. This left the trade with a profit of $180—a 100 percent return—which is calculated by taking the value of the long option ($180) and subtracting any options that had to be purchased. However, no additional options had to be purchased because the 90 options were out-of-the-money at expiration.

LONG CONDOR

Like the butterfly, a condor is composed of a body and wings. In the case of the long condor, the wings are composed of two long options—one in-the-money and one out-of-the-money. The body includes two short inner or middle options. Again, this type of strategy works well when the strategist expects the stock or market to remain range-bound.

Most often, the long condor is constructed using four strike prices. For example, a strategist might buy one in-the-money call, sell two calls with different strike prices (one at-the-money and one out-of-the-money), and buy one deeply out-of-the-money. Since this trade involves four separate options contracts, managing commissions is an important aspect of this trade—the lower the commissions, the better.

The goal of the long condor is to see the short options expire worthless, but also see the in-the-money option retain most of its value. The maximum potential reward is calculated by subtracting the net debit of the trade from the difference between the strike prices. If the underlying security makes a dramatic move higher or lower, the long condor generally yields poor results. The upside breakeven is equal to the highest strike price minus the debit. The downside breakeven is equal to the lowest strike prices plus the debit. The maximum risk associated with this trade is limited to the net debit.

Long Condor Mechanics

In order to see how the long condor works, let's say XYZ is trading for $66.40 a share on May 10. We expect the stock to stay within a trading range of $65 and $70 a share for the next several months. Consequently, a long condor is examined using October call options.

To create the trade, we first go long one October XYZ 60 call at $8 and long one October XYZ 75 call at $1. Next, we go short the October XYZ 65 call at $5 and short the October XYZ 70 call for $2. The net debit on this trade is $200, which is also the maximum risk. The maximum reward is equal to the difference between the strike prices minus the debit, or $300 per contract: $[(75 - 70) - 2] \times 100 = \$300$. The upside breakeven equals the highest strike prices minus the net debit, or 73 ($75 - 2 = 73$). The downside breakeven is computed as the lowest strike price plus the net debit, or 62 ($60 + 2 = 62$). The risk graph of this trade is shown in Figure 10.3.

Ideally, with this trade, the strategist will see the short options lose value, but the deeply-in-the-money call will retain its value. For instance, if the stock price is equal to $65 a share at expiration, the only option with any remaining intrinsic value will be the October 65 call. In that case, three of the options expire worthless, but the October 60 call is worth $5. The October 60 can then be exercised or closed. If so, the net profit from the trade will be the profit earned from the October 60 call minus the debit.

Exiting the Position

Exit strategies for the condor are similar to the butterfly spreads.

- *XYZ falls below the lower breakeven (62):* This is the maximum risk range for this trade. The strategist will probably let the options expire worthless and incur the maximum risk. Make sure to salvage any remaining value of the October 60 call if the stock price is below $62, but above the October 60 strike price at expiration.

- *XYZ remains between the downside (62) and upside (73) breakevens:* Ideally, the stock price will fall near the strike price of the first short option at expiration. Let the out-of-the-money options expire worthless and close the positions involving the in-the-money-options.

- *XYZ rises above higher breakeven (73):* Close the position to avoid assignment and incur the maximum risk.

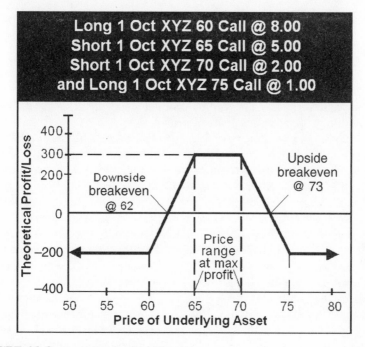

Long 1 Oct XYZ 60 Call @ 8.00
Short 1 Oct XYZ 65 Call @ 5.00
Short 1 Oct XYZ 70 Call @ 2.00
and Long 1 Oct XYZ 75 Call @ 1.00

FIGURE 10.3 Long Condor Risk Graph

Long Condor

Strategy: Buy lower strike option, sell higher strike option, sell an even higher strike option, and buy and even higher strike option with the same expiration date (all calls or all puts).

Market Opportunity: Look for a range-bound market that is expected to stay between the breakeven points for an extended period of time.

Maximum Risk: Limited to the net debit paid. (Long premiums – short premiums) × 100.

Maximum Profit: Limited. (Difference between strike prices – net debit) × 100. The profit range occurs between the breakevens.

Upside Breakeven: Highest strike price – net debit.

Downside Breakeven: Lowest strike price + net debit.

Margin: Subject to brokerage firm policy. Could be treated as a bull call spread and a bear call spread.

Long Condor Case Study

A condor is similar to a butterfly, but this strategy widens out the maximum reward. A condor is still a sideways trading strategy that takes advantage of time erosion. Choosing between a condor and a butterfly has to do with the range the stock is expected to trade and the risk graph. Remember, a butterfly has a maximum profit at a specific price. A condor has a maximum profit across a range of prices.

A condor is a limited risk, limited reward strategy. The initial entry into a condor creates a net debit, which is also the maximum risk. The maximum reward is the difference between strikes less the initial debit. For example, if we enter a 30-35-40-45 condor, we would buy a 30 put (call), sell a 35 put (call), sell a 40 put (call) and buy a 45 put (call). If our initial debit were $2, our maximum risk would be $200. The maximum profit occurs if the underlying security closes between the two sold strikes at expiration. This is the main attraction of a condor, as it has a larger maximum profit zone than a regular butterfly. However, the risk also increases with the added reward.

As in the long butterfly case study, in mid-October 2003, a trader might have looked at IBM and expected it to trade sideways through November's option expiration on the 21st. On October 16, IBM closed at $89.28 and it seemed likely that the stock would consolidate near $90 after a significant decline. As a result, we could have entered a condor using the 80-85-90-95 put options. All calls could also be used, with the best reward-to-risk ratio being the one that should be used. Since we benefit from time erosion and because we don't want to give the stock too much time to move out of its range, it's normally best to use front month options when trading a condor.

The November 80 puts could be purchased for $0.30, with the 85 puts selling for $0.90. The 90 puts could be sold for $2.80, with the 95 puts costing $6.50. This created a debit of $3.10 per contract, with five contracts for a total of $1,550, which is also the maximum risk. The maximum reward is calculated by subtracting the net debit from the difference in strikes (5 points). In this trade, if IBM were to close anywhere between $85 and $90 on expiration, the maximum profit of $190 [(5 − 3.10) × 100 = $190] per contract, or $950 (5 × 190 = $950), could be kept. The breakeven points were at 83.10 and 91.90 and are found by taking the net debit of $3.10 and adding it to the lower strike for the downside breakeven: (80 + 3.10 = 83.10). The upside breakeven is found by subtracting the $3.10 debit from the higher option strike: (95 − 3.10 = 91.90).

Notice how the risk graph (see Figure 10.4) shows the trade's limited reward and limited risk. The risk graph also points out that the maximum profit is impossible to achieve until expiration. This strategy rarely sees a

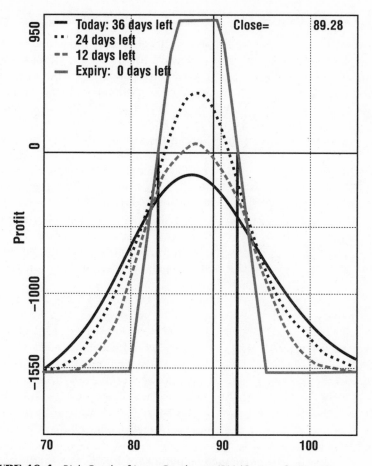

FIGURE 10.4 Risk Graph of Long Condor on IBM (*Source:* Optionetics Platinum © 2004)

trader get out with a profit at the beginning of the trade. This is because a condor benefits from time erosion. We aren't going to see as high a reward-to-risk ratio trading a condor as trading a butterfly, but our maximum profit is more likely to be achieved because of the wider maximum profit range.

IBM shares did indeed trade sideways through November expiration, closing at $88.63 on November 21. This left this trade with the maximum profit of $950. If the stock had closed above 95 or below 80, the maximum loss would have occurred.

Long Condor Case Study

Strategy: With the security trading at $89.28 a share on October 16, 2003, go long 5 November IBM 80 puts @ .30, go short 5 November IBM 85 puts @ .90, go short 5 November IBM 90 puts @ 2.80, and go long 5 November IBM 95 puts @ 6.50.

Market Opportunity: Expect stock to stay in narrow range through November expiration.

Maximum Risk: Limited to the net debit. In this case, the max risk is $1,550: [(6.50 + .30) − (.90 + 2.80)] = 3.10; (3.10 × 5) × 100.

Maximum Profit: Limited. (Difference in strikes − the net debit) × 100. In this case, the max reward is $950: [(85 − 80) − 3.10] × 5 × 100.

Downside Breakeven: Lower strike plus the net debit. In this case, the DB is 83.10: (80 + 3.10).

Upside Breakeven: Higher strike minus the net debit. In this case, the UB is 91.90: (95 − 3.10).

Margin: None.

LONG IRON BUTTERFLY

The long iron butterfly is another strategy that works well in range-bound markets. It's actually a combination of a bear call spread, with (a short ATM call and a long OTM call), along with a bull put spread (a long OTM put and a short ATM put). The short put can have a lower strike price than the short call. Therefore, unlike the long butterfly with only puts or only calls, the iron butterfly includes both puts and calls, as well as four different options contracts instead of three.

To structure the trade, the strategist will buy an OTM call and an OTM put. At the same time, they will sell an ATM call. In general, the short call will have a strike price in the middle of the stock's recent trading range. Finally, an ATM or slightly OTM put is also sold. In contrast to the long butterfly, which is established for a debit, the iron butterfly is done for a credit because the strategist is buying two out-of-the-money options and selling two at-the-money options.

Both the risks and the rewards of the long iron butterfly are limited. The success of the trade depends on the stock staying in between the upside and downside breakevens. The upside breakeven is computed as the strike price of the short call plus the net credit received for the trade. The downside breakeven is equal to the short put strike price minus the net credit. The maximum reward is the total credit received on the trade. The greatest risk is equal to the difference between the strike prices minus the net credit. Also, importantly, since this trade involves four contracts, the commissions can be significant. For that reason, although the risks are generally limited, keeping commissions low will greatly improve the reward potential of the iron butterfly trade.

Long Iron Butterfly Mechanics

Let's say you've been watching XYZ Corporation and believe the company's share price will stay in a range for the next several months. The stock is currently trading for $70.75 a share. Consequently, in the month of May, you decide to create a long iron butterfly by going long one October XYZ 75 call at $2.50 and going short one October XYZ 70 call at $5, which is the bear call spread of the trade. At the same time, you go long one October XYZ 60 put at $1 and go short one October XYZ 65 put at $2—the bull put spread side of the trade. All told, the sale from the short options equals $7 and the cost of the long options is $3.50. So, this trade fetches a net credit of $3.50, or $350 per spread.

The maximum profit from the long iron butterfly is equal to the credit and will occur if the stock is between the strike prices of the two short options at expiration. If so, all the options expire worthless and the strategist will keep the premium earned from both the bull put spread and the bear call spread. In this example, the maximum profit is $350. The risk graph of this trade is shown in Figure 10.5.

Ultimately, the strategist wants the stock to trade sideways. If XYZ makes a dramatic move higher or lower, above or below the breakevens, the long iron butterfly will probably result in a loss. To compute the downside breakeven, subtract the net credit from the strike price of the short put, or 61.50: (65 − 3.50 = 61.50). The upside breakeven equals the short call strike price plus the net credit or, in this example, 73.50: (70 + 3.50 = 73.50). A move above or below the breakeven can result in the maximum possible risk, which is equal to the difference between the strike prices minus the net credit. In this case, the maximum risk is $150 per spread: (5 − 3.50) × 100.

Exiting the Position

In the case of the iron butterfly, the strategist wants the underlying stock to remain between the two breakevens at expiration. Moreover, if the stock falls between the two strike prices of the short options, all of

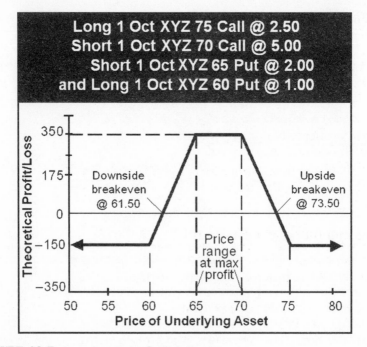

Long 1 Oct XYZ 75 Call @ 2.50
Short 1 Oct XYZ 70 Call @ 5.00
Short 1 Oct XYZ 65 Put @ 2.00
and Long 1 Oct XYZ 60 Put @ 1.00

FIGURE 10.5 Long Iron Butterfly Risk Graph

Long Iron Butterfly

Strategy: Buy a higher strike call, sell a lower strike call, sell a higher strike put, and buy a lower strike put all with the same expiration date.

Market Opportunity: Look for a range-bound market that is expected to remain quiet until expiration.

Maximum Risk: (Difference in strike prices × 100) – net credit received.

Maximum Profit: Net credit. (Short premiums – long premiums) × 100. The profit range occurs between the breakevens.

Upside Breakeven: Strike price of middle short call + net credit.

Downside Breakeven: Strike price of middle short put – net credit.

Margin: Check with broker. Some brokerage firms treat the long iron butterfly as a short straddle and a long strangle. If so, the margin requirements can be significant. Look for a broker that treats them as a combination of a bull put spread and a bear call spread.

the options expire worthless and the trade yields the maximum profit—the net credit.

- *XYZ falls below the lower breakeven (61.50):* Let the call options expire worthless. Exit the bull put spread in order to avoid assignment.
- *XYZ remains between the downside (61.50) and upside (73.50) breakevens:* Ideally, the stock price will land between the strike prices of the short options at expiration. Let the options expire worthless and keep the credit.
- *XYZ rises above higher breakeven (73.50):* Let the put options expire worthless. Exit the bear call spread in order to avoid assignment.

Long Iron Butterfly Case Study

A long iron butterfly is a strategy best used when a trader expects sideways movement in a stock or index. A long iron butterfly has the same risk graph as a condor, but is composed of a bull put spread and a bear call spread. This strategy combination creates a net credit instead of a debit. However, the same risks and rewards as a condor are present. Some traders call this a long iron condor, which has the same characteristics.

Let's review: An iron butterfly is a limited risk, limited reward strategy. The initial entry into an iron butterfly creates a net credit, which is the maximum reward. The maximum risk is the difference between strikes less the initial credit. For example, if we enter a 30-35-40-45 iron butterfly, we would buy a 30 put, sell a 35 put, sell a 40 call, and buy a 45 call. If our initial credit were $300, our maximum risk would be $200. The maximum profit occurs if the underlying security closes between the two sold strikes at expiration. This is the main attraction of an iron butterfly, as it has a larger maximum profit zone than a regular butterfly. However, the risk also increases with the added reward.

As in the previous two case studies, in mid-October 2003, a trader might have looked at IBM and expected it to trade sideways through November's option expiration on the 21st. On October 16, IBM closed at $89.28 and it seemed likely that the stock would consolidate near $90 after a significant decline. As a result, we could have entered an iron butterfly using the 80-85-90-95 put and call options. Since a long iron butterfly benefits from time erosion and we don't want to give the stock too much time to move out of its range, it's normally best to use front month options.

The November 80 puts could be purchased for $0.35, with the 85 puts selling for $0.95. The 90 calls could be sold for $2, with the 95 calls costing $0.60 creating a net credit of $200 per contract: (.95 + 2.00) – (.35 + .60) × 100. Thus, a total of five contracts bring in a net credit of

$1,000, which is also the maximum reward. The maximum risk is calculated by subtracting the net credit ($200) from the difference in strikes (95 – 90 = 5). This creates a maximum risk of $300: (5 – 2) × 100 = $300. If IBM were to close anywhere between $85 and $90 on expiration, the maximum profit of $200 per contract, or $1,000 (for five contracts), could be kept. The breakeven points were at $83 and $92 and are found by taking the net credit of $2 and subtracting it from the lower sold strike for the lower breakeven. The upper breakeven is found by adding the $2 credit to the higher sold option strike.

Notice how the risk graph (see Figure 10.6) shows limited reward and limited risk. The risk graph also points out that the maximum profit is impossible to achieve until expiration. This strategy rarely sees a

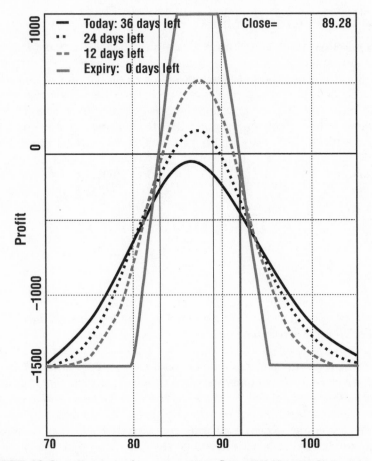

FIGURE 10.6 Risk Graph of Long Iron Butterfly on IBM (*Source:* Optionetics Platinum © 2004)

Long Iron Butterfly Case Study

Strategy: With the security trading at $89.28 a share on October 16, 2003, Long 5 November IBM 80 Puts @ 0.35, Short 5 November IBM 85 Puts @ 0.95, Short 5 November IBM 90 Calls @ 2, and Long 5 November IBM 95 Calls @ 0.60.

Market Opportunity: Expect stock to stay in narrow range through November expiration.

Maximum Profit: Limited to the net credit. In this case, $1,000: {5 × [(.95 + 2.00) − (.35 + .60)]} × 100.

Maximum Risk: Limited to difference in strikes minus the net credit. In this case, $1,500: 5 × [(5 − 2) × 100].

Lower Breakeven: Lower short strike minus the net credit. In this case, 83: (85 − 2).

Upper Breakeven: Higher short strike plus the net credit. In this case, 92: (90 + 2).

Margin: Minimal—just enough to cover the broker's risk.

trader get out with a profit at the beginning of the trade. This is because an iron butterfly benefits from time erosion. We aren't going to see as high a reward-to-risk ratio trading an iron butterfly, but our maximum profit is more likely to be achieved because of the wider maximum profit range.

IBM shares did indeed trade sideways through November expiration, closing at $88.63 on November 21. This left this trade with the maximum profit of $1,000. If the stock had closed above 95 or below 80, the maximum loss would have occurred.

CALENDAR SPREAD

A calendar spread is a trade that can be used when the trader expects a gradual or sideways move in the stock. Sometimes called the horizontal spread, it uses two options with the same strike prices and different expiration dates. It can be created with puts or calls. Generally, with the calendar spread, the option strategist is buying a longer-term option and selling a shorter-term option. Unlike the vertical spreads like bull call spreads, bear put spreads, and other trades that are directional in nature (i.e., they require the shares to move higher or lower), calendar spreads can be created when the strategist is neutral on the shares. Basically, in a neutral calendar spread, the trader wants the short-term option to decay at a faster rate than the long-term option. However, strategists can also create both bullish and bearish calendar spreads depending on their outlook for the shares.

Calendar Spread Mechanics

Let's consider an example of the calendar spread using XYZ at $50 a share in March. In this case, we expect the shares to stay at roughly the same levels or move modestly higher. Consequently, we decide to purchase a LEAPS long-term option and offset some of the cost of that option with the sale of a shorter-term option. In this case, we buy the XYZ 60 LEAPS at $4 and sell an XYZ 60 call with two months of life remaining at $1. The cost of the trade is $300 [(4 – 1) × 100 = $300], which is also the maximum risk associated with this trade. The maximum profit is unlimited once the short-term option expires. At that point, the trade is simply a long call.

Prior to the expiration of the short call, the maximum profit and breakeven will depend on a number of factors including volatility, the stock price, and the amount of time decay suffered by the long call. Basically, it is impossible to determine how much value the long call will gain or lose during the life of the short option. Options trading software, such as the Optionetics.com Platinum site, can help give a better sense of the risk, rewards, and breakevens associated with any particular calendar spread. For now, suffice it to say that the risk is limited to the net debit. In addition, time decay is not linear. That is, an option with 30 days until expiration will lose value more rapidly than an option with six months until expiration. Calendar spreads attempt to take advantage of the fact that short-term options suffer time decay at a faster rate than long-term options.

Computing breakeven prices for complex trades requires the use of computer software. To understand why, let's consider a bullish calendar spread. In this case, we are buying a longer-term call and selling a shorter-term call with the same strike price. The trade is placed for a debit and closed for a credit. Ideally, the short-term call will expire worthless, but the longer-term call will retain most or all of its value. In that case, we can sell another call or close the trade at a profit. The breakeven price for the calendar spread will depend on the value of the long call when the short option expires. The value of the long call will, in turn, depend on several factors. Say, for example, the stock price falls and the short call expires worthless. The long-term option might still have value, but we don't know exactly how much value because of changes in implied volatility and time decay. To break even, the value of the long call when it is sold must be equal to the debit paid for the calendar spread. If the call is worth more, and the spread is closed when the short option expires, the trade yields a profit. However, it is impossible to calculate the exact value of the long call, and therefore, the breakeven when the short call expires. It is possible to get an idea or rough guess, but it is better to use computer software to plot the risk graph and see where the potential breakeven points might be.

Exiting the Position

The exit strategy for the calendar spread is extremely important in determining the trade's success. Specifically, if the shares remain range-bound and the short call expires worthless, the strategist must make a decision: (1) to exit the position, (2) to sell another call, or (3) to roll up to another strike price. Generally, if the shares are stable as anticipated, the best approach is to sell another shorter-term option. In our example, the long call has 18 months until expiration and was purchased for $4. A call with three months can be sold for $1. If, over the course of 18 months, calls with three months until expiration can be sold for $1 five times, the credit received from selling those calls totals $5. The cost of the long option is only $4. Therefore, the trade yields a $1 profit on a $4 investment, or 25 percent over the course of 15 months. Furthermore, after 15 months, the long call, which has been fully paid for, will still have three months of life remaining and can offer upside rewards in case XYZ marches higher.

Sometimes, however, it is not possible to sell another call. Instead, the share price jumps too high and the risk profile associated with selling another call is not attractive. In that case, the strategist might simply want to close the position by selling the long call. Or another calendar spread can be established on the same shares by rolling up to a higher strike price. In that case, the strategist closes the long call, buys back another long call with a higher strike price, and then sells a shorter-term call with the same strike price. If the shares move against the strategist during the life of the short call, the best approach is probably to exit the entire position once the short call has little time value remaining. If the shares jump higher and the long call has significant time value, it is better to close the position rather than face assignment or buy back the short option. If assigned and forced to exercise the long option to cover the assignment, the strategist will lose the time value still left in the long contract.

Calendar Spread

Strategy: Sell a short-term option and buy a long-term option using ATM options with as small a net debit as possible (all calls or all puts). Calls can be used for a more bullish bias and puts can be used for a more bearish bias.

Market Opportunity: Look for a range-bound market that is expected to stay between the breakeven points for an extended period of time.

Maximum Risk: Limited to the net debit paid. (Long premium – short premium) × 100.

Maximum Profit: Limited. Use software for accurate calculation.

Breakeven: Use software for accurate calculation.

Margin: Amount subject to broker's discretion.

Calendar Spread Case Study

Shares of Johnson & Johnson (JNJ) are trading for $51.75 during the month of February and the strategist expects the shares to make a move higher. A bullish calendar spread is created by purchasing a JNJ January 2005 60 call for $4 and selling an April 2003 60 call for $1. The trade costs $300: $(4 - 1) \times 100 = \$300$. Therefore, the initial debit in the account is equal to $300. The debit is also the maximum risk associated with this trade. As the price of the shares rises, the trade makes money.

As we can see from the risk graph in Figure 10.7, the maximum profit occurs when the shares reach $60 at April expiration and is equal to roughly $570. At that point, the short call expires worthless, but the long

Calendar Spread Case Study

Market Opportunity: JNJ is expected to trade moderately higher. With shares near $51.75 in February, the strategist sells an April 60 call for $1 and buys a January 2005 60 call for $4.

Maximum Risk: Limited to the net debit. In this case, $300: $(4 - 1) \times 100$.

Maximum Profit: Limited due to the fact that the short call is subject to assignment risk if shares rise above $60.

Upside Breakeven: Use options software to calculate. In this case, roughly $47.

Downside Breakeven: Use options software to calculate. In this case, same as upside breakeven.

Margin: Theoretically, zero. The short call is covered by the long call. Check with your broker.

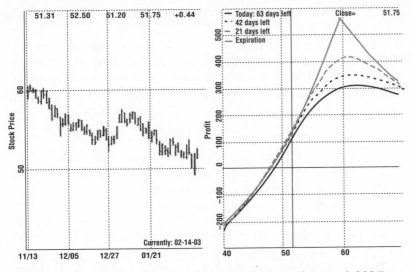

FIGURE 10.7 JNJ Calendar Spread (*Source:* Optionetics Platinum © 2004)

call has appreciated in value and can be sold at a profit. If the strategist elects to hold the long call instead, another calendar spread can be established by selling a shorter-term call. At that point, the risk curve will probably look different. The downside breakeven is 46.80. Below that, the trade begins to lose money. An options trading software program like Platinum can be used to compute the maximum gain and the breakevens.

In this case study, the stock did indeed move in the desired direction. By April expiration, shares of JNJ fetched $55.35 a share. At that point, the short call would expire worthless and the strategist would keep the entire premium received for selling the April 60 call. Meanwhile, the January 60 call has not only retained all of its value, but it is currently offered for $5.10. Therefore, the strategist's earnings are $210 of profit per spread ($1 received for the premium and $1.10 profit for the appreciation in the January 60 call), for a five-month 70 percent gain. On the other hand, the strategist could also hold the long call and sell another short-term call with the same or higher strike price. If the strategist chooses to sell a call with a higher strike price, the position becomes a diagonal spread, which is also our next subject of discussion.

VOLATILITY SKEWS REVISITED

As we have seen, calendar spreads are trades that involve the purchase and sale of options on the same shares, with the same strike price, but different expiration dates. One thing to look for when searching for calendar spreads is a volatility skew. A volatility skew is created when one or more options have a seeable difference in implied volatility (IV). Implied volatility, as mentioned in Chapter 9, is a factor that contributes to an option's price. All else being equal, an option with high IV is more expensive than an option with low IV. In addition, two options on the same underlying asset can sometimes have dramatically different levels of volatility. When this happens, it is known as volatility skew. Looking at various quotes of options and looking at each option's IV will reveal potential volatility skews.

As previously mentioned, there are two types of volatility skews present in today's markets: volatility price skews and volatility time skews. Volatility price skews exist when two options with the same expiration date have very different levels of implied volatility. For example, if XYZ is trading at $50, the XYZ March 55 call has an implied volatility of 80 percent and the XYZ March 60 call has implied volatility of only 40 percent. Sometimes this happens when there is strong demand for short-term at-the-money or near-the-money call (due to takeover rumors, an earnings report, management shake-up, etc.). In that case, the 55 calls have become much more expensive (higher IV) than the 60 calls.

Calendar spreads can be used to take advantage of the other type of volatility skew: time skews. This type of skew exists when two options on the same underlying asset with the same strike prices have different levels of implied volatility. For example, in January, the XYZ April 60 call has implied volatility of 80 percent and the XYZ December 60 call has implied volatility of only 40 percent. In that case, the short-term option is more expensive relative to the long-term call and the calendar spread becomes more appealing (although the premium will still be greater for the long call because there will be less time value in the short-term option). The idea is for the strategist to get more premiums for selling the option with the higher IV than he or she is paying for the option with the low IV.

DIAGONAL SPREAD

There are a significant number of different ways to structure diagonal spreads. Diagonal spreads include two options with different expiration dates and different strike prices. For example, buying a longer-term call option and selling a shorter-term call option with a higher strike price can be a way of betting on a rise in the price of the shares. The idea would be for the shares to rise and cause the long-term option to increase in value. The short-term call option, which is sold to offset the cost of the long-term option, will also increase in value. But if the shares stay below the short strike price, the short option expires worthless. In this type of trade, the longer-term option should have some intrinsic or real value, but the option sold should have only about 30 days or so to expiration and consist of nothing but time value. This strategy profits if the shares make a gradual rise. Similar diagonal spreads can be structured with puts and generate profits if the shares fall.

Diagonal Spread Example

Diagonal spreads are a common way of taking advantage of volatility skews. Let's consider an example to see how. The rumor mill is churning and there is talk that XYZ is going to be the subject of a hostile takeover. With shares trading at $50 a share, the rumor is that XYZ will be purchased for $60 a share. At this point, you have done a lot of research on XYZ and you believe that the rumor is bogus. Furthermore, you notice that the talk has created a time volatility skew between the short-term and the long-term options. In this case, the March 55 call has seen a jump in implied volatility to 100 percent and trades for $1.50. Meanwhile, the December contract has seen no change in IV and the December 50 call currently trades for $6.50.

To take advantage of this skew, the strategist sets up a diagonal spread by purchasing the December 50 call and selling the March 55 call. The idea is for the short call to lose value due to time decay and a drop in implied volatility. Meanwhile, the long-term option will retain most of its value. The cost of the trade is $5 a contract or $500: (6.50 − 1.50) × 100. This is the maximum risk associated with the trade.

There are no hard-and-fast rules for computing breakevens and maximum profits for diagonal spreads. In our example, the ideal scenario would be for the short option to lose value much faster than the long option due to both falling IV and time decay. However, the term *diagonal spread* refers to any trade that combines different strike prices and different expiration dates. Therefore, the potential combinations are vast. However, it is possible to compute the breakevens, risks, and rewards for any trade using options trading software like the one available at Optionetics.com Platinum site.

Exiting the Position

The same principles that were discussed with respect to calendar spreads apply to diagonal spreads. If the shares move dramatically higher, the short option has a greater chance of assignment when it moves in-the-money and time decay diminishes to a quarter of a point or less. If the long call has significant time value, it is better to close the position than face assignment. If assigned and forced to exercise the long option, the strategist will lose the time value still left in the long contract. If the short option expires as antic-ipated, the strategist can close the position, roll up to a higher strike price, or simply hold on to the long call.

In the previous example, a diagonal spread was designed to take ad-vantage of a volatility skew. Once the skew has disappeared and the ob-jective is achieved the strategist can exit the position by selling the long call and buying back the short call. However, it generally takes a relatively large volatility skew in order to profit from changes in implied volatility alone. Therefore, strategists generally use time decay to their advantage as well, which, as we saw earlier, impacts shorter-term options to a greater degree than longer-term options.

In the example, the idea was to take in the expensive (high IV) premium of the short option and benefit from time decay. As a result, once the short option expires, there is no reason to keep the long option. Thus, selling an identical call can close the position. If the shares fall sharply, the trade will lose value and the strategist wants to begin thinking about mitigating losses. A sharp move higher could result in assignment on the short call as expira-tion approaches. Again, it is better to close the position than face assign-ment because the long option will still have considerable time value, which would be lost if the long call is exercised to cover the short call.

Breakeven Conundrums

While the risk to the diagonal spread is easy to compute because it is lim-ited to the net debit paid, and the reward is known in advance because it is unlimited after the short-term option expires, the breakeven point is a bit more difficult to calculate. Often, traders first look at the breakeven price when the short-term option expires. However, at that point in time, the longer-term option will probably still have value. In addition, the value of that long option will be difficult to predict ahead of time due to changes in implied volatility and the impact of time decay.

For example, assume we set up a diagonal spread on XYZ when it is trading for $53 a share. We buy a long-term call option with a strike price of 60 for $3 and sell a shorter-term call with a strike price of 55 for $1. The net debit is $200. Now, let's assume that at the first expiration the stock is trading for $54.75 and the short-term option expires worthless. How much is the longer-term option worth, and what is the breakeven? It is difficult to predict what the longer-term option will be worth because of the im-pact of time decay and changes in implied volatility. So, it is impossible to know the breakeven when the short-term option expires because it will also depend on the future value of the longer-term option. If the longer-term option has appreciated enough to cover the cost of the debit when the short-term option expires, the trade breaks even.

Diagonal Spread

Strategy: Sell a short-term option and buy a long-term option with different strikes and as small a net debit as possible (use all calls or all puts).

- A **bullish diagonal spread** employs a long call with a distant expiration and a lower strike price, along with a short call with a closer expiration date and higher strike price.

- A **bearish diagonal spread** combines a long put with a distant expiration date and a higher strike price along with a short put with a closer expiration date and lower strike price.

Market Opportunity: Look for a range-bound market exhibiting a time volatility skew that is expected to stay between the breakeven points for an extended period of time.

Maximum Risk: Limited to the net debit paid. (Long premium – short premium) × 100.

Maximum Profit/Upside Breakeven/Downside Breakeven: Use options software for accurate calculation, such as the Platinum site at Optionetics.com.

After the short-term option expires, the breakeven shifts to the expiration of the longer-term option. In this case, the breakeven price becomes the debit plus the strike price, or $62 a share. However, the breakeven will change again if we take follow-up action like selling another short-term call option.

In sum, it is difficult to know exactly what the breakeven stock price will be for the diagonal or calendar spread because we are dealing with options with different expiration dates. In these situations, the best approach is to use options-trading software to get a general idea. However, even software is not perfect because it can't predict future changes in an option's future implied volatility. The best we can do is to calculate an approximate breakeven and then plan our exit strategies accordingly.

Diagonal Spread Case Study

For the diagonal spread case study, let's consider Johnson & Johnson (JNJ) trading for $51.75 a share in early February 2003. The strategist sets up a diagonal spread by purchasing a January 2005 50 call for $6.50 and selling the March 2003 55 call for $1.50. Again, there is time volatility skew when purchasing these contracts and the long call has lower IV compared to the short call. This type of time volatility skew is a favorable characteristic when setting up this type of diagonal spread.

The risk, profit, and breakevens for this trade are relatively straight-forward. The cost of the trade is $500 and is equal to the premium of the long call minus the short call times 100: [(6.50 − 1.50) × 100]. The debit is also the maximum risk associated with this trade. Profits arise if the shares move higher. The maximum profit during the life of the short call equals $374.45. After the short call expires, the position is no longer a di-agonal spread. It is simply a long call. At that point, the strategist can sell, exercise, or hold the long call.

The risk curve of the diagonal spread is plotted in Figure 10.8. It is similar to the calendar spread. In both cases, the strategist wants the share price to move higher, but not rise above the strike price of the short call. A move lower will result in losses. If the stock rises and equals $55 a share at the March expiration, the short call will expire worthless. The strategist will keep the premium received from selling the short call and will have a profit from an increase in the value of the call. At that point, he or she can sell, exercise, or hold the long call. If the trader elects to hold the long call, another diagonal spread can be established by selling another shorter-term call.

So, what happened with our JNJ calendar spread? Shortly after the trade was initiated, shares rallied sharply and, in the week before expiration, the stock was well above the March 55 strike price. At that point, we would be forced into follow-up action because assignment was all but assured. For example, the week just before expiration, the stock was making its move above $55 a share. Seeing this, the strategist would probably

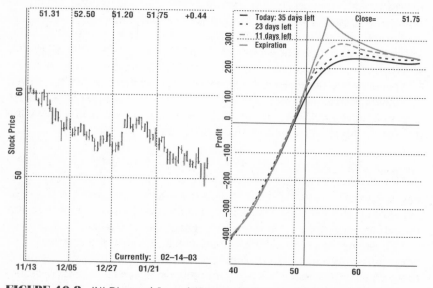

FIGURE 10.8 JNJ Diagonal Spread (*Source:* Optionetics Platinum © 2004)

want to buy the short-term call to close because assignment would force him or her either to buy the stock in the market for more than $55 a share and sell it at the strike price or cover with the long call, which still has a significant amount of time value.

So, facing the risk of assignment, the position is closed when the stock moves toward the strike price of the short call. The Friday before expiration, the January 2004 50 call was quoted for $8.50 bid. Therefore, the strategist would book a $2 profit on that side of the trade. At the same time, he or she would want to buy to close the short March 55 call, which was offered for $1. That side of the trade would yield a 50-cent profit. Therefore, taken together, the strategist makes $250 on a $500 investment. Time decay has indeed worked in this trade's favor.

The reason I like trading diagonal spreads is that they lend themselves to numerous position adjustments during the trade process. For example, say we initiate a diagonal calendar spread on stock XYZ by purchasing a longer-term ITM call option and writing a shorter-term slightly OTM call option. This position can be put on at a lower cost than the traditional covered call and with a subsequent lower risk. It also has a higher-percentage return than a covered call but still profits from time decay. However, the real advantage of the position in my view is its inherent flexibility. Consider just some of the adjustments afforded the options trader with the diagonal spread position:

- *XYZ is below the strike price that we initially sold:* Let it expire worthless and realize the short-term call premium as a profit. We can then exit the long position, or sell another short-term call for the next month out.
- *XYZ is near or above the short strike price by the expiration date:* Buy the short option back and sell back the long position to close the trade, or sell the next month calls of the same strike or even a higher strike if the underlying stock has an upward directional bias.
- *XYZ is deep in-the-money:* Exit the entire position and rebracket the diagonal spread at the new trading range.

In addition, we can convert from a diagonal spread to a horizontal if more than 60 days are still left until expiration. If we are going into the final 30 days of the long position we can transform this position into a vertical spread. Even though our XYZ example was created using calls, the trader can also construct this position using put options.

These are just a handful of adjustments afforded the options trader when managing a diagonal spread. I encourage you to test and paper trade these types of positions. The adjustment possibilities are virtually endless and for my money that makes for a terrific options strategy.

Diagonal Spread Case Study

Strategy: With JNJ trading for $51.75 in February, set up a bullish diagonal spread by selling a March 55 call at $1.50 and buying a January 50 call at $6.50.

Market Opportunity: Anticipate a short-term move higher in a trending stock. Look for time volatility skew to increase odds of success.

Maximum Risk: Limited to the net debit. In this case, the risk is losing the premium paid for the long call ($650) minus the premium received for the short put ($150) for a maximum risk of $500.

Maximum Profit: During the life of the short option, the profit is limited due to the possibility of assignment. In this case, above $55 a share, the strategist will be forced to engage in follow-up action.

Upside Breakeven: No set formula. Will vary based on IV assumptions.

Downside Breakeven: No set formula. Will vary based on IV assumptions.

Margin: Amount subject to broker's discretion.

COLLAR SPREAD

Collar spreads are usually one of the first combination option trades a person is exposed to after getting a grasp of what basic puts and calls are all about. They are usually presented as appreciating collars or protective collars. However, not much mention is given to the inherent flexibility of this position and how, as a trader, if you want to put just a little bit more effort into the trade, you can increase your returns.

There are two types of collar trades: the protective collar and the appreciating collar. The protective collar is chosen when a person already owns the stock and has a bearish outlook but still wants to hold the stock. In this case, the trader would purchase an at-the-money put and at the same time sell an at-the-money call to finance that put. This essentially locks in the current price and protects the trade from losses until such time when the bearish scenario changes.

The other type of collar is an appreciating collar. This is the one where you can make money and indeed trade dynamically if you desire. The appreciating collar involves buying stock and for every 100 shares of stock purchased buying an at-the-money put and selling an out-of-the-money call to finance the put. The key to this strategy is selecting a stock that has been in the news, whose volatility is high, and for which a type skew exists (a type skew is when a volatility skew exists between the put purchased and the call sold). By doing so you will find that your risk will be reduced to virtually nothing.

Now what if the stock you have chosen gets on a nice steady run and is at or goes above your appreciating collar strike price? If it is at the strike price, you can continue to hold and eventually let the calls and puts expire worthless, and then sell the stock to take your profits. If it is above the strike price, the calls you sold will carry away the stock and the put expires worthless; you garner the maximum profit potential of this position.

To establish a collar, many strategists buy (or already own) the actual shares, buy an at-the-money LEAPS put, and sell an out-of-the-money LEAPS call. Doing so combines the covered call with a protective put. In theory, the call and put that are equidistant from the share price should carry the same premium. So, if you own a stock at $50 a share and want to protect the downside risk, you could buy a put. However, the put will cost money and the premium would be deducted from your account. Another option is to buy a 45 put and sell a 55 call. The sale of the call will reduce the cost of the purchase of the put.

Collar Mechanics

Let's consider an example of a collar using XYZ. During the month of February, XYZ is trading for $50 a share and an investor has been holding the shares for some time. She doesn't expect much movement in the stock, but believes that there is a 10 percent chance that the price will decline during the next four months and wants to hedge her exposure to all stocks—including XYZ. Therefore, with the stock trading for $50, she buys an August 45 put with six months left until expiration and sells an August 55 call. The options are both five points out-of-the-money (OTM).

Since both the put and the call are five points OTM, they have similar premiums. In this case, each option trades for roughly $3. Luckily, with the stock trading for $50, the strategist is able to buy the put and sell the call at the same price. The cost of the trade is therefore zero because the shares are already held in the portfolio and the cost of the put is offset by the sale of the call. The risk to this trade is to the downside, but is limited to the strike price of the put. The maximum risk is equal to the initial stock price minus the strike price of the put plus the net debit (or minus the net credit). In this case, the maximum risk equals $500: $[(50 - 45) + (3 - 3)] \times 100 = \$500$. The maximum risk occurs if the stock price falls to or below the lower strike price (i.e., $45). Therefore, this strategy offers the trader a limited risk approach that makes money in either direction. The risk graph of this trade is shown in Figure 10.9.

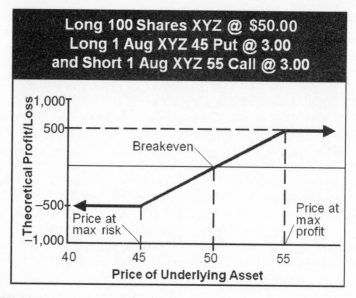

FIGURE 10.9 Collar Spread Risk Graph

While there is limited risk associated with the collar, there is also limited reward. If the stock price moves higher, the position begins to make money. However, the maximum reward is capped by the strike price of the call. If the stock price moves above the strike price of the call, the chances of assignment will increase. In other words, there is a greater probability that the stock will be called away at $55 a share. At that point, the maximum profit is realized. Namely, the higher strike price minus the stock price minus the debit (or plus the credit) is the maximum gain associated with the collar. In this case, it equals $500: $(55 - 50 + 0) \times 100 = \$500$. The maximum profit levels off at $55 a share, which is the point that assignment becomes likely. The breakeven is equal to the stock price plus the net debit (or minus the net credit). In this case, it is simply the price of the stock at the time the collar was established, or $50 a share.

What are the risks associated with buying a put and selling a call on shares that we already own? First, the stock could move above $55, requiring us to sell it at a price lower than the current value; and second, the stock could still trade as low as $45 without seeing any profit from the put. However, this is also the case if we just held the stock as well. Much like catastrophe insurance, the idea behind a collar is that we don't want to be stuck holding a stock as it falls into a tailspin. The collar is a form of disaster insurance.

Exiting the Position

While a collar can be tailored to make money when shares move higher, it is normally used for protection. It does not require a lot of attention. If the shares shoot higher, the stock will probably be called (due to assignment) when the time premium has fallen to a quarter of a point or less. Therefore, if the price of the stock has risen above the strike price of the short call and the strategist does not want to lose the shares, it is better to close the short call by buying it back. If not, the call will be assigned and the trader will make the profit equal to the difference between the exercise price and the original purchase price of the stock minus any debits (or plus any credits). The put, on the other hand, will protect the stock if it falls. If the stock drops sharply, the strategist will want to buy back the long call and then exercise the put. If the short call is not closed and the put is exercised, the strategist will be naked a short call. Although it will be deep OTM, it will still expose the trader to risk. Therefore, it is better to buy back the short call and close the entire position. If the stock stay in between the two strike prices, the trader can roll the position out using longer-term options or do nothing and let both options expire worthless.

In addition, if you can monitor your collar trade a bit more closely, you can significantly enhance your returns when the stock in your appreciating collar rallies to your strike price. How can you do this? By rebracketing your collar. To rebracket the trader first would sell the put and buy back the call, then would recollar or create a new collar by buying a new at-the-money put and selling a new out-of-the-money call to create a new appreciating collar at the higher strike price. This is far better than just sitting and waiting for everything to expire after you already have capped your profits.

Let's look at a quick example for stock XYZ. We buy 100 shares of the stock at $50. We then buy the 50 put and sell the 55 call with a year still to go before expiration. Just a few months into the trade, the stock is trading at the $55 level. Now to lock in profits and pursue further appreciation in the stock, we would sell the 50 put and buy back the 55 call. We then would create another appreciating collar by buying the 55 put and selling the 60 call—locking in profits as well as being able to participate in further gains. This can be done over and over again throughout the year as the stock continues to climb. This technique gets around the capped profits limitation the standard appreciating collar possesses.

If you have the time, the dynamic trading of collars might be something of interest. However, the traditional collar is still an excellent low- or no-risk strategy, which, if placed correctly, offers an excellent return. In fact, the return is enhanced even more if done in a margin account.

Collar Spread

Strategy: Buy (or already own) 100 shares of stock, buy an OTM put, and sell an OTM call. Try to offset the cost of the put with the premium from the short call.

Market Opportunity: Protect a stock holding from a sharp drop for a specific period of time and still participate in a modest increase in the stock price.

Maximum Risk: [Initial stock price – put strike price + net debit (or – net credit)] × 100.

Maximum Profit: [(Call strike price – initial stock price) – net debit (or + net credit)] × 100.

Breakeven: Initial stock price + [(put premium – call premium) ÷ number of shares (100)].

Collar Case Study

As we have seen, collars are combination stock and option strategies that have limited risk and limited reward. With this strategy, the strategist buys (or owns) the shares, sells out-of-the-money calls, and buys out-of-the-money puts. It is a covered call and a protective put (which involves the purchase of shares and the purchase of puts) wrapped into one. The idea is to have the downside protection similar to the put, but to offset the cost of that put with the sale of a call. As with the covered call, however, the sale of a call will limit the reward associated with owning the stock. If the stock price moves higher, the short call will probably be assigned and the strategist must sell the shares at the short strike price. This strategy is generally implemented when the trader is moderately bullish or neutral on a stock, but wants protection in case of a bearish move to the downside.

Let's consider a collar example using shares of American International Group (AIG), which are trading for $50.18 during the month of February 2003. In this example, the strategist buys 100 shares, buys an August 45 put for $3.30, and sells the August 55 call for $3. The sale of the call nearly offsets the purchase of the put and the debit is only $0.30, or $30 a contract. One hundred shares of stock cost $5,018 and the total trade results in a debit equal to the cost of the shares plus the net debit or $5,048: ($30 + $5,018). The maximum risk is limited also due to the protective put. No matter what, until the options expire, the stock can be sold for the strike price of the put, or $4,500 per 100 shares. The upside profit is also limited. If the stock price moves above $55, the call will probably be exercised. In that case, the stock is sold for

$5,500 per 100 shares and the trader makes a profit. The breakevens are equal to the total cost of the trade per share. In this case, the breakeven occurs at 50.48.

The risk curve in Figure 10.10 shows the profit/loss possibilities for the collar. Notice that the trade generates profits if the stock moves higher, but the gains are limited by the strike price of the call. At $55 a share, profits level off. In between the breakeven and the upper strike price, the trade is profitable. On the other hand, if the stock falls below $50.48, the trade begins to lose money. The losses are capped by the lower strike price of the put, or $45 a share. Therefore, the collar carries some upside rewards, but also limited risks. For that reason, many traders view the strategy as a form of low-cost disaster insurance.

So, what happened to our AIG August 45 put/55 call collar? Well, three months later, in mid-May 2003, shares of AIG rose to $56 a share. At that point, the maximum gain had been recorded and, if the call had not been assigned (which it probably would not have due to the remaining time value), the position could be closed at a profit. The August 45 put is sold at a loss for the bid price of 60 cents a share. The August 55 call is bought back (buy to close) for the offering price of $3 and AIG is closed for $56. As a result, the call is a wash. The put results in a $270 loss and the stock is sold at $5.82 a share for a $582 profit. The total profit on the trade is $312: ($582 − $270). Excluding commissions, this collar generated a three-month 6.2 percent profit.

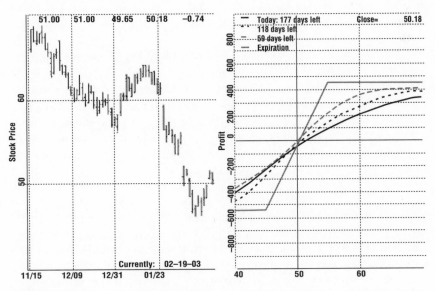

FIGURE 10.10 AIG Collar Spread (*Source:* Optionetics Platinum © 2004)

Collar Case Study

Strategy: With AIG stock trading at $50.18 a share in February 2003, buy one August AIG 45 put at $3.30, sell one August AIG 55 call at $3, and buy 100 shares of AIG stock. Total cost of trade is $5,048.

Market Opportunity: The stock is expected to make a modestly bullish move higher before expiration.

Maximum Risk: Limited to initial stock price − (put strike price × 100) + net debit. In this case, $548: [5,018 − (45 × 100)] + 30.

Maximum Profit: Limited as the stock price moves higher as the short call may be assigned. [(Call strike price − initial stock price) − net debit] × 100. In this example, the maximum profit is $452: [(55 − 50.18) − .30] × 100. However, the final profit is $312.

Breakeven: Initial stock price + [(put premium − call premium) ÷ number of shares]. In this case, 50.48: 50.18 + [(330 − 300) ÷ 100].

Margin: Check with broker.

STRATEGY ROAD MAPS

Long Butterfly Spread Road Map

In order to place a long butterfly spread, the following 14 guidelines should be observed:

1. Look for a sideways-moving market that is expected to remain within the breakeven points.
2. Check to see if this stock has options available.
3. Review options premiums per expiration dates and strike prices. Make sure you have enough option premium to make the trade worthwhile, especially considering the commission fees of a multicontract spread.
4. Investigate implied volatility values to see if the options are overpriced or undervalued.
5. Explore past price trends and liquidity by reviewing price and volume charts over the past year.
6. A long butterfly is composed of all calls or all puts with the same expiration. Buy a lower strike option (at the support level), sell two higher strike options (at the equilibrium point), and buy one even higher option (at the resistance level).

7. Look at options with 45 days or less until expiration.

8. Determine the best possible spread to place by calculating:

   - **Limited Risk:** Limited to the net debit paid on the options.
   - **Limited Reward:** Difference between highest strike and the short strike minus the net debit. Maximum profit is realized when the stock price equals the short strike.
   - **Upside Breakeven:** Highest strike price – net debit paid.
   - **Downside Breakeven:** Lowest strike price + net debit paid.
   - **Return on Investment:** Reward/risk ratio.

9. Create a risk profile of the most promising option combination and graphically determine the trade's feasibility. The risk curve of a long butterfly shows a limited reward inside the breakevens and limited risk outside the breakevens.

10. Write down the trade in your trader's journal before placing the trade with your broker to minimize mistakes made in placing the order and to keep a record of the trade.

11. Make an exit plan before you place the trade. For example, if the stock begins to move outside the breakevens, consider cutting your losses. You want the stock price to stay within a range so that you get to keep most or all of the credit.

12. Contact your broker to buy and sell the chosen options. Place the trade as a limit order so that you limit the net debit of the trade.

13. Watch the market closely as it fluctuates. The profit on this strategy is limited—a loss occurs if the underlying stock closes outside the breakeven points.

14. Choose an exit strategy based on the price movement of the underlying stock:

   - *XYZ falls below the downside breakeven:* Let your position expire worthless. The cost for this trade will be the net premium paid (plus commissions).
   - *XYZ falls within the downside and upside breakevens:* This is the range of profitability. Ideally you want to sell the long options and let the short options expire worthless. The maximum profit occurs when the underlying stock is equal to the short strike price.
   - *XYZ rises above the upside breakeven:* Either exit the trade or if you are assigned the short options, exercise your long options to counter.

Long Condor Spread Road Map

In order to place a long condor spread, the following 14 guidelines should be observed:

1. Look for a sideways-moving market that is expected to remain within the breakeven points.
2. Check to see if this stock has options available.
3. Review options premiums per expiration dates and strike prices. Make sure you have enough option premium to make the trade worthwhile, especially considering the commission fees of a multi-contract spread.
4. Investigate implied volatility values to see if the options are over-priced or undervalued.
5. Explore past price trends and liquidity by reviewing price and volume charts over the past year.
6. A long condor is composed of all calls or all puts with the same expiration. Buy a lower strike option (at the support level), sell one higher strike option, sell a higher strike option, and buy one even higher option (at the resistance level).
7. Look at options with 45 days or less until expiration.
8. Determine the best possible spread to place by calculating:

   - **Limited Risk:** Limited to the net debit when the position is placed.
   - **Limited Reward:** Difference in strike prices minus the net debit × 100. The profit range is between the breakevens.
   - **Upside Breakeven:** Highest strike price – net debit paid.
   - **Downside Breakeven:** Lowest strike price + net debit paid.
   - **Return on Investment:** Reward/risk ratio.

9. Create a risk profile of the most promising option combination and graphically determine the trade's feasibility. The risk curve of a long condor is similar to the long iron butterfly; the limited profit zone exists between the breakevens and the limited risk occurs outside of the breakevens, as shown in Figure 10.3.
10. Write down the trade in your trader's journal before placing the trade with your broker to minimize mistakes made in placing the order and to keep a record of the trade.
11. Make an exit plan before you place the trade. For example, if the stock begins to move outside the breakevens, consider cutting your

losses. You want the stock price to stay within a range so that you get to keep most or all of the credit.

12. Contact your broker to buy and sell the chosen options. Place the trade as a limit order so that you limit the net debit of the trade.

13. Watch the market closely as it fluctuates. The profit on this strategy is limited—a loss occurs if the underlying stock closes outside the breakeven points.

14. Choose an exit strategy based on the price movement of the underlying stock:

- *XYZ falls below the downside breakeven:* This is in the maximum risk range. Let the options expire worthless.
- *XYZ falls within the downside and upside breakevens:* This is your profit zone with maximum profit being at the short strikes.
- *XYZ rises above the upside breakeven:* You will need to close out the position to ensure you are not assigned.

Long Iron Butterfly Spread Road Map

In order to place a long iron butterfly spread, the following 14 guidelines should be observed:

1. Look for a sideways-moving market that is expected to remain within the breakeven points.

2. Check to see if this stock has options available.

3. Review options premiums per expiration dates and strike prices. Make sure you have enough option premium to make the trade worthwhile, especially considering the commission fees of a multicontract spread.

4. Investigate implied volatility values to see if the options are overpriced or undervalued.

5. Explore past price trends and liquidity by reviewing price and volume charts over the past year.

6. A long iron butterfly is composed of four options with the same expiration. Buy one higher strike OTM call (at the resistance level), sell one ATM lower strike call, sell one slightly OTM lower strike put, and buy one even lower strike put (at the support level).

7. Look at options with 45 days or less until expiration.

8. Determine the best possible spread to place by calculating:

- **Limited Risk:** The difference in strikes minus the net credit received for placing the position. This is usually a small value and is the reason why this trade is attractive. Realize that commissions are not calculated in this example and can really eat into the profits.
- **Limited Reward:** Net credit received on placing the position. The profit range occurs between the breakevens.
- **Upside Breakeven:** Middle short call strike price + net credit.
- **Downside Breakeven:** Middle short put strike price – net credit.
- **Return on Investment:** Reward/risk ratio.

9. Create a risk profile of the most promising option combination and graphically determine the trade's feasibility. A risk graph for a long iron butterfly is very similar to the risk curve of a long butterfly, once again showing a limited reward inside of the breakevens and a limited risk outside the breakevens.

10. Write down the trade in your trader's journal before placing the trade with your broker to minimize mistakes made in placing the order and to keep a record of the trade.

11. Make an exit plan before you place the trade. For example, if the stock begins to move outside the breakevens, consider cutting your losses. You want the stock to stay within a range so that you get to keep most or all of the credit.

12. Contact your broker to buy and sell the chosen options. Place the trade as a limit order so that you limit the net debit of the trade.

13. Watch the market closely as it fluctuates. The profit on this strategy is limited—a loss occurs if the underlying stock closes outside the breakeven points.

14. Choose an exit strategy based on the price movement of the underlying stock:

- *XYZ falls below the downside breakeven:* You should exit the trade to make sure you are not assigned the put side of your position. The calls can expire worthless. You're in the maximum risk range.
- *XYZ falls within the downside and upside breakevens:* This is the profit range and ideally the position expires near the short strike prices.

- *XYZ rises above the upside breakeven:* Similar to the lower breakeven, you should exit the trade to make sure you are not assigned the call side of your position. The put options can expire worthless.

Calendar Spread Road Map

In order to place a calendar spread, the following 14 guidelines should be observed:

1. Look for a market that has been range-trading for at least three months and is expected to remain within a range for an extended period of time. A dramatic move by the underlying shares in either direction could unbalance the spread, causing it to widen.
2. Check to see if this stock has options available.
3. Review options premiums per expiration dates and strike prices.
4. Investigate implied volatility to look for a time volatility skew where short-term options have a higher volatility (causing you to receive higher premiums) than the longer-term options (the ones you will purchase).
5. Explore past price trends and liquidity by reviewing price and volume charts over the past year.
6. A calendar spread can be bullish or bearish in bias.

   - A slightly **bullish calendar spread** employs an ATM long call with a distant expiration date and an ATM short call with a closer expiration date.
   - A slightly **bearish calendar spread** combines an ATM long put with a distant expiration date and an ATM short put with a closer expiration date.

7. Look at a variety of options with at least 90 days until expiration for the long option and less than 45 days for the short option.
8. Determine the best possible spread to place by calculating:

   - **Limited Risk:** Limited to the net debit when the position is placed. If you replay the long leg, then your limited risk continues to decrease because you take in additional credit for replaying this strategy.
   - **Limited Reward:** Use options software for calculation. The reward is limited but the exact maximum potential varies based on

several factors including volatility, expiration months, and stock prices.

- **Breakevens:** Since this is a more complex trade you must have an options software package available to calculate your maximum risk, breakevens, and your return on investment. The Platinum site at Optionetics.com provides this service.

9. Create a risk profile of the most promising option combination and graphically determine the trade's feasibility. A calendar spread has limited risk and limited reward. Since it is a complicated strategy, a computerized risk graph is necessary to determine the needed variables of maximum profit and breakevens.

10. Write the trade in your trader's journal before placing the trade with your broker to minimize mistakes made in placing the order and to keep a record of the trade.

11. Make an exit plan before establishing a calendar spread. If the stock makes a dramatic move in the wrong direction, consider cutting your losses rather than hoping for a turnaround. If the stock goes through the short option's strike price sooner than expected, close the trade to avoid assignment. Ideally, the stock will make a gradual move in the appropriate direction and the short option will expire worthless. Then another short option can be sold against the long option or the trade can be closed for a profit.

12. Contact your broker to buy and sell the chosen options. Place the trade as a limit order so that you limit the net debit of the trade.

13. Watch the market closely as it fluctuates. The profit on this strategy is limited—a loss occurs if the underlying stock makes a dramatic move higher or lower.

14. Choose an exit strategy based on the price movement of the underlying stock and the effects of changes in implied volatility on the prices of the options.

For a bearish calendar spread:

- *The underlying stock falls sharply to the downside:* Both puts would increase in value one-for-one so they would offset each other. The most you would lose is the net debit.

- *The underlying stock stays within a trading range:* If the shares fall within the desired range, you will make a profit. The largest profit potential occurs if the shares expire at the ATM strike price. You can then sell another short-term put option.

- *The underlying stock makes a significant move higher:* Both puts would expire worthless and you would lose the premium paid.

For a bullish calendar spread:

- *The underlying stock makes a significant move to the downside:* You are in the maximum risk range. Exit the position for the loss on the short call and hold the long call in case of a reversal.

- *The underlying stock stays within the desired trading range:* If the stock falls within a range as expected, you will make a profit. The largest profit potential occurs if the shares expire at the ATM strike price.

- *The underlying stock rises above the desired trading range:* Your short call is in-the-money and possibly subject to assignment. Close the trade by purchasing the short-term call.

Diagonal Spread Road Map

In order to place a diagonal spread, the following 14 guidelines should be observed:

1. Look for a market that has been range-bound for at least three months and is expected to remain within a range or move modestly higher or lower over an extended period of time. A dramatic move by the underlying shares in either direction could unbalance the spread, causing it to widen.

2. Check to see whether this stock has options available.

3. Review the option premiums for different expiration dates and strike prices.

4. Investigate implied volatility to look for short-term options with a higher volatility (causing you to receive higher premiums) than the longer-term options (the ones you will purchase). Unlike the calendar spread, look for different strike prices between the long-term option and the short-term option.

5. Explore past price trends and liquidity by reviewing price and volume charts over the past year.

6. A diagonal spread can be bullish or bearish in bias.

   - A **bullish diagonal spread** employs a long call with a distant expiration and a lower strike price, along with a short call with a closer expiration date and higher strike price.

   - A **bearish diagonal spread** combines a long put with a distant expiration date and a higher strike price along with a short put with a closer expiration date and lower strike price.

7. Look at a variety of options with at least 90 days until expiration for the long option and less than 45 days for the short option.

8. Determine the best possible spread to place. To do this, look at:

   - **Limited Risk:** Limited to the net debit when the position is placed. If you sell more than one short option then your limited risk continues to decrease because you take in additional credit for replaying this strategy.

   - **Limited Reward:** Use software for calculation. The reward is limited but the exact maximum potential varies based on several factors including volatility, expiration months, and stock price.

   - **Breakevens and Return on Investment:** Since this is a more complex trade you should have a software package available to calculate your maximum risk, breakevens, and return on investment. The Platinum site at Optionetics.com provides this service.

9. Create a risk profile of the most promising option combination and graphically determine the trade's feasibility. A diagonal spread (see Figure 10.8) has limited risk and limited reward. It is a more complicated strategy, so a computerized risk graph is required to determine the maximum profit and breakevens.

10. Write the trade in your trader's journal before placing the trade with your broker to minimize mistakes made in placing the order and to keep a record of the trade.

11. In most cases, the srategist wants to see the underlying asset make a gradual move higher or lower when using the diagonal spread. If the stock makes a dramatic move in the wrong direction, consider cutting losses rather than hoping for a reversal. If the stock goes through the short option's strike price sooner than expected, close the trade to avoid assignment. Ideally, the stock will make a gradual move in the appropriate direction and another short option can be sold against the long option or the trade can be closed at a profit.

12. Contact your broker to buy and sell the chosen options. Place the trade as a limit order so that you limit the net debit of the trade.

13. Watch the market closely as it fluctuates. The profit on this strategy is limited—a loss occurs if the underlying stock moves too far in one direction or the other.

14. Choose an exit strategy based on the price movement of the underlying stock and the effects of changes in implied volatility on the prices of the options.

   For a bearish diagonal spread:

   - *The underlying stock falls below the lower strike:* Both puts will increase in value and offset each other. The most you would lose is the premium. Avoid assignment by closing the trade.

- *The underlying stock falls between the two strike prices:* If the shares fall within this range, you will make a profit. The largest profit occurs if the shares fall to the lower strike price (but not below) and the short put expires worthless. At that point, the long put will still have intrinsic and time value. Close the position, or sell another short-term put. Check the implied volatility first.

- *The underlying stock rises above the higher strike:* Both puts could expire worthless and you would lose the premium paid.

For a bullish diagonal spread:

- *The underlying stock falls below the short strike:* You are in the maximum risk range. Exit the position for the loss.

- *The underlying stock falls between the two strike prices:* If the shares trade at the higher of the two strikes at expiration, then the maximum profit is attained. In that case, the long call retains most of its value, but the short-term option expires worthless. At that point, the position should be closed or another call can be sold.

- *The underlying stock rises above the higher strike:* You are at risk of assignment on the short call. Close the trade for a loss.

Collar Spread Road Map

In order to place a collar spread, the following 13 guidelines should be observed:

1. A collar is utilized to protect a stock holding against market declines for a specific period of time and still participate in a modest increase in the stock price.
2. Check to see if this stock has options.
3. Review out-of-the-money LEAPS call and at-the-money LEAPS put premiums at various strike prices.
4. Explore past price trends and liquidity by reviewing price and volume charts over the past year.
5. Investigate implied volatility values to see if the options are overpriced or undervalued.
6. This strategy is created by purchasing an ATM put and selling an OTM call against 100 shares of stock. The idea is to provide protection for the long shares and to offset the cost of the put with the premium from the short call.

7. Determine the best possible trade to place. To do this, calculate the following:

   - **Limited Risk:** [(Initial stock price − put strike price) + net debit (or − net credit)] × 100.
   - **Limited Profit:** [(Call strike price − initial stock price) − net debit (or + net credit)] × 100.
   - **Breakeven:** Initial stock price + [(put premium − call premium) ÷ total number of shares (100)].

8. Risk is limited to the downside by the long put. Upside reward is also limited by the short call. Create a risk profile for the trade to graphically determine the trade's feasibility.

9. Write down the trade in your trader's journal before placing the trade with your broker to minimize mistakes made in placing the order and to keep a record of the trade.

10. The collar is known as a vacation trade. It is designed to provide low-cost protection when the strategist expects a gradual move in the underlying asset. If the stock trades sideways, do nothing and let the options expire or roll out to a more distant expiration month. If the stock makes a considerable move lower and is trading below the put strike price at expiration, exercise the put option and sell the stock at the strike price. If it makes a sharp move higher, do nothing and the call option will be assigned. To avoid assignment, buy back the call to close.

11. Contact your broker to buy the put and sell the call. Choose the most appropriate type of order (market order, limit order, etc.).

12. Watch the market closely as it fluctuates. The profit and loss on this strategy is limited.

13. Choose an exit strategy based on price movement of the underlying stock and the effects of changes in implied volatility on option prices.

    - *The underlying stock falls below the put strike price:* Do nothing. The shares are covered by the long put. If you exercise the put and sell the stock, also sell the call to close because it is no longer covered once the stock is sold. If you hold the short call without owning the stock, you are naked a call and are exposed to unlimited risk to the upside.
    - *The underlying stock rises above the short call strike price:* Do nothing. If the calls are assigned to an option holder, when exercised the shares will have to be delivered to the option holder to fulfill the obligation that comes with the short call. Hold the put and let it expire worthless or try to sell it for any remaining value.
    - *The underlying stock closes at the initial stock price:* Call and put expire worthless. Sell the stock or create a new collar.

CONCLUSION

When trading stocks, we can profit in two kinds of markets: when stocks move up or when they move down. However, with options, we can also profit in sideways-trading markets that occur quite often. This chapter introduced an array of innovative strategies that are designed to profit in sideways markets, which are more common than one might think. Just take a look at a long-term chart of a stock or index and notice how many times they see little net movement over time. Instead of sitting out during times of consolidation, you may want to look at sideways-trading strategies like calendar and diagonal spreads, butterflies and condors, and collars. These strategies take advantage of sideways trading in different ways, with each having its place.

Regardless of the market environment, there are always numerous stocks trading in a channel. These are quickly recognized when viewing charts, as they have distinct support and resistance points. We can also use ascending or descending channels by extrapolating where the stock will be by expiration.

However, we have a dilemma when looking for good butterfly and condor candidates. This dilemma develops because we want high IV to get a better entry price, but IV is normally low on stocks in a trading range. However, when a stock is making numerous sharp moves within its channel, we can get a high IV reading even though a trading range has developed. A drop in IV helps our trade, so we would like to use options that are showing relatively high IV, which is expected to drop. One way to find these trades is to look at a list of the largest declining stocks during a trading session. When a stock drops dramatically in one or two sessions, it often enters a consolidation phase. This is the best of both worlds: First we have a stock that has had a spike in its options' IV, but IV should fall sharply as the stock consolidates.

Another way to find candidates for this strategy is to get a list of high-IV stocks and look at their charts. The easiest chart pattern to see is a stock in a trading range. By eyeballing dozens of stocks that have high-IV options, we can often find great candidates to use for a butterfly strategy. When looking at a chart with moving average convergence/divergence (MACD), look for a MACD pattern that is moving sideways near the zero line. This is also a sign of a consolidating stock.

As with any strategy, there are ways to make a butterfly more profitable, albeit with higher risk. The one thing to remember when trading a butterfly is that it is hard to make a profit until expiration or near it. Thus, be aware when entering long-term butterfly trades that it will be tough to see a profit in the short term. Nonetheless, a butterfly spread is an excellent strategy for making a profit in a sideways-trading market, but make sure you understand the risks and are willing to accept the possible consequences if the stock does not stay within your channel.

This chapter also took a good look at calendar and diagonal spreads. These versatile spreads can be constructed using calls or puts. I usually base my selections by calculating the best possible reward-to-risk ratios. To accurately assess the situation, you have to be willing to do the calculations. The same holds true for collars. I look for the right market by scanning charts until I locate one with strong support and resistance levels. Collars, or hedge wrappers, can be used either to hedge a stock you already own or to enter a new strategy, looking to profit from the move of an underlying security. The strategy consists of buying actual stock (we'll assume 100 shares), buying a put, and selling a call. This combines the effects of a covered call with a protective put kicker. Depending on what strikes a trader uses, a collar can be neutral, bearish, or bullish.

When I see a market with strong support and resistance levels, I take a ruler and draw the lines before choosing which options to buy and sell. In many cases, I am willing to accept a lower profit potential for an expanded profit zone. Although you can calculate these risk/reward scenarios by hand, a good options analysis program is worth the investment. It will save you a great deal of time and avoid costly errors. Besides, one good trade could certainly pay for the software.

These strategies can be exited by simply doing the opposite of the original trade. If you bought options, you sell them; and if you sold options, you buy them back. If you are exiting at expiration, then you can let the short options that are worthless simply expire. If any of the short options have value, you can buy them back for a profit. Try to limit your commissions when you are placing and exiting these trades, as commissions can be a big part of the cost of trading.

Trading sideways markets can be a very conservative specialty. If you decide to trade markets that have established strong support and resistance levels, never forget that markets can change erratically. Always be vigilant to the changing nature of the markets you are trading. If the market starts to move above the option strikes you purchased, make a bullish adjustment. If the market appears to be making a real move downward, make a bearish adjustment. Learning to be flexible in your trading approach will lead to longer-term success.

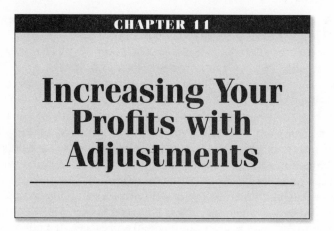

CHAPTER 11

Increasing Your Profits with Adjustments

You can create the best trade in the world, but what you do *after* the trade is placed is crucial to your success. When you put on a trade that is perfectly delta neutral and the market makes a move, it changes your overall position delta. Your trade is no longer delta neutral. At this point, you can choose to maintain or exit the trade, or return to delta neutral by making adjustments. To bring a trade back to delta neutral (a position delta of zero), an adjustment can be made by purchasing or selling options and stocks (or futures) to offset your position. Determining which adjustment to make is a decision dependent on analysis and market experience.

In general, when delta neutral trading guides your decision-making process, you know when and how to make an adjustment to your position. To a certain extent, adjustments are the real meat of delta neutral trading. As you become more experienced with this process, your profits will reflect your increased proficiency. This is where the professional floor trader needs to excel to survive. Off-floor traders have more time to think about and execute the optimal hedge.

When you are trading delta neutral, it can be helpful to think of one side of the trade as your hedge and the other side as your directional bet. In many cases, even if you are 100 percent wrong about market direction you can still make a profit. I prefer to hedge with the options and bet on the direction of the stock (or the futures). Theoretically speaking, if the market moves 10 points up or down, you should be able to squeeze the same amount of profit out of the trade. However, when you start factoring in things like time decay and volatility, this figure may change. For that reason, the trader will often adjust the position in order to shift back to neutral. Let's consider some examples.

VARIABLE DELTAS

Before we show some working examples of adjustments, keep in mind that there are two types of deltas: fixed deltas and variable deltas. A fixed delta means something that never changes, something that always stays the same. For example, if you buy 100 shares of XYZ selling at $25 per share and then sell it for $30, you will have 5 points deposited into your account, or $500. Conversely, if you buy 100 shares at $25 a share and it goes down to $20, you lose 5 points—$500 will be drained out of your brokerage account. Either way, the delta of the shares remains the same. This is a fixed delta. Buying and selling futures is also an example of fixed deltas. The deltas will remain at +100 for each 100 shares of stock you are long and –100 for every 100 shares you short sell.

What is a variable delta? Deltas change because of the passing of time and due to market movement, which also changes prices. Options at different strikes have different deltas that vary as the underlying security changes.

If you buy 500 shares and sell 500 shares at $25 per share, your overall position is delta neutral. But there's something faulty in this reasoning. This kind of trade goes flat. Although this combination creates an overall position delta of zero, since both deltas are fixed, this trade cannot be adjusted, and will not increase or decrease in value. Options, in contrast, have variable deltas that change as the underlying price moves. When the overall position delta moves away from zero, you can apply adjustments to bring the trade back to delta neutral and thereby generate additional profits.

As we have already discussed, delta is at the cornerstone of learning delta neutral trading. As previously shown, one future or 100 shares of stock has a fixed delta of plus or minus 100 while ATM options have a delta of plus or minus 50. If you buy 200 shares and get a delta of +200, you can buy four ATM puts or sell four ATM calls to create a delta neutral trade: $200 + (4 \times -50) = 0$. The type of options you choose determines whether the position has a long or a short focus. The plus or minus sign of the delta depends on which direction best takes advantage of the market circumstances. Buying a call or selling a put takes advantage of a rising market and therefore has a corresponding plus sign. Buying a put or selling a call takes advantage of a decreasing market and therefore has a minus sign.

Mathematically, this is quite easy to understand. But why do deltas act the way they do? Perhaps a simple analogy will convey the meaning of a delta. When you slam on the brakes of your car, the process from the time you hit the brakes until the time your car stops is like a delta curve. Near the end of the stopping, you tend to experience more deceleration than when you first hit the brakes—even with antilock brakes. Right at the precise point where you completely stop, everybody kind of jogs forward a bit for a little whiplash action. This is exactly like the movement of a delta at expiration.

ADJUSTING A STRADDLE

One of the advantages of trading straddles is the ability to easily adjust them. The adjustment process is designed to bring in additional profits while maintaining the delta neutral status of the trade. The adjustment strategy used depends on a wide variety of trade specifics. This chapter is designed to explore the reasons why adjustments are an effective trading tool.

A delta neutral trade is one in which the overall delta of the combined position equals zero. This means that both sides of a delta neutral trade balance each other out, thereby reducing the overall risk of the trade. The trade makes money when one leg of the trade moves in-the-money enough to pay for the cost of placing the overall trade.

Straddles and strangles are nondirectional delta neutral trades that rely on increases and decreases in volatility movement to make a profit. Straddles use ATM options with identical strike prices and expiration dates. A long straddle is usually applied in markets where a large price movement is anticipated; but the direction of the move is unclear. Upon entering a straddle, the underlying stock price changes to some degree in one direction or the other. As the price fluctuates, the position is no longer delta neutral. An increase in the underlying stock price creates a positive delta, and a decrease creates a negative delta. The trade thereby changes its nature to becoming either bullish or bearish, and the resulting profit becomes more reliant on the future direction of the underlying stock.

Let's look at an example to see how an adjustment can change this scenario. If you're holding a straddle and the price of the underlying stock rises, the delta becomes positive and you have a profit on the call side of the position. At this point you may not want to lose the profit you already have, so you have three choices:

1. *Close the position, take your profits and move on.* Although this may be the most prudent move to make, you can no longer participate in any future moves. You have put a limit on your gains, as well as your losses.

2. *Sit tight and do nothing.* Just continue the trade, hoping the price will continue to rise and your profits will increase. If the price goes up, the trade is a winner. If the stock takes a nosedive, you are risking your profits. If the price of the stock declines, you may lose your profits, and perhaps some of the original premium due to time decay.

3. *Adjust the position.* There are several ways to do this. The idea is to continue in the trade while simultaneously capturing profits and returning the overall position delta to zero.

These three alternatives possess their own respective advantages and disadvantages. Often the best choice can only be determined by hindsight. But since the key to profitable trading lies in assessing the available choices, learning the benefits of adjusting can help you to become a more profitable trader.

Options with various strikes have different deltas, and these delta amounts change as the underlying asset's price fluctuates. The object of the delta neutral game is to keep your trade as close to zero deltas as possible. When the next uptick changes the market you are trading, you are no longer neutral. That means that you may be able to make an adjustment by purchasing or selling calls, puts, or stock shares to get the trade back to delta neutral.

Adjustments are much easier to make when you have placed a trade with multiple contracts. They enable traders to lower the overall risk of the trade, and in some cases, start the spread over again at a new price. If there's a profit on the table, an adjustment can allow you to take it and still keep the overall risk of a trade low. If the price continues to rise, you can still benefit from the bullish movement. Conversely, if the price declines, there are ways to profit from a reversal rather than lose. As a delta neutral trader, I have often found it profitable to adjust my straddle positions.

Since a straddle is already a combination trade consisting of at-the-money (ATM) puts and calls, there are many alternatives by which adjustments can be made. All adjustments, however, fit into two categories: adjusting with options or stock. The adjustments further break down into positive or negative changes depending on what is needed to bring position delta back to zero.

Adjusting with Options

Straddles have a large theta risk because the time value of the options is constantly declining, which results in lost premium. Since adding more options increases the theta decay, you can decrease it by making adjustments through selling options that are already owned. If the price of the stock has increased since the last adjustment, you can reduce the delta by selling some of the calls and taking profits. If the price of the stock declines, simply sell some puts to increase the overall position delta. Selling options provides an additional major advantage: You can put your cash back to work by investing in new positions.

The number of options to be sold depends on the overall position delta in relation to the deltas of the specific options. All options are provided a delta relative to the 100 deltas of the underlying security. If 100 shares of stock are equal to 100 deltas, then the corresponding options must have delta values of less than 100. You can estimate an options delta using Table B.3 in Appendix B.

Selling options does have two basic disadvantages: commissions and slippage. Most traders pay a certain minimum commission when trading options—typically $10 to $30. If the adjustment involves the sale of only one or two options, this can become a significant amount. In addition, the bid/ask spread on options is an eighth or higher, sometimes as much as a whole point. This can also have a detrimental effect on the profitability of the position. Since you are working with a spread, it can be difficult to be precise with adjustments because the calculations involved in trying to pinpoint the price at which the contract should be sold are often problematic.

Adjusting with Stock

Adjusting a straddle with stock is a fairly easy to understand process and usually less difficult to execute. If the straddle becomes too delta positive (long), shares of stock can be sold. If the straddle becomes too short, stock can be purchased to easily adjust the delta. The calculations of when to make an adjustment are much easier: When delta gets to 100, a sale of 100 shares of stock will bring it back to zero.

Commissions on buying and selling stocks have become so low, thanks to the advent of online brokerages, as to hardly be of any concern. Many online brokers will execute a trade for less than $10. The bid-ask spread is typically a sixteenth and the savvy trader can get a price executed exactly when the trader wants.

Although selling options might appear at first to be the best way to make adjustments, for the reasons just mentioned, many traders have found that adjusting with stock is the most efficient way. Option software and spreadsheets can be produced that can very easily indicate all of the possible adjustments needed in the trading day, before the market opens.

Adjustment Targets

There are three main triggers or targets that you might consider using to make adjustments in a spread position: delta-based, time-based, and event-based targets. Each one has a unique set of advantages and disadvantages that can be employed to advance your profitability.

Delta-Based Adjustments   The straddle is constantly monitored for its position delta. Using option software, you can watch how the price of the stock changes, which triggers market makers to change implied volatility. In the process, the delta of your position is recalculated. When the delta reaches a predetermined level—usually 100—you can adjust the position by buying or selling stock or options to return it to delta neutral.

Many traders do their calculations at the beginning of each day, identifying the exact stock prices at which the delta will change by 100, and place orders to buy or sell stock at that point. This allows the orders to be placed in advance and automatically executed at the proper levels. The trader does not have to follow the stock tick-by-tick to find the adjustments; they will just happen.

The major advantage of this method is that it is exact and mechanical. The position never acquires more than plus or minus 100 deltas, thereby capturing profits as they occur. You can also take advantage of intraday swings in price. No judgment or decisions are necessary because the adjustments are automatic.

The main disadvantage used to be the time it took to do the calculations. But technology rules the day. This process can be computerized into a spreadsheet, even the number of trades that are made and the resulting commissions. But another disadvantage rears its ugly head: Delta-based electronic trading does not allow for positions to spontaneously "run" or take advantage of the higher deltas from a large move in the stock. This, however, is the type of directional risk that we are seeking to avoid.

Time-Based Adjustments   A simple method is to make delta adjustments according to a time schedule. At the end of the morning, the day, or the week, a calculation is made to bring the position back to delta neutral. The major advantage is simplicity, but many opportunities for adjustments between the scheduled times might be missed.

Event-Based Adjustments   This method is used quite frequently to adjust positions that would not ordinarily be adjusted. A special event makes such an adjustment important in preserving profits.

For example, the release of an earnings report increases a stock's market volatility. In fact, stock prices often run up or down in anticipation of the upcoming report, and if the report catches Wall Street by surprise, the stock might reverse direction altogether. In this case, just before the report, an adjustment can be made to capture the profits in the straddle that have resulted from the preannouncement volatility increase and resulting move in the stock. By returning the straddle to delta neutral, you can benefit from a continued run, or even more important, from the reversal that seems to occur frequently around these reports.

For example, let's say you have a straddle on a stock, with a strike of 50. The earnings report will be on Monday, and the stock has moved to 60 in anticipation of a great report. You could choose to be optimistic and hope that the report will be a surprise to the upside, and the stock will increase even more. But what if the report triggers a sell-off? You'll lose your profits. If you do your delta calculations—sell some stock or options to bring the position back to delta neutral—by Monday you won't care which way the stock moves; you will benefit either way!

Bottom line: Adjustments can be excellent ways to reduce your risk of losing hard-earned profits, and even increase them further by benefiting from reversals.

ADJUSTING LONG SYNTHETIC STRADDLES

You can create a long synthetic straddle by selling 500 shares of XYZ at $25 and buying 10 June XYZ 25 calls at $2.20. This is a perfectly hedged delta neutral position that enables you to make money in either direction (with calls to the upside and the short shares to the downside). Remember, as long as you use *long* options—puts or calls—it is a long synthetic straddle.

I prefer to use ATM options because they have high liquidity and are easy to work with. High liquidity increases the probability of profit and fosters better pricing because the price spreads are thinner. Price spreads are the difference between the bid price and the ask price for which you, as a trader, can buy and sell options, futures, or shares. As an off-floor trader you will typically buy at the higher price (the ask) and sell at the lower price (the bid). Meanwhile, floor traders typically make their money by purchasing from you at the bid, and selling to someone else at the ask, or vice versa. In other words, when we refer to price spreads, we are really talking about the bid and ask prices.

In the last 30 days before expiration, an ATM option is actually the most liquid option out there. Although ATM options have the highest liquidity, liquidity tends to taper off similar to a bell curve; the further out-of-the-money or deeper in-the-money you go, the less buying and selling occurs. The spreads become a lot wider. You can look at something that is two strikes out-of-the-money and there could be half a point difference between buying and selling it. This means that you are automatically down half a point in your position as soon as you initiate the trade. That's why I highly recommend initiating a delta neutral trade by using ATM options to offset stock positions. They are more liquid and should have a narrower spread between the bids and asks (offers).

Let's return to the long synthetic straddle example composed of the sale of 500 shares of XYZ at $25 and the purchase of 10 June XYZ 25 calls at $2.20. In this trade, you have –500 (5 × –100) deltas on the short stock side and +500 (10 × +50) deltas on the options side for an overall position delta of zero. If the stock moves up 5 points, its delta is still –500. It doesn't change, because it's fixed. The only time it changes is when you alter the position by selling existing, or purchasing additional, shares.

The variable deltas are your option deltas. The ATM calls are +50 each. If the underlying stock moves up 5 points, the calls become in-the-money with a higher delta of approximately +70 each for a total of +700 deltas. This means that your overall position delta is +200. To bring the trade back to delta neutral, you can make an adjustment by either selling 200 shares or selling three of the ATM calls you already own. Either choice realizes an increased credit into your account. If the market makes another move, you will be able to make another adjustment to increase your profit even more. This adjustment process locks in profits.

Adjustment Example #1

Let's explore another example using XYZ. Suppose the stock is about to break out or move above its all-time high of $90 a share. You decide to place a long synthetic straddle. With XYZ trading for $90, the July 90 calls are priced at $3.75 and the July 90 puts are priced at $2.75. You decide to initiate a 5 × 10 position (i.e., 500 shares of XYZ stock and 10 XYZ options). Once again, you have to choose which options have a better profit potential: puts or calls. You decide to purchase the shares and buy ATM puts. On the stock side, you have +500 deltas, which will be offset by 10 long ATM July 90 puts for a total of –500. The overall position delta going into this trade is a perfect zero. The total risk is the premium paid for the 10 put options, or $2,750.

On April 14, XYZ closes at $95. The July 90 calls close at $6.875 and the July 90 puts close at $2. The positive delta is still +500. Since you are one strike out-of-the-money, the negative deltas have moved to –35 each for total deltas of –350. Your overall position delta is now +150. You make an adjustment to get back to delta neutral by selling 150 XYZ shares for a profit. Now you own 350 shares of XYZ and the 10 puts originally purchased.

What is your cash settlement up to this point? Right now, it is relatively easy to calculate the cash settlement. You started with 500 shares of XYZ at $90. Then the price went up 5 points and you sold 150 shares for a $750 profit. The puts are now at $2. You lost .75 point on the puts, which equals $750. That means you have broken even on this trade so far, but still have 350 shares of XYZ at $90 showing an open position profit of $1,750.

Market Opportunity: On April 11, XYZ breaks out of its all-time high of $90.

Strategy: Long synthetic straddle—limited risk and unlimited profit potential.

Initial Trade: Long 500 Shares of XYZ @ 90, Long 10 July XYZ 90 Puts @ 2.75.

Initial Deltas: +500 and –500 = zero.

Move #1: April 14—XYZ moves to $95. July 90 puts close at $2.

Consequence #1: Puts are now one strike out-of-the-money for a total of –350 deltas. Overall position is now +150 deltas.

Adjustment #1: Sell 150 shares of XYZ at $95.

Cash Settlement: Selling 150 XYZ shares at $95 translates to a profit of $750. The long puts are now at $2, which is a loss of $.75 each. This equates to a loss of $750. The total cash profit so far is zero; however, the 350 shares of XYZ at $90 do have an open position profit of $1,750.

Move #2: On April 26, XYZ hits $105 a share. July 90 puts close at $1.625.

Consequence #2: Puts are now three strikes out-of-the-money for a total of –250 deltas. Overall position delta is now +100.

Adjustment #2: Sell 100 shares of XYZ at $105.

Cash Settlement: Selling 100 XYZ shares at $105 translates to a profit of $1,500. The 10 long puts are now at $1.625, which translates to $1,625, a net loss of $1,125.

Total Cash: The additional open position profit on the 250 shares purchased at $90 that are now worth $105 translates to $3,750 profit. Adding this to the previous profits creates a total of $6,000. The total put loss is $1,125. The total profit on this trade equals $4,875.

On April 26, XYZ hits $105 a share. The July 90 calls are now at
$11.50 and the July 90 puts are now going for $1.625. Your 350 XYZ
shares have a positive delta of 350. The puts are now at –250 because
you're three strikes out or –25 each. That gives you a position delta
of +100. Let's make another adjustment by selling 100 more shares of
XYZ at 105.

What is your cash settlement to date? You started with 500 shares of
XYZ at $90. You sold 150 at $95. You made $750 on that one trade. You still
own a lot more that have incurred profits as well. You just haven't sold
them yet. Then, you sold another 100 shares at $105 making 15 points on
each. That gives you another $1,500. Now, you are still holding 250 shares
of XYZ stock at $90. If you bought 250 shares at $90 and now XYZ is at
$105, you have $3,750 in an open position profit. This adds up to $6,000 on
the stock side of the straddle. Let's take a look at the put side of the trade.
You bought the puts for $2.75, which translates to $2,750. They are worth
only $1,625 now, which means you have lost $1,125. That creates a net
profit of $4,875—a pretty healthy profit.

Adjustment Example #2

Since a large trade ratio allows us to make even more adjustments, let's
try a 10 × 20 long synthetic straddle. On March 25, using XYZ trading at 30,
we initiate the following trade: short 1,000 shares of XYZ at $30 and long
20 June XYZ 30 calls at $3.50. Each call option costs $350 (3.50 × 100) for a
total debit of $7,000 (350 × 20).

Four days later, the market moves to $35. The calls are now worth
$11.25 each and are now one strike in-the-money. This means that the 20
long calls now have a total delta of +1,300, creating an overall position
delta of +300. To return to delta neutral, we make an adjustment by selling
300 more shares. We now have a position that is short 1,300 shares of XYZ
and long 20 June XYZ 30 calls.

Two days later, the market rises to $40. Once again, the long deltas
increase another +300. We sell 300 more shares to adjust the trade back
to delta neutral. That gives us an open position of long 20 calls at $19,
short 1,000 shares at $30, short 300 shares at $35, and short 300 shares
at $40.

Let's take a look at the cash settlement to date. We originally sold
1,000 shares at $30, incurring a credit of $30,000. We made our first adjustment by selling 300 more shares at $35 for an additional credit of $10,500.
Then we sold 300 shares at $40 or $12,000. This creates a total credit of
$52,500. However, since the price of XYZ has been increasing, we have
lost the following on the shares with XYZ trading at $40.

1,000 shares @ 30 = $30,000 = Loss of $10,000 @ 40.

300 shares @ 35 = $10,500 = Loss of $1,500 @ 40.

300 shares @ 40 = $12,000 = Loss of 0 @ 40.

Total loss on the shares = $11,500 @ 40.

On the other side, the long calls originally cost us $3.50 each for a total debit of $7,000. They have increased in value to $19 or $1,900 each, for a total of $38,000. This creates a profit on the call side of $31,000. If we reconcile this with our loss on the stock side, we have total profit of $19,500 ($31,000 – $11,500 = $19,500).

Market Opportunity: On March 25, XYZ is ready for a breakout move above $40.

Strategy: Long synthetic straddle—limited risk and unlimited profit potential.

Initial Trade: Short 1,000 Shares of XYZ @ 30 (Credit = $30,000), Long 20 June XYZ 30 Calls @ 3.50 (Total debit = $7,000).

Initial Deltas: –1,000 and +1,000 = zero.

Move #1: March 29, XYZ moves to $35.

Consequence #1: The calls are now one strike in-the-money, which means that the 20 long calls now have a total delta of +1,300. Overall position delta is now +300.

Adjustment #1: To make an adjustment, sell 300 shares of XYZ at $35. The trade is now short 1,300 shares of XYZ and long 20 calls.

Move #2: On April 1, XYZ moves to $40.

Consequence #2: Long call deltas increase another +300.

Adjustment #2: Sell 300 shares of XYZ at $40. The trade is now long 20 June XYZ calls at $19, short 1,000 shares of XYZ at $30, short 300 shares of XYZ at $35, and short 300 shares of XYZ at $40.

Total Cash: We originally sold 1,000 shares of XYZ, incurring a loss of $10,000. We made our first adjustment by selling 300 more shares at $35 for a loss of $1,500. We also sold 300 shares of XYZ at $40, but since shares are still trading at $40, we have not incurred a profit or a loss yet. This creates a total loss of $11,500. The long calls originally cost us $350 each for a total debit of $7,000. They have increased in value to $19 or $1,900 each. That gives us a total of $38,000 for a profit on the call side of $31,000. If we reconcile this with our losses on the stock side, we have total profit of $19,500 ($31,000 – $11,500 = $19,500).

ADDITIONAL ISSUES

Can you make adjustments on 1×2 trades? Approximately 90 percent of the time, a 1×2 trader will not make any adjustments. The trade is simply placed and exited when the market moves. If an adjustment is possible, it will most likely be made on the option side.

Frequently, when the market moves up fast and you see a dramatic increase in volatility, it can be better to get out of the trade altogether. Why? Because when you have an increase in the volatility, the premium on an option is going to pump up. I recommend exiting the trade, waiting for volatility to collapse a little, and then getting back in.

For example, if you have a 1×2 (100 shares $\times 2$ options) or 2×4 (200 shares $\times 4$ options) trade, you have to have some decent-sized market movement, and a good profit (i.e., 20 percent), before you even consider making an adjustment. Why make an adjustment at all when you can just get out of the trade and then get back into the trade when the market calms down? If you can make a 20 percent return on your risk capital, you are on your way to healthy, consistent profits.

What determines whether you initially go short or long the underlying stock with the corresponding long two puts or long two calls? The way to decide is to look at the prices of the puts and calls and buy the ATM options that are the cheapest. You could be looking at a computer or you could be looking at the newspaper at the end of the night. Let's say XYZ shares are trading at $48 and the 50 puts are $3.25. There is a $0.75 difference between the price of the puts and the price of the calls. Therefore, I would rather pay $2.50 for the calls and buy two for each I sell. But it really doesn't matter which way you go to get to delta neutral. It is safe to assume that you want to take the less expensive of the two options and thereby pay less money out-of-pocket. Taking less money out of your account initially is a good technique to use if you want to dramatically increase your account size. That's where the real buried treasure lies, and it's just waiting for you to discover it.

USING ADJUSTMENTS TO REPAIR A TRADE

The type of strategies that traders implement is a major factor that determines their success or failure in this business; however, the ability to adjust positions to obtain maximum profitability is what separates the professionals from the average trader. There have been situations where I have made changes to a position and then within in a couple of days realized that I had made the wrong decision. When you are faced with these

---

types of circumstances, it is important to be able to think outside of the box in order to create a new position or fix the mistake that you made. Let's review how to fix a trade when mistakes have been made and where revisions will improve the risk/reward profile. Let's use an example of a long synthetic straddle using Nortel Systems (NT). The price chart of the stock is shown in Figure 11.1.

My original assumption in 2000 was that NT was consolidating to go higher, so the trade was placed in anticipation of making a profit from the increase but was hedged just in case things went differently. The original trade was composed of going long 1,000 shares of NT at $81.50 and long 20 January 85 puts at $11. This long synthetic straddle was pretty close to delta neutral with an overall position delta of +50. The original risk profile for this position is shown in Figure 11.2.

Unfortunately, the market assumptions on NT were completely wrong. In addition, some mistakes were made when adjusting this trade that turned this relatively good trade into somewhat of a problem—the cause of great frustration.

A couple days after putting this position on, NT began to fall and it started to fall hard. After the third day of the stock falling, it closed above its low from the day before. This seemed like a reversal and since the shares seemed headed to go higher from that point, I reacted by selling off five of my puts and taking some profits. At that point in time, this seemed like a great idea, because I was booking some profits, increasing the delta of my position, and setting myself up for the big run-up the shares were going to make. Unfortunately, the shares continued to fall and fall and fall!

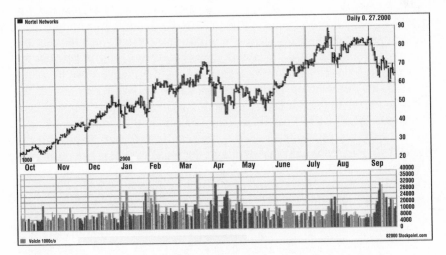

FIGURE 11.1 NT Price and Volume Chart (*Source*: Optionetics © 2004)

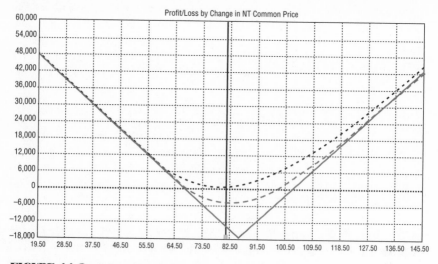

FIGURE 11.2 Original NT Risk Profile

What a terrible decision it was to sell off part of my protection (the puts); but it wasn't a complete disaster. I was still long 15 puts against the long 1,000 shares; however, it would have been much more profitable to have held on to the puts that I sold. This left me just about breakeven in a trade that could have been far more profitable. Figure 11.3 shows the risk profile after selling the five puts and the shares falling to $60.

After viewing the risk profile in Figure 11.3, I decided that something had to be done with this position. I simply didn't feel comfortable with the risk profile anymore. The shares would have to continue lower or really ramp in order for this trade to turn green for me. Even though the options didn't expire until January, I was still fighting with the issue of time decay. In reality, the shares could remain range-bound for a while. It was time to consider my alternatives. I could exit the whole trade and continue to remain angry for making a costly mistake, or I could think creatively and change the whole profile of my original position. I opted to do the latter.

My longer-term assumptions for this security had not changed. I still thought the shares would eventually go higher. Let's take inventory and see what we have to work with. We have 1,000 shares of stock and 15 puts. The problem is that if the shares remain in a range from this point, I will lose the time value that I paid for in the options. There are a number of different changes that can be made to this position; but I prefer to turn the synthetic straddle into a collar. This is accomplished by purchasing 500 more shares of stock at $60 and selling 15 January 90 calls at $1.50. These adjustments decrease the maximum risk on the entire trade and relieve

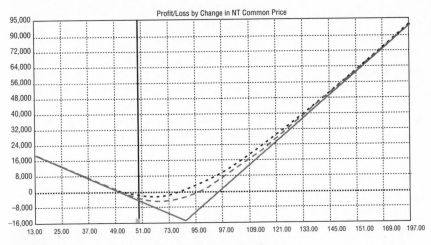

FIGURE 11.3 NT Risk Profile after Selling Five Puts

my mind of the time decay problem. Additionally, I still have a nice profit potential if the shares do head higher. The risk profile of the new position (collar) is shown in Figure 11.4.

The maximum risk on this trade has been reduced to $2,000. The maximum reward is approximately $20,000, which is realized if the shares climb to the mid 90s by January expiration. As you can see, this position begins to react immediately if the shares begin to climb; and even if I'm wrong again

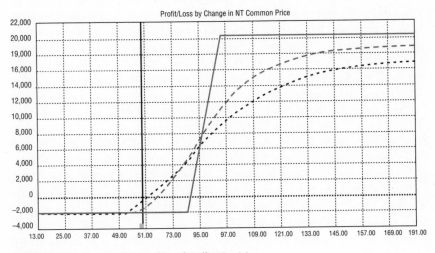

FIGURE 11.4 NT Risk Profile of Collar Position

and the stock heads south, I am limited to a small loss at January expiration. If the stock does not move in my favor within the time frame needed, then I can readjust the positions and give myself more time to be right.

The process of adjusting positions is just as much an art as it is a science. There are usually many different courses of action that you can take. Sometimes you will be right on the first try. Other times you will be wrong or maybe your market assumptions change while being in a trade, requiring you to change the profile of the position. The key to successful trading is to be able to creatively make changes that enable you to obtain a risk profile that makes you feel comfortable.

911 STRATEGIES

Here's a dose of reality to those who are reading this book! You can have the best trading system in the world that works 90 percent of the time, with low drawdowns and big gains; but if you don't have an exit plan or an adjustment plan when things don't go your way, that great system isn't going to help you at all. Optionetics 911 strategies are designed to teach you various techniques that focus on teaching you how to fix losing positions.

Seminar students frequently ask, "Is there any possible way to fix a losing stock or option trade?" Rest assured that our Optionetics team of traders has found some viable answers. However, I want to first point out a mistake made by many traders—a mistake I used to make myself until I gained some other tools that work in these types of situations.

We've all taken directional stock trades in which the particular stock has gone 5 to10 points against us. Many traders assume that the only way to fix a losing position is to average up or down, depending on the directional bias of the initial trade. Averaging down is put into practice by purchasing more of a stock at a lower price in order to reduce the average cost per share. Averaging up consists of selling more shares at a higher price. These types of approaches not only require more capital, but also increases the risk of the trade.

For example, if you were to buy 100 shares of XYZ at $100, the cost of the trade would be $10,000. If XYZ stock fell to $90, the trade would have an open position loss of $1,000. Buying 100 more shares of XYZ at $90 would require another $9,000. Although it lowers the breakeven on the trade to 95, you have doubled your risk if the stock continues to decline. This is a very dangerous strategy in some cases, especially when markets are in a free-fall. Many traders have used this strategy only to find that they regretted averaging down later. Just imagine if you had done this with an Internet stock that was trading at $420 per share and now trades at $5.

Some traders may choose to buy an at-the-money (ATM) call on XYZ. This approach ties up less capital, reduces the breakeven to 95, and is less risky than averaging down on the stock. However, this solution still requires additional trading capital for the cost of the option. If XYZ were to stay at 90 or below, the option expires worthless, meaning you lose the additional money paid to purchase the option. This is a more sophisticated approach but also has its perils.

Let's say you get a hot tip on a stock, and you decide to position yourself for a big gain if the stock moves up. You place the order and wait, and wait, and wait! The stock does nothing. You may think the option is going to do nothing as well, but unfortunately the option loses value while you're just sitting there like a deer in the headlights. The options drop to half their original value and you're stuck wondering why you got into this position in the first place. But there are ways to repair this position. Learning what they are, and how they are applied is the key to reducing your losses and increasing your returns.

Our Optionetics team has researched and discovered many ways to fix long and short positions, as well as spread positions on stock, options, and futures. Each Optionetics 911 strategy fulfills three basic criteria that make up a good trade by:

1. Reducing the breakeven of the position.
2. Tying up no additional capital.
3. Allowing the trade to still have profit potential without any additional risk.

CONCLUSION

When I see people, including my colleagues, who make their living by navigating the markets, I feel very fortunate that options play such an integral role in my trading process. The simple reason is that options are the most flexible financial instruments that exist in the markets today. They provide unique investment opportunities and advantages to the knowledgeable trader on a regular basis. Yes, the entire options arena can be a very complex and confusing place to venture—especially for the novice trader—but the rewards far outweigh the sacrifices of getting there. One of those rewards is that you never have to be stagnant. There is always something that you can do to make the risk/reward characteristics of your trade fit your objectives. Remember Legos, those building toys you used to play with as a kid? Well, options are very similar; they let you build to your heart's content.

As we all know, this market can be one tough cookie to beat. Sometimes the best approaches have been nondirectional in nature. Add the critical levels we're currently trading to this difficult environment and you have a recipe for some serious fireworks, one way or the other. I'm a big believer in protecting profits by making adjustments.

This is where the major dilemma comes in and where the flexibility of options provides us with many advantages over other techniques. When taking profits, the major emotion that we have to deal with is greed. Have you ever caught yourself thinking, "Well, I'm just going to capture those last couple of points I'm entitled to on my bull call spread"? I used to think this way all the time—until that time the stock came crashing down and my profits faded away in the blink of an eye.

There are a couple of ways to protect yourself from this scenario. First, if you've already doubled your money in the trade, it may make sense to take half of the position off for a no-risk trade. It may also make sense to take the entire position off and make 100 percent! This is a great situation to be in, but not one in which we always find ourselves. For example, positions that are constructed with LEAPS take more time to mature (depending on the type of trade). Therefore, you may not have doubled your money, even though the security has moved big in your direction. Let's say you're up 15 percent in your trade, but it will be quite some time before the profits really kick in. You don't want to exit the entire trade because your profit potential is much higher; but at the same time, you don't want to give up the gains you've already earned. What can you do?

When I'm in this situation, I adjust the position so that I keep my original upside and protect my profits on the downside or even make money on the downside. One way to achieve this is to simply purchase puts against the position. You want to minimize the time value you pay for these puts, so going in-the-money is a good idea. The number of contracts that you would purchase is subjective and dependent on the risk profile you want. The best thing to do is look at a number of different alternatives by checking out what the Optionetics.com Platinum site has to say. The objective here is to protect the profits you've already made and not take the upside (or downside) out of your position. If you adjust the trade correctly, you lock in profits, keep upside reward potential, and have the ability to make money on the downside. Talk about a stress reliever! Incorporating these types of adjustment strategies into your trading approach is vital to your success as a trader.

The more contracts you have to buy and sell (i.e., 2×3, 3×5, 5×10), the more profitable adjustments you can make. It's somewhat like being in Atlantic City or at the racetrack. If you are betting on a horse with 2-to-1 odds, you know you have a pretty decent chance of winning. If you bet on a horse that has 100-to-1 odds, your chances of winning are slim, but the payoff would be enormous.

Consistent returns on your investments lead to the gradual accumulation of wealth. The accounts I trade have increased dramatically over the years because I take profits on a consistent basis. You, too, will be able to increase your account size dramatically. Did you ever lose everything you had in the futures or stock market? I have, more than once. But I persevered in the face of what seemed impossible odds and bounced back into prosperity. It can happen to anybody. With delta neutral trading, you have a much better chance of succeeding. I tell a lot of traders that if they cannot trade delta neutral, then it's better not to trade at all. I believe that trading without visualizing the risk and subsequently limiting that risk is akin to gambling at a Las Vegas craps table—the house eventually wins.

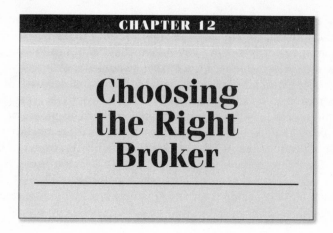

CHAPTER 12

Choosing the Right Broker

S electing the right broker and placing orders correctly are essential elements in your development as a successful trader. In the beginning, the entire process may seem quite complex and perhaps more complicated than you thought. Don't waste time worrying about all the different issues involved. It all boils down to one intention: You contact your broker and explain to him or her what you want to do. That's it.

However, it is important to realize that each step leaves room for error to occur. You can't control all the steps, because once you place your order the rest of the process is handled by your brokerage firm and the exchanges. At the same time, however, you can control which broker you've selected to help you. Remember, a good broker is an asset and a bad broker is a liability. It is vital to take the selection process very seriously because you don't want your broker to make you broker!

A major mistake many people make when they first begin investing is to listen to their broker's advice without question. Why do they do this? Perhaps because many people have been brainwashed to believe that just because a broker has a license, he or she must know how to make profitable investment decisions. As in any profession, there are top-notch professionals as well as others who have missed their calling and should not be offering their services. The best advice I can give you is to be very selective in finding your broker. The first step is to decide what kind of trader or investor you want to be.

No two investors are exactly alike. Some prefer to trade actively while others simply want to buy stocks and hold them for many years.

Still others rely heavily on options. Trading and investing attracts all sorts of people, and each person has a unique approach to the market.

What type of investor are you? Answering that question is an important first step when looking for a broker—someone who meets your specific trading needs. After all, there are more than 200 different brokers to choose from and each is unique in terms of commissions, choices of investments, research, and so on. There are, however, only a handful of brokerage firms that most options traders choose to deal with regularly (check the Optionetics.com Broker Review section for a current list).

WHAT IS A BROKER?

A broker is an individual or entity who is licensed to buy and sell marketplace securities and/or derivatives to traders and investors. In addition, brokerage firms must also be licensed and insured to accept customer deposits. A word of caution: It is a major misconception to believe that just because someone is licensed to take an order they have the knowledge to invest your money wisely. Just like there are bad doctors out there practicing medicine, there are many brokers who are not good at making investment decisions.

If you're reading this book, chances are that you don't need the help of a *full-service* broker, which is a type of broker that receives relatively high commissions or fees for offering investment advice. Instead, most options traders use *self-directed* brokerage accounts, or brokerage firms that serve as order takers rather than investment advisers. Commissions and fees will be greater at a full-service broker.

A reliable broker is worth a great deal whether he or she is offering advice or merely executing trades. Finding a broker who understands a wide variety of markets and your trading strategies is relatively difficult, but, when possible, the relationship between client and customer can develop into a long-term and successful one. Remember, successful traders develop profitable trading strategies that require a broker who can execute orders with precision. Brokers are the intermediaries of trading. Building profits is the name of the game. The broker makes money whether you win or lose—the brokerage commissions will always be paid.

Many traders choose to trade with discount brokers; this can be profitable as long as they are getting good executions on their orders. Brokers get paid to provide this service. They execute your orders and protect your interests. Many investors, especially beginners, try to find a broker with the lowest commission cost. However, an inexpensive broker can become an expensive broker overnight if mistakes are made each time the broker places your trade. It is imperative to balance low-cost commissions with prompt service and good execution.

Until 1975, the brokerage business was dominated by a relatively small number of large firms. But in May of that year, deregulation loosened the commission fee structures and discount brokerages began setting up shop. Since then three main kinds of brokers have dominated the playing field: full-service, discount, and deep-discount.

All brokers get paid a commission each time you place a trade. The amount of this commission depends on what kind of service they provide. Full-service brokers have higher commissions because they spend considerable time researching markets in order to advise their clients. Discount brokers have lower commissions because they simply act as an agent placing the trader's order as well as facilitating the exit. Deep-discount brokers primarily trade for investors who trade in large blocks. They offer the lowest commission rates of the three. In the 1990s, online electronic brokers burst upon the scene offering the lowest commission costs ever via easy computer access.

THE RISE OF ONLINE BROKERAGES

The way people use the Internet to make investment decisions continues to evolve. It all started with the appearance of a handful of online discount brokers in the late 1990s. Now a large number of online brokers are battling for traders' orders. Full-service firms, which have seen an increasing number of clients gravitate toward do-it-yourself investing and online trading, have responded by launching their own web sites and recapturing some of those lost accounts.

But the way people use the Internet to handle investments goes beyond the battle of full-service and online brokers. A number of new and innovative products have been launched and more are expected in the near future. Some products are designed to help investors make better asset allocation decisions and others are designed merely to simplify the investment process. Regardless of the specific purpose, the new Web-based financial services are all designed to profit from the increasing use of technology by the individual investor. The result has been a proliferation of new online products and an evolution in the way the Internet is used for investment decisions.

Online brokerages provide a number of advantages over traditional full-service and discount brokerages. First and foremost, online brokerages have severely reduced their commission costs from the lofty levels set by traditional brokers. All brokers get paid a commission fee each time you place an order (or exit an option position). The amount of this commission depends on what kind of service they provide. Each transaction is called a round turn and costs as little as $10 (and the cost is getting lower) at an online brokerage and more than $100 at a full-service brokerage.

Although generally much lower than their predecessors, online brokerage commissions and margin amounts vary. But don't waste too much time fretting over a couple of dollars of commission when evaluating online brokers. Small difference in prices due to poor trade executions can cost you a great deal more, and an inexpensive broker can become an expensive broker overnight if they lose money each time they place your trade. Broker responsibilities may differ, but timely executions and good fills are still the most important part of a broker's services. Bottom line: It may be desirable to match low cost with prompt service and good execution; but it is not always profitable to use the cheapest broker just to save a few bucks on commissions.

Another major improvement comes in the form of information. Online brokerages offer real-time quotes, charts, news, and analysis as well as the ability to customize this information to fit your portfolio. Now you have the means to research stock tips immediately, read up-to-the-minute news as it happens, monitor the mood of markets throughout the day, and access option premiums for price fluctuations. The marketplace is alive and you're right there with it. You no longer have to sit on hold waiting for your broker to tell you he'll get back to you on that.

Given the Internet revolution that has permeated almost every aspect of our lives, it is likely that you will consider using an online broker. To help you make the most of this decision, pay attention to the following points:

- *Trade online, but have a broker on standby.* Some investors want the convenience of being able to make some trades online, but also have a specific broker to bounce ideas off. Full-service firms have answered their call. Responding to the increasing popularity of online trading and its low commissions, many of Wall Street's big names are rolling out services that let investors trade online for discount commissions or a flat fee, but at the same time offer the services of a live broker for higher commissions. Similarly, many online firms provide clients with the ability to trade over the Internet or with a broker for an additional fee.
- *Online brokers are also recognizing the importance of having an online and traditional brick and mortar presence.* Some firms like E*Trade and Charles Schwab have developed online trading platforms and physical locations that investors can visit and do business. If you're the type of person who likes to go into the bank rather than use the ATM, you might want to check in the yellow pages to see which brokers have branches in your area.

- *Options specialists.* Some brokerage firms like Thinkorswim, Wall Street*E, and OptionsXpress specialize in dealing with options traders. These firms provide sophisticated trading platforms with the ability to execute almost any conceivable options strategy on- or off-line.
- *Screen for trades.* Are you looking for a site that will help you find that next big winner? Some web sites, such as the Platinum site at Optionetics.com, now offer investors a way of screening for stocks based on a number of variables (P/E ratios, price-to-book, market value, etc.) in a matter of seconds.

Many brokers and other financial services firms are recognizing the changing needs of online investors. In response, some of Wall Street's big names are using a combination of both online and full-service amenities to woo investors. Others are hoping to attract new accounts by offering financial planning as well as an amazing array of portfolio building services. The ongoing evolution in web-based financial services continues and serves as further evidence of how technology is changing our everyday lives.

QUESTIONS FOR POTENTIAL BROKERS

Remember, your broker is in the business of looking after your interests. Make sure you find a broker that is licensed to execute stocks and options or futures transactions. Most brokerage firms provide either stocks and options or futures, not both, because futures are regulated separately from stocks and options. Some firms, like Cybertrader, allow you to trade both, but you must maintain two separate accounts in order to do so. In either case, your chief concern as a trader should be to get the transaction executed as you desire and at the best price possible. Choosing the right broker is essential to your success. But how do you find the right one? When choosing a broker, review the following four points:

1. *Does your broker really know more than you do?* Your broker should be an asset to you, should have sufficient knowledge of the markets you trade and invest in, and be able to make first-rate suggestions to help you increase your profitability. As a novice investor, be very careful with your broker selection. Look for a broker who has knowledge about a wide variety of option markets, including margins, spread strategies, volatility, points, strikes, and so on. Interview potential brokers by presenting a specific trade to see if she or he can talk intelligently about it. Can she or he define the market conditions, risk, potential return, breakevens, and so on? Ask the broker how much of a

percentage of their revenue comes from options. Look for a broker with a similar risk profile as yours. Most importantly, make sure your personality fits the broker's personality—you really have to be comfortable with their style and time availability. You should also find out if your broker's backup assistants understand options as well. Inevitably, you will end up dealing with assistants, and they need to be knowledgeable about options or you will find frustration down the road.

2. *Invest your own account.* Information from your broker should be viewed as a potential opportunity, not as advice. Once again, ask your broker for suggestions, not advice. It is very important that you always take responsibility for your own profitability.

3. *Do your own homework.* Study, study, study. Continue to do your homework even after you've achieved success, because the learning process never ends when you're in the investment field. The day you think you have learned it all is the day you should retire. Overconfidence leads to complacency and losses.

4. *Always listen and digest before making any investment decisions. Remember, you can always call your broker back.* When you call, listen to what your broker has to say, but never make an investment while still on the phone. End the call and put the phone down. Think about the information you have received and then do an analysis of risk and reward. If you still find the suggestion to be valuable, then call back and make the investment. My biggest mistakes were hasty investment decisions.

WHAT MAKES A GOOD BROKER?

Much advice has been given as to just what makes a good broker, and just what one must look for in opening a brokerage account. The key elements of most advice come down to the following issues:

- *Commissions.* You want them as low as possible, but be careful—a low commission structure may mean that you don't get the level of service you may want and need.
- *Minimum account size requirements.* This can vary anywhere from $500 up to and above $25,000 to open an account. While the size of your trading account may limit you to certain low-requirement brokers, keep in mind that to open a marginable account (required for spread trading) there is a minimum $2,000 balance requirement beyond any options you own. Thus you must have a minimum of $2,000

in cash or nonmargined securities available before you even start to trade. Hence, a $2,500 opening balance would only permit you to enter a trade (or trades) with a net $500 debit position. Needless to say, this will severely restrict what trades can be placed.

- *Other requirements of the brokerage house.* Check to see what other requirements may be in effect. For instance, how are good till canceled (GTC) orders handled, if at all? For instance, many houses will not enter a GTC order on a spread trade. If you want to trade this way, then special arrangements will have to be made for you (the broker will automatically reenter the trade each morning, etc.). You'll need to adjust your trading style or find a different broker.
- *Speed and accuracy of fills.* This is something that is very difficult to determine before opening an account, other than by talking with other traders. However, "good" is really in the eye of the beholder—if it is profitable for you, then it is good, regardless of what others may think.
- *Optionable and spreadable accounts available.* In particular, make sure that in calculating margin requirements on your account that the brokerage house gives you credit for your long position as an offset to your short. You do not want the house to be calculating margin based on the short position only!
- *Experience in trading options in general and combination trades in particular.* You will want your broker familiar with options, and hopefully, with option strategies, so that they can anticipate your needs.
- *Ability to fill the order between the spread.* If you place your buy orders at the ask and sell orders at the bid prices, will the broker routinely get you a better price? If so, you can then place an order such that you will be filled, with the broker working the difference to get you the best price. Online brokers typically do not do this, as everything is placed electronically.
- *General comfort level with the broker.* This is a very subjective point, but probably the most important. You must feel that the broker is looking out for your interests. After all, your broker has your money. Even if you're only placing trades online, it is important to feel comfortable about the firm you are dealing with on a regular basis.

Once you have chosen a broker, however, the fun begins. As you are likely aware from your own business, there are customers or clients that you enjoy dealing with and others whose call you dread taking. Obviously, those whom you enjoy dealing with will get service beyond the minimum and will generally be happier with their experience than will the troublesome customers—so, too, in the world of brokers.

Two personal experiences come to mind when thinking of good

brokers. In one case, we had been discussing exiting a trade for several weeks. Finally, I put the order in. About three minutes later, I got a phone call from my broker, saying that no, she hadn't filled the order, but rather had pulled it. It seems that after sending the trade to the floor, she overheard someone talking about a takeover rumor. On checking, she found that the stock was indeed in play, and in fact trading had been halted. On reopening, the shares gapped up about $5, and that is where I would have been filled had she not pulled the trade. By pulling it, she enabled me to watch the stock drift up about $15 over the next week, which turned an otherwise small loss into a very profitable trade. The second example is a situation where I got a call back from the broker checking to see if my trade was accurate. I normally use bull positions when trading, and I had inadvertently entered a bear spread on this particular trade. Upon checking, I found that indeed I had transposed my buy and sell options on the trade. It was my error, and could have been quite expensive.

So, what will get you the best treatment? Besides common courtesy, the key factor mentioned by various brokers in an informal survey I conducted was that the customer has to have a plan, and has to articulate the plan with them. What do you expect from the account? What are your goals—retirement portfolio, current income, and so on? What risks are you willing to take? What types of trades do you like or dislike? Are there industries you want to avoid or to specialize in? Such information can obviously help them to recognize situations that may interest you.

Reviewing your account periodically with your broker is also important. Obviously, as a trader, you will be in frequent contact with your broker regarding your trades, but periodically you should review your goals with your broker. If your trades are then deviating from your stated goals, the broker can better question if indeed this is what you really want to be doing. This, of course, would not apply if you were dealing only with an online broker. In that case, it will be up to you to review your goals and your trades to make sure you are staying on track.

Knowing what you need from the broker and asking for specific information also looms high on the list of good customer traits. If you are on a fishing expedition and don't know exactly what you need, or what you need is not absolutely critical for this instant, wait until after market hours for such discussions. In other words, be judicious with your broker's time. In this same vein, ask questions when you are unsure. Whether it is a definition (a "chocolate milkshake" in Chicago is a different beverage than one in New York—i.e., different terms are frequently used for the same concept) or it is a new strategy, ask your broker to explain it. Don't make guesses; your broker is willing to help. It is a lot easier to spend 30 seconds in explanation up front rather than trying to unwind some position you got into by not understanding what was happening.

The most surprising comment of my informal survey came from a brokerage dealing primarily in options, one where all of the brokers have actual trading-floor experience. The comment was that this broker preferred longer-term investors. He much preferred customers who had 90 percent of their investments in long-term positions and limited their short-term plays to less than 10 percent of their portfolio. "Short-term traders don't last."

The worst type of account, according to one full-service broker, is the customer simply handing them a check and saying to "make me money." With no direction, no understanding of risk tolerances, and no clear goals, it is almost impossible to satisfy such a client.

Decision making is important on the part of the client. Clients who cannot make up their minds, clients who ask for advice and then go away to "think about it," never returning with an answer, lead to frustration on the part of the broker. A final problem client is the one who expects much service, but then doesn't trade with that broker—and instead goes elsewhere. Obviously this is a problem faced much more frequently by the full-service broker, but even the discount brokers seem to have such problems. Obviously the broker understands that they won't get every trade, nor does every request for information result in a trade, but commissions pay them, so they expect some reasonable relationship between the amount of service delivered and the amount of trading through your account.

Finally, talk to your broker. We will assume that you let them know when they make a mistake, but also let them know when they do a good job. Recommend them to friends and family when appropriate. Remember that by being a good client, you will soon find that most brokers suddenly get better. After all, "brokers are people, too."

QUALITY OF EXECUTION

While many investors focus solely on the dollar costs of commissions when choosing brokers, there are other less obvious costs to be wary of. Specifically, when investors place buy and sell orders, the quality of the execution and the subsequent price at which the stock trade takes place are equally important to consider.

For instance, if you place a market order to sell 500 shares of a stock and the broker fails to act promptly, the order might get filled for, hypothetically, $50 rather than $50.25 a share. In other words, a delay in executing an order when a stock is falling can cost you 25 cents a share. Meaningless? Well, that amounts to $125 on your 500-share order. So if you are consistently losing eighths and quarters on share trades, who cares if the trades are commission-free?

Arguably, the quality of a broker's execution is more important than the commissions on trades. In fact, under federal securities laws, all brokers have a duty to execute orders at the best possible price. It is called the "duty of best execution." Consequently, the Securities and Exchange Commission (SEC) has stepped up surveillance of online brokers because of concern over the quality of their executions. Some of the concern stems from a practice known as payment for order flow.

In order to understand how payment for order flow works, consider what happens from the time you submit your stock order until the time it is executed. Once the broker receives the order, they have a responsibility under the "duty of fair dealing" provision of the Securities Exchange Act to proceed promptly. At the same time, under the "duty of best execution" provision of the same Act, the broker is obligated to fulfill the order at the best possible price.

With payment for order flow, this isn't always the case. Rather than shopping the order around to competing market makers or electronic communication networks (ECNs), the order is sent to a wholesale market maker who, in turn, pays the broker for sending orders in their direction. In short, brokers are increasingly using preferred market makers who pay them for the buy and sell orders. Such arrangements allow online brokers to offer cheap automated trades because they also make money off the order flow.

At the same time, large market makers, such as Knight/Trimark, sometimes handle more than 30 percent of the orders in a particular stock. As the high volume of orders comes through, the market makers generate profits from the difference between the bids and offers. There is no incentive for them to beat the prevailing market price. Therefore, by directing trades to market makers who pay for order flow rather than shopping the order around to competing market makers, the broker is not assuring clients execution at the best possible price.

During a speech to the Securities Industry Association in November 1999, SEC governor Arthur Levitt noted, "I worry that best execution may be comprised by payment for order flow, internalization, and certain other practices that can present conflicts between the interests of brokers and their customers."

Some brokers are responding to critics of payment for order flow by offering rebates to clients. A few brokerages, for example, do not prearrange to generate payments for order flow. Instead, when they receive an order, it is routed to the best execution point. If the best price happens to be with a market maker that does pay for orders, the brokerage passes the payment to its customers in the form of monthly rebates.

The practice of paying for order flow is providing ammunition for firms that allow customers to bypass the traditional role of the broker. So-called direct-access firms are attacking Web-based brokers head-on by offering technology that takes orders directly to the marketplace, rather than through a broker. With direct-access firms, investors execute orders directly with market makers, exchanges, or ECNs—wherever the best price exists. Cybertrader, Edgetrade, and E*Trade Professional are the latest to offer the individual investor direct access to the stock market by eliminating the role of the broker. Direct-access firms are appealing in that they offer the individual investor a higher probability of better execution. These firms cater primarily to active traders, however. Often, their commissions are based on the number of trades executed monthly, with more frequent traders getting cheaper commissions and access to services like research and quotes. Bottom line: If you are an active trader, direct access can greatly increase the efficiency and effectiveness of your orders.

INVESTOR SAFEGUARDS

When investing in the stock market, your fiduciary—the financial agent you trust with your money—is your broker. The SEC and the exchanges are diligent in their regulation of both brokers and their firms, but you still need to be aware of some of the possible indiscretions to protect against fiduciary fraud. First we will delineate these improper deeds and then provide the reader with six ways to self-protect one's account. Some of the most common improprieties include:

- *Embezzlement.* Usually a matter of a salesperson misappropriating your assets without the firm's knowledge.
- *Misuse of assets.* Using customer equity or cash to cover operating expenses, or as collateral for the firm.
- *Kickbacks.* When order takers take bribes to direct trades to certain market makers, you end up paying for the bribe through higher customer prices.
- *Misuse of discretionary authority.* Trading without customer approval, or without the best interests of the client in mind.
- *Churning.* Increasing commissions by recommending excessive trading.
- *Front running.* Trading for the firm or selected clients with advance knowledge of forthcoming research recommendations.

- *Conflict of interest.* Arising from the brokerage firm's role as market maker, underwriter, mutual fund manager, or investment adviser.

There a number of things you can do to protect your account. Use the following six guidelines to safeguard your stock market profits:

1. *Do your own research before you invest.* Don't invest in companies that minimize or avoid disclosure of their financial condition. Always read the fine print in your information sources, and avoid hot tips.

2. *Deal with major brokerage firms and reputable brokers.* Know your brokerage firm's financial condition and who owns the firm. Be sure you know exactly what your agreement specifies.

3. *Keep a written record of all trades.* Write your orders in advance. When you receive trading confirmations, be sure to compare them with your written records.

4. *Put your broker to work.* If trading confirmations are slow in coming, complain to your broker. Balance all monthly statements. Ask your broker to explain any discrepancies. If trouble persists, go to a supervisor. If it continues, change firms.

5. *Change brokers who talk about sure winners.* Resist all sales manipulation emphasizing double-digit rates of return, stocks that will double, hot stocks, and guaranteed profits.

6. *Never put greed before safety.* Sometimes you have to protect yourself against yourself, and that can be the most difficult job of all. Remember the stock market will be here tomorrow—but to use it, you need investment capital.

Hopefully this information will help you avoid or deal effectively with any account issues that you might experience. Investors who know how to choose a good broker, how to analyze information, how to order skillfully, and how to protect themselves are investors who know how to make money.

OPENING AN ACCOUNT

The first step on the road to being a trader is opening an account with a broker. This can be done using an online broker, over the telephone, or visiting a brokerage in your area. Today, I find that most traders prefer the online route. In any event, whether you use a broker on- or off-line, you start by signing a new account agreement. This somewhat legal-looking document may have you wondering if you are setting up an account or applying for a job. Nevertheless, the new account agreement is important for two reasons:

1. The new account form enables the brokerage firm to find out about you and your financial resources, including your assets, liabilities, income, net worth, and the like.
2. It spells out the terms and conditions that the broker imposes on you.

Therefore, while not particularly interesting, the new account agreement is your first look at the broker and, because it stipulates the terms of your relationship with that firm, is worth reading in detail.

As soon as the account form is reviewed and approved by the brokerage firm, you can begin trading. Based on your experience level and financial profile, the broker may impose limits on your trading (e.g., limit the use of credit, limit specific option strategies, or prohibit the purchase of certain speculative investments). In most cases, however, that will not pose a problem.

While the actual process of setting up a brokerage account is relatively easy, in the long run finding the right broker who meets your specific investment goals can be quite difficult. After all, there are a large number of online brokers out there these days. Determining which one is right for you can be a long and arduous process.

One of the most important considerations when evaluating various brokers is: What type of brokerage firm is it? In turn, in order to understand the differences between brokers, it is important to understand how they make money. Specifically, most of a brokerage firm's revenues come from the trading activity of its clients. In other words, each time an investor buys or sells an investment security, the broker makes money through commissions.

Today, due to the sheer number of firms in existence, commissions (and/or sometimes fees) vary wildly. Furthermore, with the recent growth in online trading and subsequent competition, commissions have reached historical lows. Some firms even let certain wealthy clients trade for free. Others, however, provide specific investment advice and, therefore, require that investors pay higher fees and commissions for doing business with them.

As a generalization, commissions will be higher for brokers who offer specific advice to the investor. So-called full-service firms have financial consultants or financial advisers who not only buy and sell shares on your behalf, but also gather information about your financial resources and make specific recommendations. Other firms, sometimes called discount brokers, do not offer any sort of financial advice. They simply execute buy and sell orders on your behalf at the lowest cost possible.

For instance, to buy 100 shares of a stock trading for $55, a full-service broker will charge between $75 and $200, while a discount broker charges only $10 to $20. At the same time, a full-service broker will place the order in context of your personal financial situation and, if you request, offer advice as to whether it is a suitable investment for you. A discount broker will simply complete the transaction according to your instructions. Charles Schwab and E*Trade are examples of discount brokers. If you are reading this book, chances are you will be a self-directed investor and it will not make much sense to use a high-priced broker. Instead, you will focus on online firms that specialize in options trading and have relatively low commission schedules.

THE OPTIONS ACCOUNT

Believe it or not, one problem new traders sometimes face is not being able to obtain permission to trade options from a broker. Clients of brokerage firms who want to trade options are required to complete an options approval form when opening new accounts. The options approval form is designed to provide the brokerage firm with information about the customer's experience, knowledge, and financial resources. According to the "know your customer" rule, options trading firms must ensure that clients are not taking inappropriate risks. Therefore, the new account form and the options approval document gather appropriate background information about each customer.

Once the documents are submitted, the compliance officers within the brokerage firm determine which specific strategies are appropriate for the client. The process is designed to ensure that inexperienced traders do not take inappropriate risks. For example, if the option approval form reveals that the client has little or no options trading experience, and then the client goes on to lose large sums of money via complex high-risk trades, the brokerage firm could potentially face regulatory and legal troubles for not knowing its customer. So, each brokerage firm is required to understand the client's experience level and financial background to ensure that the customer is not trading outside of certain parameters of suitability.

An individual's past options trading experience and financial resources will allow him or her to trade within certain strategy levels. For instance, level 1 strategies include relatively straightforward approaches like covered calls and protective puts. More complicated trades, however, require a higher level of approval. Table 12.1 shows a typical breakdown a

TABLE 12.1   Typical Brokerage Firm Breakdown

Strategy	Options Trading Level				
	Level 1	Level 2	Level 3	Level 4	Level 5
Covered call writing	✔	✔	✔	✔	✔
Protective puts	✔	✔	✔	✔	✔
Buying stock or index puts and calls		✔	✔	✔	✔
Covered put writing			✔	✔	✔
Spreads			✔	✔	✔
Uncovered put and call writing				✔	✔
Uncovered writing of straddles and strangles				✔	✔
Uncovered writing of index puts and calls					✔

brokerage firm might use to group strategies by levels. Traders with a great deal of experience and significant financial resources can generally receive approval for level 5 trading. This would allow them to implement any type of trading strategy, including high-risk trades like naked calls and uncovered straddles.

Although the options approval levels can vary from one broker to the next, level 3 is enough for most readers following the strategies in this book. Since we do not recommend uncovered selling of options, approval beyond level 3 is unnecessary. At that point, traders can use a variety of simple strategies like straight calls and puts, as well as more complex trades such as spreads, straddles, and collars.

In order to avoid the frustration of opening an account with a firm that will not allow trading in more advanced levels, new traders will want to find out the brokerage firm's policy regarding options approval before funding an account. The best way to do this is to contact the firm's options approval department by phone. If you have little or no experience, ask them what steps you need to take in order to trade the more complex options strategies (level 3). It sometimes helps to specify which trades (i.e., spreads, straddles, collars, etc.) you intend to trade. Often, the firm will ask you to write a letter or somehow demonstrate that you understand the risks of trading options. After that, most firms will allow you to fund the account and to begin implementing those options trading strategies that interest you.

ROLES AND RESPONSIBILITIES OF ALL BROKERS

Regardless of whether the broker charges high or low commissions, all brokers are regulated by the Securities and Exchange Commission (SEC) and are required to meet certain standards when dealing with customers. Specifically, the Securities Exchange Act of 1934 puts forth certain provisions that all brokers must adhere to.

- *Duty of fair dealing.* This includes the duty to execute orders promptly, disclosing material information (information that a broker's client would consider relevant as an investor), and charge prices that are in line with those of competitors.
- *Duty of best execution.* The broker has a responsibility to complete customer orders at the most favorable market prices possible.
- *Customer confirmation rule.* The broker must provide the investor with certain information at or before the execution of the order (i.e., date, time, price, number of shares, commission, and other information).
- *Disclosure of credit terms.* At the time an account is opened, a broker must provide the customer with the credit terms and, in addition, provide credit customers with account statements quarterly.
- *Restriction of short sales.* This rule bars an investor from selling an exchange-listed security that they do not own (in other words, sell a stock short) unless the sale is above the price of the last trade.
- *Trading during offerings.* Rule 101 prohibits the broker from buying a stock that is being offered during the "quiet period"—one to five days before and up to the offering.
- *Restrictions on insider trading.* Brokers have to establish written policies and procedures to ensure that employees do not misuse material nonpublic (or inside) information.

WHY PAY HIGH COMMISSIONS?

In a world of low-cost (in some cases, no-cost) trading and strict government regulation of brokers, does it ever make sense to pay the high commissions of a full-service broker? Sometimes it does. While investors are protected to an extent by federal securities laws, they are not protected from poor investment decisions. Investors often lose money in the stock market. There are risks and, in a world of do-it-yourself investing, the investor is ultimately responsible for ensuring that investment decisions are wise.

The ultimate goal in investing is to preserve capital and improve your financial well-being. Investors are sometimes uncertain about the risks associated with an investment. If you are reading this book, you are probably not one of them. But, at times, a full-service firm can be helpful. For instance, firms like Merrill Lynch, Morgan Stanley Dean Witter, and Prudential have financial advisers or consultants who offer investment advice for a commission or fee. Sometimes paying a higher commission in exchange for objective financial advice is sensible. The important element in the equation, of course, is being confident that the information is objective and worthwhile. To find out, you can ask the perspective financial consultant a number of questions. The SEC has compiled a list of helpful questions to ask which can be accessed at its web site (www.sec.gov).

Sometimes it makes sense to do both—that is, open an account with a brokerage firm to handle some of your retirement savings, money you have saved for an education, or other aspects of your portfolio, and then take a smaller percentage to trade options in a self-directed online account. For example, you might split your portfolio into 75 percent conservative investments and 25 percent with more aggressive options trades like long-term bull call spreads.

CONCLUSION

If you are motivated to the point that you want to invest in stocks, finding a broker and opening an account are relatively straightforward tasks. Over the long run, however, finding a broker to meet your particular investment needs can prove complicated. If you plan on doing one or two trades and are not seeking help with respect to your overall financial plan, a discount broker who simply executes your orders is appropriate. However, if you are not sure about whether the investment is a wise one, a full-service broker, while charging higher commissions, may offer you objective and worthwhile information. Therefore, the first step in selecting a broker is determining the level of financial advice you need, if any.

Regardless of whether you trade one or a hundred times a month, brokers have a duty to execute orders promptly and at the best possible price. While it is difficult to monitor the brokerage firm from the time your order is submitted until the time it is executed, there are some things you can do. If you trade actively, monitor the market in real time and watch your trade take place. In addition, consider submitting limit orders (priced between the bid and the offer). Finally, if you have a bad trade—or in Street parlance, a bad fill—contact your broker's customer service department and find out what happened. If the problem persists, remind them of their "duty of best execution." If that doesn't work, change brokers.

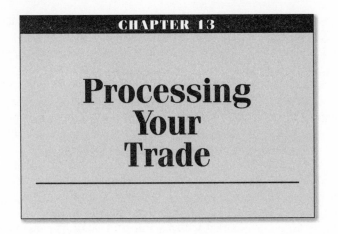

CHAPTER 13

Processing Your Trade

M ost investors never realize the number of steps required for a trade to occur and the incredible speed involved. Technology has made this process almost unnoticeable to the average investor. When you contact your stock or futures broker, you begin a process that, in many cases, can be completed in 10 seconds or less, depending on the type of trade you want to execute. There are various types of orders that are placed between customers and brokerage firms. The faster technology becomes, the faster a trader's order gets filled. Let's take a closer look at what happens when you place an order.

EXCHANGES

Stocks, futures, and options are traded on organized exchanges throughout the world, 24 hours a day. These exchanges establish rules and procedures that foster a safe and fair method of determining the price of a security. They also provide an arena for the trading of securities. Over the years, the various exchanges have had to update themselves with the ever-increasing demands made by huge increases in trading volume. The New York Stock Exchange (NYSE)—probably the best known of the exchanges—not too long ago traded 100 million shares as a high. Today we see 700, 800, 900 million, and even 1 billion shares trading in a day.

Stocks, futures, and options exchanges are businesses. They provide the public with a place to trade. Each exchange has a unique personality and competes with other exchanges for business. This competitiveness keeps the exchanges on their toes. Exchanges sell memberships on the exchange floor to brokerage firms and specialists. They must be able to react to the demands of the marketplace with innovative products, services, and technological innovations. If everyone does his or her job, then you won't even know where your trade was executed.

In addition, exchanges all over the world are linked together regardless of different time zones. Prices shift as trading ends in one time zone, moving activity to the next. This global dynamic explains why shares close at one price and open the next day at a completely different price at the same exchange. With the increased use of electronic trading in global markets, these price movements are more unpredictable than ever before.

The primary U.S. stock exchanges are the New York Stock Exchange, the American Stock Exchange (Amex), and Nasdaq. There is a host of others that do not get as much publicity as the big three. However, each exchange certainly produces its share of activity. These include the Pacific Exchange in San Francisco, the Chicago Stock Exchange, the Boston Stock Exchange, and the Philadelphia Stock Exchange. The major international exchanges are in Tokyo, London, Frankfurt, Johannesburg, Sydney, Hong Kong, and Singapore.

The primary commodities exchanges include: Chicago Mercantile Exchange (CME); Chicago Board of Trade (CBOT); New York Mercantile Exchange (NYMEX); COMEX (New York); Kansas City Board of Trade; Coffee, Cocoa and Sugar Exchange (New York); and the Commodity Exchange (CEC). The Commodity Futures Trading Commission (CFTC) and the National Futures Association (NFA) currently regulate the nation's commodity futures industry. Created by the Commodity Futures Trading Commission Act of 1974, the CFTC has five futures markets commissioners who are appointed by the U.S. President and subject to Senate approval. The rules of the SEC and the CFTC differ in some areas, but their goals remain similar. They are both charged with ensuring the open and efficient operation of exchanges.

EXPLORING THE FOREX

The term FOREX is derived from "foreign exchange" and is the largest financial market in the world. Unlike most markets, the FOREX market is open 24 hours per day and has an estimated 1.2 trillion in turnover every day. The FOREX market does not have a fixed exchange. It is primarily traded through banks, brokers, dealers, financial institutions, and private individuals.

A common term in the FOREX arena you will run into is "Interbank."

Originally this was just banks and large institutions exchanging information about the current rate at which their clients or themselves were prepared to buy or sell a currency. Now it means anyone who is prepared to buy or sell a currency. It could be two individuals or your local travel agent offering to exchange euros for U.S. dollars.

However, you will find that most of the brokers and banks use centralized feeds to ensure the reliability of a quote. The quotes for bid (buy) and offer (sell) will all be from reliable sources. These quotes are normally made up of the top 300 or so large institutions. This ensures that if they place an order on your behalf that the institutions they have placed the order with are capable of fulfilling the order.

Just as with other securities on other exchanges, you will see two numbers. The first number is called the bid and the second number is called the ask. For example, using the euro against the U.S. dollar you might see 0.9550/0.9955. The first number is the bid price and is the price at which traders are prepared to buy euros against the U.S. dollar.

Spot or cash market FOREX is traditionally traded in lots, also referred to as contracts. The standard size for a lot is $100,000. In the past few years, a mini-lot size has been introduced of $10,000 and this again may change in the years to come. They are measured in pips, which is the smallest increment of that currency. To take advantage of these tiny increments it is desirable to trade large amounts of a particular currency in order to see any significant profit or loss.

Leverage financed with credit, such as that purchased on a margin account, is very common in FOREX. A margined account is a leverageable account in which FOREX can be purchased for a combination of cash or collateral depending what your broker will accept. The loan in the margined account is collateralized by your initial margin or deposit. If the value of the trade drops sufficiently, the broker will ask you to either put in more cash, sell a portion of your position, or even close your position. Margin rules may be regulated in some countries, but margin requirements and interest vary among broker/dealers; so always check with the company you are dealing with to ensure you understand its policy.

Although the movement today is toward all transactions eventually finishing with a profit or loss in U.S. dollars, it is important to realize that your profit or loss may not actually be in U.S. dollars. This trend toward U.S. dollars is more pronounced in the United States, as you would expect. Most U.S.-based traders assume they will see their balance at the end of each day in U.S. dollars

Preferably you want a company that is regulated in the country in which it operates, is insured or bonded, and has an excellent track record. As a rule of thumb, nearly all countries have some kind of regulatory authority that will be able to advise you. Most of the regulatory authorities will have a list of brokers who fall within their jurisdiction and may provide you with a list. They probably will not tell you who to use but at least if the list came from them, you can have some confidence in those companies.

Just as with a bank, you are entitled to interest on the money you have on deposit. Some brokers may stipulate that interest is payable only on accounts over a certain amount, but the trend today is that you will earn interest on any amount you have that is not being used to cover your margin. Your broker is probably not the most competitive place to earn interest, but that should not be the point of having your money with them in the first place. Payment on the portion of your account that is not being used, and segregation of funds all go to show the reputability of the company you are dealing with.

Policies that are implemented by governments and central banks can play a major role in the FOREX market. Central banks can play an important part in controlling the country's money supply to ensure financial stability.

A large part of FOREX turnover is from banks. Large banks can literally trade billions of dollars daily. This can take the form of a service to their customers, or they themselves might speculate on the FOREX market.

The FOREX market can be extremely liquid, which is why it can be desirable to trade. Hedge funds have increasingly allocated portions of their portfolios to speculate on the FOREX market. Another advantage hedge funds can utilize is a much higher degree of leverage than would typically be found in the equity markets.

The FOREX market mainstay is that of international trade. Many companies have to import or export goods to different countries all around the world. Payment for these goods and services may be made and received in different currencies. Many billions of dollars are exchanged daily to facilitate trade. The timing of those transactions can dramatically affect a company's balance sheet.

Although you may not think it, the man in the street also plays a part in today's FOREX world. Every time he goes on holiday overseas he normally needs to purchase that country's currency and again change it back into his own currency once he returns. Unwittingly, he is in fact trading currencies. He may also purchase goods and services while overseas and his credit card company has to convert those sales back into his base currency in order to charge him.

The key impression I would like to leave you with about the FOREX is that it is more than the combined turnover of all the world's stock markets on any given day. This makes it a very liquid market and thus an extremely attractive market to trade.

HISTORY OF OPTIONS

Stock options have been trading on organized exchanges for more than 30 years. In 1973, the first U.S. options exchange was founded and call options on 16 securities started trading. A few years later, put options began trading. A decade later, index options appeared on the scene. Today, five exchanges are active in trading options, and annual options trading volumes continue to set records. Indeed, over the course of 30 years, from the early 1970s until now, a great deal has changed in the world of options trading. What was once the domain of mostly sophisticated professional investors has turned into a vibrant and dynamic marketplace for investors of all shapes and sizes.

The history of organized options trading dates back to the founding of the Chicago Board Options Exchange (CBOE) in 1973. By the end of that year, options had traded on a total of 32 different issues and a little over 1 million contracts traded hands. In 1975, the Securities and Exchange Commission (SEC) approved the Options Clearing Corporation (OCC), which is still the clearing agent for all U.S.-based options exchanges. As clearing agent, the OCC facilitates the execution of options trades by transferring funds, assigning deliveries, and guaranteeing the performance of all obligations. The Securities and Exchange Commission approved the OCC roughly two years after the founding of the first U.S.-based options exchange.

The early 1970s also witnessed other important events related to options trading. For instance, in 1973, Fischer Black and Myron Scholes prepared a research paper that outlined an analytic model that would determine the fair market value of call options. Their findings were published in the *Journal of Political Economy* and the model became known as the Black-Scholes option pricing model. Today it is still the option pricing model most widely used by traders.

As more investors began to embrace the use of stock options, other exchanges started trading these investment vehicles. In 1975, both the Philadelphia Stock Exchange (PHLX) and the American Stock Exchange (AMEX) began trading stock options. In 1976, the Pacific Stock Exchange (PCX) entered the options-trading scene. All three became members of the OCC, and all three still trade options today. In addition, in 1977, the SEC permitted the trading of put options for the first time. In 1975, 18 million option contracts were traded. By 1978, the number had soared to nearly 60 million.

The 1980s also saw an explosion in the use of options, which eventually peaked with the great stock market crash of 1987. The Chicago Board Options Exchange launched the first cash-based index in the early 1980s. In 1983, the exchange began trading options on the S&P 100 index (OEX).

The OEX was the first index to have listed options. In 1986, the CBOE Volatility Index (VIX) became the market's first real-time volatility index. VIX was based on the option prices of the OEX. In 2003, it was modified and is now based on S&P 500 Index (SPX) options.

The early 1980s saw a growing interest in both stock and index options. From 1980 until 1987, annual options volume rose from just under 100 million contracts to just over 300 million. After the market crash in October 1987, however, investor enthusiasm for options trading waned and less than 200 million contracts traded in the year 1991, or roughly two-thirds of the peak levels witnessed in 1987.

Throughout most of the 1990s, trading activity in the options market improved. In 1990, long-term equity anticipation securities (LEAPS) were introduced. The OCC and the options exchanges created the Options Industry Council (OIC) in 1992. The OIC is a nonprofit association created to educate the investing public and brokers about the benefits and risks of exchange-traded options. In 1998, the options industry celebrated its 25th anniversary. In 1999, the American Stock Exchange began trading options on the Nasdaq 100 QQQ (QQQ)—an exchange-traded fund that is among the most actively traded in the marketplace today. That same year, total options volume surpassed one-half million contracts for the first time ever.

In the year 2000, a new options exchange arrived on the scene. On May 26, 2000, the International Securities Exchange (ISE) opened for business. It was the first new U.S. exchange in 27 years. In addition, ISE became the first all-electronic U.S. options exchange. In 2001, the options exchanges converted prices from fractions to decimals. In 2003, more than 900 million contracts traded, nearly four times greater than 10 years before. Therefore, despite the three-year downturn in the U.S. stock market, options trading continued to grow.

On February 6, 2004, the Boston Options Exchange (BOX) made its debut as the sixth options exchange and began trading a handful of options contracts. The exchange was the second all-electronic exchange and is already another key player in the burgeoning options market.

EVOLUTION OF THE CHICAGO BOARD OPTIONS EXCHANGE

The CBOE has had quite an impact on the financial world over the past 31 years. Formed on April 26, 1973, the CBOE changed this country's and the world's approach to the markets forever. This new organization introduced the trading universe to standardized options contracts. The contract represented 100 shares of stocks with expiration dates attached using various months as their basis.

Today the CBOE is the largest options exchange in the United States, trading more than half of all U.S. options and accounting for over 90 percent of all index trading. To get to this point, the CBOE has been through many changes and has had a very interesting historical time line.

When the Chicago Board of Trade first opened the CBOE, it traded only call options on 16 equities. After four years of operation, put options were finally offered. This caused quite an explosion in option trading activity in 1977 and moved the SEC to bring to a halt any further options expansion until a formal review could take place. The review, which was designed to protect the customer, lasted until March of 1980. From there the CBOE quickly added option coverage to include 120 equities. Later in that same year (1980) the CBOE and the Midwest Stock Exchange merged their options operations.

In March 1983, one of the biggest developments in the CBOE's history took place. This involved introducing the trading public to options on broad-based stock indexes. The impact was enormous, with the first such index traded being the Standard & Poor's 100 Index (OEX). This proved to be a very active index, trading an average of more than 130,000 contracts per day in 1983.

This surge in trading volume prompted the CBOE to move into its own facilities in 1984, leaving the CBOT behind. The move allowed the CBOE to implement key trading floor technologies enhancing customer service. The major innovation was what was known as the Retail Automatic Execution System that facilitated the filling of customer orders at the current bid or ask and reported back all within a matter of seconds.

The CBOE launched the Options Institute in 1985 to educate its major customers such as retail account executives and institutional money managers. In 1989 options on Treasury securities were introduced. The option values were pegged to changes in the U.S. Treasury yield curve.

In 1990, the needs of the conservative options investor were addressed by introducing long-term equity anticipation securities (LEAPS) to the trading public. LEAPS allow investors to create positions that have up to three years until expiration, which makes them particularly attractive to the traditional buy-and-hold investor. In 1992 the CBOE expanded its coverage to include various sectors and foreign markets. This new development helped customers to better hedge their exposure to these areas as well as allowing investors to participate in different market spaces and the continued globalization of the markets.

The growth continued in 1997, adding another cash-settled index based on the Dow Jones Industrial Average, which quickly became the CBOE's most popular new product. At the same time options on the

Dow Jones Transportation Average and Dow Jones Utility Average were introduced.

Of course, there are indeed other option exchanges that do exist in the United States such as the American Stock Exchange, the Philadelphia Stock Exchange, and the Pacific Exchange. However, by far the CBOE is the options-trading king when one just looks at sheer volume. Going forward, the CBOE will continue to innovate and bring even more products to the investment community, especially given the continued and growing popularity of options.

STOCK AND STOCK OPTION ORDERS

If you are trading the stock market, you begin by placing an order with your broker, who passes it along to a floor broker, who then takes it to the appropriate specialist. At this time, the floor broker may or may not find another floor broker who wants to buy or sell your order. If your broker cannot fill your order, it is left with the specialist who keeps a list of all the unfilled orders, matching them up as prices fluctuate. In this way, specialists are brokers to the floor brokers and receive a commission for every transaction they carry out. Groups of specialists trading similar markets are located near one another. These areas are referred to as trading pits.

Once your order has been filled, the floor trader contacts your broker, who in turn contacts you to confirm that your order has been placed. The amazing part of this process is that a market order—one that is to be executed immediately—can take only seconds to complete. Today, electronic exchanges like the International Securities Exchange handle a large number of options orders and offer an electronic platform to match option buyers and sellers.

Your broker, as your intermediary, is paid a commission for his or her efforts. Each completed trade costs $10 on the low end and $100 or more on the high end. Stock commissions may also be based on a percentage value of the securities bought or sold. Remember, your broker should be in the business of looking after your interests, not generating commissions for the broker's own pockets. Since your chief concern as a trader should be to get the transactions executed as you desire and at the best price possible, choosing the right broker is essential to your success.

Let's review the stock market order process. The seven steps are:

1. You call your broker.
2. The broker writes your order.
3. Broker transmits your order to an exchange.

4. Floor broker tries to immediately fill your order or takes it to a specialist.
5. A specialist matches your order.
   - If your order is placed as a market order, you get an (almost) immediate fill.
   - If placed as a limit order, you have to wait until you get the price you want.
6. Confirmation is sent back to the broker.
7. Broker contacts you to confirm that your order has been executed.

This is the process for most transactions. In addition to the specialists, there are also market makers who are there to create liquidity and narrow the spread. Market makers trade for themselves or for a firm. Once an order "hits the floor," the market makers can participate with the other players on a competitive basis.

Stock orders are handled in a similar manner. For example, orders for a stock trading on the New York Stock Exchange or the American Stock Exchange are routed to the floor electronically or to a floor broker by phone.

In contrast, Nasdaq—also referred to as the over-the-counter (OTC) market—is an electronic computerized matching system that lists more than 5,000 companies, including a large number of high-tech firms. Brokers can trade directly from their offices using telephones and continuously revised computerized prices. Since they completely bypass the floor traders, they get to keep more of their commissions. There are no specialists, either—but there are market makers. Their role is to bid and offer certain shares they specialize in, thereby creating liquidity. They make their money on the spread—the difference between the bid price and the offer price—as well as on longer-term plays. This difference may be only $0.25 or less. However, when you trade a large number of shares this adds up very quickly.

FUTURES (COMMODITY) ORDERS

Futures contracts are traded at commodity exchanges. The exchanges are divided into trading pits that are sometimes subdivided into sections of smaller commodities. Individual trades are recorded on trading cards that are turned in to the pit recorder, who time-stamps and keys the transaction into a computer. Some exchanges prefer the use of handheld computers that instantly record the transactions.

Orders are filled using an open-outcry system in which the buyers (who make bids) and the sellers (who make offers, otherwise known as the ask) come together to execute trades. For example, in the gold market, if gold is trading at $300 per ounce, you may get a price of $299.50 to $300.50. This means that you would be buying the gold futures contract at $300.50 and you would be selling at $299.50. You may ask, "Why can't I buy for the lower price and sell for the higher price?" You can try, but the trade will probably not be executed. The floor traders make their living off this spread. They won't want to give it up to you.

Let's review the futures market order process. The six steps are:

1. Call your commodity broker (or call direct to the trading floor for large accounts).

2. The broker writes an order ticket or sends your order via computer or calls the trading floor.

3. Floor broker will bid or offer.

4. When your order is matched, the fill is signaled to the desk.

5. The desk calls your broker.

6. Broker contacts you to confirm trade execution.

Floor traders primarily make their money on the bid/ask spread. They are the ones who spend (in many cases) thousands of dollars each month for the privilege of being on the floor of the exchange (or hundreds of thousands to buy a seat). They can either lease the seats—gaining the right to trade as an exchange member—or purchase the seats. In addition, they spend each and every day creating liquidity for the investor who is not trading on the exchange floor. For this they want something in return—the right to make money on the spread. The money to be made on the spread comes from the difference between the bid and offer price. In the gold example, the reward is $1.00 ($300.50 − $299.50 = $1.00).

In addition, being right where the action is allows them to see the order flow. Order flow is the buying and selling happening around them. They can spot when large traders are trading. This does give them an advantage, but there are negatives. These include the following five aspects:

1. High monthly expenses.

2. The need to always be in the market to cover costs.

3. Sometimes getting caught up in emotion, not fact.

4. Missed opportunities in other markets.

5. Very physically and mentally demanding work.

You probably have watched scenes of the trading pits on television or in movies. You see lots of people yelling and screaming. Is this the way it really is? Yes, when there is action in the market, it can be extremely volatile. If it is slow, people will read newspapers or just stay away. I do suggest that you visit a commodity exchange if you get the chance. It is very exciting and enlightening to experience what really goes on there.

Commodity exchanges have to provide safeguards for the public trader. For every buyer there is a matching seller. Clearing firms—where the funds are held—must guarantee that each person trading through them has the available funds to meet that trader's financial obligations, or they are responsible for the integrity of the transaction. This system of checks and balances has never failed, no matter how crazy the markets have become. Public investors can feel secure that they will not lose their money due to the system failing.

PLACING AN ORDER

One of the most stressful functions of the new trader is actually to place that first trade. Picking up the phone or turning to the broker's web site is, without a doubt, a time of considerable angst. After all, you are trying something totally new. There is seemingly an endless number of choices, you are on your own, and, if you mess it up, it could conceivably cost you a lot of money—your money.

As you gain experience, you will settle into a style of order placing that works for you and your broker, often forgetting that there are many other ways that might possibly solve a particular problem. This section covers the basics of how to place a trade, as well as some of the available options that even the more experienced trader may have forgotten.

To place a trade, you need to communicate several specifics to your broker. The following list is designed to introduce you to these specifics, although in no particular order. This list can be applied to a single asset trade (stock, call, or put), but will work just as well for any of the Optionetics-style combination (or hedge) trades. You will need to provide your broker with seven items of information:

1. Whether you want to buy (go long) or sell (go short) the security.
2. The underlying stock (and possibly ticker symbol).
3. The actual investment vehicle (stock, call, or put).
4. For an option, the particular month and strike (and possibly the appropriate symbol).

5. The number of shares or contracts.

6. The type of trade (market, limit—and if so, what limit).

7. Whether you are "opening" a position (initially setting up the position—long or short) or you are "closing" a position (selling an existing long position or buying back an existing short position).

Some brokers and most web sites require you to provide the exact ticker symbol for your transaction. Other brokers will accept an order using a plain English description of your transaction. Personally, I much prefer to give the plain English description, as then I am exactly sure of what I am saying. Using the coded description (which you can search for on Optionetics.com) is just too easy to mess up, especially for a beginning trader or a semiactive trader (one who "remembers" the code from last week or month). For instance, "AEQFI" and "AEQRI" appear to be almost identical (at least with my handwriting!) and in fact are both options for Adobe Systems, ADBE. However, the "FI" is the descriptor for the June 45 call, while the "RI" is the descriptor for the June 45 put—both fine options, but hardly interchangeable. If you are using a broker that cannot look up the symbols (or remember them—they, after all, do this many, many times per day), then be very careful that you in fact have the correct symbol—it is your money that is on the line.

ELECTRONIC ORDER ROUTING SYSTEMS

In a relative sense, electronic communication networks (ECNs) are fairly new. Changes in the 1990s made it possible for the small investor to get access to Level II data and compete with market makers through the use of ECNs. Level II quotes are one of three levels of the National Association of Securities Dealers Automated Quotations System (Nasdaq). Level I quotes provide basic information such as the best bids and asks for Nasdaq-listed stocks. Level II data provides investors with more detailed quotes and information, including access to current bids and offers for all market makers in a given Nasdaq-listed stock. Level III is the most advanced level and is used by market makers to enter their own quotes to the system. In order to utilize ECNs you need to use a broker who provides direct access to them. Most traditional online brokerages offer Level I quotes; only direct-access brokers provide Level II quotes.

ECNs are little exchanges themselves. There are many competing bids and offers from every single stock on each ECN. This depends a lot on the interest in the stock you are following. For example, you might find little interest from ECNs in particular stocks and sometimes find no interest at all for certain issues. By default, you will find only the best bid and ask from every ECN displayed in the Level II window.

Generally each ECN is able to communicate only within the same ECN. There are some "intelligent" ECNs, though, that take all other ECNs into account. You are, however, able to display your own bids and offers through ECNs.

The major advantage of these networks is that your orders are sent directly to the market, with no intermediary involved. They are kept in an electronic environment. For example, assume you are attempting to buy 600 shares of Cisco on an ECN and someone is willing to sell 600 shares or more for $17. If you enter an order for $17, your order gets executed immediately since there is a matching sell order. If the seller would be willing to sell only 300 shares, then you would get executed on only 300 shares. Also, since ECN orders are kept in an electronic environment they can be immediately changed or canceled at any time.

The electronic Island network is the most popular order route among day traders. It is very inexpensive and amazingly fast and offers tremendous liquidity. Some of the major rules applying to the Island network are that you can place your own bids and offers, there is no limit to the amount of shares you can trade, and you can place only limit orders. Also, Island allows you to enter price limits with less than one-cent increments. Some of the bigger stocks can be traded on the network as well as Island, accounting for a large percentage of the total trades made on Nasdaq.

Archipelago is an intelligent order routing system. It has its own order book but is also able to communicate with other market participants. Archipelago is a very useful system for day traders. Whenever there are ECNs inside of your price limit, Archipelago is generally a very good choice. If there is a better price coming into the market, Archipelago tries to target that price. The network can only accept round lots for smart order routing, and if you get a partial fill it will keep resending your order until it is completely filled or you become the bid or ask yourself.

The small order execution system (SOES) was developed in the 1980s and was made mandatory after the 1987 stock market crash. During the crash, market makers were ignoring their posted prices and therefore clients weren't able to execute their orders. This system made it mandatory for market makers to execute orders at the market maker's displayed price. It is for trading with the market makers only and cannot execute to ECNs.

The small order execution system used to have many limitations to it, such as maximum number of shares that one could execute, as well as a time restriction for executing orders on the same stock. The biggest problem with it was that a market maker was required to execute only one SOES order every 15 seconds.

However, with the introduction of the new super SOES system these rules have changed significantly. Market makers are now required to execute every order they receive up to the size they are displaying, unless they decide to change their offer. You can now execute up to 999.999 shares via the new SOES.

Since market makers now have to execute every SOES order they receive it has made SOES executions much faster and it has become a very interesting route for day traders again. You cannot display your own bids and offers through SOES, and the old SOES system still exists for small-cap stocks.

The other ordering system worthy of a mention is the Selectnet system, also known as SNET. SNET was developed by market makers in order to execute their trades electronically and to avoid the verbal communication process via telephone. Today Selectnet is available to direct-access traders as well. Using an SNET preference order you can send your order to every market participant available on the Nasdaq.

As you evaluate any of these systems for your own trading, just remember order entry rules change quite frequently. Make sure to study your broker's manual very carefully before making any trades.

ORDER MECHANICS

When you call your broker to place an order, it is a good idea to have all of the important information written down in front of you. What factors are important to this process? You have to know the quantity, the month, and the commodity. If there are options, you have to know the strike price, whether you want calls or puts, and if there is a price. A fill refers to the price at which an order is executed. Let's review the important items that need to be specified depending on the type of order you are placing.

1. *Order type.* The kind of order you wish to place. For example, a delta neutral spread order.

2. *Exchange.* Sometimes you will choose the exchange where the order is to be placed (for futures and options). Often, however, you will simply choose "best," which instructs the broker to send the order to the exchange showing the best price. The default in most cases is "best."

3. *Quantity.* Number of contracts.

4. *Buy/sell.* Puts or calls (also include the strike price and expiration).

5. *Contract.* Name of the contract (e.g., T-bond futures).

6. *Month.* Expiration month of the contract.

7. *Price.* Instructions regarding price execution.

Types of Orders

Once you've decided to place a trade, you have to choose the type of order to place. There are two basic order types: market orders and limit orders.

Market orders are generally not the preferred way to trade when you are trading options. By placing a market order, you are assured of getting the trade executed immediately, but at whatever price the floor chooses to charge you! You are, in effect, handing them a blank check. In reality, if you are trading a stock or option with much activity, the price that the broker gives you on the phone and the price the stock is trading at by the time the order reaches the floor (a few seconds or minutes later) will not be much different. However, thinly traded stocks and options may find a fairly large swing. Also, if your broker happened to give you a bad quote or you didn't hear it correctly and you place a market order expecting a similar price, you may be quite disappointed. You would choose a market order only if you absolutely, positively had to have the trade consummated right now, no matter what. Therefore, under most circumstances, the limit order is the preferred way to trade.

Limit orders come in many forms, but the basic concept is that you want the trade filled only if it meets your requirements (primarily a price that you have set). This protects you in several ways, not the least being that it protects you from the floor traders (manipulating the prices just as your trade reaches the floor) and from yourself (making an error in calculation, reading, hearing, or whatever). In a limit order, you will typically give the broker a price for the trade. If it is a debit trade (you are paying money out of your account) that price is the maximum price that you pay, and if the trade is a credit trade (you are receiving money into your account), that price is the minimum amount you will accept. *Note:* If the stock is moving rapidly, you can always set a limit outside the bid-ask spread.

For instance, if the stock is moving up and you want to be sure to buy it, you can set a buy price of $55, even if the bid-ask quote is $49–$50. Your broker should be able to get the stock (or option) even if it is moving, but you are protected from finding that the price is $60 or $70 by the time your order is filled. If the stock price does jump up to $70 by the time your order hits the floor, you, of course, will not be filled. But then not getting filled is probably a good thing, especially if it was trading at $50 only moments before.

From that basic setup, there are a number of additional choices that can be made. The first set of choices revolves around the duration of your limit order. There are basically three choices at this time:

1. *Fill or kill.* The broker is instructed to fill the order immediately, or kill (cancel) the order.

2. *Day order.* This tells the broker to put the order in for the day; if it is not filled by the close of the market today, then cancel the order. This is by far the most common type of limit order for two reasons. First, if you don't otherwise specify, the broker will automatically place the order as a day order. Second, it protects you from forgetting that you have the order placed with the broker, and being surprised somewhere down the road when you get a fill notice on that trade you placed weeks or months before. There is nothing stopping you from placing a series of day orders, if the original order was not filled. If you forget to replace the order and circumstances change dramatically in your security, you will not be adversely surprised.

3. *Good till cancelled (GTC).* When you place such an order, your broker will simply put it into the system and forget about it until your criteria are met. At that time, the order will be filled. Most brokers do have a limit on GTC orders, and will automatically cancel them after some period of time—two months, six months, and so on. You should inquire of your broker as to what their standards are. For instance, one of the brokerage houses I use will accept day orders only for spread trades. However, my particular broker will automatically replace a spread order each morning if I have entered it as a GTC order. (I've been told this has something to do with their computer systems!)

Beyond the basic formats, there are numerous specialized order formats that could be useful for the trader in given circumstances. The following list details a few of these formats, and the reasons for using them:

1. *At-the-opening order.* If you want to make sure that you buy or sell a stock or option at the beginning of the day, you would place an at-the-opening order. Whatever price is set at the opening is the price at which your order will be filled. Typically, you would place this order if you were expecting a large move in the stock based on overnight news.

2. *Buy on close.* If you want to buy the security for the closing price of the day, you would place a buy on close order. This is often used if you are short a put or call on expiration day, there is a lot of time value still remaining in the option, and you don't want to either purchase or deliver the actual stock. By placing a buy on close order, you will suck out the entire premium, and avoid being assigned on your short option position.

2. *Buy on opening.* The buy side of the at-the-opening order.

3. *Cancel former order.* If you have previously placed a limit order, it hasn't yet been filled, and you now want to cancel it, you would place a cancel former order.

4. *Exercise.* If you are long an option and you either want the stock (if you are long the call) or you want to sell stock you own (if you are long the put), you would exercise your option. You would choose to exercise the option as opposed to either buying the stock and selling the call or selling the stock and selling the put if there was no time value in the option (typically if the option is deep in-the-money). You will then get the strike price of the option (buying or selling) no matter where the stock is presently trading, and with no slippage for the spread between the bid and ask prices. The exercise of the option takes place after the market has closed for the day—it doesn't happen immediately.

5. *Market-if-touched (MIT).* This is an order that automatically becomes a market order if the specified price is reached. This is frequently done as a form of protection for falling prices if you are long the stock or call, or rising prices if you are short the stock or long a put. Although it will not absolutely protect you (the market price could slam down through your price and keep on going before it can be executed, or conversely it could touch the price and then rebound, but still force you out of that trade), it can be useful in some instances. This order can be used either to close out an existing long or short position or to create a new position (if you only want to buy XYZ Corporation if the price dips to $X).

6. *Buy stop order.* Set a price (usually lower) than the current price, and if the market price falls to that specified price, the order becomes a market buy order. This is the same as the market-if-touched order, but specifically to repurchase a short position.

7. *Sell on opening.* The sell side of the at-the-opening order.

8. *Sell stop order.* Set a price lower (as protection) or higher (to capture a profit) than the current price, and if the market price reaches that price, the order becomes a market sell order. This is the same as the market-if-touched order, but specifically to sell your position.

Placing an order is not a simple process, especially for the beginner. The variations are many, and the consequences of being wrong are great. This is why, when asked by new traders about the type of broker to get, I strongly recommend a full-service broker—they can and will take the time to walk the novice trader through the intricacies of the system, generally protecting the traders from themselves. Even after many years of trading, I still find a full-service broker very helpful, especially when I am trying to do anything out of the ordinary, anything that is new to me, or something that I haven't done in some time.

HOW TO PLACE A DELTA NEUTRAL TRADE

To demonstrate this process, let's take a look at a few delta neutral orders.

Straddle Example

Trade: 1 Long June XYZ 50 Call @ 3.50 and 1 Long June XYZ 50 Put @ 4.
Place the order by saying: "I have a delta neutral spread order. I want to buy one June XYZ 50 call. I want to buy one June XYZ 50 put."
Explanation: You then have to decide if you want to place the order at-the-market or as a limit order. A market order must be executed immediately at the best available price. It is the only order that guarantees execution. In contrast, a limit order is an order to buy or sell stocks, futures, or option contracts at, below, or above a specified price. If you want a limit order, you would say, "I want to do the straddle as a limit order at a debit of 7.50 to the buy side."

If you place each part of the spread as a separate order, you run the risk of getting filled on one side and not the other; and there goes your risk curve. If you are going to do this, you need to carefully pick some period of low volatility in the middle of a very fast market. You need to wait until things settle down a little bit. What happens if your chosen market is between two strike prices? Be clear! State the strike prices you want.

Those of you who have traded before probably already know why clarity is so important. Most orders consist of buying the stock and selling the puts. This buy-sell combination on a spread is pretty normal. You have to be explicit when you place an order to make sure you get what you want. Before calling your broker, always write orders down on paper or, better yet, in a trading journal. Every order you place with a broker is recorded on tape. If you make a mistake in the order process, you are responsible for that trade no matter what. By writing down exactly what you are going to say to your broker, you can avoid making costly mistakes. In addition, keeping a trading journal is an excellent way of learning from your successes and mistakes as well as staying organized.

Long Synthetic Straddle Example

Trade: 2 Long September XYZ 40 Calls and Short 100 Shares of XYZ Stock.
Place the order by saying: "I have a delta neutral spread order. Shares with options. I am buying two Labor Day September XYZ 40 calls and I am selling 100 shares of XYZ stock at the market."

Explanation: We say "Labor Day" because "September" and "December" sometimes sound alike, especially when spoken loudly. You also want to request that the order be placed as one ticket to give you a better chance of execution. Whenever you use ATM calls, you will probably find it easier to get the order filled.

These examples are simply guides for entering delta neutral trades. Remember, the ratio does not make any difference. You could be doing 2 calls and 100 shares or 20 calls and 1,000 shares. Although you need to specify the number, all the other important factors remain the same. Again, it does not make a difference what kind of order you wish to enter. Just specify the quantity, the month, the commodity, and then if there is an option, what kind and the price. These examples are basic market orders. Let's switch gears and try something a little more complicated.

Bull Call Spread Example

Trade: Long 1 June XYZ 35 Call @ 13.95 and Short 1 June XYZ 40 Call @ 11.05.

Place the order by saying: "I have a spread order. I am buying one June XYZ 35 call and selling one June XYZ 40 call at a debit of 2.90 to the buy side."

Explanation: A plain old bull call spread will enable you to understand the debit and credit side of a trade. In this example, we are going to place the order as a limit order. We are not going to do it at-the-market. Just for a little calculation, let's say the premium on the buy side was 13.95 and the premium on the sell side was 11.05. This is where they closed. We come in and want to do it at whatever price they closed at. On the buy side, we are out-of-pocket paying 13.95; and on the sell side, we are receiving 11.05. What is the point difference? We are paying 2.90 more than we are getting. This is just an ordinary bull call spread where we buy the lower strike call and sell the higher strike call. The trick is to figure out an acceptable limit order based on the premium on the buy side (debit) and the premium on the sell side (credit).

This process is pretty easy and would be the same if you were doing a 10×10, a 20×20, a 100×100, or a 2×2, as long as it is a 1-to-1 ratio. There is no other calculation than just doing the simple math. This would be the same process if you were doing a put spread. You would need to determine both the debit and the credit and net them out. If you are taking money out-of-pocket, it is a debit to the buy side. If you are receiving money, it is a credit to the sell side.

Put Ratio Backspread Example

Trade: Long 10 July XYZ 35 Puts @ 11.05 and Short 5 July XYZ 40 Puts @ 13.95.

Place the order by saying: "This is a put ratio backspread. I am buying 10 July XYZ 35 puts. I am selling 5 July XYZ 40 puts for a 8.15 debit to the buy side."

Explanation: Perhaps you have a specific idea—particularly when you are doing ratios—of a certain price you are willing to pay. Maybe this spread is trading at 8.15 but you are only willing to pay 7.50. You can put that order in; however, it may not get filled. The point is that you can enter a trade at whatever prices you like. The previous prices were just used to demonstrate the calculations. If you are debiting the buy side, you don't say "credit" because you are actually taking money out-of-pocket. This is a debit. A credit means that you are taking money in. It is something that goes on the sell side of the ticket. A debit means that you are taking money out. It is something you are paying on the buy side.

Don't worry about the prices. Just make sure you get the right spread to make the trade work the way you want it to. If you want to do a credit of 5, do you care whether you do it at 15 and 20 or 5 and 10? No, you don't care what those prices are. All you care about is the differential between the two prices. The floor will not fill a limit order if you give them premium prices on each side.

Before you place a trade, write the order in a trading journal to keep an accurate account of every trade you make and glean as much knowledge as possible from your trading experiences.

AVOIDING COSTLY ORDERING MISTAKES

Option trading can sometimes be very complex; some positions may be constructed using a couple of different instruments. If adjustments are added to an existing position, then the complexity of the matter can become even greater. Even seasoned traders can become confused when dealing with the trades that they have created. It's just the nature of the beast. But confusion can lead to placing a trade incorrectly. You may end up putting yourself in a position where you are exposed to a greater amount of risk than what you originally intended. The severity of the mistake will determine the course of action that is required to fix it. This topic really hits home with me since I just went through an experience of confusing strike prices, which caused me to make a mistake on the long and short options that I wanted to trade. If I had followed the advice in this chapter, perhaps the mistake could have been avoided completely.

Let's go through a couple of different scenarios. Let's say you receive the confirmation from your brokerage firm and then realize that you placed the wrong trade. Unfortunately, in this business you can't go back and say, "Hey, "I really didn't mean to place the trade this way." However, if you are able to call your broker immediately after the trade was executed and tell him or her that you need to "bust" the trade, then they may be able to accommodate you; but that certainly is not the norm. Fortunately, I was able to have my trade busted and I certainly learned my lesson!

Scenario #1

Let's say that you intended to get into a Cisco Systems (CSCO) bull call spread using the 20/40 strike prices for a small debit. However, the symbols that you gave your broker were incorrect and you ended up with the 20/30 bull call spread for that same debit. This is not a complete disaster because the risk profile is going to be similar to what you originally wanted. You have a couple of different actions that you can take in this situation. First, you can just sit with the trade and see what happens. If your original assumptions were correct and the stock moves higher, then you should be okay. The position just won't move as quickly as the intended trade. Another alternative is just to exit the trade immediately and realize the loss that you will incur because of the bid-ask spread. All other things being equal, I would probably stick with the erroneous trade, since there is plenty of time for the trade to work out.

Scenario #2

Now let's look at a situation that's a little more serious that requires immediate attention. Let's say that you had a synthetic straddle on Best Buy (BBY), and you have been trading it very aggressively—as the stock moves, you are buying and selling off shares in order to lock in profits and remain delta neutral. Another adjustment that you could make to the position is to sell calls against the long stock. In the process of doing this, you neglect to double-check the number of shares that you were long. You end up selling more calls than you have long stock. This is a very serious situation, because the position now has an unlimited amount of risk due to the greater number of short calls compared to the number of long shares available to hedge the trade. The reason to trade a synthetic straddle is to limit risk, not create an unlimited liability. The action to take here is to immediately buy back the appropriate number of calls that were sold short. This action eliminates the unlimited risk that became part of the position, which is exactly the goal when dealing with this type of scenario.

As you can imagine, there are many different types of mistakes that can be made when placing orders; some mistakes are more serious than others. It is up to the trader to discern what has happened and determine how the risk characteristics of the position have changed, and then act accordingly. Maybe you will just stick with the trade or maybe something will need to be done immediately.

The best way to keep yourself from getting into these problem situations is to be well prepared when you trade. There are five steps that I always go through before placing a trade. This process should help you catch any of the possible mistakes that are easy to make.

1. Write out the trade exactly that you want to place, including the appropriate actions (buy/sell), the number of contracts, the months, the strike prices, the appropriate option symbols, as well as the net price for the overall trade.
2. Write out the various characteristics of the trade. Know and understand the margin requirements that the brokerage firm is going to require once you're in the trade.
3. Use an options analysis software package to view the risk profile.
4. Know your exit strategy or at what point the next adjustment will need to be made.
5. Place the trade with confidence.

Hopefully, some of these ideas will help you to avoid panicking if you realize that a mistake has been made with one of your trades, as well as to provide some ideas on how to prevent mistakes from occurring.

POINTS TO REMEMBER

The typical brokerage firm ticket has the buy side of the trade on the left and the sell on the right. Generally, we would always start from left to right, writing down your buy side first. You would say, "I have a straddle order. I am going to buy three of the June XYZ 45 calls and buy three June XYZ 45 puts at _____" at the market or as a limit order with a certain number of points to the buy side.

With a spread order, always give the quantity, the month, the underlying instrument, the price, and the strategy: "I am buying three [quantity] June [month] XYZ (stock) 45 [strike price] straddles [strategy]." The other half of the order would be, "I am buying three June XYZ 45 puts. I am buying three June XYZ 45 calls."

Now we have to calculate the cost. It is either a debit, a credit, or at even. If it is at even, you do not want to receive a debit or a credit. You want to stay at net cost of zero. I prefer to do my trades at even or better. However, a straddle is a debit strategy because you are buying both legs.

If you are not comfortable with the specific language of straddles and spreads, then state each part of the trade instead. Tell your broker, "I want to buy three of the June XYZ 45 puts. I want to buy three of the June XYZ 45 calls." Spell out the whole thing if you are more comfortable doing it that way. In fact, you don't even have to say "straddle" and "strangle" if you are not comfortable with those terms. In the beginning, it is a good idea to be specific about each leg to make sure you get it right. Once you have experience in these types of trades, it will become second nature to properly state your orders correctly.

If you are trying to get a credit, do not state the credit as a dollar value. You do not say, "I want $200." You specify the credit, if that is what you desire, at the point level you want. So $200 is actually 2 points. You need to specify the trade in the terminology used by the floor. Most importantly, it has to always be in tick values or point values, not in dollar terms of how much you want to spend or take in.

You can go into any market at whatever price you want. The floor will either execute the trade at that price or it won't. You could say that you want the trade at even, but if the market is not at even, your order will not get filled. At one point during the day, perhaps the market does get to even and you finally get what you want. Bottom line: If you don't enter, you can't win. If you want it at a certain price, put the order in as a limit order. Then wait to see if you get the trade filled. If you do not get your credit price or at even, try the trade at some other time. Do not chase the trade.

The more volatile the market is, the wider the bid-ask spread will be. If the market is pretty quiet that day, the bid-ask spread will be smaller. The bid-ask will be smaller for the at-the-money (ATM) options and for the body of the trade and greater for the wings. Floor prices primarily depend on volatility and liquidity. In addition, the longer the time your options have until expiration, the wider the spread. Floor traders will widen the spread when there is a greater chance of their being wrong due to time, volatility, and volume.

CONCLUSION

The progression of an order through the trading system is a fascinating process. It has come a long way from the days in the late 1700s when traders met under a buttonwood tree on Wall Street. Today's floor traders run an average of 12 miles each trading day just to get the job done. Although many traders never set foot in an exchange, it is important to understand the process your order goes through before returning to you as a profit or a loss. As we progress further into the twenty-first century, this process will undoubtedly become even more electronically synchronized. As the information superhighway speeds up, it will be very interesting to see how it changes and if the nature of the game itself remains the same.

CHAPTER 14

Margin and Risk

W hen we refer to risk management, we speak of the ability to handle with a degree of skill the possibility of loss. Of course, when dealing with trading and the market, there are many kinds of risks. Overall, what we are trying to do is make money while at the same time managing the possibility of loss. This definition could be considered the Optionetics motto.

Risk management isn't the sexiest of terms; people don't run out and study everything they can on the subject when they hear it. This has to do with the fact that risk management often discusses how to avoid losses, not how to make huge returns. Newsletters and stock-picking sites post claims of high returns on individual plays, but rarely state they controlled their losses with proper risk management. It just doesn't sell. Baseball has taught us that people prefer a home run to four straight base hits, but a knowledgeable coach or trader knows that it's the base hits that win games.

Everyone wants to talk about the option play that made him or her 1,000 percent. But do these same people tell you about the other five plays that they lost everything on? Of course they don't. Does risk management mean you can't make large returns on your money? No, it does not. It means avoiding risks that do not make sense over the long term. Maybe the most common reason why option traders don't last long is because they take too many risks. Even though they win occasionally, they end up running out of capital before the next home run is hit. Once you are down 5–0 in the ninth inning, that one home run is not going to win the game for you.

I believe one of the most helpful concepts to understand is compound interest. Most of us profess to understand this concept, but if we did, we wouldn't be so quick to take the risks we often do. Let me explain this with an example.

If I put $1,000 in a trade and it returns 1,000 percent, I now have $10,000. Now that I have this extra capital, I decide to place $2,500 in four different trades, but each of these loses 50 percent of their value. I now have $5,000 left. If I had made just a 50 percent profit on each trade and compounded this growth each time, I would have more than $11,000. This is because of the compounding effect on my money. This is a very rough example. Obviously, taking all your winnings and playing it on one trade is not advised; but the point is that smaller profits that are compounded will create a larger account than risking too much to hit the home run. When was the last time you got a 1,000 percent return, anyway? In order to accomplish this task, too much risk is normally taken.

At Optionetics, we teach that hedging in case of a loss is as important as getting out with a profit. None of us want to entertain the thought that we might be wrong about a trade, but the fact is that we will be wrong sometime and we need to be prepared for that event. On every trade we place, we should figure what our risk/reward ratio is. If we are risking $500 to make $100, is that a good risk/reward ratio? In general, the answer would be no. However, it really depends on the probability that the $100 would be made or the $500 would be lost. For example, what if you see an option trade that has a risk of $500, but this would occur only if a stock at 50 drops all the way to 35 in the next two weeks? The odds would probably say this risk is worth the reward because this drop is not likely to happen. This same philosophy holds true when looking at risk/reward of, let's say, 10–1. This looks great, but if the stock needs to move 75 percent in a month to get this reward, is it really a promising risk?

Clearly, there is a lot to risk management. The underlying theme is to make certain you analyze the relationship between risk and reward. Understand that taking fewer risks and not holding on for the home run will benefit each of you in the long run. The Optionetics Platinum site has tools to help traders figure probabilities and risk/reward ratios that can make better traders of us all.

So before you start visualizing that new car from the profits of one trade, realistically analyze the situation and make sure it really is the best move to make.

THE CONTEXT OF RISK

When you put on a trade, you need to look at the worst-case scenario to determine just how much your investment could possibly lose. Then you have to decide just how much you are willing to risk—$100, $1,000, or $10,000? When professional traders put on a trade, the first thing they look at (if they know what they're doing) is the risk.

For example, if you're a trader with a large bank trading in currencies, you're not trading just $100. You're trading $10 million per contract. To be able to profitably handle such sums, these traders have to be able to manage their risk. The most profitable trades have two key elements: limited risk and unlimited reward. After all, you can create trades with limited risk all day long, but most of them will also have a limited reward. A $100 risk for a $100 reward is simply not acceptable. No one wants to risk $100 to get $100, even if you win 50 percent of the time. Only if you increase your winning percentage will it be an acceptable risk-to-reward ratio. Would you take a $100 risk for a $500 reward? I would. But how many times are you going to be right? That's why it's imperative to find trades with limited risk and strong rewards with a high probability of being correct.

I am frequently asked, "What will it cost me to invest?" This is a difficult question to answer. The necessary amount depends on a number of factors. The most important factors are the size of the transaction (number of shares/futures or options) and the risk calculated on the trade.

As we discussed briefly in an earlier chapter, there are two types of transactions—cash and margin. Cash trades require you to put up 100 percent of the money. Margin trades allow you to put up a percentage of the calculated amount in cash, and the rest is on account. Both types of accounts are set up to settle trades and payments for trades, yet they are quite different. With a cash account, all transactions are paid in full by settlement day. Most of the time, the cash is already in the account before the trade is placed. If you bought 100 shares of IBM at $100, this trade would cost $10,000 plus commissions paid out of your cash account. If IBM were to rise to $110, your account would then show an open position profit of $1,000, or a 10 percent rise in the account. Let's take a closer look at margin and how it can help improve the risk-reward ratio.

WHAT IS MARGIN?

Margin is defined as the required amount of cash on deposit with your clearing firm to secure the integrity of a trade. Most traders and investors prefer margin accounts in order to leverage their assets to produce a higher return. The amount of margin required on every trade is the calculated figure required by securities and commodities regulators, exchanges, and brokers to protect them from default. Margin is the amount required to protect these various parties against your "falling off the face of the earth."

A margin account allows the trader to borrow against the securities owned. In order to set up a margin account, you are required to fill out additional applications with your broker. You can use the money for anything you want; however, many traders use it as a type of leveraging vehicle with which to buy more stock. Margin accounts allow a trader to extract up to 50 percent of the cash value of securities, or to have two-to-one leverage in buying stocks. This means that for every share of stock you own, the brokerage firm will lend you money to buy another share. This doubles your reward, but also *doubles your risk*.

If you buy 200 shares of IBM at $100 using a margin account, this trade will cost $10,000 plus commissions ($20,000 ÷ 2), since the brokerage firm loans you the money to purchase half of this position. If IBM were to rise to $110, the margin account would show an open position profit of $2,000, or a 20 percent rise in the account, while you still have only $10,000 invested in this position.

The margins on futures are significantly lower than the margins on stocks. The increased leverage that futures markets offer has contributed to their rise in popularity. As previously discussed, the margin requirements for futures vary from market to market. These requirements change frequently as the price of the commodity fluctuates. You should check with your broker to determine the current margin requirement for any futures you are considering trading. In most cases, if your trade starts to lose money, you will receive a margin call from your broker, which requires you to increase your margin deposit to maintain your position.

When trading a margin account, brokerage firms charge interest against the cash loaned to the trader. The interest rate is usually broker call rate plus the firm's add-on points. The rate is lower than for most loans due to the fact that it is a secure loan. The broker has your stock, and in most cases will get cash back before you get your stock back.

Keeping your margin requirement low is essential to lowering stress. Many people find it difficult to stay in a high-stress trade. They think about it too much, fretting about how they might lose $5,000. After all, it took them two months to earn that $5,000. Suddenly, they're out of the game. Lowering your stress gives you a clear mind with which to make good decisions. When you put on a trade, try to keep the cost of capital as low as possible and the return on your investment as high as possible. Maintaining a low margin is the natural extension of limiting your risk.

If you are buying options as part of your delta neutral strategy, or doing futures with options, your margins should be pretty close to zero. You will, however, have to pay for the options in full. Now, as the trade starts working, if your futures side makes money, you shouldn't really have to add any more money to your margin account. However, if your futures side is losing money, you may have to. There's nothing like receiving a margin call in the early hours of the morning to ruin your whole day.

If you have a $100,000 account and you spend $50,000 on your options, there is still $50,000 in your account to support a losing futures position. The problem is that in the options market you cannot touch your long option value, although it is probably keeping pace with the futures loss. It is almost like it's in escrow. It's there, but you cannot touch it. The only way you can get to it is to exit your position. You may have to add more money temporarily to your account to stay in the trade.

If money were absolutely no object whatsoever—go ahead and dream big—then you wouldn't care if you had to feed your account. You'd probably be better off if your option side was the one working because of the long gamma. For example, let's say you initiate a delta neutral trade with ATM options. As the market goes up, your options are getting longer and longer, which is definitely the preferable position to be in. Unfortunately, for most of us money is not only an object, but also the driving force behind many of our decisions each and every day.

When you are choosing which side to concentrate on—the long side or the short side for your futures—keep in mind that you may have to add more money. This is why it is sometimes beneficial to try to forecast market direction. Loans against your securities do not have any scheduled payments. Therefore, you can pay back your loan on your terms. Borrowing from your margin account also has tax considerations if you have stock that you do not want to sell.

If the perceived risk of your trade increases, then the margin requirement will also increase. If you have enough money in your account to cover the increased perceived risk, then you won't be required to put up any additional cash. However, if you do not have the cash required to cover this additional perceived risk, then you will get a margin call. A margin call is a call from your broker requiring you to place additional funds in your account. If you do not place these additional funds in your account, your position will be liquidated. (If you bought something it will be sold, and if you sold something it will be repurchased. This will close out your position.)

Why should you be concerned about margin? Most new investors and traders rarely consider the margin other than from the standpoint of how much money they have to put up initially. However, an investor or trader should look at margin as a cost of doing business. There may also be opportunity costs incurred by placing a trade. In other words, the best way to make money over the long term is to use limited resources (capital) to achieve the highest return with the lowest risk over the shortest period of time. You may have a chance to put on 10 different trades, each with different risk/reward and timing profiles. Each potential trade should be placed in order of the highest return on capital with the least risk.

New investors or traders need time to figure this out. However, once you reach a level of proficiency sufficient to understand and numerically calculate these levels and categorize them, you will achieve your goal of generating the highest return while minimizing your risk.

Let's take a look at the established general margin requirements. Then we will explore some examples of capital analysis.

MARGIN REQUIREMENTS

One of the most common questions asked by new traders when opening up a trading account deals with margin requirements. However, before we get started, let me state that there are minimum rules set by the NASD that govern margin accounts. Each firm, however, can set more stringent rules, so it is important that traders check with the brokerage firm they are opening an account with to find out its specific rules.

As previously mentioned, a margin account is a type of account that allows traders to borrow money from the broker to leverage their trades. This seems like a great thing, and it can be; but margin can also work in reverse. It also means that a margin call might be made to tell you to put more money in to cover the losses. This is where margin accounts can become dangerous. If the stocks in your account drop sharply, like during a market crash, you can lose more money than you originally invested. This was one of the main causes of the stock market crash in 1929, because the margin requirement was only 10 percent at the time.

Some traders might notice that even retirement accounts sometimes use margin accounts. This isn't because you have the ability to borrow money in these accounts, but because a margin account is needed to place the capital to trade strategies that have higher risk than the initial debit. This is another reason why I teach traders not to use naked option strategies. Not only is the risk unlimited with these strategies, but also the amount of capital needed to trade them is very high.

Many traders might wonder what the margin requirements are for different strategies. This varies according to broker, but the easiest way to figure it is to calculate the risk the broker has. Whatever the maximum risk is will be the minimum amount of money the broker will want in your margin account. If you have any specific questions about the margin needed, just pick up the phone and call your broker.

Stocks

Based on the rules of the Securities and Exchange Commission and the clearing firms, margin equals 50 percent of the amount of the trade using stock. For example, if 100 shares of IBM at $100 cost $10,000, then you are required to have a minimum of $5,000 on deposit in your margin account. There are other levels, but the general public rule of thumb is leverage equals two to one. If the price of the stock rises, then everyone wins. If the price of the stock falls below 75 percent of the total value of the investment, the trader receives a margin call from the broker requesting additional funds to be placed in the margin account. Brokerages may set their own margin requirements, but it is never less than 75 percent, which is the amount required by the Fed.

Margin on selling stocks short is extremely expensive. You have to be able to cover the entire cost of the stock plus 50 percent more. This value will change as the market price fluctuates. For example, if you wanted to short sell 100 shares of IBM at $100 each, you would need to have $15,000 as margin in your account—that's $10,000 plus 50 percent more. If the market price falls, you can buy back the shares at the lower price to repay the loan from your broker and pocket the difference. If the stock price rises, you will be required to post additional margin. Exactly how much is up to the discretion of your broker.

Futures

Margin requirements for futures vary significantly from market to market due to the volatility of the markets as well as the current price. A comprehensive margin commodity table detailing a variety of futures margins can be found at the Chicago Board of Trade (www.cbot.com) and the Chicago Mercantile Exchange (www.cme.com) web sites. You can also consult your broker for current margin requirements.

Options

Margin is used in a slightly different manner by options traders. Options are not marginable, meaning that the broker requires payment in full for an option purchase. However, when we trade a strategy that could cost us more than the original debit, we must have a margin account. The easiest way to look at this is to figure what the risk is to the broker. For example, let's say that I want to enter a bear call spread using 40 and 50 strike calls. I would sell the 40 call and buy the 50 call for a credit. Let's assume this credit is $2. This means that if the stock stays below $40 at expiration, I get to keep the entire premium. However, if the stock rises above $40 and ultimately moves above $50, I have reached my maximum loss, which is figured by taking the difference in strikes minus the initial credit. Thus, my maximum loss would be 8 points or $800 per contract. If I don't want to put this money in the account up front, I can use a margin account. However, the margin requirement should not be very large because the broker is at risk for only $800. This is where it is important to choose an appropriate broker. There are many brokers who will require an account value of $50,000 or more just to give you margin on an $800 trade. Most brokers who cater to option traders have less stringent demands; but it's important to find out ahead of time how much the broker you are investigating requires to open a brokerage account.

Selling naked options—placing a trade with unlimited risk—has the highest margin requirements. (I highly recommend that you never sell naked options. All short options should have a corresponding long option or stock to cover you against unlimited risk.)

Combination Trades

If you are hedging options, then the use of margin is up to your broker's discretion. While combining the buying and selling of options, stocks, and/or futures creates a more complex calculation, it can also reduce your margin requirements dramatically. These days, you have to find a broker who caters to option traders to make it in the volatile twenty-first century markets. An important rule of thumb: If you're worried about the margin at the onset of the trade, you should not be doing the trade. This rule keeps me away from putting on positions that are much larger than I can really handle. Obviously, the larger your capital base becomes, the less you worry about margin. However, it's always in your best interest to look for the best trade—one with the highest return and the lowest risk—no matter how much money you have available in your account. Individuals with large investment accounts may be tempted to make trades that are too big for their knowledge level. Start small. Build your account intelligently as you build your knowledge base.

RISK, CONTROL, AND BALANCE

When we have positions in the markets, we usually want to have a way of protecting ourselves from the worst possible scenario that could occur. The reason is so that we can preserve our capital and manage our risk exposure to the markets. But, why do we want to do this? Do we trade so that we can have an added element of risk in our lives? And, if the answer were yes, why would we want to limit that amount of risk? I think the answer may lie in what I call the balance between risk and control. This may also provide some insight into what compels a person to trade the markets.

I remember as a child hearing stories about wild animals that, for one reason or another, came into the custodial care of a person. Maybe the person was trying to nurse the animal back to health or turn the animal into a pet. The thing that interested me most about these stories was that the animals would sometimes starve to death even though they had food to eat in front of them. One of reasons was that the animals needed to hunt their own food. Why? To me, it seemed obvious that it would be easier for the animal to eat the food in front of it than it would be to have to go through the difficulties of hunting for its food in the wild. Is the animal's need to hunt greater than its need for food? I will leave that last question for the psychologists to answer. However, I think that we could agree that the animal would experience a higher degree of uncertainty and risk if it had to search for its own food.

I think this need for the element of risk extends to people, but we also want to have a degree of control. I remember watching a television program several years ago about people bungee jumping off a bridge. A few months later, some entrepreneurs had set up platforms for bungee jumping in vacant lots of large cities. For a small fee, the thrill seeker would get a few moments of an adrenaline rush and the experience was over. While many of my friends classified this as a "faked suicide attempt," I wondered if there was much difference between this and a roller coaster ride at an amusement park. There was an element of risk and control that each participant agreed to before either event occurred.

Why is all of this important to trading? Most traders do not consider their reasons for trading. This is probably because they have never considered what their values and beliefs are about taking financial risks. They also seem to pay little attention to the parts of trading that they have control over. I am usually reminded of this fact when I talk with a trader about his methodology for trading. When the subject of risk and stop-losses comes up, there may be some element of apprehension that develops. This usually means that their stop-loss rules change from day-to-day or that no rules exist in their methodology. As a result, the limit for risk that the trader has is left for the markets to decide. This is because the trader has made a decision not to exercise control over the only thing that can be controlled once he or she is in the market: the protective stop-loss order. The only things that you have control over in the markets are your orders to enter or exit the markets and when you place the orders. Unless you have a risk-free options trade, there is never a guarantee of profits.

There are three basic types of protective stop-losses for options traders: time, premium, and the price related to the stock. Most options traders should consider using all three techniques for each of their positions. Also, you should note that these techniques are elements of a trading plan that a trader has to act on. In that respect, these parameters are different than the typical stop-loss orders for buying or selling stocks. The protective stop-loss order for a stock may be placed immediately after the position is entered and may get automatically triggered days or weeks later if the market moves against his position. This is different from the type of stop-loss protection that I am talking about for options. For the option's protective stop-loss, the order to exit the option's position is placed with the broker after the stop-loss parameter is exceeded.

The time stop-loss may be triggered when you have purchased an option and you want to exit the position in the last 30 to 45 days before expiration. This approach helps a trader exit the position when the options will experience the most time decay. However, this would probably not apply for all options spreads. For example, you would likely want a credit spread to expire in order to receive the full credit potential of the spread. If you are trading debit and credit spreads, you will likely have different time stop-loss parameters for both in your trading plan.

Stop-loss parameters may also be based on options premium. When you have purchased an option or an option spread, you may want to exit the spread if the value of the position depreciates to a certain level. Also, you may want to distinguish between making this decision based on the option's theoretical value or its actual value. If the option that you traded last week is no longer at-the-money, there may not be a lot of volume traded on the day you look at the markets. As a result the last traded price may not be relevant to the current market conditions.

The third method would be based on the value of underlying stock. This method is usually employed when the trader has used some element of technical analysis in his or her decision to trade the stock. Since technical analysis is based on the stock price, the trader is able to determine the price at which the decision to trade the stock is no longer valid. This decision could be related to a moving average or a particular chart pattern. It helps the trader to quantify the price where the trader should exit the options spread.

The effective use of protective stop-loss parameters in a trading plan has a correlation to the beliefs and values that the trader has about risk and control. When traders begin learning about the markets, they tend to look at the analysis part of the endeavor and as a result have a very left-brain approach to trading. This leaves the trader open to self-sabotage because the very emotions, beliefs, and values that compel him or her to trade are not included in the initial training and assessment of the trading plan. We have all heard that trading is both an art and a science. Integration of the right-brain beliefs and values with the left-brain analytics helps the trader to create a trading plan where success is a function of technical decisions more closely aligned with their tolerance for risk.

A final consideration when trying to mitigate risk is to avoid investing all or even half of your trading capital to one trade—even if you're certain that it's a sure thing. Allocate maybe 5 or 10 percent to each trade. That way, by diversifying and spreading your risk across many different strategies, one bad trade or idea will not clean out your whole account.

CONCLUSION

As a trader you must be aware of all the risks—as well as potential rewards—of every trade you place. Understanding the risks, and most importantly, learning how to intelligently protect yourself are essential to successful investing and trading. To achieve success, you must become an avid risk manager. In the beginning, this will not be easy. That's why it's so important to start small. Mistakes will be made and you don't want your account to be wiped out before you get the chance to spread your wings. Since learning to protect yourself through creative risk management is the most vital part of successful trading, take the time to practice the art of risk management by setting up paper trades.

Options are one of the most flexible financial instruments ever invented. They can be employed to reduce your risk exposure and potentially increase your returns, especially when playing the securities that have been beaten up without mercy. As Calvin Coolidge once said, "Those who trust to chance must abide by the results of chance." Understanding how options interrelate and respond in different scenarios is the first step to managing risk while taking advantage of the opportunities that the current market presents.

CHAPTER 15

A Short Course in Economic Analyses

The global financial marketplace strikes a delicate balance between a vast network of business interests. Fascinating events in one area of the global economy, such as energy prices, can trigger a reaction in other markets, like bonds, and the ripple effect can spread to other commodities and stocks. With technology helping to speed up the decision-making process and allowing traders to execute trades at the speed of light, capital can and often does shift from one country's financial markets to the next. All of this movement in money and investments securities is often based on international events, the global economy, and the outlook for various financial markets around the world.

Understanding the relationship among stocks, bonds, and economic events helps traders to obtain a better understanding of what is happening in the world, the daily movements in the financial markets as well as the long-term trends. This type of broad market analysis allows us to better understand the risk-reward profiles of various directional trades before we actually put money on the line and pull the trigger. This chapter seeks to assess the general behavior of and interrelationships among stocks, bonds, and interest rates and how various economic conditions impact all three.

Historically, two factors have caused the stock market to crash: war and long-term interest rates. If bond prices drop too much, interest rates can climb too high because there is an inverse relationship between bonds and interest rates, or yields. If so, it can devastate the stock market. A 7.5 percent yield on the benchmark long-term Treasury bond has been a catalyst for a decline in the stock market, because it creates competition for investor money. For example, if bonds offer an attractive yield, a large institution might change its asset allocation from 60 percent of the money invested in stocks and 40 percent in bonds to 60 percent in bonds and 40 percent in shares.

In addition, when bond yields go up, companies have to pay more to borrow from banks, which hurts their profits. As a result, the stock market is affected. In addition to bond yield concerns, investors also worry about the earnings of a company. If earnings are better than expected, they can override rising bond yields, which can cause stocks to go up. When stocks aren't focused on earnings, which are released quarterly, they sometimes focus on bond yields.

These interrelationships are both dynamic and constantly evolving. Here are 11 salient relationships I look for when developing a broad market analysis:

1. Lower bond rates help companies make more profits.

2. Short covering in the bond market can boost the Dow Jones Industrial Average.

3. Falling bond yields can contribute to strength in financial stocks.

4. Bond yields follow the economy. If the economic indicators are coming in strong, bond yields will rise; if they are coming in weak, bond yields will fall.

5. Inflation is not only the enemy of the bond market—it's also the enemy of the stock market because a rise in prices affects corporate profits.

6. Shares are driven by corporate profits, and profits are driven by a healthy economy with low inflation.

7. The inflation reports such as the Producer Price Index and the Consumer Price Index will affect both stocks and bonds the same way.

8. With steady economic growth, stocks can increase even if earnings aren't outstanding.

9. When the Fed hikes interest rates, this can cause the yield on the long bond to increase, which will create competition for shares.

10. If the Fed raises rates too high, this can cause a recession and can reduce inflation, during which time, bonds, and interest rate–sensitive stocks will rise.

11. When the dollar is strong, U.S. exports cost more; as the dollar falls, import prices rise, which is inflationary.

If some of these relationships do not hold, then it behooves the trader to analyze the reasons for this divergence and look for opportunities to make money under the circumstances. Dissecting these 11 factors will give the trader a good feel for the current environment as we develop our broad market analysis scenario, which is always an excellent first step before implementing a particular directional strategy at the micro level.

INTEREST RATES, BONDS, AND STOCKS

Forecasting market direction is never a sure thing. Luckily, there are a few economic interrelationships that can help you to make consistent profits. One of the most important of these is the relationship between interest rates and bond prices. The following table illustrates the typical interrelationship of the change in interest rates to the price of a bond and the subsequent effect on the stock market.

Interest Rates	Bond Prices	Stock Prices
Up	Down	Down
Down	Up	Up
Sideways	Sideways	Up

Although these relationships are relatively stable, occasionally there are deviations from typical economic behavior, referred to as divergences. This table, however, illustrates the *normal* expected action based on economic theory.

A bond is a debt instrument sold by governments or corporations to raise money for various reasons. The bond most widely considered by investors and traders is the 30-year Treasury bond. It has a corresponding futures contract that is traded at the Chicago Board of Trade and reflects one very important aspect of many Americans' lives: mortgage interest rates. Bonds are rarely held by the same buyer until maturity. Instead, they are traded at a price that fluctuates according to interest rates and inflation. Since a bond's interest rate stays the same until maturity, its real value at maturity depends on inflation's actual value of the dollars at repayment. In general, interest rates are also tied to inflation.

According to economic theory, if interest rates go up, bond prices go down; and if interest rates go down, bond prices rise. Why does this inverse relationship hold true? Let's say that you decide you are going to lend me $1,000 for a five-year period. I agree to pay you interest at a rate of 8 percent each year, which happens to be the market rate for interest charges. Therefore, I will pay you $80 per year interest. The very next day, interest rates jump to 10 percent. Now you could lend $1,000 and receive 10 percent interest, which would bring in $100 per year, but you have lost the opportunity of lending that first $1,000 at the higher rate of interest. Did the value of the first loan go up or down with the rise in interest rates? The first loan's value went down. If you want to sell that 8 percent loan as an investment to someone else, you will find that its value has decreased. A loan with a 10 percent interest rate has a greater value than one with 8 percent. Therefore, when interest rates go up, bond (loan) prices fall.

Let's examine the converse situation: When interest rates go down, bond prices rise. If interest rates drop from 8 percent to 5 percent, an investor could receive only $50 on the $1,000 investment. A previous loan with an 8 percent interest rate would now increase in value, because it would make the investor $80 a year instead of just $50. In general, fluctuations in interest rates stimulate the bond market. Trading bond options can also be quite lucrative if you pay close attention to interest rates and inflation.

It is also a good practice to monitor certain bond markets' yield to maturity. This measurement predicts a bond's return over time by assessing its interest rate, price, par value, and time until maturity. To access this information, please consult our web site at www.optionetics.com.

In general terms, the same inverse relationship exists between interest rates and shares as between interest rates and bond prices. Thus, bond prices and the stock market usually move in the same direction. Assume your company has to buy $10,000 worth of equipment. You don't want to pay cash for the equipment; therefore, you have to finance the purchase. In this case, you will pay 8 percent interest—$800 per year. Interest is an expense that gets subtracted from what you earn. Therefore, if you earn $20,000 before interest, you will have earned $19,200 after interest is paid. If the interest rate were 10 percent for the same $10,000 loan you would pay $1,000 per year and your earnings would drop to $19,000 after you subtracted interest. Once again, we see an inverse relationship, this time between interest rates and earnings—the higher your interest rate, the less money flows to your earnings. If your company has reduced its earnings due to a higher interest expense, then your company's value decreases. This affects your company's stock price. Therefore, an interest rate increase (bond prices fall) usually decreases stock prices.

This inverse relationship does not *always* hold. There are periods when a divergence will occur and a company's earnings will increase regardless of whether interest rates go up or down. However, these divergences are generally short-term in nature. You can usually count on the market coming back, reacting to the change in interest rates.

If you watch the day-to-day price changes in the stock market, you may find that investors and traders are watching bond prices and interest rates very closely. Changes in either may determine whether it is a good time to buy or to sell bonds. In addition, if you see interest rates increasing quickly, you don't want to be a buyer of stocks. An increase in interest rates signals a time of caution due to the negative bias for individual stocks and the stock market in general. However, if you find that interest rates are stable or decreasing, being a buyer of stocks is a good idea because the stock market has an upward bias.

Historically, the general bias of the stock market is to rise. Investors usually push markets up. Even after stock market crashes, the market usually rebounds strongly. The stock market's cyclical movement is directly related to economic, social, and political factors, with bull markets lasting longer than bear markets—dropping quickly and then rising slowly but steadily. However, when it comes to the stock market, there are no absolutes. Since no one has a crystal ball with which to see the future, I prefer to create trades that are nondirectional in nature using delta neutral strategies that reap consistent profits.

KEY INTEREST RATE INDICATORS

Putting together a broad market analysis requires a feeling for where interest rates might be headed. In order to do this, the analyst needs a clear understanding of three key indicators: the prime rate indicator, the Federal Reserve indicator, and the installment debt indicator. Each indicator provides important clues pertaining to future interest rate trends.

The prime rate indicator represents the interest rate that banking institutions require their very best customers to pay which more often than not are the top corporations in the country. The majority of bank loans actually made are pegged to the prime rate with a premium being charged relative to the degree of risk of the loan. So, the worse off the borrower's credit rating, the more the borrower will pay above the prime rate.

Following prime rate changes is relatively easy since it does not change every day, as do other interest rates. In addition, when the prime rate indeed does change it is hard to miss it since it is plastered all over the news. Also, this indicator lags behind other interest rates. For example, the prime rate typically declines only well after a decrease in the federal funds rate or certificates of deposit yields. But these prime rate changes should be monitored closely because many times when a distinct trend can be identified then this can translate into corresponding movement in the equity markets.

The Federal Reserve indicator consists of two of its primary monetary policy tools: the discount rate and reserve requirements. The discount rate is how much the Federal Reserve charges banking institutions that wish to borrow from it. And why would banks ever want to borrow from the Federal Reserve? The answer is to satisfy their reserve requirements, which are also controlled by the Fed. These requirement levels basically determine the bank's loan making ability.

Just like the prime rate, the Fed's adjustments to the discount rate and/or reserve requirements garner a lot of media attention, which makes changes quite easy to track. These two data points are rarely changed within the course of a year. The key information that is critical for the analyst to capture is the directional change in either of these two key monetary tools.

Finally, the other key piece of information in determining interest rate trends is the installment debt indicator. This indicator gauges the level of loan demand in the country. This demand has a large impact on the direction of interest rates. If loan demand increases significantly interest rates tend to increase. When loan demand decreases at a sharp level the interest rates are likely to decline.

Loan demand is measured from a variety of sources, which include state, federal, and local governments; corporations using short-term commercial loans and longer-term bond market monies; mortgage debt; and consumer installment debt.

Again, just like the other indicators, this data is simple to track. Keep in mind that when the monthly total of this debt is released by the Federal Reserve it is about six weeks late; however, the important thing to note is how this figure is trending. This can gives us a keen insight into the future direction of interest rates.

All three of these interest rate forecasting tools are not only extremely easy to track but easy to interpret as well. And as indicators go, that is exactly how they should be if they are going to be effective. If you are a fundamental analyst who likes to adopt a broad market view before investing, then I suggest adopting these tools as part of your overall approach.

THE ECONOMIC DATA

Since traders are constantly trying to predict the next direction of interest rates, the economic news can have a significant effect on the financial markets. Often, signs of a strong economy can trigger concerns about the prospect of inflation, which has historically led to higher interest rates. In addition, inflation is also a concern due to its adverse impact on corporate profits.

There are several pieces of economic data that can give clues regarding the trends in inflation. For instance, the prices-paid element of the Institute of Supply Management (ISM) manufacturing report, which is released monthly, can serve as a guide report that gauges inflation. If prices paid are too strong, stocks and bonds might react negatively to the news.

The Consumer Price Index (CPI) measures prices on consumer goods and services, and the Producer Price Index (PPI) gauges prices on various goods such as commodities, capital items, automobiles, and textiles. Both should be watched for inflationary pressures. Some traders also watch trends in the commodities market for signs of inflation. The Commodity Research Bureau provides an index of commodity prices known as the CRB. When it is rising, it is a sign of rising commodity prices and, sometimes, mounting inflationary pressures.

A host of other economic reports receive the market's attention on a regular basis. Bond traders sometimes call the monthly unemployment report from the Labor Department the "unenjoyment" report because stocks and bonds sometimes slide following the release of the monthly numbers. It is released on the first Friday of every month. Figures on retail sales, housing, motor vehicle sales, and consumer sentiment numbers can also cause a reaction on the financial markets. Table 15.1 shows a list of important economic indicators.

THE IMPORTANT ROLE OF THE FEDERAL RESERVE

Another major reason you should keep track of economic reports is because they can influence the decisions at the Federal Reserve. Just what is the Federal Reserve? Most people believe that it is the branch of the U.S. government charged with making monetary policy decisions. Most people are wrong. While it's true that the Federal Reserve makes U.S. monetary policy, it is an independent group. The U.S. government was on the verge of bankruptcy back in the early 19-teens. Twelve very wealthy families actually stepped forward to bail out the government, and Congress officially created the Federal Reserve in 1913. Today, the Federal Reserve consists of 12 district banks as well as a board of governors. Alan Greenspan is currently the Fed chairman.

Today, the Federal Reserve works more like a government agency than a corporation. The chairman of the Federal Reserve and his fellow central bankers play a key role in influencing the money supply. As a trader, it is vital to examine how open market operations are one of the primary tools used by the Federal Reserve to implement U.S. monetary policy. You can also track the profound impacts these decisions have on the U.S. economy, as well as the key reports that are monitored to determine if the Fed is indeed meeting its intended goals.

TABLE 15.1 Important Economic Indicators

Component	Release Date	Advancing Numbers	Declining Numbers
Employment report	First Friday of the month	A rise in unemployment rate is often seen as a negative for stocks but a positive for bonds.	A decrease in unemployment numbers is a positive sign for the economy.
Wholesale trade	Second week of each month	If the wholesale trade inventories number rises, consumption is slowing. Rising inventory-to-sales ratio reflects a slowdown in the economy.	If wholesale trade inventories are falling, consumption is on the rise. If this inventory to sales ratio begins to fall, consumer spending increases (more confidence).
Import and export prices	Around mid-month	Imports constitute 15 percent of U.S. consumption, and also directly affect the profitability of U.S. companies. Higher prices for imports translate to higher prices for domestic goods. This is good news for businesses; bad for the consumer.	If import prices fall, U.S. companies must lower prices to compete. This is bad for businesses, good for the consumer.
Employment Cost Index (ECI)	Once a quarter, toward end of month, for preceding quarter	Analyzes wages and fringe benefits. Rising wages alone have less meaning, but are used in conjunction with other reports, like housing starts.	Lower wages mean a slowing economy, and will be used in conjunction with other economic measurements to gauge the economy's strength.
Consumer Price Index (CPI)	Around the 15th of each month, 8:30 A.M., EST	Since the CPI describes price changes of a basket of consumer goods. A rising number means inflationary pressures at work. This is bad for the market because inflation is held in check with rising interest rates.	A drop in prices is generally considered a good sign for consumers and good for the market. Too much of a drop is a negative, or a sign of possible deflation.

(continues)

TABLE 15.1 *(Continued)*

Component	Release Date	Advancing Numbers	Declining Numbers
Producer Price Index (PPI)	Previous month's data released during second full week of current month	Increases may or may not be good news. If interest rates are declining then a rising PPI number means the economy is reacting to the rate cuts. If rates are increasing, this is bad because further rate hikes may be required.	Decreases mean the economy is slowing. It is best to look at trends. Prolonged slowing may lead to deflation and a recession.
Institute of Supply Management Index (ISM)	First of month	Above 50 percent indicates economic expansion.	Below 50 percent suggests economic contraction.
Retail sales	Midmonth	If people are spending more and confidence is high, it's a good sign for the market.	If people spend less and confidence shrinks, it's a bad sign for the market, especially retail stocks.
Gross Domestic Product (GDP)	One month after end of quarter	GDP takes into account consumer demand, trade balance, and so on. Economy expanding is good news, but not too fast—the Fed raises rates when that happens.	Economy slowing. If it continues Fed will (possibly) lower rates, which is good for the market.
Housing starts and sales of new and existing homes	Third week of month	Increasing starts indicate confidence—a good sign for the market.	Decreasing starts indicate economy slowing. Red flag for Fed to be on lookout for downturn in economy. Market reaction is anybody's guess.
Construction spending	First of month	Lagging indicator. Reports come in only after building is finished. An increase in numbers is a good sign.	Since it's a lagging indicator, it may serve to confirm the economy is slowing and rates need to be lowered. Good for the market.

TABLE 15.1 *(Continued)*

Component	Release Date	Advancing Numbers	Declining Numbers
Industrial Production Index	Midmonth, 9:15 A.M., EST	Increasing numbers would indicate the slack is being taken out of the economy; we're maxing out.	Decreasing numbers indicate factories are slowing down. Might be considered bad for the market, is considered bad for the economy.
Personal income and consumption expenditures	Third or fourth week after month it reports on.	Not much effect as it reports after other key data (employment and retail sales).	Prolonged decrease in consumer demand is definitely bad for consumer stocks.
Factory orders— durable goods and nondurable goods	Four weeks from end of reporting month (8:30 A.M. EST). However, everyone keys off of the advance release one week prior.	Leading indicator of industrial demand. Numbers going up are generally a positive for the markets.	Slowing demand means a slowing economy, if it stays in a declining mode for several months. Might adversely affect markets, but if it prompts interest rate reductions it could be good.

The Federal Reserve actually has three tools at its disposal to carry out monetary policy: open market operations, discount rate, and reserve requirements. Open market operations are by far the most widely used mechanism. When the economy is growing too fast and the inflation rate is high, the Federal Reserve will sell government securities from its portfolio to the open market. This decreases bank reserves, which means the money supply decreases. When there are less bank reserves, short-term interest rates increase. This means consumers and businesses have to pay the bank more in order to borrow money. Less borrowing means less spending, which slows the economy and eventually can reduce price pressures.

However, if the economy is growing too slowly and the inflation rate is low, the Federal Reserve will buy government securities, such as Treasury bills and notes. This increases bank reserves, which increases the money supply and causes short-term interest rates to decrease. Reduced rates induce consumers and businesses to borrow. Consumers will borrow money for items such as automobiles or homes. Businesses borrow to build their inventories or finance new factories. As a result, economic growth will accelerate.

The Federal Reserve will also leave rates unchanged if the economy is growing at a moderate pace with low inflation or if they feel the economy will slow down by itself. They will even take a wait-and-see approach with regard to how fast or how slowly the economy is growing and the rate of inflation, before determining monetary policy.

The major goals of the Federal Reserve include moderate growth, low unemployment, and low inflation. To determine how these open market operations have been impacting these areas, the Fed monitors the key related reports for feedback.

Economic growth is measured by the gross domestic product, which consists of consumption, investment, government, and exports. The retail sales report would fall under consumption. Business inventories and housing starts would fall under investment. Construction spending would fall under government, and international trade would fall under exports. Other reports include the employment report, which includes the unemployment rate and is also closely monitored by the Federal Reserve. Finally, the Producer Price Index, Consumer Price Index, capacity utilization rates, and Employment Cost Index are all monitored to determine the current inflation outlook.

As these reports are released week-by-week, a consensus is developed among policy makers as to whether the economy and the inflation rate are growing too fast, too slow, or just right. They look for the evidence and then they take a vote on whether to raise or lower rates or leave them unchanged. The bottom line is that the Federal Reserve chairman and fellow central bankers have a great influence on our economy and should be watched closely.

The primary goals of the Federal Reserve are to stabilize prices, promote economic growth, and strive for full employment. These goals are pursued through managing monetary policy, which is implemented by the Federal Open Market Committee (FOMC). The FOMC includes seven Fed governors as well five presidents of the district banks. Four of the presidents serve on a rotating basis. The FOMC's most frequently used tool to control monetary policy is open market operations. Open market operations means the buying or selling of government securities to control liquidity in the economy. That's what is happening when you hear that liquidity is going up or down in the economy. When liquidity is high, it makes it easier for businesses to borrow money, which in turn leads to more research and development (R&D) spending, which leads to growth.

Have you ever really looked at a dollar bill? Across the top it says "Federal Reserve Note." It didn't always. I actually have a 1917 United States dollar framed on the wall in my office; it was the last year they were printed. How about the back of the current dollar bill? There is a pyramid with an eye on the top and a banner along the bottom with a slogan that stands for "New World Order." (That's the original name the 12 families who bailed out the government in 1913 coined for themselves.) Our old money had an "X" across the back with the words "United States of America" embodied in the "X."

That's enough history and economics; now let's examine more recent Fed moves. As the market was racing forward at the end of the 1990s, many may remember the famous "irrational exuberance" speech from Fed Chairman Alan Greenspan. The sad thing is that the Fed helped create that exuberance. In 1999, the Fed began injecting massive doses of liquidity into the economy in anticipation of Y2K. It wanted to make sure businesses had plenty of easily available money. Banks actually had more money than they could lend. So where did all this money end up? That's right, the stock market. And what was in vogue at the time? The unknown Internet sector. This just further fueled the raging bull market that already existed. After Y2K arrived with few problems, the Fed began rapidly draining that liquidity back out of the market. At the same time, the Fed was concerned about the rapid growth of our economy. Surely, an economy growing at 6 to 7 percent would spur wild inflation, even though there were no signs of it anywhere. So at the same time the Fed was withdrawing liquidity, it was raising interest rates to "tap the brakes" on the economy. What is so frustrating is that everyone knows that interest rate cuts or hikes take time to affect the economy. The Fed kept pressing that brake with more rate hikes because the economy still looked so healthy.

We now see the results of what withdrawing liquidity combined with rate hikes can do to businesses and a healthy economy. The effect has been more of slamming on the brakes and jamming the gears into reverse. Was there an Internet bubble? Sure there was: It would have eventually become apparent anyway that all those dot-coms were never going to make a profit. The bubble would have suffered a slow leak until it disappeared altogether. Instead, we got a painful "pop." Could our economy have continued to grow at such a rapid pace without rampant inflation? If you believe in the free enterprise system, supply will always meet demand. Take away the demand and look what happens.

SECURITIES AND EXCHANGE COMMISSION

In the United States, stock exchanges are regulated by the Securities and Exchange Commission (SEC), which was created by Congress in 1934 during the Depression. It is composed of five commissioners appointed by the President of the United States and approved by the Senate and a team of lawyers, investigators, and accountants. The SEC is charged with making sure that security markets operate fairly and with protecting investors. Among other acts, they enforce the Securities Act of 1933, the Securities

Exchange Act of 1934, the Trust Indenture Act of 1939, the Investment Company Act of 1940, and the Investment Advisers Act of 1940.

The SEC is also in charge of monitoring insider trading as well as detecting corporate fraud. Insider trading is a form of trading in which corporate officers buy and sell shares within their own companies. This type of trading is widely influenced by inside information that only corporate officers have access to. Many off-floor traders keep track of insider trading to gauge the movement of a specific stock. In addition, there are a multitude of regulations aimed at preventing corporate officers from profiting from information not released to the general public during mergers or takeovers.

Corporate Fraud

Corporate fraud has been in the news a great deal in the United States since the accounting scandals of 2002 rocked Wall Street and the U.S. economy. The collapse of Enron, the bankruptcy of WorldCom, and a series of lawsuits against high-profile executives, including Martha Stewart, give the impression that global corporate fraud and misconduct are rampant. This, of course, occurred during the second year of a bear market—a period that saw some stocks lose 50, 60, and sometimes 70 percent or more of their values, Since stocks were already reeling, the exact impact on the stock market as a whole is difficult to determine. Therefore, the exact impact of the corporate misconduct remains difficult to quantify.

While the exact impact of accounting scandals and corporate fraud is difficult to measure, without question the fact remains: The Enron debacle and subsequent bankruptcies have eroded investor confidence in U.S. financial markets. They also dealt a financial blow to the shareholders of bankrupt companies like WorldCom, Enron, and Adelphia Communications. On a national level, the scandals and fraud left many investors wondering, who is next? When will the next shoe drop? Those concerns served to keep many investors away from stocks. Unfortunately, there is little hope for a market rebound during an absence of prospective buyers.

Eventually, some of the concern faded. On February 11, 2003, Federal Reserve Chairman Alan Greenspan said that he believed that the corporate scandals that shook Wall Street in the summer of 2002 were reaching an end. "I would be very surprised if it were initiated beyond mid-2003," the Fed chairman said in a speech to the Senate Banking Committee. "It is not a problem for the immediate future." One reason for his optimism stemmed from the passage of the Sarbanes-Oxley legislation approved by Congress in 2002. The new law restored some of the lost investor confidence.

Yet investor confidence can prove fragile. While it is hard to tell just what impact corporate scandals had on the stock market, it is clear that investors have begun to recognize it as an additional risk. As time passed, some of the fears and uncertainty began to fade. Stricter regulation and greater enforcement by the Securities and Exchange Commission have played important roles in shoring up investor confidence in financial markets. Still, believing that every issue related to corporate malfeasance and accounting scandal has been solved would be naive. In fact, such problems might resurface at any time and rekindle investor jitters. If and when this scenario will play out again is unpredictable.

Nevertheless, corporate misconduct is an important factor to consider before stepping into the financial world. Make sure that all your trades consider the possibility that such problems could resurface anytime in the not too distant future. Manage your risk!

INFLATION CATEGORIES AND GOVERNMENT IMPACT

Economists recognize two principal types of inflation: cost-push inflation, in which increases in the cost of raw materials and/or labor are reflected in higher prices, and demand-pull inflation, which is caused by the demand for goods increasing faster than the supply.

Cost-push inflation usually results from a chain of related events. For example, if the labor costs involved in producing a specific raw material rise, the supplier of that material will pass on the increase to the manufacturer who uses the material in a finished product. The manufacturer, in turn, raises prices on the finished product in order to protect their profit margin.

The consumer who buys the product ultimately pays for the higher cost of labor in the price of the product. When this happens in several industries at once, consumers who are also workers demand higher wages to help meet the increased prices. This, in turn, sets off another round of price increases as manufacturers and retailers attempt to recoup their higher labor costs. As the cycle continues, it raises the cost of living for everyone.

Demand-pull inflation, in contrast, is caused by increased demand for a product or material, or by scarcity of that commodity. During the 1970s, many of the world's oil-producing nations held their product back from the market at a time when demand for petroleum was increasing rapidly. The results were across-the-board increases in the prices of oil, gasoline, and synthetic materials made from petroleum. In turn, refiners, power generating companies, and manufacturers passed along the higher prices of crude oil to consumers. In addition, the fuel costs of freight haulers who delivered goods rose, and these, too, were passed on to consumers.

In some instances, demand for goods is stimulated by the availability of extra dollars. The amount of money in circulation increases faster than productivity in the economy, leading to greater demand. In effect, money chases supply. For example, during the 1960s, the government increased the amount of money in the economy rather than raising taxes to pay for the war in Vietnam. The resulting inflation was, in effect, a hidden tax to pay for government operations, because wage earners were pushed into higher tax brackets.

The federal government can impact inflation and the overall economy in three major ways. First, the government can spend more money than it collects in taxes, duties, and fees. Such deficit spending tends to stimulate the economy. But the government must borrow the difference between its income and expenditures, usually by selling Treasury bonds or bills.

When the government enters the credit markets, it competes with other big borrowers, such as corporations, for the dollars that are available. The resulting increase in demand for money tends to raise the interest rate. Rising interest rates reduce the overall demand for many goods and services, particularly those that are financed, such as housing, durable goods, and plant and equipment. Thus, initially deficit spending tends to increase overall demand, while borrowing to finance the deficit tends eventually to decrease such demand. The net inflationary impact depends on the state of the economy and the relative effects of these two forces.

If the economy has slack in it, additional stimulation has little or no inflationary impact. If the economy is already booming, further stimulation can push up prices dramatically. The relative effect of the deficit depends on how it is financed. This always prompts an economic debate on how best to impact our economy: balanced budgets versus deficit financing.

The second way in which government can affect the economy is through its taxing policies. By raising taxes, government can slow the rate of growth in the economy. By reducing taxes, it can provide more money for economic growth. Over the years, the Congress has tended to use this technique to stimulate specific areas of the economy.

For example, the deduction for mortgage interest payments on personal residences was designed to boost the home-building industry and the many other industries it influences. The investment tax credit, which was repealed in 1986, was instituted to encourage businesses to expand their plants and buy new equipment. Other tax measures have targeted areas in similar ways.

Finally, the third major government influence on inflation and the economy is the Federal Reserve. One of its jobs is to regulate the supply of money in the economy. If the money supply grows too quickly, prices will rise faster than productivity, which fuels inflationary pressures. If the Federal Reserve tightens up on the money supply too much, it could throttle a growing economy.

Despite the fact that the Federal Reserve is a government-chartered corporation, it is not required to work with other branches of the government to coordinate action affecting the economy. However, the Federal Reserve is required to report to Congress, and Congress can change the laws affecting it. In addition, the President appoints its membership. In some cases, actions by the Federal Reserve may be opposite those of the Administration and Congress, causing mixed economic results.

Regardless of the current political environment a savvy investor must be keenly aware of the current inflation trend and the impact it has on the investor's savings, income, and portfolio. This understanding can make a major difference in an investor's financial future.

FED FUNDS FUTURES CONTRACT AND MONETARY POLICY

The federal funds rate is the interest rate banks pay when they borrow Federal Reserve deposits from other banks, usually overnight. It is closely watched in financial markets because the level of the funds rate can be immediately and purposefully affected by Federal Reserve open market operations.

The Federal Open Market Committee, the main policy-making arm of the Federal Reserve, communicates an objective for the fed funds rate in a directive to the trading desk at the Federal Reserve Bank of New York. Actions taken to change an intended level of the fed funds rate are motivated by a desire to accomplish ultimate policy objectives, especially price stability. Permanent changes in the fed funds rate level are thus the consequence of deliberate policy decisions.

The fed funds contract, also known as 30-day fed funds futures, calls for delivery of interest paid on a principal amount of $5 million in overnight fed funds. In practice, the total interest is not really paid, but is cash-settled daily. This means that payments are made whenever the futures contract settlement price changes.

The futures settlement price is calculated as 100 minus the monthly arithmetic average of the daily effective fed funds rate that the Federal Reserve Bank trading desk reports for each day of the contract month. Payments are made through margin accounts that sellers and holders have with their brokers. At the end of the trading day, sellers' and holders' accounts are debited or credited to facilitate payments.

Fed funds futures are a convenient tool for hedging against future interest-rate changes. To illustrate, consider a regional bank that consistently buys $100 million in fed funds. Suppose the bank's analysts believe that economic data to be released in the upcoming week will induce the FOMC to increase the objective of the fed funds rate by 50 basis points at its next meeting.

If the contract settle price (for the meeting month) implies no change from the current rate, the bank may choose to lock in its current cost by selling 20 contracts (or taking a short position) and holding the position to expiration. Conversely, suppose that a net lender of funds expects a policy action to lower the fed funds rate. It can protect its return by purchasing futures contracts (or taking a long position).

Participants in the fed funds futures market need not be banks that borrow in the fed funds market. Anyone who can satisfy margin requirements may participate. Thus, traders who make their living as "Fed watchers" may speculate with fed funds futures. This would suggest that to the extent Fed policy is predictable, speculators would drive futures prices to embody expectations of future policy actions. Since the level of the fed funds rate is essentially determined by deliberative policy decisions, the fed funds futures rate should have predictable value for the size and timing of future policy actions.

Given that the trading desk may face systematic problems that hinder its ability to achieve its objective, the consequences for the funds rate may be predictable. Speculators who anticipate such effects may find it profitable to buy or sell current contracts.

In the case of fed funds, the rate is essentially determined by a deliberative decision of the FOMC, the main policy-making arm of the Federal Reserve System. Hence, the fed funds futures markets must anticipate actions taken by the FOMC. In short, through the fed funds futures markets, one can place a bet on what future monetary policy will be. The committee then can get a clear reading of what these market participants expect them to do, which may at times be helpful for FOMC members who place great weight on knowing if a policy choice would surprise the market.

If they are to be instructive for policymakers, the fed funds rate should have some predictive content. The predictive accuracy of futures rates historically improves over the two-month period leading up to the contract's expiration, providing some evidence that the market is efficient in incorporating new information into its pricing. The largest prediction errors have occurred around policy turning points. Nevertheless, there is considerable evidence to suggest that the fed funds futures markets are efficient processors of information concerning the future path of the fed funds rate.

U.S. DOLLAR'S IMPACT ON GLOBAL COMMERCE

The rate of economic growth—meaning the rate of gross national product (GNP) growth—is determined by three key rates: the interest rate, the tax rate, and exchange rates. The business cycle is influenced by those rates, which in turn are shaped by monetary, fiscal, and trade policy. Given the global economic environment that we live in, it's important to understand world trade basics and how the dollar actually impacts global commerce.

Assume that you buy a Japanese-made car. The dealer who imported the car has to pay an exporter in Japan for the cost of the vehicle that's been sent over. The exporter wants to be paid in yen, the Japanese currency. So the importer takes his dollars and buys yen from a currency dealer or bank. The number of dollars he pays for the amount of yen he gets is determined by the exchange rate. He then sends the yen to the exporter in Japan and sells you the car he's purchased.

The same thing happens in reverse when a Japanese consumer buys an American-made product. A U.S. export turns into a Japanese import just the way a Japanese export becomes a U.S. import. All things being equal, if imports and exports occur in the same total amount, the balance of trade will be equal.

Simply put, if the balance of trade between two countries is equal, then the rate of exchange between the currencies of those two countries will also be equal. That may be hard to grasp, because many investors think that currency has intrinsic value. But currency is only worth what it will buy. Ask yourself how much value a U.S. dollar has in a land where goods are bought and sold in yen. If the Japanese have no U.S. imports, they'll need no dollars, and the dollar will be nothing more than a souvenir.

The same is true of the yen's value in the reverse situation. In Houston, where goods are paid for in dollars, a yen is worthless unless it's needed to pay for a Japanese import. And if you need it because you're taking a trip to Japan, that's also counted as an import. When Americans spend abroad, they have the same effect on the balance of trade as an importer. In both cases, yen must be bought, and dollars flow out. But if no trade takes place, there is no need for currency exchange. When it does take place, if the Japanese need as many dollars as Americans need yen, the dollar and the yen will be equal in value. That's how the dollar shapes up when all things are equal. But things are never equal, and that means you've got to think about the shape the dollar's in when you're trying to stay ahead of economic trends.

The problem is that the United States is now the world's largest debtor nation. If we exported more than we imported, our trade account would have a surplus. But because we import much more than we export, we now have a hefty yearly trade deficit. The more we import, the more foreign currency we have to buy to pay for it. Since we need more foreign currency and our trading partners need fewer dollars because they have fewer U.S. imports to pay for, demand for dollars is less than demand for yen and German marks, for example. That means a strong yen, or mark, and a weak dollar.

Trade imbalance normally works itself out. As we import more and more Japanese goods, the dollar will weaken against the yen. That will make Japanese goods more expensive, which will reduce our imports of them. On the other side, a weakening dollar makes our exports less expensive. So the Japanese should buy more of them. As they import more and we import less, trade will eventually balance. The difficulty is that countries erect barriers to trade, and these barriers act to strengthen or weaken currency, which in turn affects economic growth.

The U.S. can regulate the strength of the dollar in several ways. On the fiscal side it can enact protectionist legislation and impose traffic and import quotas on foreign goods. Or it can push for international trade agreements, which require its partners to export less and import more. The United States can also adjust exchange rates by using monetary policy. If the dollar is falling or rising sharply, the Fed, acting with foreign central banks, can buy or sell dollars in the currency markets. This is known as intervention to either support or weaken the dollar, a result that can be achieved in the short run only. In the long run, no amount of intervention can overcome the balance of trade when it comes to determining the dollar's exchange value. Hopefully, this discussion has given you a greater appreciation of the intimate nature of the U.S. dollar and world trade.

CONCLUSION

Many traders ignore the macro-type analysis for the stock market that can be put together using various forms of economic and bond data. This big picture provides the trader and investor alike a very important starting point before they hone in on potential trading opportunities.

There is an abundance of economic data that has an inextricable linkage to the stock market. For instance, when bond prices drop too much, forcing yields higher, this often has a devastating impact on the stock market. In general, bond yields have more of an effect on the financial sector versus other sectors such as the food service stocks, for example. To this point you will see that when there is overall strength in the financial stocks, bond yields will drop.

Keep in mind that many times declining long-term interest rates fuel a stock market rally and this is why when stocks are not focusing on quarterly earnings they focus on bond yields. If bond yields reach too high a level, companies may have to start paying more to borrow money, which adversely impacts profits. Of course, declining profits in turn lead to declining stock prices. To overcome rising bond yields, earnings have to come in better than expected to see appreciation in the stock price.

Another trend to watch closely is when investors leave stocks to go into bonds, making it difficult for companies to raise money. This also indicates what is known as a "flight to quality" where investors decrease the money flow into stocks to pursue safer investments.

Due to its adverse impact on corporate profits, inflation is another key factor that needs to be monitored. For example, the prices-paid element of the Institute of Supply Management report gauges inflation. If prices-paid come in too strong, not only will bonds sell off, but stocks will sell off as well.

For these same reasons the Consumer Price Index, which measures prices on consumer goods and services, and the Producer Price Index, which calibrates prices on various goods such as commodities, capital items, automobiles, and textiles, should also be watched closely for inflationary pressures.

Another report that can impact the inflationary outlook is the retail sales report. If this report, for example, experiences an upward revision from the previous month this can cause both the stock and bond market to sell off. Basically, these four inflation-type reports impact both the stock market and the bond market in the same way. The bottom line here is that the primary stock market catalyst is corporate profits. A major factor for profitability is having an economy that shows low inflation.

Overall, if the economic reports are coming in strong, the bond market will begin to be concerned about the Fed increasing interest rates to derail possible inflation. This will in turn cause bond yields to rise and foster an environment where stocks are more than likely going to decline because of the increased competition among the investment community on where to get the best return.

Another major reason you should track these reports is that just like corporate earnings, economic reports and Federal Reserve decisions also come with their own expectations. For example, if the stock market is anticipating a raise in rates by the Federal Reserve and it doesn't happen, then expect the stocks to decline across the board because stocks will reprice themselves to reflect the higher rates. These higher rates dampen both business and consumer spending due to the fact that borrowing costs are now higher. The higher rates can sometimes actually spur a recession and can reduce inflation with interest rate–sensitive stocks being the beneficiary.

Now of course, when the Federal Reserve cuts rates this can have a very positive impact on both the stock and bond market. Also, if rates are unchanged then more often than not this generates a positive signal to the equities market. In this same vein, there is always a concern that the Fed can reduce interest rates too much, pumping too much money into our economic system, which can fuel stock prices, resulting in asset inflation.

Another more cryptic thing to monitor is certain chatter that occasionally comes out of the Federal Reserve. For instance, a news story about a key Federal Reserve official warning about possible inflation or Alan Greenspan talking about overvalued assets could ignite a stock market sell-off.

The point I want to leave you with is that this type of macroanalysis of the economic environment is an essential starting point when developing a general bullish or bearish scenario. This analytical backdrop has always given me the extra confidence I needed to pull the trigger based on Elliott wave, MACD, or any other technical tool I choose to employ before making a trading decision based on a directional bias.

Additionally, paying close attention to interest rates can help you to forecast market direction. Although many delta neutral strategies are not dependent on market direction, it never hurts to be able to anticipate movement. Since prices have extremely erratic fluctuation patterns, monitoring interest rates is a relatively consistent method that can help you to find profitable trading opportunities.

You don't have to become an expert in economics to gauge market performance; but you do need to know what you're looking for and how to use the information that's out there. Part of a trader's learning curve depends on his or her ability to integrate an understanding of the big picture with the multitude of details that trading individual stocks requires. Since money is the lifeblood of the stock market, understanding how it moves and where it moves to is a major key to financial success. Not only events move the markets, but also the international flow of money as investors seek the highest possible rate of return. The thought of international money flow may be overwhelming to many of us, but it is an important part of the big picture. So put on your high waders, the water's just fine.

CHAPTER 16

Mastering the Market

In the previous chapter, we examined some of the macroeconomic events that can cause changes in the stock market. Rising interest rates, comments from the Federal Reserve, and economic reports can all cause changes in the economic outlook, which can cause stock prices to move sharply higher or lower. When one examines the economic outlook in order to make investment decisions, it is known as a *top-down* approach to investing.

Some traders prefer to take a *bottom-up* approach. In this case, you are more concerned about the individual investment. For example, you might start by studying an individual company and understand its details before making a decision.

In this chapter, we take more of a bottom-up approach. We want to help you identify the fundamentals of profitable investment. You will have to decide, probably by trial and error, which of the many analytical techniques and market-forecasting methods work well for you. I find many investment tactics to be irrelevant to profit making, preferring to use strategies that are nondirectional in nature. However, there are a few basic guidelines that will enhance your ability to increase your account size consistently by making good investment selections.

DESIRABLE INVESTMENT CHARACTERISTICS

Finding promising trades is perhaps the most difficult issue to address when first starting out in the investment arena. While there are no absolutes, there

403

are a few guidelines that will enhance your ability to identify profit-making opportunities. A desirable investment has the following characteristics:

- Involves low risk.
- Has a favorable risk profile.
- Offers high potential return.
- Meets your time requirements.
- Meets your risk tolerance level.
- Can be understood by you, the trader.
- Meets your investment criteria.
- Meets your investment capital constraints.

Involves Low Risk

First and foremost, a good investment must have low risk. What does low risk really mean? The term's significance may vary with each person. You may be able to accept a risk level of $5,000 per trade based on the capital you have available. However, an elderly person on a fixed income may find $100 to be too much to risk. Acceptable risk is based on your available investment capital as well as your tolerance for uncertainty. You should trade only with money you can afford to lose, as there is risk of loss in all forms of trading.

Has a Favorable Risk Profile

Every time you contemplate placing a trade, you need to create a corresponding risk profile. Whether you trade shares or commodities, invest in real estate, or put your money in the bank, every investment has a certain potential risk/reward profile. Some are more favorable than others. Studying a risk profile can show you the potential increasing or decreasing profit and loss of a trade relative to the underlying asset's price over a specific period of time. As the variables change, the risk curve changes accordingly.

In order to find the best investment, you have to look for trades that offer optimal risk-to-reward ratios. For example, which of the following investment choices has the better risk-to-reward ratio?

- Trade A: potential risk of $1,000; potential reward of $1,000.
- Trade B: potential risk of $1,000; potential reward of $5,000.

Anyone would rather make $5,000 than $1,000. However, to actually make a good decision, you must also have enough knowledge to discern which trade has the greater probability of working out. Another key ingredient is time frame—the time it takes to make the money. If trade A can make me $1,000 in one month with a 75 percent chance of winning, and trade B takes a year to make $5,000 with a 75 percent chance of winning, I would rather go with trade A. In one year, I could potentially make $9,000 [(12 × 1,000) × .75] repeating trade A, and only $3,750 ($5,000 × .75) using trade B. This is referred to as an expected value calculation.

The risk/reward profile of any investment must take into account the following elements:

- Potential risk.
- Potential reward.
- Probability of success.
- How long the investment takes to make a return.

Offers High Potential Return

Risk comes hand-in-hand with reward. A trader cannot be expected to take a risk unless reward is also in the equation. Believe it or not, I have seen countless investors make foolish investments where the risk outweighs the reward many times over. Why would they do such a thing? Usually because they simply haven't taken the time to verify the potential risk and reward of the trade or they are taking advice from someone who doesn't know any better.

The best investments have an opportunity for high reward with acceptable risk. In addition, the good trades have a high probability of winning on a consistent basis. I consider 75 percent an acceptable winning percentage. This means I win three out of four times I place a trade. A baseball player who could do this would have a .750 batting average—which is unprecedented in baseball history.

Meets Your Time Requirements

The process of locating and monitoring your investments must meet your time constraints if you are to be successful. In other words, if you do not have the time to sit in front of a computer day in and day out, then your best investments will not be day trades (entering and exiting a position in the same day). If you don't even have the time or inclination to look at your investments over a one-week period, then you have to take this into consideration. The time you have available for making investment decisions and monitoring those investments will affect the types of investments you should make. If you don't have enough time to pay attention to a trade that needs to be closely monitored, chances are you'll lose money on it. The best investments will match your time availability.

THE OPTIONS COURSE

Meets Your Risk Tolerance Level

Your risk tolerance level is directly proportional to your available investment capital. Risking more than you can afford to lose creates stress that impairs your ability to make clear decisions. Some people have the ability to handle uncertainty better than others. It is important to accurately assess your own risk tolerance levels and stay within those boundaries as you progress up your own trading learning curve. As experience in the markets naturally develops your confidence level, your risk tolerance level will increase.

Can Be Understood by You, the Trader

One of my most basic investment rules is as follows: If you don't know how hot the fire is, don't stick your hand into it. This rule is broken on a consistent basis by many beginning and intermediate traders. In addition, many seasoned traders singe their fingers as well. Basically, if you don't understand the exact characteristics of a trade, it is better to walk away from it.

It is imperative that you familiarize yourself with the trades you place. Each trade has a unique personality. Your personality and your trade's personality have to match for you to be successful over the long run.

Meets Your Investment Criteria

Your personal investment criteria can come in many shapes and sizes. Each individual has personal goals, expectations, and objectives when making investments. When I ask my students what they want out of their investments, the typical response is to make money. However, there are a number of related issues that also must be evaluated, including:

1. *Capital gains* (stocks—medium- to high-risk securities). What are the tax implications of your investing and trading practices?

2. *Interest income* (fixed income securities—medium-risk bonds and lowest-risk U.S. government securities). Is your objective to earn interest income?

3. *Security* (government securities—lowest-risk securities). Do you want to invest in only low-interest, low-return investments such as U.S. government securities (e.g., Treasury bonds)?

Meets Your Investment Capital Constraints

Do the investment requirements match your capital available for investment? Just as your investment strategy must meet your personality and time constraints, the capital you have available will have a major impact on what you invest in, how often you invest, and the number of contracts you can afford to trade. For example, if you have a small account (less than $10,000), you will invest very differently from someone with $1 million. In addition, if you're trading commodities with a small account, you should trade in markets that have low margin requirements and good return potential. You should stay away from the high-margin markets such as the S&P 500 stock index futures.

No matter how much money you have to invest, start small. I have taught a variety of people over the years with a very wide range of capital available for investment. I advise them all to start by trading small until they figure out what they're doing. Whether you have $1,000 or $1 million, you have to learn to walk before you can run. In the beginning, I recommend risking only 5 percent of your account on any one trade. In this way, you can afford to learn from your mistakes as a novice trader.

Often, having too much money as a beginner can be detrimental. The more money you have, the greater the chance of overinvesting and making costly mistakes. I find that the best long-term investors are very cautious early on. However, they systematically increase the size of their trades based on the steady increase in capital in their accounts. For example, you may begin with $5,000 and choose to invest 100 shares at a time, then not increase to 200 shares until such time as your account has doubled to $10,000.

IMPORTANCE OF TARGETED EXIT POINTS

One of the most important decisions a trader must make when entering a position is determining when to sell or close out the trade. It is imperative to set a target exit point for each trade. A target exit point is an option price that would result in a substantial, yet attainable, profit.

By setting your profit objectives in advance and determining your target exit point before you trade or at the time you make your option purchase, you avoid the consequences of one of the major stumbling blocks to achieving trading profits: greed. It is very hard for most investors to set reasonable profit goals once an option has jumped substantially in price. That extra point becomes a moving target with each advance in the option's price. Therefore, it is not surprising that a reasonable profit is not achieved when the investor is forced to bail out because of tumbling prices.

Although setting profit goals in advance may be simplistic and not the most flexible approach to option trading, the target exit point approach to taking profits is a necessary compromise. This is especially true for the options trader who has neither the savvy nor the emotional control to know when to hold and when to fold in the heat of battle, and who is also unable to stay tuned to the markets throughout the trading day.

Note also that the profit objective should be substantial, meaning at least 100 percent, or double your initial investment, so you will not be walking away with small profits by using this approach. With this approach, you will miss out on those 1,000 percent gains that are the options equivalent of hitting the jackpot; but much more important, you will minimize the instances of solid profits becoming painful losses and you will regularly be taking respectable gains off the table.

Once you have entered the heat of battle, the tendency will be to base your decisions upon emotion, and therefore your decisions will tend to be incorrect. To avoid this pitfall, set a closeout date based on the amount of time you expect the option needs to reach its target exit point. If that profit level has not been reached by the closeout date, exit the position on that date. Closeout dates should be set so that there is still enough time until expiration to salvage some time value from the option if the underlying stock has failed to move.

Resist the temptation to sell at a small loss prior to your closeout date. You will be yielding to fear, robbing yourself of some potential gains. Also, resist the temptation to raise your profit objective as the price of the option nears your target exit point. You will then be yielding to greed, and your profits will slip away.

Another important question that needs to be addressed is when should you not sell? You should not sell a position the instant it moves against you. There is never a need to engage in panic selling if it is assumed that your original conditions for opening the position still hold true (e.g., your market outlook and your outlook for the stock on which you own options have not changed); also, that you are not committing an excess amount of trading capital and you are still operating within your own risk tolerance.

As option traders we create option positions for their huge profit potential, which can be fully realized only by allowing positions to remain open for a reasonable period of time. Setting predefined exit points goes a long way to facilitate this task.

TIPS FOR SPOTTING AN EMERGING BULL MARKET

Although no two bulls or bears are exactly alike, and sometimes their signals may be a bit obscure, eventually the indicators will pile up and a trend will become evident. As you analyze the stock market for signs of shifting trends, be cautious. Each market is different from its previous cousins, so not all the warning signs will be present each time. If you notice only one or two of the telltale clues, some fleeting business or economic event temporarily may be tilting the market. However, if you detect four, five, or more of these signs appearing all at once, you've probably discovered a major new market phase.

Before the bull begins to charge ahead, you will find six major signs that the bear has retreated into hibernation. Most of these signs apply to stocks, but often they readily relate to other investment markets as well.

One of the signs is that the market has undergone a mature decline. Naturally, if you want to determine whether a new market is on its way up, one of the first things you'll do is determine what activity has come before. If the market has undergone a mature decline then a bull may not be far off.

Second, look for a market that is dull and boring. Historically, bear markets generally storm onto the market scene, but they depart extremely quietly. This kind of lackluster activity is one of the most common signs that a bear market is losing strength. Such sluggishness may go on for weeks or even months, but stock prices do not necessarily tumble along with trading volumes. When this scenario occurs, professional investors might say the market has been seized by a complacent attitude.

The next possible sign is when the market resists bad news. Generally, financial and even some sociopolitical news has a marked effect on the markets. When the markets refuse to budge, despite significant developments, you definitely should take notice.

Another sign is when the gloom is so deep that even the top-quality investments are sold. As a severe bear market grinds on for what seems like forever, stock investors, for example, often sell their blue-chip securities in one last brief selling period. These probably are the last stocks to go, as investors will have unloaded their lower-quality holdings at the start of the bear.

When the market has fallen to an uncomfortable degree, and investors believe hope for a quick recovery is gone, blue chips hit the market with a sudden decline. Not surprisingly, that tends to reinforce the bleak market mood, as investors begin to think that if even the best stocks are acting this way, then something really must be wrong with the market.

Next, as a bear market begins to fade, stocks that once sold at price-earnings ratios of, say, 18 to 20 times earnings often are selling at unusually low P/Es, perhaps less than half their former figures. When those stocks once regarded as must-have securities lose all their appeal, the change from the normal situation should cause investors to take notice. Those who have a chance to purchase bargain stocks before the next bull market should swing into gear.

Finally, high dividend yields offer a key signal. Like low price-earnings ratios, the often high-dividend yields to be found at the tail end of a bear market represent a market reversal in market psychology. Although yields in a bear market typically are higher than those for the same stock at the peak of a bull market, you can look for this phenomenon to alert you that a bear market has run its course.

What does it mean when you can identify several of these indicators? Obviously, the bear market has begun to fade and the bull market slowly is taking shape. More and more trading occurs daily, and the number of advances, the upward movements in the prices of the individual investments, outpace the declines. The volume of trading and the number of advances and declines indicates the market breadth.

To summarize, be aware of the following key signals that a bear market is approaching a bottom. First, market prices have been declining for more than 12 months. Second, the volume of trading declines and you start to observe a very boring market. Third, bad news makes no impression on the markets. Fourth, investors start unloading top-quality investments by heavily selling many of the blue chips. Fifth, investments that once were stars are now on the skids, selling at undervalued prices. With stocks, price-earnings ratios are unusually low. And finally, sixth, stock dividend yields rise abruptly. The bottom line is if you observe most or all of these signs, the bear market is probably coming to an end and a new bull may not be far behind.

TAKE A LOOK BEHIND THE ANALYST CURTAIN

How many times have you placed a trade that you thought was perfectly set up only to have an unforeseen or unexpected event cause the trade to go bad? The technicals all looked good; maybe even the fundamentals were all in place. To all intents and purposes, the trade looked like a winner. Then all of a sudden out of nowhere comes a comment from one of the "guru goons" (my term for analysts), the company announces an acquisition that the Street doesn't like, or maybe even a bizarre incident like an earthquake in Taiwan! The underlying then reverses and the trade moves against you. Let's look behind the scenes of how analysts and institutions really work.

It's amazing how many individual investors and traders still live and die by analysts' recommendations. Many people actually still think that analysts make recommendations for the good of investors. Think about it, who do the analysts work for? They work for the institutions. Why do analysts continue to rate a stock a "strong buy" while the underlying is bleeding a slow death? Why do the same analysts raise a stock's rating that has clearly been in an extended uptrend? Institutions build inventories in stocks that they then allocate to their brokers to sell to investors. In some cases, it is nothing more than a quota that the broker is expected to sell. The analyst from the institution will then focus on some piece of positive data regarding the stock and raise the ratings on the same. This causes a short-term buying interest in the stock by retail investors and usually a bump up in the price as well. Who are the retail investors buying from? Their institution! The institution has been accumulating inventory in a stock, so then it manufactures a buying spurt and depletes its inventory at a higher price. Many times this occurs as the stock is showing signs of topping out. The institution makes money, and who is left holding the "bag" or stock?

Institutions are in the business to make money, and that consists of more than just broker commissions. If the investors make money, then that's okay, too, but it's not the priority. In fact, in some cases your own institution will actually take a position against your trade! It goes even deeper. If an institution is dumping an inventory and you have purchased the stock and later decide that you want to sell, the institution won't buy your stock back! It will execute your trade only after it finds some other patsy to take it off your hands.

Have you ever wondered why analysts always seem to be a step behind? When a company announces something negative, if it's a stock that the institutions are interested in, the analysts all jump on the bandwagon with downgrades. As retail investors are dumping the stock based on the downgrades, the institutions are sitting back and waiting for the downdraft to subside and then they begin to start accumulating again. The whole process starts all over again. How about raising a stock to a "strong buy" once it appears ready to break out of a long-term consolidation or basing pattern? Wouldn't that be a novel idea? That would mean that analysts were really employed to help investors, however.

Then there are all of the amazing abuses of investors by analysts regarding initial public offerings (IPOs). How many investors own Internet stocks that were priced at ridiculous price multiples due to continued upgrades by analysts as the stock prices went into the stratosphere? How many investors still own those stocks today under $10 a share? Do you think the institutions feel bad that they sold investors those stocks at ridiculous multiples? Believe me, they will only feel bad until they look at their bottom lines.

Some of these longtime abuses are finally beginning to surface in the media, both on the television networks as well as in the print media. Some investors have even sued the analysts. Okay, so what's my point in all this? We are on our own out here and have only ourselves to hold accountable when investing our hard-earned money. Optionetics exists because no matter how much research we do, no matter how good a trade looks when we place it, things happen that are out of our control and can cause trades to go against us. Hedging all trades is crucial. When an unforeseen event does happen, we can employ a creative options strategy to take advantage of it. Even in our worst-case scenarios, our losses are minimal and we live to fight another day. Option strategies are designed not only to aid your research, but also to help hedge the trades you make, regardless of existing market conditions or directional bias.

COMPUTERIZED TRADING SYSTEMS

Trading systems facilitate trader discipline. Computerized systems offer additional advantages. The speed and efficiency with which a computer identifies patterns and generates signals is one obvious advantage. Computers can quickly achieve the number crunching necessary to recognize trading signals. However, it is possible for a trader to calculate these signals manually (in the time required), and the trader's ability to evaluate a complete rule-based system is limited as well. Computer systems offer direction and suggestions about what to do in a given market and help limit the range of choices. This makes the trader's task less overwhelming, because the possibilities and opportunities become more clearly defined.

Trading systems approach the market consistently and objectively. Programs are designed logically. Rules are uniformly applied to defined market conditions. Trading systems are effective since rules are not the victims of trader judgment. The whimsical nature of a trader is diminished by a system.

The emotional aspect of trading can be significantly reduced as well since systems are void of emotion and judgment. Unfortunately, the emotional tendency of a trader is to outguess the system, even when it's producing profitable trades. If a trader can discipline himself or herself to follow a system with rigor, emotions will not rule the decision-making process. Trading systems are designed to think, not to feel. Another positive feature of trading systems is that they generally include money management rules that help to facilitate trading discipline.

One of the more common arguments against trading systems is that they can become popular enough to influence the underlying price. This concern has been voiced both by the market federal regulatory agencies and by individual traders. The concern is that the similarity of computer-based systems used to manage large positions may cause large traders to respond in the same way at the same time, thereby causing distortion in the markets.

While it is not guaranteed that past price patterns guarantee future price patterns, it is also not true that markets are random. Another argument against the use of trading systems is they define market behavior in limited ways when the market can, in fact, behave in an infinite number of ways. It is believed that because systems are mathematically or mechanically defined, this reduces relationships of events to percentage odds of what could happen next. While the criticism is valid in that systems do capture a very limited number of possibilities, this characteristic is also what makes systems useful. The ability to reduce information to observable patterns gives the trader some semblance of order and direction. Without this, many traders feel overwhelmed and directionless.

One of the more controversial techniques to develop from computerized trading is the concept of optimization. Optimization is a process by which data is repeatedly tested to find the best results. The best moving average size, point and figure method, or other parameters are made to fit the raw data. It is important to understand the methods of optimization and to provide proper precautions regarding optimized trading systems. Performed properly, extensive testing can reveal a great deal. However, excessive optimizing can be misleading, deceptive, and costly.

Trading systems give the trader a way to interpret, quantify, and classify market behavior. Since trading systems define potential opportunity and provide specific trading signals, following these signals can facilitate the development of profit-making trading skills as well as strong exit and entrance discipline.

Computerized trading systems have vastly expanded the scope of information available to today's traders. Systems can now be thoroughly back-tested and perfected using the computer to test many if-then scenarios. Trading systems offer a way to define and categorize market behavior by reducing information to patterns that generate trading signals. While systems are without emotion, traders are not and often try to outguess a system. Misuse and lack of discipline are major causes of losses in trading systems.

CONCLUSION

The investment elements mentioned in this chapter are designed to guide you on the road to trading success. Trading can be a humbling experience. It can also be highly profitable. Perhaps it is human nature to get a little overconfident and cocky when the money starts rolling in. But that's the time when you need to fight against your own bravado. Remember, it takes only one big mistake to send you back to ground zero. Start small and let your account grow consistently. There's always more to be learned and a better trade down the road.

In addition, there a number of things you can do to protect your account. Use the following six guidelines to safeguard your share of market profits:

1. Do your own research before you invest. Don't invest in companies that minimize or avoid disclosure of their financial condition. Always read the fine print in your information sources and avoid hot tips.

2. Deal with major brokerage firms and reputable brokers. Know your brokerage firm's financial condition and who owns the firm. Be sure you know what your agreement specifies.

3. Keep a written record of all trades. Write your orders in advance. When you receive trading confirmations, make sure to compare them with your written records.

4. Put your broker to work. If trading confirmations are slow in coming, complain to your broker. Balance all monthly statements. Ask your broker to explain any discrepancies. If trouble persists, go to a supervisor. If it continues, change firms.

5. Change brokers who talk about sure winners. Resist all sales manipulation emphasizing double-digit rates of return, shares that will double, hot stocks, and guaranteed profits.

6. Never put greed before safety. Sometimes you have to protect yourself against yourself, and that can be the most difficult job of all. Remember the market will be here tomorrow—but to use it, you need investment capital.

Hopefully, this information will help you avoid or deal effectively with many of the issues that you might experience. Investors who know how to choose a good broker, how to analyze information, how to order skillfully, and how to protect themselves are investors who know how to make money.

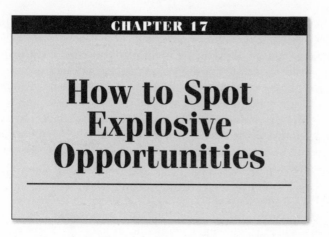

CHAPTER 17

How to Spot Explosive Opportunities

L ocating exceptional investment opportunities is the key to successful trading. The main objective is to discover opportunities that:

- Meet all the criteria for a good investment.
- Use your investment capital in the most efficient manner.
- Produce substantial returns in a relatively short period of time.

Throughout the years I have been investing and trading, I have thought of myself as being fairly successful, while in the eyes of others, I have been perceived as extremely successful. However, contrary to popular belief, I know that deep down inside I still have more room to grow. Over the past few years, I have been able to accelerate my profitability by being patient (as much as I could be) and by being *selective* when I made an investment.

I have to admit that I love the day-to-day excitement and the financial rewards of trading. However, I make a great deal more money by looking for opportunity intelligently. In other words, instead of being in the markets just because I feel I need to be, now I wait like a cheetah in the jungle, looking for a wounded animal to pounce upon. Although the cheetah can catch any animal, wounded or not, it preys on the sure thing. I have learned that this is the best way to trade—wait for everything to look right, then attack with speed and confidence.

Initially it may not be easy for you to do the same. However, this confidence and patience will come over time as you build up experience and increase your investment account through successful trades. How do you spot explosive profit opportunities? It's an awareness that needs to be developed, and if done correctly will enable you to make 100 percent on your money, sometimes in minutes, hours, or days, instead of years.

How do you find the growing money trees hidden deep within the information forest? Simply use the vast amounts of information available to you; learn to filter the data and find the best investments. The problem is that there is so much information. This can be overwhelming and quite confusing. Many would-be investors pick up a newspaper, look at the financial section, quickly decide that they can't make heads or tails out of the information, and promptly give up. The general feeling is that anything this complicated must be extremely difficult to succeed in.

What if you gave up the first time you fell off a bicycle? What if you gave up the first time you sat behind the wheel of a car to learn to drive? What if you gave up on anything halfway challenging? You wouldn't get anywhere—which is why many people never succeed. Successful individuals persevere. This also is true in learning the financial markets. It may seem difficult at first; but once you know the basics about how to ride the bike, it gets easier. After a while, you're cruising down the road yelling, "Look, Mom—no hands!"

Recognizing an excellent trade when you see it is just half the battle. As a trader, you must know how to go about finding explosive profit opportunities. There are an overwhelming number of methods used by the investment community to evaluate trading opportunities. I will not attempt to impart an exhaustive study of analysis techniques—there are far too many of them, and most do not work on a long-term basis. However, there are two basic categories that should be included as basic components of a trader's arsenal: fundamental analysis and technical analysis.

FUNDAMENTAL ANALYSIS

Fundamental analysis is a trading approach used to predict the future price movements of a market based on the careful analysis of an investment's true worth. Various economic data—including income statements, past records of earnings, sales, assets, management, and product development—assist in predicting the future success or failure of the company. Thus, a fundamental analyst studies the fundamentals of a business—its products, customers, consumption, profit outlook, management strength, and supply of and demand for outputs (i.e., oil, soybeans, wheat, etc.). Fundamental analysts use this data to anticipate price transitions. They see a company or market as it is now in the present, and they attempt to forecast where it is going in the future.

Annual reports and quarterly financial statements (and their close government-mandated cousins for publicly traded companies, the 10-K and 10-Q, respectively) are part of the information used in fundamental analysis. The first question is, "Why should we be concerned about financial statements?" They are, after all, simply a restatement of the past, not a road map to the future. There are two primary reasons. The first reason for looking at financial statements is to determine how well management has handled the affairs of the company, because if you own shares or have a bullish position on the stock using options, these people are handling your investments. Is management operating the company well or poorly? Is management efficient or inefficient? How is this firm's management as compared to its competitors?

The second reason for looking at financial statements is to determine if the firm is positioned to carry out the goals of management. For instance, if they are about to run out of cash, expansion projects are probably not going to be realized.

The first step in studying financial statements is to get one's hands on the items from the annual or quarterly report. There are many sources for acquiring an annual report. The most direct way is to call or write the investor relations department of the firm you are interested in analyzing, and simply ask them to send you one. If you already own one or more shares in the firm, they will automatically send you both the annual report and the quarterly financial information. Another location for financial information is the firm's own web site.

Most companies will post at least the numbers from their financial statement on their web site. Your local library will often have copies of firms of local interest. In addition, there are a number of web sites, including EDGAR Online, that will give you access to a firm's 10-K statement and other financial information. Libraries also carry many other sources of financial data on a firm.

One final bit of housekeeping: Which is better, a 10-K or an annual report? A 10-K is a financial statement required by the Securities and Exchange Commission to be filed with the SEC by every publicly traded company on an annual basis. The report is a comprehensive look at the financial dealings of the firm throughout the year. The difference between the 10-K and the annual report is that the 10-K requires all firms to file certain detailed information and to list it in a specific order. The annual report will often include the 10-K, but even if it doesn't, it has basically all the information required in the 10-K, and sometimes with even more detail. Personally, I prefer an annual report because I like to look at all the photos of smiling employees and happy customers, as well as the management discussions that usually accompany the dry numbers.

Okay, say you have an annual report in front of you. Where do you start? The first thing you should realize is that there are no absolutes in financial statements. Unlike the basic laws of physics, what you see is not necessarily what you get; and everything is always open to interpretation. What we will be concerned with is not necessarily in coming to a conclusion on a particular annual report, but rather to point out the pitfalls and areas to be aware of when you start to analyze a statement.

Remember: First, foremost, and always, an annual report is often a sales pitch—management pays for the annual report, and they will be putting their best foot forward in the presentation. Therefore, don't let subjective statements sway your opinion of the company too much. Most fundamental analysts dig deeper inside the report and study the actual numbers.

Some traders overlook fundamental analysis. However, as most trades are not totally neutral (in other words you have a bias as to whether you would prefer the shares to go up or down), studying the fundamentals of a firm should at least help you to be in front of the trend. If you are looking at a strong company in a strong industry, you should think twice before putting a bearish trade on that stock and vice versa. This is especially true for longer-term trades.

There are three important factors to consider when studying the income statement and also three from the balance sheet. On the income statement, you want to look at sales, gross profit (or operating income), and net income. From the balance sheet, you need current assets, current liabilities, and total assets. In addition to these six numbers, the curious investor will have to do a couple of divisions to glean about 80 percent of the information available.

Sales are good. They are necessary to generate income, so more is generally better than less. In addition to the raw number, most investors divide this year's sales by last year's sales to look at the rate of growth. Increasing growth is generally better than decreasing growth, providing each sale is generating more revenue than it costs to produce it.

To determine if a firm is generating profitable sales, we use the second number from the income statement, the gross profit. Dividing gross profit by sales gives the gross profit margin, a number that describes what percent of each sales dollar is available (after the direct costs of producing that sale) to pay for overhead, debt repayment, taxes, and, of course, dividends. Larger is better. A gross profit margin that is deteriorating from prior years is generally not so good. It may not be a problem, but a deteriorating number should raise a red flag so that your antennae are tuned into looking for the reasons when you read articles about that company. The reasons for a deteriorating gross profit margin can come from many things. Raw material and employee costs can escalate faster than the firm is able to raise prices; this is typically not a very good situation. On the other hand, the firm could simply be changing its sales mix (selling a larger percentage of low-margin products) or be going after sales that are less profitable (possibly large orders with associated discounts, etc.), which could be a good strategy. The idea, here, is for the investor to simply be aware that there is something happening.

Finally, the net profit line on the income statement is important. As a bullish investor, you want to see this number positive and increasing. If you are looking for a bearish position, negative and decreasing is your ideal. However, remember that net profit is a result of many things, not just the operations of the company. From your perusal of the footnotes and the auditor's letter, you should be able to judge just how much confidence you can place on this particular number.

While the income statement gives us a picture of just how well the firm prospered over the past year, the balance sheet gives us a glimpse as to how conservative the firm is with its assets and how efficiently it is using them. Current assets and current liabilities are defined as those assets and liabilities that either are or will, in the normal course of business, be turned into cash over the next 12 months. Thus, receivables will be collected, inventory will be sold, prepaid expenses will be utilized (et cetera) in the upcoming year. Similarly, all accounts will be paid, notes and loans will be paid, and unpaid taxes will, by definition, be paid during the upcoming year. Thus, if current assets are greater than current liabilities, there should be no trouble (barring some unforeseen circumstance) meeting all obligations with cash collected from various accounts, even if there are temporary glitches in sales, collections, or production. Obviously, the larger the difference in those two numbers (current assets and current liabilities), the better.

The final number that we are concerned with on the balance sheet is total assets. By dividing "net income" by "total assets," we get return on assets (ROA). This is a measure of just how efficient management is in utilizing the assets at its disposal. This is a more accurate measure of management efficiency than is the return on equity (ROE) that many investors utilize. ROE is a direct result of ROA, adjusted for the amount of debt management has assumed. By simply borrowing more money, management can usually increase the ROE without doing anything better operationally. In fact, the total profit will decrease, as additional funds will be needed to pay the interest costs of the new debt. If carried to the extreme, or if the firm hits a patch of trouble, the increased leverage of the additional debt will become critical.

The standard income statement is generally constructed utilizing what is called "accrual basis accounting." In layman's terms, this means that management chooses when a sale is final and then records it, regardless of when the firm actually receives cash for that good or service. This gives rise to the balance sheet account called "accounts receivable," or the amount of money owed the firm by its customers for goods and services delivered but not yet paid for. To fairly represent the true profitability of the firm, the costs of those raw materials used in the products delivered are then listed on the income statement as a cost, regardless of when they are paid for. Similarly, assets such as buildings and equipment are depreciated, or expensed a little bit each year as management feels they are used up, again regardless of when they are actually paid for.

The statement of cash flows, then, is the vehicle that converts accrual accounting back to a cash basis, and hence is far more critical than most investors give it credit for being. If the firm cannot generate enough cash from its operations to pay for those operations, it will never be able to pay for new investments needed for continuing operations nor be able to repay debt previously borrowed nor pay dividends to shareholders. Thus, the "net cash provided by operating activities" should always be positive (if the company is going to prosper), and the second major category (investing activities) should not always be negative. A negative number in this category is fine if the firm is doing major expansions, but it should, after a few years, turn positive. Finally, a glance at the financing activities section should clue you in on how the firm is paying for all the cash needs it has. Is it raising cash through debt (adding risk) or through the sale of more equity (diluting the shareholder's position)? Or, as one would hope in a mature company, is it repaying past borrowings?

The final section of numbers that the trader should look at is the "Reconciliation of Retained Earnings." This statement is a detailed look at the depreciation and other noncash adjustments that resulted in the final balance of the shareholders' equity account on the balance sheet. This account lists extraordinary items that have taken place during the accounting period as well as adjustments to prior years' statements that do not directly flow through the income statement or any of the other balance sheet accounts. This statement should tie in with your investigation of the footnotes. While you are not looking for anything specific, strange entries should raise questions.

Again, there is no right or wrong answer to any of these particular categories. You are just trying to get a feel for the general health of the firm. If too many of the numbers turn up negative, then you should recognize that this firm is not a slam-dunk gold-plated investment, and appropriate precautions must be taken in your trading efforts.

Entire industries are built around fundamental analysis. Every major brokerage firm has armies of analysts to review industries, companies, and commodities markets. The majority of what you see and hear on television or read in the newspapers is fundamental analysis.

Fundamental analysis comes in many shapes and forms. For example, you may hear that a company's product is selling like hotcakes, or perhaps there has been a management change. Maybe the weather is killing the orange juice crop. It's up to you to learn how to apply this information to making money in the markets. Typically, I don't listen to others, because too often they are wrong. On the other hand, I love to find opportunities to do the opposite of everyone else. This is known as the contrarian approach—when all the information is too positive, look for an opportunity to sell, and when it is too negative, look for an opportunity to buy. Moral of the story: Listen to the market. It will tell you a great deal. Use a discerning ear when listening to anyone else.

TECHNICAL ANALYSIS

Technical analysis evaluates securities by analyzing statistics generated from market activity, such as past prices and volume, to gauge the forces of supply and demand. Furthermore, technical analysis is built in part on the theory that prices display repetitive patterns. These patterns can be utilized to forecast future price movement and potential profit opportunities.

Technical analysts study the markets using graphs and charts to determine price trends and gauge the strength or weakness of an investment (stock, futures, index, etc.). The technical analyst is trying to understand the past price trends of the stock or commodity in order to try to determine price patterns that will forecast future price movements. The type of analysts that use this method of predicting stock movements are sometimes called *technicians* or *chartists*.

Do I believe in technical analysis? Absolutely. I believe a good technician can look at many factors and determine future price action with a certain degree of accuracy. In fact, since many option strategies are relatively short-term in nature, it's important to use technical trading tools to help improve the timing of certain trades. Many options traders use technical analysis more than fundamental analysis for that reason.

However, no person or computer can predict the future 100 percent of the time. We need to use all the information available about the markets in the past and present to attempt to forecast the future. Although many a profit has been made from complex technical charts, there are no crystal balls. Therefore, we recommend studying technical analysis and using it when implementing trading strategies, but don't rely exclusively on charts, patterns, or other technical trading tools.

The simplest and most widely used technical analysis tool is a moving average. A moving average is the analysis of price action over a specified period of time on an average basis. This typically includes two variables (more can be used). For example, we may look at the price of gold trading right now and how that price compares to the average over the past 10 days and the average price over the past 30 days. When the 10-day average goes below the 30-day average, you sell; and, conversely, when the 10-day average goes above the 30-day average, you buy. Technicians go to great lengths to fine-tune which time spans and averages to use. When you find the right time frames, the moving average is probably the simplest and most effective technical tool.

Moving averages and crossovers can be very useful tools. To keep their strengths and benefits in perspective follow these five suggestions regarding their use:

1. If you get a buy or sell signal and you take on a position, keep that position until the 18-day line goes flat or changes direction. Do not take on a new position until there is a proper realignment of all three averages.

2. To protect accumulated profits along the way use the 50-day moving average as an exit point.

3. Think of the 50-day moving average as a support or resistance line.

4. Moving averages work very well in uptrends and downtrends and not as well in sideways markets. That's because in sideways markets, you can get buy signals near tops and sell signals near the bottom. If you trade on those signals, you will more than likely incur losses.

5. Finally, because moving averages do not work that well in sideways markets, which can occur a fair amount of time, use caution. Try to find stocks that trend a great deal if you plan to rely on this tool.

Moving averages are a time-tested tool, and I would urge any new market technician to understand their proper use and application.

Another technique is to use a momentum indicator. This technical market indicator utilizes price and volume statistics for predicting the strength or weakness of a current market and any overbought or over-sold conditions, and can also note turning points within the market. This can be used to initiate momentum investing, a strategy in which you trade with (or against) the momentum of the market in hopes of profiting from it. It's one of my favorite ways to trade because I can spot stocks, futures, and options with the potential to make money on an accelerated basis. Finding these explosive profit opportunities is the key to highly profitable trading.

Briefly, a momentum investor looks for a market that is making a fast move up or down at a specific point in time, or there is an indication of an impending movement. Like a volcano about to erupt, a great deal of pressure starts to build, followed by an explosion for some time, with a calm thereafter. A momentum investor might miss the eruption but be able to catch the market move right after the eruption. Different techniques are used in each case. To catch the first move (another example is that of a surfer trying to ride a wave), you have to see the signs, place the appropriate strategy, and then get ready to get off when the momentum (or eruption, or wave) fizzles. This can be hours, days, or weeks. If you miss the first move, it's best to wait until the movement fizzles and then look to place a contrarian trade. If you wait until there is a slowdown, you can then anticipate a reversal. If you employ a contrarian approach, you will be trading against the majority view of the marketplace. A contrarian is said to fade the trend (which suits me just fine). Very fast moves up lead to very fast moves down, and vice versa.

Trading, investing, and price action are driven by two elements—fear and greed. If you can learn to identify both, you can profit handsomely. Momentum investing plays off of these two human emotions perfectly: greed not to miss a profit opportunity and fear that profits made will be lost if the market reverses course, thus intensifying the reversal in many cases.

There are hundreds of technical analysis tools out in the marketplace. Be very cautious with those that you decide to use. Make sure you thoroughly test these systems over a long period of time (i.e., 10 years or more).

Both fundamental and technical analyses have their proponents. Some traders swear by one and hold great disdain for the other method. Other traders integrate both methods successfully. For example, fundamental analysis can be used to forecast market direction while technical analysis prompts profitable trading entrances and exits. Most investors have had to use trial and error to determine which methods work best for them. Ultimately, it depends on what kind of trading you are more inclined to use, and which methods you are most comfortable employing.

When you begin to select investment methods, try to determine why they work, when they work best, and when they are not effective. Test each method over a sufficient period of time and keep an accurate account of your experiences. If possible, you should always back-test systems as well. You can use trading software to back-test almost any technical analysis technique available. Inevitably, as the markets change, suitable methods of analysis will change also. The key is to remain open-minded and flexible so that you can take advantage of what works.

SENTIMENTAL ANALYSIS

The stock market is a fascinating place. It is particularly interesting in that the day-to-day fluctuations reflect the views, expectations, and forecasts of investors around the world. Indeed, it is an arena in which the final outcome depends not on one individual decision maker, but on the activity of millions of investors.

Given that market moves are due to decisions of a mass of market participants, or the *crowd* and not one individual decision maker, history is replete with episodes of crowd or mob behavior. Basically, under certain decision-making situations, the individual may act quite rationally, but as part of a crowd, will act based on feelings and emotion. In the words of Humphrey B. Neill:

> *Because a crowd does not think, but acts on impulses, public opinions are frequently wrong. By the same token, because a crowd is carried away by feeling, or sentiment, you will find the public participating enthusiastically in various manias after the mania has got well under momentum. This is illustrated in the stock market. The crowd—the public—will remain indifferent when prices are low and fluctuating but little. The public is attracted by activity and by the movement of prices. It is especially attracted to rising prices.* (The Art of Contrary Thinking, *1963*).

As an example, take the contagion that spread throughout global financial markets in the fall of 1998. The fact that the sell-off of one stock market in one country eventually led to a drop in another, and then another, was an example of extreme crowd behavior. It was labeled contagion: defined as the ready transmission of an idea, response, emotion, and so on. However, given that global financial markets recovered toward the end of 1998 and early 1999, obviously the panic selling and drop in global financial markets was overdone. In that case, it was the opposite of a *mania*, but still an example of crowd psychology in its worst form—fear, panic, and disengagement.

Given the nature and impact of crowd psychology on financial markets, many traders use sentiment analysis to gauge the overall attitude of the mass of investors, or the crowd. Studying market sentiment, in turn, is an endeavor in contrary thinking. In other words, one of the premises underlying the study of sentiment data is that, during certain periods of time, it pays to go against the masses. Specifically, when market sentiment becomes extreme in one direction or another, the contrary thinker will act in a manner opposite to the crowd. For example, at the apex of panic selling during the global financial crisis of 1998, the contrary thinker armed with an understanding of sentiment data may well have turned into a buyer: just as the crowd was getting rid of shares. Indeed, when the market is gripped with fear and panic, it usually turns out to be the best buying opportunity.

An often-heard saying in the stock market is that investors are "right on the trend, but wrong at both ends." In a rising or bull market, investors are better served buying shares. In a declining or bear market, the trend is downward and it is a better time to sell. In short, during significant market trends, it is more profitable to go in the direction of the market rather than contrary to it. So the crowd is not always wrong. The turning points, however, often catch investors unaware. Sentiment analysis offers a variety of tools for identifying the extreme crowd behavior or "the ends." Let's start by taking a closer look at put/call ratios.

Put/call ratios are widely used and easy to obtain. All of the necessary data is available on the Chicago Board Options Exchange web site (www.cboe.com). As the name implies, the put/call ratio is computed by dividing puts by calls. It can be done for shares or index options. I focus on two put/call ratios: the CBOE total put-to-call and index put-to-call ratios. While the CBOE put/call ratio uses the total of all option trades on the Chicago Board Options Exchange, the index ratio considers only index trading. For example, February 12, 2004, 508,743 put options and 916,360 calls traded on the CBOE. So the put-to-call ratio was .56 (or 508,743/916,360). The same analysis is repeated for the CBOE index put-to-call ratio, but the equation considers only index options. The ratios are available daily at the CBOE web site.

Put/call ratios are used as a contrary indicator. Since calls make money when shares or indexes rise, they often represent bullish bets on the part of investors. Conversely, puts increase in value when a stock or index moves lower and, therefore, reflect bearish bets. So when the put/call ratio increases, it suggests that there are a greater number of puts traded relative to calls, and market sentiment is turning bearish. When it falls, call buying is increasing in comparison to put buying. Again, studying put/call ratios is an exercise in contrary thinking. Specifically, if most market participants, or the crowd, are buying puts, it is a sign of negative sentiment and reason to turn bullish. Conversely, a low put/call ratio is interpreted as a market negative since the crowd is excessively bullish, but probably wrong.

In practice, readings of .50 or less from the total put-to-call ratio are a sign of heavy call activity and extremely bullish sentiment. In that case, the contrarian would turn more cautious or bearish. On the other hand, readings of 1.00 or more are a sign of excessive bearishness and reason to be bullish. The index put-to-call ratio will rise above 2.00 when investors are too bearish and drop below 1.00 when bullish sentiment is extreme.

Adviser sentiment, which is used to measure excessive bearish and bullish positions, is one of the more popular contrarian indicators and is certainly one I employ. If adviser bearish sentiment is greater than 60 percent, this is a signal that a possible bottom is forming. If adviser optimism is greater than 70 percent, this signals a market top.

The mutual fund liquid assets ratio is based on the premise that cash balances rise as the trend nears a bottom when increased buying power exerts a bullish effect. If buying power is greater than 10 percent of balances, this is bullish. The Investment Company Institute (ICI) releases the number monthly. The first cousin of this indicator is customer credit balances and is based on the fact that the cash balances rise or fall as the market bottoms or peaks.

The short interest ratio indicator consists of ratios of short interest to average daily trading volume. Readings above 1.75 are bullish and ratios under 1.0 are bearish. A related indicator is odd-lot short sales, which typically are wildly speculative in the wrong direction.

The final three contrarian indicators I look at are the over-the-counter (OTC) relative volume, market P/E ratio, and the Dow Jones Industrial Average dividend yield. OTC volume breakouts above 80 percent provide bearish signals of excessive speculation. Price-earnings ratios of 5 and 25 are approximate lower- and upper-trend boundaries. DJIA yields get as low as 3 percent at market tops and as high as 18 percent at market bottoms.

The different numbers I have used for quantification purposes are typical rules of thumb used by most contrarian traders. I basically use them as a ballpark figure versus an absolute. They will change through time and should be considered in light of their long-term trends. As far as finding the latest readings for these indicators, information can be found in *Barron's*, *Value Line*, and *Investor's Business Daily*, as well as on a multitude of Internet sites.

In conclusion, there is a wide variety of sentiment tools that can be used to enhance your trading, especially if you are interested in becoming a contrarian trader. The premise holds that the crowd is not always wrong, but invariably on the wrong side of the market during major turning points. The goal behind using sentiment analysis, therefore, is to identify extreme cases of bullishness or bearishness and then trade in the opposite direction because the major turning points generally turn out to be the most profitable trading opportunities.

Table 17.1 lists key contrary indicators and other technical trading tools. The rightmost column shows how each indicator can be used by market technicians to keep up with changing market trends.

The market is always going to bounce around, and this constant fluctuation may indicate that there's never an exactly right time to enter a trade, but there will always be a time that's better than another. Professional traders

TABLE 17.1 Key Contrary Indicators

Indicator	Type	Trend	Usage
Confidence index	Sentiment	Parallel	Index rises as investors shift from high-grade to lower-grade bonds with bullish expectations.
Adviser sentiment	Sentiment	Contrary	Excessive adviser bearishness (60 percent) signals bottoms; optimism (10 percent bearish) signals tops.
Put/call ratio	Sentiment	Contrary	Excessive puts (70/100) or calls (40/100) signal bottoms or tops early.
Odd-lot trading	Sentiment	Parallel	Odd-lot investors step up their buying at bottoms and sell into market tops.
Specialist trading	Sentiment	Parallel	Specialists buy and sell ahead of the trend, using nonpublic information.
Money-fund balances	Cash flow	Contrary	Rising balances draw money from shares; declining balances are bullish.
Mutual-fund liquid assets ratio	Cash flow	Contrary	Cash balances rise as the trend nears a bottom, when increased buying power exerts a bullish effect.
Customer credit balances	Cash flow	Contrary	Cash balances rise or fall as the market bottoms or peaks.
Customer margin debt	Cash flow	Parallel	Margin buyers are half as much in debt at tops as at bottoms.
Short interest	Short sale	Contrary	Increased short selling fuels rallies, and at extremes signals trend turning points.
Short interest ratio	Short sale	Contrary	Ratios of short interest to average daily trading volume above 1.75 are bullish; ratios under 1.0 are bearish for the market.
Odd-lot short sales	Short sale	Contrary	Odd-lot short sellers are wildly speculative in the wrong direction.
Specialist short-sale ratio	Short sale	Parallel	Ratios of specialist short sales to public short sales above 3.5 percent are bearish; ratios below 1.8 percent are bullish.
Up/down volume	Breadth	Parallel	Daily volume change of 90 percent or more signal trend reversal.

(continues)

TABLE 17.1 *(Continued)*

Indicator	Type	Trend	Usage
OTC relative volume	Breadth	Contrary	OTC volume breakouts above 80 percent provide bearish signals of excessive speculation.
Advance/ decline line	Breadth	Parallel	The broad market peaks and bottoms ahead of the indexes; divergence signals turning points.
TRIN (short-term trading or ARMS index)	Breadth	Parallel	Measures average volume of advancers relative to decliners; readings above 1.5 are bullish, below 0.7 are bearish.
Market P/E ratio	Breadth	Contrary	Price-earnings ratios of 5 and 25 are approximate lower and upper trend boundaries.
DJIA dividend yield	Breadth	Contrary	DJIA yield gets as low as 3 percent at market tops and as high as 18 percent at bottoms.

use timing and technical indicators to secure the best moment of entry and exit. They take advantage of the market's swings rather than letting volatility take advantage of them. That's why it is so important to learn how to use timing indicators—to put the odds in your favor and dollars in your trading account.

OPTIONS AND THEIR BUILT-IN SENTIMENT INDICATORS

The utilization of sentiment indicators has been common in the stock, futures, and options market for a long time. However, the difference for the options market is that it inherently possesses its own sentiment indicators and does not have to look outside to gauge or measure investor feelings. The inherent sentiment indicators I am referring to come in the form of implied volatility, option trading volume, option open interest, and put/call ratios. All of these reveal important sentiment type information about the markets.

First, implied volatility is a calibration of a stock's volatility as implied by the current price of the option. Many times it is referred to as the *fear factor* as it gauges the level of concern investors might have in the markets at a particular time. An option's implied volatility is an approximation of the underlying equity's volatility in the future. Estimating the level required to arrive at the option's current value gives us implied volatility.

To determine whether implied volatility is exhibiting investor fear or complacency, we compare it against its historical volatility levels. Historical volatility, also known as statistical volatility, gauges a stock's volatility based on the equity's past price action. Historical volatility is constructed using the standard deviation of a stock's price changes from close-to-close of trading for a specified time period.

If an option's implied volatility is greater than the statistical volatility, the option is considered expensive or overvalued. The type of sentiment reading would indicate to the option strategist that they should consider selling options. If an option's implied volatility is less than historical volatility then the option is considered cheap or undervalued. In this scenario, the options trader would pursue a strategy where he or she would buy options. This comparison is necessary because just relying on implied volatility alone doesn't really provide you with enough information.

Additionally, there are two other perplexing ways to use options for ascertaining investor sentiment: option trading volume and open interest. Option trading volume is the amount of option contracts traded in one day recorded at the market close. The interpretation is based on the idea that put purchasing is bearish and buying calls is bullish. Put volume divided by call volume determines if a specific market has a bullish or bearish sentiment.

Option open interest is the number of outstanding contracts that are available on a specific option series. Monitoring the open interest statistics of an option allows an investor to judge the relative demand of an option. An increase in an option's open interest means there are additional purchasers for that option. On the other hand, a reduction in the open interest of an option indicates fewer buyers and more sellers than previously. Just as with option volume comparing the put option's open interest with the call option's open interest generally indicates the underlying equity's bullish or bearish bias.

Finally, you can look at how bearish or bullish a particular market is by monitoring the ratio between put premiums and call premiums. This is by far the most popular option sentiment tool of the mix. In general, if there is a lot of put buying compared to call buying the premium on puts will be higher, which signals a bearish environment. Conversely, if call buying exceeds put buying, this increased demand pushes call prices higher signaling a bullish sentiment.

These inherent sentiment indicators are yet another illustration of the amazing flexibility of an option. One thing to note though before employing the indicators as definite buy and sell signals: Sometimes an upsurge in open interest can be attributed to a large institution hedging a position. As with any technical tool, look to get confirmation from one or two additional indicators before locking yourself into a directional bias.

VIX AND VXN

The Chicago Board Options Exchange created the CBOE Volatility Index, or VIX, in 1986. VIX has become the number one gauge of market volatility available today. Computed throughout the trading day, it is unique in that it offers up-to-the-minute or real-time information regarding market volatility. Therefore, there are no cumbersome calculations and the information is available at the click of the mouse. (For example, go to the Optionetics.com home page and enter $VIX in the quote box.)

VIX gives up-to-the-minute readings of market volatility. At the same time, it is not a gauge of actual volatility, but a measure of implied volatility. Implied volatility is derived using an option valuation model. In the case of VIX, the options are on the S&P 500, or SPX index, which is an index of 500 large companies with stocks trading on the U.S. exchanges. Therefore, VIX represents the market consensus view regarding the future volatility of 500 of the largest and most actively traded stocks.

So, as VIX measures the implied volatility of SPX options, it will begin to rise when traders expect volatility to increase. During times of uncertainty and market turmoil, VIX will move higher to reflect expectations regarding future volatility going forward. For that reason, it is often referred to as the "fear gauge." However, during times of relative tranquility in the U.S. stock market, VIX will move lower to reflect investor expectations that market volatility will remain low.

The chart shown in Figure 17.1 details the performance of VIX from 1999 to early 2004. During the fifth year, beginning in March 2003, the market performed well and stocks moved broadly higher. During that time, the CBOE Volatility Index edged lower. In fact, VIX fell to seven-year lows of 14.3 percent in early 2004. There was no fear reflected in the market's "fear gauge."

Another interesting aspect of the chart is the periodic spikes in the volatility index. This happens during periods of panic in the market. For instance, shortly after its inception, during the market crash in October 1987, VIX hit a record high of 173 percent, which has never been surpassed. In the mini-crash of 1989 after the problems associated with UAL and its restructuring, VIX spiked again. In 1990, when Iraq invaded Kuwait and the United States became embroiled in a war in the Middle East, the

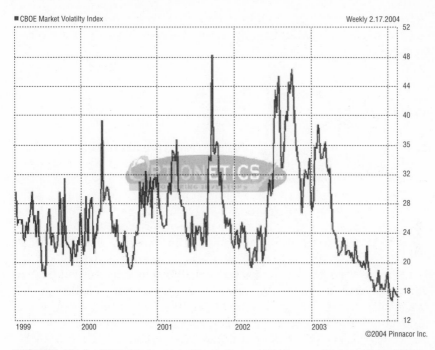

FIGURE 17.1 CBOE Market Volatility Index or VIX (*Source:* Optionetics © 2004)

volatility index spiked twice: once when Iraq moved into Kuwait in 1990 and again in 1991 after the United Nations attacked Iraq.

More recently, in October 1997, investors were spooked when the Dow Jones Industrial Average tumbled 555 points. VIX jumped to 55.5 percent. In the fall of 1998, as the impact of the global financial crisis was beginning to shake U.S. markets, market anxiety once again picked up. The volatility index soared above 65 percent in October 1998. On the chart, we can see VIX spiking again in September 2001 when the terrorist attacks rocked the financial center on Wall Street. Since that time, VIX has traded below 50 percent.

In response to the growing interest in Nasdaq 100 options, the Chicago Board Options Exchange launched an implied volatility indicator on the Nasdaq 100 Index in January 2001. Known by its ticker symbol, VXN, the new implied volatility indicator was created to track the implied volatility of the popular NDX options contract. Like VIX, it is updated continually throughout the trading day.

In addition, traders can also plot the index's long-term movement in order to identify the extremes. As we can see from Figure 17.2, VXN has

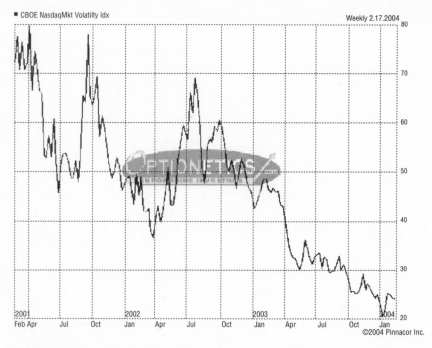

FIGURE 17.2 CBOE Nasdaq Volatility Index or VXN (*Source:* Optionetics © 2004)

been in a long-term decline since its inception. However, there are times when it spikes higher, like in September 2001 and July 2002. A move higher in the Nasdaq volatility index tells us that the implied volatility of Nasdaq 100 Index options is on the rise. Therefore, traders are expecting market volatility to increase going forward, which generally occurs when investor anxiety levels and fear are on the rise.

Using VIX and VXN as sentiment indicators requires a bit of contrary thinking. An adage among options traders says, "When VIX is high, it's time to buy. When VIX is low, it's time to go." This tells us that when VIX is high, it is time to buy into the stock market with long strategies such as bull call spreads or other bullish strategies. During these times, market anxiety levels and pessimism are high. In that case, investors, or the crowd, have probably overreacted and driven stock prices to bargain basement levels. When VIX is low, it is time to go, or get out of the market. During those times, investors are probably complacent or too bullish on the stock market. So the contrarian thinker will get out of bullish positions, or even set up some bearish trades.

A NOTE ON BEING A CONTRARIAN

Taking action contrary to the crowd will always feel uncomfortable. At the actual time you must decide and act, you will never have all the information you'll want because gauging market psychology is more of an art than a precise science. Furthermore, your countertrend decision will make you feel lonely, and we humans are social animals who seek comfort and approval from others. Always remain tight-lipped about your investment moves. If you're a talking contrarian, people hearing of your views and behavior will exert immense pressure and may convince you to abandon your thinking at precisely the wrong times.

Successful trading, contrarian-style, requires observation, understanding, and, finally, action. First, you must see facts: events, trends, and rates of growth or decline. It is imperative that the contrarian trader develops a sense of history, an ability to put things together in context, and a good feel for when a trend is moving to an extreme. But even all that will do you no good if you don't take action. Acting is usually the most difficult skill to master.

Being a contrarian requires that you identify the market's situation, whether that be broad averages or the market of opinion. The factual and emotional states of the economy and the market can be observed at any time. Successful investment behavior requires patience so that you don't pull the trigger at the very first observation of important elements; you need to wait for an accumulation of evidence that an extreme is developing.

Trying to play contrarian on a short-term basis creates what is known on the street as *whipsawed* traders. Given that the public is usually right during the trends but wrong at both ends, we should not get impatient at the first sign of extreme behavior in others. Let a trend run for a while and watch the evidence accumulate.

This approach can be profitable due to the bipolar nature of market dynamics. The trick is to recognize a market's turning points by monitoring psychological market indicators to assess your next move and then trade with or against the majority's view of the market. One indicator alone, like VIX, will not necessarily help you time the turning points. To invest contrary to the crowd, you need to consider a broad range of indicators, the big picture, and sometimes exercise a great deal of patience.

NONANALYTICAL METHODS

There are many other ways to find a good investment. However, the two most common are probably the most unreliable. It is important that you use discretion as you make investment decisions.

Reliance on Others

The biggest mistake most people make in the field of investing is relying on others. This includes consulting brokers, listening to friends, receiving tips, or even calling psychic hotlines. Professional money managers (mutual fund managers) also must be selected with care. Be careful whom you listen to. You are the only person who is ultimately responsible for your own profitability. Make a strong commitment to relying on your own initiative.

Religious Experience

From long observation, it seems to me that prayer is truly the method most often used by traders and investors. Most traders and investors do very little analysis and have no idea as to what is going on; still they go ahead and trade. Then, they just pray that they will be right. Even when their initial position goes against them, they just stay in the bad trade praying the market will come back. They continue to pray until they can't take the loss anymore or they lose all their money.

Nick Leeson, the trader who allegedly lost $1 billion for Barings Bank—a loss that brought down the 200-year-old institution—got himself into a bad position and kept adding to that bad position praying that the market would indeed turn around and make him right. It never happened. Seize the day!

CREATING A TRADING FILTER

After years of investing and trading, I came to the realization that to become good at this business I had to keep my eyes and ears open. I then set myself up to be able to accept both visual and audio information and to filter out useless information. Peter Lynch, former manager of the Fidelity Magellan mutual fund, is one of the best money managers of our time. In his books, he clearly states this principle of accepting all available information. Although the Magellan Fund, like many other funds, focuses on longer-term investments, the principles stated in Peter Lynch's books—as well as books by other great investors—can also be applied on a short-term trading basis. I focus my attention on these principles of "intelligent investing" to get both the long-term and short-term perspectives.

Many investors may be satisfied with a 10 percent return on their money compared to 4 percent interest for a certificate of deposit. I prefer to work a little harder in order to get a much higher percentage return. After all, this is the business I choose to be in. I want my trades and investments to make me a very good living no matter how much money I started with. Remember, the only way to build your account up quickly is to spot the consistently profitable opportunities and to use your money efficiently.

Most investors and traders have very little idea how to find explosive opportunities. It's not that they're not smart enough. It's just that they haven't been made aware of the effectiveness of these techniques. During each trading day, I can work as little as five minutes and still make more money (with a much higher return) than investors who work all day. This is not to say that I spend only five minutes a day trading. I enjoy this business way too much. In fact, I don't even see what I do as work. I am sometimes even a little disappointed when the trading day is over. Believe it or not, weekends can be my most difficult periods.

However, explosive opportunities can be found every day. To gain true opportunity insight, open yourself up to receive information from the perspective of a trader. Don't let important information slip through your fingers as many people do. Filtering information correctly can be the key to making money. Years of experience have shown me that the mega-successful investors are unique individuals who have developed approaches to finding opportunities others may be missing. Let's take a closer look at where these chances to make a very high return on your money in the short term—minutes, hours, or days—can be found.

Remember That Stocks Follow Bonds

If you keep your eyes on how interest rates are moving, you can determine where shares are likely to go. When interest rates are going up, bond prices are going down and shares will likely go down also. Conversely, if interest rates are decreasing, then bond prices are rising and shares should also be rising. If interest rates are stable, shares will have a tendency to go up. You can use these insights to create consistent profits in your account. However, there are points in time when this relationship does not hold. When this occurs, take the time to discern what has affected this relationship. For example, in 1998 turmoil broke out in the Asian markets which changed this relationship. Foreign investors bought bonds, which increased the price of bonds and lowered yields while the stock market moved downward.

Stay Informed on Seasonal and Event-Driven Markets

Event-driven markets are exactly that: markets that are driven by events—seasonal, political, or otherwise. For instance, the energy markets are seriously affected not only by war in the Middle East, but by scheduled meetings of the Organization of Petroleum Exporting Countries

(OPEC). The agriculturals are directly impacted by seasonal weather changes. Bonds are tied to changes in interest rates and the monthly release of the government's unemployment report. In essence, look for markets that have an event that triggers a specific trade strategy once or twice a month, or maybe once every three months.

To keep up with these important market factors, you must keep abreast of daily news by watching television and reading mainstream and alternative newspapers and magazines in hard copy and on the Internet. It can also be important to listen to what key people in specific markets have to say. Typically, you need to come home from work and study what the markets are doing from many angles. In the beginning, it can be empowering to keep a journal of daily events and their effect on various markets you are actively watching. If a market's going to move, then it's more likely that you can make money from it. By studying the daily reactions of specific markets to events, you can begin to forecast which strategy can be used to make the largest potential profit.

Always keep an eye on markets that are dependent on the weather (oil, soybeans, wheat, etc.). See how they are reacting to seasonal factors. The tougher the winter, the higher the price of heating oil. The longer the drought, the higher the price of soybeans. All of this information can be used to find highly profitable trades.

Walk around Retail Stores

You can even make money while you are spending it. Just open your eyes and ears when you are shopping and see if you can spot an interesting investment.

- Find out what products are hot.
- Notice which products have the most store shelf exposure.
- Ask a clerk which products are literally flying off the shelf.

On a shopping trip to a local toy store at Christmastime, I noticed that not only was the store filled to capacity, but people were fighting over the last items of one obviously hot product. Instead of jumping into the battle to fight for a toy, I picked up a box to find out the manufacturer. In addition, I asked a clerk at the store about the frenzy over this one product. She stated that this was almost a daily occurrence and then told me about a number of other items that were also flying off the shelf.

This is not to say that everyone will be this helpful, but I was able to spot some particular potential investment opportunities by just asking questions of a store clerk. I then called my broker and investigated whether these particular companies were doing well. The next time you are shopping, take a look around and see if you can spot hot products or hot companies.

Look for Opportunities When Driving

Even when you're driving your car, you can spot opportunities. Once again, all you have to do is keep your eyes and ears open. For example, a few years ago I found a new restaurant—at least it was new when I found it—by the name of Boston Chicken. I first visited the place because I was hungry. However, when I saw the food and tasted the meals, I realized that this was a different kind of fast-food restaurant. I was given large portions of delicious food at a good price. I was not only satisfied with the food quality, but I felt that I got a good deal as to price and quantity as well. I returned on several occasions with others and everyone had the same impression. In addition, the counters displayed information on franchise opportunities. Although I was not interested in becoming a franchisee, it was clear this concept had to take off. Sure enough, these restaurants started popping up all over Boston, and the list of franchises exploded nationwide. When the company went public, I knew I had to get in on this. The company's public offering was a smash success. Now the company is known as Boston Market with stores all over the country and entrées in supermarkets as well.

When driving, always look for trends. Years ago I spotted a number of cars and trucks that had some interesting designs. It surprised me that they were Dodge products—I had never been a big fan of Dodge or any U.S. manufacturer's automobiles. However, I kept seeing television commercials about the "new Dodge." Well, I knew the old Dodge was not very exciting; but as a car fan—I love sports cars—I kept reading about their newest "super car," the Dodge Viper.

Luckily for me, a friend ended up buying one and I had the privilege of driving the Viper in the Nevada deserts. If you've ever driven in the desert, you know you can drive really fast out there. After all, there's nothing there but hard-packed sand. I won't tell you how fast I was going; but I was beyond merely being impressed with this car. At that time, I owned some other sports cars (Porsche and Ferrari) but I found the Dodge Viper to be much more exciting and fun to drive. Thereafter, I sold the Ferrari and bought the Viper, remaining to this day one of the Viper's biggest fans. Years later, I still get a thrill out of driving this car and so does anyone I know who drives one. It is by far the best sports car I have ever owned.

This very positive impression of the car—a Chrysler product—led me to change my opinion of Chrysler products and American automobiles in general. Since then, I have bought two other Chrysler products (Jeep Cherokees), and I love them just as much. Such a positive experience on my part and the number of Dodge Ram pickups I saw on the road led me to believe that Chrysler had nowhere to go but up. The company has since reported record earnings. Indications are that this trend will continue and the stock will be a good long-term investment.

Critique That Which You Already Own

If you like a certain product, others probably do also. You can then look at this product as a potential investment. In addition, if you have a problem with a product and you feel dissatisfied, then others will likely have the same opinion. This may be a good selling opportunity for the stock (using a strategy that makes money when the price drops). Most of us have had a lot of both good and bad experiences. It is up to you to figure out how to translate these experiences into profit opportunities.

If you buy an item and then are dissatisfied, can't get anyone to help you, or can't exchange the product, you're probably not the only one. This happened to me recently. I kept hearing about a certain computer product and how great it was. I subsequently purchased it and found installing it to be extremely difficult. The product was supposed to be easily installed, especially for a computer-literate person like myself. I contacted the customer support line and was put on hold for 20 minutes. I hung up out of frustration and called a second time determined to get through. After being kept on hold for 45 minutes (a very expensive long-distance call), I finally got a representative who knew less about the hardware and computers than I did. I asked for someone else, who ended up giving me information that crashed my computer.

I quickly returned the product and went back to a reliable company that I have never had any problems with—Hewlett-Packard. I figured that everyone was having the same problems I was and that the product would flop as the hype about the product fizzled. The stock of this overhyped company was trading at around $50—it had made a very fast move up from around $5 in less than a year. I immediately put on a bearish position to make money when the shares went down. The shares fell in less than four months to around $15, and I smugly changed my dissatisfaction and frustration with the company into cash.

I didn't have to be a genius to figure this one out. All I had to do was translate a personal experience into what other people's experience was likely to be and pinpoint a way to make money from this information. You can do this on a daily basis with items you own or have purchased and returned.

Ask Your Children

Yes, even children can be a good source of spotting new trends. What new movie do they want to see? What new toys do they want to purchase? What clothes styles are all the rage? What sports are popular?

Children offer a wealth of information especially because they are greatly influenced by what other kids are doing as well as by what they see on television, in the movies, or anywhere. They can alert you to new trends that can affect the bottom line of a company. These pieces of information are valuable to the establishment of a winning investment perspective.

Look Around Where You Work

Opportunities can also be spotted directly from where you work, your spouse works, or a friend works. For example, a friend of mine who was working at a pharmacy told me that one of her favorite customers sadly has AIDS. One day, he came into the pharmacy looking much better. He credited a new experimental drug from a company called Nexstar Pharmaceutical with helping him feel better than he had in years. My friend had an article from the local newspaper that her customer had shown her (he was mentioned in the article). I called my broker to ask about the stock. It was trading around $9 a share. I bought some shares in the company and within a few months it was well over $20 per share. (I'll give my friend credit for this one.) I sold the shares for a large return, and now I keep asking pharmacists what they consider to be exciting products. By going directly to the people who know a lot about a particular industry, I can leverage their years of education and experience into another profit-making opportunity.

Subscribe to a Data Service Provider

Data service providers can furnish you with current prices on shares, futures, and options. In addition, you can receive up-to-the-minute news and market analyses. This information comes in a variety of ways, including the Internet, cable, FM radio, satellite, and wireless networks, and can receive price quotes that are real-time (as the prices change on the exchanges they are transmitted to you), delayed (typically 15 to 20 minutes after the prices change), or end-of-day (after the markets close).

Your service fees are based on the kind of service you choose to receive. The faster you get your data, the more costly it will be to obtain; however, it will also be more accurate for making your investment decisions. If you are not going to sit in front of a computer all day long, then you don't really need real-time feeds; you can easily get away with delayed or end-of-day quotes. Subscribing to only what you need keeps your cost as low as possible—you can upgrade later as your trading progresses.

Depending on the data you want and the exchanges you sign up to, data feeds can cost you from $20 to $400 per month. There are even feeds used by the large institutional firms (big trading firms) that can run thousands of dollars per month. If you want to place longer-term trades, delayed or end-of-day quotes should be sufficient for your needs. In many cases, if you sign up to trade with an online brokerage firm, they will provide real-time quotes for you at no cost or for a very small fee. Some other web sites, like www.cboe.com, have real-time quotes available for a relatively small monthly fee. Remember, if you are just starting out, keep your overhead as low as possible. Request information on only the markets you initially want to trade. Too much information can be overwhelming if you don't know how to use it. It is essential to start small and build your profits systematically. A detailed account of data providers can be found in Appendix A.

Watch Television with an Investor's Eye

Television is one of the best sources of beneficial investment ideas. Commercials can give you a greater awareness as to who is doing what, and who is competing with whom. Television is not just a source of daily entertainment; it is an exceptional medium for distributing information to the masses, much of which is useful for spotting investment opportunities. Specifically, you should watch commercials to discover which products you see over and over again and which products have been newly introduced.

However, you can also use this powerful medium in other ways. CNBC and CNN Business are shown in many areas on cable. These are the primary channels watched by traders and investors throughout the trading day. CNBC was born from the Financial News Network (FNN), which was watched widely by the investment community. Before, during, and after trading hours, CNBC broadcasts market information on many issues, including stocks and futures. Expert commentators and guests give market summaries and opinions throughout the day.

As a professional trader, I leave CNBC on with just enough volume to overhear any piece of information that might have a bearing on an investment decision. I typically do not watch any particular show unless something strikes me as intriguing, but I do listen to the commentary all day long. As with any news organization, they report on stories they believe to be interesting to their target audience—the investment community. They talk about what is hot and what is not. They focus on the most market-moving information they can find, because that's the business they are in.

What kind of information do I listen for? Extremely good news and extremely bad news. This is where you can make explosive profits. For example, one day CNBC reported about a company that had a drug use test using a strand of hair. My broker informed me the stock was trading around $6 per share. I bought some shares knowing the news would get out overnight and create buying interest in the stock. As I predicted, the shares opened the next day at around $9.50. I sold my shares immediately, because stocks with this kind of run-up often come down quickly. The shares closed that day at around the same level I bought in at, leaving me with a 50 percent profit on an overnight investment.

To give you another example, CNBC reported about a stock that had dropped from around $12 per share to about $3.50 overnight due to "accounting irregularities." I called my broker and found that there were options available on the stock to trade. Seeing less risk in the options than the shares, I bought out-of-the-money (OTM) call options at $50 each. These I sold 27 days later at $150 apiece for a 200 percent profit in less than a month.

My mother used to complain that I watched too much television. Well, watching TV for me now has become a profitable experience. Looking at CNBC or CNN Business, one can have a 15-minute delay of price quotes all at the touch of a remote (some prices are actually real-time). But what does this TV ticker tape tell me? Let's forget for the moment about the men and women at the anchor desks in the flashy studio, and concentrate on the bottom of the screen. This is referred to as a ticker tape.

Before the market opens, you will see a recap of stocks using the closing prices of the previous trading day. Also, futures prices are mixed in every few minutes. At 8:30 A.M., after a government or economic report, bond prices are shown in the lower right-hand corner for 10 minutes or so. Beginning at 9:30 A.M. and until 9:45 A.M. Eastern standard time (EST), the market averages run real-time across your screen. The top line usually represents the NYSE stocks, and from time to time futures will appear. The bottom line represents the AMEX and OTC stocks as well as real-time market averages that appear about every minute. Throughout the day, from 9:45 A.M. until 4:15 P.M., stock prices are quoted on the screen. These are displayed as the ticker symbol, followed by shares traded, followed by the last trade and the change in price since yesterday's close (on some stations)—for example:

IBM *10000.00 88 + .50*

The stock symbol is IBM, which last traded 10,000 shares at $88 each, up $.50 from yesterday. If you see only the symbol and the price, then that was the last quoted price of the shares and no shares having been traded.

Averages that are quoted include the Dow Jones Industrial Average (DJIA) and the Standard & Poor's 500 Cash Index (SPX), followed by the daily change of the index. This information is useful to anyone who has the time to watch the markets on a daily basis.

There are many more examples of how I've been able to use television, especially CNBC, to make money. You can do the same. In some cases, I have been able to apply the contrarian approach to accelerate my profits even further.

Local television programming is certainly not as concise as CNBC; however, you can pick up information on local companies and futures markets that are pertinent to the local community. There are also several national television shows that have segments on investing and trading, such as CNN and the *Nightly Business Report*. Unfortunately, most of them lack a great deal of specialized information; either they do not focus on the investment community or they intersperse business news with general news stories.

Read Newspapers Attentively

The first task is to learn how to read a newspaper efficiently and intelligently. A successful investor can scan a newspaper in about five minutes and spot potential opportunities. You must be able to pass by all the fluff and get to the meat of the information.

You can start by picking up copies of newspapers that specialize in financial news, such as *Investor's Business Daily* and *The Wall Street Journal*. (See Appendix A for a breakdown of investment terms found in these two papers.) It's also important to keep tabs on what is happening locally by scanning the local papers that highlight regional companies. This gives you an opportunity to get a better understanding of these potential investments. For example, if you live in the San Francisco Bay Area, you will find a great deal of news about the Silicon Valley companies (e.g., Intel, Oracle, Hewlett-Packard, Yahoo!, etc.). These companies employ a great many individuals in the region, so both good and bad news often leaks out. If you don't live in the Bay Area, you can locate information about Silicon Valley's high-tech companies by using the various resources found on the Internet, including our web site (www.optionetics.com).

Since local newspapers are in the business of finding and reporting news that has an impact on the people in the area, they look for any chance to report on developments both positive and negative on major companies. Therefore, you can usually find a much wider variety of pertinent information in local papers than in a national newspaper. It is a wise practice to research the major employers in your area and then look for news that can directly affect the performance of these companies' stocks.

A number of periodicals and magazines are also available to help you spot good investment opportunities and educate yourself further regarding shares, options, and futures including *Futures* magazine, *Technical Analysis of Stocks and Commodities*, and *Commodity Price Charts*. However, make no mistake, both *The Wall Street Journal* and *Investor's Business Daily* are essential weapons in the battle to locate investment opportunities. When looking at the first page of the *Journal*'s Money & Investing section, you can scan the left-hand side of the page to gauge what the markets look like. Focus on the interest and stock charts. See if they are moving in the same direction, or if interest rates are stable and stock prices are moving up, down, or sideways. See if the interrelationship follows what is expected.

In addition to reviewing the tables in *The Wall Street Journal* and *Investor's Business Daily*, I like to look at the charts—graphical representations of price movement—found in the *IBD*. These charts are almost like looking at an electrocardiogram (EKG) of your heart. This EKG-like analysis does not require you to overstudy the chart. With a quick glance, a knowledgeable investor or trader can visualize the health or weakness of a stock or a commodity. New investors can look at a chart and easily ascertain one of three scenarios:

1. Is the price of the security (shares or futures) going up?
2. Is the price of the security going down?
3. Is the price of the security going sideways?

The best investments will have momentum. This momentum should be monitored over both a short and long period of time. You want to make short-term investments by looking at short-term price momentum (daily or weekly) and long-term investments by looking at the investment from a long-term perspective (each quarter or yearly). If a stock's volume is low, it isn't likely to go anywhere. Look for increasing volume in a stock to signal movement. The best investments will have a reasonable price-earnings (P/E) ratio compared to the industry average. All of this information can be obtained by studying the investment sections in *The Wall Street Journal* or *Investor's Business Daily*, or by consulting your broker or the Optionetics.com web site.

To locate the best potential investment opportunities in a newspaper, you should focus on the following information for stocks:

- Stocks with the greatest percentage rise in volume.
- Stocks with an increase in price greater than 30 percent.

- Stocks with a decrease in price greater than 30 percent.
- Stocks with strong (buying) or weak (selling) earnings per share (EPS) growth.
- Stocks with strong (buying) or weak (selling) relative strength.
- Stocks making a new 52-week high or new 52-week low.

Many people think that it takes years of practice to become a good chart reader. Some experts on technical analysis—the study of price movement through numerical analysis—tend to make the process look more difficult than it really is, so that many individuals give up in their quest to be good investors or traders before they have given themselves a chance to succeed. Many times, information from traders and analysts with accurate knowledge often gets lost in the abundance of useless investing debris.

I have often mentioned that sometimes the best investment approach is to become a contrarian and do the opposite of what the crowd does. You may find local newspapers (depending on where you live) reporting on a number of issues that can affect commodity prices. For example, if you live in the farm belt of the United States, you will read many articles on the weather, crop expectations, and livestock outlooks. These tidbits of information get filtered to the investment community. Investors and traders then make investment decisions based on their perceptions of the impact of these tidbits of information on the prices of the various commodities.

For example, on a trip to the farm belt, I noticed that everyone was talking about the skyrocketing prices of wheat and soybeans. I heard this in stores and restaurants, and it was front-page news in the local papers. I could tell—even though I wasn't from the area—that there was a feeling of frenzy. No one thought prices could fall. When people who probably don't monitor investment prices make them a topic of conversation, I sense a frenzy. That's when I know the end is near for that movement. I sold both contracts, knowing that on a very fast move up in prices, on any sign of weakness all those who thought the markets were shooting up to the moon will realize the party is over and have to sell in a panic. The same holds true for markets that move quickly to the downside. Sellers will become panic buyers.

One of the most successful trading techniques is to look for markets that have made very fast moves to the upside or downside and watch for the momentum to change. You can then place a trade that benefits from a reversal. This accelerates profits, as a frenzied movement in one direction will move even faster (in many cases) in the opposite direction when the move is over.

Look for Good and Bad News Concerning Specific Companies

Explosive opportunities can often be found when specific companies are the subject of extremely good or bad news. There is tremendous financial loss for millions of shareholders when stocks drop like a rock. When such a stock dropped to around $4 per share overnight from $12 (not to mention a previous high of $35 about nine months earlier), this signaled a buying opportunity. With the shares this low, I bought call options that would make money when the stock moved back up. They cost only $25 apiece, and they doubled in value in a day. I sold my position a few days later for a profit of over 400 percent. You can find extreme examples almost daily and super investment opportunities at least twice a week. If you wait for these opportunities, you can become much more successful.

For example, keep an eye out for bad earnings reports or news from a company that the earnings will not be as had been expected. As mentioned earlier, the value of a company's shares is determined by many factors. However, the most significant factor is expected future earnings as forecast by brokerage company analysts. If a company begins to give these analysts any information that is viewed as hurting a company's next earnings release, then they will quickly downgrade their forecasts. This turn of events can trigger a major selling frenzy.

Back in August of 1996, the Medaphis Corporation, a leading provider of management services to physicians and hospitals, let out that there was a significant underperformance of the quarterly results compared to analysts' expectations. The share price, which had been steadily advancing over the previous year and was trading at around $36 the day before, dropped overnight to around $12. That was a $24 drop—representing two-thirds of the value—lost overnight. If you owned the shares, how would you feel? Devastated. I would feel the same way. If I had invested $1,000 in this supposedly safe stock, I would have only $333 the next day. I would jump ship just like the other owners that day. However, after a fast move down like this there is usually a bounce back in price (which happened) for a short period of time. Then the shares usually continue down until a new support level is reached.

After many years of trading, you learn that reactions are very similar in extreme situations. A good trader and investor will immediately react to this situation and place a trade that will benefit from this situation. What would I do? I'd buy out-of-the-money (OTM) calls and OTM puts—a spread—at a cheap enough price so that I would risk very little, with enough time for me to be proven right (three months or so).

Watch for New Product Developments

There can be numerous investment opportunities when pharmaceutical companies and biotech research and development companies announce successful trials of new drugs and approvals from the Food and Drug Administration (FDA). If you ask your broker to notify you of these types of situations, this alone can present tremendous opportunities.

Bet on Smart People

This is an easy one that many people overlook. Why not invest your money with smart, successful people? My theory is that someone who has been successful in the past will be successful in the future. There are many examples of this around you. Why not let a billionaire invest your money for you? Billionaires do not become billionaires without investing their money very wisely. Jump on the bandwagon and join them. Let Bill Gates of Microsoft invest for you. How do you do this? Just invest money in Microsoft shares.

Many of you may not know his name yet, but let me tell you, he can make you wealthy. I am referring to Wayne Huzienga. Perhaps you have heard of two companies—Waste Management and Blockbuster—he built and sold successfully. I am sure you have spent a few nights in front of a television set after visiting one of his stores. There are a number of other individuals you might want to follow. Guess where I put my longer-term investment dollars? I just ride the wave with other successful people.

Look for Low-Priced Shares

I define low-priced shares as those trading at $20 or less. It's a lot easier to make a high return on low-priced shares than high-priced shares. If I buy a stock that is trading at $100 per share, how long will it take to double my money? Although anything can happen in this business, most likely high-priced shares like this could take years to double in value. In addition, there is a greater chance of losing a lot of money. If I take a stock that is $10 per share, how long might it take for this stock to double in value? Many times I have seen it happen in a day. Also, if the shares become worthless, I lose only $10. Bottom line: Placing a low-priced stock trade gives you the following benefits:

- You can make a high return faster.
- You have less money invested to lose.
- You can play more stocks with $100 (10 different stocks if they average $10 each).

This last point is very important. If I have $100 to invest, I will—in many cases—pick a few stocks that allow me to average my risk. This is referred to as a portfolio. A broad portfolio is the basis of a mutual fund. The basic theory is that a larger group of stocks will even out the chances of winning in the long run. This, in turn, reduces your risk.

If I put my $100 into one stock, there is a 50 percent chance of these shares losing money (50 percent up, 50 percent down). If I buy 10 stocks (average price of $10), then if one stock loses 100 percent of its value, I have nine stocks to carry the portfolio and can still make money. A mutual fund may have hundreds of stocks. Some may be terrible investments, but overall the fund may still do very well as it diversifies its risk. Let's take another example: If I feel that a particular $100 stock may make a large move up in price, instead of buying the stock, I would buy a $4 OTM call option giving me control of 100 shares for $400. If the shares now move up from $100 to $105 (a 5 percent price increase), these options may go up 50 percent in price to $600, because a move in the price of a stock will typically have a magnified effect on the price of the options. This magnification is due to a number of factors, including the leverage the options provide you. Therefore, it's a lot easier to make a 100 percent return on your money using options on stocks (as well as options on futures). However, I have to caution you: It is also easier to lose 100 percent of your investment with options. If you want to trade options, never underestimate how important it is to keep learning as much as you can about them.

Look for Price Increases or Decreases of More Than 20 Percent in the Past 60 Days

Momentum creates opportunities for both buying and selling. Momentum investors are very widespread; however, they are a very fickle group. When a stock (or future) gains momentum and then starts to lose momentum, there is usually a flurry of activity to take the market in the other direction. I like to invest when the momentum is strengthening or weakening, because these are the best short-term opportunities and they often create longer-term opportunities.

Momentum investors are much shorter-term-oriented than mutual fund investors or money managers. A momentum investor may be looking for momentum over the next few seconds, minutes, days, weeks, or even months. This creates many different time frames in which investors and traders are viewing the markets. When a market starts to move quickly, then all these players may jump aboard. The momentum may last, but usually, on a short-term basis, prices will reverse as investors become disappointed when the market dies.

How do I measure momentum? I look for a change in the price of the
stock over the previous 60 or 90 days. I use this as my long-term indicator.
If I am building a longer-term portfolio of stocks, I want stocks that are
showing a minimum of 60-day strength.

As previously mentioned, many technical analysts use momentum indicators. These indicators are very specific. They might show the change
in stock price relative to a set prior period (i.e., five minutes, one day,
etc.). Perhaps they use a moving average to locate a change in momentum. When the current price moves below the moving average, they sell;
when it moves above, they buy.

Look for Price Increases or Decreases of More Than 30 Percent since Yesterday

This is the most important indicator I use for momentum investments.
The 30 percent rule is the minimum. I prefer a much higher number to
show even stronger momentum. Typically, the higher the percentage, the
stronger the momentum. How does this work? You can either look at the
price percentage gainers and losers lists from the newspapers or check
out our web site to access this information from your computer terminal.
If you are receiving real-time or delayed quotes, then you can get this
information from your data feeds during the day.

When I look at the lists, I look for the stocks that have gone up the
most in price over the previous day's closing price—the basis for the percentage gain or loss. However, it is important to note that stocks with the
highest percentages do not necessarily have the most interest or momentum. Sometimes a stock that was trading for only $1 moves up to $1.75. Although that's a 75 percent increase, it doesn't always mean high profits.

In order to get a better understanding of a stock's profitability, I also
look at price range and trading volume. I typically trade only stocks starting at $5; however, sometimes I do trade lower-priced stocks if they show
significant trading volume. Generally, I trade stocks that have increased in
volume significantly. If a stock trades less than 300,000 shares a day, I
avoid it. Maybe it will make a move, but there is not enough interest from
other investors for me to believe the trade will be profitable. I like to see
more than one million shares trading. This shows commitment on the part
of the investors. Once again, the more volume the better. When buying
shares, I want them to be on the price percentage gainers list.

I consult the price percentage losers list to find shares that have made
major moves down (30 percent or more) and then look for a rebound. This
is when I find buying opportunities. This may sound strange, as most investors may think this shows more weakness coming, but remember that I
like the contrarian approach. Also, understand that when a stock moves

so far down so fast there is usually negative news regarding the company. Perhaps the quarterly financial results are disappointing Wall Street, or the company has presented information that future earnings will be disappointing. Most importantly, this usually creates a panic and what is called a blow-off bottom. This means that the fast move down has made every potential seller panic. After the sellers have all sold, buyers tend to produce a rebound.

How often does this occur? Sometimes on a daily basis I find at least one stock that has dropped at least 30 percent (50 percent or more is even better). These declines appear to come in spurts, especially around the time in each fiscal quarter when companies are reporting earnings. When the market opens, I watch these shares closely and wait for them to start gaining momentum to the upside before buying. I wait for a movement of at least a 20 percent price move off the lows, with heavy volume of at least 300,000 shares. I like to see large blocks (5,000 shares or more) increasing, as this shows the institutions are buying.

When this scenario occurs, I look to buy the shares, but prefer to buy the call options (if there are options available). Remember, I get more leverage with options and also have the benefit of limited risk. All I can lose is the amount I paid for the options.

Let's take an example of a trade using SyQuest Technology, Inc. SyQuest's stock price was increasing on heavier-than-average volume and had an average daily volume of around 200,000 shares. One day, the stock price moved from $5 to $6 (a 20 percent increase) on volume of more than 1 million shares trading. This was an obvious clue that something was happening that was creating a great deal of interest. I contacted my broker to see if there was any news to account for this movement. There was none. The shares price had been much higher before dipping to trade just around $5 for the past few months. I considered buying it. However, 2,000 shares would cost me $12,000 (2,000 × 6 = $12,000). Instead, I decided to buy the 7.50 (strike price) call options at .875 each, making sure there was plenty of time left to expiration. I prefer to buy options with at least three months remaining, especially on momentum investments. Thus, I paid $87.50 for each option representing control of 100 shares of stock. In comparison, buying 100 shares of the stock would have cost $6,000.

Although the options did not represent the shares on a one-to-one basis, any move up in the price of the shares would double the value of the options quickly. Approximately four days later, the shares had doubled in value (a 100 percent move). This enabled me to sell each option for $537.50—a profit of $450 per option. My choice to buy call options instead of purchasing the shares straight out led to a 500 percent return in just four days!

Let's review this trade:

Trade Initiation

Current stock price:	$6 per share
Previous stock close:	$5
Percent increase:	20 percent
Average daily trading volume:	200,000 shares
Most recent day's volume:	1,000,000+ shares
Margin required:	Zero (cost of options)
Option price:	$87.50

Note: I used a 20 percent rule in this example due to the dramatic increase in trading volume.

Trade Closing

Shares price:	$12
Option price:	$537.50
Shares price up:	100 percent
Option price up:	500+ percent

This simple technique can provide you with profits greater than you ever imagined could be made in such a short period of time.

Look for Shares Reaching New Highs or Coming Off New Lows

When used in conjunction with lists of price percentage gainers and losers, this is one of the most powerful indicators. When a stock is on one of the gainers lists and it's making new highs as calculated over the previous 52 weeks, then it may be a buy (especially if it's making new historical highs). Also, when the stock has made new lows and is coming off new lows, the blow-off bottom may have occurred.

Buy a Small Number of Shares or Contracts

Until you have the experience to make money consistently in the markets, start off as a small investor. Regardless of whether you have a thousand dollars or a million, until you really understand what you're doing, you'll be much better off with small investments. How small is small? This question is virtually impossible to answer. Just be cautious when you start out, until such time as you are a consistent winner. Then build up slowly.

Build Your Confidence

It is important to earn your confidence through winning investments. However, be vigilant that you do not build a false sense of confidence. Although I have been investing for many years, I still spend considerable time figuring out ways to improve my trading. If you develop a sense of temperate confidence, you will most likely be a survivor. That means you'll actually be around to enjoy the benefits of this business.

Often, when a trader starts to make a little money in the markets, a false sense of confidence drives them to make much bigger trades. This is a big mistake. As they say on Wall Street, "Pigs get fat, hogs get slaughtered."

When You Make a Good Return, Sell

What is a good return? Every trader or investor will probably tell you something different. I like to make 100 percent on my money when trading stock options, and a minimum of 20 percent when making commodity trades. With stocks you usually have to settle for a lower return (10+ percent). These are the numbers I use based on my experience with winning trades; however, these are benchmarks, not hard-and-fast rules. My exit strategies are usually based on momentum shifts, which means that some of my trades have returns much higher than 100 percent.

I also have losing trades (nobody's perfect). However, a disciplined trader will get out of losing trades quickly and learn how to stay with the winners. It's very much like being a surfer waiting for the big wave. A wave might approach that has the characteristics of a winner but then starts to look like a loser. Instead of wasting time riding the loser to shore, the experienced surfer will get off that wave and look for another opportunity. You too are looking for the big winners. So don't forget to get out of the losers quickly so that you can use your capital in the most efficient manner possible.

CONCLUSION

Profitable trading opportunities come from an infinite number of sources. The trick is to foster the growth of your own personal trading antennae through cultivating a variety of sources. Remember, you will never have as much time as you would like to study the markets. You have to use your time efficiently to find the best possibilities for profitable trades.

In many ways, the maxim "in on greed, out on fear" captures the essence of traditional trading methodologies by cutting through the hype and complexity that drives market momentum. This emotional motivation sets up quite a paradox. On the one hand, trading appears to be a very dry business. However, the emotions of hope and fear impel traders to place trades and exit them creating erratic market swings. These swings can be devastating to traders who simply buy stocks hoping prices will rise. In fact, directional traders are always at risk of losing money when markets reverse course in the middle of a trend. That's because directional trends depend on trader optimism—as unlikely a source for stability as you can find, especially these days.

As sellers scramble to exit a market, fear drives prices down until a new low inspires buyers to get involved again. This cycle feeds on itself— winners and losers trading back and forth at the whim of human emotion. Meanwhile, thousands of analysts spend countless hours poring over fundamental, technical, and sentiment data looking for clues to price movement. Analyzing markets can be overwhelming, especially to traders who are just getting their feet wet for the first time.

To trade successfully, it is essential to develop comprehensive market insight and the moral conviction to stand strong against the mass psychology that drives market behavior. Market insight comes from studying market movement and a certain familiarity with trading strategies that take advantage of specific conditions. Market movement is an extremely complex subject. There seems to be an endless stream of directional analysis techniques. Each may offer a piece of the greater puzzle—but no technique holds all the answers.

Trading might as well be a foreign country to the uninitiated. It has its own language and its own customs. It's up to you to find your favorite haunts by exploring the territory and finding out what suits you best. If technical analysis feels comfortable and fits in with the rest of your lifestyle, then read all you can about it. Trading is a game of odds, and though no one can be 100 percent correct in their decisions, by using the data available and then placing hedged positions, traders can see nice profits without the risk of losing everything in their portfolios. Whatever you choose, make sure you dedicate yourself to really understanding it. Familiarity may breed contempt, but when it comes to trading, familiarity breeds prosperity.

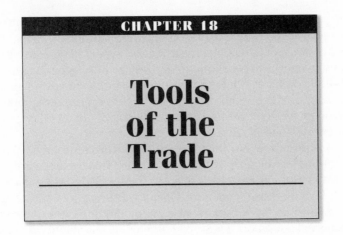

Tools
of the
Trade

Options traders today have a wide array of tools at their disposal. Thanks to the Internet and the proliferation of finance-related web sites, a great deal of information is available at no cost at all. In addition, many online brokerage firms today provide a large amount of research, information, and analytical tools to their customers. At the same time, software and premium services like Optionetics.com Platinum are available for a fee and can greatly speed up the decision making process. However, the abundance of tools and information can also be a double-edged sword when traders get bogged down by information overload and subsequently lose sight of the real objective of options trading—making profits.

In this chapter, we examine some of the tools traders use. Not all of them are necessary. Some, like stock charts, may seem essential; but a number of successful traders can even get by without those. So, when reading through this chapter, and learning about some of the featured tools of the trade, keep in mind that not all of them are absolutely necessary. Instead, think of them as shortcuts that are designed to make your trading life a great deal easier.

WHAT YOU REALLY NEED TO KNOW

Successful options trading requires a certain level of knowledge that is generally not taught in schools or universities. Options traders should know the basics of the stock market like understanding stock symbols, quotes, placing orders, and the factors that cause prices to rise and fall. In addition, traders should also understand options basics like the difference between puts and calls, the relationship between the strike price of an option and the price of the underlying asset, the impact of time decay, expiration dates, and the difference between opening and closing transactions. In short, trading options requires a basic understanding of how the stock and options markets function. The first few chapters of this book should have helped you to develop such an understanding.

In addition to this book, a visit to the library or a bookstore can help traders acquire a basic knowledge of options trading. A visit to the local library will produce hundreds of books on the stock market and options trading. Watching financial television such as CNBC during the day and the *Nightly Business Report* in the evening can help you get a better understanding of the financial markets. Doing a search on the Internet will yield thousands of free articles that cover the markets and trading strategies. Optionetics offers free trading education, brokerage reviews, articles, commentary, and market data information on its web site.

Once a certain foundation of trading knowledge has been attained, and an individual wants to begin trading, most brokerage firms will provide the required tools including the ability to place orders, assistance from a broker, and price quotes. So since learning the essentials of options trading can be done for a small cost, it is possible to become a successful options trader through self-learning.

While much of the information and tools required to successfully trade options is widely available at no cost, some products and services can increase the odds of success by making life easier. For example, attending a seminar can save an enormous amount of studying time by providing a structured set of courses of proven strategies. In addition, students can ask their instructors questions directly before, during, and after the seminars.

Technology and the Internet have also helped immensely. When I started teaching options trading strategies more than 10 years ago, most traders relied on magazines and newspapers to make trading decisions. More experienced traders knew how to use options pricing models, the Internet, and charting software, but the process of finding trades and creating risk graphs was extremely costly and time consuming. Today, a number of software programs greatly simplify the process of creating hypothetical trades, viewing variables (such as implied volatility, delta, and theta), and creating risk graphs. Again, using computer software is not essential to trading success, but it greatly simplifies the decision-making process—especially as traders become more experienced and develop a greater need for more sophisticated information.

In order to determine what type of information they need, we encourage new students to focus on one or two strategies and paper trade them until they feel comfortable enough to create trades with real money on the line. The initial first step should be to develop a basic understanding of the market and options trading. The fact that you have made it this far in this book indicates that you are, or already have, accomplished the first step. From there, new students can begin creating hypothetical trades on paper using one or two strategies. In the beginning, the goal should be to master a small number of strategies. Don't try to become a "jack-of-all-trades" too quickly. Too many products and too many strategies in the early stages of this process can prove to be a distraction rather than an aid.

Stock options trading in the United States began in the early 1970s. Obviously, many of the tools and services that exist today were not available to those early traders. So, if you are not sure what type of information you need, put yourself in their shoes for a few months. Rely almost exclusively on the resources available in your local library like *Value Line Investment Survey*, *The Wall Street Journal*, and *Investor's Business Daily*. Do the math by hand and paper trade one or two strategies. Doing so will help you better understand the calculations and get a better feel for how option prices change on a daily basis. From that point, you can use an online portfolio service to track your paper trades. Paper trading will help you to understand which tools, products, and services you might need to foster consistent options trading success.

CHARTS

Technical traders rely heavily on charts and indicators. In today's market, most of this is done with computers and trading software. We will examine some of the software programs available to traders later in the chapter. For now, let's examine the three most commonly used chart types: the line chart, the open-high-low-close (OHLC), and Japanese candlesticks.

The simplest type of chart is the line chart. This type of chart is plotted using only closing prices over a period of time. On the vertical axis, we have the underlying asset's price. The horizontal axis plots the time used—daily, weekly, monthly or annually. Figure 18.1 provides an example of a line chart using the PHLX Bank Sector Index. When the graph moves higher, it tells us that the bank index, which is an index consisting of 24 banks, is increasing in price. When the chart moves lower, the BKW is losing value. Simple enough.

The open-high-low-close (OHLC) chart (see Figure 18.2) is the one I use most often and is a common way of viewing the performance of a stock, index, or futures chart. Also known as the range bar chart, the graph provides the technical analyst with a great deal more information than the line chart because it includes more than just the closing price.

Weekly 1.15 2004

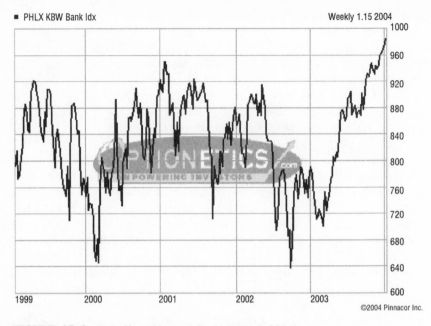

FIGURE 18.1 Line Chart (*Source:* Optionetics © 2004)

It is constructed using the high of the day and the low of the day, along with the closing price.

The chart shown in Figure 18.2 provides an example of an HLC for Microsoft (MSFT). In this example, we have created a daily range bar chart, which means that each bar (vertical line) represents one day of trading data. The length of the bar, or the highest and lowest points, reflect the high and low prices of the stock on each day. When the bars are long, it suggests that the stock traded in a wide range and when the vertical bar is short, the stock traded in a narrow range. Finally, a small horizontal line on the right side of each bar indicates the close, which is the last trade of the day. Some charting software allows traders to create OHLC charts, which include the opening price as well. In that case, the open appears as a small horizontal dash on the left side of the chart.

Each OHLC bar gives a better idea of whether bulls or bears are in control of a stock or market. In a healthy advance, the bulls are firmly in control and driving prices higher. As evidence, the technical analyst wants to see the stock closing near the highs of the day. This is easy to do with an OHLC chart. Recall that the right horizontal on each OHLC bar represents the closing price. When these closing lines appear near the top of each vertical bar on the chart, it suggests that the bulls have the stock in

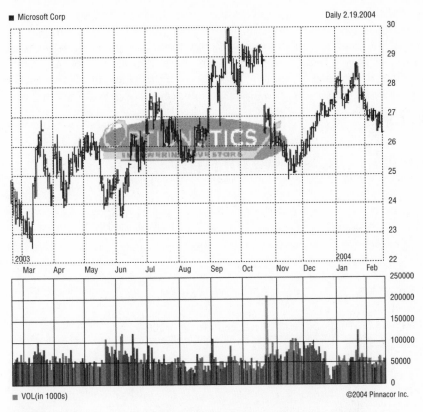

■ Microsoft Corp Daily 2.19.2004

■ VOL(in 1000s) ©2004 Pinnacor Inc.

FIGURE 18.2 High-Low-Close Bar Chart (*Source:* Optionetics © 2004)

control. However, when the bears seize a stock, the chartist is looking to see if the stock is closing near the low price of the day. For example, on the MSFT chart, during the decline in mid-October, the stock was finishing most trading sessions near the lows of the day, which was a sign that bears were firmly in control of MSFT during that time.

The third type of chart that has become popular among traders is the Japanese candlestick chart. A candlestick is composed of two parts known as the body and the shadows. The body represents the range between the opening and closing prices. The shadow is the thin vertical line that can project outward above or below the body and represents the full price range for the stock, index, or futures contract. As a result, if there were no prices outside the range of the open to close, then there would be no shadows.

If the market closed above the opening price, the body is often colored green or left blank (white). If the price closes below the opening price, the body is colored black or red. The colors will vary from one charting software package to the next, but green and red seem to be the most common. This color-coding of the body makes it easy to immediately see if the market closed above or below the opening price for the given time period. An OHLC bar gives you the same information, but the color-coding of the candlestick bar can be a bit more convenient. Figure 18.3 provides an example of a six-month candlestick chart using Microsoft rendered in black, white, and grey.

CHARTS, VOLUME, AND VOLATILITY

A visual look at a chart can also give important information regarding a stock's volatility and, for that reason, it is extremely important to option traders. Since the length of each bar in an OHLC chart is determined by the high and low prices of the day, short bars suggest that the stock is

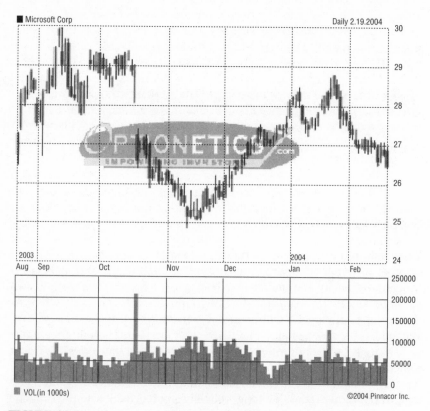

FIGURE 18.3 Six-Month Candlestick Chart (*Source:* Optionetics © 2004)

exhibiting low volatility. In that case, the trading ranges between the daily high and low prices are small. On the other hand, when the bars are longer, it means that there is a bigger difference between the highs and lows of the day. Therefore, longer bars suggest greater volatility.

Most charts will also plot volume underneath the price area. Volume refers to the total activity in the underlying asset during the course of a day, week, month, and so on. For a stock, the volume refers to the number of shares traded.

To some traders, volume is the single most important indicator used in technical analysis. When a stock is rising and volume increases, it suggests that buyers are actively bidding the price higher and shorts are running for cover. Strong volume during an advance is considered a bullish sign. On the other hand, when volume swells during a decline, bears are driving prices lower, bulls are in pain, and the action of the stock is considered poor. Therefore, studying volume gives the analyst a better sense of whether the bulls or bears are in control of the stock.

Volume is the total number of shares associated with a specific stock or market. Also known as turnover, it reflects the number of shares bought or sold relative to a specific security. For instance, if you purchase 100 shares of Microsoft, the volume of that trade is equal to 100. Volume is considered during daily time periods. For instance, on Wednesday, February 18, 2004, total volume on the Nasdaq Stock Market equaled 1,777,995,664 shares. Therefore, daily volume is generally defined as the number of shares traded in one day and can be considered for one individual stock, an options contract, or an entire market. On a chart, volume is plotted as a histogram such as can be seen in Figures 18.2 and 18.3. Tall bars suggest heavy volume while short bars indicate periods of low trading volume.

COMPUTER SOFTWARE

When I started trading, the charts we had available to us were newspapers or other print publications. Today, however, charting software makes the process extremely fast and easy. While there are a large number of great packages out there, we will just mention the three that our students seem to use most often: The Optionetics Platinum site, ProfitSource and Advanced GET from eSignal.

Optionetics Platinum site is a web-based computer software program designed for options traders. Access is available for an annual fee. Once inside the site, traders can perform a host of options related studies including creating hypothetical trades, plotting volatility charts, back-testing strategies, viewing historical prices and implied volatility levels, monitoring put/call ratios, initiating trade searches based on specific parameters, and plotting risk graphs. Many of the case study examples in this book were created using Optionetics.com Platinum.

ProfitSource is a market analysis program that combines a fully featured technical analysis suite with a comprehensive set of special market direction tools such as Elliott wave, trend filters, and gap filters. These tools enable the user to adopt a rule-oriented approach to trading. In addition, it has the ability to scan for potentially profitable opportunities such as Wave 4 and Wave 5 trades, a state-of-the-art "Walk Through Mode" for learning how to apply concepts such as Elliott wave, alerts functionality for price, indicator and Elliott wave parameters, and a complete portfolio management package. ProfitSource can be used in multiple markets including stocks, indexes, futures, and foreign exchange and gives the user access to international markets.

Advanced GET from eSignal has also gained popularity among options traders. It is a graphical charting package that gives traders access to a full set of technical analysis tools, specialty tools and indicators based on Elliott waves and Gann theory, and also one of the most complete sets of standard studies available in the market today. Many options traders use these three software packages to enhance their ability to confidently use options strategies.

PUTTING IT ALL TOGETHER

In order to get a better understanding of how traders combine trading tools to create a promising trade, let's work through a simple example. The first thing we need to employ is a method of finding stocks that are expected to make a strong directional move to the upside or the downside. In this case, we are looking for an explosive move higher.

There are several tools on Platinum that help us find stocks, but for this example we will use the Candlestick I tool. This tool searches for stocks based on candlestick formations. (There is a wide array of different candlestick formations that go well beyond the scope of this book. Traders interested in the topic are encouraged to visit Optionetics.com and look through the article archives for a complete discussion of the various patterns.) In this case, we chose the Bullish Patterns search using stocks that were trading above $12.50 and that had volume above 300,000. Once a list of stocks appears, we need to look at various price charts and implied volatilities.

To keep things simple, suppose we find a bullish stock and decide to buy a long call. When buying a call, we want the implied volatility to be below the average IV for at least six months. Remember, when IV is low, the options are cheaper. After eyeballing the charts, we found that Lehman Brothers (LEH) looked like a strong candidate. Figure 18.4 is a chart of LEH on May 20, 2003 showing the candlestick pattern known as Red Candle + Doji that flagged the stock.

Not only did the stock form a bullish pattern known as a Harami, but it also bounced off support at its ascending trend line. Once we find a stock that looks promising, we want to check IV to make sure it isn't too high. Figure 18.5 is an IV chart of the stock on May 20, 2003, the day it came up on the Candlestick I search.

We can see by looking at this chart that IV was definitely low on a historic basis. This is important because the higher the IV, the more the option will cost. IV also acts like elastic, stretching to extremes, but ultimately coming back to its mean. If we buy a call and IV increases, it raises the price of the option.

Now that we have a stock picked out that fits our criteria, we can enter the data into Platinum to view the risk graph. Before we actually enter the data into the Create Trade screen, we need to first decide which option strike and expiration month we want to test. Of course, after this is entered into the graph, we can view it to see if the trade makes sense given our outlook and resources.

Since we are buying an option, we want to give the trade enough time

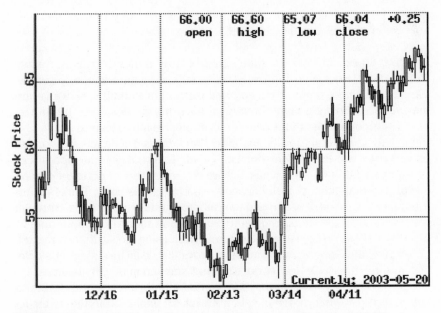

FIGURE 18.4 Daily Chart of LEH (*Source:* Optionetics Platinum © 2004)

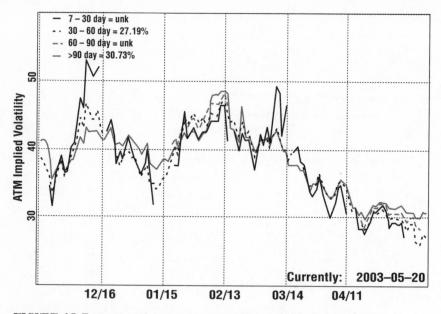

FIGURE 18.5   IV Chart for LEH (*Source:* Optionetics Platinum © 2004)

to work in our favor. Mainly, we don't want to hold long options that expire in less than 30 days because time erosion picks up the last month of an option's life. The stock closed the session at $66.04 and since we don't normally want to use too far out-of-the-money options, let's look at the October 70 call. We choose the October expiry month because June and July are too close and there aren't any August or September options on May 20 to choose from. After entering the data into Platinum, we get the information shown in Figure 18.6 from the program.

This screen is just part of what Platinum tells us about the trade, but there is plenty to see from just this information. First, we see that the model price is between our bid-ask spread, so we know that option isn't overpriced. Second, we can see our breakeven point at expiration. It is important to remember that the breakeven point here is figured as of expiration. Usually, we will see a profit well before this point. This screen also gives us the Greeks and the specific option information. The next thing we want to look at is the risk graph (Figure 18.7).

This graph gives us a visual of what the profit or loss would be given a move in the stock and using different time frames. Obviously, if the stock moves up in the short term, we will see higher profits than if it takes three months to occur. Our initial debit was $340 in this trade for buying one long October 70 call. By looking at the chart, we can see that

Lehman Brothers Holdings, Inc (LEH) Option Trade												
Log Date	Position	Num	OptSym	Expire	Strike	Type	Entry	Bid/Ask	Model	IV %	Vol	01	Days
2003-05-20	Bought	1	LEHIN	OCT03	70	Call	3.4	3.2/3.4	3.314	28.1	0	2569	150

Entry DB	Profit	Max Profit	Max Risk	Delta (Shares)	Gamma	Vega	Theta
$340.00	$-20.00	Unlimited	$-340.00	41.8	3.2692	$16.46	$-1.53

Downside Breakeven	Upside Breakeven	Max Profit/Max Risk	Max Profit/Debit
73.40	73.40	Unlimited%	Unlimited%

FIGURE 18.6 Trade Data for LEH Call (*Source:* Optionetics Platinum © 2004)

the stock would need to move to approximately $72 for our call option to double in price.

Another tool we can use to assess the trade is the implied volatility chart. The IV chart shown in Figure 18.8 details the profits we would achieve on a move in IV alone. This graph assumes the stock stays at the same price. We can see that a rise in IV can affect the trade drastically, and that is why we want IV in our favor.

Before we enter the trade, we should have already decided on our exit points. The price we decide to sell at should be based on our outlook and money management. Remember that it's always important to have a set exit point before entering a trade to take the emotion out of it. An oft-used

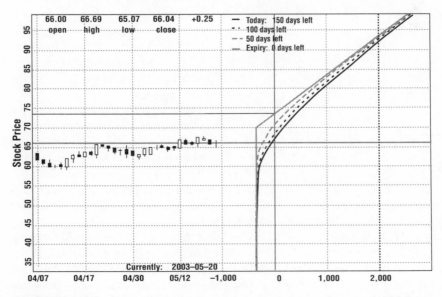

FIGURE 18.7 Risk Graph for LEH Call (*Source:* Optionetics Platinum © 2004)

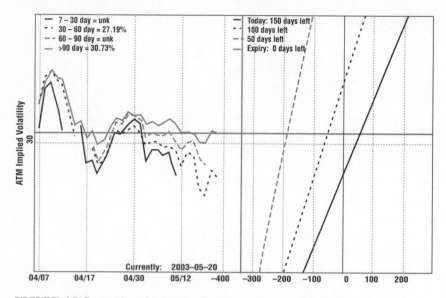

FIGURE 18.8 IV Chart for LEH Trade (*Source:* Optionetics Platinum © 2004)

exit strategy for a long call is to sell if the option loses half its value to the downside or when the option doubles in price to the upside. Of course, we can always set stops once our price target is achieved to let our profits run, but the last thing we want to do is see a profitable trade turn into a loser.

This trade did indeed work out well, with LEH shares moving up following this bullish sign. As originally expected, the stock went higher and our option was at a double on June 2 with the stock trading near $72.50. At this point, either the option could be closed or the trader could set a stop to make sure that if the stock were to move lower, the option would be sold before the profits were lost. Keep in mind that buying long calls is a great way to use leverage, but it is also a high-risk one. When the strategist identifies an explosive situation like in the Lehman Brothers example, he or she might want to consider other trades like bull call spreads, call ratio backspreads, or some of the other bullish strategies discussed in the earlier chapters of this book.

CONCLUSION

Not all traders use charts or computers. In fact, 20 years ago much of this information was either not available or extremely expensive. So, traders do not need to spend a lot of money on research and analytical tools. A high-speed Internet connection, a brokerage firm that specializes in options trading, and access to research can produce enough information to trade successfully.

Hopefully, this chapter has helped to expand your knowledge regarding the tools that are available and how a trader uses information to create a trade. The example toward the end of the chapter explained how to find an explosive opportunity and how to analyze the situation to find the best options contract for the given strategy. Not all successful traders use the same approach. Through time, you will undoubtedly develop your own tools and methods for picking winning trades. Hopefully, the chapters in this book are helping you along the way.

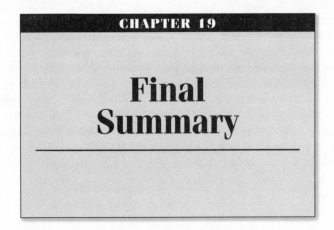

CHAPTER 19

Final
Summary

This book has reviewed a variety of strategies that can be applied in various markets. It has avoided trying to forecast market direction or analyzing charts with detailed market patterns, and has not referenced highly technical data or difficult-to-interpret fundamental information. Although these trading tools may have their place in your trading arsenal, they are exhaustively studied in many other publications. The purpose of this book is to focus on options trading strategies and to demonstrate how professionals trade without overanalyzing the markets. When traders get bogged down in trying to process too much information, the result is what I often call "analysis paralysis."

I have tried to make the information contained in this book as straightforward as possible. Learning to trade can be quite difficult and perplexing. Each strategy has an infinite number of possibilities when applied to the markets. Each trade is unique, and your task as a trader is to learn from your achievements and your mistakes. There are no absolutes in trading.

However, I do believe that you will be able to build a solid trading foundation based on the delta neutral strategies explored in this book. This approach to trading comes from years of experience from my trading team and my own endeavors. To become successful, it's up to you to take a systematic approach to becoming a confident market player. However, you must be willing to spend the time and energy it takes to study the markets if you want to learn how to trade successfully.

In late October of 1997, the Dow Jones Industrial Average dropped 554 points or 7 percent. By most people's standards, this constitutes a mini-crash. It was not as severe as the 1987 crash when there was a 22 percent drop, but it definitely shook up the markets. Throughout the day of the mini-crash, I talked with a number of traders and investors to discuss our views on this market decline. At many brokerage firms, clients were being forced to meet margin calls as their positions declined. Eventually, there were more sell orders than the markets could bear and trading closed early at the New York Stock Exchange. Compared to the millions of individuals who lost a great deal of money, traders who were using the strategies included in this book fared much better. They knew how to hedge their positions and either made money or at least minimized the losses to their accounts. This approach to trading offers protection and enables players to keep playing the game.

To get started, find one market you like and get to know it very well. Find out how many shares or contracts are traded. What is the tick value? What are the support and resistance levels? What are the strike prices of the available options? How many months of options should be analyzed? Is this a volatile market? Does it have high liquidity? Do you have enough capital to play this market?

Once you determine the right market for you, focus your efforts on evaluating which strategies best take advantage of this market's unique characteristics. This can be accomplished by paying close attention to market movement trends. For example, stock shares tend to go up in price over the long run. This means that in many cases I take a bullish bias over the long run in top stocks. Since many futures markets go sideways, I like to apply the appropriate range-bound strategies.

By concentrating your attention on one market, you will become familiar with that market's personality. When change occurs, this familiarity will enable you to profit the most from the change. Practice these strategies by paper trading your market until you get the hang of it. I recommend three to six months of paper trading before investing a dime. For every great trade you missed, there will be mistakes that could have wiped out your whole account. Take small steps up the ladder of experience and you'll learn what you need to master along the way.

In addition, you need to determine what influences a specific market. Markets have spheres of influences. You need to get to know what internal and external forces drive your chosen market. For example, the bond market affects the S&Ps. What affects Dell, Intel, Microsoft, gold, and silver? All of this research combines to increase your overall knowledge of trading, which will help to make you a more successful trader in the years to come.

During one of my two-day Optionetics seminars, I kept saying that very few traders and investors really know what is going on in the markets. The very next day, as if by magic, the following article appeared in *USA Today*. I promptly revealed it to the students at my seminar.

Garbagemen Good at Predicting Economy

In December of 1994, the economists sent a questionnaire to four chairmen of multinational companies, former finance ministers from four countries, four Oxford University students, and four garbagemen. They were asked to predict average economic prospects including world economic growth, inflation, the price of oil, and the pound's exchange rate against the dollar in the ten years following 1994. The economists said the garbagemen and company bosses tied for first with the predictions. The finance ministers came in last.

So, let me get this straight. Politicians supposedly run entire countries, right? Then how come their own finance ministers cannot beat garbagemen at predicting economic prospects? This only emphasizes the point that the markets are great equalizers of education. It is irrelevant whether you have an MBA or a PhD or are a rocket scientist. High school dropouts can do just as well at trading, if not better, if they are disciplined and have the skills and knowledge to succeed. It is actually easier for me to train individuals with very little experience or none whatsoever than those who have years of experience. This is due to the fact that many experienced traders have developed bad habits that need to be broken.

Approximately 99 percent of the time that I trade delta neutral, I am able to manage my risk on entering the trade and monitor it each day as the market moves. Delta neutral trading is a scientific system that significantly reduces your stress level. It provides you with the means to limit your risk and make a consistent profit. It directs you to take advantage of market movement by making adjustments. By learning to trade using delta neutral strategies, traders have the opportunity to maximize profits by making consistent returns.

OPTIONS-TRADING DISCIPLINE

Proper money management and patience in options trading are the cornerstones to success. The key to this winning combination is discipline. Now, discipline is not something that we apply only during the hours of trading, opening it up like bottled water at the opening bell and storing it away at the closing. Discipline is a way of life, a method of thinking. It is, most of all, a serious approach. A consistent and methodical, or disciplined, system leads to profits in trading. On one hand, it means taking a quick, predefined loss because the first loss is always the best. On the other hand, discipline gives you the impenetrable strength to keep holding on to an options position when success is at hand or passing on the trade or an adjustment when you don't have a signal. It also entails doing all our preparatory work before market hours. It is getting ourselves ready and situated before the trade goes off so that, in a focused state, we can monitor market events as they unfold.

Discipline can sometimes have a negative sound, but the way to freedom and prosperity is an organized, focused, and responsive process of trading. With that, and an arsenal of low-risk/high-profit options strategies, profits can indeed flow profusely. The consistent disciplined application of these strategies is essential to your success as a professional trader.

Finally, as option traders, in order to improve in the area of discipline, we must identify, change, or rid ourselves of anything in our mental environment that doesn't contribute to the strictest execution of our well-planned trading approach. We need to stay focused on what we need to learn and do the work that is necessary. Your belief in what is possible will continue to evolve as a function of your propensity to adapt. On a cautionary note, avoid high commissions, brokers soliciting business, and software that promises or boasts impossible results. High turnaround fees can really eat into your profits. Remember, nothing beats your own ability to trade effectively. No one wants to take better care of your money than you do.

CHOOSING THE OPTIMUM OPTION STRATEGY

For the skilled investor, stock options can be a very powerful tool. Whether they are used alone or in combination with other options or stock, options offer the flexibility to address any number of unique investment goals and parameters. However, before the search for a suitable strategy can even begin, the investor needs a solid understanding of how option investments work.

The options strategist is always faced with a variety of alternatives. To determine which one is best you must consider your investment goals, market outlook, and risk tolerance all of which are key in narrowing down the list of reasonable candidates. The same goals and predictions can also limit the choice of suitable strike prices and expiration dates. Each strategy and each contract has its own advantages and drawbacks.

Forecasting the price of the underlying equity is a prime motive behind directional option strategies. Whether the goal is profit or protection, the market outlook certainly narrows the list of strategic alternatives.

More often than not directional strategies require the investor to make at least three assessments about the future price of the stock. The first one is obviously direction itself. Based on our market analysis, we need to determine if we expect the price of the stock to rise, fall, or stay at the current level. The second judgment is about the size of the move. This will have a distinct bearing on the choice of strike prices.

For some option strategies, it is not enough to decide on a direction. The magnitude of the projected price move may determine which strike prices are suitable candidates. For instance, when analyzing a call option with an out-of-the-money strike price, you will need to determine how high would the underlying stock have to rise to make the position profitable as well as how realistic this move would be based on your research.

The third decision concerns the time frame in which the stock price forecast must take place. Options have a limited time span. If both the projected direction and size of the move come true, but only after the option expires, the option strategist still would not have achieved the intended goal. That is why timing is just as crucial in strategy selection as it is for everyday life.

So, option strategists who are making a directional call must be right on three levels; the stock price must move in the right direction, by a sufficient amount, and by the expiration date. If the trader is wrong about any of the three projections, it could have an adverse impact on the success of the strategy.

For some strategies, it is enough for XYZ to reach a certain level at some point before expiration, but the exact timing is less important. The consequences for being a bit off the mark are much more serious in other cases. There are some that succeed only if the stock price behaves correctly for the duration of the contract. A clear idea about where the underlying equity is likely to move and when, should improve the option strategist's chances of success with selecting and implementing an appropriate directional strategy.

Finally, even when two traders' forecasts are exactly the same, different goals may dictate two very different approaches. For example, is the trade intended primarily to generate income or is it to protect an existing position in the same stock? Or is it a way to set a price objective for entering or exiting a stock position? The answers to these kinds of questions will guide the trader in ruling in some strategies and ruling out others when attempting to select the optimum options strategy.

IMPLIED VOLATILITY AND TRADE SELECTION

When it comes to professionally trading options, there is no more important component than volatility. As discussed in earlier chapters, volatility will often dictate which strategy is best in any given situation. We have already explored what volatility is and the relationship between two types of volatility: implied and historical volatility. Now let us correlate the relative implied volatility levels to the inventory of available option strategies using a strategy matrix. It will provide some guidelines on how to best use this valuable strategy-driving indicator.

Before presenting a comprehensive table of implied volatility levels and option strategies, let's review the definitions of each strategy. These definitions serve only to facilitate an understanding of the table so that you may refer to it when needed with clarity. Although most of the strategies have been covered in this book, the reader is encouraged to investigate additional educational resources that offer a more in-depth analysis on any or all of the strategies. You may want to find one or two that seem to make the most sense to you, and start paper trading them until you understand them thoroughly. For now, here are some basic definitions of the option strategies covered in this book:

Call Gives the buyer the right, but not the obligation, to buy the underlying stock at a certain price on or before a specific date. The seller of a call option is obligated to deliver 100 shares of the underlying stock at a certain price on or before a specific date if the call is assigned.

Put Gives the buyer the right, but not the obligation, to sell the underlying stock at a specific price on or before a specific date. The seller of a put option is obligated to buy a stock at a specific price if the put is assigned.

Covered call Sell an out-of-the-money call option while simultaneously owning 100 shares of the underlying stock.

Covered put Sell an out-of-the-money put option while simultaneously selling 100 shares of the underlying stock.

Bull put spread Long the lower strike puts and short the higher strike puts with the same expiration date using the same number of contracts, all done for a net credit.

Bull call spread Short the higher strike calls and long the lower strike calls with the same expiration date using the same number of contracts, all done for a net debit.

Bear put spread Long the higher strike puts and short the lower strike puts with the same expiration date using the same number of contracts, all done for a net debit.

Bear call spread Long the higher strike calls and short the lower strike calls with the same expiration date using the same number of contracts, all done for a net credit.

Long straddle Long both an at-the-money call and an at-the-money put with the same number of contracts, identical strike price and expiration date.

Long strangle Long both a higher strike OTM call and a lower strike OTM put with the same number of contracts and same expiration date.

Call ratio backspread Short the lower strike calls that are at-the-money or in-the-money and simultaneously buy multiple higher strike calls with the same expiration date in a ratio less than .67.

Put ratio backspread Short the higher strike puts that are at-the-money or in-the-money and simultaneously buy multiple lower strike puts with the same expiration date in a ratio less than .67.

Call butterfly spread Sell two at-the-money middle strike calls and buy one call on each wing. The trade is a combination of a bull call spread and a bear call spread.

Put butterfly spread Sell two at-the-money middle strike puts and buy one put on each wing. The trade is a combination of a bull put spread and a bear put spread.

Long iron butterfly Long a lower strike out-of-the-money put; long a higher strike out-of-the-money call; short a middle strike at-the-money call; short a middle strike at-the-money put.

Condor Long a lower strike option at support; sell a higher strike option, and an even higher strike option; and buy an even higher strike option at resistance (all calls or all puts).

Call calendar spread Buy a long-term call and sell a short-term call against it for the same strike price and same number of contracts, using different expiration months.

Put calendar spread Buy a long-term put and sell a short-term put against it for the same strike price and same number of contracts, using different expiration months.

Diagonal spread Buy a long-term option and sell a short-term option with different strikes and as small a net debit as possible.

Collar Purchase stock and sell a call against it usually for a year or longer. With the premium received for selling the call, buy a protective put.

In order to determine which strategy is best in any given situation, it is useful to consider volatility. Recall that there are two types:

1. *Historical volatility*. Measures a stock's tendency for movement based on the stock's past price action during a specific time period.

2. *Implied volatility.* Approximates how much the marketplace thinks prices will move. It is derived from the option prices in the market and an option pricing model.

Option strategists often use historical volatility as a guide, or a barometer, to determine if implied volatility is high or low. Table 19.1 shows the various strategies that can be used in high and low implied volatility situations. In this case, the implied volatility level column on the right-hand side of the table is referring to the relationship of the current implied volatility reading to the stock's historical volatility. If it is low, this suggests that implied volatility is less than statistical volatility. If it is high, this suggests that implied volatility is greater than historical volatility.

Current Implied Volatility Level
- High—Current implied volatility is significantly above historical volatility.
- Low—Current implied volatility is significantly below historical volatility.
- Average—Current implied volatility is at or near historical volatility.

To use the strategy matrix effectively, the trader needs to select the directional bias of the stock, evaluate the implied volatility level, and then match this information up with the available strategies. For example, if I am bullish and the underlying stock has an average implied volatility level, then by using the selection matrix, I can select either a long call or a short put for my options strategy. On the other hand, if I am bearish and implied volatility is high, I might consider a bear call spread or a bear put spread.

In conclusion, the table is a guide to help you understand your alternatives and subsequently determine which strategy works best in any implied volatility situation: high, average, or low. Use it not only as a quick reference chart convenient for choosing the appropriate strategy, but also to develop a fundamental appreciation for the role implied volatility plays in the selection process.

SUCCESSFUL INVESTMENT MAXIMS FROM WALL STREET LEGENDS

Let's take a look at the various investment principles, practices, and philosophies of some of the most successful equity investors on Wall Street. Most of these names you have certainly heard of; however, there are others who do not have quite as much notoriety. But as you will see,

TABLE 19.1 Strategies for High, Low, and Average Implied Volatility Situations

Directional Bias			Implied Volatility Level
Bullish	**Neutral**	**Bearish**	
Buy call	Buy straddle	Buy put	Low
Protective put	Buy strangle	Protective call	Low
Bull call spread	Short ATM call butterfly	Bear call spread	Low
Bull put spread	Short ATM put butterfly	Bear put spread	Low
Short ITM call butterfly spread	Call ratio backspread	Short OTM call butterfly	Low
Short OTM put butterfly spread	Put ratio backspread	Short ITM put butterfly	Low
Long OTM call calendar spread	Short ATM call calendar spread	Long ITM call calendar spread	Low
Long ITM put calendar spread	Short ATM put calendar spread	Long OTM put calendar spread	Low
Long call	No trade	Long put	Average
Short put	No trade	Short call	Average
Short put	Short straddle	Short call	High
Covered call	Long ATM call calendar spread	Covered put	High
Bull call spread	Short strangle	Bear call spread	High
Bull put spread	Long ATM call butterfly spread	Bear put spread	High
Long OTM call butterfly spread	Long ATM put butterfly spread	Long ITM call butterfly spread	High
Long ITM put butterfly spread	Iron butterfly spread	Long OTM put butterfly spread	High
Short ITM call calendar spread	Condor spread	Short OTM call calendar spread	High
Short OTM put calendar spread	Put and call ratio spreads	Short ITM put calendar spread	High
Collar spread	Long ATM put calendar spread	No trade	High

Note: The following abbreviations are used in the table: ATM = At-the-money, ITM = In-the-money, OTM = Out-of-the-money.

they all offer something valuable and different that can be applied to your own equity investing.

The first legendary investor I am sure most of you have heard of is Warren Buffett. Buffett has a famous quote when describing his approach to the market: "Rule number 1: Never lose money. Rule number 2: Never forget rule number 1." Buffett has often said when entering a stock trade that he is not attempting to make money but operates on the assumption that they could close the market the next day and not reopen it for five years. He asserts that he does not invest in stocks but rather in businesses and feels that one of the dumbest reasons to purchase a stock is because it is going up.

Buffett feels that investors should draw a circle around the businesses they understand and then filter out those that fail to qualify on the basis of value, good management, and ability to endure hard times. This classic fundamentalist has another famous quote that drives home his philosophy: "You should invest in a business that even a fool can run, because someday a fool will."

Another Wall Street legend for whom even Warren Buffett has a lot of praise is Phillip Carret. Carret lived from 1896 to 1998. He founded one of the first mutual fund, the Pioneer fund, in 1928. Carret insisted an investor should never hold fewer than 10 different securities covering five different business sectors and at least once in six months should reappraise every security held. He maintained if one were to do it more frequently one would be more apt to sell it sooner than one should because many times it takes years for a stock price to reflect the value of the company.

Carret always was aware of his surroundings when trying to uncover profitable opportunities. For example, when staying at a hotel in Boston he used Neutrogena soap and was so elated with the product that he purchased the stock. A few years later Johnson & Johnson bought Neutrogena and Carret made a fortune from his original investment. He also liked options and felt that an investor should set aside a small proportion of available funds for the purchase of long-term stock options of promising companies whenever available.

Peter Lynch is also an investor who has had a fabulous career on Wall Street. One of his key rules is to absolutely understand the nature of the companies you own as well as the specific reasons for holding the equity. He maintains that if investors would put their stocks into categories they would have a better idea of what to expect from them. Even though Peter Lynch might visit more than 400 companies in a year, some of his best investments have come from using the company's product. For example, he purchased Taco Bell after trying and enjoying one of their burritos during his travels.

Some of his other investment maxims include the observation that big companies have small moves and small companies have big moves. Also, he says it's better to miss the first move in a stock and wait to see if a company's plans are actually working out. Mr. Lynch likes to invest in simple companies that appear dull and out of favor with Wall Street.

He asserts that you should look for companies that consistently buy back their own shares and views insider buying as a positive sign, especially when several individuals are buying at once. As a true fundamentalist, he carefully considers the price-earnings ratio. It is his belief that if the stock is extremely overpriced, even if everything else goes right, you won't make any money.

Another Wall Street wizard is Sir John Templeton, who is an expert at uncovering international investment opportunities. To illustrate, by the mid-1960s, Templeton and his famous Templeton Funds were invested in Japan, where stocks were trading at 4 times earnings whereas U.S. stocks were at 16. He believes that for all long-term investors, there is only one objective: maximum total return after taxes.

Much of his investment philosophy is predicated on the belief that it is impossible to produce a superior performance unless you do something different from the majority. He goes on to explain that a time of extreme pessimism is a great buying opportunity, and a time of extreme optimism is the best time to sell. He is indeed a classic contrarian. The crux of his approach is that if you search for investments worldwide, you will find more deals and better bargains than by analyzing only one country. In addition, you gain the safety of diversification.

One very colorful figure who had an exceptional career on Wall Street was Bernard Baruch, who lived from 1870 to 1965. In his investments he adopted a skeptical philosophy, always trying to separate facts from emotion. He insisted that to successfully speculate in the markets it must be a full-time job. Baruch viewed relying on inside information or hot stock tips as a very dangerous way to invest.

Before purchasing any stock, Baruch would make sure he knew everything he could about the company: its competitors, its management, and its earnings growth potential. He never attempted to pick tops and bottoms and was always quick to take losses. In addition, Mr. Baruch tried to be in just a few investments at one time so the trades could be better managed. He would periodically analyze all of his investments to see if new developments had changed his original outlook.

One of his key habits to which he attributed much of his success was that he constantly would analyze his losses to determine his mistakes. He would often get away from the hustle and bustle of Wall Street to perform this review. He always concluded this exercise with a self-examination of his trading decisions to better understand his own failings.

Another impressive investment guru is John Bogle, who founded the Vanguard Group, a mutual funds company in 1974. The cornerstone of his investment approach is that investing is not complicated and can be done quite successfully by just employing a little common sense. He contends the investor can do very well by doing just a few things right and avoiding serious mistakes.

He believes in taking reasonable risks to achieve higher long-term rates of return and that one's portfolio should be well diversified. This diversification maxim is why Bogle feels that mutual funds are so valuable. He contends that a set of diversified investments in stocks and bonds only has market risk versus the greater risk of being in just one or two stocks. Finally, he emphasizes thinking for the long term and that stocks may remain overvalued or undervalued for years, so staying the course is one of his key trading rules. He feels that patience and consistency are the most valuable assets an investor can possess.

Henry Clews, a famous investor who lived from 1834 to 1923, was a very successful trader who practiced his craft in the very early days of Wall Street after coming to New York from England in 1850. Mr. Clews always felt investment experts should be sought out to manage portfolios, asserting that if one needed legal help one would see a lawyer and if one needed medical help one would not hesitate to see a doctor; thus if needing investment advice one should seek out a professional.

Much of Mr. Clews' advice centers on what types of people to avoid when seeking your investment fortune. Some of the characteristics he cites include individuals who unjustly accuse others of bad deeds, who never have a good word for anybody, who won't work for an honest living, or who run into debt with no apparent intention of repaying. He asserts that by prudently avoiding these types of people and selecting only associates without these characteristics your life and fortune will be a lot better off.

I am sure most of you have heard of this next investment legend, Charles Schwab. He founded Charles Schwab & Company in 1974. After selling a controlling interest in the firm to BankAmerica in 1983, he bought it back in 1987 and took the company public that same year. Some of his investment wisdom for selecting stocks and mutual funds includes when reading financial papers to always pay attention to the advertisements as there might be an investing opportunity behind the ad.

Mr. Schwab considers mutual funds to be the best investment for most people and claims index funds are a great way to invest for both the novice and the veteran investor. In addition, he feels that one should consider only no-load mutual funds with good performance records, not only for the current year but also over the life of the fund. Mr. Schwab strongly recommends that investors include an international component in their asset allocation plan.

Another brilliant trader, Linda Bradford Raschke, currently the president of LBRGroup, began her professional trading career in 1981 as a market maker in equity options. After seven years on the trading floor, she left the exchange to expand her trading program in the futures markets. Linda Raschke has since been a principal trader for several hedge funds and runs commercial hedging programs in the metals markets. She has pioneered work on volatility-based trading indicators, which were incorporated into her daily trading programs and her overall approach to the markets.

Linda Raschke is a very successful short-term trader who uses a swing trading methodology as the cornerstone of her success. Her approach is a combination of monitoring intraday news and economic reports along with pattern recognition on charts that signal potentially explosive moves. Linda use the Average Directional Index (ADX) as her core indicator to signal direction and examines market volatility to determine where best to apply her ADX tool.

Traders who have employed these short-term tools have increased the profit probability of their positions dramatically. In fact, this is the main theme of Linda's trading philosophy. She requires that the probability of profit for any trade she considers placing is definitely in her corner before ever pulling the trigger. The effectiveness of this approach is obvious, given her long-term success in the business and that she was featured in Jack Schwager's book, *The New Market Wizards* (HarperBusiness, 1992). Linda Raschke's high-probability short-term trading strategies are worth learning for any trader wishing to profit from swings and volatility in the marketplace. As a technical trader, she has contributed a wealth of knowledge in this area and through her lectures and publications has helped many people become better market timers.

I hope you have enjoyed this information about these Wall Street gurus. Even though they have different styles and have invested in different eras, each one has some very invaluable investment insights that can be integrated into your own approach to the markets.

TRADING PERFECTIONISM

In the trading arena, you will find endless sources of financial achievement and accolades, which often go hand-in-hand. In general, our culture respects achievement. Our daily lives are full of pressures to be better, faster, and more accurate. Of course the ultimate achievement would be to attain total perfection. The logical extension of better is best, and the ultimate best is perfect. Many times we carry this burden of impossible expectations into our trading, where it can be quite detrimental.

Knowing and understanding these self-imposed problems might not banish your temptation to seek unrealistic goals, but awareness of forces working on you can help you develop emotional discipline. For example, many people allow others to define their expectations and goals—the old "keeping up with the Joneses" syndrome. Many people often care way too much about what others think about their trading. Instead you should spend your time determining your own personal financial goals. Trading is challenging enough without loading it up with this type of emotional baggage.

Also, people have widely differing levels of comfort with uncertainty. Some people have no fear and will try just about anything. There are others for whom making decisions without 100 percent certainty is a nightmare.

Trading decisions are made emotionally difficult because we:

- Are keenly aware of our chancy surroundings;
- Accurately predict that waiting will afford us some additional information;
- Our precision-dominated world makes us believe a perfect answer might actually exist.

So we recoil from decisions in the realization that our odds of less than ideal results are high. It seems we must always fight our aversion to uncertainty and get on with our investment lives as best we can.

Which brings us to envy. This major enemy is constantly poised to defeat our trading endeavors. We see the rich and famous and read of the fabulous successes of a very few traders, but we fail to focus on their status as exceptions to the norm. By allowing envy to define the exceptional performance of others as our own standard, we help to defeat ourselves. Such self-imposed frustration leaves us concentrating on the difficulty of our task rather on the task itself.

For many traders, for whom no amount of gain is enough, greed is a success killer. Whether by long actual experience or merely by considering the odds, we know that we will not sell at the highest price. And yet we seem to always hold on for that last extra point. Are we greedy in our trading because we think that an even bigger gain will stroke our egos and pad our pockets even more? Do we hold on because this particular stock has treated us well and we are willing to stay in the trade rather than risk selecting another trade? Whatever the reasons for and operating dynamics of our greed, it will defeat us. Greed is merely another way of expressing a driving need for perfectionism.

Ego is another key barrier to trading success. We seem to want to be right and be the best even if there are no other observers. Our egos feel better when we are right and worse when we are wrong. So, in thinking about buying, we become frozen into indecision by realizing we might make a mistake, which would in turn injure our egos. When looking at holding versus selling, we subconsciously provide our egos with more chances for stroking and forestall the known immediate pain of an ego injury by doing nothing. That way, our possibilities for further gain, for reducing or recovering a loss, and for avoiding the pain of not selling at the top are left open.

Here we have perfectionism again making our ego feel good and urging us to do nothing. Knowing your ego's tendency to get in the way, and observing in real time your own behaviors that indicate this is happening, can help you to come to terms with perfectionism. It is probably not totally curable, but can be managed by constant attention.

There are some trading tips one can follow to minimize the occurrence of these self-imposed problems. Databases and experts are wonderful sources of financial information. However, the more sources you consult, the higher the likelihood that the information will conflict. Such conflicts will confuse you, allowing information overload to drive up your anxiety level. It is important for you to use as much information as you can easily handle. You need to develop a trading approach that feels comfortable and then stick to it. For example, if you are more attracted to value than growth investing then go for it. If fundamentals make more sense intuitively than technical analysis, so be it, and vice versa. Go with what you can reasonably handle and ignore the latest fundamental or technical tools that come out. As a trader, this will help you to stay focused, follow your plan, and concentrate on making consistent profits.

TRADING TIPS FOR SUCCESS

Becoming a trader who consistently wins in the options market requires three key elements:

1. A bargain-hunting instinct with the ability to identify undervalued and overvalued options.

2. A sound and well-designed game plan that provides consistent action over time and that prospers in all market conditions.

3. The discipline to follow the game plan. (Plan your trade and trade your plan.)

In applying this formula for success in the options market, the first element is simple: You must always seek to buy underpriced options and sell overpriced options. Most option investors do not follow this basic rule of option investing. They spend far too much time studying the underlying stocks and following the market, and base their option purchases only on these factors, ignoring the price and implied volatility of the option. If you do not buy underpriced options or sell overpriced options, you are going to lose eventually.

You must also create a good game plan. In the options market, the game plan is far more important than in other markets because things happen so quickly that you must be prepared before you play. Then, you have to follow your game plan.

A good trading plan involves a gradual program for investing in the options market versus the elephant approach, where you take all of your money and invest it all at one time, all on one side of the market. In addition, your portfolio must be balanced, investing money in both puts and calls. As you become more familiar with the different trading tactics, you can further diversify among directional, sideways, and delta neutral strategies. Also, be sure to diversify among different sectors over time.

Set aside a speculative fund for options, realizing you could lose everything because of the short-term expiring nature of these investment vehicles. Most importantly, this speculative cash must be money you can afford to lose. If you play in the options market with money you cannot afford to lose, your emotions are guaranteed to overwhelm you and you will be forced into bad trading decisions.

Finally, the most important part of your game plan is not how many positions to take and when to take them, but once you are in a position—when do you take profits and when do you cut losses? Here you must clearly define when to take profits or cut losses before you place the trade, or your emotions will force you to do the wrong thing at the wrong time. Try to be consistent. Don't keep changing the rules of your game plan in the middle of the strategy.

The last ingredient to success is ironclad discipline. You may think that this step is the easiest one to implement, but discipline can be difficult to maintain, especially in the midst of the battle when you may be incurring losses and have to make some tough decisions. If you don't have your trading plan written down on paper, and instead decide in your head what moves will be made at each point, your lack of discipline will catch up with you sooner or later. If you find yourself straying from your game plan, you are doomed, and you might as well liquidate all your positions and invest in some Treasury bills. Without discipline, you will simply never win the options game.

Options traders lose when they follow the crowd because the crowd feeds on emotions. To profit consistently, you must stand alone and act rationally. In the options markets, this means buying underpriced options/selling overpriced options, and having a well-designed trading plan—one that shuns your emotions, forces you to be consistent, and keeps you with a balanced, diversified portfolio.

THE HEART OF MY TRADING APPROACH: OPTIONETICS

Over the years, I have taught my trading approach—which I call Optionetics—to thousands of people all over the world. The Optionetics philosophy of trading is not just valuable to beginners; long-time professionals benefit as well. Overlaying the Optionetics way of trading with any trading system that trades liquid markets can significantly enhance that system's performance. The Optionetics methodology facilitates the implementation of a system's money management rules using a trading technique worthy of application.

To validate this assertion, I want to briefly review the Optionetics philosophy, trading system basics, and money management approaches and conclude with the beneficial impacts the Optionetics philosophy can have on a trader's current trading system.

So just what do the Optionetics philosophies encompass? The absolute crux of this approach can be classified as a scientific method of analysis that utilizes options as tools to minimize risk exposure. Since risk is directly correlated to a trader's number one nemesis—stress—it stands to reason that if you can get a good handle on risk, your ability to execute your trading plan will accelerate.

The Optionetics approach to the markets predefines the risk and reward of each and every trade to determine its feasibility. Once the risk/reward ratio has been revealed and the maximum loss position is clearly defined, a natural calm comes over the trader that triggers a very pronounced stress level reduction. The results are much better decision making during the trade execution and management phase.

Another major benefit of trading the Optionetics way is that it surrounds your core trading or belief system with a flexible investment plan. This flexibility allows the traders to employ a variety of option strategies that best exploit the current market environment. For long-term survival in the trading business, the ability to change directions is absolutely essential. This attribute, which is at the heart of the Optionetics philosophy, turns the naturally dynamic trading environment of the markets into extremely profitable opportunities.

Now let's take a look at what constitutes a typical trading system. There are three building blocks in any system: market entry, exit with a profit, and exit with a loss. Identifying these and making decisions about them is a key element in a successful trading system. Before you trade, your system should tell you: Where should I get into the market? Where should I get out with a profit? And where should I get out with a loss? You need to know the answer to all three of these questions before you trade. If you know the answer to only one or two, you do not have a complete trading system. An effective trading system has to clearly delineate the market entry price, the exit with a loss price, and finally the exit with a profit price.

Of course, with all sound trading system approaches, the trader must have some complementary money management rules that can be effectively applied. Money management takes the trader past the point of no return. For example, a trader who makes $100,000 over the next two years and then loses the $100,000 during the following two years has a return of zero dollars.

Had the trader used proper money management, the $100,000 could have grown to $500,000 at the end of two years. Then, during a large losing period as much as $100,000 could have been protected. After the trader made it to $500,000, the account was in a position to withstand just about any size drawdown, as long as the trader continued to apply money management rules without going back down to zero.

This is why money management is so important. There is no need for your account to reach the point of no return. Proper money management discounts all factors that cannot be mathematically proven. In addition, proper money management takes into account both risk and reward.

Now let's examine how the Optionetics approach can enhance the implementation of both the trading system being employed as well as the accompanying money management rules that are to be applied. The use of puts and calls to hedge against long and short stock positions offers the following four benefits:

1. Greater protection than stop losses.
2. Protection of stock positions from major losses.
3. Elimination of the risk of receiving a margin call.
4. Low maintenance requirement, allowing you to lock in profits.

Given the fact that stop losses are essential components of a good money management system, the Optionetics approach provides a far superior method of protection through the utilization of options. For example, with the distinct possibility of a major gap down or up the traditional stop loss can encounter major slippage. Employing an option as your risk reduction strategy eliminates this negative slippage impact.

Also, by clearly delineating the risk and reward picture of every trade, the Optionetics discipline automatically enforces the most important money management rules of them all. When a trading system generates the market entry, market exit with loss, and market exit with profit price levels the Optionetics methodology can really go to work. The approach allows you to apply the optimum options strategy based on the system's forecasted price levels as well as the underlying option's current and forecasted volatility.

Furthermore, the trader can be as flexible as each trade demands. The Optionetics approach enables traders to make adjustments based on market flow, keep their positions intact by locking in profits, continue to minimize risk, and provide the staying power to see the trade to fruition versus being continually whipsawed in and out of the market.

With so many benefits of applying the Optionetics trading philosophy, it behooves the trader to master these trading principles and use them faithfully in conjunction with one's current trading system. The improvement—not only in the system's profitability but also with better risk-to-reward profiles—makes it a very worthwhile endeavor indeed.

CONCLUSION

The markets by their very nature have multiple personalities. Perhaps the only way to beat them is to get to know their personalities and learn how best to use the right tools to help make winning decisions. In order to do well in this business, you need to cultivate patience, pursue knowledge, garner experience, and always persevere.

By reading this book, you are opening yourself to a veritable anthology of knowledge that has taken years to accumulate. Just remember, there are a million trades out there every day. It's just you and your trading savvy against the world! The many tools and strategies discussed in this book are your biggest allies. The more you get to know them, the better equipped you'll be to profit in the highly volatile markets of the twenty-first century.

Perhaps we all have a fear of failure and the ever-pressing need to become successful. Accomplishing these very human goals usually takes a lifetime. Along the way, I have found it absolutely necessary to nourish my self-confidence by cultivating the disciplines that I seek to master. Trading is one of those disciplines. Getting good at it has entailed developing discriminatory good taste as well as impeccable timing when it comes to the buying and selling of options. And yes, timing really is everything in the markets. But getting good at timing is more than an art; it's also a science—the science of Optionetics—and through it you can develop real trading savvy. All it takes is a lot of practice and a little courage.

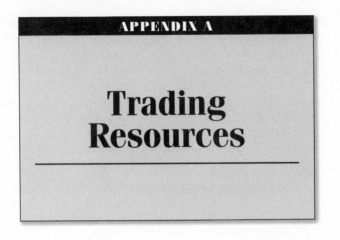

APPENDIX A

Trading Resources

TRADING MEDIA SOURCES

Futures Magazine

This top-notch monthly magazine as well as its online counterpart is a must-read for finding great futures investment opportunities, understanding the markets, and learning all aspects of successful futures trading. It has an excellent editorial staff and offers in-depth analysis of futures markets, trends, seasonal forecasting, and individual commodities.

www.futuresmag.com
Phone: (888) 804-6612

Technical Analysis of Stocks & Commodities

This insightful monthly offers a good cross section of stock and commodity information. In some ways, it is more technical than other periodicals, but it's a very good source of interesting trading ideas.

www.traders.com
Phone: (800) 832-4642; (206) 938-0570

The Wall Street Journal

It is a rare event to find anyone who has not heard of *The Wall Street Journal* (the *Journal*). This publication seems to have been around forever and will undoubtedly be around for many years to come. With worldwide distribution and a wide readership in the United States, it has the ability to influence the markets. If a company is mentioned in *The Wall Street Journal*, it is news. The *Journal* is packed with information—some useful to the investor, some not. The following areas are the most useful for spotting investment opportunities, as well as providing a perspective of what is happening in the markets.

www.wsj.com
Phone: (800) 568-7625

"What's News—Business and Finance" (Front Page)   This section is the first read of the day. In just a few minutes, you can scan summaries of the most important information you need. You can then turn to the detailed article if you find something that interests you.

"Money & Investing" (Main Investment Section)   On the first page of this section, you will find the Markets Diary containing the following series of graphs: stocks, international stocks, bonds and interest, U.S. dollar and currencies. These charts are placed here purposely. A knowledgeable investor can look at these charts individually and collectively to get a very good idea as to the outlook for the U.S. economy, the stock market's strengths or weaknesses, and even what the world may think of U.S. economic prospects.

The second page of this section provides some valuable information that many investors tend to overlook. This includes the following:

- **Most Active Issues** (Various Exchanges). Many stocks show up here day after day. To spot profitable trade opportunities, you want to locate those that are new to the list. For example, while you may see Wal-Mart and Intel on the list each day, it's important to concentrate on finding the new stocks. These new stocks have increased in volume for a reason. You may also ask your broker if any new stocks came out. If there isn't anything new, then this may be a good momentum investment time since there may be news that hasn't leaked out yet. Does this happen? Yes. It happens all the time, even though it's not supposed to happen.
- **Price Percentage Gainers . . . and Losers.** This is my favorite listing. If there were only two pieces of information I could look at to make a smart investment, I would pick these two because they reveal the stocks with the greatest momentum (up or down). The best investments are based on momentum, at least in the short term. I watch these stocks like a hawk to see if they have momentum that is continuing (good or bad) or momentum that is slowing and reversing. I look for a chance to do the opposite on fast movers down (price percentage losers) by looking for buying opportunities. I also like to buy on a fast mover up (price

percentage gainers). If a move up is missed, I look to sell as soon as the momentum starts slowing or reversing. Bottom line: Focus on the information in the Price Percentage Gainers and Losers columns and learn how to use it intelligently (as described in this course) to make money.

"Marketplace" (Review Front Page) This column can be used effectively if you scan for news that is dramatically bullish (good news that should help a stock price go up) or excessively bearish (bad news that should make a stock price go down). One of the best ways to use much of this information is to do the opposite of the crowd by employing the contrarian approach to investing. The theory behind this approach is that the majority of the investors will be wrong a majority of the time (i.e., most people lose money when they invest). Look for information that sounds very optimistic or very pessimistic then watch these stocks to see how they react once the information is in the marketplace.

Stock Page Headings Many people look at these tiny numbers and become overwhelmed. This section of the paper is easier to read once you know which information is important to focus on.

- **52 Weeks Hi/Lo:** High and Low Prices for the Past 52 Weeks. *Important:* This figure tells you the price change of a stock over the past year. The difference between the high and low is called the range. If a stock has moved only $1 in the past year, it is likely to stay in this range. Also, if a stock is at its 52-week high, it may be ready to make new highs. This is one you want to look at as a potential buy. If a stock is at a 52-week low, it could break down and go lower, which may be a selling opportunity (going short). It is generally stated on Wall Street that strength leads to strength and weakness leads to weakness. Since many investors use this information to make investment decisions, it can have great influence on the directions of many stocks.
- **Stock:** Name of the Company. *Important:* Obviously, you need to know the name of the company and its abbreviation to trade it.
- **Yld Div/%:** Dividend Yield. *Not Too Important:* Unless you are buying stocks based on dividend yield (the return you make on a dividend payout) and earnings, this is not a critical number. If you are building a long-term portfolio based on yields, then you will want to compare one stock versus another using this information. Many stocks—especially high-tech stocks—will have a low dividend yield yet are still good investments.
- **PE:** Price-to-Earnings Ratio. *Important:* The price-to-earnings ratio tells you how many times the earnings a stock is trading at. For example, a stock with earnings of $1 per share and a price of $20 has a P/E of

20. If the industry average is a P/E of 40, then this stock may be under-valued. If the stock is trading at a P/E of 100 ($100 per share) with the industry average being a P/E of 40, then the stock is likely overvalued; on any sign of weakness, the stock will come tumbling down. Broker-age firm analysts establish guidelines for each industry. For example, a slow-growth industry, such as the steel industry, may have a P/E of only 10, while a high-growth industry, such as the Internet businesses, may have a P/E of 40 or higher. These range significantly. There are a num-ber of publications that list this information, including *Value Line*.

- **Vol:** Number of Shares of Stock Traded per Day. *Important:* This num-ber is important when the volume is increasing significantly. For exam-ple, when a stock has an average share volume of 100,000 shares and the stock trades five times that high (500,000), this information is use-ful. If the stock has a high trading volume and is found on the Price Percentage Gainers . . . and Losers list, then you have a confirmation signal that the stock is making a move. When volume is decreasing or stable, the stock will likely go nowhere as interest in the stock is dwin-dling. It is important to watch the volume of the stocks you own or are trading to see whether there is a momentum increase or decrease.
- **Hi/Lo:** High and Low Prices Yesterday. *Not Critical:* Unless you are day trading (going in and out during one trading session), this infor-mation is not critical. Investors and traders look at this information to signal if stock traders will be running stops. This technique can also be used to look for orders from public traders. For example, if a trader sold a stock yesterday, he or she may place a buy stop (to cover losses) above yesterday's high. This is referred to as a resis-tance point. If the trader bought a stock, he or she may place a sell stop (to sell the stock purchased) below yesterday's low. This is re-ferred to as a support point. These techniques are used frequently for protection if the market moves against the original position. *Note:* The technique of running stops is used by many investors and traders; however, it is not what I recommend. I prefer to use options to protect my investments, because I find them to be more profitable and safer in the long run.
- **Close:** Closing Price Yesterday; **Net Chg:** Change in Price Yester-day. *Important:* These two points are important as they represent the dollar value a stock has changed. The net change value is based on where the price of the stock is today relative to yesterday's close. If a stock is trading at $10 today, and it closed yesterday at $8, then the stock has a net change of +$2. This 20 percent increase is significant (30 percent is even better). If a stock is trading today at $10 and closed yesterday at $20, this $10 drop in value (50 per-cent) is very significant.

Note: The Wall Street Journal contains a great deal of information. Each day, I scan the newspaper and look for clues to make intelligent investment decisions. If you make an effort to learn to use *The Wall Street Journal* to its fullest, you will have made a significant investment in your own trading education.

Investor's Business Daily

Investor's Business Daily (IBD) was started with the intent to add a new dimension of information to the investment community. *IBD* focuses on concise investment news information—including sophisticated charts, tables, and analytical tools—with the hope of adding valuable information that *The Wall Street Journal* may not provide. As the name implies, *Investor's Business Daily* is published for the investor. *IBD* is an exceptional daily newspaper for an investor to learn about the markets and locate profitable investment opportunities. It is an excellent publication for spotting stock patterns that can produce excellent trading profits. It's well worth the investment.

www.investors.com
Phone: (800) 831-2525

Note: Since some of the information included in *IBD* has already been explained in the previous *Wall Street Journal* description, I will refer to this information when applicable.

"Executive News Summary"   Located on the very first page, this section is a brief, yet useful summary of the important news of the day. Once again, you want to focus on news events that are either extremely bullish (positive for the market or an individual stock) or very bearish (negative for the market or an individual stock). If you find an article worth exploring, you can go to the details within the article.

Stock Tables: Intelligent Tables   One of the most interesting features in *IBD* is its "intelligent" tables developed for the major stock markets. These contain some of the most important information on stocks based on a number of technical indicators. *IBD* uses a number of standard technical indicators that will be reviewed in detail.

Note: Once again, you need to focus on the movers and shakers in the market. If you focus on ordinary stocks you will produce ordinary financial returns. As discussed in *The Wall Street Journal* section, you need to focus on the stocks that have a reason to move. Stocks move on momentum either due to technical factors or because they are being watched by a large number of investors.

You will find Intelligent Tables that list selected stocks with the following indicators:

* Greatest % Rise in Volume.
* Most Active.
* Most % Up in Price.
* Most % Down in Price.

You will also find Intelligent Tables for the three major exchanges:

* New York Stock Exchange (NYSE).
* Nasdaq over-the-counter issues.
* American Stock Exchange (AMEX).

Table Column Headings

* **EPS Rnk.:** Earnings per Share Growth Rank. *Important:* This number is calculated as an average of five-year earnings per share growth and stability and the EPS growth the last two quarters. The resulting number is compared to other companies in the table and given a rank of 1 (lowest) to 99 (highest). Focus on companies with an EPS ranking of 95 or better when buying and 20 or lower when selling (i.e., buy stocks with the greatest strength and sell the weakest). It is a good idea to track the EPS rank of your stocks on at least a weekly basis so you have a chance to make changes to your portfolio if there is a dramatic change in the character of your investments.
* **Rel. Str.:** Relative Price Strength. *Important:* A relative strength weighting is used to compare one company to another, or one industry to another. This *IBD* table is an analysis of a stock's price change relative to other stocks in the table over a 12-month period. When buying options, I focus on stocks with a relative strength weighting of 80 or better, and 40 or lower when selling stock short.
* **Acc. Dis.:** Accumulation Distribution Rating. *Important:* This indicator reflects the percentage change of a stock's price and its volume, two of the most important indicators of strength or weakness in a stock. *IBD* uses the rating A (strongest) to E (weakest). I like to focus on As only for buying and Es only for selling stock short or taking a bearish perspective on the stock.
* **Vol. % Chg.:** Percent Change in Volume. *Important:* This is an interesting addition to the table of information. *IBD* highlights stocks that have prices greater than $10 when the volume increases by 50 percent or greater than the average volume over the last 50 trading days. Why is this important? Volatility. Always look for large increases in volume. I look for increases that are at least double (200 percent) in average volume because the larger the increase in volume, the more likely some-

thing important may be happening. This is a typical signal of momentum change, which indicates strong impending moves either up or down in the price of a stock.

Note: Look for stocks that are lower than $10 in price that have volume percentage changes of 200 percent or greater. These could signal the beginning of explosive growth in the price of a stock.

• Other table column headings include:

  • 52-Week High.
  • 52-Week Low.
  • Closing Price.
  • Price Change.
  • PE Ratio: price-to-earnings ratio.
  • Float (mil): number of shares outstanding.
  • Vol. (100s): number of hundreds of shares traded on the session.

Investor's Business Daily— Option Guide from Daily Graphs

This exceptional publication can help you spot stocks and futures with options ready to make a big move. This periodical reviews every stock that has options, complete with the related charts and graphs. This publication and its online counterpart is worth its weight in gold many times over once you understand the risks and rewards associated with options strategies.

www.dailygraphs.com
Phone: (800) 472-7479

DATA SERVICE PROVIDERS

As an investor or trader, you can access sources of information that provide you with current data as to prices on stocks, futures, and options. In addition to prices, you can also receive up-to-the-minute news and market analyses. This information can be accessed in a variety of ways including the Internet, cable, FM, satellite, and wireless networks. Which kind of service you need depends on what kind of trading you are involved with. Real-time data is as close to the actual prices as you can get. As the prices change at the exchange, the data is transmitted directly to you, thereby minimizing price discrepancies. Delayed prices are typically transmitted 15 to 20 minutes after the prices have changed at the exchanges. End-of-day prices are transmitted at the close of the market each day. The faster you receive your data, the more costly it is to obtain; however, the level of accuracy can be a significant contributing factor in the kind of trading you choose to pursue.

eSignal
Product of Data Broadcasting Company
www.esignal.com
Phone: (800) 322-1339

- Fundamental information on more than 150,000 stocks, futures, options, bonds, mutual funds, indexes, fixed income, FOREX, and statistics direct from the exchange floors.
- Compatible with a wide variety of software packages.
- Discrimination between day and night sessions.
- Complete news stories to keep you informed of continual changes in market conditions.
- Data is available via Internet.
- Real-time, delayed, or end-of-day quotes 24 hours a day.
- Stock market information from NYSE, AMEX, Nasdaq, regional exchanges, and European, Asian, and Canadian stocks and futures.
- Commodity and futures option information from CBT, CME, NYBOT, NYMEX, KCBT, MGE, MidAm, and COMEX.
- Quotes on stock and currency options from the Option Price Authority Exchange.
- Money market funds, mutual funds, and indices direct from the exchange floors.
- A variety of news services including the Dow Jones News Service and Broadtape.
- Market commentary, fundamental analysis, historical charting, and company research are prepared daily by leading experts and wire services.
- Advanced GET—Advanced charting package, including indicators such as Elliott waves for Types One and Two Trades, Ellipse, Make-or-Break, Expert Trend Locator, and False Bar Stochastics.
- Market Scanner—Powerful tools that screen the market in real-time including:

  - PreMarket Scan: Focuses on the best trading opportunities before the opening bell.
  - Rally Scan: Captures every big move as it happens.
  - Hot Groups Scan: Points to sector investment opportunities.
  - Power Scan: Tracks trading opportunities throughout the market day.
  - End-of-Day: Scans user's entire database of issues on any number of simple or complex triggers.

Provider Costs

Your service fees are based on the kind of service you choose to receive. If you are not going to sit in front of a computer all day long, then you don't really need real-time feeds. You can easily get away with delayed or end-of-day quotes. Depending on the kind of data you choose and the exchanges that you sign up for, data feeds can cost you anywhere from $25 to $400 per month. Subscribing to only what you need could keep your costs as low as possible. You can always upgrade later as your trading progresses.

For instance, a basic real-time subscription from eSignal that gives you access to all exchanges starts at around $185 per month. It goes up from this price depending on a variety of criteria, including how you want to receive the data. If you want to place longer-term trades, delayed or end-of-day quotes should be sufficient for your needs. Remember: If you are just starting out, keep your overhead as low as possible. Only request information on the markets you want to initially trade. Too much information can create "analysis paralysis." It is essential to start small and build your profits systematically.

INTERNET SITES

Optionetics.com

www.optionetics.com

Learning about options and various innovative strategies is the key to trading success in today's volatile markets. The Optionetics.com web site offers traders an exciting journey into the world of options trading. It provides comprehensive information detailing the interactive nature of stocks and options, as well as options strategies that enable traders to navigate the markets successfully. Optionetics.com features the following areas:

- **Stock and Option Quotes and Charts:** Find delayed stock and option quotes and charts, most active gainers and losers lists, market analysis, index charts, research, bond quotes, and updates on all major markets. Use the free Options Ranker to sort through the universe of options to find the cheapest and most expensive contracts.
- **Educational Articles:** The Optionetics trading team provides insightful articles and monthly columns to a variety of newspapers, magazines, and e-zines. Now you can read them before they hit the newsstand!
- **Market Commentary:** Get the lowdown on the mood of the marketplace three times a day with specific tips on stocks on the move and profitable market strategies from the Optionetics trading team.

- **Stock and Options Portfolios:** A portfolio is an electronic method of tracking stocks and trades as they change value due to market movement. Track hypothetical paper trades for the purpose of learning; or monitor real trades by receiving daily updates and news alerts concerning the stocks you are watching.
- **Discussion Boards:** Chat with other traders from around the world to hear what they think about specific stocks, options strategies, or upcoming events that could rock the marketplace.
- **Broker Review:** See how various brokerage firms stack up in the broker review section. In addition, compare options services, commissions, fees, and more from one broker to the next.
- **Trader's Resource Store:** An electronic store featuring videos, books, newsletters, and software applications for the avid trader.
- **A Comprehensive Trading Bookstore:** Utilize the extensive scope of Trader's Library to find the latest best-sellers, hard-to-find investment must-reads, and find out what critics have to say about each book.
- **Seminar Information:** Find out where, when, and how you can attend the next Optionetics.com seminar in your area. Learn to manage risk the Optionetics way!

Platinum Site at Optionetics

www.platinum.optionetics.com

Platinum is an online software analysis program that enables traders to select from millions of possible trades. In just a matter of seconds, you can look for single-option or combination trades that meet your strict criteria! Platinum provide options traders with:

- Risk graph analysis of your own personal trades!
- Implied volatility rankings tailored to any and every option you choose. Find the right skew for the trade.
- The Trade Selection Matrix, which allows you to match trades with your market preferences.
- Option trade portfolio management with nightly e-mail of profit/loss performance. Paper trading made easy!
- Historical back-testing capabilities on options going back more than two and a half years!
- Access to the Greeks for any option position including delta, vega, gamma, and theta.
- If you use the volatility of options and stocks to locate promising trades, this site is a must-have.

Educational Web Sites

InvestorWords.com
www.investorwords.com
A comprehensive financial glossary that allows participants to browse by letter and to receive a daily e-mail containing the "Term of the Day."

The Motley Fool
www.fool.com
The Motley Fool site was created to educate, amuse, and enrich, and contains quotes, charts, financials, education, portfolios, news, and ideas, as well as some of the most heavily trafficked bulletin boards on the Internet. Also, check out their Broker Center. Don't be fooled by their foolish bravado—this site has plenty of investor clout.

Options Clearing Corporation
www.optionsclearing.com
As the largest clearing organization in the world for financial derivatives, the OCC web site offers a wealth of options-education information. OCC issues put and call options on several types of underlying assets including stocks, stock indexes, foreign currencies, and interest rate composites.

Options Industry Council
www.optionscentral.com
The OIC is a nonprofit organization dedicated to educating the public about options through seminars, videos, and brochures. Its web site serves as an educational arm offering free educational material to help you learn about trading options.

Securities and Exchange Commission
www.sec.com
The Securities and Exchange Commission (SEC) is the regulatory entity that supervises U.S. financial markets. On its web site, readers will find a lot of detailed securities-related information. SEC has reports on listed companies, investor guides, and EDGAR—a database that performs automated collection of corporate information and financial statements.

Stock-Trak
www.stocktrak.com
Stock-Trak provides portfolio simulations featuring stocks, options, futures, bonds, and more. This terrific educational site is used by more than 10,000 college students each semester in their finance and investment courses. Stock-Trak is now available to anyone, allowing you to manage a

fake brokerage account of $100,000 in order to test strategies, place trades, and learn about the financial markets.

Exchanges

American Stock Exchange

www.amex.com

The American Stock Exchange (AMEX) is comprised of companies that were too small to be listed on the New York Stock Exchange. Requirements include a pretax income of $750,000 in two of the past three years, stockholders' equity of $4 million and a minimum market capitalization of $3 million.

Chicago Board of Trade

www.cbot.com

The Chicago Board of Trade (CBOT) is primarily a futures and options exchange, where the Dow Jones Industrial Averages (DJIA) futures trade. The CBOT also has a trading simulation through the Auditrade system. There is a charge of $10 per month to participate in Auditrade's simulated trading. This will allow you to practice trading, using a fake account and real prices until you get comfortable with the strategies and their results.

Chicago Board Options Exchange

www.cboe.com

The Chicago Board Options Exchange (CBOE) has news, new option listings, and exchange information on equities, options, and LEAPS. Specialization includes calls and puts on NYSE stocks, the S&P 500, U.S. Treasury bonds, and other indexes.

International Securities Exchange

www.iseoptions.com

As the newest U.S. exchange, the ISE is the first all-electronic network for trading stock and index options. Since its first day of trading on May 26, 2000, ISE has grown into the third largest options exchange.

Nasdaq

www.nasdaq.com

The Nasdaq is the over-the-counter market where, via online computer transactions, securities are bought and sold through licensed securities brokers and dealers. The web site includes indexes, quotes, charts, and individual company news, as well as updated stories from Reuters.

New York Stock Exchange

www.nyse.com

The New York Stock Exchange (NYSE), or the Big Board, is the world's largest equities market with a capitalization of more than $12 trillion. A tremendous amount of information is available about new and previously listed companies, with annual reports, research, publications, and news. The NYSE ensures marketplace integrity by taking disciplinary actions when necessary and is considered the international market of choice.

Pacific Exchange

www.pacificex.com

The Pacific Exchange (PCX) is the third most active stock exchange in the country and the third largest stock options exchange in the world. More than 2,600 stocks, bonds, and other securities issued by publicly traded companies as well as options on more than 550 stocks are traded on the PCX, along with a variety of indexes. Quotes on equities and options are delayed 20 minutes.

Philadelphia Stock Exchange

www.phlx.com

Founded in 1790, the PHLX trades more than 2,800 stocks, 700 equity options, 12 index options, and 100 currency options. Fifteen-minute delayed quotes and volatility charts are available, along with news, research, and daily market analysis.

Charts and Quotes

BigCharts

www.bigcharts.com

BigCharts is sure to become one of your favorite sites with intraday charts, historical quotes, and quotes on more than 34,000 stocks, mutual funds and indexes. It provides an excellent array of information on the big movers and losers in the main markets, momentum charts, and other goodies.

eSignal

www.esignal.com

eSignal is a leading real-time quote service that delivers continuously updated, time-sensitive financial data over the Internet. The web site offers market quotes for stocks, options, and futures, as well as charts, news, research and alerts to the growing base of online investors.

North American Quotations
www.naq.com
One of the top preferred data suppliers to brokerage firms, web sites, corporations, and private investors, this site offers real-time quotes and charts for a premium.

PC Quote
www.pcquote.com
One of the world's premier electronic providers of real-time securities quotations, news and investment tools, PC Quote hosts a multitude of innovative investment tools, software applications and excellent articles.

Quicken
www.quicken.com
In addition to its TurboTax products, the Quicken site has quotes, advanced charting, portfolio information, news, analysis, profiles, SEC filings and reports.

StockMaster
www.stockmaster.com
StockMaster is another excellent site that includes quotes and clear daily price charts with separate volume charts. Check out its investor sentiment surveys.

News Sources

Bloomberg
www.bloomberg.com
Bloomberg's site has a staggering selection of financial information including headlines, market updates, and equity indexes. Currency calculators and cross-currency rates are useful bonuses. Real audio sound bites are available for up-to-the-minute updates.

BusinessWeek
www.businessweek.com
BusinessWeek Online has daily briefings, quotes and portfolio information. Many interesting and well-written articles make this a worthwhile site, while the banking, technology and education centers are interesting. The searchable archives date back to January 1991.

CBS MarketWatch

www.cbs.marketwatch.com

CBS MarketWatch is sure to be on everyone's bookmark list, with comprehensive coverage of news, headlines, and market data. Delayed quotes are supplied by eSignal.

CNBC

www.moneycentral.msn.com

The CNBC television news channel is the leader in business news. The CNBC site has programming information for CNBC in the United States, Europe, and Asia. Biographies for the CNBC staff are also online. Extensive executive and job search Web listings and phone numbers are available.

Dow Jones

www.dowjones.com

The Dow Jones site has global market updates, economic indicators, quotes, and the newswires. Access to other business publications is also available.

Dun & Bradstreet

www.dnb.com

Dun & Bradstreet specializes in press releases and company profiles, focusing on news, views and trends.

The Economist

www.economist.com

The *Economist* is the international journal of news, ideas, and opinions. Thought-provoking analysis and articles abound on its web site, as well as access to archived editions.

Forbes

www.forbes.com

Forbes Digital Toolbox is a great site that offers the popular *Forbes* lists, interesting commentary, and quotes. Includes several key sections including Manufacturing, Technology, Commerce, Services, Energy, HealthCare, Bonds, Emerging Markets, Enterprise Tech, Future Tech, Networks, E-Business, and Sciences and Medicine. The site also has links to their magazine.

Investor's Business Daily

www.investors.com

IBD's site has incorporated many topical daily news articles from sections such as Inside Today, Front Page, Computers & Tech, the Economy, the Markets and Vital Signs.

Kiplinger

www.kiplinger.com

Kiplinger online is an excellent source of business forecasts and personal financial advice. The PAWWS Financial Network provides 20-minute delayed quotes.

Moody's

www.moodys.com

Moody's Investors Service is the leading provider of credit ratings, research, and financial information to the capital markets.

Nasdaq Trader

www.nasdaqtrader.com

The Nasdaq Trader has trading and market data services, volume reports on shares, lists share volume leaders, trading halts, and timely access to Nasdaq news.

Pathfinder

www.pathfinder.com

Time Warner's Pathfinder site has links to all the online publications in the Time Warner family, such as *Time, People, Money, Fortune,* and *Entertainment Weekly.* The scrolling newswire is useful, as are the other links to CNN types of news sites.

Red Herring

www.redherring.com

One of the most popular financial e-zines, this site offers a multitude of insider news, analysis, and commentary by highly respected journalists primarily focused on the business of technology.

Reuters

www.reuters.com

Reuters has market briefs, indexes updates, the market snapshot, business news, company news, quotes, and top stories.

Technical Analysis of Stocks & Commodities

www.traders.com

The online site of *Technical Analysis of Stocks & Commodities* magazine has monthly featured articles and excellent educational information for the novice trader. A wide variety of links and resources make this a useful site.

The Wall Street Journal

www.wsj.com

The Wall Street Journal requires a small fee for its online subscription. You'll find all the bells and whistles on this comprehensive site that the *Journal* is famous for worldwide. There is also an updated job and career search section with technical, professional, and management positions listed.

Zacks

www.zacks.com

Zacks is a very popular financial site that offers a variety of free and subscription services. It provides access to research produced by more than 3,000 analysts and approximately 240 brokerage firms. It also features a vast array of brokerage and equity research, screening, and advisory tools. Check out the daily "Bull of the Day" and "Bear of the Day."

Analysis Tools

iVolatility.com

www.ivolatility.com

An options-related web site that offers subscribers the ability to rank and search options based on different variables. This site offers daily implied volatilities and catalogs this information in a powerful database. Traders can utilize this database to scan for a variety of opportunities based on historical and implied volatility and to evaluate overbought/oversold options.

VectorVest

www.vectorvest.com

The VectorVest site provides services that integrate fundamental and technical analysis to sort, screen, rank, graph, and analyze more than 6,500 stocks, industry groups, and industry sectors for price, value, safety, timing, and more. If you're not ready for a subscription, you may want to take advantage of their free in-depth stock analysis service—just click on the "Free Stock Analysis" box on the upper left-hand corner of the home page screen.

Informative Sites

Briefing

www.briefing.com

Briefing's site has live market commentary, stock analysis, quotes and charts, sector ratings, and an economic calendar. Other premium services are available.

Daytraders
www.daytraders.com
A day trader's paradise, full of news and resources. Delayed quotes are supplied by Quote.com. The trading strategies section has some wonderful commonsense information for all traders.

ICLUBCentral
www.iclub.com
Serves as an online clearinghouse for all the communicative and administrative needs of investment clubs including products and services targeted to both new and established investment clubs such as the National Association of Investors Corporation (NAIC). It recently acquired Doug Gerlach's Investorama, a wonderfully comprehensive directory for investors.

Investor Guide
www.investorguide.com
Investor Guide is a tremendous resource for personal investing on the Web. In addition to quotes and news, it has more than 1,000 responses to investment questions. This excellent, comprehensive site focuses on investing, personal finance, and education. It also runs the Hedgehog Investment Competition. Have you ever wanted to create and manage your own $1 million hedge fund? Here's your chance.

Investor Home
www.investorhome.com
The Investor Home page is a treasure trove of links, quotes, charts, research, profiles, and earnings estimates. This site had won 12 honors and awards the last time we checked.

TheStreet
www.thestreet.com
Controversial analyst Jim Cramer hosts this extremely popular and influential site. TheStreet.com's engaging articles and perceptive market analyses no doubt help to shape the mass psychology of the marketplace.

World Wide Financial Network
www.wwfn.com
The World Wide Financial Network has an excellent variety of investor resources, including indexes, charts and quotes, extensive research tools, feature articles, and access to online brokers. Overall, a great site.

Yahoo!
finance.yahoo.com
The Yahoo! Finance site has a wealth of information including top news headlines, market overviews, stock and index quotes, economic indicators, and a host of excellent articles on national and international business.

APPENDIX B

Important Charts and Tables

TABLE B.1 Option Expiration Month Codes

	Jan	Feb	Mar	Apr	May	Jun	Jul	Aug	Sep	Oct	Nov	Dec
Calls	A	B	C	D	E	F	G	H	I	J	K	L
Puts	M	N	O	P	Q	R	S	T	U	V	W	X

TABLE B.2 Strike Price Codes

A	B	C	D	E	F	G	H	I
5	10	15	20	25	30	35	40	45
105	110	115	120	125	130	135	140	145

J	K	L	M	N	O	P	Q	R
50	55	60	65	70	75	80	85	90
150	155	160	165	170	175	180	185	190

S	T	U	V	W	X	Y	Z
95	100	7.50	12.50	17.50	22.50	27.50	32.50
195	200	37.50	42.50	47.50	52.50	57.50	62.50

TABLE B.3 Option Delta Value

	Calls		Puts	
	Long	**Short**	**Long**	**Short**
At-the-Money	+50	−50	−50	+50
In-the-Money				
1 Strike	+60 to +65	−60 to −65	−60 to −65	+60 to +65
2 Strikes	+70 to +75	−70 to −75	−70 to −75	+70 to +75
3 Strikes	+80 to +85	−80 to −85	−80 to −85	+80 to +85
Out-of-the-Money				
1 Strike	+35 to +40	−35 to −40	−35 to −40	+35 to +40
2 Strikes	+25 to +30	−25 to −30	−25 to −30	+25 to +30
3 Strikes	+15 to +20	−15 to −20	−15 to −20	+15 to +20

TABLE B.4 Option Quote Terms

Data	Definition
Last	The last price that the option traded for at the exchange. For delayed quotes, this price may not reflect the actual price of the option at the time you view the quote.
Open	The price of the first transaction of the current trading day.
Change	The amount the last sale differs from the previous trading day's closing price.
% Change	The percentage the price has changed since the previous day's closing price.
High	The high price for the current trading day.
Low	The low price for the current trading day.
Bid	The bid is the highest price a prospective buyer (floor trader) is prepared to pay for a specified time for a trading unit of a specified security. If there is a high demand for the underlying asset, the prices are bid up to a higher level. Off-floor traders buy at the ask price.
Ask	The ask is the lowest price acceptable to a prospective seller (floor trader) of the same security. A low demand for a stock translates to the market being offered down to the lowest price at which a person is willing to sell. Off-floor traders sell at the bid price. Together, the bid and ask prices constitute a quotation or quote and the difference between the two prices is the bid-ask spread. The bid and asked dynamic is common to all stocks and options.
52-Week High	The highest price the stock traded at in the past 52-week period.
52-Week Low	The lowest price the stock traded at in the past 52-week period.
Earnings per Share	The bottom line (net pretax profit) divided by the number of shares outstanding.
Volume	The total number of shares traded that day.
Shares Outstanding	The total number of shares the company has issued.
Market Cap	Shares outstanding multiplied by the closing stock price.
P/E Ratio	Stock price divided by the earnings per share; P = price/E = earnings per share.
Exchange	This indicates where a company lists, or registers its shares (e.g., New York Stock Exchange).

TABLE B.5 Exchange-Traded Funds

Exchange-Traded Fund Type	Exchange-Traded Fund Description	Market Representation
DIAMONDS	Diamonds Trust Series	Dow Jones Industrial Average
FITRS	Fixed Income Exchange Traded Securities	Various Treasuries
HOLDRS	Holding Company Depositary Receipts	Very narrow industry sectors
iShares	Index Shares	Various countries and market sectors
QUBEs	Nasdaq 100 Tracking Stock (QQQ)	Nasdaq 100 Index
Spiders	Standard & Poor's Depositary Receipts (SPDRS)	Various Standard & Poor's indexes
StreetTracks	State Street Global Advisor ETFs	Various Dow Jones style indexes
VIPERs	Vanguard Index Participation Receipts	Several Vanguard index funds

Year	Key Event

TABLE B.6 Time Line of the Stock Market

Year	Key Event
1791	Brokers meet at an outdoor marketplace in Philadelphia to buy and sell securities issued by the new U.S. government.
1792	Merchants who used to meet under a buttonwood tree on Wall Street in New York City organize America's first formal exchange with membership requirements, giving birth to the New York Stock Exchange (NYSE).
1829	Trading volume reaches 50,000 shares a day.
1836	Trading moves inside, but the fixtures over the trading posts are still modeled after streetlights.
1867	Edward Calahan invents the stock ticker, displaying current market prices with each company represented by a symbol based on Morse code—a tradition that continues today.
1871	Continuous trading replaces the old roll call system, which gave investors just two chances to trade during the day; one in the morning and one in the afternoon. Brokers are positioned by company in fixed places—the start of modern-day trading and specialists' trading posts.
1882	Charles Dow and Edward Jones start Dow Jones & Company and are the first to create an index measuring the activity of the New York Stock Exchange. The original 11 companies in this first Dow Jones Index were Western Union, Pacific Mail Steamship, and nine railroads.
1886	Trading volume hits 1 million shares per day.
1896	Dow Jones begins publishing a daily paper: *The Wall Street Journal*. It also creates four averages to measure market performance as a whole. These averages include the Dow Jones Industrial Average (DJIA), the Transportation Average, the Utility Average, and the Composite Average.
1920–1929	After World War I, the stock market sees substantial gains during a long-term bull market.
1929	On October 29, 1929, the rally of the 1920s ends when the stock market crashes, falling more than 12.8 percent in one day. After the largest stock market rally in history, the market crashed 33 points from 263 to 230.
1930–1944	Securities prices languish as the deepening global depression is followed by the outbreak of World War II. In the last years of World War II, the American stock markets finally begin to recuperate.

(continues)

TABLE B.6 *(Continued)*

Year	Key Event
1945–1972	After the end of the war, the stock market rallies to new highs. This rally continues, with some intermissions, until the early 1970s. In 1972 the Dow Jones Industrial Average rises to 1,000 before falling back. Volume increases from an average of 1 million shares a day to about 15 million shares a day.
1954	The Ford Foundation sells $657 million worth of Ford Motor Company stock, the largest secondary offering of stock up to that time.
1957	Prior to 1957, the S&P Corporation calculated a weekly 480-stock average and a daily 90-stock average. Spurred by advancing technology, S&P decides to calculate the S&P 500 Index on an hourly basis. S&P believes that this index, which includes more stocks and a different mathematical formula than the Dow Jones Industrial Average, better reflects market movement.
1964	The National Association of Securities Dealers (NASD) is reorganized to consolidate, regulate, and automate the over-the-counter (OTC) securities market where trades from around the world are made via computer and telephone.
1971	The National Association of Securities Dealers Automated Quotation (NASDAQ) system officially opens, displaying quotes for more than 2,500 securities.
1972–1982	During this period, known as the bear market of the 1970s, the stock market retreats. This occurs as the oil crisis, inflation, and unemployment stifle the U.S. and world economies.
1973	The Chicago Board of Trade forms the first listed options exchange, the Chicago Board Options Exchange (CBOE). This exchange is quickly copied by other exchanges around the world.
1987	The stock market crashes in October, sending the Dow nose-diving 22.6 percent. The DJIA drops 508 points from 2,246 to 1,738. Program trading restrictions and automatic trading curbs are instituted in an attempt to prevent future crashes.
1994	Online trading is launched over the Internet.
1995	Andrew D. Klein launches the first initial public offering (IPO) over the Internet for his microbrewery, Spring Street Brewing Company.
2000	Dow Jones hits all-time high of 11,722 on January 14, 2000. Nasdaq peaks at 5,048 on March 10, 2000.

TABLE B.7 Popular Indexes

Symbol	Index	Symbol	Index
$XAL	Airline Index	$NYA	NYSE Composite Index
$ISSA	AMEX Advance/Decline Issues	$TRIN	NYSE Short-Term Trade Index
$XAX	AMEX Composite Index	$XOI	Oil Index
$XMI	AMEX Major Market Index	$DRG	Pharmaceutical Index
$XOI	AMEX Oil & Gas	$BKX	PHLX Bank Sector Index
$AVOL	AMEX Volume	$BMX	PHLX Computer Box Maker
$BTK	Biotechnology Index		Sector
$MNX	CBOE Mini-NDX Index	$XAU	PHLX Gold and Silver Index
$DDX	Disk Drive Index	$OSX	PHLX Oil Service Sector Index
$COMP	Dow Jones Composite Index	$SOX	PHLX Semiconductor Sector
$DJC	Dow Jones Composite Index		Index
$INDU	Dow Jones Industrial Average	$DOT	PHLX TheStreet.com Internet
$DJI	Dow Jones Industrial Index	$PSE	PSE High Technology Index
$DJT	Dow Jones Transportation Index	$RUI	Russell 1000
$DJU	Dow Jones Utilities Index	$RUT	Russell 2000
$FCHI	France Cac-40 Index	$RUA	Russell 3000
$FTSE	FTSE-100 Index	$OEX	S&P 100 Index
$GDAX	Germany DAX Index	$SPX	S&P 500 Index
$GNX	Goldman Sachs Index	$SGX	S&P Barra Growth Index
$GSO	GSTI Software Index	$SVX	S&P Barra Value Index
$JPN	Japan Index	$CEX	S&P Chemical Index
$VIX	Market Volatility Index	$IUX	S&P Insurance Index
$MEX	Mexico Index	$MID	S&P MidCap 400 Index
$CMR	Morgan Stanley Consumer Index	$RLX	S&P Retail Index
$CYC	Morgan Stanley Cyclical Index	$XBD	Securities Broker Dealer Index
$MSH	Morgan Stanley High Tech Index	$SOX	Semiconductor Index
$ISSQ	Nasdaq Advance/Decline Issues	$TSE-TC	Toronto 35 Index
$COMPQ	Nasdaq Composite	$TOP-TC	TSE 100 Index
$IXCO	NASDAQ High Tech Index	$UTY	Utility Sector Index
$NDX	Nasdaq 100 Index	$XVG	Value Line Index (Geometric)
$QQV	Nasdaq QQQ Volatility Index	$WSX	Wilshire Composite Index
$VXN	Nasdaq Volatility Index	$FVX	5-Year T-Note Index
$QVOL	Nasdaq Volume	$TNX	10-Year T-Note Index
$XNG	Natural Gas Index	$IRX	13-Week T-Bill Index
$ISSU	NYSE Advance/Decline Issues	$TYX	30-Year T-Bond Index

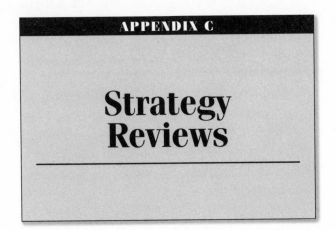

APPENDIX C

Strategy Reviews

TABLE C.1 Quick Option Strategy Reference Guide

Strategy	Trade	Market Outlook	Profit Potential	Risk Potential	Time Decay Effects
Long call	B1-C	Bullish	Unlimited	Limited	Detrimental
Short call	S1-C	Bearish	Limited	Unlimited	Helpful
Covered call	B100-U S1-C	Slightly bullish to neutral	Limited	Limited	Helpful
Long put	B1-P	Bearish	Limited	Limited	Detrimental
Short put	S1-P	Bullish	Limited	Limited	Helpful
Covered put	S100-U	Slightly bearish to neutral	Limited	Unlimited	Helpful
Bull call spread	B1-LC S1-HC	Bullish	Limited	Limited	Mixed
Bear put spread	S1-LP B1-HP	Bearish	Limited	Limited	Mixed
Bull put spread	B1-LP S1-HP	Moderately bullish	Limited	Limited	Mixed
Bear call spread	S1-LC BI-HC	Moderately bearish	Limited	Limited	Mixed
Long straddle	B1-ATM-C B1-ATM-P	Volatile	Unlimited	Limited	Detrimental
Long strangle	B1-OTM-C B1-OTM-P	Volatile	Unlimited	Limited	Detrimental

(Continued)

511

TABLE C.1 *(Continued)*

Strategy	Trade	Market Outlook	Profit Potential	Risk Potential	Time Decay Effects
Long synthetic straddle with puts	B100-U B2-ATM-P	Volatile	Unlimited	Limited	Detrimental
Long synthetic straddle with calls	S100-U B2-ATM-C	Volatile	Unlimited	Limited	Detrimental
Ratio call spread	B1-LC S2-HC	Bearish/ stable	Limited	Unlimited	Mixed
Ratio put spread	B1-HP S2-LP	Bullish/ stable	Limited	Limited	Mixed
Call ratio backspread	S1-LC B2-HC	Very bullish	Unlimited	Limited	Mixed
Put ratio backspread	S1-HP B2-LP	Very bearish	Limited	Limited	Mixed
Long butterfly	B1-LC/P S2-HC/P B1-HP/P	Stable	Limited	Limited	Helpful
Long condor	B1-LC/P S1-HC/P S1-HC/P B1-HC/P	Stable	Limited	Limited	Helpful
Long iron butterfly	S1-ATM-C B1-OTM-C S1-ATM-P B1-OTM-P	Stable	Limited	Limited	Helpful
Calendar spread	B1-LT-C/P S1-ST-C/P Same Strikes	Stable	Limited	Limited	Helpful
Diagonal spread	B1-LT-C/P S1-ST-C/P Different Strikes	Stable	Limited	Limited	Helpful
Collar spread	B100-U B1-ATM-P S1-OTM-C	Volatile	Limited	Limited	Helpful

B = Buy/S = Sell	P = Put option	ATM = At-the-money
1 = 1 Contract	HC = Higher strike call	OTM = Out-of-the-money
100 = 100 shares	LC = Lower strike call	ITM = In-the-money
U = Underlying stock	HP = Higher strike put	LT = Long-term
C = Call option	LP = Lower strike put	ST = Short-term

DETAILED STRATEGY REVIEWS

Long Stock

Strategy: Buy shares of stock.

Market Opportunity: Look for a bullish market where a rise in the price of the stock is anticipated.

Maximum Risk: Limited to the price of the stock as it falls to zero.

Maximum Profit: Unlimited as the stock price rises above the initial entry price.

Breakeven: Price of the stock at initiation.

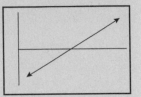

FIGURE C.1 Long Stock

Short Stock

Strategy: Sell shares of stock.

Market Opportunity: Look for a bearish market where a fall in the price of the stock is anticipated.

Maximum Risk: Unlimited as the stock price rises.

Maximum Profit: Limited to the full price of the stock shares as they fall to zero.

Breakeven: Price of the stock at initiation.

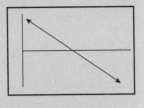

FIGURE C.2 Short Stock

Long Call

Strategy: Buy a call option.

Market Opportunity: Look for a bullish market where a rise above the breakeven is anticipated.

Maximum Risk: Limited to the amount paid for the call.

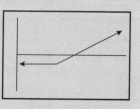

Maximum Profit: Unlimited as the price of the underlying instrument rises above the breakeven.

FIGURE C.3   Long Call

Breakeven: Call strike + call premium.

Short Call

Strategy: Sell a call option.

Market Opportunity: Look for a bearish or stable market where you anticipate a fall in the price of the underlying below the breakeven.

Maximum Risk: Unlimited as the stock price rises above the breakeven.

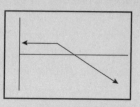

Maximum Profit: Limited to the credit received from the call option premium.

FIGURE C.4   Short Call

Breakeven: Call strike + call premium.

Long Put

Strategy: Buy a put option.

Market Opportunity: Look for a bearish market where you anticipate a fall in the price of the underlying below the breakeven.

Maximum Risk: Limited to the price paid for the put premium.

Maximum Profit: Limited as the stock price falls below the breakeven to zero.

Breakeven: Put strike – put premium.

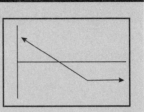

FIGURE C.5 Long Put

Short Put

Strategy: Sell a put option.

Market Opportunity: Look for a bullish or stable market where a rise above the breakeven is anticipated.

Maximum Risk: Limited as the stock price falls below the breakeven until reaching a price of zero.

Maximum Profit: Limited to the credit received from the put premium.

Breakeven: Put strike – put premium.

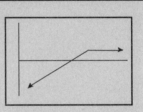

FIGURE C.6 Short Put

Covered Call

Strategy: Buy the underlying security and sell an OTM call option.

Market Opportunity: Look for a slightly bullish to neutral market where a slow rise in the price of the underlying is anticipated with little risk of decline.

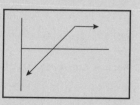

FIGURE C.7 Covered Call

Maximum Risk: Limited below the downside breakeven as it falls to zero.

Maximum Profit: Limited. [Short call premium + (short call strike – price of long underlying asset) × 100].

Breakeven: Price of the underlying at initiation – short call premium.

Covered Put

Strategy: Sell the underlying security and sell an OTM put option.

Market Opportunity: Look for a slightly bearish or stable market where a decline or stability in the price of the underlying is anticipated with little risk of the market rising.

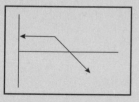

FIGURE C.8 Covered Put

Maximum Risk: Unlimited above the upside breakeven.

Maximum Profit: Limited. [Short put premium + (price of underlying asset at initiation – put option strike) × 100].

Breakeven: Price of the underlying at trade initiation + short put premium.

Bull Call Spread

Strategy: Buy a lower strike call and sell a higher strike call with the same expiration dates.

Market Opportunity: Look for a bullish market where you anticipate a modest increase in the price of the underlying above the price of the short call option.

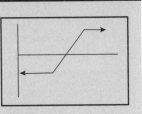

FIGURE C.9 Bull Call Spread

Maximum Risk: Limited to the net debit paid for the spread.

Maximum Profit: Limited. [(Difference in strikes – net debit) × 100].

Breakeven: Lower (long) call strike price + net debit.

Bear Put Spread

Strategy: Buy a higher strike put and sell a lower strike put with the same expiration date.

Market Opportunity: Look for a bearish market where you anticipate a modest decrease in the price of the underlying asset below the strike price of the short put option.

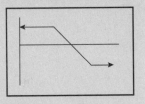

FIGURE C.10 Bear Put Spread

Maximum Risk: Limited to the net debit paid.

Maximum Profit: Limited. [(Difference in strikes – net debit) × 100].

Breakeven: Higher (long) strike – net debit.

Bull Put Spread

Strategy: Buy a lower strike put and sell a higher strike put with the same expiration date.

Market Opportunity: Look for a bullish market where you anticipate an increase in the price of the underlying asset above the strike price of the short put option.

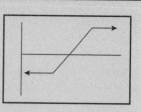

FIGURE C.11 Bull Put Spread

Maximum Risk: Limited. [(Difference in strikes – net credit) × 100].

Maximum Profit: Limited to the net credit received when the market closes above the strike price of the short put option.

Breakeven: Higher (short) strike – net credit.

Bear Call Spread

Strategy: Buy a higher strike call and sell a lower strike call with the same expiration date.

Market Opportunity: Look for a bearish market where you anticipate a decrease in the price of the underlying asset below the strike price of the short call option.

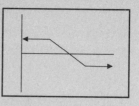

FIGURE C.12 Bear Call Spread

Maximum Risk: Limited. [(Difference in strikes – net credit) × 100].

Maximum Profit: Limited to the net credit.

Breakeven: Lower (short) strike price + net credit.

Long Straddle

Strategy: Purchase an ATM call and an ATM put with the same strike price and the same expiration date.

Market Opportunity: Look for a market with low implied volatility options where a sharp volatility increase is anticipated.

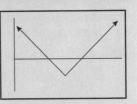

Maximum Risk: Limited to the net debit.

FIGURE C.13 Long Straddle

Maximum Profit: Unlimited to the upside and limited to the downside (as the underlying can only fall to zero). Profit requires sufficient market movement but does not depend on market direction.

Upside Breakeven: ATM strike price + net debit.

Downside Breakeven: ATM strike price − net debit.

Short Straddle

Strategy: Sell an ATM call and an ATM put with the same strike price and the same expiration date.

Market Opportunity: Look for a wildly volatile market where you anticipate a period of low volatility.

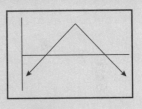

Maximum Risk: Unlimited to the upside and limited to the downside (as the underlying can only fall to zero) beyond the breakevens.

FIGURE C.14 Short Straddle

Maximum Profit: Limited to the net credit. Profit is possible if the market stays between the breakevens.

Upside Breakeven: ATM strike price + net credit.

Downside Breakeven: ATM strike price − net credit.

Long Strangle

Strategy: Buy an OTM call and an OTM put with the same expiration date.

Market Opportunity: Look for a stable market where you anticipate a large volatility spike.

Maximum Risk: Limited to the net debit paid.

Maximum Profit: Unlimited to the upside and limited to the downside (as the underlying can only fall to zero).

Upside Breakeven: Call strike price + net debit.

Downside Breakeven: Put strike price – net debit.

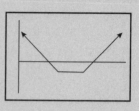

FIGURE C.15 Long Strangle

Short Strangle

Strategy: Sell an OTM call and an OTM put with the same expiration date.

Market Opportunity: Look for a wildly volatile market where you anticipate a drop-off into a very stable market with low volatility.

Maximum Risk: Unlimited to the upside and limited to the downside (as the underlying can only fall to zero).

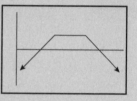

FIGURE C.16 Short Strangle

Maximum Profit: Limited to the net credit. Profit occurs when the underlying trades between the breakevens.

Upside Breakeven: Call strike price + net credit.

Downside Breakeven: Put strike price – net credit.

Long Synthetic Straddle

Market Opportunity: Look for a market with low volatility where you anticipate a volatility increase resulting in stock price movement in either direction beyond the breakevens.

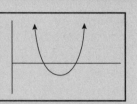

FIGURE C.17 Long Synthetic Straddle

Long Stock and Long Puts

Strategy: Buy 100 shares of underlying stock and buy 2 long ATM puts.

Maximum Risk: Net debit of options + [(Price of underlying stock at initiation – option strike price) × number of shares].

Maximum Profit: Unlimited above the upside breakeven and limited as the underlying falls to zero below the downside breakeven.

Upside Breakeven: Price of the underlying at initiation + net debit of options.

Downside Breakeven: [(2 × option strike) – price of the underlying at initiation] – net debit of options.

Short Stock and Long Calls

Strategy: Sell 100 shares of underlying stock and buy 2 long ATM calls.

Maximum Risk: [Net debit of options + (option strike price – price of underlying at initiation)] × number of shares.

Maximum Profit: Unlimited above the upside breakeven and limited as the underlying falls to zero below downside breakeven.

Upside Breakeven: [(2 × option strike) – price of the underlying at initiation] + net debit of options.

Downside Breakeven: Price of the underlying at initiation – net debit of options.

Ratio Call Spread

Strategy: Buy a lower strike call and sell a greater number of higher strike calls.

Market Opportunity: Look for a volatile market where you expect a slight decline or a small rise not to exceed the strike price of the short options.

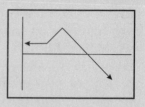

Maximum Risk: Unlimited above the upside breakeven.

FIGURE C.18 Ratio Call Spread

Maximum Profit: Limited. [Number of long contracts × (difference in strike prices × 100) + net credit (or – net debit)].

Upside Breakeven: Lower strike + [(difference in strikes × number of short contracts) ÷ (number of short calls – number of long calls)] + net credit (or – net debit).

Ratio Put Spread

Strategy: Buy a higher strike put and sell a greater number of lower strike puts.

Market Opportunity: Look for a market where you expect a rise or slight fall not to exceed the strike price of the short options.

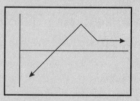

Maximum Risk: Limited to the downside below the downside breakeven (as the stock can only fall to zero). Lower strike – (difference in strikes × 100) – net credit (or + net debit).

FIGURE C.19 Ratio Put Spread

Maximum Profit: Limited. (Difference in strike prices × 100) + net credit (or – net debit).

Downside Breakeven: Higher strike – [(difference in strike prices × number of short puts) ÷ (number of short puts – number of long puts)] – net credit (or + net debit).

Call Ratio Backspread

Strategy: Sell lower strike calls and buy a greater number of higher strike calls (the ratio must be less than .67).

Market Opportunity: Look for a market where you anticipate a sharp rise with increasing volatility; place as a credit or at even.

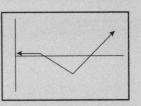

Maximum Risk: Limited. [(Number of short calls × difference in strikes) × 100] – net credit (or + net debit).

FIGURE C.20 Call Ratio Backspread

Maximum Profit: Unlimited to the upside above the upside breakeven.

Upside Breakeven: Higher strike + [(difference in strikes × number of short calls) ÷ (number of long calls – number of short calls)] – net credit (or + net debit).

Downside Breakeven: Lower strike + (net credit ÷ number of short calls). No downside breakeven exists if the trade is entered with a net debit.

Put Ratio Backspread

Strategy: Sell higher strike puts and buy a greater number of lower strike puts (the ratio must be less than .67).

Market Opportunity: Look for a market where you anticipate a sharp decline with increased volatility; place as a credit or at even.

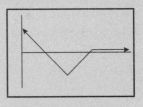

Maximum Risk: Limited. [(Number of short puts × difference in strikes) × 100] – net credit (or + net debit).

FIGURE C.21 Put Ratio Backspread

Maximum Profit: Limited to the downside (as the underlying can only fall to zero) below the breakeven.

Upside Breakeven: Higher strike – (net credit ÷ number of short puts). No upside breakeven exists if the trade is entered with a new debit.

Downside Breakeven: Lower strike – [(number of short puts × difference in strikes) ÷ (number of long puts – number of short puts)] + net credit (or – net debit).

Long Butterfly

Strategy: Buy lower strike option, sell 2 higher strike options, and buy a higher strike option with the same expiration date (all calls or all puts).

Market Opportunity: Look for a range-bound market that is expected to stay between the breakeven points.

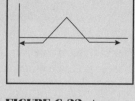

FIGURE C.22 Long Butterfly Spread

Maximum Risk: Limited to the net debit paid.

Maximum Profit: Limited. (Difference between strikes − net debit) × 100. Profit exists between breakevens.

Upside Breakeven: Highest strike − net debit.

Downside Breakeven: Lowest strike + net debit.

Long Condor

Strategy: Buy lower strike option, sell higher strike option, sell an even higher strike option, and buy an even higher strike option with the same expiration date (all calls or all puts).

Market Opportunity: Look for a range-bound market that is expected to stay between the breakeven points.

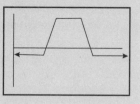

FIGURE C.23 Long Condor Spread

Maximum Risk: Limited to the net debit paid.

Maximum Profit: Limited. (Difference between strikes − net debit) × 100. Profit exists between breakevens.

Upside Breakeven: Highest strike − net debit.

Downside Breakeven: Lowest strike + net debit.

Long Iron Butterfly

Strategy: Buy a higher strike call, sell a lower strike call, sell a higher strike put, and buy a lower strike put with the same expiration date.

Market Opportunity: Look for a range-bound market that you anticipate to stay between the breakeven points.

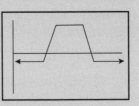

FIGURE C.24 Long Iron Butterfly Spread

Maximum Risk: Limited. (Difference between strikes × 100) – net credit.

Maximum Profit: Limited to the net credit received. Profit occurs between the breakevens.

Upside Breakeven: Strike price of middle short call + net credit.

Downside Breakeven: Strike price of middle short put – net credit.

Calendar Spread

Strategy: Sell a short-term option and buy a long-term option using at-the-money options with as small a net debit as possible (use all calls or all puts). Calls can be used for a more bullish bias and puts can be used for a more bearish bias.

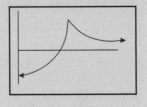

FIGURE C.25 Calendar Spread

Market Opportunity: Look for a range-bound market that is expected to stay between the breakeven points for an extended period of time.

Maximum Risk: Limited to the net debit paid.

Maximum Profit: Limited. Use software for accurate calculation.

Breakeven: Use options analysis software for accurate calculation.

Diagonal Spread

Strategy: Sell a short-term option and buy a long-term option with different strikes and as small a net debit as possible (use all calls or all puts).

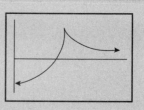

- A **bullish diagonal spread** employs a long call with a distant expiration and a lower strike price, along with a short call with a closer expiration date and higher strike price.

FIGURE C.26 Diagonal Spread

- A **bearish diagonal spread** combines a long put with a distant expiration date and a higher strike price along with a short put with a closer expiration date and lower strike price.

Market Opportunity: Look for a range-bound market that is expected to stay between the breakeven points for an extended period of time.

Maximum Risk: Limited to the net debit paid.

Maximum Profit: Limited. Use software for accurate calculation.

Breakevens: Use options analysis software for accurate calculation.

Collar Spread

Strategy: Buy (or already own) 100 shares of stock, buy an ATM put, and sell an OTM call. Try to offset the cost of the put with the premium from the short call.

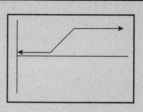

Market Opportunity: Protect a stock holding from a sharp drop for a specific period of time and still participate in a modest increase in the stock price.

FIGURE C.27 Collar Spread

Maximum Risk: Initial stock price – put strike + net debit (or – net credit).

Maximum Profit: (Call strike – initial stock price) – net debit (or + net credit).

Breakeven: Initial stock price + [(put premium – call premium) ÷ number of shares].

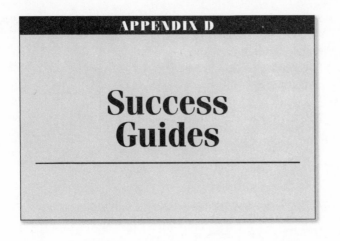

Success Guides

FIVE MINUTE SUCCESS FORMULA: A QUICK METHOD FOR FINDING PROMISING TRADES

1. *Look for stocks that are up (+) or down (–) at least 30 percent in value for the day.*

   • You are looking for good momentum trades (where fear and greed are really driving the market).

2. *From these, choose those with volume greater than 300,000 shares for the day.*

   • Greater than 1 million shares a day is better; 10 million is best.

   • Look for volume spikes (market moves generally begin or end on volume spikes).

   • Call your broker twice a day to check on potential movers (call a half hour after the market opens and 15 minutes prior to market close).

3. *Try to find out/ask your broker why each of these stocks is moving.*

   • Usually movement is based on really good news or really bad news, including:

      • Earnings releases.
      • Earnings upgrades/downgrades.
      • New product announcements.

- New agency approvals.
- Stock splits.
- Merger announcements.
- Friendly or hostile takeovers.
- Litigation.
- Accounting irregularities.
- No news (can mean insider buying/selling).

- Good reasons can indicate big moves.

- Takeovers that are done deals produce little movement and are generally not good plays.

4. Determine which of these stocks has options.

- Forget those stocks that don't have any options.

- Consider only those stocks that have liquid options available.

- If none exist, try again tomorrow.

5. Choose a low cost/low risk strategy.

- A good goal is to find trades that cost less than $100 for each position.

- Cheapest play for an up move? Buy calls, bull call spreads, or call ratio backspreads.

- Cheapest play for an down move? Buy puts, bear put spreads, or put ratio backspreads.

- Cheapest play for a neutral move? Straddles, strangles, or long synthetic straddles.

- Calculate the maximum risk, maximum reward, and upside and downside breakevens for each possible position to find the trade with the best probability of profitability.

6. Find out/ask your broker how many block trades (institutional trades of more than 5,000 shares in size) have traded in these stocks.

- Choose only those stocks that have 10 or more block trades on a volume of greater than 300,000 shares for the day.

7. Find out/ask your broker how many blocks are trading on the upticks or downticks (i.e., how many institutions are buying or selling).

- Blocks trading on upticks—stock is moving higher.
- Blocks trading on downticks—stock is moving lower.

8. Select your entry strategy.

- Put the trade on in the last 15 minutes before the market closes (provides the best fills and prices).

- Buy options with at least 90 days till expiration (six months or more is even better).

- Consider multiple positions so that you can eventually create a free trade.

- If you miss the first big move, try to position yourself for the rebound (wait for one "ugly" day, one reversal from the top or bottom, and then place the trade).

9. Select your exit strategy.

- *General Rule:* You should exit the trade 30 days prior to expiration, unless the profit on the trade depends on a short option expiring OTM.

- If you hold multiple positions, sell off half when they double in value to produce a free trade. Ride the free trade to maximize profits.

- In an up move, if the stock breaks 20 percent in price from a new high, then close out the position.

- In a down move, if the stock breaks 20 percent in price from a new low, then close out the position.

RULES FOR TRADING SUCCESS

1. Use a reliable and knowledgeable broker who offers a balance between low commission rates and fast and accurate fills.

2. Research all aspects of a trade using your favorite techniques—fundamental and technical analysis—as well as sentiment and broad market analysis, and scheduled and breaking news.

3. Know what you are trying to do: Define your goals. Select your time frame and availability. Create a risk graph for your position.

4. Look for trades with a reward/risk ratio that is greater than 2 to 1.

5. Buy low volatility and sell high volatility.

6. Do not leg into or out of a spread. Place all sides of the trade at the same time as a single order

7. Write down all orders and read them to your broker to make sure you call your orders in correctly.

8. To get the price you want, the best time to place your order is at the end of the day about 15 minutes before the close.

9. Risk no more than 5 percent of your trading account on any one trade.

10. Risk no more than 50 percent of your total trading account at any one time.

11. Keep a record of all your trades and review them periodically.

12. Review all your trades every six months, especially the ones you lost money on; identify bad trading habits/patterns, and try not to repeat them!

TABLE D.1 Market Acronyms

AAF—asset allocation fund	CD—certificate of deposit
AAGR—average annual growth rate	CEO—chief executive officer
AAR—average annual return	CFA—chartered financial analyst
ABS—automated bond system	CFO—chief financial officer
AD Line—advance/decline line	CFP—certified financial planner
ADR—American Depositary Receipt	CFPS—cash flow per share
ADX—Average Directional Movement Index	CFTC—Commodity Futures Trading Commission
AGI—adjusted gross income	COGS—cost of goods sold
AMEX—American Stock Exchange	COO—chief operating officer
AMT—Alternative Minimum Tax	CPA—certified public accountant
AON—all or none	CPI—consumer price index
APR—annual percentage rate	CPM—cost per thousand
APV—adjusted present value	CSI—Commodity Selection Index
APY—annual percentage yield	CUSIP—Committee on Uniform Securities Identification Procedures
AR—accounts receivable	
ARM—adjustable rate mortgage	DAT—direct-access trading
ASX—Australian Stock Exchange	DD—due diligence
ATM—at-the-money	DI—disposable income
ATP—arbitrage trading program	DJIA—Dow Jones Industrial Average
ATR—average true range	DJTA—Dow Jones Transportation Average
BIC—bank investment contract	DJUA—Dow Jones Utility Average
BIS—Bank for International Settlements	DMI—Directional Movement Index
BOP—balance of payments	DPSP—deferred profit sharing plan
BOT—balance of trade	DRIP—dividend reinvestment plan
BP—basis point	EAFE—European, Australasian, Far East Equity Index
CAPEX—capital expenditure	
CAPM—capital asset pricing model	EBIT—earnings before interest and taxes
CAPS—convertible adjustable preferred stock	EBITDA—earnings before interest, taxes, depreciation, and amortization
CBOE—Chicago Board Options Exchange	ECN—electronic communication network
CBOT—Chicago Board of Trade	EDGAR—Electronic Data Gathering Analysis and Retrieval
CCE—cash and cash equivalents	
CCI—Commodity Channel Index	EMA—exponential moving average

TABLE D.1 *(Continued)*

EPS—earnings per share
ERISA—Employee Retirement Income
 Security Act
ESO—employee stock option
ETF—exchange-traded fund
FAD—funds available for distribution
FASB—Financial Accounting Standards
 Board
FDIC—Federal Deposit Insurance
 Corporation
FFO—funds from operations
FIFO—first in, first out
FHLMC—Federal Home Loan Mortgage
 Corporation (Freddie Mac)
FNMA—Federal National Mortgage
 Association (Fannie Mae)
FOMC—Federal Open Market Committee
FRA—forward-rate agreement
FRB—Federal Reserve Board
FRS—Federal Reserve System
GAAP—generally accepted accounting
 principles
GARP—growth at a reasonable price
GDP—gross domestic product
GIC—guaranteed investment certificate
GNMA—Government National Mortgage
 Association (Ginnie Mae)
GO—general obligation bond
GSE—government-sponsored enterprise
GTC—good till canceled order
HOLDRS—Holding Company Depositary
 Receipts
HTML—hypertext markup language
IFCI—International Finance Corporation
 Investable Index
IPO—initial public offering
IRA—individual retirement account
IRR—internal rate of return
ISO—International Organization for
 Standardization
ITM—in-the-money
IV—implied volatility
JSE—Johannesburg Stock Exchange
KCBT—Kansas City Board of Trade
LBO—leveraged buyout
LEAPS—long-term equity anticipation
 securities
LIFO—last in, first out

LLC—limited liability company
LP—limited partnership
MA—moving average
MACD—moving average
convergence/divergence
MEM—maximum entropy method
MER—management expense ratio
MIPS—Monthly Income Preferred
 Securities
MIT—market if touched
MPT—modern portfolio theory
MSCI—Morgan Stanley Capital
 International
NASD—National Association of Securities
 Dealers
NASDAQ—National Association of
 Securities Dealers Automated
 Quotations
NAV—net asset value
NMS—normal market size
NOI—net operating income
NPV—net present value
NSO—nonqualified stock options
NYSE—New York Stock Exchange
OBV—on-balance volume
OI—open interest
OID—original issue discount
OPEC—Organization of Petroleum
 Exporting Countries
OTC—over-the-counter
OTM—out-of-the-money
PDF—portable document format
P/E—price-earnings ratio
PEG—price/earnings to growth
POP—public offering price
PPI—producer price index
QQQ—ticker symbol for Nasdaq 100
 Trust
R&D—research and development
REIT—real estate investment trust
RIC—return on invested capital
ROA—return on assets
ROE—return on equity
ROI—return on investment
RPI—Retail Price Index
RSI—Relative Strength Index
SAI—Statement of Additional Information
SAR—stop and reverse

(continues)

TABLE D.1 *(Continued)*	
SEC—Securities and Exchange Commission	SV—statistical volatility
SEMI—Semiconductor Equipment and Materials International	SWIFT—Society for Worldwide Interbank Financial Telecommunication
SEP—simplified employee pension	TPO—time price opportunity
SIC—Standard Industrial Classification	TRIN—trading Index
SIPC—Securities Investor Protection Corporation	TSE—Toronto Stock Exchange
SMA—simple moving average	UN—United Nations
SOES—small order execution system	VIX—CBOE Market Volatility Index
SOX—Philadelphia Semiconductor Index	VPT—volume price trend
S&P—Standard & Poor's	VXN—Nasdaq Volatility Index
SPDRs—Standard & Poor's Depositary Receipts (ETF)	WSE—Winnipeg Commodity Exchange
SSR—sum of squared residuals	XD—ex-dividend
	XR—ex-rights
	XY—ex-warrants
	YTD—year-to-date
	YTM—yield to maturity

Glossary

ABC wave Elliott wave terminology for a three-wave countertrend price movement. Wave A is the first price wave against the trend of the market. Wave B is a corrective wave to Wave A. Wave C is the final price move to complete the countertrend price action.

adjustment The process of buying or selling instruments to bring a position delta back to zero and increase profits.

All Ordinaries Index The major index of Australian stocks. This index represents 280 of the most active listed companies or the majority of the equity capitalization (excluding foreign companies) listed on the Australian Stock Exchange (ASX).

American Stock Exchange (AMEX) A private, not-for-profit corporation, located in New York City, that handles approximately one-fifth of all securities trades within the United States.

American-style option An option contract that can be exercised at any time between the date of purchase and the expiration date. Most exchange-traded options are American-style.

amortization The paying off of debt in regular installments over a period of time.

analyst Employee of a brokerage or fund management house who studies companies and makes buy and sell recommendations on their stocks. Most specialize in a specific industry.

annual earnings change (percent) The historical earnings change between the most recently reported fiscal year earnings and the preceding year earnings.

annual net profit margin (percent) The percentage that the company earned from gross sales for the most recently reported fiscal year.

annual percentage rate (APR) The cost of credit that the consumer pays, expressed as a simple annual percentage.

annual rate of return The simple rate of return earned by an investor for each year.

annual report   A report issued by a company to its shareholders at the end of the fiscal year, containing a description of the firm's operations and financial statements.

annuity   A series of constant payments at uniform time intervals (for example, periodic interest payments on a bond).

appreciation   The increase in value of an asset.

arbitrage   The simultaneous purchase and sale of identical financial instruments or commodity futures in order to make a profit, where the selling price is higher than the buying price.

arbitrageur   An individual or company who takes advantage of momentary disparities in prices between markets to lock in profits because the selling price is higher than the buying price.

ascending triangle   A sideways price pattern with two converging trend lines; the top trend line is relatively flat (resistance), while the bottom trend line (support) is rising. This is generally considered a bullish formation, since most of the time it will break out to the upside.

ask   The lowest price of a specific market that market makers, floor brokers, or specialists are willing to sell at.

assignment   When the short option position is notified of the long position's intent to exercise. The long position exercises and the short position is assigned. The long position has the right to exercise; if the trader chooses to exercise, the short position must oblige.

at-the-money (ATM)   When the strike price of an option is the same as the current price of the underlying instrument.

at-the-opening order   An order that specifies execution at the opening of the market or else it is canceled.

auction market   A market in which buyers enter competitive bids and sellers enter competitive offers simultaneously. Most stock and bond markets, including those on the NYSE, function this way.

automatic exercise   The automatic exercise of an in-the-money option at expiration by the clearing firm.

Average Directional Index (ADX)   Developed by Welles Wilder, the ADX indicates the degree in which a security is trending. It is a normalized index that uses the components of the Directional Movement Indicator (DMI). It is typically calculated for a 14-period time frame and does not usually move into extreme ranges. The ADX indicates a trending market when the indicator is rising and a nontrending market when the indicator is falling. Standard use of the ADX includes the following: an ADX line rising above 20, signals a trending market, while an ADX line falling below 40, signals the start of a nontrending environment.

back months   The futures or options on futures months being traded that are furthest from expiration.

backspread   A spread in which more options are purchased than sold and where all options have the same underlying asset and expiration date. Backspreads are usually delta neutral.

back-testing   The testing of a strategy based on historical data to see if the results are consistent.

balance sheet   A financial statement providing an instant picture of a firm's or individual's financial position; lists assets, liabilities, and net worth.

bar chart   A chart composed of a vertical bar in the center that shows the price range for the period, as well as a horizontal hash mark that identifies the opening price. By reviewing the chart alone, a trader can determine the high and low trades for the time period designated on the chart.

bear   An investor who believes that a security or the market is falling or is expected to fall.

bear call spread   A strategy in which a trader sells a lower strike call and buys a higher strike call to create a trade with limited profit and limited risk. A fall in the price of the underlying asset increases the value of the spread. Net credit transaction; maximum loss = difference between the strike prices less net credit; maximum gain = net credit.

bear market   A declining stock market over a prolonged period of time, usually caused by a weak economy and subsequent decreased corporate profits.

bear put spread   A strategy in which a trader sells a lower strike put and buys a higher strike put to create a trade with limited profit and limited risk. A fall in the price of the underlying asset increases the value of the spread. Net debit transaction; maximum gain = difference between strike prices less the net debit; maximum loss = net debit.

bid   The highest price at which a floor broker, trader, or dealer is willing to buy a security or commodity for a specified time.

bid and asked   The bid (the highest price a buyer is prepared to pay for a trading asset) and the asked (the lowest price acceptable to a prospective seller of the same security) together comprise a quotation or quote.

bid-asked spread   The difference between bid and asked prices.

bid up   When demand for an asset drives up the price paid by buyers.

block trade   A trade so large (for example, 5,000 shares of stock or $200,000 worth of bonds) that the normal auction market cannot absorb it in a reasonable time at a reasonable price.

blow-off top   A steep and rapid increase in price followed by a steep and rapid drop in price. This indicator is often used in technical analysis.

blue-chip stock   A stock with solid value, good security, and a record of dividend payments or other desirable investment characteristics with the best market capitalization in the marketplace. Many times these stocks have a record of consistent dividend payments, receive extensive media coverage, and offer a host of other beneficial investment attributes. This term is derived from poker, where blue chips hold the most value. On the downside, blue-chip stocks tend to be quite expensive and often have little room for growth.

board lot   The smallest quantity of shares traded on an exchange at standard commission rates.

Bollinger bands   Specific types of envelopes that use expanding and contracting values employed as a lagging indicator. This is accomplished by setting the envelope lines above and below the moving average equal to a value that varies with price. Commonly used settings for Bollinger bands include the 20-period exponential moving average, plus or minus two standard deviations, to create the envelope channels.

bond   Financial instruments representing debt obligations issued by the government or corporations traded in the futures market. A bond promises to pay its holders periodic interest at a fixed rate (the coupon), and to repay the principal of the loan at maturity. Bonds are issued with a par or face value of $1,000 and are traded based on their interest rates—if the bond pays more interest than available elsewhere, its worth increases.

breakeven   (1) The point at which gains equal losses; (2) the market price that a stock or futures contract must reach for an option to avoid loss if exercised; for a call, the breakeven equals the strike price plus the premium paid; for a put, the breakeven equals the strike price minus the premium paid.

break out   A rise in the price of an underlying instrument above its resistance level or a drop below the support level.

broad-based index   An index designed to reflect the movement of the market as a whole (for example, the S&P 100, the S&P 500, and the Amex Major Market Index).

broker   An individual or firm that charges a commission for executing buy and sell orders.

bull   An investor who believes that a market is rising or is expected to rise.

bull call spread   A strategy in which a trader buys a lower strike call and sells a higher strike call to create a trade with limited profit and limited risk. A rise in the price of the underlying asset increases the value of the spread. Net debit transaction; maximum loss = net debit; maximum gain = difference between strike prices less the net debit.

bull market   A rising stock market over a prolonged period of time, usually caused by a strong economy and subsequent increased corporate profits.

bull put spread   A strategy in which a trader sells a higher strike put and buys a lower strike put to create a trade with limited profit and limited risk. A rise in the price of the underlying asset increases the value of the spread. Net credit transaction; maximum loss = difference between strike prices less net credit; maximum gain = net credit.

butterfly spread   The sale (or purchase) of two identical options, together with the purchase (or sale) of one option with an immediately higher strike, and one option with an immediately lower strike. All options must be the same type, have the same underlying asset, and have the same expiration date.

buy on close   To buy at the end of a trading session at a price within the closing range.

buy on opening   To buy at the beginning of a trading session at a price within the opening range.

buy stop order   An order to purchase a security entered at a price above the current offering price, triggered when the market hits a specified price.

CAC 40 Index   A broad-based index of 40 common stocks on the Paris Bourse.

calendar spread   A spread consisting of one long option with a far off expiration month and one short option with 30 to 45 days until expiration. Both options must be the same type and have the same exercise price.

call option   An option contract which gives the holder the right, but not the obligation, to buy a specified amount of an underlying security at a specified price within a specified time in exchange for paying a premium.

call premium   The amount a call option costs.

candlestick chart   Chart that includes the price range for the day, as well as the opening and closing price. A candlestick bar includes a "body" bounded by the open and close for the period and "shadows" which extend above and below the body to the high and low prices for the period. When the "body" of the candlestick is dark (or red in color charts), the closing price was below the opening. When the body of the candlestick is white (or green in color charts), the closing price was higher than the opening.

cancel (CXL) order   An order is used to eliminate a prior order that has not yet been executed. A canceled order must be communicated by a trader to the broker and such an order is not executed or confirmed until the floor broker reports back that the trader is out of the trade. Understand that once an order has been filled, it cannot be canceled, so a CXL order is really only a *request* to cancel. Therefore, you should not assume an order has been canceled just because you enter a request to do so—wait for the confirmation.

capital   The amount of money an individual or business has available.

capital gain   The profit realized when a capital asset is sold for a higher price than the purchase price.

capitalization   Refers to the current value of a corporation's outstanding shares in dollars.

capital loss   The loss incurred when a capital asset is sold for a lower price than the purchase price.

capped-style option   An option with an established profit cap or cap price.

cash account   An account in which the customer is required to pay in full for all purchased securities.

cash dividend   A dividend paid in cash to a shareholder out of a corporation's profits.

change   The difference between the current price of a security and the price of the previous day.

Chicago Board of Trade (CBOT)   Established in 1886, the CBOT is the oldest commodity exchange in the United States and primarily lists grains, Treasury-bonds and notes, metals, and indexes.

Chicago Board Options Exchange (CBOE)   The largest options exchange in the United States.

churning   When a registered representative performs excessive trading in a customer's account to increase commissions. This is deemed illegal by the SEC and exchange rules, since the registered representative is not seeking improved returns and does not have the customer's interests in mind.

class of options   Option contracts of the same type (call or put), style, and underlying security.

clearinghouse   An institution established separately from the exchanges to ensure timely payment and delivery of securities.

close   The price of the last transaction for a particular security each day.

closing purchase   A transaction to eliminate a short position.

closing range   The high and low prices recorded during the period designated as the official close.

closing sale   A transaction to eliminate a long position.

commission   A service charge assessed by a broker and his/her investment company in return for arranging the purchase or sale of a security.

commodity   Any bulk good traded on an exchange (for example, metals, grains, and meats).

Commodity Futures Trading Commission (CFTC)   A commission created by the Commodity Futures Trading Commission Act of 1974 to ensure the open and efficient operation of the futures markets.

condor The sale or purchase of two options with consecutive exercise prices, together with the sale or purchase of one option with an immediately lower exercise price and one option with an immediately higher exercise price.

consolidation pattern A resting period where the price action is in equilibrium. Typically, price action narrows and the volume drops off while investors and traders attempt to get a better sense of the next move, up or down. Visually, a consolidating market may resemble a triangle or a rectangle.

consumer price index (CPI) A measure of price changes in consumer goods and services. This index is used to identify periods of economic inflation or deflation.

contract A unit of trading for a financial or commodity future, or option.

contrarian approach Trading against the majority view of the marketplace.

correction A sudden decline in the price of a security or securities after a period of market strength.

covered call A short call option position against a long position in an underlying stock or future.

covered put A short put option position against a short position in an underlying stock or future.

cover the short To buy shares of stock to replenish those borrowed from your brokerage to place a short sale.

credit spread The difference in value between two options, where the value of the short position exceeds the value of the long position.

cross rate The current exchange rate between differing currencies.

cycle The tendency for price action to repeat uptrends and downtrends in a relatively predictable fashion over a prescribed period of time. Price cycles are measured low to low, high to high, or low to high. Various types of measurements are possible.

daily range The difference between the high and low price of a security in one trading day.

day order An order to buy or sell a security that expires if not filled by the end of the day.

day trade The purchase and sale of a position in the same day.

day trading An approach to trading in which the same position is entered and exited within one day.

debit spread The difference in value between two options, where the value of the long position exceeds the value of the short position.

deep in-the-money A deep in-the-money call option has a strike price well below the current price of the underlying instrument. A deep in-the-money put option has a strike price well above the current price of the underlying instrument. Both primarily consist of intrinsic value.

delayed-time quotes   Quotes from a data service provider that are delayed up to 20 minutes from real-time quotes.

delta   The amount by which the price (premium) of an option changes for every dollar move in the underlying instrument.

delta-hedged   An options strategy protecting an option against price changes in the option's underlying instrument by balancing the overall position delta to zero.

delta neutral   A position arranged by selecting a calculated ratio of short and long positions that balance out to an overall position delta of zero.

delta position   A measure of option or underlying securities delta.

derivative   Financial instruments based on the market value of an underlying asset.

descending triangle   A sideways price pattern with two converging trend lines; the top trend line is declining (resistance), while the bottom trend line is relatively flat (support). This is generally considered a bearish formation, since most of the time it will break out to the downside.

discount brokers   Brokerage firms that offer lower commission rates than full-service brokers, but do not offer services such as advice, research, and portfolio planning.

divergence   When two or more averages or indexes fail to show confirming trends.

dividend   A sum of money paid out to a shareholder from the stock's profits.

Dow Jones Industrial Average (DJIA)   Used as an overall indicator of market performance, this average is composed of 30 blue-chip stocks that are traded daily on the New York Stock Exchange.

downside   The potential for prices to decrease.

downside breakeven   The lower price at which a trade breaks even.

downside risk   The potential risk one takes if prices decrease in directional trading.

each way   The commission made by a broker for the purchase and sale sides of a trade.

earnings   The net profit for a company after all expenses are deducted.

earnings per share (EPS)   The net profit for a company allocated on an individual share of stock basis.

Elliott wave theory   A technical tool based on R. N. Elliott's work in the 1930s. Elliott believed the charted price activity of a market is the graphical representation of mass psychology. In other words, the Elliott wave theory organizes the seemingly random flow of market price action into identifiable, predictable patterns based on the natural progression of crowd psychology. Elliott wave theory is based on the premise that markets will move in ratios and patterns that reflect human nature. The classic Elliott wave pattern consists of two different types of waves. The first consists of a five-wave sequence called an impulse wave and the second is a three-wave sequence called a corrective wave. Usually, but not always, the market will move in a corrective wave after a five-wave move in the other direction.

end of day   The close of the trading day when market prices settle.

EPS Rank   An *Investor's Business Daily* list of companies ranked from 0 to 100 by the strength of each company's earnings per share.

equilibrium   A price level in a sideways market equidistant from the resistance and support levels.

Eurodollars   Dollars deposited in foreign banks, with the futures contract reflecting the rates offered between U.S. banks and foreign banks.

European-style option   An option contract that can be exercised only on the expiration date.

exchange   The location where an asset, option, future, stock, or derivative is bought and sold.

exchange rate   The price at which one country's currency can be converted into another country's currency.

exercise   The process of implementing an option's right to buy or sell the underlying security.

exercise price   A price at which the stock or commodity underlying a call or put option can be purchased (call) or sold (put) over the specified period. (Same as **strike price**.)

expiration   The date and time after which an option may no longer be exercised.

expiration date   The last day on which an option may be exercised.

explosive   Refers to an opportunity that can yield large profits with usually a limited risk in a short amount of time.

extrinsic value   The price of an option less its intrinsic value. An out-of-the-money option's worth consists of nothing but extrinsic or time value. (Same as **time value**.)

fade   Refers to selling a rising price or buying a falling price.

failed rally   The inability of a market to sustain an upward move, often associated with a pattern that does not resolve itself in an expected upward direction. The most typical evidence of a failed rally is diminishing volume.

fair market value   The value of an asset under normal conditions.

fair value   The theoretical value of what an option should be worth, usually generated by an option pricing model such as the Black-Scholes.

fast market   A stock with so much volume that the order entry systems have difficulty processing all of the orders.

Federal Reserve System   The independent central bank that influences the supply of money and credit in the United States through its control of bank reserves.

Fibonacci series   A mathematical series used in the markets that is produced by adding two sequential numbers to arrive at the next number in the series. Starting with 1, the series is: 1, 1, 2, 3, 5, 8, 13, 21, 34, 55, 89, 144, 233, . . . This series represents common naturally occurring phenomena such as the reproduction rate of a pair of rabbits and decay relationships, among others.

fill   An executed order.

fill order   An order that must be filled or canceled immediately.

fill or kill   An order to buy or sell an exact number of units or none at all.

financial instruments   The term used for debt instruments.

fixed delta   A delta figure that does not change with the change in the underlying asset. A futures contract has a fixed delta of plus or minus 100.

flags   Relatively short-lived, sideways patterns that form after a sharp rise or decline in price. They represent a pause in the current move that occurs at the approximate midpoint. As a result, these formations have measuring implications. By definition, flags are continuation patterns. The flag resembles a rectangle that is slightly trending up or down (similar to a parallelogram). The slope's direction is often the opposite of the move prior to formation. These formations typically take one to three weeks to form, with volume diminishing into the pattern.

float   The number of shares available for public trading in the markets.

floor broker   An exchange member who is paid a fee for executing orders.

floor ticket   A summary of the information on an order ticket.

floor trader   An exchange member who executes orders from the floor of the exchange only for his or her own account.

front month   The first expiration month in a series of months.

fundamental analysis   An approach to trading research that aims to predict futures and stock price movements based on balance sheets, income statements, past records of earnings, sales, assets, management, products, and services.

futures contract   Agreement to buy or sell a set number of shares of a commodity or financial instruments in a designated future month at a price agreed on by the buyer and seller.

gamma   The degree by which the delta changes with respect to changes in the underlying instrument's price.

gap When the daily range is completely above or below the previous day's daily range.

going ahead Unethical brokerage activity whereby the broker trades first for his or her own account before filling the customer's order(s).

go long To buy securities, options, or futures.

good till canceled order (GTC) An order to buy or sell stock that is good until the trader cancels it.

go short To sell securities, options, or futures.

gross domestic product (GDP) The total value of goods and services produced in a country during one year. It includes consumption, government purchases, investments, and exports minus imports.

guts A strangle where the call and the put are in-the-money.

hammering the market The intense selling of stocks by speculators who think the market is about to drop because they believe prices are inflated.

head and shoulders (H&S) The head and shoulders pattern is probably one of the best-known, most reliable patterns. The pattern resembles the silhouette of a head with shrugged shoulders. Each outside peak, or shoulder, is about the same height, with the middle peak, or head, higher than both shoulders. All three peaks use the same support line (the neckline) and a specific volume pattern is seen when this reversal is valid. The pattern is not complete until there is a close below the neckline accompanied by increased volume. These reversals occur at market tops and are bearish. Price projections are possible with valid H&S patterns.

hedge Reducing the risk of loss on an outright directional move by taking a position through options or futures opposite to the current position held in the market.

high The highest price that was paid for a stock during a certain period.

high and low Refers to the high and low transaction prices that occur each trading day.

highflier A speculative high-priced stock that moves up and down sharply over a short period of time.

high-tech stock Stock of companies involved in high-technology industries, such as computers, biotechnology, robotics, electronics, and semiconductors.

historical volatility A measurement of how much a contract's price has fluctuated over a period of time in the past; usually calculated by taking a standard deviation of price changes over a time period.

holder One who purchases an option.

HOLDRS Stands for Holding Company Depositary Receipts, which are exchange-traded funds that hold baskets of stocks from specific industry groups. HOLDRS trade on the American Stock Exchange and can be bought or sold in lots of 100 shares. For example, investors can buy or sell Biotechnology HOLDRS

(BBH), Semiconductor HOLDRS (SMH), or Oil Service HOLDRS (OIH). In all, the American Stock Exchange offers trading in 17 different HOLDRS. Options are also available on these exchange-trade funds and can be used to profit from trends related to specific sectors or industry groups.

illiquid market   A market that has no volume; slippage is subsequently created due to lack of trading volume.

immediate/cancel order   An order that must be filled immediately or canceled.

income statement   A financial statement that shows a company's revenues and expenditures over a stated period (usually one quarter or year) resulting in either a profit or a loss.

index   A group of stocks that can be traded as one portfolio, such as the S&P 500. Broad-based indexes cover a wide range of industries and companies, and narrow-based indexes cover stocks in one industry or economic sector.

index options   Call options and put options on indexes of stocks are designed to reflect and fluctuate with market conditions. Index options allow investors to trade in a specific industry group or market without having to buy all the stocks individually.

inflation   Increases in the general price level of goods and services; it is commonly reported using the consumer price index as a measure. Inflation is one of the major risks to investors over the long term as savings may actually buy less in the future if they do not return an amount in excess of price increases.

inside information   Material information that has not been disseminated to, or is not readily available to, the general public.

institutional investor   A person or organization that trades securities in large enough share quantities or dollar amounts that it qualifies for preferential treatment and lower commissions. These entities are assumed to be more knowledgeable investors who are better able to protect themselves from risk.

interest rate   The charge for the privilege of borrowing money, usually expressed as an annual percentage rate.

interest rate–driven   Refers to a point in the business cycle when interest rates are declining and bond prices are rising.

intermarket analysis   Observing the price movement of one market for the purpose of evaluating a different market.

intermarket spread   A spread consisting of opposing positions in instruments with two different markets.

in-the-money (ITM)   When exercising an option would generate a profit at the time. A call option is in-the-money if the strike price is less than the market price of the underlying security. A put option is in-the-money if the strike price is greater than the market price of the underlying security.

intrinsic value The amount by which an option is in-the-money. Out-of-the-money options have no intrinsic value. Calls = underlying asset less strike price. Puts = strike price less underlying asset.

inverse relationship Two or more markets that act totally opposite to one another, producing negative correlations.

investment Any purchase of an asset to increase future income.

iron butterfly The combination of a long (or short) straddle and a short (or long) strangle. All options must have the same underlying asset and the same expiration.

lagging indicator A technical indicator can lead or follow price action. A lagging indicator will move in a bullish or bearish direction after the same bullish or bearish price move. The extent to which an indicator lags is dependent upon the "speed" of the indicator. Lagging indicators include moving averages, envelopes, and channels. Many economic indicators are also considered lagging indicators that follow the overall pace of the economy.

leading indicator Technical indicators can precede or lag price action. A leading indicator will move in a bullish or bearish direction prior to the same bullish or bearish price move. It is important to note that leading indicators can provide false signals; therefore, price confirmation is important. Leading indicators include volume and momentum, among other oscillators.

leg One side of a spread.

Level II quotes One of three levels of the National Association of Securities Dealers Automated Quotations System (Nasdaq). Level I quotes provide basic information such as the best bids and asks for Nasdaq-listed stocks. Level II data provides investors with more detailed quotes and information. Level II users have access to current bids and offers for all market makers in a given Nasdaq-listed stock. Level III is the most advanced level and is used by market makers to enter their own quotes to the system.

limit move The maximum daily price limit for an exchange-traded contract.

limit order An order to buy a stock at or below a specified price or to sell a stock at or above a specified price.

limit up, limit down Commodity exchange restrictions on the maximum upward or downward movements permitted in the price for a commodity during any trading session day.

line chart Line charts "connect the dots" of the closing prices. They offer nothing as to the price action in any given time period, but are useful in looking at the overall price direction of a stock or index.

liquidity The ease with which an asset can be converted to cash in the marketplace. A large number of buyers and sellers and a high volume of trading activity provide high liquidity.

locked market   A market where trading has been halted because prices have reached their daily trading limit.

long   The term used to describe the buying of a security, contract, commodity, or option.

long-term equity anticipation securities (LEAPS)   Long-term stock or index options that are available with expiration dates up to three years in the future.

low   The lowest price paid for a stock during a certain period.

low-risk investing   A trade that is hedged for purposes of limiting price loss, as opposed to a directional trade where loss is unlimited.

make a market   A market maker stands ready to buy or sell a particular security for his or her own account to keep the market liquid.

margin   A deposit contributed by a customer as a percentage of the current market value of the securities held in a margin account. This amount changes as the price of the investment changes.

margin account   A customer account in which a brokerage firm lends the customer part of the purchase price of a trade.

margin call   A call from a broker signaling the need for a trader to deposit additional money into a margin account to maintain a trade.

margin requirements of options   The amount of cash the writer of an uncovered (naked) option is required to deposit and maintain to cover his or her daily position price changes.

marked to market   At the end of each business day the open positions carried in an account held at a brokerage firm are credited or debited funds based on the settlement prices of the open positions that day.

market   Used to refer to the entire stock market, a specific sector, or a specific asset, security, or commodity that is traded at an exchange.

market-if-touched (MIT) order   A price order that automatically becomes a market order if the price is reached.

market maker   An independent trader or trading firm that is prepared to buy and sell shares or contracts in a designated market. Market makers must make a two-sided market (bid and ask) in order to facilitate trading.

market on close   An order specification that requires the broker to get the best price available on the close of trading, usually during the last five minutes of trading.

market on open   An order that must be executed during the opening of trading.

market order   Buying or selling securities at the price given at the time the order reaches the market. A market order is to be executed immediately at the best available price, and is the only order that guarantees execution.

market price The most recent price at which a security transaction has taken place.

market value The price at which investors buy or sell a share of common stock or a bond at a given time. Market value is determined by the interaction between buyers and sellers.

mark to market Refers to the daily adjustment of margin accounts to reflect profits and losses. In this way, losses are never allowed to accumulate.

mid-cap stocks Usually solidly established medium-growth firms with less than $100 billion in assets. They provide better growth potential than blue-chip stocks, but do not offer as wide a variety of investment attributes.

momentum A measure of the rate (velocity) at which a security is rising or falling. When a market continues in the same direction for a certain time frame, the market is said to have momentum.

momentum indicator A technical indicator utilizing price and volume statistics for predicting the strength or weakness of a current market.

momentum trading Investing with (or against) the momentum of the market in hopes of profiting from it.

moving average Probably the best known and most versatile technical indicator, this is a mathematical procedure in which the sum of a value plus a selected number of previous values is divided by the total number of values. Used to smooth or eliminate the fluctuations in data and to assist in determining when to buy and sell.

moving average convergence/divergence (MACD) This popular lagging indicator, also known as the "Mack-D," represents the difference between two moving averages with differing time periods. One is shorter (commonly 12 days) while the other is longer (commonly 26 days). The shorter one is referred to as the fast line while the longer one is termed the slow line. When a stock is in an uptrend, the fast line will cross over the slow line. If a stock is trending down, the fast line will cross under the slow line.

mutual fund An open-end investment company that pools investors' money to invest in a variety of stocks, bonds, or other securities.

naked option An option written (sold) without an underlying hedge position.

naked position A securities position not hedged from market risk.

narrowing the spread Refers to lessening the gap between the bid and asked prices of a security as a result of bidding and offering.

Nasdaq National Association of Securities Dealers Automated Quotations system is a computerized system that provides brokers and dealers with the ability to trade approximately 3,300 securities over-the-counter. On average, Nasdaq trades more shares than any other exchange.

near-the-money   An option with a strike price close to the current price of the underlying tradable.

net change   The daily change from time frame to time frame—for example, the change from the close of yesterday to the close of today.

net profit   The overall profit of a trade.

New York Stock Exchange (NYSE)   The trademarked name of the largest and oldest stock exchange in the United States. The NYSE operates as an auction market in which orders are brought to the trading floor for execution.

note   A short-term debt security, usually maturing in five years or less.

OEX   This term, pronounced as three separate letters, is Wall Street shorthand for the Standard & Poor's 100 index.

offer   The lowest price at which a person is willing to sell.

offer down   The change of the offer of the market related to a downward price movement at that specific time.

off-floor trader   A trader who does not trade on the actual floor of an organized futures or stock exchange.

offset   To liquidate a futures position by entering an equivalent but opposite transaction. To offset a long position, a sale is made; to offset a short position, a purchase is made.

on-the-money   When the option in question is trading at its exercise price. (Same as **at-the-money**.)

open interest   The number of total outstanding contracts for a specific option or futures contract.

opening   The period at the beginning of the trading session at an exchange.

opening call   A period at the opening of a futures market in which the price for each contract is established by outcry.

opening range   The range of prices at which the first bids and offers are made or first transactions are completed.

open order   An order to buy or sell a security at a specified price, valid until executed or canceled.

open outcry   A system of trading where an auction of verbal bids and offers is performed on the trading floor. This method is slowly disappearing as exchanges become automated.

open trade   A current trade that is still held active in a customer's account.

opportunity costs   The theoretical cost of using capital for one investment versus another.

option   A security that represents the right, but not the obligation, to buy or sell a specified amount of an underlying security (stock, bond, futures contract, etc.) at a specified price within a specified time.

option holder   The buyer of either a call or a put option.

option premium   The price of an option.

option writer   The seller of either a call or a put option.

order   A ticket or voucher representing long or short securities or options.

order flow   The volume of orders being bought or sold on the exchanges.

oscillators   Technical indicators that focus on a variety of chart data, including price and volume. Oscillators provide insight on trending markets and are most closely associated with determining overbought and oversold conditions. Upper and lower fixed bands are incorporated into an oscillator graph, and these bands warn of extreme market conditions. Oscillators are also useful in sideways-trending markets since certain oscillators will lead the price action and provide clues about a potential move from the sideways pattern, as well as the direction of that move. Oscillator movement relative to a midpoint line can provide trading alerts and signals.

out-of-the-money (OTM)   When an options exercise price has no intrinsic value.

out-of-the-money (OTM) option   A call option is out-of-the-money if its exercise or strike price is above the current market price of the underlying security. A put option is out-of-the-money if its exercise or strike price is below the current market price of the underlying security.

overbought   A term used to describe a security or option in which more and stronger buying has occurred than the fundamentals justify.

oversold   A technical term used to describe a market or security in which more and stronger selling has occurred than the fundamentals justify.

paper trading   Simulating a trade without actually putting up the money, for the purpose of gaining additional trading experience.

par   The stated or nominal value of a bond (typically $1,000) that is paid to the bondholder at maturity.

perceived risk   The theoretical risk of a trade in a specific time frame.

performance-based   A system of compensation in which a broker receives fees based on performance in the marketplace.

points   In the case of shares, one point indicates $1 per share. For bonds, one point means 1 percent of par value. Commodities differ from market to market.

point spread   The price movement required for a security to go from one full point level to another (e.g., for a stock to go up or down $1).

position   The total of a trader's open contracts.

position delta   The sum of all positive and negative deltas in a hedged position.

position limit   The maximum number of open contracts in a single underlying instrument.

premium   The amount of cash that an option buyer pays to an option seller.

price   Price of a share of common stock on the date shown. Highs and lows are based on the highest and lowest intraday trading prices.

price-earnings (P/E) ratio   A technical analysis tool for comparing the prices of different common stocks by assessing how much the market is willing to pay for a share of each corporation's earnings. P/E is calculated by dividing the current market price of a stock by the earnings per share.

principal   The initial purchase price of a bond on which interest is earned.

private company   A company that issues private stock and is not publicly traded.

public company   A company that issues shares of stock to be traded on the public market.

put option   An option contract giving the owner the right, but not the obligation, to sell a specified amount of an underlying security at a specified price within a specified time. The put option buyer hopes the price of the shares will drop by a specific date, while the put option seller (writer) hopes that by the specified date the price of the shares will rise, remain stable, or drop by an amount less than the seller's profit on the premium.

quickie   An order that must be filled as soon as it reaches the trading floor at the price specified, or be canceled immediately.

quotation or quote   The price being offered or bid by a market maker or broker-dealer for a particular security.

quoted price   Refers to the price at which the last sale and purchase of a particular security or commodity took place.

rally   A brisk rise in the general price level of the market or an individual security.

ratio backspread   A delta neutral spread where an uneven amount of contracts are bought and sold with a ratio less than 2 to 3. Optimally, a backspread is placed at even or for a net credit.

ratio call spread   A bearish or stable strategy in which a trader sells two higher strike calls and buys one lower strike call. This strategy offers unlimited risk and limited profit potential.

ratio put spread   A bullish or stable strategy in which a trader buys one higher-strike put and sells two lower-strike puts. This strategy offers unlimited risk and limited profit potential.

real-time quotes   Data received from a quote service as the prices change.

relative strength   A stock's price movement over the past year as compared to a market index.

Relative Strength Index (RSI)   Developed by Welles Wilder, this oscillator is used to measure the strength of a security's recent price relative to less recent price moves it has completed. It is often used to identify price tops and bottoms.

resistance   A price level the market has a hard time breaking through to the upside.

retracement   The amount in which a market move is corrected. A retracement is usually expressed in percentage terms, so if the original move was 60 points and a 30-point correction occurred, we would say there was a 50 percent retracement of the original move (30/60).

return on investment   The income profit made on an investment, calculated by dividing the net gain or loss by the total cost of the investment.

reversal stop   A stop that, when hit, is a signal to reverse the current trading position (i.e., from long to short); also known as stop and reverse.

rich   Priced higher than expected.

risk   The potential financial loss inherent in the investment.

risk graph   A graphic representation of risk and reward on a given trade as prices change.

risk manager   A person who manages risk of trades in a portfolio by hedging the trades.

risk profile   A graphic determination of risk on a trade. This would include the profit and loss of a trade at any given point for any given time frame.

risk-to-reward ratio   The mathematical relationship between the maximum potential risk and maximum potential reward of a trade.

round turn   Procedure by which a long or short position is offset by an opposite transaction.

running stops   When quoted, floor traders use these to move the market. When stops are bunched together, traders may move the market in order to activate stop orders and propel the market further.

seasonal market   A market with a consistent but short-lived rise or drop in market activity due to predictable changes in climate or calendar.

seat   The traditional term for membership in a stock or futures exchange.

securities and commodities exchanges   Organized exchanges where securities, options, and futures contracts are traded.

Securities and Exchange Commission (SEC)   Commission created by Congress to regulate the securities markets and protect investors.

security   A trading instrument such as a stock, bond, and short-term investment.

selling short   The practice of borrowing a stock, future, or option from a broker and selling it because the investor forecasts that the price of a stock is going down. Same as *short selling*.

sentiment analysis   An attempt to gauge investor sentiment by analyzing the subconscious of the marketplace through the use of specific psychological market criteria.

shares   Certificates representing ownership of stock in a corporation or company.

short   The selling of a security, contract, commodity, or option not owned by the seller.

short premium   Expectation that a move of the underlying asset in either direction will result in a theoretical decrease of the value of an option.

short selling   The sale of shares or futures that a seller does not currently own. The seller borrows them (usually from a broker) and sells them with the intent to replace what he or she has sold through later repurchase in the market at a lower price. Same as **selling short**.

single-stock futures (SSF)   An agreement between two parties that commits one party to buy a stock and one party to sell a stock at a given price and on a specified date. They are similar to existing futures contracts for gold, crude oil, bonds, and stock indexes. Unlike actual stock, there is no ownership or voting rights contained in an SSF.

slippage   The cost of the trade that is lost due to commissions and because of the spread between the bid price and ask price. Traders try to keep slippage to a minimum, which can be done by using brokerage firms with low commissions and by sometimes placing orders between the bid and ask price.

small-cap stocks   Up-and-comer companies that offer big rewards and higher risks. They tend to cost less than mid-caps and have lower liquidity. However, small amounts of media coverage can prompt big gains.

smoothing   In trading, a mathematical technique that removes excess data in order to maintain a correct evaluation of the underlying trend.

specialist   A member of the securities exchange who is a market maker trader on the exchange floor assigned to fill bids/orders in a specific stock out of his or her own account.

speculator   A trader who hopes to profit from a directional move in the underlying instrument. The speculator has no interest in making or taking delivery.

spike   A sharp price rise in one or two days indicating the time for an immediate sale.

spread   (1) The difference between the bid and the ask prices of a security.

(2) A trading strategy in which a trader offsets the purchase of one trading unit against another.

Standard & Poor's Corporation (S&P)   A company that rates stocks and corporate and municipal bonds according to risk profiles and that produces and tracks the S&P indexes.

stochastic indicator   An indicator based on the observation that as prices increase, closing prices tend to accumulate ever closer to the highs for the period. Its goal is to identify where the price closes relative to the high and low for the day.

stock   A share of a company's stock translates into ownership of part of the company.

stock exchange or **stock market**   An organized marketplace where buyers and sellers are brought together to buy and sell stocks.

stock split   An increase in the number of a stock's shares that results in decreasing the par value of each share.

stops   Buy stops are orders that are placed at a specified price over the current price of the market. Sell stops are orders that are placed with a specified price below the current price.

straddle   A position consisting of a long (or short) ATM call and a long (or short) ATM put, where both options have the same strike price and expiration date.

strangle   A position consisting of a long (or short) call and a long (or short) put where both options have the same underlying asset and the same expiration date, but different strike prices. Most strangles involve OTM options.

strike price   A price at which the stock or commodity underlying a call or put option can be purchased (call) or sold (put) over the specified period. (Same as **exercise price**.)

support   A historical price level at which falling prices have stopped falling and either moved sideways or reversed direction.

swings   The measurement of price movement between extreme highs and lows.

synthetic long call   A long put and a long stock or future.

synthetic long put   A long call and a short stock or future.

synthetic long stock   A short put and a long call.

synthetic short call   A short put and a short stock or future.

synthetic short put   A short call and a long stock or future.

synthetic short stock   A short call and a long put.

synthetic straddle   Futures and options combined to create a delta neutral trade.

synthetic underlying   A long (or short) call together with a short (or long) put.

Both options have the same underlying asset, the same strike price, and the same expiration date.

technical analysis   A method of evaluating securities and commodities by analyzing statistics generated by market activity, such as past prices, volume, momentum, and stochastics.

theoretical value   An option value generated by a mathematical option pricing model to determine what an option is really worth.

theta   The Greek measurement of the time decay of an option.

tick   A minimum upward or downward movement in the price of a security. For example, bond futures trade in 32nds, while most stocks trade in 8ths.

time decay   The amount of time premium movement within a certain time frame on an option due to the passage of time in relation to the expiration of the option itself.

time premium   The additional value of an option due to the volatility of the market and the time remaining until expiration.

time value   The amount by which the current market price of a right, warrant, or option exceeds its intrinsic value. (Same as **extrinsic value**.)

trader   A client who buys and sells frequently with the objective of short-term profit.

trading account   An account opened with a brokerage firm from which to place trades.

Treasury bill (T-bill)   A short-term U.S. government security with a maturity of no more than a year.

Treasury bond (T-bond)   A fixed-interest U.S. government debt security with a maturity of 10 years or more.

Treasury note (T-note)   A fixed-interest U.S. government debt security with a maturity of between 1 and 10 years.

trend   The general direction of the market. Markets have three trends: up, down, and sideways. These trends can be major (primary) trends, corrective (secondary) trends, or minor trends. Primary trends typically extend for a year or longer; secondary trends extend for three weeks to six months; and minor trends extend for two to three days to two to three weeks. Typically the closing price is used for the trend line.

triangles   A sideways price pattern in which prices fluctuate within converging trend lines. When a stock enters one of these patterns it is likely to experience a decline in volume as the pattern progresses. As the price range gets tighter, the ensuing move is likely to be explosive. Common triangle patterns include symmetrical triangle, ascending and descending triangles, and pennants.

Triple Witching Day   The third Friday in March, June, September, and December when U.S. options, index options, and futures contracts all expire simultaneously, often resulting in massive trades.

type   The classification of an option contract as either a put or a call.

uncovered option   A short option position, also called a naked option, in which the writer does not own shares of the underlying stock. This is a much riskier strategy than a covered option.

underlying asset   A trading instrument subject to purchase or sale upon exercise.

undervalued   A security selling below the value the market value analysts believe it is worth.

upside   The potential for prices to move up.

upside breakeven   The upper price at which a trade breaks even.

value stocks   Stocks that appear to be bargains because they are price lower than their calculated worth.

variable delta   A delta that can change due to the change of an underlying asset or a change in time expiration of an option.

vega   The amount by which the price of an option changes when the volatility changes. Also referred to as volatility.

VIX   The CBOE Volatility Index measures the implied volatility of S&P 500 Index options. When it rises, traders are becoming more bearish and are worried about future market volatility. For that reason, VIX is sometimes called the "fear gauge." Low VIX readings are a sign of bullishness or complacency among traders.

VXN   The ticker symbol for the Nasdaq 100 Volatility Index ($VXN). The index tracks the expected (or implied) volatility of options on the Nasdaq 100 Index ($NDX).

volatility   A measure of the amount by which an underlying asset is expected to fluctuate in a given period of time. Volatility is a primary determinant in the valuation of option premiums and time value. There are two basic kinds of volatility—implied and historical (statistical). Implied volatility is calculated by using an option pricing model (Black-Scholes for stocks and indexes and Black for futures). Historical volatility is calculated by using the standard deviation of underlying asset price changes from close to close of trading going back 21 to 23 days.

volatility skew   The theory that options that are deeply out-of-the-money tend to have higher implied volatility levels than at-the-money options. Volatility skew measures and accounts for the limitation found in most option pricing models and uses it to give the trader an edge in estimating an option's worth.

volume   The number of shares bought and sold on a stock exchange. Volume should increase as a stock breaks through a support or resistance level.

whipsaw   Losing money on both sides of a price swing.

wide opening   Refers to an unusually large spread between the bid and asked prices.

Wilshire 5000 Equity Index   A market index of approximately 7,000 U.S.-based equities traded on the American Stock Exchange, the New York Stock Exchange, and the Nasdaq Stock Market.

Witching Day   A day on which two or more classes of options and futures expire.

writer   An individual who sells an option.

Yellow Sheets   A daily publication of the National Quotation Bureau detailing bid and asked prices.

yield   The rate of return on an investment.

zeta   The percentage change in an option's price per 1 percent change in implied volatility.

Index